# The Complete Annotated

# Durham 'Russiagate' Report:

*A Corrupt, Cruel Fraud*

**Andrew Kreig**

Also by Andrew Kreig:

*Spiked: How Chain Managem* [illegible] *Americ* [illegible]

*Presidential Puppetry: Obam* [illegible] *Their* [illegible]

**Eagle View Books**
**Washington, DC**

First Edition 2023
Second Edition, Updated Hardcover, September 2024



*Publishing Note:* The text of Special Counsel John H. Durham's report to the Attorney General was published on May 12, 2023, and included such related materials as the report's Introduction and Table of Contents. This book has left that report as is, without corrections or any other modifications.

The publication of that report, which is in the public domain as a government document, in no way implies any kind of relationship between Eagle View Books or Andrew Kreig and the United States Government, including the U.S. Department of Justice, John H. Durham or any of the government's employees or contractors.



For information about author lectures and interviews, bulk discounts, educational discounts, electronic sales, and excerpts contact Eagle View Books. The address is 701 Pennsylvania Ave., NW, PH 8, Washington, DC. Tel: (202) 638-0070. Email: info@EagleViewDC.com.

*Library of Congress Control Number Has Been Applied For.*

Names: Kreig, Andrew, author (1949)

Title: *The Complete Durham 'Russiagate' Report: A Corrupt, Cruel Fraud*

Subjects: Trump, Donald, 1946. Durham, John, 1950. Clinton, Hillary, 1947. Barr, William, 1950. U.S. Law. U.S. Election Law. FBI. U.S. Justice Department. U.S. Political Activity. U.S. Intelligence Services. U.S. Foreign Relations. Russia (Federation).

Printed in the United States of America.

Trade Paperback ISBN: 978-0-9886728-6-4
Trade Hardcover ISBN: 978-0-9886728-7-1

*For those who seek justice, not mere "truths"*

*and half-truths easily manipulated*

# Table of Contents

# Author-Editor's Preface

*U.S. Justice Department Special Counsel John H. Durham testifying before the House Judiciary Committee about his "Russiagate" report on June 21, 2023 (Photo by Michael Brochstein via Split Stone Media).*

This book is a practical guide for those who want to understand the news, not just to watch it. Provided here is the complete final report that U.S. Department of Justice Special Counsel John Durham and the Department, dated May 12, 2023, regarding his four-year investigation of potential criminal wrongdoing by the FBI and its sources regarding allegations of Russian interference in the 2016 U.S. presidential election to help Republican candidate Donald J. Trump.

More important than the report itself are its omissions and distortions, which are reported here as well because conventional political punditry, with few exceptions noted, does not tell us what we need to know about the Durham investigation and its massive fraudulent aspects and cruel impacts on victims.

The report's continui[illegible] Wa[illegible] media illustrate a theme that cannot be repeated too often: Histori[illegible] aten [illegible] civic life — and impact everyone's future. These changes dir[illegible] ier nati[illegible] emocratic functions of fair elections, freedom of information an[illegible] war[illegible] reported below.

Previewing that, we r[illegible] the [illegible] leading their country's armies in the invasion of Ukraine, had [illegible] also i[illegible] U.S. [illegible] Western elections via Internet-based hackers, social media infl[illegible] fro[illegible] on-military methods. That pattern of activity and threat — illust[illegible] er Gr[illegible] and Russian Armed Forces General Staff Chief Valery Gerasi[illegible] ves fa[illegible] ves. So does Russian interference in elections in Western Euro[illegible] Russia[illegible]'s recent bellicosity and an ongoing series of coups in Western [illegible]

These events are root[illegible] succ[illegible] ions in the United States and United Kingdom, among other p[illegible] he [illegible] mp "investigative" efforts as John Durham's to explore the m[illegible] thre[illegible] lly stunning omission from Durham's report are the documented [illegible] and in[illegible] archs and pro-Trump Republicans in the 2016 campaign season.

Among the more nota[illegible] was [illegible] family members and Roger Stone to obtain from Russians inf[illegible] ed fr[illegible] linton and the Democratic National Committee, much of which [illegible] semin[illegible] included WikiLeaks, Guccifer 2.0 and DC Leaks. Missing also fr[illegible] Repor[illegible] of Trump pardons for those convicted of conspiring with Russia[illegible] the [illegible] mp Campaign Chief Executive Paul Manafort, his fabulously w[illegible] Oleg [illegible] s of highly-paid operatives. Durham focused discussion of M[illegible] eripa[illegible] memos written in 2016 by analyst Christopher Steele instead [illegible] ostan[illegible] one such matter, the FBI indicted in early 2023 Charles McGo[illegible] r hea[illegible] FBI's New York office, for work he performed for Deripaska, [illegible] whom [illegible] ed for interfering in the 2016 U.S. presidential election. McG[illegible] rged [illegible], conspiracy, and money laundering for working in 2021 with [illegible] separ[illegible] McGonigal with concealing $225,000 he allegedly received from [illegible] anian [illegible] rth underscoring that FBI executives like McGonigal are supp[illegible] Ameri[illegible] nd a special counsel like Durham is supposed to alert the publ[illegible] imina[illegible] not cherry-pick targets and topics that help his own patrons.

As for this reporter's [illegible] cover[illegible] with a tip in the year 2010 about how Durham had handled and [illegible] gnific[illegible] ecticut-based federal prosecutor. In a pattern familiar to most ex[illegible] rters, [illegible] sions benefited from an encouraging, experienced editor. In this [illegible] timat[illegible] sity's *Neiman Watchdog* Editor Barry Sussman, a noted journal[illegible] the [illegible] itor of its Watergate coverage. His encouragement and adep[illegible] e earl[illegible] helped sustain research momentum overcoming obstacles even [illegible] And, [illegible] les, which is not surprising regarding national security and gra[illegible] inher[illegible] s and their importance surrounding Durham's work proved s[illegible] e ori[illegible]'s publication originally planned for spring 2023 was postpone[illegible] inclu[illegible] Report — because of its omissions and other flaws — turns [illegible] essa[illegible] urney of discovery, not the ultimate destination.

*Explosive 2024 Developme[illegible]*

Important revelations rel[illegible] ok's [illegible] rds in Western democracies became increasingly apparent to th[illegible] late 20[illegible] e available for sale but before it was formally launched with an [illegible] and [illegible] ich was postponed until the spring of 2024 to enable treatment i[illegible] expa[illegible]

The major change is t[illegible] sclos[illegible] two other Justice Department special counsels who had been ap[illegible] ttorn[illegible] ion and then appointed by the Biden Administration to investiga[illegible] imes b[illegible] son Hunter Biden. More specifically,

Biden Attorney General Merrick Garland named former Maryland U.S. Attorney Robert K. Hur to investigate whether Joe Biden had broken laws in retaining documents following the end of his vice presidency in 2017. Separately, Garland retained David Weiss as U.S. Attorney for Delaware and then augmented his powers in 2023 by naming him as a special counsel to probe disputed claims that the Bidens had engaged in illegal influence peddling involving businesses in Ukraine and China, and that the younger Biden had also criminally violated U.S. gun possession and income tax laws. In announcing the appointments of Hur and Weiss, Garland reassured the public that their long careers as prosecutors provided well for capable and fair investigations of inherently explosive allegations. Public confidence in their integrity was particularly important because congressional Republicans and their allied media networks repeatedly smeared the Bidens in advance of the reports to prepare for President Biden's impeachment in 2024 before the presidential elections, thereby neutralizing as an election issue President Trump's two House impeachments (without Senate convictions) during his term.

The work of both Hur and Weiss, however, was revealed in early 2024 to have been exceptionally controversial and partisan and shoddy in the mode of Durham's, thus illustrating a pattern.

More specifically, Hur found in his 300-page report no basis to prosecute President Biden criminally. But Hur used the opportunity provided by his investigation, much like former FBI Director James Comey did in maligning Democratic Presidential nominee Hillary Clinton in 2016 without bringing any charges, to assert at length that Biden had failing mental capacities. This claim matched closely with a major Republican campaign talking point and was regarded by many scholars as outside a prosecutor's mandate of either making criminal charges or closing an investigation with minimal comment.

Similarly, Weiss seemed on the verge of closing the major parts of his investigation in mid-2023 with a plea bargain with Hunter Biden that called for no prison time. But news reports enraged Republican officials and media and prompted sharp questions from the presiding judge on whether the agreement foreclosed any future charges. Weiss regrouped and led an effort to bring felony tax and gun charges against the President's son. Also, the continuing investigation by the special counsel and his team fostered expectations that their narrow House majority could proceed with an impeachment of the president in early 2024, based in significant part on an unnamed source who had been alleging for years to law enforcement and to Republicans via leaked documents that the Bidens had received bribes, including a $5 million payoff via Ukraine.

Yet experts following the prosecution of the younger Biden documented numerous irregularities and suspected irregularities in his gun and tax prosecutions, including the government's reliance on evidence private parties took from his electronic devices without his knowledge or consent before using it for political and law enforcement purposes. Part of the complex and inherently secret pre-indictment and pre-trial investigatory process required both prosecutors and defense to evaluate whether electronic messages supposedly found on the younger Biden's devices or server records was actually his and legally obtained – or whether some represents theft, sabotage and electronic planting of suspicious words by either American political opponents of Biden and/or Russian operatives with similar political goals of ruining the Bidens. As Bidens defense and independent experts unveiled new findings during the late 2023, a question front-and-center during the Durham probe remained unanswered: Why shouldn't it be a priority to investigate whether Russian agents and their allies are hacking high-profile Democrats and using the findings, real or imagined, to undermine presidential campaigns?

In one alleged error rare if not unique for federal prosecutors in a major case, the younger Biden's defense counsel argued that a photo of purported cocaine on a table that prosecutors used to indict Hunter Biden in 2023 for gun possession while using drugs was actually a photo of sawdust on someone else's wood-working table — a that Biden's psychiatrist had sent him.

Even more shocking, Weiss obtained a false statement indictment in early 2024 Alexander Smirnov, revealed as the government's main secret witness for years on the corruption claims smearing the Bidens regarding Ukraine. Furthermore, Smirnov's indictment stated that he had been working with Russian intelligence for years regarding those kinds of allegations.

The implications are enormous, of course, and help illustrate in ways amplified below how accountability problems with prosecutors can extend far beyond a case study of the Durham Report. Before reaching any such conclusions, however, we resume our narrative about John Durham and his work.

*Durham's Day*

To begin in the middle of things as narrators have done since ancient times, we start with Durham's hearing before the U.S. House Judiciary Committee, illustrated above. His testimony and reactions illustrated certain of these themes in extraordinary fashion on June 21, 2023.

Committee Chairman Jim Jordan, an Ohio Republican, and nearly all of the rest of the GOP majority ranted about alleged outrageous smears inflicted on Trump via the FBI while ignoring more documented threats to United States law, freedoms and national security, including Russian spies like the late FBI Special Agent Robert Hanssen who had actually worked for the FBI while delivering vital U.S. secrets.

A few Republicans saved their invective for Durham for not successfully prosecuting and jailing any Democrats or FBI personnel during his four-year investigation. Rep. Matt Gaetz, a Republican from Florida, unloaded a surprise tirade as one of the hearing's final speakers. Gaetz accused Durham, a Trump-appointee, of running a "cover-up" to protect the guilty.

Democrats, by contrast, were united in picking apart Durham's report in blunt language for omissions and pro-Trump bias casting unmerited aspersions on Durham's targets.

This reporter had a ringside seat to this circus, as illustrated by the photo on the left I took of Durham from my perch just behind him as he responded to a Democrat's questions nearly four hours after the hearing began. First-term U.S. Rep. Wesley Hunt, a Republican from Texas, is shown at center awaiting his turn to defend Trump and denounce Democrats and FBI personnel for reports showing Trump encouraging Russian interference in elections.

Trump's supporters in Congress and in the media are determined to use Durham's report to keep conspiracy allegations alive against the FBI and anyone else who questions the 2016 election despite Durham's losses in court trying to prove to juries in 2022 that Democrats worked with the FBI to make false allegations claiming Russian help for the 2016 Trump presidential campaign. Indeed, Durham is listed as the author of two separate books advertised on Amazon.com selling his report in book form. The books were published within days of its publication, one on May 14, suggesting close coordination of the book publishing with the government release of the taxpayer-paid report.

It's high time to cut through the back-and-forth of accusations. National security analyst Marcy Wheeler, blogging under the pen name Emptywheel, aptly summed up the controversy this way: "John Durham's investigation was a four-year effort to flip the script: to make Hillary Clinton — the victim of a nation-state attack in 2016 — its villain." Wheeler, entitled her predictions, "A Guide to the False Claims John Durham Will Tell Congress," and published them the day before the hearing.

She referenced the well-documented sabotage of the Clinton campaign by stolen emails that Russians and their assets used to create months of controversies for her Clinton and other Democrats beginning in mid-2016. That surely should have been part of the context for Durham's probe but is missing. Those kinds of omissions are explored below in this Preface and in a Bibliography that cites expert commentaries about the Durham Report.

Wheeler's summation recalls the iconic moment in the third Trump-Clinton 2016 presidential debates when Trump said of Clinton with a sneer, "Putin, from everything I can see, has no respect for this person."

"Well," Clinton responded, "that's because he'd rather have a puppet as president..."

Trump interrupted to exclaim, "No puppet! No puppet! You're the puppet!!"

That debate helps explain the seven years of follow ups including this Durham probe, that reached a climax of sorts in that wild Judiciary Committee hearing in June while causing enormous damage to American institutions and to those falsely accused.

We shall explore these mysteries in the pages that follow, first with this overview. Then comes the Durham Report and finally an Appendix containing expert commentaries that pick it apart and provide more general context, plus a roster (with photos) showing key figures in this "Russiagate," both those mentioned in the Durham report and those (including convicted Russian spies) curiously omitted.

*Eight Things Not Mentioned in the Durham Report*, a May 16 column by Wheeler excerpted with a link in the Bibliography here, exemplifies the brutal criticism Durham deserves for avoiding evidence that implicates the Trump team and Russians, and focusing firepower on trivial side-issues and players. Her first example was a description of how Durham and his boss, U.S. Attorney Gen. William Barr, traveled to Italy in search of evidence for their theories but were told instead by Italian authorities of their suspicions about crimes Trump may have committed. "Mr. Durham never filed charges," Wheeler wrote, "and it remains unclear what level of an investigation it was, what steps he took, what he learned and whether anyone at the White House ever found out. The extraordinary fact that Mr. Durham opened a criminal investigation that included scrutinizing Mr. Trump has remained secret."

There's more, much more.

First, though, I would like to reassure readers: These topics are not just complex, but important. They are not just important but interesting. And part of the interest, I hope, is that the conclusions are simple once the reader gets the clues and sees the evidence, as in all good mystery stories. Think of the popular Sherlock Holmes 1892 story of a Silver Blaze, a famed racehorse that disappeared with its trainer found dead as an apparent murder victim. Holmes solved the mysteries by noting "the curious incident of the dog," which failed to bark. That clue informed Holmes that the perpetrator kidnapping the racehorse must have been someone whom the watchdog knew well: The trainer, as it turned out, whom Silver Blaze kicked in the head when he tried to wound the horse to fix a race.

This case before us now provides its own share of mysteries, including spies, secrets, sex scandal, and almost non-stop sensationalism that for years has distracted many from focusing on actual threats to the United States.

But in the end, the facts point the way to conclusions that are not very complicated. So, stay the course as a reader and you'll be rewarded.

*A Journalist's Journey*

Why did I start researching and reporting on the career of John Durham in 2008? The reasons having nothing to do with Russia or Trump.

As a Washington, DC-based reporter covering the justice system, I thought newsworthy his 2008 appointment by the Bush Administration to serve as special counsel investigating potential criminal wrongdoing in CIA destruction of evidence after revelations of CIA waterboarding of terror suspects.

My interest deepened upon learning that Nora Dannehy, Durham's longtime prosecutorial colleague in Connecticut's U.S. Attorney office, had received a similar appointment as special counsel to conduct a nationwide investigation of the so-called "U.S. Attorney Firing Scandal." This was a major scandal whereby the Justice Department had fired eight (or by some counts nine) of the nation's presidentially appointed U.S. attorneys in the 2006 period, allegedly for reluctance to use their law enforcement powers for White House-directed political reasons, such as criminally prosecuting prominent Democrats in dubious cases.

The Brandeis University Schuster Institute for Investigative Journalism had named me as a senior fellow to study those firings, as well as the related issue that seemed ripe to explore: What kind of potentially politically motivated decisions, compromising their oaths to administer justice fairly, were other U.S. attorneys around the nation forced to make to avoid getting fired? Plenty, as it turned out, causing enormous harm to defendants, families and communities. But that's another story.

My interest in Durham's then-role as an accountability enforcer was enhanced further because I had received a tip that Durham's record as a federal prosecutor was marred by several admonishments from federal judges reviewing Connecticut prosecutions, an aspect of his career unknown to the media and public. I was especially interested since I had previously covered the Justice Department full-time for five years as a reporter for the *Hartford Courant*, Connecticut's largest news organization. The beat required a special focus on the U.S. attorney's office in Connecticut, responsible for all federal civil and criminal litigation. Durham and Dannehy had both led that office at different times as interim U.S. attorneys. It was long after my coverage and so I had met neither in person. But one of my memorable moments in my years covering courts came when a high-ranking federal prosecutor familiar with the media explained to me how political smears can work if FBI agents, prosecutors and journalists get careless, break rules and otherwise lose sight dangers. He said explained that authorities will take an initial look at serious allegations that might be credible but that does not mean that they are credible and prosecutable even if the claims are leaked to the media, often for political purposes in the guises of good government.

Those 2008 appointments for Durham and Dannehy temporarily attracted considerable congressional and national media attention before their probes faded from the news. In the end, neither Durham nor Dannehy found any cause for any significant accountability for what were obvious scandals. Dannehy apparently interviewed only one of the "fired" presidentially appointed prosecutors, David Iglesias from New Mexico, and none of the victims of the scandal.

One such victim we co [illegible] ate U.S. [illegible] Ste[illegible] [illegible]lican from Alaska who was convicted on questionable corruptio[illegible] before [illegible] 2008, leading to a narrow loss before the Justice Department wit[illegible] ges [illegible] judge [illegible] conduct.

Another victim was [illegible] a Go[illegible] Siegelm[illegible] [illegible]rat convicted of dubious corruption charges and promptly sent[illegible] ears in [illegible] [illegible]p protested by many whistleblowers. Also protesting was an unp[illegible] ray o[illegible] stat[illegible] [illegible]enerals, the chief law enforcers from more than 40 states, who [illegible] ccessful[illegible] U.S. [illegible] [illegible]urt that Siegelman's alleged crime, reappointing to a state boar[illegible] a non-[illegible] [illegible]ported, was not a crime but instead a fairly routine practice at [illegible] d fe[illegible] The [illegible] [illegible]behind the Siegelman frame-up was heightened because whistle[illegible] aled th[illegible] judge [illegible] [illegible]trolled a defense contracting company that had received $300 mil[illegible] federal [illegible] while [illegible] [illegible]as issuing numerous pro-prosecution rulings against a defendant [illegible] to have [illegible] because [illegible] [illegible]ad sought to expose the judge's own corruption in trying to loot [illegible] funds [illegible] [illegible]

In sum, Dannehy's s[illegible] probe [illegible] [illegible]tter[illegible] [illegible]n's of the CIA waterboard evidence-destroyers, reeked of white[illegible]

In 2010, I reported th[illegible] Durham [illegible] Harvard [illegible]'s *Nieman Watchdog*. The column — "New Questions Raised [illegible] ctor [illegible] Bu[illegible] in U.S. Attorney Firings." *Nieman Watchdog*, an adjunct to [illegible] an Fel[illegible] ogram [illegible] [illegible]lication for journalists closely edited by the late Barry Sussman, [illegible] guishe[illegible] editi[illegible] [illegible]r included serving as the *Washington Post's* primary editor for it[illegible] coverage [illegible] 70s.

I had researched the [illegible] rt bec[illegible] [illegible] [illegible]rosecutorial zealousness and lack of accountability demonstrate[illegible] and [illegible] le t[illegible] [illegible]rney Generals at the time, the Bush-nominated Michael Mukas[illegible] can, a[illegible] a-no[illegible] [illegible]cessor Eric Holder, a Democrat, also entrusted them with speci[illegible] of n[illegible] orta[illegible] [illegible]ting suspected lawbreaking by other federal law enforcement a[illegible] ce off[illegible] [illegible]d of [illegible]or waterboarding. The lack of news reporting and Justice Depa[illegible] ntabili[illegible] [illegible] [illegible] from the higher standards of justice that I had witnessed, in ge[illegible] ter c[illegible] the Justic[illegible] [illegible]nt and later as a law clerk to a Boston federal judge, U.S. District [illegible] L. Wolf [illegible] well-kn[illegible] [illegible]ularly in the Boston area, for holding to high ethical standards a[illegible] ring [illegible] Ora[illegible] [illegible]e federal prosecution on racketeering charges of seven leaders o[illegible] gland [illegible] [illegible]mounting his own investigation of the investigators, resulting in [illegible] fact" [illegible] FB[illegible] [illegible] prosecutors of misconduct in their handling of sources, inclu[illegible] notor[illegible] Jam[illegible] " Bulger, later convicted of multiple murders.

It happened that one o[illegible] signm[illegible] Justic[illegible] [illegible] in the 1990s was to reinvestigate the misconduct allegations. H[illegible] most [illegible] form[illegible] [illegible]visor John "Zip" Connolly, who was sentenced to life in prison [illegible] ng, obs[illegible] murd[illegible] [illegible]cy charges stemming from protecting informants including Bulg[illegible] inter Hi[illegible] wa[illegible] [illegible]g major crimes while also informing on rival criminals. Curio[illegible] supe[illegible] that [illegible] Fitzpatrick, co-authored a memoir, *Betrayal*, that contained s[illegible] of D[illegible] fede[illegible] [illegible]ies promptly accused and convicted Fitzgerald of perjury relate[illegible] aspe[illegible] rupti[illegible] [illegible]wing. After his plea deal and sentence he was unresponsive befor[illegible] follow[illegible] abo[illegible] [illegible]t of his experiences.

After my *Nieman Wa*[illegible], my r[illegible] Durhan[illegible] [illegible]y by *Connecticut Law Tribune* staff writer Kellie A. Wagner u[illegible] line "[illegible] ial T[illegible] [illegible]gned." She reported that Connecticut U.S. District Judge Janet [illegible] had [illegible] the extra[illegible] [illegible]p of overturning a weapons charge conviction largely on acco[illegible] torial [illegible] by [illegible] [illegible]e specifically, the Connecticut judge had ruled that Durham ha[illegible] vouched [illegible] prosecu[illegible] [illegible]ses while maligning defense counsel and his arguments, and tha[illegible] alluded [illegible] prej[illegible] [illegible]ot in evidence.

In sum, portents of D[illegible] vided [illegible] de[illegible] [illegible]unded abuses were visible more than a decade ago but essential[illegible] and un[illegible] news [illegible]rving general audiences. That is yet another consequence of th[illegible] spin [illegible] region[illegible] [illegible]edia, which have undergone massive layoffs of reporters coverin[illegible] stitu[illegible] [illegible]s, lea[illegible] [illegible]ters adrift amidst partisan propaganda battles.

After the election President Trump and his colleagues denied and deplored suggestions of foreign influence. Among their main targets were then-FBI Director James Comey, who had allowed the FBI Crossfire Hurricane probe to start in the summer of 2016 (albeit without public disclosure) and then had tried to warn the president-elect in January 2017 about opposition research known as "The Steele Dossier" being privately circulated in Washington, DC containing negative claims about Trump.

The Steele Dossier, a series of memos named after their author, former British M6 Russian spy expert Christopher Steele, was unknown to the public until *Buzzfeed News* published it in January 2017. The materials included a claim, never verified, that Trump had once hired prostitutes to watch them pee on a bed in a Moscow hotel suite where Barack Obama and his wife had once stayed, and that the hotel might possess a surveillance videotape. Discussions of Steele Dossier and its unverified "pee tape" claim have received enormous news coverage, in effect dwarfing coverage of documented Russian interference during the election.

Here's the history of the Steele Dossier: A Washington, DC-based newspaper, the *Beacon Free Press*, heavily funded by the conservative hedge fund tycoon and activist Paul Singer, had originally hired the research consultancy Fusion GPS in the fall of 2015 as part of a "stop-Trump" effort within the Republican Party. That funding stopped in early 2016 because of Trump's victories in GOP primaries.

Fusion GPS, co-founded by former *Wall Street Journal* reporters Glenn Simpson and Peter Fritsch, then marketed its services to the law firm Perkins Coie, which represented Democratic clients. Fusion GPS next hired Steele as a consultant via his firm Orbis Business Intelligence. Orbis then hired the Russian-born Virginia consultant Igor Danchenko, who has said he never saw the "dossier" until BuzzFeed published it and never thought his information certain enough for publication. The "pee tape" has never surfaced and may have been the kind of made-up story that political operatives spin to each other.

Fusion GPS and Steele argued in 2016 along with certain Perkins Coie staff that their raw findings might prove valuable to the FBI in a probe the agency had begun independently of Trump campaign ties to Russians. But it was highly disputed how much or even whether the Clinton campaign knew specifics of the lawyer Sussmann's and GPS outreach efforts.

Continuing controversies after the 2016 election regarding potential Russian influence, involvement by members of the Trump campaign team, the Trump firing of FBI Director James Comey and FBI responses led Deputy Attorney Gen. Rod Rosenstein to appoint former FBI Director Robert S. Mueller as Special Counsel on May 17, 2017. With bipartisan support from Congressional leaders, Mueller's mandate was to oversee a probe into "any links and/or coordination between the Russian government and individuals associated with the campaign of President Donald Trump, and any matters that arose or may arise directly from the investigation."

Continuing also were investigations by the Department of Justice Inspector General and Congressional committees. In June 2018, Inspector General Michael Horowitz released a report finding that FBI supervisor Peter Strzok and other employees brought discredit to themselves" and to the agency. Horowitz found also that former FBI Director James Comey failed to follow FBI procedures in publicly describing investigations, but Horowitz did not find that Comey was motivated by political bias.

Mueller delivered his much-anticipated report to Attorney General William Barr in March 2019. Barr took two actions that undermined the report's conclusions and Barr's own longtime credibility.

First, Barr publicized his own a pro-Trump interpretation of the report in a four-page letter while withholding the report's public release, thereby fostering a deceptive narrative for the media and public about the report's findings when interest was most intense.

Andrew Weissmann, Mueller's lead prosecutor, more than four pages of his memoir *Where Law Ends* to describing devotes Barr's misleading statements, including the claims that Mueller's investigation was "comprehensive" and obtained cooperation from Trump and his administration. Weissmann describes reading the Barr letter as a "gut-punch" in trying to deceive the public about Russia's intention to tilt the election toward Trump illegally and Trump's active encouragement for such help. "Barr's conduct after we submitted our report," Weissmann wrote, "proves why a special counsel was so necessary in the first place — how crucial it is for our government to have a mechanism for independently investigating allegations of criminality by a president. But it also exposes why that mechanism is not strong enough."

Second, Barr secretly met with John Durham, the Trump-appointed U.S. attorney for Connecticut, to discuss as yet-unknown matters. Durham evaded specifics under questioning at the House hearing on June 20, 2023. Whatever the topics were, Barr soon granted Durham authority in April 2019 to begin investigating the beginnings of the FBI inquiry into the 2016, thereby providing an opportunity for an alternative public narrative about matters that Mueller had been investigating.

The Mueller Report found considerable evidence of Russian involvement in the U.S. elections and complicity in various ways by members of Trump's circle. It set the stage of federal charges against more than thirty individuals and organizations. Mueller, citing a Justice Department policy stemming from the 1970s, said also that his investigation was foreclosed from investigating potential criminal liability regarding President Trump and so the report neither exonerated nor implicated the President.

My focus on Justice Department actions and accountability, primarily via the Justice Integrity Project founded in 2010, led me to attend a number of pre-trial and trial proceedings arising out of Mueller's investigation.

Among the trials and pre-trial matters I covered were those involving such Trump associates as former National Security Advisor Michael Flynn, former Campaign Manager Paul Manafort, and longtime Trump advisor and friend Roger Stone, whom I had gotten to know through shared interest in other Washington-related stories, including President Kennedy's assassination, Watergate and the seldom-reported intelligence connections of a number of prominent officials and their supporters.

Later, I would cover the Durham-led trials of his two major targets, cyberlaw attorney Michael Sussmann, whose clientele included Democratic organizations, and Igor Danchenko, a consultant who worked at various times for both former British spy Christopher Steele and for the FBI.

*The Durham Probe*

Barr's mandate to Durham, whom Trump had nominated in 2017 to become U.S. attorney for Connecticut following work as a federal prosecutor beginning in 1982, was to oversee a review of the Russia investigation's origins and to determine if the FBI's probe was "lawful and appropriate." That Durham mission overlapped with several other inquiries, including the just-ended Mueller probe that had found sufficient evidence for more than 30 indictments and an ongoing Senate Intelligence Committee probe that was in the process of documenting massive Russian interference.

Durham's mandate also overlapped with the Inspector General's work ending nearly a year previously and allowed its focus on FBI procedures to continue in parallel, it turns out, with a four-page memo that had been issued by House Intelligence Committee Chairman Devin Nunes, a Republican from California, describing claims from George Papadopoulos, an indicted former Trump foreign policy adviser who claimed that authorities were mistreating him and colleagues

Trump called Durham "Bull Durham," thereby touting Durham as an exceptionally determined and skilled prosecutor who would vindicate Trump from claims in the Steele Dossier and implicate Clinton and FBI personnel in crime.

Durham, a career prosecutor reared in southeastern Connecticut, had achieved among other things a reputation as extremely guarded in public statements outside of court. He made only one significant public lecture appearance aside from official duties, some Connecticut news reporters have said. This was at the University of St. Joseph in West Hartford in 2018. There he presented a slide show about his successful prosecution of corrupt FBI personnel in the Whitey Bulger case in Boston.

During most of the Durham investigation, few in the public knew how the investigation was proceeding aside from Durham's misdemeanor prosecution of a junior FBI lawyer Kevin Clinesmith, whom the Inspector General had identified in 2018 as exaggerating the basis for a surveillance warrant, albeit with a finding that Clinesmith had not done so for political reasons.

Most public attention for the Durham probe came from Trump and right-wing media, including the Murdoch-owned *Wall Street Journal*, *New York Post* and Fox News who hit different audiences with overlapping coverage of how Durham was uncovering a "Russiagate" scandal. *National Review* contributor Andrew McCarthy, a former federal prosecutor, also published many commentaries (some excerpted in this book's Bibliography) touting the importance of Durham's work.

Public confusion was inevitable when several probes overlapped and most research proceeded in secret. Any findings were hotly disputed on a partisan basis that recalled the original "puppet" insults during the Trump-Clinton 2016 debate.

Several propaganda techniques fostered confusion in ways too subtle to merit widely read news reports but proved very powerful in the long run.

For one thing, many conservatives started calling Durham's target "Russiagate," a term derived from the "Watergate" scandal that toppled President Nixon in 1974. The implication is that "Russiagate" is a phony claim of Russian interference designed by Democrats, the media and certain FBI personnel to recreate the ouster of a Republican President unfairly. But Trump critics who assert that solid evidence shows illegal Russian help for Trump also use the "Russiagate" term, creating a confusion for the public because of the two contradictory meanings.

Another major misdirection by Trump advocates was to sidestep the massive evidence of Russian intervention in the election and instead focus on flaws in the work of the strategic consultancy Global GPS and part of its work product, the so-called Steele Dossier citing unverifiable raw intelligence gathered by former British spy Christopher Steele via his consulting firm Orbis Business.

The conservative hedge fund tycoon Paul Singer originally hired the research consultancy Fusion GPS in 2015 as part of a "stop-Trump" effort within the Republican Party. Singer stopped his funding in early 2016 because of Trump's victories in GOP primaries.

Fusion GPS, co-founded by former *Wall Street Journal* reporters Glenn Simpson and Peter Fritsch, then marketed its services to the law firm Perkins Coie, which represented Democratic clients. Fusion GPS then hired as a consultant Christopher Steele, a former top Russian expert for the British spy agency MI6, who in turn drew on help from Igor Danchenko, a Russian-born consultant living in Virginia.

The Steele Dossier, a collection of separate bulletins totaling about 34 pages conveyed to Perkins Coie beginning in mid-2016, played no role in the FBI's launch of its "Crossfire Hurricane" probe of Russian interference in July 2016.

But that fact has never stopped either officials or pundits from magnifying its importance, particularly the unfairness of its inclusion of a supposed lewd anecdote – that Trump supposedly watched prostitutes urinating in a Moscow hotel room – that is likely untrue and largely irrelevant to any serious issue, especially since Trump was already well-known through the *Access Hollywood* tape in 2016 to having bragged about seizing women's genitals when possible and also to have had an affair with porn actress Stormy Daniels, etc., etc.

Fusion GPS and Steele argued in 2016 along with certain Perkins Coie staff that their raw findings might prove valuable to the FBI in a probe the agency had begun independently of Trump campaign ties to Russians. But it was highly disputed how much or even whether the Clinton campaign knew specifics of the lawyer Sussmann's and GPS outreach efforts.

And while Trump partisans correctly note that the Steele Dossier was subcontracted via the strategic consultancy Fusion GPS hired by the Clinton campaign the links between the raw research and the candidate's top staff would remain extremely hard to prove. Clinton Campaign Manager Robby Mook, for example, testified that he never heard of the dossier or its contents during the campaign or authorized payment for anything like it since the campaign paid a monthly retainer to its main law firm, Perkins Coie, whose billable expenses were typically so far over the retainer that Mook did not check the details.

Even more dramatically, the most partisan Republican critics of the FBI investigation would simplify all these factors into a description of a supposed "Clinton Plan" to unfairly tarnish Trump with claims of cooperation with Russian interference, validated improperly by the FBI. The concept had its roots in Trump's 2016 debate outburst "No Puppet!" and then in independent research by House Intelligence Committee Chairman Devin Nunes and finally in the Durham Report. Durham's report made 65 references to a "Clinton Plan" without a providing any substantial proof that such a plan existed, according to commentator Daniel Friedman writing on May 25 for *Mother Jones* and noting that Durham's source his repeated claim was "Russian intelligence," which had every motive to smear Clinton once again.

*Durham's Sussmann Trial*

In the spring of 2022, the Durham prosecution team brought to trial cyberlaw expert Michael Sussmann on a false statement charge stemming from Michael Sussmann's 2016 tip to FBI General Counsel James Baker, a former colleague of Sussmann's at the Justice Department, about suspected Russian help for Trump during that year's presidential campaign. A jury promptly acquitted Sussmann, who was no relation to the editor Barry Sussman.

The Durham team had hoped to tie Sussmann's actions to the Democratic Party and the Hillary for President campaign that used Sussmann's then-law firm Perkins Coie for political and cybersecurity work.

Sussmann's partner at Perkins Coie, Marc Elias, was a major outside counsel for both the Democratic National Committee (DNC) and the Hillary Clinton campaign. Sussmann, as a partner, thus represented both entities in a general sense, and more specifically in certain other respects, such as his experience as a former federal prosecutor with expertise in cybersecurity to work on behalf of his client, the Democratic National Committee to solve a hack of DNC comp [illegible] the ca[illegible] DNC al[illegible]ngly suspected during the summer of 2016 that Russian assets a[illegible] or a[illegible] operat[illegible] a role in the disclosures. A website called *DCLeaks* and an enti[illegible] ccifer [illegible] cutouts for Russian trolls, and activist site WikiLeaks were major [illegible] stole[illegible]

Durham's efforts to li[illegible] nton to [illegible] headlines during the trial in the pro-Trump media. The biggest [illegible] onally [illegible] the trial stemmed from a supposedly accidental revelation of par[illegible] rt men[illegible] ary C[illegible] public testimony, Durham's team asked former Clinton Campaign [illegible] e M[illegible] th[illegible] excerpt that mentioned Clinton, even though the trial judge out[illegible] aring [illegible] usly [illegible]secutors not to include the part about Clinton.

That led to the headli[illegible] ervat[illegible] sugge[illegible]al complicity by Clinton in nefarious deeds. That led next to a lit[illegible] licial r[illegible] ham [illegible]t at a sidebar out of the jury's hearing – but reported by the *Empty*[illegible] the e[illegible] cer[illegible] Marcy Wheeler, who had purchased transcripts to enable more [illegible] ting [illegible] by [illegible] journalists (such as me) who would not be able to hear sideb[illegible] being [illegible] in[illegible]vent jurors from hearing disallowed discussions.

Moreover, the conser[illegible] ailed to [illegible] took[illegible]ted in his testimony that the campaign paid Perkins Coie a flat m[illegible] for se[illegible] seem[illegible]th so much more than the number of hours billed that he had no[illegible] read de[illegible] bil[illegible] of other campaign obligations, much less to notify Clinton of the [illegible] e bil[illegible]

Mook testified also th[illegible] ton no[illegible]'s firm had hired Fusion GPS to draw on Steele's research. Neith[illegible] know, [illegible] that [illegible]as planning to provide the FBI with a tip about another matter in[illegible] a.

The Durham team's a[illegible] ness [illegible] the forbidden Clinton reference and similar trial disputes beca[illegible] ffect, [illegible] caus[illegible] promptly acquitted Sussmann, thereby dealing a major public rela[illegible] Durham [illegible] ation [illegible] supporters such as Trump and Barr.

*Danchenko's Acquittal: An[illegible] Deb[illegible]*

In the fall of 2022, Durha[illegible] ecution [illegible] brought [illegible]or Danchenko, the U.S.-based Russia expert who had helped St[illegible] FBI p[illegible] fiv[illegible] making false statements to the FBIs. Durham's supporters antic[illegible] chenk[illegible] con[illegible]ate Durham's team, especially after its embarrassing loss in May [illegible] r the [illegible] Suss[illegible] though Danchenko was even farther removed from the world o[illegible] paign [illegible] Su[illegible]

Durham's conservati[illegible] in the [illegible] ed [illegible]th previews of the Danchenko trial, which was to be held in the [illegible] suburb[illegible] VA.

U.S. District Judge A[illegible], a R[illegible] mine[illegible]nt George W. Bush, denied a defense motion to dismiss the indic[illegible] of evi[illegible] the [illegible]at his decision to permit the trial was a close call legally, a warn[illegible] concer[illegible]

The indictment's five [illegible] on w[illegible] henk[illegible] lied to the FBI when he stated he had never "talked" during his r[illegible] Democra[illegible] tant [illegible]uck" Dolan, Jr. After the prosecution rested its case the judge di[illegible] unt f[illegible] der[illegible]chenko had ever "talked" with Dolan since they communicated b[illegible] Durha[illegible] fail[illegible]wn the difference.

That left four counts [illegible] state[illegible] de[illegible] involving Sergei Millian, then head of the Russian-American C[illegible] Commer[illegible] ko sa[illegible]17 conversations with FBI personnel that in July 2016 he had c[illegible] by phon[illegible] th Mil[illegible]one else pretending to be Millian.

Prosecutors argued th[illegible] must [illegible] lying [illegible]four criminal counts. They said their search records for listed ph[illegible] the tw[illegible] not [illegible]ers for Danchenko, who did not take the witness stand, argued t[illegible] could [illegible] rec[illegible] Internet application not listed in the searched records. Pundit M[illegible] who r[illegible] dept[illegible]ham's probe on her *Emptywheel* blog, mocked him and his team [illegible] ng that [illegible] elling [illegible]al consultants often use mobile apps, often with security features, [illegible] taking [illegible] scuss[illegible]

The defense argued a[illegible] s "d[illegible] mining [illegible]'s research was shared with the FBI after the agency had alrea[illegible] s "C[illegible] alleged Russian ties based on other information not part of the trial. Also, Danchenko had told his FBI interviewers that he regarded some of the Steele dossier information as unreliable raw intelligence although he asserted responsibility for passing on most of it.

Durham's team failed to present as witnesses either Steele or Millian, both of whom were last known to live overseas.

Jurors witnessed the unusual spectacle of Durham jousting with two of his own witnesses, the two key FBI agents who had interviewed Danchenko. The prosecutor suggested that they unduly sympathized with the defendant, to whom the FBI had paid more than $200,000 as a consultant.

In a striking assertion, longtime FBI counterintelligence agent Kevin Helson said Danchenko's prosecution was "dangerous" and had hurt the nation's ability to gather intelligence because Danchenko was providing useful information about Russian activities.

Durham's dispute with FBI agents reassured some pro-Trump, anti-FBI commentators outside of court as confirming their suspicions of the agency.

But the display could hardly have helped the prosecution with the jury since neither Danchenko nor FBI agents were accused of conspiring with each other. More generally, the disputes illustrated how Durham's team had repeatedly threatened FBI witnesses and consultants with criminal prosecution in the Sussmann and Danchenko cases if they failed to shade the prosecution's theories sufficiently with their testimony.

The jury spent about nine hours deliberating (including meal breaks) before acquitting Danchenko on all four charges on Oct. 18, 2022.

With the expiration of a Virginia grand jury, the tally for the then-3.5-year Durham investigation was grim: Acquittals for the two major defendants, Sussmann and Danchenko, and a plea bargain with a sentence of probation for the only other defendant, former FBI lawyer Kevin Clinesmith, whom Inspector General Michael Horowitz had exposed in 2018.

The *Washington Post* editorial board opined that Durham-Barr track record showed that they pursued a partisan, pro-Trump agenda. Pro-Trump media differed, saying the verdicts showed that Trump cannot obtain justice and that the public's best hope was the prosecutor's written report. Thus: "The special counsel's looming report is the only chance the American people will ever get to hold the Clinton campaign and the FBI accountable for Russiagate," former prosecutor Andrew C. McCarthy wrote in the *National Review* after Durham lost the Danchenko verdict. That was the prompt acquittal of former FBI consultant Igor Danchenko.

Terms of the special counsel appointment by Barr specified that Durham should prepare a report on his investigation for submission to the U.S. Attorney General. That office is now held by Merrick Garland, a Democrat nominated by President Biden. Republicans in Congress and former President Donald Trump have already begun to tout its release in May 2023 and whatever statements Durham can further generate for a massive display of hearings and media appearances claiming vindication for their views.

The acquittals capped one stage of a sad, shocking tale, and one that justifies a description of Durham's work – and the applause of his backers -- as both fraudulent and cruel.

Missing from mainstream newspaper, broadcast, cable and academic analysis, however, is that Durham's prosecution track record includes rulings by at least four federal judges throwing out convictions in which he played a key prosecution role. Largely missing also is reporting on disturbing pressure tactics against FBI agents and other witnesses to create pro-prosecution testimony to vindicate Durham's theories.

Aside from those shortfalls in Durham's performance, the prosecutor enjoyed a reputation in Connecticut and elsewhere as a capable career professional who inexplicably ruined his reputation.

*Newsweek* published the headline, "Durham Blasted by Experts After New Acquittal: 'Laughed Out of Court Twice'" by Aila Slisco, who reported mockery of Dunham elsewhere in the legal community for not fulfilling Trump's prediction that the prosecutor would prove "the crime of the century" in a massive conspiracy.

Other comments:

Laurence Tribe, professor emeritus of constitutional law at Harvard University, told *Newsweek* that the acquittal was evidence Durham's "groundless mission has now failed yet again, putting yet another dismal marker on William Barr's shameful record as Trumps henchman and the worst Attorney General in our nation's history."

"John Durham racks up another acquittal, this time on a case he tried personally," legal analyst and former federal prosecutor Elie Honig tweeted. "His investigation will go down as a shameful abuse of prosecutorial power in service of political vengeance. Juries -- our most basic civilian bulwark -- have firmly rebuked this abuse of power."

Claims of liberal bias by the FBI are undercut by the history: Neither the FBI nor its predecessor have ever been led by a Democrat during the entire near-century of their existence. The FBI's overwhelming institutional ethos tilts right, as is commonly the case with law enforcement bodies.

As for the those acquitted or otherwise investigated at great fanfare? Few express any concern about those like Sussmann, Danchenko, the accused FBI personnel and their family hardships. Defendants and many witnesses often lose their jobs and must spend vast amounts on defense lawyers, with seldom any accountability for prosecutors. That's all part of what we accept as the "justice" process.

Regarding battles to come? Pro-Trump pundit McCarthy is looking forward to new fights and disclosures. "The report has always been John Durham's primary job," he wrote for the *National Review*. "There was never a realistic chance that he could make a comprehensive Russiagate record in a major prosecution. "He took a calculated risk by bringing comparatively trivial cases against minor players, before what were sure to be hostile jury pools," McCarthy continued, illustrating the notion in some circles that suspects must be guilty even if proof is lacking. Of Durham, McCarthy wrote, "He has gotten the predictable results: acquittals across the board."

A different view came from former federal prosecutor Dennis Aftergut, later counsel to the group Lawyers Defending American Democracy. He targeted Barr and Durham more personally in a column for NBC News: "Barr's attempts to rehabilitate his image cannot erase his sad final legacy as a Trump enabler," Aftergut wrote. "Special counsel John Durham, who once enjoyed a solid reputation as a prosecutor, now owns what may be the worst trial record of any special counsel or independent prosecutor in American history ..."

*Time For Blunt Talk*

In previewing events and players described at greater length in the following pages, we have so far kept within the bounds of official reports and mainstream commentary. But that fails to convey all the relevant information and informed speculation, particularly when the topics involve spies, scandals, election dirty tricks funded by oligarchs and other billionaires — and the formidable rivalries of major nations, which have track records of spying, regime-change and assassination.

As a guide to this world, this reporter would be remiss in not sharing certain background that may prove instructive in assessing motivations and goals of officials, particularly when they conduct much of their activity in secret or in well-orchestrated public displays knowing that they are highly unlikely ever to have answer unwelcome questions in a meaningful way.

Durham's responses to Democratic questions during his June 21 hearing illustrated the point. He repeatedly declined to answer questions on the grounds that they were "beyond the scope" of his report. Regarding the question of why his longtime colleague Nora Dannehy resigned from his investigative team shortly before the 2016 election, he responded that it was a "personnel matter" he would not discuss — even when questioners repeatedly cited seeking confirmation of a *New York Times* report that she resigned in protest over a purported plan by Durham to make news about his investigation just before the 2020 presidential election.

This reporter has twice unsuccessfully requested comment from Durham, both after the June 21 hearing and previously during Sussmann trial coverage. The offer still stands, of course. But it is impractical to stop reporting simply because the subject declines to comment.

So let's dig deeper, starting with Durham's boss and enabler, then-Attorney General Barr. Our reporting so far has focused solely on their legal posts and law-related actions, including what Weissmann had called Barr's "gut-wrenching" deception of the public.

The conventional path in news commentary is to suggest that such differences in opinion might stem from political partisanship. That seems true up to a point. But there are likely additional factors suggested by an in-depth look at Barr's background.

Barr's late father, Donald Barr, had been an Office of Strategic Services (OSS) officer during World War II and it has been reported that William Barr aspired to become CIA director while still in high school.

Donald Barr's eclectic and impressive career included the position of headmaster during the early 1970s at the Dalton School, an elite private school in Manhattan. On Jan. 1, 1973, Donald Barr published *Space Relations*, a futuristic science fiction novel portraying elites maintaining child sex slaves in Outer Space. That is a curious theme, to say the least. Curious also is that future high-rolling financier and notorious sex trafficker Jeffrey Epstein would be hired by the Dalton School to teach beginning in the fall of 1974. Donald Barr retired earlier in 1974 and died in 2004. It remains publicly unknown whether he played a role in hiring Epstein, who was 21 and with no college degree when hired.

In the absence of solid information, most reporters understandably skip such matters entirely. An exception has been investigative reporter Wayne Madsen, a former Navy intelligence officer whose experiences included helping investigate the notorious spy Jonathan Pollard. Madsen, once a frequent national security commentator on major television and cable networks and many international ones, has sometimes described in his commentaries complex situations in the words of Ian Fleming, who had been a high-ranking British Navy intelligence officer during World War II before authoring the James Bond books. One of Fleming's spy-world sayings, voiced by Bond in *Goldfinger,* was, "Once is happenstance. Twice is coincidence. Three times is enemy action."

For the younger Barr, a devout Roman Catholic after his father converted from Judaism to Catholicism, the worlds of spies and intrigue held enduring allure. He worked for the CIA for seven years after graduating with a master's degree from Columbia University with expertise in China. Madsen has reported (and another independent, Republican source has confirmed to this reporter) that Barr's career was advanced by assisting then U.S. Envoy to China George H.W. Bush, a future CIA director, out of an embarrassing lewd scandal arising from a public display during Bush's year as envoy in China.

Barr enrolled in law school while continuing to work at the CIA, thus embarking on the legal path for which he is best known to the public. But it takes only a superficial review of the public record to determine that one of his major functions during his government posts during the 1980s was helping the Reagan-Bush administrations suppress embarrassing information, particularly regarding the Iran-Contra arms-narcotics scandal being investigated by Independent Counsel Lawrence Walsh. Walsh's memoir *Firewall* makes clear Barr's role as Bush Attorney General in recommending pardons for major defendants, who included former Secretary of Defense Casper Weinberger. Therefore, Barr's similar role regarding the Mueller Report should be no surprise even if it is rarely reported. Curious also, but seldom reported, is Barr's coincidental visit to New York City's Metropolitan Correction Center shortly before Epstein died there, taking his secrets with him.

More generally, the Durham Report to follow describes, often in an incomplete manner, many professionals in the world of espionage, intelligence, law enforcement and consultancy. We attempt to supplement the Special Counsel's report with an appended "Roster of Key Individuals" derived from mainstream sources, not original reporting. Those names include high-level FBI and CIA personnel such as Robert Hanssen convicted of spying for Russians. These spies are not featured in the Durham Report but are included to illustrate that inexplicable perfidy can occur in respected institutions when the stakes are high enough.

Sex scandal is a topic that deserves to be addressed in blunt terms, particularly after the pearl-grabbing antics of Republicans in voicing horror over the unverified "Pee-tape" reference in the Steele Dossier. One Republican congressman at the June 21 hearing made a great show of warning the video audience to protect children from hearing what he was about to say about the vile subject matter, which he went on to describe in vivid terms. "Parents, if you're watching: Ear muffs for your kids!" said Rep. Troy Nehls of Texas, before launching into a description of a supposed "pee tape" of prostitutes mentioned in the Steele Dossier and, separately, what Nehls asserted (without evidence) was an "affair" by a Democratic colleague with "a Chinese spy."

Let's get real.

Nehls, in an all-too-common posture, was trumping outrage for rhetorical and partisan purposes with no indication of interest uncovering wrongdoing wherever it might occur.

Actual sex scandal is commonplace in espionage undertaken by all countries. It is pervasive also in the U.S. House of Representatives among other locales in the nation's Capital, as elsewhere around the United States and the world. And while such scandals usually involve a powerful older man exploiting subordinates, more detailed reporting shows a wide variety of situations, including ambitious youths of both sexes advancing their careers and other finances by working with patrons to entrap the powerful, ideally with hidden video footage. The Justice Integrity Project publishes a near-daily update of #MeToo scandals, sex-related blackmail efforts and related topics, including those on abortion policies.

Scandal?

That's why Craig Unger named his important book about the KGB and Trump *American Kompromat*.

That's why convicted Russian spy Maria Butina was traipsing around the United States during the 2016 campaign cycle flirting, shall we say, with Republican money-men, attending gun shows and voicing gun rights rhetoric as if Russia would welcome private gun rights there, where she now serves post-imprisonment in its Duma.

That's why over 200 former Ohio State University wrestlers have persisted in winning a U.S. Supreme Court decision on June 26, 2023, which permitted their sexual abuse lawsuit to move forward against the university based on the conduct of the late Dr. Richard Strauss. Several of the litigants have said House Judiciary Committee Chairman Jim Jordan (shown in an official photo), a wrestling coach at Ohio State during relevant years, knew of the abuses and did nothing to stop it.

And that's why the a[illegible] Way[illegible] wr[illegible]rt series in 2006 reporting that U.S. House Speaker Dennis Has[illegible] an sex[illegible] und[illegible] when he was a high school wrestling coach and that he continu[illegible] ble [illegible] ngto[illegible] ng to foster a culture whereby House colleagues so motivated co[illegible] ouse [illegible] Ma[illegible] helped sustain an eco-system that is useful to DC insiders who k[illegible] shar[illegible] the[illegible] sible to others, the better — generate powerful political loyalties.

The facts were not re[illegible] re b[illegible] clu[illegible] rps until Hastert's federal arrest and imprisonment years later f[illegible] -up [illegible] alistic risk to write the story because the nation's third-highest [illegible] a had [illegible] a "family values" Republican from Illinois trying to make it s[illegible] ne c[illegible] Flo[illegible] an Mark Foley, had been improperly grooming pages when a sc[illegible] pro[illegible] ng [illegible].

As a result of all this, [illegible] ge pro[illegible] ns de[illegible] one can be confident that the reasons for its demise and for self-r[illegible] oating [illegible] ality [illegible] ent in the nation's Capital, as so often in its history.

*What's Next?*

Trump supporters such as [illegible] y Ch[illegible] that Durham could use his report and hearing appearance to reliti[illegible] s tha[illegible] Pla[illegible] false "Russiagate" scandal whereby by Trump and Russia were [illegible] sed of [illegible] ot[illegible] activities regarding the 2016 election and beyond.

Not one of the Republi[illegible] mem[illegible] led [illegible] any significant dangers to the United States from the Russian ac[illegible] even [illegible] 's [illegible] still raging and just months after the arrest on money laundering [illegible] arge[illegible] McG[illegible] rmer head of counterintelligence in the FBI New York City field [illegible] charg[illegible] spi[illegible] defendant Sergey Shestakov, a former Soviet and Russian diplom[illegible] S. citiz[illegible] le s[illegible] sian oligarch Oleg Deripaska in 2021, in violation of U.S. sanctio[illegible] n Deri[illegible] 8.

Durham himself repe[illegible] ed his [illegible] ait[illegible] ing his probe and his support for his conclusions. Yet analyst M[illegible] noted [illegible] m[illegible] back some of his more inflammatory claims in his report, perhap[illegible] a priva[illegible] J[illegible] t have been so well protected against a defamation suit as he w[illegible] rment [illegible] ssui[illegible] in May. And she skewered him for focusing so much attention [illegible] his o[illegible] pros[illegible] n the relatively low-level FBI lawyer Kevin Clinesmith while ne[illegible] ng in [illegible] mach[illegible] Deripaska, one of the world's richest men and one whose hidden [illegible] acc[illegible] behi[illegible] ost sinister activities of former Trump Campaign Manager Paul M[illegible] Manaf[illegible] Kor[illegible] ik, an accused spy for Russia, as well as the accused FBI agent M[illegible]

The House Judiciary C[illegible] ne 2[illegible] ari[illegible] e a debacle for Republicans and their agenda, even with Repub[illegible] lling [illegible] ist [illegible] rpretation, and numbering six more committee members (with [illegible] ing [illegible] emo[illegible]

Democrats forced sev[illegible] ns fro[illegible] ion that his investigation incurred no interference whatsoever f[illegible] Gen[illegible] G[illegible] her Biden appointees at the Justice Department. Also, Durham [illegible] gges[illegible] was [illegible] with findings of Russian interference contained in the Mueller R[illegible] eated [illegible] ould [illegible] pointed questions about his methods because the questions pert[illegible] s he [illegible] ts[illegible]" of his report and his willingness to respond.

He invoked that excus[illegible] or ex[illegible] whether his longtime colleague Nora Dannehy had resigned in [illegible] rted b[illegible] *York* [illegible] nuary, over his intention to issue an interim report shortly befo[illegible] esiden[illegible] ndard Justice Department procedures forbidding actions that mi[illegible] nent [illegible] nec[illegible]

Likely to be especiall[illegible] g for D[illegible] back[illegible] harsh final rebukes of his conduct by Republican Judiciary Com[illegible] s Ma[illegible] Flori[illegible] t Hageman of Wyoming.

All in all, the question[illegible] spar[illegible] sa[illegible] forget even though he boasted at the end to congressional critic[illegible] friend[illegible] mily [illegible] his work — and only that matters to him. So much for accounta[illegible]

*Horrid Revelations, Threats*

Financial, sex, blackmail and cover-up scandals are bad enough. But they have existed in world capitals, as elsewhere, throughout recorded history. The latter part of this research into the Durham investigation, however, revealed how its deliberate omissions of national security threats against the United States and its allies helped empower unaccountable enemies of Western democracies whose sinister activities threaten our societies in ongoing, unpredictable ways.

Most obviously, the Russian interference in the 2016 U.S. presidential election helping Trump documented by Special Counsel Robert Mueller, among others, surely helped embolden Russia's leadership to pursue other such election interference using similar methods in other nations, including Great Britain and France, then invade Ukraine in 2022 with the view that NATO nations were too weak and divided to stand up against Russia. The grievous suffering and death from that invasion and war is still ongoing as of this writing. Aside from dead, wounded and displaced on each side, the toll of suffering includes Russia's mass kidnapping of Ukrainian children in forced culture-destruction reeducation programs (prompting charges against Putin by the International Criminal Court). Suffering includes also Russian blockades of Ukrainian grain exports globally, thereby use starvation of Third World populations as a quasi-military weapon to try to build global pressure against Ukraine and the West.

Notable also are Russia's threats, veiled and direct, that if Ukraine continues to resist Russia nuclear fallout might devastate Ukraine, either through a potential "accident" to Europe's largest reactor (now located under Russian control near the war's front line) or via Russian tactical weapons used against Ukraine. The seriousness of such threats can be assessed in part via Russia's track record, it is credibly alleged, of continued bombing of civilian targets in Ukraine and blowing up Ukraine's major dam to lessen the risk of further Ukrainian ground gains in Kherson region.

Alarming also is the renewed activity of Russia's Wagner Group mercenary army in supporting the anti-West, pro-Russia coup in Niger to overthrow an elected government that occurred in July 2023 following a pattern of similar Wagner-supported coups in a belt stretching across sub-Saharan Africa.

Add to those global security threats American public opinion polling. It shows that a third of the American public professes to believe pro-Trump lies and deceptions fostered in part by the Durham Report that Democrats and Hillary Clinton used a supposed plan to falsely blame Russians and Trump for any 2016 election interference. That hardly bodes well for the future of American elections and democracy, particularly since wealthy and otherwise powerful institutions foster such attacks in both Western nations and Russia during an era when Artificial Intelligence increasingly enables creation of fake photos, videos, voice recordings and other "evidence" supporting almost any theme that election disrupters might want to prove to a befuddled and otherwise hapless public.

Proving such themes beyond doubt is obviously impossible here. The bulk of this book consists of Durham's own arguments and evidence, provided in full.

What is vital about this book, however, is not so much his deflections, exaggerations and biased analysis but the contrary evidence here in appendices citing books, official reports and news reports up to March 2024. Durham's omission of these well-researched threats is not the end of the story.

The Durham Report, far from being a one-of-a-kind disgrace, remains an important case study of similarly politicized recent Special Counsel probes whose perpetrators ascend to greater power facilitated by their backers and unwitting cheerleaders. This kind of scandal extends into the future as of this writing with the new Special Counsel probe of Hunter Biden, President Joe Biden's son, among other developments.

To recap this larger pattern, Durham and his longtime Connecticut colleague Dannehy were each named as a Special Counsel by the Bush Administration in 2008 to investigate, respectively, CIA destruction of waterboarding evidence and the 2006 U.S. attorney firing scandal. Each official provided career-enhancing reports that found no grounds for anyone to be prosecuted. Critics aptly described the Durham and Danney reports as whitewashes.

On Sept. 1, 2023, Connecticut Gov. Ned Lamont, a Democrat, nominated Dannehy to the Connecticut Supreme Court, with no apparent political or media pushback on her Bush-era appointment and the underlying scandals.

Yet the harms from the unresolved abuses remain readily apparent. Evidence includes memoirs by former Alabama Gov. Don Siegelman (*Stealing Our Democracy*, 2020), his co-defendant businessman Richard Scrushy (*It Should Not Happen In America*, 2021) and Trump-nominated New York Southern District U.S. Attorney Geoffrey Berman (*Holding the Line*, 2022). Beman documents immense pressure by the Trump Justice

Department for him to make politically motivated prosecution decisions, including those involving Trump advisor Rudoph Giuliani and his Ukraine-related allegations against former Vice President Joe Biden and his son, Hunter Biden.

Durham's Report gave scant attention to scandals that benefited Trump, as readers will see in the pages that follow, even though the Giuliani-Biden-Ukraine controversies had by then resulted in Trump's first impeachment. That was for his refusal to supply Ukraine with congressionally authorized weapons to defend itself against Russia unless Ukraine cooperated in launching a pre-election investigation of the Bidens that Ukraine's president, Volodymyr Zelensky, insisted was not justified.

Instead of a Ukraine-initiated investigation that could be used by the Trump Campaign to help its 2020 reelection effort, the Trump Campaign and its allies floated via cooperative media allegations and political fixers claims of criminal conduct by the Bidens, with sensational material derived from a purported Hunter Biden "laptop." Material supposedly derived accurately from a laptop's hard drive was reportedly delivered from a computer repair shop to Giuliani's network, including Russian and Ukrainian allies, and then publicized well into 2023 as part of alleged criminal activity by the Bidens. To investigate, the Biden administration kept in office the Trump-appointed U.S. Attorney for Delaware David Weiss, who then successfully obtained status as a Special Counsel to enhance his prosecution powers in related matters. These matters resulted in federal gun possession and income tax charges against Hunter Biden. House Republicans were seeking impeachment of President Joe Biden on related charges unspecified as of this publication date.

Meanwhile, independent national security analyst Marcy Wheeler, who earned a relevant doctorate at the University of Michigan, has taken the lead in extensive commentaries on her Emptywheel blog in showing that materials ascribed to the so-called "laptop" may have been derived in part from hacked materials and then disseminated in gross violation of privacy laws. She has suggested that the materials were enhanced by fabricated material supplied by Russian experts to foster impeachment advocacy and otherwise smear President Biden and his 2024 re-election campaign via the Special Counsel process.

In a related filing on Sept. 13, 2023, Biden's attorney Lowell filed a federal lawsuit naming as defendant former Trump Administration appointee Garrett Ziegler as a defendant in such privacy-related violations along with 10 others, not identified. Ziegler formerly worked for White House Assistant to the President Peter Navarro, the Director of the Office of Trade and Manufacturing Policy. Politico reporter Betsy Woodruff Swan then collected these materials and others from Biden's legal team in an important column, "Hunter Biden's lawyer accuses House Republicans of 'congressional manipulation,'" excerpted in our Appendix chronology in this book following the Durham Report.

That Appendix includes also a sample of Wheeler's hard-hitting reporting asserting that some of the so-called "laptop" materials include obvious privacy violations.

Any such Russian-assisted hacking and smear tactics against Democrats are clearly intended to affect the 2024 U.S. presidential election. The smear efforts have been fostered with scant apparent concern under the Trump holdover Special Counsel Weiss and his team. They are eerily reminiscent of how Durham's focus during his four-year probe was to target Democrats and FBI investigators after Russians had hacked Democratic National Committee and Hillary Clinton Campaign Chairman John Podesta's electronic devices during the 2016 campaign.

*Shocking 2024 Revelations*

This book's official launch was delayed several times into 2024 to enable inclusion of deeply disturbing revelations illustrating how the Durham probe's partisan abuses and slipshod methods found parallels in two other probes by Special Counsels originally appointed during the Trump Administration and held over by the Biden Justice Department.

Most shocking was the federal indictment on perjury and fraud charges of longtime FBI informant Alexander Smirnov, the chief witness in long-running smears by Congressional Republicans and Justice Department investigators into Smirnov's claims that Hunter Biden and President Biden had each received five million dollar bribes from the Ukraine energy company Burisma Holdings. The 2024 federal indictment accused Smirnov of falsifying the claim and also working with Russian intelligence in a plot to concoct the allegations. Special Counsel David Weiss protected his credibility by announcing the charges in February 2024. Yet his actions came only after an aggressive defense by Hunter Biden was revealing massive flaws in the prosecution's case and the parallel impeachment efforts by House Republicans. The flaws, which might more aptly be described as scandals given the government's obligation to disclose evidence to defendants, included evidence that at least some federal investigators for years had doubted Smirnoff's credibility while he attempted to change world history by his claims against the Bidens.

A similar pro-Trump partisan approach came from another Republican-appointed Special Counsel, Robert Hur, a former Maryland U.S. Attorney nominated by Trump, when Hur issued a report in early 2024 on whether the elder Biden should be criminally charged with illegal possession of government documents following the end of his vice-presidency in 2017. Hur's report found no grounds for prosecution but went far beyond normal Justice Department practices by portraying Biden as elderly and confused. That portrayal precisely matched Republican campaign rhetoric attacking the president as too old for reelection but violated Justice Department standard operating procedures that generally forbid derogatory comments against those not indicted.

Although a book can never keep up with daily headlines there is value in illustrating by these new developments that our Durham case study is part of an important, continuing pattern. As indicated by this book's appendix, U.S. House Republicans showcased Hur's report and slurs against the president in a congressional hearing on March 12, 2024, much as they did with Durham's report in 2023.

The lesson? Partisan prosecutors and their enablers do not believe it necessary to win convictions or even bring charges to weaponize the Justice Department against desired targets when the stakes are high, as in a presidential election.

That lesson's importance became stunningly clear in a Feb. 26 report by *Politico*, headlined, "The prospect of a second Trump presidency has the intelligence community on edge," based on interviews with 18 former officials and analysist who had worked in the Trump administration, "some of who still speak to the former president and his aides and had insight into conversations about his potential second term."

The gist? "Former top officials from Donald Trump's administration are warning," according to the report, "he is likely to use a second term to overhaul the nation's spy agencies in a way that could lead to an unprecedented level of politicization of intelligence." That warning is echoed by similar reporting about plans to politicize much of the rest of the federal civil service created in the 1880s, including the Justice Department, to enhance presidential power to control events and spending.

Especially frightening is new reporting of how Russian operatives have expanded their efforts, visible as early as 2016, to create fake "news" organizations in major U.S. cities just in time for the 2024 elections, as reported by the *New York Times* in "Mock News Sites With Russian Ties Pop Up in U.S." Disinformation expert Steven Lee Myers wrote, "Into the depleted field of journalism in America, a handful of websites have appeared in recent weeks with names suggesting a focus on news close to home: *D.C. Weekly*, the *New York News Daily*, the *Chicago Chronicle* and a newer sister publication, the *Miami Chronicle*. In fact, they are not local news organizations at all. They are Russian creations, researchers and government officials say, meant to mimic actual news organizations to push Kremlin propaganda by interspersing it among an at-times odd mix of stories about crime, politics and culture."

Similarly ominous, investigative reporter and author Seth Abramson documented on his *Proof* site how a powerful Russian-linked banking and insurance family appeared poised to bankroll the presumed Republican presidential nominee Donald Trump's major legal costs, creating what Abramson called a "national security crisis" whose implications were being overlooked by major mainstream media.

His investigative commentary "Politics Experts Said for Weeks That Trump Might Get Bonded By Kremlin Allies. Now It's Happening—Causing a National Security Crisis," excerpted in this book's bibliography, is subtitled "So Why Is Media So Silent About the Greenberg Family? Former Russian bank co-owner Maurice "Hank" Greenberg is the father and former boss of new Trump financial patron Evan Greenberg, whose Chubb Limited now hopes to back the nearly bankrupt criminal defendant to the tune of over $91 million dollars."

Before ending this Preface, [illegible] reporter [illegible] ry, readers can see how this reporter's initial suspicion in 2010 tha[illegible] fall[illegible] g prosecutor's *persona* led to a book rooted in traditional, albeit [illegible] ed, sta[illegible] orting.

Regarding journalism, [illegible] s appa[illegible] d have occurred if the nation still had a healthy eco-system of ne[illegible] partic[illegible] evels where system aberrations could be reported at an early stag[illegible] ften [illegible] uded 14 years as a *Hartford Courant* reporter.

This is not just a probl[illegible] ists b[illegible] nembers of the public when decisions, whether in court or politics, [illegible] mir[illegible] y answers to problems in journalism. But any improvements mu[illegible] ublic [illegible] ing.

Another of my concer[illegible] ng [illegible] many Americans may be playing by two sets of rules regarding [illegible] s em.

For most citizens bus[illegible] ncern[illegible] an abstraction whereby courts, trials, hearings seem at least inte[illegible] for jus[illegible] d other such democratic goals, even if they often fall short in pra[illegible] ass, [illegible] ne every day across the country with that comforting ideal.

Yet there may be ano[illegible] ith dif[illegible] y minority but a powerful one: In this the justice system, big cas[illegible] d for [illegible] nts in a controlled setting, regardless of the merit of claims, with [illegible] ng al[illegible] power and augment their power. This method of justice is best kn[illegible] n's [illegible] in the Soviet Union. That system still exists there, at least to som[illegible] lustra[illegible] dissidents and kidnapped Americans subjected to kangaroo cour[illegible] d lon[illegible] m is admired and copied also in other sections of the world, and [illegible] nd No[illegible] autocrats and would-be autocrats.

Here are questions fo[illegible] Do w[illegible] ited States? If not, what are we going to do about it?

[illegible] DC

***"It's clear that Tru[illegible] hole [illegible] in the Justice Department."***

— MSNBC "Deadlin[illegible] e" Ho[illegible] 024, responding to California U.S. Senator-elect Ada[illegible] nocr[illegible] President-elect Donald Trump's next attorney general [illegible] r gran[illegible] states and the District of Columbia to indict Trump afte[illegible] able c[illegible] ad engaged in multiple serious crimes.

**United States Department of Justice**

*Office of Special Counsel*
*John H. Durham*

*Department of Justice, 2CON*
*145 N Street, NE*
*Washington, D.C. 20002*

May 12, 2023

TO: ATTORNEY GENERAL MERRICK B. GARLAND

FROM: JOHN H. DURHAM
SPECIAL COUNSEL

SUBJECT: REPORT ON MATTERS RELATED TO INTELLIGENCE ACTIVITIES AND INVESTIGATIONS ARISING OUT OF THE 2016 PRESIDENTIAL CAMPAIGNS

The attached report is submitted to the Attorney General pursuant to 28 C.F.R. § 600.8(c), which states that, "[a]t the conclusion of the Special Counsel's work, he . . . shall provide the Attorney General a confidential report explaining the prosecution or declination decisions reached by the Special Counsel." In addition to the confidential report required by section 600.8(c), the Attorney General has directed that the Special Counsel, "to the maximum extent possible and consistent with the law and the policies and practices of the Department of Justice, shall submit to the Attorney General a final report . . . in a form that will permit public dissemination."[1] This two-part report (Unclassified Report and Classified Appendix) is presented in fulfillment of these requirements and sets forth our principal findings and recommendations concerning the matters that were the subject of our review. The principal report is confidential, but contains no classified information based on thorough, coordinated reviews of the information contained therein by the appropriate authorities within the Federal Bureau of Investigation, the Central Intelligence Agency, and the National Security Agency. The Classified Appendix likewise has been coordinated with those same agencies for classification purposes.

We note that the Classified Appendix contains some information that is derived from Foreign Intelligence Surveillance Act ("FISA") authorities. Accordingly, to the extent the Department determines that it is appropriate to share information contained in the Classified Appendix with congressional or other government entities outside of the Department, steps will need to be taken in accordance with that Act and any relevant Orders that have been issued by the Foreign Intelligence Surveillance Court.

---

[1] Office of the Att'y Gen., Order No. 4878-2020, Appointment of Special Counsel to Investigate Matters Related to Intelligence Activities and Investigations Arising Out of the 2016 Presidential Campaigns ¶ (f) (Oct. 19, 2020).

Finally, we want to thank you and your Office for permitting our inquiry to proceed independently and without interference as you assured the members of the Senate Judiciary Committee would be the case during your confirmation hearings to become Attorney General of the United States.

# Report on Matters Related to Intelligence Activities and Investigations Arising Out of the 2016 Presidential Campaigns

Special Counsel John H. Durham

*Submitted Pursuant to 28 C.F.R. § 600.8(c)*

Washington, D.C.

May 12, 2023

[illegible] Con[illegible]

## INTRODUCTION

This report is submitted to the Attorney General pursuant to 28 C.F.R. § 600.8(c), which states that, "[a]t the conclusion of the Special Counsel's work, he . . . shall provide the Attorney General a confidential report explaining the prosecution or declination decisions reached by the Special Counsel." In addition to the confidential report required by section 600.8(c), the Attorney General has directed that the Special Counsel, "to the maximum extent possible and consistent with the law and the policies and practices of the Department of Justice, shall submit to the Attorney General a final report, and such interim reports as he deems appropriate, in a form that will permit public dissemination."[1] This report is in fulfillment of these requirements and sets forth our principal findings and recommendations concerning the matters that were the subject of our review. Section I briefly describes the scope of our investigation, and Section II is an Executive Summary of this report. Section III describes the laws and Department and Federal Bureau of Investigation ("FBI") policies that applied to, or were addressed in, our investigation. Section IV summarizes the facts and evidence that we found and describes our prosecution and declination decisions. In Section V, we provide some observations on issues pertinent to our areas of inquiry.

## I. THE SPECIAL COUNSEL'S INVESTIGATION

In March 2019, Special Counsel Robert S. Mueller, III concluded his investigation into the Russian government's efforts to interfere in the 2016 presidential election, "including any links or coordination between the Russian government and individuals associated with the Trump Campaign." That investigation "did not establish that members of the Trump Campaign conspired or coordinated with the Russian government in its election interference activities."[2] Following Special Counsel Mueller's report, on May 13, 2019, Attorney General Barr "directed United States Attorney John Durham to conduct a preliminary review into certain matters related to the 2016 presidential election campaigns," and that review "subsequently developed into a criminal investigation."[3] On February 6, 2020, the Attorney General appointed Mr. Durham "as Special Attorney to the Attorney General pursuant to 28 U.S.C. § 515."[4] On October 19, 2020, the Attorney General determined that, "in light of the extraordinary circumstances relating to these matters, the public interest warrants Mr. Durham continuing this investigation pursuant to the powers and independence afforded by the Special Counsel regulations." Relying on "the authority vested" in the Attorney General, "including 28 U.S.C. §§ 509, 510, and 515," the

---

[1] Office of the Att'y Gen., Order No. 4878-2020, Appointment of Special Counsel to Investigate Matters Related to Intelligence Activities and Investigations Arising Out of the 2016 Presidential Campaigns ¶ (f) (Oct. 19, 2020) (hereinafter "Appointment Order").

[2] 1 Robert Mueller, *Report on the Investigation into Russian Interference in the 2016 Presidential Election* 1-2 (2019) (hereinafter "*Mueller Report*"); *see also id.* at 173.

[3] *Appointment Order* (introduction). When Mr. Durham was asked to lead the review, he was serving as the United States Attorney for the District of Connecticut. Before May 2019, Mr. Durham had been asked by Attorneys General of both major political parties, namely Janet Reno, Judge Michael Mukasey, Eric Holder, and Senator Jeff Sessions, to conduct other sensitive investigations for the Department.

[4] Letter from the Attorney General to United States Attorney John Durham (Feb. 6, 2020).

Attorney Gene[illegible] the appo[illegible] he Sp[illegible]sel "in order to discharge the [Attorney Gene[illegible] bility [illegible] supe[illegible] management of the Department of Justice, and to [illegible] and th[illegible] stigati[illegible] matters."[5] The Order stated:

> The Spe[illegible] is auth[illegible] investi[illegible] er any federal official, employe[illegible] er per[illegible] violat[illegible] in connection with the intellige[illegible] -intelli[illegible] w-en[illegible] ctivities directed at the 2016 pr[illegible] rpaigns, [illegible] ls as[illegible] th those campaigns, and individu[illegible] with [illegible] stratio[illegible] ent Donald J. Trump, includin[illegible] ed to [illegible] furth[illegible] investigation of Special Counse[illegible] Mueller.[illegible]

"If the Special C[illegible] es it [illegible] ar[illegible]" the Order further provided, "the Special Counse[illegible] to pro[illegible] eral [illegible] ng from his investigation of these matters." The [illegible] ovide[illegible] F.R.[illegible] 600.10 are applicable to the Special Counse[illegible]

[5] *Appointment* [illegible] ction [illegible]

[6] *Appointment* [illegible]

[7] *Id.* ¶¶ (c)-(d). [illegible] t interpr[illegible] rder [illegible] us to investigate the Department's handling of ma[illegible] ed wit[illegible] igatio[illegible] Secretary of State Hillary Clinton's use o[illegible] nail se[illegible] revie[illegible] matters, *see* Office of the Inspector General, U.S. D[illegible] f Justic[illegible] *ons by the Federal Bureau of Investigation a*[illegible] *nt of J*[illegible] *6 Election* (June 2018). We also have not interp[illegible] er as [illegible] to c[illegible] andling of the investigation into President Trum[illegible] the FBI [illegible] 6, 20[illegible] EC from Counterintelligence, *Re: [Redacted]* [illegible] *nts Re*[illegible] *ct –* [illegible] *sitive Investigative Matter* (May 16, 2017). (Th[illegible] y, the [illegible] torne[illegible] ppointed Special Counsel Mueller "to investigate [illegible] feren[illegible] 2016 [illegible] election and related matters." *See* 1 *Mueller Rep*[illegible] describ[illegible] hority [illegible] Special Counsel Mueller). Finally, we have not int[illegible] Order [illegible] us t[illegible] matters addressed by the former United States A[illegible] he Distri[illegible] or [illegible] United States Attorney for the Eastern Distric[illegible] other [illegible] relat[illegible] fire Hurricane or the FISA applications ta[illegible] Page. [illegible] nts [illegible] ers in the news media, *see* Thomas Burr & Pamela [illegible] *S. Atto*[illegible] *ng GOP-Raised Concerns About the FBI Survei*[illegible] *de a*[illegible] *Ties*, Salt Lake Tribune (Mar. 29, 2018), https://[illegible] m/new[illegible] 29/[illegible] r-utah-huber-probing-gop-raised-concerns-abou[illegible] illing[illegible] -igno[illegible] n-uranium-ties/; Charlie Savage et al., *Barr Instal*[illegible] *secu*[illegible] *Michael Flynn, Ex-Trump Adviser*, N.Y. Times (F[illegible] , https:[illegible] me[illegible] 2/14/us/politics/michael-flynn-prosecutors-ba[illegible]

On December 21, 2020, the Attorney General delegated certain authority to use classified information to the Special Counsel.[8]

After the inauguration of President Biden, Attorney General Garland met with the Office of Special Counsel ("OSC" or "the Office"). The Office very much appreciates the support, consistent with his testimony during his confirmation hearings, that the Attorney General has provided to our efforts and the Department's willingness to allow us to operate independently.

The Special Counsel structured the investigation in view of his power and authority "to exercise all investigative and prosecutorial functions of any United States Attorney."[9] Like a U.S. Attorney's Office, the Special Counsel's Office considered in the course of its investigation a range of classified and unclassified information available to the FBI and other government agencies. A substantial amount of information and evidence was immediately available to the Office at the inception of the investigation as a result of numerous congressional investigations[10] and Special Counsel Mueller's investigation. The examinations by the Office of the Inspector General ("OIG") of the Crossfire Hurricane investigation, the Foreign Intelligence Surveillance Act ("FISA") applications targeting Carter Page, and other matters provided additional evidence and information,[11] as did an internal report prepared by the FBI's Inspection Division.[12] The Office reviewed the intelligence, counterintelligence, and law-enforcement activities directed at the 2016 Trump campaign and individuals associated either with the campaign or with the Trump administration in its early stages. The Office structured its work around evidence for possible use in prosecutions of federal crimes (assuming that one or more crimes were identified that warranted prosecution). The Office exercised its judgment regarding what to investigate but

---

[8] Office of the Att'y Gen., Order No. 4942-2020, *Delegation to John Durham, Special Counsel, Authority to Use Classified Information* (Dec. 21, 2020). The Special Counsel has not used this authority.

[9] 28 C.F.R. § 600.6.

[10] *See, e.g.*, Senate Select Committee on Intelligence, S. Rep. No. 116-290, 116th Cong., 2d Sess. (2020) (hereinafter "*SSCI Russia Report*").

[11] *See* OIG, U.S. Department of Justice, *Review of Four FISA Applications and Other Aspects of the FBI's Crossfire Hurricane Investigation* at xiii-xiv, 414 (Dec. 8, 2019) (redacted version) (hereinafter "*OIG Review*" or "*Redacted OIG Review*"), https://www.justice.gov/storage/120919-examination.pdf; OIG, U.S. Department of Justice, *Management Advisory Memorandum for the Director of the Federal Bureau of Investigation Regarding the Execution of Woods Procedures for Applications Filed with the Foreign Intelligence Surveillance Court Relating to U.S. Persons* (Mar. 30, 2020) (hereinafter "*OIG Management Advisory Memorandum*"); OIG, U.S. Department of Justice, *Audit of the Federal Bureau of Investigation's Execution of Its Woods Procedures for Applications Filed with the Foreign Intelligence Surveillance Court Relating to U.S. Persons* (Sept. 2021) (hereinafter "*Audit of 29 Applications*").

[12] FBI Inspection Division, Internal Affairs Section, *Closing Electronic Communication for Case ID # [redacted]* (Nov. 15, 2021) (hereinafter "*Inspection Division Report*" or "*FBI Inspection Division Report*").

did not investigate every public report of an alleged violation of law in connection with the intelligence and law enforcement activities directed at the 2016 presidential campaigns.

In addition to the Special Counsel, the Office has been staffed by experienced FBI and Internal Revenue Service Criminal Investigation Division Agents; Department attorneys and prosecutors; support personnel; and contractor employees.

The Office's investigation was broad and extensive. It included investigative work both domestically and overseas. It entailed obtaining large document productions from businesses, firms, government agencies, universities, political campaigns, internet service providers, telephone companies, and individuals. The Office interviewed hundreds of individuals, many on multiple occasions. The Office conducted the majority of interviews in classified settings; for some interviewees and their counsel security clearances needed to be obtained. The Office conducted interviews in person and via video link, with the vast majority of the latter occurring after the COVID-19 pandemic-related closures began in March 2020. Although a substantial majority of individuals voluntarily cooperated with the Office, some only provided information under a subpoena or grant of immunity. Some individuals who, in our view, had important and relevant information about the topics under investigation refused to be interviewed or otherwise cooperate with the Office. As of April 2023, with two trials completed, the Office has conducted more than 480 interviews; obtained and reviewed more than one million documents consisting of more than six million pages; served more than 190 subpoenas under the auspices of grand juries; executed seven search warrants; obtained five orders for communications records under 18 U.S.C. § 2703(d); and made one request to a foreign government under a Mutual Legal Assistance Treaty.

The Office would like to express its appreciation to, among others, the FBI's Office of General Counsel ("OGC")[13] and Inspection Division; the Litigation Technology Support Services Unit in the National Security Division ("NSD"); the eDiscovery Team in the Office of the Chief Information Officer of the Justice Management Division ("JMD"); and JMD's Service Delivery Staff. The NSD and JMD entities created and maintained the databases and technology infrastructure needed to organize and review the large amount of data we obtained. The Office would also like to express its appreciation to the Department's Office of Privacy and Civil Liberties for its guidance on appropriate information to include in a public report.

---

[13] The FBI's OGC produced more than 6,580,000 pages of documentation in response to our multiple requests. We note that it did so at the same time it was coping with the personnel shortages brought about by the COVID-19 crisis, working to comply with various production demands from congressional committees, and addressing requests from other government entities. Moreover, FBI leadership made it clear to its personnel that they were to cooperate fully with our inquiry, which, in all but a few instances involving some personnel in the Counterintelligence Division, proved to be the case. In those few instances in which individuals refused to cooperate, FBI leadership intervened to urge those individuals to agree to be interviewed. Similarly, both the Central Intelligence Agency ("CIA") and the National Security Agency ("NSA") made their employees available for interview, including former CIA Director John Brennan and former NSA Director Mike Rogers, who voluntarily made themselves available for interviews.

The Office has concluded its investigation into whether "any federal official, employee, or any other person or entity violated the law in connection with the intelligence, counter-intelligence, or law-enforcement activities directed at the 2016 presidential campaigns, individuals associated with those campaigns, and individuals associated with the administration of President Donald J. Trump."

This report is a summary. It contains, in the Office's judgment, that information necessary to account for the Special Counsel's prosecution and declination decisions and describe the investigation's main factual results. It then sets forth some additional observations.

The Office made its criminal charging decisions based solely on the facts and evidence developed in the investigation and without fear of, or favor to, any person. What is stated below in the *Mueller Report* is equally true for our investigation:

> This report describes actions and events that the Special Counsel's Office found to be supported by the evidence collected in our investigation. In some instances, the report points out the absence of evidence or conflicts in the evidence about a particular fact or event. In other instances, when substantial, credible evidence enabled the Office to reach a conclusion with confidence, the report states that the investigation established that certain actions or events occurred. A statement that the investigation did not establish particular facts does not mean there was no evidence of those facts.[14]

Conducting this investigation required us to consider U.S. criminal laws, the Constitutional protections our system provides to individuals, and the high burden placed on the government to prove every element of a crime "beyond a reasonable doubt." Moreover, the law does not always make a person's bad judgment, even horribly bad judgment, standing alone, a crime. Nor does the law criminalize all unseemly or unethical conduct that political campaigns might undertake for tactical advantage, absent a violation of a particular federal criminal statute. Finally, in almost all cases, the government is required to prove a person's actual criminal intent – not mere negligence or recklessness – before that person's fellow citizens can lawfully find him or her guilty of a crime. The Office's adherence to these principles explains, in numerous instances, why conduct deserving of censure or disciplinary action did not lead the Office to seek criminal charges.

There are also reasons why, in examining politically-charged and high-profile issues such as these, the Office must exercise – and has exercised – special care. First, juries can bring strongly held views to the courtroom in criminal trials involving political subject matters, and those views can, in turn, affect the likelihood of obtaining a conviction, separate and apart from the strength of the actual evidence and despite a court's best efforts to empanel a fair and impartial jury. Second, even when prosecutors believe that they can obtain a conviction, there are some instances in which it may not be advisable to expend government time and resources on a criminal prosecution, particularly where it would create the appearance – even if unfounded – that the government is seeking to criminalize the behavior of political opponents or punish the activities of a specific political party or campaign. At the same time, prosecutors should not shy

---

[14] 1 *Mueller Report* at 2.

away from purs[illegible] cas[illegible] y of the defendant or the controversial na[illegible] overnm[illegible]

The *Pri*[illegible] *eral P*[illegible] pro[illegible] wing pertinent guidance on this point, which in[illegible] cial [illegible] harg[illegible] ination decisions:

> Where t[illegible] fact[illegible] und, [illegible] case, the likelihood of an acquitta[illegible] pularit[illegible] spec[illegible] ecution or because of the overwh[illegible] rity o[illegible] ant o[illegible] use is not a factor prohibit[illegible] n. F[illegible] ase or a case involving an extreme[illegible] litical [illegible] ight [illegible] the evidence of guilt— viewed [illegible] y an u[illegible] finde[illegible] sufficient to obtain and sustain [illegible] yet th[illegible] migh[illegible] y doubt, based on the circums[illegible] jury [illegible] vict[illegible] ase, despite his/her negativ[illegible] of the [illegible] f a g[illegible] (based on factors extrane[illegible] tive [illegible] aw [illegible], the prosecutor may properly [illegible] it is [illegible] nd ap[illegible] commence or recomm[illegible] ion an[illegible] crimi[illegible] to operate in accordance with the [illegible] forth [illegible]

The dec[illegible] her to [illegible] nal c[illegible] y given matter thus is a complicated one [illegible] rent [illegible] ive [illegible] stic. If this report and the outcome of the [illegible] sel's [illegible] lea[illegible] h the impression that injustices or misconduct hav[illegible] resse[illegible] ca[illegible] concluded that no such injustices or misconduct [illegible] s rath[illegible] not [illegible] e or transgression amounts to a criminal offens[illegible] al pro[illegible] tas[illegible] y with investigating and prosecuting vio[illegible] S crim[illegible] And [illegible] prosecutors believe a crime occurred based [illegible] facts a[illegible] ion [illegible] hered, it is their duty only to bring criminal [illegible] he e[illegible] the [illegible] easonably believes is *admissible in court* proves [illegible] yond [illegible] e co[illegible]

Both At[illegible] al B[illegible] nd [illegible] hat one of their most important priorities is to [illegible] per fu[illegible] nc[illegible] of federal law by government agencies. Inde[illegible] al of [illegible] ent's [illegible] *ategic Plan* is to uphold the rule of law:

> We wil[illegible] work [illegible] at [illegible] ws the Department as objectiv[illegible] and in[illegible] pe[illegible] nce. . . .
>
> The Jus[illegible] ent['s] [illegible] tions [illegible] include the principled exercis[illegible] inde[illegible] om [illegible] uence; treating like cases alike; a[illegible] ing co[illegible] to f[illegible] facts and the law. Reaffir[illegible] ere ne[illegible] ng[illegible] stice Department policies

[15] *Principles o*[illegible] *secutio*[illegible] 9-27.[illegible]

that are foundational to the rule of law – many of which were initially adopted in the aftermath of Watergate – is essential to this effort.[16]

In the aftermath of Crossfire Hurricane and the FISA surveillances of Page, the Department has adopted other important policies. We discuss them, and possible additional changes, in portions of the report that follow.

## II. Executive Summary

The public record contains a substantial body of information relating to former President Trump's and the Trump Organization's relationships with Russian businesses, Russian business people, and Russian officials, as well as separate evidence of Russia's attempts to interfere in the 2016 presidential election. These and related subjects are well-documented in the careful examinations undertaken by (i) the Department's Office of the Inspector General of issues related to the FBI's Crossfire Hurricane investigation and its use of Foreign Intelligence Surveillance Act ("FISA") authorities,[17] (ii) former FBI Director Robert Mueller as detailed in his report entitled "*Report on the Investigation into Russian Interference in the 2016 Presidential Election,*" issued in March 2019,[18] and (iii) the *Senate Select Committee on Intelligence entitled, "Russian Active Measures Campaigns and Interference in the 2016 U.S. Election."*[19] The scope of these earlier inquiries, the amount of important information gathered, and the contributions they have made to our understanding of Russian election interference efforts are a tribute to the diligent work and dedication of those charged with the responsibility of conducting them. Our review and investigation, in turn has focused on separate but related questions, including the following:

- Was there adequate predication for the FBI to open the Crossfire Hurricane investigation from its inception on July 31, 2016 as a full counterintelligence and Foreign Agents

[16] U.S. Department of Justice, *FYs 2022 – 2026 Strategic Plan* at 15. *See* Attorney General Message – DOJ Strategic Plan (July 1, 2022), https://www.justice.gov/opa/pr/attorney-general-merrick-b-garland-announces-department-justice-2022-26-strategic-plan. *See also* U.S. Department of Justice, OIG, *Department of Justice Top Management and Performance Challenges 2021* ("One important strategy that can build public trust in the Department is to ensure adherence to policies and procedures designed to protect DOJ from accusations of political influence or partial application of the law"), https://oig.justice.gov/reports/top-management-and-performance-challenges-facing-department-justice-2021; Attorney General Memorandum, *Additional Requirements for the Opening of Certain Sensitive Investigations* at 1 (Feb. 5, 2020) ("While the Department must respond swiftly and decisively when faced with credible threats to our democratic processes, we also must be sensitive to safeguarding the Department's reputation for fairness, neutrality, and nonpartisanship") (hereinafter "*Sensitive Investigations Memorandum*").

[17] *See supra* footnote 11.

[18] *See supra* footnote 2.

[19] *See supra* footnote 10; *see also* Intelligence Community Assessment, *Assessing Russian Activities and Intentions in Recent U.S. Elections* (Jan. 6, 2017).

Registration Act ("FARA") investigation given the requirements of *The Attorney General's Guidelines for FBI Domestic Operations* and FBI policies relating to the use of the least intrusive investigative tools necessary?[20]

- Was the opening of Crossfire Hurricane as a full investigation on July 31, 2016 consistent with how the FBI handled other intelligence it had received *prior to* July 31, 2016 concerning attempts by foreign interests to influence the Clinton and other campaigns?

- Similarly, did the FBI properly consider other highly significant intelligence it received at virtually the same time as that used to predicate Crossfire Hurricane, but which related not to the Trump campaign, but rather to a purported Clinton campaign plan "to vilify Donald Trump by stirring up a scandal claiming interference by Russian security services," which might have shed light on some of the Russia information the FBI was receiving from third parties, including the Steele Dossier, the Alfa Bank allegations and confidential human source ("CHS") reporting? If not, were any provable federal crimes committed in failing to do so?

- Was there evidence that the actions of any FBI personnel or third parties relating to the Crossfire Hurricane investigation violated any federal criminal statutes, including the prohibition against making false statements to federal officials? If so, was that evidence sufficient to prove guilt beyond a reasonable doubt?

- Was there evidence that the actions of the FBI or Department personnel in providing false or incomplete information to the Foreign Intelligence Surveillance Court ("FISC") violated any federal criminal statutes? If so, was there evidence sufficient to prove guilt beyond a reasonable doubt?

Our findings and conclusions regarding these and related questions are sobering.

State of Intelligence Community Information Regarding Trump and Russia Prior to the Opening of Crossfire Hurricane

As set forth in greater detail in Section IV.A.3.b, before the initial receipt by FBI Headquarters of information from Australia on July 28, 2016 concerning comments reportedly made in a tavern on May 6, 2016 by George Papadopoulos, an unpaid foreign policy advisor to the Trump campaign, the government possessed no verified intelligence reflecting that Trump or the Trump campaign was involved in a conspiracy or collaborative relationship with officials of the Russian government.[21] Indeed, based on the evidence gathered in the multiple exhaustive and costly federal investigations of these matters, including the instant investigation, neither U.S. law enforcement nor the Intelligence Community appears to have possessed any actual evidence of collusion in their holdings at the commencement of the Crossfire Hurricane investigation.

---

[20] *See The Attorney General's Guidelines for FBI Domestic Operations* § I.C.2 (Sept. 29, 2008) (hereinafter "*AGG-Dom*"); FBI, *Domestic Investigations and Operations Guide* § 4.4 (Mar. 3, 2016) (hereinafter "*DIOG*").

[21] *See infra* § IV.A.3.b.

The Opening of Crossfire Hurricane

As set forth in greater detail in Section IV, the record in this matter reflects that upon receipt of unevaluated intelligence information from Australia, the FBI swiftly opened the Crossfire Hurricane investigation. In particular, at the direction of Deputy Director Andrew McCabe, Deputy Assistant Director for Counterintelligence Peter Strzok opened Crossfire Hurricane immediately.[22] Strzok, at a minimum, had pronounced hostile feelings toward Trump.[23] The matter was opened as a full investigation without ever having spoken to the persons who provided the information. Further, the FBI did so without (i) any significant review of its own intelligence databases, (ii) collection and examination of any relevant intelligence from other U.S. intelligence entities, (iii) interviews of witnesses essential to understand the raw information it had received or (iv) using any of the standard analytical tools typically employed by the FBI in evaluating raw intelligence. Had it done so, again as set out in Sections IV.A.3.b and c, the FBI would have learned that their own experienced Russia analysts had no information about Trump being involved with Russian leadership officials, nor were others in sensitive positions at the CIA, the NSA, and the Department of State aware of such evidence concerning the subject. In addition, FBI records prepared by Strzok in February and March 2017 show that at the time of the opening of Crossfire Hurricane, the FBI had no information in its holdings indicating that at any time during the campaign anyone in the Trump campaign had been in contact with any Russian intelligence officials.[24]

The speed and manner in which the FBI opened and investigated Crossfire Hurricane during the presidential election season based on raw, unanalyzed, and uncorroborated intelligence also reflected a noticeable departure from how it approached prior matters involving possible attempted foreign election interference plans aimed at the Clinton campaign. As described in Section IV.B, in the eighteen months leading up to the 2016 election, the FBI was required to deal with a number of proposed investigations that had the potential of affecting the election. In each of those instances, the FBI moved with considerable caution. In one such matter discussed in Section IV.B.1, FBI Headquarters and Department officials required defensive briefings to be provided to Clinton and other officials or candidates who appeared to be the targets of foreign interference. In another, the FBI elected to end an investigation after one of its longtime and valuable CHSs went beyond what was authorized and made an improper

---

[22] Peter Strzok, *Compromised: Counterintelligence and the Threat of Donald J. Trump* at 115 (Houghton Mifflin Harcourt 2020) (hereinafter "Strzok, *Compromised*").

[23] Strzok and Deputy Director McCabe's Special Assistant had pronounced hostile feelings toward Trump. As explained later in this report, in text messages before and after the opening of Crossfire Hurricane, the two had referred to him as "loathsome," "an idiot," someone who should lose to Clinton "100,000,000 – 0," and a person who Strzok wrote "[w]e'll stop" from becoming President. Indeed, the day before the Australian information was received at FBI Headquarters, Page sent a text message to Strzok stating, "Have we opened on him yet? [angry-faced emoji]" and referenced an article titled *Trump & Putin. Yes, It's Really a Thing.*

[24] *See* SENATE-FISA2020-001163 (Annotated version of article titled *Trump Campaign Aides Had Repeated Contacts With Russian Intelligence,* N.Y. Times (February 14, 2017); FBI-EMAIL-428172 (Annotated version of article titled *Obama Administration Rushed to Preserve Intelligence of Russian Election Hacking,* N.Y. Times (Mar. 1, 2017).

and possibly ill[illegible] l contri[illegible] the Cli[illegible]aign on behalf of a foreign entity as a precursor [illegible] ger do[illegible] cou[illegible] And in a third, the Clinton Foundation ma[illegible] for FBI [illegible] aced restrictions on how those matters were t[illegible] such th[illegible] activities occurred for months leading up to th[illegible] hese [illegible] also [illegible] different from the FBI's actions with respect to [illegible] signif[illegible] from a trusted foreign source pointing to a C[illegible] ign pl[illegible] Trump [illegible] im to Vladimir Putin so as to divert attentio[illegible] con[illegible] g to [illegible] private email server. Unlike the FBI's opening [illegible] igati[illegible] wn [illegible] the Trump campaign based on raw, uncorroborated [illegible] n th[illegible] purported Clinton campaign plan, the FBI never [illegible] pe of i[illegible] ed a[illegible] employed any analytical personnel, or p[illegible] analyt[illegible] in [illegible] with the information. This lack of action was desp[illegible] at th[illegible] e o[illegible] plan intelligence was such as to have prompted [illegible] of the [illegible] the [illegible] Vice President, Attorney General, Director of the [illegible] er sen[illegible] ent [illegible] ut its content within days of its receipt. It was [illegible] g impo[illegible] the [illegible] a formal written referral memorandum [illegible] Comey an[illegible] uty [illegible] rector of the FBI's Counterintellig[illegible] n, Peter [illegible] r the [illegible] tion and action.[25] The investigative re[illegible] ed exa[illegible] forma[illegible] ossfire Hurricane fusion cell had "gleaned to da[illegible]

The [illegible] urr[illegible] gation

Within [illegible] ening [illegible] urr[illegible] I opened full investigations on four members of th[illegible] paign [illegible] e Pap[illegible], Carter Page, Paul Manafort, and Michael Flynn [illegible] ve b[illegible] provid[illegible] p or anyone in the campaign concerning the [illegible] received [illegible] ral [illegible] sted there might be some type of collusion betw[illegible] camp[illegible] the R[illegible] er prior to or after these investigations [illegible] Instea[illegible] began [illegible] n requests for the use of FISA authorities aga[illegible] Papa[illegible] he [illegible] ed to Papadopoulos proved

---

[25] Memorandu[illegible] IA to [illegible] of th[illegible] Bureau of Investigation, *Re: [Redacted] C[illegible]* [illegible] *RRIC[illegible]* [illegible] 16) (sent to the Director of the FBI and to the [illegible] Peter S[illegible] ty [illegible] ector for Operations Branch I, Counterintelli[illegible] r)) (re[illegible] on) [illegible] "*Referral Memo*").

[26] The *Referra[illegible]* [illegible] that th[illegible] a [illegible] t for examples of relevant information th[illegible] had ob[illegible] 2[illegible] 26, 2021 interview with the Office, Supervisory A[illegible] Auten [illegible] or [illegible] efore Labor Day, which was September 2, 2[illegible] onnel [illegible] ter[illegible] ence Section Chief Moffa (and possibly FBI [illegible] ef-1) [illegible] q[illegible] Clinton intelligence plan. Auten advised that at [illegible] wanted [illegible] e referral memo on the information. [illegible] Inte[illegible] an [illegible] July 26, 2021 at 7.

Separately, we [illegible] masked [illegible] used [illegible] ort do not necessarily correspond to those used in [illegible] ment [illegible] *OIG* [illegible]

[27] *See infra* §§ [illegible]

unsuccessful.[28] Similarly, the initial effort directed at Page was unsuccessful until the Crossfire Hurricane investigators first obtained what were designated as "Company Intelligence Reports" generated by Christopher Steele. As set forth in Sections IV.D.1.b.ii and iii and in brief below, the Steele Reports were first provided to the FBI in early July 2016 but, for unexplained reasons, only made their way to the Crossfire Hurricane investigators in mid-September. The reports were ostensibly assembled based on information provided to Steele and his company by a "primary sub source," who the FBI eventually determined in December 2016 was Igor Danchenko.

Our investigation determined that the Crossfire Hurricane investigators did not and could not corroborate any of the substantive allegations contained in the Steele reporting. Nor was Steele able to produce corroboration for any of the reported allegations, even after being offered $1 million or more by the FBI for such corroboration.[29] Further, when interviewed by the FBI in January 2017, Danchenko also was unable to corroborate any of the substantive allegations in the Reports. Rather, Danchenko characterized the information he provided to Steele as "rumor and speculation"[30] and the product of casual conversation.[31]

Section IV.D.1.h describes other efforts undertaken by the Crossfire Hurricane investigators working on the Page FISA application. Those efforts included having CHSs record conversations with Page, Papadopoulos and a senior Trump foreign policy advisor. The FBI's own records and the recordings establish that Page made multiple exculpatory statements to the individual identified as CHS-1, but the Crossfire Hurricane investigators failed to make that information known to the Department attorneys or to the FISC. Page also made explicit statements refuting allegations contained in the Steele reporting about his lack of any relationship with Paul Manafort, but the FBI failed to follow logical investigative leads related to those statements and to report to Department lawyers what they found. Similarly, multiple recordings of Papadopoulos were made by CHS-1 and a second CHS, in which Papadopoulos also made multiple exculpatory statements that were not brought to the attention of the Department lawyers or the FISC.

Furthermore, our investigation resulted in the prosecution and conviction of an FBI OGC attorney for intentionally falsifying a document that was material to the FISC's consideration of one of the Page FISA applications.[32]

<u>The Steele Dossier</u>

In the spring of 2016, Perkins Coie, a U.S.-based international law firm, acting as counsel to the Clinton campaign, retained Fusion GPS, a U.S.-based investigative firm, to conduct

---

[28] OSC Report of Interview of Chicago Agent-1 on Aug. 7, 2019 at 4.

[29] SCO-101648 (Email from Special Agent-2 to Supervisory Special Agent-1, Strzok, Auten, Case Agent-1, Acting Section Chief-1 & Handling Agent-1 dated Oct. 4, 2016); *United States v. Igor Danchenko*, 21-CR-245 (E.D. Va.) Trial Transcript 10/11/2022 PM at 81:7-20 (hereinafter "*Danchenko* Tr.").

[30] SCO_005801 (Interview of Igor Danchenko Electronic Communication dated 02/09/17) at 39.

[31] SCO_105282 (CHS Reporting Document dated 06/01/2017) at 1.

[32] *See infra* § IV.D.2.a.

opposition research on Trump and his associates. In mid-May 2016, Glenn Simpson of Fusion GPS met with Steele in the United Kingdom and subsequently retained Steele and his firm, Orbis Business Intelligence ("Orbis"), to investigate Trump's ties to Russia.[33] Steele described himself as a former intelligence official for the British government,[34] and was also at the time an FBI CHS. Beginning in July 2016 and continuing through December 2016, the FBI received a series of reports from Steele and Orbis that contained derogatory information about Trump concerning Trump's purported ties to Russia. As discussed in Section IV.D.1.b.ii, Steele provided the first of his reports to his FBI handler on July 5th. These reports were colloquially referred to as the "Steele Dossier" or "Steele Reports."

As noted, it was not until mid-September that the Crossfire Hurricane investigators received several of the Steele Reports.[35] Within days of their receipt, the unvetted and unverified Steele Reports were used to support probable cause in the FBI's FISA applications targeting Page, a U.S. citizen who, for a period of time, had been an advisor to Trump. As discussed later in the report, this was done at a time when the FBI knew that the same information Steele had provided to the FBI had also been fed to the media and others in Washington, D.C.[36]

In particular, one allegation contained in an undated Steele Report, identified as 2016/095, described a "well-developed conspiracy of co-operation" between Trump, his campaign, and senior Russian officials. This allegation would ultimately underpin the four FISA applications targeting Page. Specifically, the allegation stated:

> Speaking in confidence to a compatriot *in late July 2016, Source E, an ethnic Russian close associate of Republican US presidential candidate Donald TRUMP,* admitted that there was a well-developed conspiracy of co-operation between them and the Russian leadership. This was managed on the TRUMP side by the Republican candidate's campaign manager, Paul MANAFORT, who was using foreign policy advisor, Carter PAGE, and others as intermediaries. The two sides had a mutual interest in defeating Democratic presidential candidate Hillary CLINTON, whom President PUTIN apparently both hated and feared.[37]

---

[33] Glenn Simpson & Peter Fritsch, *Crime in Progress: Inside the Steele Dossier and the Fusion GPS Investigation of Donald Trump* at 69-70 (2019) (hereinafter "*Crime in Progress*").

[34] Steele has testified in prior legal proceedings that between 1987 and 2009 that he was an intelligence professional working for the British government. Trial Testimony of Christopher Steele, *Peter Aven, et al. v. Orbis Bus. Intel. Ltd.*, Claim No. HQ18M01646 (hereinafter "*Steele Transcript*") (Mar. 17, 2020) at 147-48.

[35] While Steele first provided several of his Reports to his FBI handler in July 2016, the transmittal of these Reports to FBI Headquarters and the Crossfire Hurricane team met an inexplicable delay. This delay is discussed in Section IV.D.1.b.iii.

[36] *See infra* § IV.D.1.

[37] SCO-105084 (Documents Known to the FBI Comprising the "Steele Dossier") at 9 ("Company Intelligence Report 2016/095") (Emphasis added, capitalization in original).

Igor Danchenko – Steele's Primary Sub-Source

As noted, the FBI attempted, over time, to investigate and analyze the Steele Reports but ultimately was not able to confirm or corroborate any of the substantive allegations contained in those reports. In the context of these efforts, and as discussed in Sections IV.D.1.b.ix and x, the FBI learned that Steele relied primarily on a U.S.-based Russian national, Igor Danchenko, to collect information that ultimately formed the core allegations found in the reports. Specifically, our investigation discovered that Danchenko himself had told another person that he (Danchenko) was responsible for 80% of the "intel" and 50% of the analysis contained in the Steele Dossier.[38] [39]

In December 2016, the FBI identified Danchenko as Steele's primary sub-source. Danchenko agreed to meet with the FBI and, under the protection of an immunity letter, he and his attorney met with the Crossfire Hurricane investigators on January 24, 25, and 26, 2017. Thereafter, from January 2017 through October 2020, and as part of its efforts to determine the truth or falsity of specific information in the Steele Reports, the FBI conducted multiple interviews of Danchenko regarding, among other things, the information he provided to Steele. As discussed in Section IV.D.1.b.ix, during these interviews, Danchenko was unable to provide any corroborating evidence to support the Steele allegations, and further, described his interactions with his sub-sources as "rumor and speculation" and conversations of a casual nature.[40] Significant parts of what Danchenko told the FBI were inconsistent with what Steele told the FBI during his prior interviews in October 2016 and September 2017. At no time, however, was the FISC informed of these inconsistencies. Moreover, notwithstanding the repeated assertions in the Page FISA applications that Steele's primary sub-source was based in Russia, Danchenko for many years had lived in the Washington, D.C. area. After learning that Danchenko continued to live in the Washington area and had not left except for domestic and foreign travel, the FBI never corrected this assertion in the three subsequent Page FISA renewal applications. Rather, beginning in March 2017, the FBI engaged Danchenko as a CHS and began making regular financial payments to him for information – none of which corroborated Steele's reporting.

---

[38] *Danchenko* Government Exhibit 1502 (LinkedIn message from Danchenko dated Oct. 11, 2020).

[39] Our investigators uncovered little evidence suggesting that, prior to the submission of the first Page FISA application, the FBI had made any serious attempts to identify Steele's primary sub-source other than asking Steele to disclose the identities of his sources, which he refused to do. The reliability of Steele's reporting depended heavily on the reliability of his primary sub-source because, as represented to the FISC, Steele's source reporting was principally derived from the primary sub-source, who purportedly was running a "network of sub-sources." *In re Carter W. Page*, Docket No. 16-1182, at 16 n.8 (FISC Oct. 21, 2016). The failure to identify the primary sub-source early in the investigation's pursuit of FISA authority prevented the FBI from properly examining the possibility that some or much of the non-open source information contained in Steele's reporting was Russian disinformation (that wittingly or unwittingly was passed along to Steele), or that the reporting was otherwise not credible.

[40] *See supra* footnotes 30 and 31.

The [illegible] Prior FBI [illegible] intell[illegible] [illegible]stigation of Danchenko

Importa[illegible] discuss[illegible] in I[illegible] [illegible]BI knew in January 2017 that Danchenko had [illegible] subject of [illegible] counterinte[illegible] investigation from 2009 to 2011. In late 2008, w[illegible]ko was [illegible] by th[illegible] Institution, he engaged two fellow employe[illegible] ther on[illegible] employ[illegible] willing or able in the future to provide classifi[illegible] in ex[illegible] mon[illegible]ing to one employee, Danchenko believed that he [illegible]ee) migh[illegible]wing [illegible] to the incoming Obama administration [illegible]s to [illegible] inform[illegible]g this exchange, Danchenko informed the em[illegible] he had [illegible] people [illegible] willing to pay for classified information. Th[illegible] employ[illegible] this in[illegible] to a U.S. government contact, and the information [illegible]quently pa[illegible] FBI. [illegible] this information, in 2009 the FBI opened a prelim[illegible]igation i[illegible]enko [illegible]onverted its investigation into a full investigatio[illegible]g that [illegible] (i) h[illegible]entified as an associate of two FBI counterintellig[illegible] and (ii) [illegible]us on[illegible] the Russian Embassy and known Russian intellig[illegible]. Also, [illegible]ed in [illegible].D.1.c, at that earlier time, Agents had interviewe[illegible]er col[illegible] Danch[illegible] raised concerns about Danchenko's p[illegible] vemen[illegible]ian i[illegible] For example, one such colleague, who had intern[illegible] intellig[illegible] office that Danchenko frequently inquired about [illegible] knowl[illegible] military matter.

Meanw[illegible] 2010, th[illegible] [illegible]ted a[illegible]use FISA authorities against Danchenko, wh[illegible]equently [illegible] Dep[illegible]orneys in August 2010. However, the investigatio[illegible]enko wa[illegible] in Ma[illegible]ter the FBI incorrectly concluded that Danchenk[illegible] country [illegible]ed [illegible]

Our rev[illegible] indica[illegible] Cro[illegible]cane investigators ever attempted to resolve the p[illegible]ko espi[illegible]g him as a paid CHS. Moreover, our investigatio[illegible]dicatio[illegible] Cross[illegible] the investigators disclosed the existence of Da[illegible] resolv[illegible] intelli[illegible]stigation to the Department attorneys who w[illegible] le fo[illegible] FIS[illegible] applications targeting Carter Page. As a result, the [illegible] ver ad[illegible] forma[illegible]ry well may have affected the FISC's view of [illegible]ary s[illegible] (and [illegible] liability and trustworthiness. Equally import[illegible]hat i[illegible]ing D[illegible] status vis-à-vis the Russian intelligence ser[illegible]ars the [illegible] gave [illegible] consideration to the possibility that the intellig[illegible]ko was [illegible] to S[illegible]h, again, according to Danchenko himself, made [illegible] major[illegible] info[illegible]e Steele Dossier reports – was, in whole or in par[illegible] inform[illegible]

[illegible] chen[illegible] [illegible]nshi[illegible] [illegible]les Dolan

During [illegible] ne p[illegible]enk[illegible] a relationship with Charles Dolan, a Virgi[illegible] c rel[illegible]ssio[illegible] previously held multiple positions and roles in the [illegible] Nation[illegible]tee ("[illegible] the Democratic Party. In his role as a public rela[illegible]onal, D[illegible]ed m[illegible]career interacting with Eurasian clients, with a [illegible]us on [illegible] desc[illegible]tion IV.D.1.d.ii, Dolan previously conducted busi[illegible] Russ[illegible] relationships with several key Russian govern[illegible]s, inc[illegible]ry P[illegible]owerful Press Secretary of the Russian Presid[illegible]istrati[illegible] er o[illegible]ian government officials with whom Dolan maintained a relationship – and was in contact with at the time Danchenko was collecting information for Steele – would later appear in the Dossier.

In the summer and fall of 2016, at the time Danchenko was collecting information for Steele, Dolan traveled to Moscow, as did Danchenko, in connection with a business conference. As discussed in Section IV.D.1.d.iii, the business conference was held at the Ritz Carlton Moscow, which, according to the Steele Reports, was allegedly the site of salacious sexual conduct on the part of Trump. Danchenko would later inform the FBI that he learned of these allegations through Ritz Carlton staff members. Our investigation, however, revealed that it was Dolan, not Danchenko, who actually interacted with the hotel staff identified in the Steele Reports, so between the two, Dolan appears the more likely source of the allegations.

As discussed in Section IV.D.1.d.vi, our investigation also uncovered that Dolan was the definitive source for at least one allegation in the Steele Reports. This allegation, contained in Steele Report 2016/105, concerned the circumstances surrounding the resignation of Paul Manafort from the Trump campaign. When interviewed by the Office, Dolan admitted that he fabricated the allegation about Manafort that appeared in the Steele Report. Our investigation also revealed that, in some instances, Dolan independently received other information strikingly similar to allegations that would later appear in the Steele Reports. Nevertheless, when interviewed by the FBI, Danchenko denied that Dolan was a source for any information in the Steele Reports.

Furthermore, as discussed in Section IV.D.1.d.iii, during the relevant time period, Dolan maintained a business relationship with Olga Galkina, a childhood friend of Danchenko, who, according to Danchenko, was a key source for many of the allegations contained in the Steele Reports. In fact, when Galkina was interviewed by the FBI in August 2017, she admitted to providing Dolan with information that would later appear in the Steele Reports.

The FBI's Failure to Interview Charles Dolan

Our investigation revealed that the Crossfire Hurricane investigators were aware of Dolan and his connections to Danchenko and the Steele Reports. In fact, as discussed in Section IV.D.1.b.v, in early October 2016, Steele informed the FBI that Dolan was a person who might have relevant information about Trump. The FBI interviewed hundreds of individuals through the course of the Crossfire Hurricane and later investigations, and yet it did not interview Dolan as a possible source of information about Trump. Our investigators interviewed Dolan on several occasions, as well as the two other persons mentioned by Steele. Dolan initially denied being a source of information for the Steele Reports. When, however, he was shown a particular Steele Report relating to Paul Manafort and his resignation as Trump's campaign manager, along with related emails between himself and Danchenko in August 2016, he acknowledged that the reporting mirrored the information he had provided to Danchenko. Dolan acknowledged to the Office that he fabricated this information. Although both Steele and Olga Galkina suggested to the FBI that Dolan may have had information related to the Steele Reports, our investigation was not able to definitively show that Dolan was the actual source – whether wittingly or unwittingly – for any additional allegations set forth in the Steele Reports. Regardless, in light of the foregoing, there does not appear to have been an objectively sound reason for the FBI's failure to interview Dolan.

Danchenko's Claims Regarding Sergei Millian

Perhaps the most damning allegation in the Steele Dossier reports was Company Report 2016/95, which Steele attributed to "Source E," one of Danchenko's supposed sub-sources. This report, portions of which were included in each of the four Page FISA applications, contributed to the public narrative of Trump's conspiring and colluding with Russian officials. As discussed in Section IV.D.1.f, Danchenko's alleged source for the information (Source E) was an individual by the name of Sergei Millian who was the president of the Russian-American Chamber of Commerce in New York City and a public Trump supporter. The evidence uncovered by the Office showed that Danchenko never spoke with Sergei Millian and simply fabricated the allegations that he attributed to Millian.

When interviewed by Crossfire Hurricane investigators in late January 2017, Danchenko said that Source E in Report 2016/95 sounded as though it was Sergei Millian. As discussed in Section IV.D.1.f.i, Danchenko stated that he never actually met Millian. Instead, he said that in late-July 2016 he received an anonymous call from a person who did not identify himself, but who spoke with a Russian accent. Danchenko further explained that he thought it might have been Millian – someone Danchenko previously had emailed twice and received no response – after watching a *YouTube* video of Millian speaking. Thus, as detailed in Section IV.D.1.f.i, the total support for the Source E information contained in Steele Report 2016/95 is a purported anonymous call from someone Danchenko had never met or spoken to but who he believed might be Sergei Millian – a Trump supporter – based on his listening to a *YouTube* video of Millian. Unfortunately, the investigation revealed that, instead of taking even basic steps, such as securing telephone call records for either Danchenko or Millian to investigate Danchenko's hard-to-believe story about Millian, the Crossfire Hurricane investigators appear to have chosen to ignore this and other red flags concerning Danchenko's credibility, as well as Steele's.[41]

The Alfa Bank Allegations

The Office also investigated the actions of Perkins Coie attorney Michael Sussmann and others in connection with Sussmann's provision of data and "white papers" to FBI General Counsel James Baker purporting to show that there existed a covert communications channel between the Trump Organization and a Russia-based bank called Alfa Bank. As set forth in Section IV.E.1.c.iii, in doing so he represented to Baker by text message and in person that he was acting on his own and was not representing any client or company in providing the information to the FBI. Our investigation showed that, in point of fact, these representations to Baker were false in that Sussmann was representing the Clinton campaign (as evidenced by, among other things, his law firm's billing records and internal communications).[42] In addition, Sussmann was representing a second client, a technology executive named Rodney Joffe (as evidenced by various written communications, Sussmann's subsequent congressional testimony, and other records).

---

[41] As noted in Section IV.D.2.f, a federal grand jury in the Eastern District of Virginia returned a five-count indictment against Danchenko charging him with making false statements. A trial jury, however, found that the evidence was not sufficient to prove his guilt beyond a reasonable doubt. *See United States v. Igor Danchenko*, 21-CR-245 (E.D. Va.).

[42] *Sussmann* Government Exhibit 553 (Perkins Coie billing records for HFA).

Cyber experts from the FBI examined the materials given to Baker and concluded that they did not establish what Sussmann claimed they showed. At a later time, Sussmann made a separate presentation regarding the Alfa Bank allegations to another U.S. government agency and it too concluded that the materials did not show what Sussmann claimed. In connection with that second presentation, Sussmann made a similar false statement to that agency, claiming that he was not providing the information on behalf of any client.

With respect to the Alfa Bank materials, our investigation established that Joffe had tasked a number of computer technology researchers who worked for companies he was affiliated with, and who had access to certain internet records, to mine the internet data to establish "an inference" and "narrative" tying then-candidate Trump to Russia. In directing these researchers to exploit their access in this manner, Joffe indicated that he was seeking to please certain "VIPs," in context referring to individuals at Perkins Coie who were involved in campaign matters and the Clinton campaign. During its investigation, the Office also learned that, after the 2016 presidential election, Joffe emailed an individual and told that person that "[he - Joffe] was tentatively offered the top [cybersecurity] job by the Democrats when it looked like they'd win."

As explained in Section IV.E.1.c.i, the evidence collected by the Office also demonstrated that, prior to providing the unfounded Alfa bank claims to the FBI, Sussmann and Fusion GPS (the Clinton campaign's opposition research firm) had provided the same information to various news organizations and were pressing reporters to write articles about the alleged secret communications channel. Moreover, during his September 2016 meeting at the FBI, Sussmann told Baker that an unnamed news outlet was in possession of the information and would soon publish a story about it. The disclosure of the media's involvement caused the FBI to contact the news outlet whose name was eventually provided by Sussmann in the hope of delaying any public reporting on the subject. In doing so it confirmed for the *New York Times* that the FBI was looking into the matter. On October 31, 2016, less than two weeks before the election, the *New York Times* and others published articles on the Alfa Bank matter and the Clinton campaign issued tweets and public statements on the allegations of a secret channel of communications being used by the Trump Organization and a Russian bank - allegations that had been provided to the media and the FBI by Fusion GPS and Sussmann, both of whom were working for the Clinton campaign.

## Conclusion

Based on the review of Crossfire Hurricane and related intelligence activities, we conclude that the Department and the FBI failed to uphold their important mission of strict fidelity to the law in connection with certain events and activities described in this report. As noted, former FBI attorney Kevin Clinesmith committed a criminal offense by fabricating language in an email that was material to the FBI obtaining a FISA surveillance order. In other instances, FBI personnel working on that same FISA application displayed, at best, a cavalier attitude towards accuracy and completeness. FBI personnel also repeatedly disregarded important requirements when they continued to seek renewals of that FISA surveillance while acknowledging – both then and in hindsight – that they did not genuinely believe there was probable cause to believe that the target was knowingly engaged in clandestine intelligence activities on beh[illegible] [illegible]gn po[illegible] [illegible]wing[illegible] [illegible] other person in such activities.[43] And certain pers[illegible] [illegible]arded [illegible] [illegible]xcu[illegible] [illegible]mation that should have prompted invest[illegible] [illegible]nt an[illegible] [illegible]ation.

Our inv[illegible] [illegible]c reve[illegible] [illegible]for F[illegible] [illegible]el displayed a serious lack of analytical rigor [illegible] [illegible]format[illegible] [illegible]ey re[illegible] [illegible]ecially information received from politically affili[illegible] [illegible]and err[illegible] [illegible]info[illegible] [illegible]art triggered and sustained Crossfire Hurri[illegible] [illegible]tribute[illegible] [illegible]sequ[illegible] Special Counsel Mueller's investigation. [illegible] there [illegible]nt rel[illegible] investigative leads provided or funded (directly [illegible]) by Tr[illegible] [illegible]tical[illegible] The Department did not adequately exa[illegible] [illegible]on th[illegible] [illegible]s and[illegible] [illegible]tions of those providing them, even when at a[illegible] [illegible]ime [illegible] [illegible]of th[illegible] [illegible]others learned of significant and potentially con[illegible] [illegible]rce.[45]

In light [illegible] [illegible]ing, the[illegible] [illegible]imu[illegible] the FBI and the Department to recognize that [illegible] [illegible]ical ri[illegible] [illegible]t [illegible] [illegible]ias, and an over-willingness to rely on informa[illegible] [illegible]lividu[illegible] [illegible]d to [illegible] [illegible]onents caused investigators to fail to adequately c[illegible] [illegible]tive [illegible] [illegible]ard [illegible] [illegible]t appropriate objectivity or restraint in purs[illegible] [illegible]ons of [illegible] [illegible]co[illegible] [illegible]veen a U.S. political campaign and a foreign power[illegible] [illegible]ecogni[illegible] [illegible] is clearer, much of this also seems to have been cle[illegible] [illegible]. We [illegible] [illegible]elieve [illegible]ant to examine past conduct to identify shortco[illegible] [illegible]nprove[illegible] [illegible]ve[illegible] [illegible]s out its most sensitive functions. Section V discu[illegible] [illegible]hese i[illegible] [illegible]ful[illegible]

This re[illegible] [illegible]recom[illegible] [illegible]vhe[illegible] [illegible]s in the guidelines and policies that the Depart[illegible] [illegible]FBI n[illegible] [illegible]place[illegible] [illegible]roper conduct and accountability in how counter[illegible] [illegible]ctiviti[illegible] [illegible]d ou[illegible] is intended to accurately describe the matters tha[illegible] [illegible]revi[illegible] [illegible]sist[illegible] General in determining how the Department an[illegible] [illegible]do a be[illegible] [illegible]cred[illegible] [illegible]ulfilling its responsibilities, and in analyzing and r[illegible] [illegible]politi[illegible] [illegible]all[illegible] [illegible]he future. Ultimately, of course, meeting those r[illegible] [illegible]com[illegible] [illegible]the i[illegible] [illegible]he people who take an oath to follow the guid[illegible] [illegible]licies [illegible] [illegible]pla[illegible] [illegible]s that date from the time of Attorney Gener[illegible] [illegible]hat ar[illegible] [illegible]en[illegible] [illegible]of law is upheld. As such, the answer is not th[illegible] [illegible]new r[illegible] [illegible]new[illegible] [illegible]o the old. The promulgation of additional rule[illegible] [illegible]ons to [illegible] [illegible]n ye[illegible] [illegible]ing sessions would likely prove to be a fruitless e[illegible] [illegible]FBI's [illegible] [illegible]cipl[illegible] [illegible]ty, Bravery and Integrity" are not

[43] *See, e.g.*, OS[illegible] [illegible]ntervi[illegible] [illegible]visor[illegible] [illegible]gent-2 on May 5, 2021 at 1-2; OSC Report of [illegible] [illegible]Super[illegible] [illegible]ial A[illegible] [illegible]ar. 18, 2021 at 2-3.

[44] *See, e.g.*, FB[illegible] [illegible]9 (L[illegible] [illegible]exch[illegible] [illegible]en Case Agent-1 and Support Operations Spe[illegible] [illegible]09/[illegible] [illegible]018[illegible] [illegible]16 (Handwritten notes of FBI OGC Unit Chi[illegible] [illegible]2/201[illegible] [illegible]-000[illegible] [illegible]ndwritten notes of Lisa Page dated 10/12/2016); C[illegible] [illegible]f Inter[illegible] [illegible]Atto[illegible] [illegible]ly 1, 2020 at 2-7.

[45] *See infra* § I[illegible]

engrained in the hearts and minds of those sworn to meet the FBI's mission of "Protect[ing] the American People and Uphold[ing] the Constitution of the United States."[46]

## III. APPLICABLE LAWS AND DEPARTMENT AND FBI POLICIES

This section begins by summarizing some of the *Principles of Federal Prosecution*, which govern all federal prosecutions. Next, this section describes the laws and policies that we considered in the course of our investigation. These include the requirements that apply to the FBI's assessments and investigations of counterintelligence matters, most of which are found in guidelines promulgated by the Attorney General and FBI policies, and the legal standards for conducting electronic surveillance under FISA. This section concludes by describing the principal statutes that we used to evaluate possible criminal conduct for prosecution: 18 U.S.C. § 1001(a)(2) (false statements); 18 U.S.C. § 1621(2) (perjury); 18 U.S.C. § 1519 (falsification of records); 18 U.S.C. § 242 (violation of civil rights); 18 U.S.C. §§ 241, 371 (conspiracy); 18 U.S.C. § 1031(a) (fraud against the United States); 52 U.S.C. §§ 30116, 30121(a) (campaign contributions); 18 U.S.C. §§ 1956-57 (money-laundering); and 18 U.S.C. § 793(d) (transmission of classified information).

### A. Principles of Federal Prosecution

In deciding whether to exercise prosecutorial authority with respect to the statutes discussed below, the Office has been guided by the *Principles of Federal Prosecution* set forth in the *Justice Manual*.[47] Those principles include:

#### *1. Determination to prosecute*

A determination to prosecute represents a policy judgment that the fundamental interests of society require the application of federal criminal law to a particular set of circumstances. The attorney for the government should commence or recommend federal prosecution if he/she believes that the person's conduct constitutes a federal offense, and that the admissible evidence will probably be sufficient to obtain and sustain a conviction, unless (i) the prosecution would serve no substantial federal interest; (ii) the person is subject to effective prosecution in another jurisdiction; or (iii) there exists an adequate non-criminal alternative to prosecution.[48]

#### *2. Substantial federal interest*

In determining whether a prosecution would serve a substantial federal interest, the attorney for the government should weigh all relevant considerations, including:

> Federal law enforcement priorities, including any federal law enforcement initiatives or operations aimed at accomplishing those priorities;
> The nature and seriousness of the offense;
> The deterrent effect of prosecution;

[46] *See* Mission Statement of the Federal Bureau of Investigation, https://www.fbi.gov/about/mission.

[47] U.S. Department of Justice, *Justice Manual* § 9-27.000 (Feb. 2018), https://www.justice.gov/jm/jm-9-27000-principles-federal-prosecution#9-27.001.

[48] *Justice Manual* §§ 9-27.001; 9-27.220.

The person's culpability in connection with the offense;
The person's history with respect to criminal activity;
The person's willingness to cooperate in the investigation or prosecution of others;
The person's personal circumstances;
The interests of any victims; and
The probable sentence or other consequences if the person is convicted.[49]

### 3. *Most serious, readily provable offense*

During our investigation, the *Justice Manual* provided that once the decision to prosecute has been made, the attorney for the government should charge and pursue the most serious, readily provable offenses. By definition, the most serious offenses are those that carry the most substantial guidelines sentence, including mandatory minimum sentences.[50]

### 4. *Unpopularity*

Where the law and the facts create a sound, prosecutable case, the likelihood of an acquittal due to unpopularity of some aspect of the prosecution or because of the overwhelming popularity of the defendant or his/her cause is not a factor prohibiting prosecution.[51] This provision from the *Justice Manual* is quoted more fully in section I.

### 5. *Interests of uncharged parties*

In all public filings and proceedings, federal prosecutors should remain sensitive to the privacy and reputation interests of uncharged third parties. In the context of public plea and sentencing proceedings, this means that, in the absence of some significant justification, it is not appropriate to identify (either by name or unnecessarily specific description), or cause a defendant to identify, a third-party wrongdoer unless that party has been officially charged with the misconduct at issue.[52]

As a series of cases makes clear, there is ordinarily "no legitimate governmental interest served" by the government's public allegation of wrongdoing by an uncharged party, and this is true "[r]egardless of what criminal charges may . . . b[e] contemplated by the Assistant United States Attorney against the [third-party] for the future."[53] Courts have applied this reasoning to preclude the public identification of unindicted third-party wrongdoers in plea hearings, sentencing memoranda, and other government pleadings.[54]

---

[49] *Id.* § 9-27.230.

[50] *Id.* § 9-27.300. This charging policy has since been revised. *See* Att'y Gen., General Department Policies Regarding Charging, Pleas, and Sentencing Memorandum (Dec. 16, 2022).

[51] *Justice Manual* § 9-27.220.

[52] *Id.* § 9-27.760.

[53] *In re Smith*, 656 F.2d 1101, 1106-07 (5th Cir. 1981).

[54] *Justice Manual* § 9-27.760. *See Finn v. Schiller*, 72 F.3d 1182, 1189 (4th Cir. 1996) ("Overzealous prosecutors must not be allowed to file sweeping statements of fact alleging violations of various laws by unindicted individuals. A primary purpose of Rule 6 is to protect

In a similar vein, Deputy Attorney General Rosenstein stated that "we do not hold press conferences to release derogatory information about the subject of a declined criminal investigation." He went on to say that "[d]erogatory information sometimes is disclosed in the course of criminal investigations and prosecutions, but we never release it gratuitously."[55]

### B. **The FBI's Assessment and Investigation of Counterintelligence Matters**

This subsection describes the requirements that apply to the FBI's assessments and investigations of counterintelligence matters. The *AGG-Dom* gives the FBI a broad mandate to "detect, obtain information about, and prevent and protect against federal crimes and threats to the national security."[56] These crimes and threats include espionage and other intelligence activities and foreign computer intrusions.[57] The *AGG-Dom* provides that "[t]hese Guidelines do not authorize investigating or collecting or maintaining information on United States persons solely for the purpose of monitoring activities protected by the First Amendment or the lawful exercise of other rights secured by the Constitution or laws of the United States."[58]

The requirements of the *AGG-Dom* are implemented and expanded upon in FBI policy.[59] In its investigative activities, the FBI is to use less intrusive investigative techniques where feasible, and investigative activity is broken down into various levels. There are also requirements in separate guidelines approved by the Attorney General governing the FBI's use of confidential human sources ("CHSs").[60] In 2020, the Department imposed additional requirements for politically sensitive assessments and investigations and for applications under FISA.

---

the unindicted . . . ."); *United States v. Anderson*, 55 F. Supp. 2d 1163 (D. Kan 1999); *United States v. Smith*, 992 F. Supp. 743 (D.N.J. 1998). The Fifth Circuit has stated:

> Nine of the ten persons named in the indictment were active in the Vietnam Veterans Against the War, an anti-war group. The naming of appellants as unindicted conspirators was not an isolated occurrence in time or context. . . . There is at least a strong suspicion that the stigmatization of appellants was part of an overall governmental tactic directed against disfavored persons and groups. Visiting opprobrium on persons by officially charging them with crimes while denying them a forum to vindicate their names, undertaken as extra-judicial punishment or to chill their expressions and associations, is not a governmental interest that we can accept or consider.

*United States v. Briggs*, 514 F.2d 794, 805-06 (5th Cir. 1975) (footnote omitted).

[55] Memorandum for the Attorney General from Rod J. Rosenstein, Deputy Attorney General, *Restoring Public Confidence in the FBI* at 1 (May 9, 2017).

[56] *AGG-Dom* § II.

[57] *Id.* § VII.S.

[58] *Id.* § I.C.3.

[59] *See* FBI, *Domestic Investigations and Operations Guide* (Mar. 3, 2016) (hereinafter "*DIOG*").

[60] These are discussed in Subsection 3 below.

*1. Use [illegible] nsive [illegible]*

The Pre[illegible] rected [illegible] Intellig[illegible]unity "shall use the least intrusive collection techn[illegible] le with[illegible] United Sta[illegible]ed against United States persons abroad."[61] The [illegible] Comm[illegible] des [illegible] ce elements of the FBI. The *AGG-Dom* imp[illegible] provis[illegible] erves[illegible]

> The co[illegible] igatio[illegible] ay present choices between [illegible] ifferen[illegible] ive m[illegible] are each operationally sound a[illegible] but th[illegible] considering such factors as the e[illegible] rivacy [illegible] bert[illegible] uals and potential damage to repu[illegible]

There is additi[illegible] of [illegible] investigative matter" or "SIM," principally in t[illegible] e cat[illegible] SIM is a[illegible] lving a political candidate or a "domestic poli[illegible] ation o[illegible] pro[illegible] h an organization."[63] The definition of a [illegible] udes "a[illegible] atte[illegible] he judgment of the official authorizing an[illegible], should[illegible] t to t[illegible] of FBI Headquarters and other Department of [illegible] ials."[64] [illegible] to e[illegible]

- In a SI[illegible] care [illegible] ken [illegible] ering whether the planned course of actio[illegible] intrus[illegible] if rea[illegible] ed on the circumstances of the investig[illegible]

---

[61] Executive O[illegible] .4 ([illegible]).

[62] *AGG-Dom* § [illegible]

[63] *DIOG* § 10.[illegible] *AGG-*[illegible]

[64] *AGG-Dom* § [illegible] *DIOG* [illegible] BI policy, 'judgment' means that the decision of [illegible] g of [illegible] § 10.1.2.1. For preliminary or full investigations [illegible] s, th[illegible] re[illegible]

> An FB[illegible] shall [illegible] lead[illegible] the United States Attorney or othe[illegible] Depa[illegible] us[illegible] f the initiation by the field office [illegible] d inve[illegible] e investigative matter. If the investig[illegible] ated b[illegible] dqua[illegible] Headquarters shall notify the United [illegible] ney or [illegible] pri[illegible] ent of Justice official of the initiati[illegible] inve[illegible] f the [illegible] ion concerns a threat to the national [illegible] offic[illegible] lation[illegible] Division must be notified. The n[illegible] entif[illegible] ive [illegible] matters involved in the investig[illegible]

*AGG-Dom* § [illegible]

[65] *DIOG* § 10.[illegible]

- More generally, "when First Amendment rights are at stake, the choice and use of investigative methods should be focused in a manner that minimizes potential infringement of those rights."[66]
- "If . . . the threat is remote, the individual's involvement is speculative, and the probability of obtaining probative information is low, intrusive methods may not be justified, and, in fact, they may do more harm than good."[67]

The *DIOG* says that the FBI will "[a]pply best judgment to the circumstances at hand to select the most appropriate investigative means to achieve the investigative goal."[68] At the same time, it "shall not hesitate to use any lawful method . . . even if intrusive, where the degree of intrusiveness is warranted in light of the seriousness of a criminal or national security threat."[69] The factors that may support the use of more intrusive collection techniques include operational security.[70]

2. ***Levels of investigation***

One significant way that the *AGG-Dom* and the *DIOG* implement the least intrusive means requirement is by describing four different levels of activity. The first is activity that the FBI may conduct without any formal opening or authorization process and is referred to as "activities authorized prior to opening an assessment."[71] The other, more formalized levels of activity are assessment, preliminary investigation, and full investigation. As the level increases, the FBI may use a broader range of techniques:

a. Activity authorized before opening an assessment

The *DIOG* states that "[w]hen initially processing a complaint, observation, or information," an FBI employee may take limited steps to evaluate the information. These include looking at government records and at commercially and publicly available information. The employee may also "[c]onduct a voluntary clarifying interview of the complainant or the person who initially furnished the information . . . for the sole purpose of eliminating confusion in the original allegation or information provided." The *DIOG* explains that "[t]hese activities may allow the FBI employee to resolve a matter without the need to conduct new investigative activity."[72] New investigative activity requires the opening of an assessment or predicated investigation.[73]

---

66 *Id.* § 4.4.4.

67 *Id.*

68 *Id.* § 4.1.1(F) (bolding omitted).

69 *AGG-Dom* § I.C.2.a.

70 *DIOG* § 4.4.4.

71 *See id.* § 5.1.

72 *DIOG* § 5.1.1.

73 *Id.*

b. Assessment

The FBI may open an assessment if it has an authorized purpose and a clearly defined objective. No particular factual predication is required, but the basis for opening an assessment "cannot be arbitrary or groundless speculation." In addition to the techniques that are authorized without opening an assessment, in an assessment the FBI may recruit and use CHSs, conduct physical surveillance in 72-hour increments, and obtain some grand jury subpoenas. An FBI employee should be able to explain the reason for the use of particular investigative methods.[74]

c. Preliminary investigation

The factual predicate required to open a preliminary investigation is "information or an allegation" that a federal crime or threat to the national security "may be" occurring. Authorized investigative methods include undercover operations, trash covers, consensual monitoring, pen registers, national security letters, and polygraphs. The FBI may also conduct physical searches and use monitoring devices that do not require judicial authorization. A preliminary investigation is to last a relatively short time and lead either to closure or a full investigation.[75]

d. Full investigation

The standard for opening a full investigation is "an articulable factual basis for the investigation that reasonably indicates that . . . [a]n activity constituting a federal crime or a threat to the national security . . . is or may be occurring . . . and the investigation may obtain information relating to the activity."[76] The *DIOG* gives as examples of sufficient predication to open a full investigation:

- "[C]orroborated information from an intelligence agency" stating "that an individual is a member of a terrorist group."
- "[A]n analyst discovers on a blog a threat to a specific home builder and additional information connecting the blogger to a known terrorist group."[77]

The FBI may use "all lawful methods" in a full investigation, including court-authorized electronic surveillance and physical searches.[78]

***3. The Confidential Human Source Guidelines***

In addition to the *AGG-Dom*, the Attorney General has approved separate guidelines governing the FBI's use of human sources. The guidelines in place at the time of Crossfire

---

[74] *Id.* §§ 5.1; 18.5; 18.5.8.3.2.

[75] *See id.* § 6.7.2 ("Extensions of preliminary investigations beyond one year are discouraged and may only be approved . . . for 'good cause'"); *see also id.* § 6.7.2.1 (describing "good cause" and focusing on need to move to a full investigation or to closure); *AGG-Dom* § II.B.4.a.ii (requiring approval to extend a preliminary investigation beyond six months).

[76] *Id.* §§ II.B.3.a; II.B.4.b.i.

[77] *DIOG* § 7.5.

[78] *AGG-Dom* § II.B.4.b.ii; *see also id.* § V.A.11-13.

Hurricane required the validation of a CHS when the person was opened as a source.[79] Validation included documenting the person's criminal record and motivation for providing information."[80] Because a source's reliability can change, the guidelines directed the FBI to review each CHS's file "at least annually" and "ensure that all available information that might materially alter a prior validation assessment . . . is promptly reported" to a supervisor and documented.[81]

The guidelines also required that an FBI agent instruct the CHS.[82] Because the instructions are important, another agent or official was to be present as a witness.[83] The agent was to direct the CHS to provide truthful information and to "abide by the instructions of the FBI."[84] If the FBI compensated the CHS, the CHS was "liable for any taxes that may be owed."[85] The guidelines explained that "[t]he content and meaning of each of the . . . instructions must be clearly conveyed" to the CHS.[86] Immediately afterward, the agent "shall require" the CHS "to acknowledge his or her receipt and understanding of the instructions."[87]

---

[79] *The Attorney General's Guidelines Regarding the Use of FBI Confidential Human Sources* § II.A (Dec. 13, 2006), *as amended by* Attorney General Orders 3019-2008 (Nov. 26, 2008) and 3596-2015 (Nov. 18, 2015) (hereinafter "*2006 CHS Guidelines*"). In 2020, the Attorney General approved new CHS guidelines. *The Attorney General's Guidelines Regarding the Use of FBI Confidential Human Sources* (Dec. 23, 2020) (hereinafter "*2020 CHS Guidelines*"). The *2020 Guidelines* are discussed below in Section III.B.5.b.

[80] The guidelines required the following information as part of the initial validation:

> whether the person has a criminal history, is reasonably believed to be the subject or target of a pending criminal investigation, is under arrest, or has been charged in a pending prosecution;
>
> the person's motivation for providing information or assistance, including any consideration sought from the government for this assistance; [and]
>
> . . . .
>
> any other information that is required to be documented . . . pursuant to . . . FBI policies.

*2006 CHS Guidelines* § II.A.3.c; A.3.d; A.3.f.

[81] *Id.* § II.C. The FBI was to establish procedures to ensure the prompt reporting of information that might alter a prior assessment. *See id.* § II.C.2.

[82] *Id.* § II.B.1.

[83] *Id.*

[84] *Id.* § II.B.1.a; B.1.d.

[85] *Id.* § II.B.2.f.

[86] *Id.* § II.B.3.

[87] *Id.*

The gui[illegible] [illegible]ot inc[illegible] [illegible]olici[illegible] [illegible]t to document whether the person had pr[illegible] [illegible] a sou[illegible] [illegible]telli[illegible] [illegible] enforcement agency.[88] Moreover, the [illegible] requ[illegible] [illegible]or [illegible] [illegible]proval of the Department before using sources [illegible] [illegible]ersa[illegible] [illegible]ta[illegible] [illegible] not only from targets of its investigations [illegible] Hurri[illegible] [illegible]s P[illegible]adopoulos) but also from a senior campai[illegible] [illegible] whom [illegible] [illegible]s ha[illegible]

*4. An[illegible]*

The FBI [illegible] [illegible]ntellig[illegible] [illegible]ion[illegible] [illegible]onal component, whereas a separate Direc[illegible] [illegible]llige[illegible] [illegible]an[illegible] [illegible]t.[90] The Counterintelligence Division's poli[illegible] [illegible]ays th[illegible] [illegible] are based on integration" of personnel from [illegible] [illegible]es wh[illegible] [illegible]ar[illegible] [illegible]als." Division personnel "must cultivate and d[illegible] [illegible]ship[illegible] [illegible]cto[illegible] [illegible]ence elements "in order to maximize ope[illegible] [illegible]nance[illegible] [illegible]nt[illegible] [illegible]on" the Directorate of Intelligence "f[illegible] [illegible]d tact[illegible] [illegible]or[illegible] [illegible]orities, *the generation of source debriefing pac[illegible]* [illegible]*uatio*[illegible] [illegible]*rep*[illegible] [illegible]ation of various raw intelligence dissemination [illegible] [illegible]he id[illegible] [illegible]of i[illegible] [illegible]aps."[91]

For the [illegible] [illegible]Comm[illegible] [illegible]hol[illegible] [illegible]has directed the Director of National Intel[illegible] [illegible]") t[illegible] [illegible]rso[illegible] [illegible]to be responsible for ensuring that finished i[illegible] [illegible]oduc[illegible] [illegible]ne[illegible] [illegible]independent of political considerations[illegible] [illegible]all s[illegible] [illegible]ail[illegible] [illegible]nce, and employ the standards of proper analyti[illegible] [illegible][92] Th[illegible] [illegible]ce C[illegible] [illegible]s Analytic Standards say that analysts "must [illegible] [illegible]ir fu[illegible] [illegible]obj[illegible] [illegible]with awareness of their own assumptions a[illegible] [illegible]."[93] T[illegible] [illegible]"em[illegible] [illegible]ing techniques and practical mechanisms th[illegible] [illegible]d miti[illegible] [illegible] M[illegible] [illegible]a]ll IC analytic products" should be "[i]ndepend[illegible] [illegible]ical co[illegible] [illegible]" a[illegible] [illegible]storted by . . . advocacy of a particular . . . [illegible] [illegible]r poli[illegible] [illegible]."[95]

Respo[illegible] [illegible]ngres[illegible] [illegible]ry, th[illegible] [illegible]ce Community's Analytic Ombudsman d[illegible] [illegible]"a fe[illegible] [illegible]from [illegible]ere individuals, or groups of

---

[88] *See id.* § II.A[illegible]

[89] *See AGG-D*[illegible] [illegible]VII.C[illegible] [illegible]g co[illegible] [illegible]nitoring as a technique and requiring Depa[illegible] [illegible]val in [illegible] [illegible]me[illegible] [illegible]umstance," but not including the monitoring of [illegible] [illegible]icials [illegible] [illegible]curre[illegible] [illegible]*also Redacted OIG Review* at 30.

[90] The Directo[illegible] [illegible]gence i[illegible] [illegible]e FBI [illegible]ence Branch. *See FBI Leadership & Structure –* [illegible]*ranch*[illegible] [illegible]w[illegible] [illegible]leadership-and-structure.

[91] FBI Counter[illegible] [illegible]Divisi[illegible] [illegible]*ntel*[illegible] [illegible]*ion Policy Directive and Policy Guide* § 5.1 (N[illegible] [illegible](empha[illegible]

[92] 50 U.S.C. § [illegible]

[93] Intelligence [illegible] [illegible]Dire[illegible] [illegible]*nal*[illegible] [illegible]*ds* at 2 (Jan. 2, 2015).

[94] *Id.*

[95] *Id.*

individuals, [took] willful actions that . . . had the effect of politicizing intelligence, hindering objective analysis, or injecting bias into the intelligence process." The Ombudsman's assessment mentioned the reluctance of China analysts "to have their analysis brought forward because they tended to disagree with the Administration's policies." On the other hand, Russia analysts were frustrated because management was "slowing down or not wanting to take their analysis to customers, claiming that it was not well received."[96] The assessment also has a section entitled "historical context." It discusses the politicization of intelligence about Iraq in 2003, but it does not mention Crossfire Hurricane or the Carter Page FISA.[97] The assessment paraphrases former intelligence official Neil Wiley:

> [I]ntelligence is the only great function of state that does not come to top decision makers with an agenda . . . . The purpose of intelligence is to provide objective, unbiased, and policy-neutral assessments. We are, perhaps, most important to decision makers when we bring to them the bad news . . . . This . . . sometimes demands moral courage to carry out. Other institutions are inherently political and are much less likely to bring bad news. If we lose that objectivity, or even are perceived to have lost it, we have endangered the entire reason for us to exist.[98]

*5. **Recently upgraded protections***

a. <u>Investigative activities</u>

The *Sensitive Investigations Memorandum*, promulgated by the Attorney General in 2020, imposes additional approval requirements for politically sensitive activities. If the FBI takes "exploratory investigative steps relating to" a presidential candidate, a senior staff member, or an advisor, it must give prompt written notice to the appropriate Assistant Attorney General and U.S. Attorney. The Attorney General explained that "this includes any person who has been publicly announced by a campaign as a staffer or member of an official campaign advisory committee or group." The same notice requirement applies if the FBI opens an assessment of such a person. If the FBI opens either a preliminary or full investigation of such a person, then

---

[96] Barry Zulauf, *Independent IC Analytic Ombudsman's [sic] on Politicization of Intelligence* at 3 (Jan. 6, 2021) (attached to letter from Zulauf to Senators Rubio and Warner (Jan. 6, 2021).

[97] *See id.* at 8.

[98] *Id.* at 9 (italics omitted).

notice to the Department is not enough; the Attorney General must approve the opening of the investigation.[99]

The memorandum also directs:

- Department components to "review their existing policies governing notification, consultation, and/or approval of politically sensitive investigations," provide a summary of those policies, and recommend "any necessary changes or updates."[100]
- The Department to study, after the 2020 elections, "its experiences and consider whether changes" to the requirements in the memorandum are necessary.[101]

The Attorney General recently reaffirmed the need to adhere to the requirements of the *Sensitive Investigations Memorandum* that govern "the opening of criminal and counter-intelligence investigations by the Department . . . related to politically sensitive individuals and entities."[102]

b. <u>CHS guidelines and policy</u>

In 2020, following various OIG reviews, the FBI undertook a "comprehensive review" of the *2006 CHS Guidelines* "to ensure that the FBI's source validation process was wholly refocused, revised, and improved across the FBI."[103] The *2020 CHS Guidelines* thus provide additional direction to the FBI in the handling of human sources. They require information about whether the CHS "is reasonably believed to be a current or former subject or target of an FBI investigation."[104] There is also a new requirement for information about a source's reporting relationship with other government agencies.[105] At the time when the Attorney General approved the *Guidelines*, he also directed that "pending further guidance" he or the Deputy Attorney General must approve "any use" of a CHS "to target a federal elected official or political campaign . . . for the purposes of investigating political or campaign activities."[106]

---

99 *Sensitive Investigations Memorandum* at 2 & n.3.

100 *Id.* at 3.

101 *Id.*

102 Attorney General Memorandum, *Election Year Sensitivities* (May 25, 2022).

103 Stephen C. Laycock, Memorandum to the Attorney General, *Re: Proposed Revisions to the Attorney General Guidelines Regarding the Use of FBI's Confidential Human Sources* (Dec. 23, 2020).

104 *2020 CHS Guidelines* § II.A.3.c.

105 *Id.* § II.A.3.d.

106 Letter from Attorney General William Barr to FBI Director Christopher Wray (Dec. 23, 2020).

The FBI's *Confidential Human Source Policy Guide*[107] also includes new or strengthened requirements and implements portions of the *Sensitive Investigations Memorandum*. Its requirements include:

- Identifying the specific source-related activities in which FBI intelligence analysts and other non-agent personnel may engage.[108] For example, an intelligence analyst may only contact a CHS or a potential CHS in the presence of a case agent, and an analyst may only accompany an agent to a debriefing of a CHS with supervisory approval.[109]
- Requiring information about "[a]ll likely motivations the CHS could have for providing information."[110]
- Enhancing the requirements for source validation reviews.
- Requiring detailed information and additional approvals in a request to reopen a CHS who was previously closed for cause, either by the FBI or another agency.[111]

Finally, the *CHS Policy Guide* requires a CHS to be treated as "sensitive" and thus subject to more controls based on *either* the position the source holds or the position held by someone the source is reporting on.[112] So, for example, even though a CHS may not hold a position in a campaign, if the source is reporting on such a person he/she would still be treated as sensitive. Post-Crossfire Hurricane, the *Guide* now provides this example:

> A CHS with indirect access to a U.S. Presidential campaign is tasked to report on campaign activities involving possible cooperation with foreign entities to influence the outcome of a U.S. Presidential election. The CHS had only indirect access, but his or her affiliation nevertheless enabled the CHS to be tasked to collect information on the campaign.[113]

c. Defensive briefings

The OIG's review of Crossfire Hurricane discusses defensive briefings for those who may be targets of nefarious activities by foreign powers and, specifically at the time of the

[107] FBI, *Confidential Human Source Policy Guide* (Dec. 15, 2021) (hereinafter "*CHS Policy Guide*").

[108] *Id.* §§ 2.2.3; 2.2.3.1.

[109] *Id.* § 2.2.3.1.

[110] *Id.*

[111] *Id.* §§ 4.3; 4.5.1; *see also* § 4.5.2 (when a closed CHS from one field office is opened in another, the new office "must promptly be provided with any information that reflects negatively upon the reliability of the CHS").

[112] *See id.* § 7.19; *see also* § 6.1 (explaining § 7.19). There is also now a requirement for approval by the Assistant Director of Intelligence. *See* § 7.19.2.1 (requiring an electronic communication to the Assistant Director of the Directorate of Intelligence before the approval request goes to the Director and the Department).

[113] *Id.* § 7.19.1.3.

investigation, th[illegible] of cond[illegible] defens[illegible] for the Trump campaign on Russian activiti[illegible] say[illegible]

> We did [illegible] ry De[illegible] FBI [illegible] applied to this decision and ther[illegible] red th[illegible] onduct defensive briefings in lieu o[illegible] invest[illegible] an investigation, was a judgmen[illegible] left to [illegible] s.

It went on to su[illegible] would [illegible] to g[illegible] Department leadership the opportunity . . . [illegible] the [illegible] whethe[illegible] ct a defensive briefing in a circumstance su[illegible]."[114]

The Dep[illegible] the FB[illegible] steps [illegible] this issue. First, the Attorney General has ins[illegible] FBI Direc[illegible] mulg[illegible] es concerning defensive briefings. The [illegible] requ[illegible] "[t]o [illegible] cerns" that U.S. persons "may become unwitti[illegible] in a[illegible] fore[illegible] influence an election or the policy or condu[illegible] ernm[illegible] nd, th[illegible] established a Foreign Influence Defensive Brie[illegible] (FIDB[illegible] is

> continu[illegible] y impl[illegible] view[illegible] malign foreign influence defensiv[illegible] d in [illegible] ative and Executive Branch [illegible] will [illegible] act[illegible] er receipt of specific threat informa[illegible] t fies [illegible] gn in[illegible] rations – that is, foreign operatio[illegible] versa[illegible] ed [illegible] criminal – including conveni[illegible] B] to [illegible] ether [illegible] provide defensive briefings [illegible] parties[illegible] *fication is warranted and appropr[illegible] ase, [illegible] standardized criteria* guided by princi[illegible] lude, [illegible] the [illegible] of sources and methods and the inte[illegible] pendence [illegible] ing [illegible] estigations and prosecu[illegible]

C. **The Fo[illegible] nce [illegible] Act**

FISA p[illegible] ernme[illegible] autho[illegible] the FISC to use a range of investigative te[illegible] or th[illegible] and [illegible] register and trap and trace devices, which [illegible] unintr[illegible] requ[illegible] information likely to be obtained

---

[114] *See Redacte*[illegible] at 34[illegible]

[115] Attorney Ge[illegible] randum[illegible] *Enhance Compliance, Oversight, and Accountab*[illegible] *pect to* [illegible] *reig*[illegible] *Activities of the Federal Bureau of Investigatio*[illegible] 1, 202[illegible] ter "[illegible] *Reforms Memorandum*").

[116] *See Redacte*[illegible] *ew*, App[illegible] The F[illegible] nse to the Report, at 433 (Dec. 6, 2019) (emphasi[illegible]

[117] FISA conta[illegible] related [illegible] us [illegible] collection activities. The principal provisions of th[illegible] codifie[illegible] U.S.C. §§ [illegible] 2; 1821-1829; 1841-1846; 1861-1864; 1871-18[illegible] 1g; 188[illegible]

is relevant to an FBI investigation.[118] For electronic surveillance, which is among the most intrusive techniques available to the FBI, the requirements are more extensive. We describe below some of the findings required by the statute, FISA's First Amendment proviso, and the certification by a high-ranking Executive Branch official.[119] This subsection concludes by summarizing some of the Executive Branch's requirements for FISA applications, many of which have been added in recent years.

### *1. Required findings*

FISA requires the government submit an application to the FISC describing the target of the surveillance, the techniques that will be used, and other matters.[120] An FBI agent or other federal official swears to the truth of the facts in the application.[121]

The FISC may authorize electronic surveillance if there is probable cause to believe that the target of the surveillance is an agent of a foreign power.[122] For a U.S. person, there are at least two additional related requirements. First, as the House Intelligence Committee's 1978 report on FISA explains, "[a]s a matter of principle . . . no United States citizen . . . should be targeted for electronic surveillance . . . absent some showing that he at least may violate the laws of our society."[123] Second, the person must be knowingly engaged in the specified conduct. Thus, a U.S. person may be an agent of a foreign power if the person is knowingly engaged in clandestine intelligence gathering activities on behalf of a foreign power, or knowingly helping another person in such activities, provided that the activities involve or may involve a violation of U.S. criminal law.[124]

The *House Report* goes on to explain how foreign powers may engage both in intelligence gathering and other nefarious intelligence activities:

---

[118] *See* 50 U.S.C. §1842(c) (requiring that the applicant certify that "the information likely to be obtained . . . is relevant to an ongoing investigation to protect against international terrorism or clandestine intelligence activities, provided that such investigation of a United States person is not conducted solely upon the basis of activities protected by the [F]irst [A]mendment").

[119] This subsection focuses on those provisions of FISA and related procedures most relevant to the Crossfire Hurricane investigation and to the observations in section V. It discusses FISA's requirements for electronic surveillance. FISA contains comparable provisions governing physical searches conducted for foreign intelligence purposes. *See* 50 U.S.C. §§ 1821-25. As pertinent to this report, Carter Page was a target of both electronic surveillance and physical search.

[120] *See* 50 U.S.C. § 1804(a).

[121] *See id.* ("Each application for an order approving electronic surveillance . . . shall be made by a Federal officer in writing upon oath or affirmation to a judge").

[122] *Id.* § 1805(a)(2)(A).

[123] H.R. Rep. No. 95-1283, 95th Cong., 2d Sess., Pt. 1, at 36 (1978) (hereinafter "*House Report*"). The *Report* also says that a citizen "should be able to know that his government cannot invade his privacy with the most intrusive techniques if he conducts himself lawfully."

[124] *See* 50 U.S.C. §§ 1801(b)(2)(A) and (E).

> Not only do foreign powers engage in spying in the United States to obtain information, they also engage in activities which are intended to harm the Nation's security by affecting the course of our Government, the course of public opinion, or the activities of individuals. Such activities may include political action (recruiting, bribery or influencing of public officials to act in favor of the foreign power), disguised propaganda (including the planting of false or misleading articles or stories), and harassment, intimidation, or even assassination of individuals who oppose the foreign power. Such activity can undermine our democratic institutions as well as directly threaten the peace and safety of our citizens.[125]

Consistent with this discussion, a U.S. person engaged in political action or other non-intelligence gathering activity also may fall within the definition of an agent of a foreign power. This is the case if the person knowingly aids or abets, or conspires with:

> any person who . . . pursuant to the direction of an intelligence service or network of a foreign power, knowingly engages in *other clandestine intelligence activities* for or on behalf of such foreign power, which activities *involve or are about to involve* a violation of the criminal statutes of the United States.[126]

Because these other activities may come closer to activity protected by the First Amendment, the required level of criminal involvement is higher in this definition. The *House Report* explains that:

> [T]he activities engaged in must presently involve or be about to involve a violation of Federal criminal law. Again, this is a higher standard than is found in the other definitions, where the activities "may" involve a violation of law. In this area where there is close [sic] line between protected First Amendment activity and the activity giving rise to surveillance, it is most important that where surveillance does occur the activity be such that it involves or is about to involve a violation of a Federal criminal statute.[127]

The *House Report* also discusses the "aiding or abetting" provision at length and says that FISA:

> allows surveillance of any person, including a U.S. person, who knowingly aids or abets any person in the conduct of activities described . . . . The knowledge requirement is applicable to both the status of the person being aided by the proposed subject of the surveillance *and the nature of the activity being promoted.* This standard requires the Government to establish probable cause that the prospective target knows both that the person with whom he is conspiring or whom he is aiding or abetting is engaged in the described activities as an agent of

---

[125] *House Report* at 41.

[126] 50 U.S.C. § 1801(b)(2)(B) (emphases added).

[127] *House Report* at 42.

> a foreign power and that his own conduct is assisting or furthering such activities.[128]

The Report goes on to explain how the earlier surveillance of Martin Luther King, which was justified based on his association with members of the Communist Party, would not meet this standard:

> An illustration of the "knowing" requirement is provided by the case of Dr. Martin Luther King. Dr. King was subjected to electronic surveillance on "national security grounds" when he continued to associate with two advisers whom the Government had apprised him were suspected of being American Communist Party members and by implication, agents of a foreign power. Dr. King's mere continued association and consultation with those advisers, despite the Government's warnings, would clearly not have been a sufficient basis under this bill to target Dr. King as the subject of electronic surveillance.
>
> Indeed, even if there had been probable cause to believe that the advisers alleged to be Communists were engaged in criminal clandestine intelligence activity for a foreign power within the meaning of this section, and even if there were probable cause to believe Dr. King was aware they were acting for a foreign power, *it would also have been necessary under this bill to establish probable cause that Dr. King was knowingly engaged in furthering his advisers' criminal clandestine intelligence activities.* Absent one or more of these required showings, Dr. King could not have been found to be one who knowingly aids or abets a foreign agent.
>
> As noted above, however, the "knowing" requirement can be satisfied by circumstantial evidence, and there is no requirement for the Government to disprove lack of knowledge where the circumstances were such that a reasonable man would know what he was doing.[129]

The King excerpt underscores the need for the target to be knowingly furthering the criminal clandestine intelligence activities of those whom he is aiding, but it also explains that such knowledge may be inferred.

### *2. Protection of First Amendment activities*

In enacting FISA, Congress recognized that "there may often be a narrow line between covert action and lawful activities undertaken by Americans in the exercise of their [F]irst [A]mendment rights."[130] FISA thus includes a provision similar to the one found in the *AGG-Dom* and prohibits any U.S. person from being "considered . . . an agent of a foreign power solely upon the basis of activities protected by the [F]irst [A]mendment."[131] The *House Report* explains that "[t]his provision is intended to reinforce the intent of the committee that lawful

---

[128] *Id.* at 44 (emphasis added).

[129] *Id.* at 44-45 (emphases added).

[130] *House Report* at 41.

[131] 50 U.S.C. § 1805(a)(2)(A); *cf. AGG-Dom* § I.C.3.

political activi[illegible] [illegible]ver be[illegible] [illegible] of probable cause to believe that a U.S. person is [illegible] of a for[illegible][132]

### 3. *Cer[illegible] Exec[illegible]*

An app[illegible] [illegible]lectron[illegible] [illegible] requires a certification by the Director of the [illegible] [illegible]ilar offi[illegible] [illegible] [illegible]ify that a significant purpose of the electronic [illegible] [illegible]s to ob[illegible] [illegible] intell[illegible] [illegible]rmation.[133] One definition of foreign intellig[illegible] [illegible] the s[illegible] [illegible] [illegible]spect to a foreign power or foreign territo[illegible] [illegible] necessar[illegible] [illegible] [illegible]e or security of the United States . . . or the cond[illegible] [illegible]eign aff[illegible] [illegible] Uni[illegible] [illegible][134] The *House Report* says that this category includ[illegible] [illegible] nec[illegible] [illegible]tional [illegible] security and the conduct of foreign affairs. [illegible] [illegible]ot inc[illegible] [illegible]ation [illegible] the views . . . or activities of . . . private citizen[illegible] [illegible] the fo[illegible] [illegible] [illegible]se of the United States."[136] Another defin[illegible] [illegible] intel[illegible] [illegible]form[illegible] [illegible]ssary . . . to protect against . . . clandestine int[illegible] [illegible]vities [illegible] [illegible]genc[illegible] network of a foreign power or by an agent of a fo[illegible][137] [illegible] [illegible]g offi[illegible] designate the type or types of foreign intellig[illegible] [illegible]ation so[illegible] [illegible]nclu[illegible] [illegible]ation of the basis for that certification.[138]

The offi[illegible] [illegible] so certi[illegible] [illegible] forei[illegible] [illegible]ce sought cannot be obtained by normal investi[illegible] [illegible]ques, a[illegible] [illegible]al m[illegible] [illegible] the basis for that certification.[139] In other words, [illegible] must e[illegible] [illegible] the g[illegible] cannot obtain the information sought throug[illegible] [illegible] [illegible]rusi[illegible] [illegible]s, su[illegible] [illegible]ng government records and publicly availa[illegible] [illegible]n, int[illegible] [illegible] the [illegible] [illegible]rveillance, or using informants. "This requirem[illegible] [illegible]use Rep[illegible] [illegible] is pa[illegible] [illegible]portant in those cases when U.S. citizens or res[illegible] [illegible] the [illegible] [illegible] surv[illegible][140]

The ce[illegible] [illegible]quirem[illegible] [illegible] [illegible]lies [illegible] [illegible]se of the surveillance and to the use of electron[illegible] [illegible] as a[illegible] [illegible]ive te[illegible] [illegible]y its terms, it does not apply to the accuracy of th[illegible] [illegible]formatio[illegible] [illegible]licati[illegible] [illegible] addressed by the sworn statement of an FBI agen[illegible] [illegible] [illegible]deral off[illegible] [illegible]d by [illegible] [illegible]ive Branch requirements described below.

---

[132] *House Rep*[illegible]

[133] 50 U.S.C. [illegible] [illegible](E).

[134] *Id.* § 1801([illegible]

[135] *House Rep*[illegible]

[136] *Id.*

[137] 50 U.S.C. [illegible] [illegible]().

[138] *Id.* §§ 1804[illegible] [illegible](a)(6[illegible]

[139] *Id.* §§ 1804[illegible] [illegible](a)(6[illegible]

[140] *House Rep*[illegible]

[141] *See supra* [illegible]

### 4. *Executive Branch requirements*

Over 20 years ago, the FBI adopted procedures designed to ensure the accuracy of the information contained in FISA applications. These are often referred to as the "Woods Procedures," after their principal author.[142] The recent OIG reviews of the Page and other FISA applications raised concerns about compliance with the Woods Procedures and the accuracy and completeness of the information in FISA applications.[143] As a result, the Department has made numerous filings with the FISC, and the FISC has also directed that changes be made:[144]

- For all applications, the FBI now requires that both an agent and a supervisor must affirm that the Office of Intelligence ("OI") of NSD, which represents the Government before the FISC, "has been apprised of all information that might reasonably call into question the accuracy of the information in the application or otherwise raise doubts about the requested probable cause findings or the theory of the case."[145]
- Before the government files an application for electronic surveillance of a federal elected official, a candidate for federal office, or a staffer of such a person, the Attorney General has directed that an FBI field office not involved in the investigation must "review[] the case file and evaluate[] the proposed filing for accuracy and completeness."[146]

The Attorney General also has imposed other limitations on applications for electronic surveillance in politically sensitive matters:

- Defensive briefings. Before the government files an application with the FISC, the FBI Director must consider "conducting a defensive briefing of the target." Then, either the FBI must conduct a briefing or, "if the Director determines that such a briefing is not appropriate," the Director must document that determination in writing.[147] This is in addition to the general requirement described above for the FBI to establish procedures for defensive briefings.
- Duration of surveillance. The maximum duration the government may seek from the FISC for a surveillance is 60 days. This is shorter than the statutorily permitted 90-day maximum for surveillance of a U.S. person. In addition, every 30 days, the government

---

[142] For a description of the Woods Procedures and a discussion of accuracy issues and the FISC, *see* 1 David Kris & Douglas Wilson, *National Security Investigations & Prosecutions* § 6.3 (2019).

[143] *E.g., Redacted OIG Review* at viii-x; *Audit of 29 Applications* at i.

[144] *See, e.g., In re Accuracy Concerns Regarding FBI Matters Submitted to the FISC*, Corrected Op. and Order at 4, Misc. No. 19-02 (FISC Mar. 5, 2020); *In re Carter W. Page,* Order Regarding Handling and Disposition of Information at 1, Nos. 16-1182, 17-52, 17-375, and 17-679 (FISC Jan. 7, 2020).

[145] Declaration of Christopher W. Wray, *In Re Accuracy Concerns*, Docket No. Misc. 19-02, at 3 (Jan. 10, 2020) (hereinafter "*Wray Declaration*").

[146] *Supplemental Reforms Memorandum* at 2.

[147] *Id.*

must report to the FISC "on the results of the approved surveillance and the continued need for such authority."[148]

## D. Statutes Used to Evaluate Possible Criminal Conduct

This section begins with a brief description of the burden of proof that the government faces in every criminal case. It then describes the principal statutes that we considered to evaluate possible criminal conduct and exactly what must be proven beyond a reasonable doubt in order for a jury to convict.

### 1. *Standard of proof beyond a reasonable doubt*

The government has the burden of proving that a defendant committed any criminal offense beyond a reasonable doubt. A standard jury instruction on reasonable doubt is:

> The government has the burden of proving [name of defendant] guilty beyond a reasonable doubt. In civil cases, it is only necessary to prove that a fact is more likely true than not, or, in some cases, that its truth is highly probable. In criminal cases such as this one, the government's proof must be more powerful than that. It must be beyond a reasonable doubt. Reasonable doubt, as the name implies, is a doubt based on reason—a doubt for which you have a reason based upon the evidence or lack of evidence in the case. If, after careful, honest, and impartial consideration of all the evidence, you cannot say that you are firmly convinced of the defendant's guilt, then you have a reasonable doubt.
>
> Reasonable doubt is the kind of doubt that would cause a reasonable person, after careful and thoughtful reflection, to hesitate to act in the graver or more important matters in life. However, it is not an imaginary doubt, nor a doubt based on speculation or guesswork; it is a doubt based on reason. The government is not required to prove guilt beyond all doubt, or to a mathematical or scientific certainty. Its burden is to prove guilt beyond a reasonable doubt.[149]

### 2. *False statements*

The principal federal statute criminalizing false statements to government investigators is 18 U.S.C. § 1001. As relevant here, subsection 1001(a)(2) makes it a crime "in any matter within the jurisdiction of the executive . . . branch of the Government" knowingly and willfully to "make [] any materially false, fictitious, or fraudulent statement or representation." The government must prove five elements beyond a reasonable doubt to obtain a conviction under this provision:

> *First*, the defendant made a statement or representation;
>
> *Second*, the statement or representation was false, fictitious or fraudulent;
>
> *Third*, this statement or representation was material;

---

[148] *Id.* at 3.

[149] *Criminal Jury Instructions for the District of Columbia* 2.108 (5th ed. 2014).

*Fourth*, the false, fictitious or fraudulent statement was made knowingly and willfully; and

*Fifth*, the statement or representation was made in a matter within the jurisdiction of the executive branch of the government.[150]

The *Mueller Report* contains additional discussion of these requirements:

> An FBI investigation is a matter within the Executive Branch's jurisdiction. *United States v. Rodgers*, 466 U.S. 475, 479 (1984). The statute also applies to a subset of legislative branch actions—*viz.*, administrative matters and "investigation[s] or review[s]" conducted by a congressional committee or subcommittee. 18 U.S.C. § 1001(c)(1) and (2); *see United States v. Pickett*, 353 F.3d 62, 66 (D.C. Cir. 2004).
>
> Whether the statement was made to law enforcement or congressional investigators, the government must prove beyond a reasonable doubt the same basic non-jurisdictional elements: the statement was false, fictitious, or fraudulent; the defendant knew both that it was false and that it was unlawful to make a false statement; and the false statement was material. *See, e.g., United States v. Smith*, 831 F.3d 1207, 1222 n.27 (9th Cir. 2017) (listing elements); *see also* Ninth Circuit Pattern Instruction 8.73 & cmt. (explaining that the section 1001 jury instruction was modified in light of the Department of Justice's position that the phrase "knowingly and willfully" in the statute requires the defendant's knowledge that his or her conduct was unlawful). In the D.C. Circuit, the government must prove that the statement was actually false; a statement that is misleading but "literally true" does not satisfy section 1001(a)(2). *See United States v. Milton*, 8 F.3d 39, 45 (D.C. Cir. 1993); *United States v. Dale*, 991 F.2d 819, 832-33 & n.22 (D.C. Cir. 1993). For that false statement to qualify as "material," it must have a natural tendency to influence, or be capable of influencing, a discrete decision or any other function of the agency to which it is addressed. *See United States v. Gaudin*, 515 U.S. 506, 509 (1995); *United States v. Moore*, 612 F.3d 698, 701 (D.C. Cir. 2010).[151]

### *3. Perjury*

18 U.S.C. § 1621 provides that:

> Whoever--
>
> (1) having taken an oath before a competent tribunal, officer, or person, in any case in which a law of the United States authorizes an oath to be administered, that he will testify, declare, depose, or certify truly, or that any written testimony, declaration, deposition, or certificate by him subscribed, is true, willfully and

[150] *See generally* 2 *Modern Federal Jury Instructions* ¶ 36.01, Instruction 36-9: "Elements of the Offense."

[151] 1 *Mueller Report* at 191-92.

> contrary [illegible] states [illegible] atter which he does not believe [illegible]
>
> (2) in [illegible] certi[illegible] ent under penalty of perjury [illegible] under [illegible] ed States Code, willfully subscrib[illegible] mate[illegible] believe to be true;
>
> is guilty [illegible].

18 U.S.C. § 16[illegible] s that:

> Whoeve[illegible] (or in [illegible] verification, or statement under pe[illegible] ury as [illegible] nder [illegible] 6 of title 28, United States Code) in [illegible] ng be[illegible] llary [illegible] or grand jury of the United [illegible] gly ma[illegible] aration or makes or uses any othe[illegible] inc[illegible] ment, record, recording, or other m[illegible] ing th[illegible] ntai[illegible] aterial declaration, shall be fine[illegible] e or in[illegible] ot m[illegible] years, or both.

The Departmen[illegible] *Resou*[illegible] ons 1621 and 1623 share four common eleme[illegible] ernme[illegible] beyond a reasonable doubt. The Manual summa[illegible] ements [illegible]

> The firs[illegible] perju[illegible] tha[illegible] ent must be under oath during [illegible], declar[illegible] tific[illegible] the perjurious statement is an uns[illegible] ation [illegible] 28 [illegible] 5.
>
> The seco[illegible] elem[illegible] the [illegible] must have made a false statemen[illegible]
>
> The thir[illegible] is pr[illegible] that the defendant made the fals[illegible] ith kn[illegible] its [illegible] than as a result of confusi[illegible] r fault[illegible]
>
> The fal[illegible] must b[illegible] the [illegible].[152]

In addition to th[illegible] above[illegible] al e[illegible] of the requirements in more detail as well as the d[illegible] ong th[illegible] prov[illegible]

*4. Fal[illegible] record[illegible]*

18 U.S.[illegible] poses [illegible] ility [illegible] son who:

> knowin[illegible] s [] [illegible] false [illegible] record, document, or tangibl[illegible] the in[illegible] e, [illegible] fluence the investigation or prop[illegible] t on of [illegible] with [illegible] liction of any department or

[152] U.S. Depart[illegible] ce, *Cri*[illegible] *rce*[illegible] 1744-48, Elements of Perjury (Dec. 7, 2018) [illegible] ent), [illegible] v.just[illegible] hives/usam/criminal-resource-manual-1744-el[illegible] ury.

> agency of the United States . . . or in relation to or contemplation of any such matter.

The government must prove three elements beyond a reasonable doubt to obtain a conviction under section 1519:

*First*, the defendant knowingly falsified a document;

*Second*, the defendant did so with the intent to impede, obstruct, or influence an investigation [or] the proper administration of a matter; and

*Third*, the investigation or matter was within the jurisdiction of the Department, the FBI, or another federal department or agency.[153]

5. ***Obstruction of justice***

There are several statutes that cover conduct intended to obstruct or impede government investigations.[154] 18 U.S.C. § 1512(c)(2) is an omnibus obstruction-of-justice provision that covers a range of obstructive acts directed at pending or contemplated official proceedings. 18 U.S.C. §§ 1503 and 1505 also offer broad protection against obstructive acts directed at pending grand jury, judicial, administrative, and congressional proceedings, and they are supplemented by a provision in section 1512(b) aimed specifically at conduct intended to prevent or hinder the communication to law enforcement of information related to a federal crime. The *Mueller Report* describes these requirements and noted that "[t]hree basic elements are common to the obstruction statutes pertinent to the Office's charging decisions: an obstructive act; some form of nexus between the obstructive act and an official proceeding; and criminal (*i.e.*, corrupt) intent."[155]

6. ***Violation of civil rights***

18 U.S.C. § 242 makes it a crime for anyone, acting under color of law, willfully to deprive any person of a right secured by the Constitution or laws of the United States. The government must prove three elements beyond a reasonable doubt to obtain a conviction under section 242:

*First*, the defendant deprived the person of an identified right, such as the right to due process of law, secured by the Constitution or laws of the United States.

*Second*, the defendant acted willfully, that is, the defendant committed such act or acts with a bad purpose to disobey or disregard the law, specifically intending to deprive the person of that right. To find that the defendant was acting willfully, it is not necessary for the government to prove that the defendant knew the specific constitutional provision or federal law that his or her conduct violated. But the defendant must have a specific intent to deprive the person of a right protected by the Constitution or federal law.

---

[153] *See generally Model Crim. Jury Instr.* 8th Cir. 6.18.1519 (2020).

[154] *See* 18 U.S.C. §§ 1503, 1505, 1512(b)(3), 1512(c)(2).

[155] 1 *Mueller Report* at 192.

*Third*, the defendant acted under color of law. Acting "under color of law" means acts done under any state law, county or city ordinance, or other governmental regulation, and acts done according to a custom of some governmental agency. It means that the defendant acted in his or her official capacity or else claimed to do so, but abused or misused his or her power by going beyond the bounds of lawful authority.[156]

### 7. *Conspiracy to violate civil rights*

18 U.S.C. § 241 makes it a crime to conspire to deprive a person of his or her civil rights. The government must prove three elements beyond a reasonable doubt to obtain a conviction under section 241:

*First*, the defendant entered into a conspiracy to injure, oppress, threaten, or intimidate a named victim;

*Second*, the defendant intended to interfere with the named victim's exercise or enjoyment of a right that is secured (or protected) by the Constitution (or laws) of the United States; and

*Third*, the named victim was present in any state, district, or territory of the United States.[157]

### 8. *General conspiracy statute*

A conspiracy under 18 U.S.C. § 371 requires the government to prove four elements beyond a reasonable doubt:

*First*, two or more persons in some way agreed to try to accomplish a shared and unlawful plan;

*Second*, the defendant knew the unlawful purpose of the plan and willfully joined in it;

*Third*, during the conspiracy, one of the conspirators knowingly engaged in at least one overt act as described in the indictment; and

*Fourth*, the overt act was committed at or about the time alleged and with the purpose of carrying out or accomplishing some object of the conspiracy.[158]

In addition to criminalizing an agreement whose object is to violate a federal criminal law, section 371 also criminalizes a conspiracy "to defraud the United States, or any agency thereof for any manner or for any purpose." This may also include interfering with the performance of official duties by government officials.[159]

---

[156] *See, e.g., Pattern Crim. Jury Instr.* 5th Cir. 2.12 (2019).

[157] *See Modern Federal Jury Instructions-Criminal*, LexisNexis Form 485-17-33 (Elements of the Offense).

[158] *See, e.g., Pattern Crim. Jury Instr.* 11th Cir. OI O13.1 (WL 2020).

[159] *See United States v. Klein*, 247 F.2d 908, 916 (2d Cir. 1957); Practical Law Securities & White Collar Crime, *Conspiracy Charges: Overview*, w-009-8988 (WL 2022).

*9. **Campaign contributions***

52 U.S.C. § 30116(a)(1)(A) provides that "no person shall make contributions to any candidate and his authorized political committees with respect to any election for Federal office which, in the aggregate, exceed $2,000." The term "person" includes "an individual, partnership, committee, association, corporation, labor organization, or any other organization or group of persons."[160] "Contributions" are defined as, "any gift . . . or deposit of . . . anything of value made by any person for the purpose of influencing any election for Federal office."[161] Contributions do not include, "the value of services provided without compensation by any individual who volunteers on behalf of a candidate or political committee."[162] Section 30116(c) provides for adjustments for inflation, stating that limitations for contributions by persons to federal candidates are adjusted every two years.[163] The limitation for an individual donor to a candidate committee for the 2015-2016 election cycle was $2,700.[164]

Violations of section 30116 by a person qualify as a crime if, (1) the violation involved at least the amount specified in a calendar year, and (2) the violation was committed knowingly and willfully.[165]

*10. **Campaign contributions by foreign nationals***

52 U.S.C. § 30121(a)(1)(A) makes it a crime for "a foreign national, directly or indirectly . . . to make a contribution or donation of money or other thing of value, or to make an express or implied promise to make a contribution or donation, in connection with a Federal . . . election." Subsection (a)(2) makes it a crime for any person to solicit, accept, or receive such a contribution or donation.

*11. **Fraud against the United States***

18 U.S.C. § 1031(a) imposes criminal liability on:

> Whoever knowingly executes, or attempts to execute, any scheme or artifice with the intent—
>
> > (1) to defraud the United States; or
> >
> > (2) to obtain money or property by means of false or fraudulent pretenses, representations, or promises,

---

[160] 52 U.S.C. § 30101(11).

[161] *Id.* § 30101(8)(A)(i).

[162] *Id.* § 30101(8)(B)(i).

[163] *Id.* § 30116(c).

[164] Federal Election Commission, *Archive of Contribution Limits*, https:www.fec.gov/help-candidates-and-committees/candidate-taking-receipts/archived-contribution-limits/.

[165] 52 U.S.C. § 30109(d)(1)(A).

> in any [illegible] . . . [illegible] of [illegible] tance . . . if the value of such gr[illegible] . or [illegible] nce . . . is $1,000,000 or more . . .

The governme[illegible] three [illegible] le doubt to obtain a conviction under section 1[illegible]

*First*, th[illegible] heme with the intent to defraud the United Sta[illegible] ney [illegible] lly false or fraudulent pretenses, representations[illegible];

*Second*[illegible] ok pl[illegible] operty, services, or money as a contractor with [illegible] tes [illegible] plier on a contract with the United States; and

*Third*, th[illegible] contr[illegible] 00,000 or more.[166]

*12. Mo[illegible]ng*

18 U.S.[illegible] 1)(A) [illegible]:

> Whoev[illegible] at the [illegible] ncial transaction represents the proc[illegible] form[illegible] ts or attempts to conduct such a fi[illegible] action [illegible] proceeds of specified unlawf[illegible]
>
> [illegible] tent to [illegible] specified unlawful [illegible];
>
> [illegible] to en[illegible] a violation of section [illegible] of the [illegible] 986.

To obta[illegible] unde[illegible] government must prove the following three [illegible] ond [illegible] doubt

*First*, th[illegible] ondu[illegible]) a financial transaction involving property consti[illegible] eeds [illegible] ty;

*Second*, [illegible] kne[illegible] in the financial transaction was the proceeds of so[illegible] awfu[illegible]

*Third*, [illegible] cted [illegible] he [illegible] note the carrying on of specified unlawful activi[illegible] inten[illegible] ng certain provisions of the Internal Reven[illegible]

18 U.S.[illegible] poses [illegible] bility

> Whoev[illegible] gly en[illegible] in a monetary transaction in crimi[illegible] prop[illegible] 10,000 and is derived from

---

[166] *See Pattern* [illegible] str. 1[illegible]

[167] *See 3 Mode*[illegible] *y In*[illegible] (Lexis).

specified unlawful activity [and does so either] in the United States or in the special maritime and territorial jurisdiction of the United States [or] outside the United States and such special jurisdiction, but the defendant is a United States person.

To obtain a conviction under section 1957, the government must prove the following five elements beyond a reasonable doubt:

*First*, the defendant engaged (or attempted to engage) in a monetary transaction in or affecting interstate commerce;

*Second*, the monetary transaction involved criminally derived property of a value greater than $10,000;

*Third*, the property was derived from specified unlawful activity;

*Fourth*, the defendant acted knowingly, that is, with knowledge that the transaction involved proceeds of a criminal offense; and

*Fifth*, the transaction took place in the United States, or the defendant is a U.S. person.[168]

Finally, 18 U.S.C. § 1956(h) imposes criminal liability on any person who conspires to commit any offense defined in section 1956 or 1957. To obtain a conviction under section 1956(h), the government must prove the following three elements beyond a reasonable doubt:

*First*, two or more persons reached an agreement to commit one of the specified offenses;

*Second*, the defendant voluntarily and intentionally joined in the agreement or understanding, either at the time it was first reached or at some later time while it was still in effect; and

*Third*, at the time the defendant joined in the agreement or understanding, he/she knew the purpose of the agreement or understanding.[169]

*13. **Disclosure of national defense information***

18 U.S.C. § 793(d) imposes criminal liability on:

Whoever, lawfully having possession of, access to, control over, or being entrusted with any document, writing, code book, signal book, sketch, photograph, photographic negative, blueprint, plan, map, model, instrument, appliance, or note relating to the national defense, or information relating to the national defense which information the possessor has reason to believe could be used to the injury of the United States or to the advantage of any foreign nation, willfully communicates, delivers, transmits or causes to be communicated, delivered, or transmitted or attempts to communicate, deliver, transmit or cause to be communicated, delivered or transmitted the same to any person not entitled to

---

[168] *See* 3 *Modern Federal Jury Instructions-Criminal* P 50A.06 (Lexis).

[169] *See Modern Federal Jury Instructions-Criminal* 6.18.1956K (8th Cir.) (Lexis 2022).

> receive it, or willfully retains the same and fails to deliver it on demand to the officer or employee of the United States entitled to receive it.

Modern Federal Jury Instructions summarizes the elements that the government must prove beyond a reasonable doubt to obtain a conviction under section 793(d):

> *First*, that the defendant had lawful . . . possession of (or access to or control over) [describe document].
>
> *Second*, that the [document] was related to the national defense.
>
> *Third*, that the defendant had reason to believe that the document could be used to the injury of the United States or to the advantage of [name of foreign country].
>
> *Fourth*, that on [insert date], the defendant willfully communicated (or delivered or transmitted or caused to be communicated, delivered, or transmitted or attempted to communicate, deliver or transmit) the document to [name of person], who was not entitled to receive it.[170]

## IV. Background Facts and Prosecution Decisions

This section begins by providing factual information about the FBI's New York Field Office ("NYFO") investigation of Carter Page in the spring of 2016 (Subsection A.1); the text messages between certain FBI officials that on their face show a predisposition to investigate Trump (Subsection A.2); and the predication, opening, and conduct of the Crossfire Hurricane investigation (Subsections A.3 through A.5). This part concludes with a comparison of some of the FBI's investigative decisions related to Clinton with some of those related to Trump (Subsection A.6). The remaining parts of this section each include a factual background and then describe the prosecutive decisions the Office made. The first addresses an investigative referral of a possible Clinton "campaign plan" (Subsection B). The next is an extensive discussion of the FISA applications targeting Page (Subsection C). The last part of this section covers conduct by private-sector actors in connection with Crossfire Hurricane and related subjects (Subsection D). In describing these matters, this section does not endeavor to repeat or restate all the information that the Office and others[171] have covered and made public. Instead, it aims to add to that body of information, include additional relevant facts, and explain the prosecutive decisions we made.

The *Appointment Order* authorized the Special Counsel "to prosecute federal crimes arising from his investigation" of the matters assigned to him.[172] What is stated in the *Mueller Report* is equally true for our investigation:

> In deciding whether to exercise this prosecutorial authority, the Office has been guided by the Principles of Federal Prosecution set forth in the Justice . . . Manual. In particular, the Office has evaluated whether the conduct of the

---

[170] 1 *Modern Federal Jury Instructions-Criminal* § 29.04 (2022).

[171] These include most notably the OIG in its comprehensive reports, the *Mueller Report*, the *SSCI Russia Report*, and the *FBI Inspection Division Report*.

[172] *Appointment Order* ¶ (b).

individuals considered for prosecution constituted a federal offense and whether admissible evidence would probably be sufficient to obtain and sustain a conviction for such an offense. Where the answer to those questions was yes, the Office further considered whether the prosecution would serve a substantial federal interest, the individuals were subject to effective prosecution in another jurisdiction, and there existed an adequate non-criminal alternative to prosecution.[173]

These considerations, as explained below, led the Office to charge three individuals with making false statements. The Office considered whether other individuals, including individuals in the government, made false statements to the FBI, the OIG, or congressional committees or whether, during the course of the Office's investigation, other individuals interviewed either omitted material information or provided false information. Again, what is stated in the *Mueller Report* is also true for our investigation:

> Applying the Principles of Federal Prosecution, the Office did not seek criminal charges against any individuals other than those listed above. In some instances, that decision was due to evidentiary hurdles to proving falsity. In others, the Office determined that the witness ultimately provided truthful information and that considerations of culpability, deterrence, and resource preservation weighed against prosecution.[174]

The Office determined that other matters it investigated either did not involve the commission of a federal crime or that our evidence was not sufficient to obtain and sustain a criminal conviction.

In addition to its prosecution and declination decisions, the Office made the following referrals to other entities:

- A referral on June 30, 2020 to the FBI's Washington Field Office ("WFO") regarding a matter related to an existing counterintelligence investigation.
- A referral in December 2020 to OI of information relevant to the accuracy of information contained in four non-Page FISA applications.
- Referrals of two matters on December 14, 2022 to the Inspector General of the Department of Defense with a copy to the General Counsel of the Defense Intelligence Agency. One matter involved the execution of a contract between DARPA and the Georgia Institute of Technology; and a separate matter involved the irregular conduct in 2016 of two former employees of the Department of Defense.
- A referral to the FBI's OGC and Inspection Division of an FBI agent for failing to document properly the known history of Igor Danchenko upon his opening as an FBI CHS.

---

[173] 1 *Mueller Report* at 174 (citations omitted). For a discussion of the *Principles of Federal Prosecution, see supra* § III.A; *Justice Manual* § 9-27.220 (2018).

[174] 1 *Mueller Report* at 198-99.

- A refer[illegible] OG[illegible] [illegible] the same FBI agent for question[illegible] [illegible]ions g[illegible] [illegible] the taxability of cash payments made to [illegible] FBI.

In addition to [illegible] escrib[illegible] [illegible] vided information to the FBI's Inspection Div[illegible] certai[illegible] former FBI employees.

## A. The Cr[illegible] icane [illegible]

### *1. Ne[illegible] Offi[illegible]*

In late [illegible] Carte[illegible] consultant, was named a foreign policy [illegible] Do[illegible] 201[illegible] al campaign. Page's prior business exper[illegible] agely [illegible] Rus[illegible] asian energy issues, and as such, he frequ[illegible] ted wi[illegible] Russi[illegible] ls. Based on his previous Russian conta[illegible] s know[illegible] interviewed on three occasions between 2009 [illegible] the [illegible] 2015, [illegible] ain interviewed by the FBI in connection wit[illegible] ent of [illegible] fficers in the Southern District of New York. A[illegible] crim[illegible] int [illegible] ntly returned indictment in that case, Page had [illegible] ed b[illegible] gence [illegible] an apparent failed recruitment effort.[175] In th[illegible] mplai[illegible] igen[illegible] ferred to Page, anonymized as "Male-1," as a[illegible] Page d[illegible] receptive to the recruitment efforts.[176] Pag[illegible] ewed [illegible] government witness in that case.[177] One defendant[illegible] akov, [illegible] ilty [illegible] and was sentenced to 30 months of imprisonment.[illegible] her [illegible] the [illegible] rotected by diplomatic immunity and are no lon[illegible] ted St[illegible]

In Apr[illegible] ty aft[illegible] nam[illegible] visor to the Trump campaign, the NYFO op[illegible] erintel[illegible] estig[illegible] n. According to the case agent in the matter ("[illegible] Agent-[illegible] ation, the FBI was not so

---

[175] *See* Sealed [illegible] *nited* [illegible] *a/k/a Zhenya," et al.* (S.D.N.Y.) ¶¶ 1-4 (Jan. 3, [illegible] after [illegible] *Buryakov Complaint* has been unsealed.); *see* [illegible] ent [illegible] ffairs, *Attorney General Holder Announces Ch*[illegible] *Russi*[illegible] *ty* (Jan. 26, 2015); *see generally Redacted OIG* [illegible] -62 (d[illegible] ussia[illegible] in New York and the FBI's interviews of [illegible]

[176] *See Buryak*[illegible] at 12-[illegible] Nakashima, Devlin Barrett & Adam Entous, [illegible] *FIS*[illegible] *Trump Advisor Carter Page*, Wash. Post (A[illegible] quot[illegible] suspects" as saying that Page was an "idiot").

[177] OSC Repo[illegible] of N[illegible] Age[illegible] 5, 2019 at 2.

[178] U.S. Depar[illegible] ice, U.S. [illegible] 's Of[illegible] rn District of New York, Russian Banker Senten[illegible] tan [illegible] t to [illegible] Prison for Conspiring to Work for Russian In[illegible] y 25, [illegible]

[179] *Id.* at 4; Na[illegible] *Russia*[illegible] *spy role gets two-and-a-half years prison*, Reuter[illegible] 016).

concerned about Page, but rather it was concerned about the Russians reaching out to Page.[180] Moreover, NYFO Case Agent-1 told the Office that there were no plans to seek FISA coverage on Page.[181] NYFO Case Agent-1 and her FBI supervisor informed the OIG that Page's role as a foreign policy advisor "did not influence their decision to open a case on Page."[182] It may, however, have affected the timing of the case opening and increased interest in him. Indeed, Director Comey had earlier in April "requested relevant information pertaining to any Presidential candidate."[183] In line with that directive, Comey was briefed on the Page investigation, which a week later was described as a "top priority" for the Director.[184] At that time, FBI personnel in Washington prepared a counterintelligence report on Page for the Director.[185] In July, the same personnel described the Page case, "and ones like it" as, "a top priority for Director Comey."[186] In any event, despite Page's role as a publicly named foreign policy advisor, the FBI did not open the investigation as a "Sensitive Investigative Matter" or SIM.[187]

A few months later, shortly after the FBI opened the Crossfire Hurricane investigation at FBI Headquarters and the four sub-files, including on Page, the NYFO's investigation of Page was transferred to the Crossfire Hurricane investigation at FBI Headquarters.[188]

2. ***Evidence of predisposition to investigate Trump***

The record reviewed by the Office demonstrated a rather clear predisposition on the part of at least certain FBI personnel at the center of Crossfire Hurricane to open an

---

180 OSC Report of Interview of NYFO Case Agent-1 on Sept. 5, 2019 at 2.

181 *Id.*

182 *Redacted OIG Review* at 63; *see also id.* at 62 (noting supervisor's view that investigation should have been opened earlier).

183 FBI-AAA-21-0000829 (Email from Headquarters Supervisory Special Agent-1 to Auten & others dated 04/01/2016). Comey declined through counsel to be interviewed by the Office. Counsel indicated his client had previously testified in various Congressional hearings and been interviewed by various government entities on all matters relating to Crossfire Hurricane.

184 *Id.*; FBI-AAA-21-0000798 (Email to Headquarters Supervisory Special Agent-1, Auten & others dated 04/07/2016); FBI-AAA-21-0000828 (Email from Headquarters Supervisory Special Agent-1 to Auten & others dated 07/01/2016).

185 FBI-AAA-21-0000798 (Email to Headquarters Supervisory Special Agent-1, Auten & others dated 04/07/2016).

186 FBI-AAA-21-0000828 (Email from Headquarters Supervisory Special Agent-1 to Auten & others dated 07/01/2016).

187 *See* OSC Report of Interview of NYFO Case Agent-1 on Sept. 5, 2019 at 3; *Redacted OIG Review* at 62-63.

188 *Redacted OIG Review* at 63.

investigation of Trump. For example, Peter Strzok [189] and Lisa Page[190] were directly involved in matters relating to the opening of Crossfire Hurricane. Strzok was the Agent who both wrote and approved the electronic communication opening the matter from the very start as a full investigation rather than an assessment or preliminary investigation. At the time, Page was serving as Deputy Director Andrew McCabe's Special Assistant, and, according to Strzok, it was McCabe who directed that the Crossfire Hurricane investigation be "opened immediately" after information described more fully below was received from Australian authorities in late July 2016.[191] Over a period of months prior to the opening of Crossfire Hurricane, Strzok and Page had exchanged numerous messages, which are already in the public domain and express a very clear prejudice against Trump. For example:

<u>August 16, 2015</u>:

| | |
|---|---|
| Strzok: | [Bernie Sanders is] an idiot like Trump.[192] |

<u>December 20, 2015</u> (After exchanging an article about Trump):

| | |
|---|---|
| Page: | What an utter idiot. |
| Strzok: | No doubt.[193] |

<u>March 3, 2016</u>:

| | |
|---|---|
| Page: | God [T]rump is a loathsome human. |
| Strzok: | Yet he may win [the Republican nomination]. Good for Hillary. |
| Page: | It is. |
| Strzok: | Would he be a worse president than [C]ruz? |
| Page: | Trump? Yes, I think so. |
| Strzok: | I'm not sure. Omg [Trump's] an idiot. |
| Page: | He's awful. |
| Strzok: | America will get what the voting public deserves. |
| Page: | That's what I'm afraid of. |

---

[189] Strzok was a Section Chief and later the Deputy Assistant Director in the FBI's Counterintelligence Division. (For the positions held by those involved in the Crossfire Hurricane investigation, see the chart in the *Redacted OIG Review* at 81-82.) Strzok agreed to provide information to the Office concerning matters related to the FBI's Alfa Bank investigation, but otherwise declined to be interviewed by the Office on matters related to his role in the Crossfire Hurricane investigation.

[190] Page was an attorney in FBI's OGC who was detailed as a Special Assistant to Deputy Director McCabe's Office.

[191] Strzok, *Compromised* at 115.

[192] FBI-0008217 (Office of Professional Responsibility [OPR] letter to Strzok dated 08/08/2016) at 4.

[193] *Id.*

Strzok: God, Hillary should win 100,000,000 – 0.[194]

May 3, 2016:

Page: And holy [expletive] Cruz just dropped out of the race. It's going to be a Clinton Trump race. Unbelievable.
Strzok: What?!?!??
Page: You heard that right my friend.
Strzok: I saw [T]rump won, figured it would be a bit. Now the pressure really starts to finish [the Clinton email investigation] . . .
Page: It sure does.[195]

July 18, 2016 (During the Republican National Convention):

Strzok: Oooh, TURN IT ON, TURN IT ON!!! THE DOUCHE BAGS ARE ABOUT TO COME OUT. You can tell by the excitable clapping.
Page: And wow, Donald Trump is an enormous d*uche.

July 19, 2016:

Strzok: Hi How was Trump, other than a douche?
Page: Trump barely spoke, but the first thing out of his mouth was "we're going to win soooo big." The whole thing is like living in a bad dream.[196]

July 21, 2016:

Strzok: Trump is a disaster. I have no idea how destabilizing his Presidency would be.[197]

July 27, 2016:

Page: Have we opened on him yet? Trump & Putin. Yes, It's Really a Thing http://talkingpointsmemo.com/edblog/trumpputin-yes-it-s-really-a-thing
Strzok: Opened on Trump? If Hillary did, you know 5 field offices would . . . [198]

---

[194] *Id.* at 5.

[195] *Id.*

[196] *Id.* at 6.

[197] *Id.*

[198] *Id.* at 7 (ellipses in original); *see also* Letter from Jill C. Tyson, Office of Congressional Affairs, FBI, to Senator Ron Johnson, Chairman of the Committee on Homeland Security and Governmental Affairs (Oct. 23, 2020) (attachment), https://www.grassley.senate.gov/imo/media/doc/lync_text_messages_of_peter_strzok_from_2-13-16_to_12-6-17.pdf.

(As discussed [illegible] elow, [illegible] FBI Headquarters received the Australian info[illegible] t formal [illegible] of Crossfire Hurricane. On Sunday, July [illegible] zok, as [illegible] tter [illegible] cted to do by McCabe, immediately op[illegible] fre Hu[illegible] le be[illegible] nd approved (with the authorization [illegible] Direct[illegible] the [illegible] urricane opening communicatio[illegible]

<u>Augus[illegible]</u>

[illegible] [Tru[illegible] going [illegible] president, right? Right?!
[illegible] No. [illegible] not. [illegible][200]

Similarly, and [illegible] l in m[illegible] elow [illegible] attorney Kevin Clinesmith made troubling state[illegible] rstrat[illegible] against Trump. Clinesmith, who played a centr[illegible] Page F[illegible] ss, a[illegible] ter Trump's election as President, stat[illegible] FBI p[illegible] among[illegible] gs, "viva le resistance,"[201] an obvious refere[illegible] individ[illegible] posed t[illegible]

Althou[illegible] olved [illegible] the C[illegible] rricane investigation denied that bias against Tr[illegible] a factor in [illegible] the in[illegible],[202] the communications quoted

---

[199] *Redacted C*[illegible] 53, 58 [illegible] g St[illegible] direct access to McCabe, when asked if he wa[illegible] ople g[illegible] him [illegible] oor, (meaning jumping the chain of command a[illegible] FBI [illegible] Off[illegible] floor), Priestap replied, "oh, yeah." While P[illegible] d he c[illegible] remb[illegible] fics, Lisa Page was a concern, without questio[illegible] pect. In [illegible] there [illegible] ple times when Strzok mentioned something to Pr[illegible] hared i[illegible] who [illegible] ared the information with Deputy Director McCa[illegible] ere als[illegible] wha[illegible] red information directly with McCabe befor[illegible] d pro[illegible] orma[illegible] Cabe himself. Priestap said these actions drove [illegible] He als[illegible] Offi[illegible] k was the worst offender in this regard and tha[illegible] occur[illegible] whe[illegible] ) wanted to go in one direction and they (Page [illegible] disagr[illegible] wa[illegible] m. *See* OSC Report of Interview of E.W. Priesta[illegible] 2021 [illegible]

Priestap agreed [illegible] nform[illegible] Offi[illegible] g matters related to the FBI's Alfa Bank investiga[illegible] erwise d[illegible] be in[illegible] y the Office on matters related to his role in the [illegible] ricane i[illegible]

[200] FBI-00082[illegible] Profes[illegible] to Strzok dated 08/08/2016 at 7); *see also* Lette[illegible] Tyson, [illegible] Cong[illegible] fairs, FBI, to Senator Ron Johnson, Chairman of th[illegible] on H[illegible] nmental Affairs (Oct. 23, 2020) (attachment).

[201] FBI-AAA-[illegible] (Lyn[illegible] exch[illegible] Clinesmith and FBI OGC Unit Chief-1 dated [illegible]

[202] *See, e.g.*, S[illegible] *omise*[illegible] OSC [illegible] Interview of Supervisory Special Agent-1 on Ju[illegible] t 5; OS[illegible] f Int[illegible] BI OGC Unit Chief-1 on Aug. 29, 2019 at 10; OS[illegible] Interv[illegible] rvis[illegible] Agent-2 on May 5, 2021 at 8; OSC Report of Inte[illegible] n Aut[illegible] 15, 20[illegible]

above quite clearly show, at least on the part of certain personnel intimately involved in the matter, a predisposition to open an investigation into Trump.

### 3. *The opening of Crossfire Hurricane*

The FBI opened Crossfire Hurricane as a full counterintelligence investigation "to determine whether individual(s) associated with the Trump campaign [were] witting of and/or coordinating activities with the Government of Russia."[203] The starting point for the Office's inquiry was to examine what information was known or available to the FBI about any such ties as of July 31, 2016, prior to opening Crossfire Hurricane. That question then divided itself into two related questions: (i) what was the information that predicated the opening of the investigation and (ii) did that information support such an investigation being opened not as an "assessment" or "preliminary" investigation, but from the start as a "full" investigation. In exploring these questions, we determined the following:

a. <u>The information used to predicate Crossfire Hurricane</u>

In March 2016, the Trump campaign identified George Papadopoulos as a foreign policy advisor.[204] Papadopoulos had previously worked as an energy consultant, with a particular focus on projects in the Eastern Mediterranean.[205] At the time of his appointment, Papadopoulos was employed in the United Kingdom at the London Center of International Law Practice.[206] Among Papadopoulos's acquaintances in London was a diplomat from another country ("Foreign Government-1 Diplomat-1"). Foreign Government-1 Diplomat-1 was familiar with an Australian diplomat ("Australian Diplomat-1").[207] On May 6, 2016, by prearrangement, Foreign Government-1 Diplomat-1 introduced Papadopoulos to Australian Diplomat-1.[208] On May 10, 2016, Papadopoulos and Australian Diplomat-1 met again, and this time they were joined by

---

[203] FBI-0002784 (FBI EC from Counterintelligence, *Re: Crossfire Hurricane* dated July 31, 2016 at 3-4) (hereinafter "*Crossfire Hurricane Opening EC*" or "*Opening EC*").

[204] Missy Ryan & Steven Mufson, *One of Trump's Foreign Policy Advisers Is a 2009 College Grad Who Lists Model UN As a Credential*, Wash. Post (Mar. 22, 2016).

[205] FBI-AAA-02-0019485 (Crossfire Hurricane Papadopoulos Profile dated 08/05/2016); *See also SSCI Russia Report*, pt. 5, at 471.

[206] FBI-AAA-02-0019485 (Crossfire Hurricane Papadopoulos Profile dated 08/05/2016); *SSCI Russia Report*, pt. 5, at 470.

[207] OSC Report of Interview of Australian Diplomat-1 on Oct. 09, 2019 at 1-2; *SSCI Russia Report*, pt. 5, at 487.

[208] OSC Report of Interview of Australian Diplomat-1 on Oct. 09, 2019 at 2; FBI-0002775 (FBI interview of Australian diplomats dated Aug. 11, 2016 at 1-2) (hereinafter "*Australia 302*").

Australian High Commissioner Alexander Downer.[209] Both meetings were over drinks in public settings.[210]

The Australian diplomats were interested in meeting with Papadopoulos because of his role in the Trump campaign, and much of the conversation centered on the upcoming U.S. election.[211] Over two months later, on July 26, 2016, Australia provided the U.S. Embassy in London certain information its diplomats had memorialized at or around the time of the meetings with Papadopoulos. The next day, the State Department passed this information on to the FBI's Legal Attaché assigned to the Embassy in London ("UK Legat-1").[212]

"Paragraph Five" was the name given to the raw information provided by the Australian government and included in a May 16, 2016 cable that documented the diplomats' encounters with Papadopoulos.[213] Paragraph Five is an abstract from the cable and was quoted verbatim in the *Crossfire Hurricane Opening EC*, stating in its entirety that:

> Mr[.] Papadopoulos was, unsurprisingly, confident that Mr[.] Trump could win the election. He commented that the Clintons had "a lot of baggage" and suggested the Trump team had plenty of material to use in its campaign. He also suggested the Trump team had received some kind of suggestion from Russia that it could assist this process with the anonymous release of information during the campaign that would be damaging to Mrs[.] Clinton (and President Obama). It was unclear whether he or the Russians were referring to material acquired publicly of [sic] through other means. It was also unclear how Mr[.] Trump's team reacted to the offer. We note the Trump

---

[209] *Australia 302* at 2-3. Australia has released a redacted version of a cable describing the meeting with Papadopoulos. Cable from London (Alexander Downer) to Canberra, *Re: UK: US: Donald Trump – Views from Trump's Adviser* (May 11, 2016), https://www.dfat.gov.au/sites/default/files/dfat-foi-1801-f1852.pdf. Sky News has also interviewed Downer about the meeting. Jack Crowe, *Ex-Australian Diplomat Explains Why He Turned Papadapoulos [sic] Info over to FBI*, Yahoo! News (May 10, 2019), https://www.yahoo.com/video/ex-australian-diplomat-explains-why-164317262.html. In its report, the SSCI includes a detailed description of the meetings between Papadopoulos and the Australian diplomats. *See SSCI Russia Report*, pt. 5, at 487-89.

The information that the Australian diplomats provided to the U.S. Embassy and the FBI is described in SCO-010930 (FBI EC from London, *Re: Legat London information from U.S. Embassy London Deputy Chief of Mission* dated July 28, 2016) (hereinafter "*London EC*").

[210] *Australia 302* at 1-2.

[211] *See London EC at 2; Australia 302* at 1; OSC Report of Interview of Alexander Downer on Oct. 09, 2019 at 1; OSC Report of Interview of Australian Diplomat-1 on Oct. 09, 2019 at 1.

[212] OSC Report of Interview of UK Legat-1 on May 28, 2019 at 1-2; *London EC* at 2; *see also Redacted OIG Review* at 50-52.

[213] OSC Report of Interview of FBI OGC Unit Chief-1 on Aug. 29, 2019 at 3.

team's reaction could, in the end, have little bearing of [sic] what Russia decides to do, with or without Mr[.] Trump's cooperation.[214]

The Australian account reflects that two meetings of a casual nature took place with Papadopoulos.[215] These meetings were documented by Downer on May 11, 2016 and by Australian Diplomat-1 later in the month.[216] Both diplomats advised that prior to the Spring of 2016, Papadopoulos was unknown to them.[217] Notably, the information in Paragraph Five does not include any mention of the hacking of the DNC, the Russians being in possession of emails, or the public release of any emails. In addition, when interviewed by the Office, Downer stated that he would have characterized the statements made by Papadopoulos differently than Australian Diplomat-1 did in Paragraph 5. According to Downer, Papadopoulos made no mention of Clinton emails, dirt or any specific approach by the Russian government to the Trump campaign team with an offer or suggestion of providing assistance. Rather, Downer's recollection was that Papadopoulos simply stated "the Russians have information" and that was all.[218]

As recounted to the FBI on August 2, 2016, by Australian Diplomat-1, the substance of Paragraph Five was written in a "purposely vague" way.[219] This was done because Papadopoulos left a number of things unexplained and "did not say he had direct contact

---

[214] *London EC*, at 2-3; *see also Crossfire Hurricane Opening EC* at 3 (also quoting the Paragraph Five information); *Redacted OIG Review* at 52, 55.

[215] We note there is an inconsistency in the statements given by Australian Diplomat-1 and former-High Commissioner Downer to the Crossfire Hurricane interviewers in August 2016 and what they told the Office when interviewed in October 2019. Australian Diplomat-1 and Downer were interviewed together in August 2016, and, according to the FD-302 prepared afterward by Supervisory Special Agent-1, Papadopoulos made the statements about the Russians during the May 6, 2016 introductory meeting when he met only with Australian Diplomat-1. When the two diplomats were interviewed separately by the Office in October 2019, investigators were advised that Papadopoulos made the statements in front of both Australian Diplomat-1 and Downer during the second meeting on May 10, 2016.

[216] The meetings with Papadopoulos took place on May 6 and 10, 2016. *Australia 302* at 1-2. The Australian diplomats documented the meetings in two cables dated May 11 and May 16, 2016; OSC Report of Interview of Alexander Downer on Oct. 9, 2019 at 2; OSC Report of Interview of Australian Diplomat-1 on Oct. 9, 2019 at 3.

[217] OSC Report of Interview of Alexander Downer on Oct. 09, 2019 at 1; OSC Report of Interview of Australian Diplomat-1 on Oct. 09, 2019 at 1-2.

[218] OSC Report of Interview of Alexander Downer on Oct. 09, 2019 at 2 (and related field notes); Downer also is reported to have stated in an interview that in talking with Papadopoulos there was "no suggestion that there was collusion between Donald Trump or Donald Trump's campaign and the Russians." Brooke Singman, *Diplomat Who Helped Launch Russia Probe Speaks Out, Defends Role*, Fox News (May 10, 2019), https://www.foxnews.com/politics/former-ausralian-diplomat-alexander-downer-defends-work-pushes-back-on-claim-he-tried-to-trap-papadopoulos.

[219] *Australia 302* at 2.

with the Russia[illegible] impr[illegible] [illegible]dopo[illegible] on the Australian diplomats was wide ranging. [illegible] hand, [illegible] inf[illegible] [illegible] self," was "insecure," and was "trying to impr[illegible] the o[illegible] [illegible] was [illegible]y," was "not negative," and "did not name [illegible] Downer [illegible]."

> was im[illegible] [illegible]adopoulo[illegible] [illegible] of expertise and felt the respons[illegible] common [illegible] los' age, political experie[illegible] someone [illegible] overnight. Many people in a sim[illegible] would [illegible] ther[illegible] [illegible]erently and [Downer] would h[illegible] them [illegible]wner] [illegible] Papadopoulos was a fraud [he] wo[illegible] record [illegible] [illegible]eting [he] had with Papado[illegible].

Downer also s[illegible] did no[illegible] [illegible]se [illegible]s was the middle-man to coordinate wit[illegible] [illegible]rs."[illegible]

The Au[illegible] [illegible]mats w[illegible] [illegible] info[illegible] [illegible]nd subsequently the Office, that the impetus for [illegible] Paragr[illegible] [illegible] format[illegible] July was the public release by WikiLeaks (on [illegible] 6) of e[illegible] [illegible] [illegible]d been hacked from the DNC servers.[225] As [illegible] [illegible]fice's i[illegible] [illegible] [illegible]etermine, Papadopoulos's comments did [illegible] any a[illegible] [illegible]alys[illegible] [illegible]y by Australian intelligence officials.

b. <u>Th[illegible] Intelligen[illegible] [illegible] [illegible]e premise of Crossfire Hurricane</u>

As an [illegible], there [illegible] [illegible] [illegible] had an affirmative obligation to closely exami[illegible] [illegible]aph Fi[illegible] [illegible]tion. [illegible]graph Five information, however, was the sole b[illegible] the FBI [illegible]ing a[illegible] [illegible]igation into individuals associated with [illegible] Tru[illegible] [illegible]gn.[226] [illegible]ntly, the FBI opened a full investigation [illegible] limi[illegible] [illegible]ions. [illegible]ws were undertaken with either the Australian [illegible] Papa[illegible] [illegible] Furth[illegible] [illegible]ening EC does not describe any collaboration [illegible] men[illegible] [illegible]ormat[illegible] [illegible]ither friendly foreign intelligence services or oth[illegible] [illegible]gen[illegible] [illegible] in three days of its receipt of the Paragraph Five [illegible] the FB[illegible] [illegible]ed,[227] [illegible]rther analysis, that the

---

[220] *Id.*

[221] *Id.* at 2-3.

[222] *Id.*

[223] *Id.*

[224] *Id.* at 3.

[225] *See Austra[illegible]* [illegible] OSC [illegible] Interv[illegible] [illegible]ander Downer on Oct. 09, 2019 at 2-3.

[226] *See supra* §§ [illegible]

[227] Regarding [illegible] floor [illegible] [illegible]ed in [illegible] making, McCabe informed the OIG that Direc[illegible] was en[illegible] [illegible]ve[illegible] [illegible]sis" with the team after the

Australian information was an adequate basis for the opening of a full investigation into whether individuals associated with an ongoing presidential campaign were "witting of and/or coordinating activities with the Government of Russia."[228]

In his interview with the Office, Executive Assistant Director for National Security Michael Steinbach commented on the sufficiency of the information in the *Opening EC*, stating that it was "poorly written."[229] Steinbach added that the EC should not be read to suggest that the FBI was investigating the Trump campaign, but only those potential subjects within the campaign whose activities justified inquiry.[230] Steinbach was also questioned separately by the OIG on the amount of information that should normally be included in an EC opening a counterintelligence case. He stated that it should be a logical summary sufficient to justify the opening. Steinbach told the OIG, by way of an example, "It's, hey look, I have Mike Steinbach on this date met with a Russian who we know is associated with this intelligence organization. And, lay that out, and open a PI (preliminary investigation)."[231]

Although not referenced in the *Opening EC*, FBI officials have later pointed to the importance of the Australian information when viewed in conjunction with Russia's likely connections to the WikiLeaks disclosures and its efforts to interfere with the 2016 U.S. elections.[232] In addition, Trump had also stated in a recently televised campaign speech, "Russia, if you're listening, I hope you're able to find the 30,000 emails that are missing,"[233]

---

Paragraph Five information had been received. OIG Interview of Andrew McCabe dated Aug. 15, 2019 at 16.

[228] *Crossfire Hurricane Opening EC* at 3-4.

[229] OSC Report of Interview of Michael Steinbach on Aug. 12, 2019 at 2.

[230] *Id.* at 3.

[231] OIG Interview of Michael Steinbach on June 20, 2019 at 22-28.

[232] *See, e.g.*, OSC Report of Interview of FBI OGC Unit Chief-1 on August 29, 2019 at 4; OSC Report of Interview of Supervisory Special Agent-1 on June 17, 2019 at 2; *see generally Redacted OIG Review* at 351-52. There were also at least some activities involving the Trump campaign and Russians that did not become public, and were not known to the FBI, until much later. For example, on June 9, 2016, senior representatives of the campaign met briefly with a private Russian lawyer, Natalia Veselnitskaya, and others at the Trump Tower. 1 *Mueller Report* at 110, 117. Veselnitskaya "had previously worked for the Russian government and maintained a relationship with that government throughout this period of time." *Id.* at 110. The initial email to Donald Trump Jr. proposing the meeting said that the Crown prosecutor of Russia was offering to provide the campaign with documents and information that would incriminate Clinton. *Id.* The meeting at the Trump Tower only became public over a year later. *Id.* at 121.

[233] *Donald Trump on Russian & Missing Hillary Clinton Emails*, YouTube Channel C-SPAN, posted 7/27/16, *available at* https://www.youtube.com/watch?v=3kxG8uJUsWU (starting at 0:41). The *Mueller Report* states that this statement was "apparently a reference" to emails stored on a personal server that Clinton used while she was Secretary of State. 1 *Mueller Report* at 49. Strzok stated in his book *Compromised: Counterintelligence and the Threat of Donald J.*

a widely reported statement that appears to have referred to emails stored on the personal server that Clinton used while Secretary of State.[234]

The evidence the Office reviewed shows that there were internal discussions with FBI Headquarters executives, including the Deputy Director, about the decision to open Crossfire Hurricane. The executives were unanimous in supporting the opening of the investigation and there is no indication that these discussions contemplated anything short of an immediate full investigation, such as an assessment or preliminary investigation, into the meaning, credibility, and underpinnings of the statements attributed to Papadopoulos.[235] The personnel involved in the decision to open a full investigation have stated that they acted within the FBI's governing principles as set forth in the *AGG-Dom* and *DIOG* that required an authorized purpose and an "articulable factual basis for the investigation that reasonably indicates" that an activity constituting a federal crime or a national security threat "may be" occurring. But notably the *DIOG* also explicitly cautions FBI employees to avoid reputational risk to those being investigated by, among other things, specifying different standards for opening an assessment, a preliminary investigation, and a full investigation, with a corresponding continuum of permissible investigative activities. That measured approach does not appear to have been followed with respect to Crossfire Hurricane. Instead, as described above, on a Sunday and just three days after receiving the unanalyzed information from Australia, Strzok authored and approved the Crossfire Hurricane opening EC.[236] Thus, a full counterintelligence investigation into a SIM[237] was triggered, at the height of a political campaign, before any dialogue with Australia or the Intelligence Community, and prior to any critical analysis of the information itself or the potential for the risk

---

*Trump* at 109, as well as to the OIG that Australian High Commissioner Downer was prompted to turn over the Paragraph Five information upon seeing Trump's televised news conference during which Trump made his "Russia, if you're listening" comment. Strzok, *Compromised* at 109; OIG Interview of Peter Strzok on May 8, 2018 at 15. Strzok's version of this is factually inaccurate and contrary to the FBI's report of the August 2, 2016 interview of Downer and Australian Diplomat-1, an interview that Strzok himself conducted. The report of interview does not refer to Trump's news conference or the missing Clinton emails. *See Australian 302.* Moreover, Downer and Australian officials came to the U.S. Embassy with the Paragraph Five information on July 26th - one day *before* Trump's televised news conference. As referenced above in footnote 189, Strzok declined to be interviewed by the Office on this and other subjects.

[234] *See* 1 *Mueller Report* at 49.

[235] *Redacted OIG Review* at 53-54.

[236] *Crossfire Hurricane Opening EC* at 1. The speed of this action sharply contrasts with Strzok's decision-making in the referral in September 2016 of a matter involving former Congressman Anthony Weiner's laptop computer. In that instance, according to the OIG, the FBI and Strzok did not act for over a month to pursue legal process to review thousands of missing Clinton emails found on Weiner's laptop. The OIG sharply criticized the FBI, and particularly Strzok, for this delay. As discussed more fully below, the immediate opening of Crossfire Hurricane as a full investigation contrasts with the care taken in connection with the investigation of the Clinton Foundation and other matters.

[237] *See supra* § III.B.1 for a discussion of the requirements for sensitive investigative matters.

of error or disinformation, issues that appropriately are addressed during assessments or preliminary investigations.

The information from Papadopoulos was, in the words of one FBI executive, "a tipping point."[238] When interviewed by the OIG, FBI Deputy General Counsel Trisha Anderson stated that it would have been a dereliction of duty had the FBI not opened Crossfire Hurricane.[239] For his part, FBI General Counsel James Baker told the OIG that "[t]he opening of an investigation . . . [a]nd doing it quickly is a good thing for oversight because it forces the institution of the FBI and eventually the Department of Justice . . . to have appropriate management controls over what's going on."[240] In this regard, the *OIG Review* found that in early August 2016, after the opening of Crossfire Hurricane, NSD officials "were briefed on at least two occasions" about the investigation.[241]

FBI officials have acknowledged that they were aware that the information concerning Papadopoulos did not come from Australia's intelligence services, but rather from Australian diplomats who were previously unknown to the FBI personnel handling the Paragraph Five information.[242] In various interviews, several FBI officials have opined that the FBI was justified in opening Crossfire Hurricane as a full investigation because, in part, the information was given to the FBI from a trusted partner and therefore was deemed reliable.[243] Although this sentiment is understandable, the FBI's well-placed trust in a foreign partner should not equate to confidence in the shared information itself. Australia could not and did not make any representation about the credibility of the information. Although the Counterintelligence Division did eventually seek information about Papadopoulos,[244] the Office found no indications from witness testimony, electronic communications, emails, calendar entries, or other documentation that, at the time, the FBI gave any consideration to the actual trustworthiness of the information the diplomats

---

238 *Redacted OIG Review* at 53.

239 *Id.* at 54.

240 *See* OIG Interview of James Baker on May 17, 2019 at 44; OSC Report of Interview of James Baker on Feb. 7, 2020 at 6. Baker's point is a reasonable one regarding the oversight value of opening an investigation, but we note that it would and should apply equally to the opening of a preliminary investigation or an assessment.

241 *Redacted OIG Review* at 58 n.176 ("Notes and testimony reflect that in early August, NSD officials were briefed on at least two occasions" about the investigation).

242 *See, e.g.*, OSC Report of Interview of Supervisory Special Agent-1 on July 22, 2020 at 1.

243 U.S. Senate Judiciary Cmte. Staff Interview of Jonathan Moffa on September 9, 2020 at 65-66, 71-72.

244 *See, e.g.*, FBI-AAA-02-0019550 (Email from Special Agent-2 to Supervisory Special Agent-1, Case Agent-1 & Laycock dated 08/05/2016); FBI-AAA-02-0019485 (Crossfire Hurricane Papadopoulos Profile dated 08/05/2016).

received from [illegible] - an [illegible] what [illegible] described as, among other things, "insecure" and [illegible] impress[illegible]

The ini[illegible] from Papa[illegible] was [illegible] and unevaluated. It was not the product of nor[illegible] Intelligence Com[illegible] collec[illegible] analysis, and it lacked the standard cave[illegible] having [illegible] from an individual whose information wa[illegible] for the [illegible] — involving an ongoing presidential ca[illegible] was pre[illegible] and [illegible] ted information that required rigorous analy[illegible] to assess [illegible] ance [illegible][246] Nevertheless, the FBI predicated Cr[illegible] cane and [illegible] quen[illegible] ive activities, including the use of CHSs, unde[illegible] ations [illegible] overt [illegible] statements attributed to Papadopoulos.

Thus, a[illegible] opening [illegible] the FBI had (i) publicly available information c[illegible] Papadopo[illegible] in [illegible] gn as a volunteer foreign policy adviser, (ii) in[illegible] obtained [illegible] Papadopou[illegible] Australian diplomats, (iii) information a[illegible] s likely [illegible] interfe[illegible] ities, (iv) Trump's public statements ab[illegible] and (v) [illegible] media [illegible] n possible ties between Trump and Russian b[illegible][247] Sig[illegible] bey[illegible] FBI's Counterintelligence Division and i[illegible] Hurricane [illegible] tors [illegible] ess any intelligence or other vetted, corrobo[illegible] mation reg[illegible] Trump [illegible] aign staff colluding with the Russian gover[illegible] FBI O[illegible] Chief [illegible] d on many Crossfire Hurricane matters and ap[illegible] be being [illegible] s a S[illegible] OGC Unit Chief-1") noted that she lacked "knowle[illegible] ed . . . [illegible] the [illegible] paign and Russia prior to the

[245] *See supra* § [illegible] discussing [illegible] of F[illegible] held by the Australian diplomats and noting his [illegible] weak[illegible] ide[illegible] noted below, when Crossfire Hurricane was [illegible] us eff[illegible] made [illegible] investigation quiet so as not to interfere with th[illegible] election [illegible] Mueller investigation reported that:

> When [illegible] Papado[illegible] the [illegible] fficials who interacted with him tol[illegible] Of[illegible] cou[illegible] Papadopoulos' sharing the informa[illegible] sia had [illegible] "dirt" [illegible] ate Clinton in the form of emails [illegible] a could [illegible] Camp[illegible] gh the anonymous release of informa[illegible] Clinton [illegible] unic[illegible] ce, and nothing in the email a[illegible] der co[illegible] ons [illegible] ewed by the [Mueller] Office, [illegible] Papadop[illegible] ed th[illegible] on with the Campaign.

1 *Mueller Repo*[illegible]

[246] *See* discuss[illegible] requi[illegible] *supra* [illegible]

[247] *See Redac*[illegible] *iew* a[illegible]

[248] In early Jul[illegible] NYFO [illegible] some [illegible] rts that later came to be known as the "Steele do[illegible] Office [illegible] evide[illegible] er, suggesting that Strzok, who wrote and app[illegible] *Crossfi*[illegible] Op[illegible] was aware of those reports when he opened the[illegible], and [illegible] ire H[illegible] investigators did not receive the reports until [illegible] r. *Se*[illegible] *OIG* [illegible]

[Crossfire Hurricane] investigation being formally opened."[249] The *FBI Inspection Division Report* describes similar statements by others. As noted in that FBI internal review, "[t]his total lack of intelligence did not appear to have been considered significant [ ]"[250] when opening a full investigation on persons associated with an active presidential campaign.

As the record now reflects, at the time of the opening of Crossfire Hurricane, the FBI did not possess any intelligence showing that anyone associated with the Trump campaign was in contact with Russian intelligence officers at any point during the campaign.[251] Moreover, the now more complete record of facts relevant to the opening of Crossfire Hurricane is illuminating. Indeed, at the time Crossfire Hurricane was opened, the FBI (albeit not the Crossfire Hurricane investigators) was in possession of some of the Steele Reports. However, even if the Crossfire Hurricane investigators were in possession of the Steele Reports earlier, they would not have been aware of the fact that the Russians were cognizant of Steele's election-related reporting. The *SSCI Russia Report* notes that "[s]ensitive reporting from June 2017 indicated that a [person affiliated] to Russian Oligarch 1 was [possibly aware] of Steele's election investigation as of early July 2016."[252] Indeed, "an early June 2017 USIC report indicated that two persons affiliated with [Russian Intelligence Services] *were aware of* Steele's election investigation in early July 2016."[253] Put more pointedly, Russian intelligence knew of Steele's election investigation for the Clinton campaign by no later than early July 2016. Thus, as discussed in Section IV.D.1.a.3, Steele's sources may have been compromised by the Russians at a time prior to the creation of the Steele Reports and throughout the FBI's Crossfire Hurricane investigation.

c. <u>Interview of the Australian diplomats</u>

On August 2, 2016, two days after opening Crossfire Hurricane, Strzok and Supervisory Special Agent-1 met in London with the Australian diplomats to assess and clarify exactly what had been said by Papadopoulos in May and provided to the U.S. government in July.

In preparation for their interview, Strzok and Supervisory Special Agent-1 sought the assistance of the FBI's Assistant Legal Attaché in London ("UK ALAT-1"). UK ALAT-1's primary FBI responsibilities in London included, among other things, collaboration and information-sharing with British Intelligence Service-1. In UK ALAT-1's interview with the Office, he pointed out the inherent importance of sharing information with the British intelligence service that related to potential Russian intelligence activity in the United Kingdom.[254] Thus, UK ALAT-1 briefed the British intelligence service about

---

[249] U.S. House of Representatives Cmte. on the Judiciary Interview of FBI OGC Unit Chief-1 on Oct. 23, 2018 at 145.

[250] *FBI Inspection Division Report* at 125.

[251] This is shown by an analysis in early 2017 of what the FBI knew about articles published in the *New York Times*. It is described later in this report in connection with other matters from that time period. *See infra* § IV.D.1.a.iii.

[252] *SSCI Russia Report* at 885 (emphasis added).

[253] *Id.*

[254] OSC Report of Interview of UK ALAT-1 on June 4, 2019 at 1.

Papadopoulos's allegations involving possible Russian influence in the Trump campaign. Given the nature of the allegations and the speed with which Strzok and Supervisory Special Agent-1 needed his assistance, UK ALAT-1 assumed that the FBI's interview of the Australian diplomats was exceptionally critical.[255] UK ALAT-1 also believed that the Crossfire Hurricane investigators likely were in possession of compelling facts beyond what UK ALAT-1 understood from the substance of Papadopoulos's claims in Paragraph Five.[256] Nevertheless, UK ALAT-1's independent impression of the predication for the investigation was echoed by Supervisory Special Agent-1 in a Lync exchange with UK ALAT-1 during which the predication was referred to as "thin."[257] UK ALAT-1 also recalled Strzok making a comment in the taxi on their way to the Australian High Commission to the effect that "there's nothing to this, but we have to run it to ground."[258] These exchanges with Supervisory Special Agent-1 and Strzok resonated with UK ALAT-1 because, in sharing the Papadopoulos information with his British Intelligence Service-1 counterparts at the time, they expressed real skepticism about the motivations and reliability of Papadopoulos.[259] UK ALAT-1 told the Office that British Intelligence Service-1 did not assess the information about the Russians and Trump, attributed to Papadopoulos, to be particularly valuable intelligence.[260] Indeed, he told the FBI's Inspection Division investigators that "the British could not believe the Papadopoulos bar conversation was all there was,"[261] and they were convinced the FBI must have had more information that it was holding back.[262]

As it relates to predication for opening Crossfire Hurricane as a full investigation, after Strzok and Supervisory Special Agent-1 had traveled to London and interviewed the Australian diplomats on August 2, 2016, the following Lync exchange between UK ALAT-1 and Supervisory Special Agent-1 on August 11, 2016 is instructive:

| | |
|---|---|
| UK ALAT-1: | Dude, are we telling them [British Intelligence Service-1] everything we know, or is there more to this? |
| Supervisory Special Agent-1: | that's all we have |
| Supervisory Special Agent-1: | not holding anything back |
| UK ALAT-1: | Damn that's thin |
| Supervisory Special Agent-1: | I know |

---

255 *Id.* at 1-2.

256 *Id.*

257 FBI-AAA-EC-00000365 (Lync exchange between Supervisory Special Agent-1 and UK ALAT-1 dated 08/11/2016).

258 OSC Report of Interview of UK ALAT-1 on June 4, 2019 at 2.

259 *Id.* at 3.

260 *Id.*

261 *FBI Inspection Division Report* at 224 (quoting UK ALAT-1).

262 *Id.* at 225.

Supervisory Special Agent-1: it sucks[263]

UK ALAT-1 went on to tell the Inspection Division that in discussing the matter with a senior British Intelligence Service-1 official, the official was openly skeptical, said the FBI's plan for an operation made no sense, and asked UK ALAT-1 why the FBI did not just go to Papadopoulos and ask him what they wanted to know,[264] a sentiment UK ALAT-1 told investigators that he shared.[265]

Later in the Fall of 2016, UK ALAT-1 was at FBI Headquarters with some of his British Intelligence Service-1 counterparts. While there, members of the Crossfire Hurricane team played the audio/visual recordings of CHS-1's August 20, 2016 meeting with Carter Page. UK ALAT-1 said the effect on the British Intelligence Service-1 personnel was not positive because of the lack of any evidence coming out of the conversation.[266] UK ALAT-1 told the OIG that after watching the video one of his British colleagues said, "For [expletive] sake, man. You went through a lot of trouble to get him to say nothing." At a later point in time, after the Mueller Special Counsel team was in place, UK ALAT-1 said that "the Brits finally had enough," and in response to a request for some assistance "[a British Intelligence Service-1 person] basically said there was no [expletive] way in hell they were going to do it."[267]

From his vantage point, UK ALAT-1 saw that FBI executive management was pushing the matter so hard that "there was no stopping the train," and he told the OIG that," I mean it was, this thing was coming. So my job was to grease the skids for it, and that's what I did."[268]

Had the Crossfire Hurricane investigators attempted to critically assess the information from Papadopoulos through FBI holdings and standard requests to other government agencies for information about Trump and Russian intelligence activities involving Trump, they would have learned:

- Jonathan Moffa served as the Chief of the FBI's Counterintelligence Analysis Section throughout 2016. Moffa was a career FBI Intelligence Analyst who began working as a full-time FBI counterespionage analyst in 2004,[269] and, prior to being selected for the Section Chief position in January 2016, had been Chief of the Russian Analysis Unit for approximately four years. Moffa advised investigators that he had heard nothing about Trump and Russia until events began to be reported in July 2016.[270]

---

[263] FBI-AAA-EC-00007239 (Aug. 11, 2016 at 14:40:27)

[264] *FBI Inspection Division Report* at 224 (quoting UK ALAT-1).

[265] *Id.* at 227.

[266] *Id.* at 208.

[267] *Id.* at 233.

[268] *Id.* at 225.

[269] The Counterintelligence Analysis Section that Moffa headed throughout 2016 had responsibility for covering Russia intelligence matters, among those of other countries.

[270] *See* Section IV.A.1 regarding pre-July 2016 efforts.

- The FBI [illegible] Analyst [illegible] in-depth knowledge of particular [illegible] Russian [illegible] FBI holdings during the relevant time period [illegible] that [illegible] any Trump election campaign [illegible] with [illegible] anything in FBI holdings regarding [illegible], Michael [illegible] Papadopoulos, or Paul Manafort[271] engaging in [illegible] of co[illegible] regarding the election.[272]
- Similarly [illegible] Clapper [illegible] on the subject of Trump and Russia [illegible] "no" [illegible] of any such evidence.[273] The former [illegible] this [illegible] by the Office and advised that he knew [illegible] evidence [illegible] standard of conspiracy or collusion [illegible] part.
- Admiral [illegible] served [illegible] during the relevant time period. When [illegible] aware [illegible] of collusion as asserted in the Steele [illegible] that [illegible] intelligence that supported the collusion [illegible] in that [illegible] discussions during the Summer of 2016 [illegible] counterparts [illegible] community about collusion between the Russian [illegible] Republican [illegible]
- Victoria [illegible] as [illegible] Affairs at the Department of State during the [illegible] time [illegible] the Department of State and one of its most [illegible] Russian [illegible] investigators that she never saw any U.S. government [illegible] of the [illegible] the Steele reporting regarding Trump [illegible] officials [illegible] to her recollection no information regarding [illegible] coordinated [illegible] and the Russians had ever come across [illegible] with one [illegible] that she had received a two-page

---

[271] The Intelligence [illegible] did, [illegible] information related to Manafort that was not connected [illegible] or the [illegible] OSC Interview Report of Headquarters A[illegible] Aug. [illegible]

[272] OSC Report [illegible] of [illegible] Aug. 14, 2019 at 4; Dec. 10, 2019 at 4; and Feb. 19, [illegible]

[273] U.S. House [illegible] Representatives [illegible] Select Committee on Intelligence Interview [illegible] James Clapper [illegible] 87-89; OSC Report of Interview of James Clapper [illegible] ber 1[illegible]

[274] OSC Report [illegible] of Mi[illegible] at 2, 5.

[275] OSC Report [illegible] of Vi[illegible] 2021 at 5-6.

[276] Nuland also [illegible] however [illegible] report [illegible] a U.S. person, "it is heavily redacted and [illegible] before [illegible] information" and that it was possible that "she would not [illegible] the in[illegible] She [illegible] [t]he masking rules are followed when it comes [illegible] intelligence [illegible] "would have had no national security reason [illegible] concerning an American businessman." [illegible] for the [illegible] not intelligence" if it pertained to U.S. persons. [illegible]

summary of the Steele allegations from Jonathan Winer, who in 2016 was serving as Secretary of State Kerry's Special Envoy to Libya.[277] Winer told Nuland that Winer had prepared the summary from his review of the Steele reporting while he was at Steele's country house in the United Kingdom. Nuland thought Winer had passed the summary to her sometime in July 2016.[278]

- CIA Director John Brennan and Deputy Director David Cohen were interviewed by the Office and were asked about their knowledge of any actual evidence of members of the Trump campaign conspiring or colluding with Russian officials. When Brennan was provided with an overview of the origins of the Attorney General's Review after Special Counsel Mueller finding a lack of evidence of collusion between the Trump campaign and Russian authorities, Brennan offered that "they found no conspiracy."[279] [280] (In fact, Special Counsel Mueller's report explicitly states that "[u]ltimately, [his] investigation did not establish that the [Trump] Campaign coordinated or conspired with the Russian government in its election-interference activities."[281]) Relatedly, however, shortly after Special Counsel Mueller delivered his report to the Attorney General and the Attorney General had issued a short summary of the Report's findings, Brennan appeared on MSNBC's *Morning Joe* program, where he stated that "[he] suspected there was more than there actually was" with regard to collusion between the Trump campaign and Russia in the 2016 election, thus suggesting that he had no actual knowledge of such information.[282] Moreover, Deputy Director Cohen advised that he had no recollection of knowing anything Trump was doing with Putin, as opposed to what Putin and the Russians were doing to interfere in the election. Cohen stated that if there were such

---

[277] Nuland thought the summary was more on the order of four pages, but others believed it was two pages. *Id.* at 4.

[278] *Id.*

[279] OSC Report of Interview of John Brennan on Aug. 21, 2020 at 1.

[280] Prior to the release of the *Mueller Report*, and specifically in an August 16, 2018 opinion piece, the former Director had characterized the claims of then-President Trump that there was no collusion with Russia as, "in a word, hogwash." https://www.nytimes.com/2018/08/16/opinion/john-brennan-trump-russia-collusion-security-clearance.html.

[281] 1 *Mueller Report* at 173; *see also* 1 *Mueller Report* at 1-2 ("Although the investigation established that the Russian government perceived it would benefit from a Trump presidency and worked to secure that outcome, and that the Campaign expected it would benefit electorally from information stolen and released through Russian efforts, the investigation did not establish that members of the Trump Campaign conspired or coordinated with the Russian government in its election interference activities."); 1 *Mueller Report* at 9 ("Further, the evidence was not sufficient to charge that any member of the Trump Campaign conspired with representatives of the Russian government to interfere in the 2016 election.")

[282] MSNBC, "Morning Joe," March 25, 2019 at 8:24 a.m. ET; *see also* RealClear Politics, *Brennan: 'Relieved' There Was Not a Criminal Conspiracy with Russia, 'Good News for the Country,'* March 25, 2019.

knowledge, it would have been included in a formal referral to the FBI. In addition, if the CIA had become aware of any U.S. person being involved in a criminal conspiracy, it would have sent the information to the FBI in a formal referral. He advised that he was not aware of any such referrals in this matter.[283]

In any event, within days after opening Crossfire Hurricane, the FBI learned from interviewing the Australian diplomats that there were reasons to be unsure about what to make of the information from Papadopoulos. Not only had Supervisory Special Agent-1 and Strzok told UK ALAT-1 that what they had was "thin," but one of the Australian diplomats had told Strzok and Supervisory Special Agent-1 in their interview that the Paragraph Five information was written in an intentionally vague way because of what Papadopoulos did and did not say. Nonetheless, shortly thereafter, the FBI opened full investigations of Papadopoulos, Carter Page, General Michael Flynn, and Paul Manafort.[284] All four were U.S. persons associated with the Trump campaign and all of them (other than Papadopoulos) had "either ties to Russia or a history of travel to Russia."[285]

In July 2016, in addition to receiving the first several Steele reports, the FBI received a separate stream of information regarding Trump from a former FBI CHS. Specifically, an FBI supervisor from a New England field office ("New England Supervisory Special Agent-1") was contacted unexpectedly by the former CHS with whom the supervisor had worked many years earlier when assigned to a different field office on matters related to Russian organized crime. New England Supervisory Special Agent-1 agreed to meet his former CHS on July 21, 2016. At that meeting, the CHS told New England Supervisory Special Agent-1 that he/she had been contacted by a colleague who owns an investigative firm and who was looking into Trump's various business contacts and ventures in Russia.[286] The former CHS did not identify the investigative firm that day, except to say that the firm had been hired by the DNC and another unnamed individual.[287] The former CHS then provided New England Supervisory Special Agent-1 with a list of approximately 45 individuals and entities who reportedly had surfaced in the firm's investigation of Trump's ties to Russia.[288]

---

[283] OSC Report of Interview of David Cohen on Feb. 2, 2022 at 7-8.

[284] FBI-0002788 (Crossfire D. Opening Electronic Communication dated 08/10/2016); FBI-0007869 (Crossfire F. Opening Electronic Communication dated 08/10/2016); FBI-0007875 (Crossfire T. Opening Electronic Communication dated 08/10/2016); FBI-0007873 (Crossfire R. Opening Electronic Communication dated 08/16/2016). As noted above, the NYFO had already opened an investigation of Page. In addition, in January 2016, the FBI's Criminal Investigation Division had opened an investigation into allegations of money laundering and tax evasion by Manafort. *Redacted OIG Review* at 291.

[285] *Redacted OIG Review* at 59-60; *see also* U.S. Senate Judiciary Cmte. Staff Interview of Jonathan Moffa on September 9, 2020 at 77-80.

[286] FBI-EMAIL-197479 (Email from New England Supervisory Special Agent-1 to New England Supervisory Special Agent-2 dated 07/29/2016).

[287] *Id.*

[288] *Id.*

The list was comprised mostly of Russian individuals and entities and immediately raised "red flags" for New England Supervisory Special Agent-1, who believed it was necessary to get the information into the right hands as soon as possible.[289] Following the July 21, 2016 meeting, New England Supervisory Special Agent-1 emailed a counterintelligence colleague about the meeting and forwarded the list of names he had received. Within a few days, New England Supervisory Special Agent-1's email and the investigative firm's list of names made its way to FBI Headquarters and to the Crossfire Hurricane investigators.[290]

The former CHS reached out to New England Supervisory Special Agent-1 again on August 23, 2016, telling him that he/she had reviewed a large volume of material that the investigative firm had compiled and the former CHS passed on more information from that effort.[291] New England Supervisory Special Agent-1 in turn passed the information directly to an Agent on the Crossfire Hurricane team ("Special Agent-2").[292] Then, one month later, on September 23, 2016,[293] the former CHS reached out yet again, prompting New England Supervisory Special Agent-1 to email the Crossfire Hurricane investigators again, to report that the CHS has more information on Trump's reported ties to Russia.[294]

Months later, on January 11, 2017, after the Steele Dossier had been made public, New England Supervisory Special Agent-1 asked Supervisory Special Agent-1 if anything was "to be gleaned from" the information he provided in July.[295] It was at that time that Supervisory Special Agent-1 let New England Supervisory Special Agent-1 know that his team had received the same information through a separate reporting stream from a different source, in context being Steele.[296] Supervisory Special Agent-1 further advised that the second source was working with the same investigative firm that had given the information to the former CHS. Sometime later, New England Supervisory Special Agent-1 had learned that his former CHS had developed the information related to Trump while working with Glenn Simpson and Fusion GPS. Thus, it appears that in July 2016 the FBI had not yet determined that the dual reporting it was receiving actually was coming from the same source – that is, Simpson and Fusion GPS.

---

[289] OSC Report of Interview of New England Supervisory Special Agent-1 on Sept. 1, 2020 at 2-3.

[290] FBI-AAA-02-0018017 (Email from Moffa to Auten, Strzok & Supervisory Special Agent-1 dated 08/02/2016).

[291] FBI-EMAIL-262171 (Email from New England Supervisory Special Agent-1 to Special Agent-2 dated 08/23/2016).

[292] *Id.*

[293] Interestingly, September 23, 2016 was the same day that Michael Isikoff's *Yahoo! News* article was published.

[294] FBI-EMAIL-242390 (Email from New England Supervisory Special Agent-1 to Supervisory Special Agent-1 dated 09/23/2016).

[295] FBI-EMAIL-038612 (Email from New England Supervisory Special Agent-1 to Supervisory Special Agent-1 dated 01/11/2017).

[296] FBI-EMAIL-028908 (Email from Supervisory Special Agent-1 to New England Supervisory Special Agent-1, Supervisory Special Agent-3, Auten, Case Agent-1 & others dated 01/11/2017).

Further, it does [illegible] that the [illegible] that essentially the same information the [illegible] was pro[illegible] New[illegible] Supervisory Special Agent-1 was being provided [illegible] by S[illegible] [illegible] was a pattern similar to that later employed in the [illegible] matter [illegible] Alfa [illegible] ons were provided to members of the media by F[illegible] and then [illegible] thro[illegible] Sussmann.[297]

*4. Oth[illegible] tive act[illegible] [illegible] f the Steele Reports*

Betwee[illegible] FBI [illegible] Cro[illegible] icane investigation and when Crossfire Hur[illegible] igators [illegible] ved [illegible] eports in mid-September 2016,[298] the F[illegible] llow[illegible] [illegible]

- As disc[illegible], Strz[illegible] [illegible] Agent-1 met with Australian official[illegible] info[illegible] [illegible] opoulos.
- Record[illegible] urce [illegible] our Crossfire Hurricane subjects.
- Travel [illegible] s wa[illegible] [illegible]
- Some r[illegible] obtai[illegible] [illegible] cies and a foreign government.
- FBI C[illegible] s we[illegible] [illegible] of the subjects.[299]

The *OIG Revi*[illegible] the fol[illegible] of the FBI's investigative activity prior [illegible] of the [illegible]

> [B]y the [illegible] Crossfir[illegible] [illegible] he six Steele reports on Septem[illegible] investi[illegible] been [illegible] for approximately 6 weeks [illegible] had [illegible] stig[illegible] ur individuals: Carter Page, G[illegible] dopoul[illegible] [illegible] chael Flynn. In addition, during [illegible] weeks, [illegible] ad [illegible] conduct operations agains[illegible] dopou[illegible] [illegible] campaign official, althou[illegible] ations [illegible] *llection of any inculpatory informa*[illegible]

FBI pe[illegible] the O[illegible] [illegible] se national security letters or compulsory p[illegible] obt[illegible] first [illegible]"[301] FBI Deputy General Counsel Ande[illegible] "ea[illegible] BI [illegible] 'took off the table any idea of legal process' [illegible] the FB[illegible] ng [illegible] quietly.'"[302] Similarly,

---

[297] *See infra* § [illegible]

[298] The Steele [illegible] scribe[illegible] Sec[illegible]

[299] *See Redact*[illegible] *ew* at [illegible]-56.

[300] *Id.* at 101 ([illegible] ed).

[301] *Id.* at 78.

[302] *Id.* (quoting [illegible] Gene[illegible] son); *see also id.* at 69 (describing statements by [illegible] Depu[illegible] Mc[illegible] importance of keeping the investigation [illegible]

"[m]embers of the Crossfire Hurricane team told [the OIG] that they avoided the use of compulsory legal process to obtain information at this time in order to prevent any public disclosure of the investigation's existence and to avoid any potential impact on the election."[303] Notably absent from the list of investigative steps taken were the following non-public, non-compulsory options:

- Interviewing Page, particularly once the FBI's interest in him was publicly disclosed by the media.[304] In fact, two days after this disclosure, Page wrote to Director Comey offering to be interviewed, but the FBI elected not to do so.[305]
- Asking Page, who volunteered to be interviewed and had spoken with the FBI when asked to do so on prior occasions, if he would consent to a polygraph exam or provide access to relevant electronic records.
- Using other standard investigative techniques not requiring a court order.
- Interviewing Papadopoulos, the actual source of the Paragraph Five information.[306] [307]

Another step that the Crossfire Hurricane investigators could have taken, but chose not to take, was the use of pen registers and trap and trace devices. Although FISA authorizes the government to obtain a pen register when "the information likely to be obtained . . . is relevant to an ongoing investigation to protect against . . . clandestine intelligence activities,[308] Case Agent-1 told the OIG that he saw pen registers as a "criminal authority."[309] FBI OGC Unit Chief-1 could not understand why investigators working on

---

[303] *Id.* at 78, 355; *see also* OIG Interview of Case Agent-1 on Aug. 28, 2018 at 69 (expressing concern about the risk of disclosure of subpoenas).

[304] *See* Michael Isikoff, *U.S. Intel Officials Probe Ties Between Trump Adviser and Kremlin*, *Yahoo! News* (Sept. 23, 2016) (hereinafter "Isikoff, *Officials Probe Ties*").

[305] Letter from Carter Page to FBI Director Comey (Sept. 25, 2016). As discussed below, the FBI did not interview Page until Comey approved the interview in March 2017. *See infra* § IV.D.1.h.ii.

[306] As noted below, when Crossfire Hurricane was opened, an important goal was to keep the investigation secret. By September 23, 2016, however, the investigation was made public via Isikoff's article attributing the information to a "senior U.S. law enforcement official." *See infra* § IV.D.1.h.ii.

[307] As noted, Australian High Commissioner Downer told Strzok and Supervisory Special Agent-1 that he did not get the sense that Papadopoulos was the middle man coordinating with the Russians. *See supra* footnote 224.

[308] *See supra* § III.C.

[309] OIG Interview of Case Agent-1 on Aug. 28, 2018 at 69.

Crossfire Hurricane were not seeking authority to use pen registers and trap and trace devices.[310]

In terms of the analytical capabilities that were applied to Crossfire Hurricane, Lisa Page testified that the FBI used "line level analysts who [were] super experts on Russia."[311] The FBI's *Inspection Division Report* found, however, that the intelligence analysts "selected for Crossfire Hurricane were uniformly inexperienced" and that "[n]one of them were subject matter expert analysts."[312] Aside from Auten, the most experienced analyst had less than nine months of experience working in that capacity, two had less than four months experience, and two came straight from analyst training.[313]

The analysis done in Crossfire Hurricane was also limited by the Counterintelligence Division's failure to integrate the Directorate of Intelligence into the investigation as required by policy.[314] Rather, in at least one instance, Assistant Director of the Counterintelligence Division Bill Priestap appears to have deliberately shut down the involvement of the Directorate of Intelligence in an enhanced validation review of Christopher Steele, a key source.[315]

### B. **The FBI's and the Department's Disparate Treatment of Candidates Clinton and Trump**

In the course of the Office's investigation, we learned of allegations involving possible attempted foreign election influence activities associated with entities related to Clinton, in addition to the allegations related to Trump. The Office sought to determine, to the extent possible, if the actions taken by the FBI (and in certain instances, the Department) to address the allegations were consistent with those taken by the FBI relating to the allegations of Russian foreign election influence attached to the Trump campaign in July 2016. Comparing the respective investigative activity was significant to the investigation since it could support or undercut allegations of institutional bias against either candidate. As an initial matter, given the

---

310 FBI-AAA-EC-00006440 (Lync message exchange between Clinesmith and FBI OGC Unit Chief-1 dated 10/03/2016). In referring to Crossfire Hurricane investigators, FBI OGC Unit Chief-1 inquired of Clinesmith "[W]hy aren't they getting PR/TTs [pen registers/trap and trace devices]? UGH!"

311 U.S. House of Representatives Cmte. on the Judiciary Interview of Lisa Page on July 16, 2018 at 157.

312 *FBI Inspection Division Report* at 17.

313 *Id.*

314 *See supra* § IV.A.3.b.

315 U.S. Senate Cmte. on the Judiciary Interview of Supervisory Special Agent-1 on Aug. 27, 2020 at 91-105 (agent left the Crossfire Hurricane investigation because he "had a professional disagreement with stopping the enhanced validation review"); *see also* OSC Report of Interview of Supervisory Special Agent-1 on July 22, 2020 at 2-3; OSC Report of Interview of Jonathan Moffa on Oct. 28, 2020 at 15; OSC Report of Interview of Supervisory Special Agent-3 on Mar. 18, 2021 at 2; OSC Report of Interview of Headquarters Analyst-1 on Dec. 16, 2020 at 2. As described above, *see supra* § III.B.3, the *CHS Policy Guide* appears to give the Assistant Director for Intelligence an approval role for a source like Steele.

particular nature of the allegations related to each campaign, attempting to view the FBI's investigative activity in an "apples to apples" approach is undoubtedly an imperfect method to analyze whether the FBI engaged in disparate treatment of the campaigns. Nevertheless, the comparisons are instructive, and below we discuss our observations regarding the investigative approach to allegations of foreign election influence against each campaign.

### 1. *The threat of foreign election influence by Foreign Government-2*

Beginning in late 2014, before Clinton formally declared her presidential candidacy, the FBI learned from a well-placed CHS ("CHS-A") that a foreign government ("Foreign Government-2") was planning to send an individual ("Non-U.S. Person-1") to contribute to Clinton's anticipated presidential campaign, as a way to gain influence with Clinton should she win the presidency.[316] The FBI's independent corroboration of this information is discussed in the Classified Appendix.

Upon receipt of this information and the predication it provided, Field Office-1 sought to have one of two other better-positioned and higher-resourced field offices open a counterintelligence or public corruption investigation into these allegations, but Counterintelligence Division Executive Management directed Field Office-1 to open a full counterintelligence investigation into the matter.[317]

Field Office-1 sought FISA coverage of Non-U.S. Person 1, almost immediately, in order to obtain access to his/her email accounts and to conduct a search of him/her as soon as he/she arrived in the United States.[318] Although Field Office-1 attempted to obtain expedited approval for the FISA authorization,[319] the certified copy of the application was sent by OI to the FBI Headquarters for final approval where it remained, according to Field Office-1 SAC-1, "in limbo" for approximately four months.[320] According to another agent, the application lingered because "everyone was 'super more careful'" and "scared with the big name [Clinton]" involved.[321] "[T]hey were pretty 'tippy-toeing' around HRC because there was a chance she would be the next President."[322] Similarly, Field Office-1 SAC-1 told investigators that, when

---

[316] *See* FBI-AAA-12-0023529 (Classified Codeword-1 Investigation Chronology); *see also*, FBI-AAA-03-0000482 (Email from Comey to Field Office-1 SAC-1 & others dated 04/14/2015); OSC Report of Interview of Headquarters Supervisory Special Agent-4 on May 28, 2020 at 5.

[317] *Id.*; OSC Report of Interview of Field Office-1 Handling Agent-1 on April 23, 2020 at 1; OSC Report of Interview of Headquarters Supervisory Special Agent-4 on May 28, 2020 at 5.

[318] FBI-AAA-03-0000482 at 0000483, Email from Field Office-1 SAC-1 to FBI Director James Comey, April 14, 2015.

[319] FBI-AAA-12-0023529 (Codename-1 Investigation Chronology).

[320] FBI-AAA-03-0000482 at 0000483, Email from Field Office-1 SAC-1 to FBI Director James Comey, April 14, 2015.

[321] OSC Report of Interview of Headquarters Supervisory Special Agent-4 dated May 28, 2020 at 8.

[322] OSC Report of Interview of Headquarters Supervisory Special Agent-4 dated May 28, 2020 at 9.

she spoke with [illegible] Intelligence [illegible] Assistant [illegible] Director and Deputy Assistant Director, they [illegible] fact that [illegible] not [illegible] presidential candidate on tape, even though Field O[illegible] believe[illegible] was a [illegible] possibility.[323] According to the records the Offi[illegible] it appear[illegible] delay [illegible] have been partially attributable to a decision to a[illegible] nation [illegible] General.[324] The FISA was ultimately conc[illegible] required [illegible] defensive briefings to the various public officials [illegible] of [illegible] Clinton, targeted by Foreign Government-2 [illegible]

On Dec[illegible] 2014, FBI [illegible] McNally summarized his conversation wi[illegible] Evans, the [illegible] Assistant [illegible] General responsible for OI, about the proposed a[illegible]

> I spoke [illegible], he sug[illegible] to him rather than calling the AAG [illegible] question [illegible] about [illegible] issue)[326] it was about what wa[illegible] thinking [illegible] case, [illegible] whether or not we think that the [illegible] staff and [illegible] politician [illegible] with the target, meaning that the [illegible] know [illegible] target is [illegible] a foreign government and has som[illegible] or alt[illegible] the pol and staff are unwitting [illegible] are [illegible] some sort of defensive brief to [illegible] or staff [illegible]

Certain [illegible] in the [illegible] for months due to, among other things, concerns [illegible] politician [illegible] and that the investigation might interfere with a [illegible] future [illegible] campaign [illegible] with the directive, the FBI ultimately provi[illegible] brie[illegible] offic[illegible] representatives, though it took

---

[323] OSC Report [illegible] of Fi[illegible] SAC [illegible] 10, 2020 at 1.

[324] *Id.* at 3.

[325] FBI-AAA-[illegible] Classified [illegible] Chronology). The need for a defensive brie[illegible] discuss[illegible] Department [illegible] the FBI even before the announcement [illegible] candidacy [illegible] 2015 [illegible] ly, one was provided to her representatives [illegible] 2015. [illegible]

[326] *See also* OSC [illegible] Interview [illegible] August 12, 2021 at 1 (probable cause was "solid" wi[illegible] corrobor[illegible] evidence [illegible] was normal to 'pause' FISAs when they involved p[illegible] because [illegible] are sensitive"); *see also* OSC Report of Inter[illegible] Evans [illegible] 7, 20[illegible]

[327] Email from [illegible] McNally to [illegible] Headquarters Supervisory Special Agent-4 & others dat[illegible] 14.

approximately 11 months from the receipt of the original allegations.[328] Clinton elected to receive the defensive briefing through her personal attorneys.[329]

The use of defensive briefings in 2015 contrasts with the FBI's failure to provide a defensive briefing to the Trump campaign approximately one year later when Australia shared the information from Papadopoulos. Significant to the question of whether a defensive briefing was appropriate here - as it was determined to be just months earlier when a defensive briefing was given to Clinton via her lawyers - is the fact that Australia had specifically noted, "[i]t was unclear whether [Papadopoulos] or the Russians were referring to material acquired publicly of [sic] through other means."[330] Further, the Office's investigation revealed that the FBI engaged in what were likely very limited discussions as to whether any such briefing was appropriate. Deputy Director McCabe informed the OIG that he did not remember participating in *any* discussions about providing a defensive briefing as an alternative to opening the full counterintelligence investigation.[331] McCabe noted that, at the time Crossfire Hurricane was opened, the FBI had "[t]o do some work to have a better understanding of what [it had] before tak[ing] a step as overt as providing a defensive briefing because the . . . briefing could . . . eliminate . . . or reduce your ability to get to the bottom of the threat."[332] On the other hand, Assistant Director for Counterintelligence Priestap said that he discussed the issue of defensive briefings with others.[333] He explained that the FBI provides

---

328 OSC Report(s) of Interview(s) of Field Office-1 Handling Agent-1 on April 23, 2020 and May 5, 2020; OSC Report of Interview of Headquarters Supervisory Special Agent-4 on May 28, 2020 at 5 – 7; OSC Report of Interview of David Archey on June 21, 2021 at 1 – 3 (discussing the rationale for the debriefings regarding the threat from Foreign Government-2 and ECs documenting the September 1, 2015 briefing to a designated staffer on behalf of an elected official within the Republican party, and the October 15, 2015 defensive briefing Archey provided to Clinton's personal attorneys).

329 *See* SENATE-FISA2020-001321 (Declassified defensive brief EC dated 10/22/2015).

330 *London EC* at 2-3.

331 OIG Interview of Andrew McCabe on Aug. 15, 2019 at 118; *see also* OSC Report of Interview of Special Agent-2 on June 25, 2020 at 2 (Special Agent-2 did not recall any internal FBI discussions suggesting a defensive briefing to the Trump campaign); OSC Report of Interview of Brian Auten on July 26, 2021 at 12 (Auten did not recall conversations about a defensive briefing regarding the information from Australia); OSC Report of Interview of Supervisory Special Agent-1 on July 22, 2020 at 5-6 (Supervisory Special Agent-1 did not recall any consideration being given to conducting straightforward defensive briefings to candidate Trump or members of his team regarding this information); OIG Interview of James Comey on Feb. 28, 2019 at 102-108 (Comey stated that he had no memory of any discussion of a defensive briefing to the Trump campaign).

332 OIG Interview of Andrew McCabe on Aug. 15, 2019 at 118-119.

333 OIG Interview of E.W. "Bill" Priestap on Aug. 22, 2018 at 4; *see also Redacted OIG Review* at 55.

> defensive briefings when we obtain information indicating a foreign adversary is trying or will try to influence a specific U.S. person and when there is no indication that that specific U.S. person could be working with the adversary.
>
> . . . [W]e had no indication as to which person in the Trump campaign allegedly received the offer from the Russians. . . .
>
> . . . . Because the possibility existed that someone on the Trump campaign could have taken the Russians up on their offer, I thought it was wise to open an investigation to look into the situation.[334]

How these observations can be reconciled with the defensive briefings previously provided to Clinton and others is unclear. The FBI's decision to conduct defensive briefings in the investigation of Foreign Government-2's foreign influence efforts is curious given that defensive briefings could reduce the likelihood of success of any investigation into the foreign influence allegations[335] and that candidates and public officials might then be less likely to interact with representatives of Foreign Government-2. The decision to provide defensive briefings to Clinton and others seems to conflict directly with McCabe's notion that providing "a defensive briefing [to the Trump campaign] . . . could . . . eliminate . . . or reduce your ability to get to the bottom of the threat."

Similarly, with respect to the Trump campaign, Priestap's twofold concern that (i) the FBI was unaware of which member of the Trump campaign allegedly received the

[334] OIG Interview of E.W. "Bill" Priestap on Aug. 22, 2018 at 4-5; *see also* OIG Interview of E.W. "Bill" Priestap on Aug. 13, 2018 at 45-48; *Redacted OIG Review* at 55. Similarly, General Counsel Baker advised that there was some limited discussion about providing a defensive briefing to the Trump campaign regarding the Papadopoulos information; however, in his words, there was also the thought that "why hasn't anyone from the Trump campaign reported this information to the FBI?" Baker advised the FBI felt it did not know to whom in the Trump campaign it could provide a defensive briefing as there was uncertainty about who could be trusted with the information. Additionally, there was some concern about tipping off the Russians if they became aware the FBI had learned of its scheme through a briefing provided to the Trump campaign. Baker advised the FBI did not wish to "mess up" the political process by going overt with its investigation. He also advised that the FBI needed to do more work, figure things out and come up with a strategic plan before deciding how to proceed. He said part of that plan may have included providing a defensive briefing to the campaign. OSC Interview Report of James Baker on Feb. 7, 2020 at 8-9; *see also* OSC Interview Report of Case Agent-1 on June 19, 2019 at 3 (Case Agent-1 recalled a "notional idea of going directly to the Trump campaign leadership with a briefing about the intelligence threats").

[335] *See* OSC Report of Interview of Headquarters Supervisory Special Agent-4 on May 28, 2020 at 6-7 ("it was important to know if the [Clinton] people being targeted for foreign influence knew of the targeting. Headquarters Supervisory Special Agent-4 did not think they had any information one way or the other on that issue."); *see also* OSC Report of Interview of Field Office-1 Handling Agent-1 on April 23, 2020 at 3 (Field Office-1 Handling Agent-1 "was ok with the defensive briefings because he felt the common goal was to neutralize [Foreign Government-2's] intent to interfere with the election.")

offer from the Russian government and (ii) the possibility existed that the campaign had ultimately taken Russia up on the purported offer is also unpersuasive when viewed in light of the planned activity of Foreign Government-2 given the unknowns that existed in that investigation. Nevertheless, the FBI went forward with defensive briefings in that investigation – an investigation predicated on the receipt of corroborated information – but failed to conduct defensive briefings to the Trump campaign, an investigation predicated on less certain information.[336]

The FBI's and the Department's measured approach to these foreign influence allegations involving Clinton also stands in stark contrast to the speed with which the FBI undertook to include the Steele Report allegations in the FISA request it submitted to OI targeting Page. Indeed, as discussed below in Section IV.D.1.b.iii, the Crossfire Hurricane investigators received the initial Steele Reports on September 19, 2016 and within two days had included portions of those allegations in the draft Page FISA submission. As noted below, approximately one month later, on October 21, 2016, the FISC signed the initial authorization.

During the period between the drafting of the initial FISA request and the approval of the application by the Deputy Attorney General, Evans (who was previously consulted regarding the allegation of Foreign Government–2's foreign influence effort directed at Clinton and others) raised concerns in a call with FBI Special Assistant Lisa Page about (among other things) Steele's personal bias, unknown sourcing, and that the use of FISA authorities was bad from a policy perspective, to which Page's notes appear to indicate in response:

> We accept info from biased people all the time.
> Would look terrible if we pull our punch due to policy/political concern.
> We believe the info & sourcing is good.
> As leaks continue to trickle, is one of the only opportunities to see reflections.[337]

Despite the concerns raised by Evans, the FBI and the Department proceeded to obtain authority from the FISC to conduct surveillance of Page slightly more than one month after the Crossfire Hurricane investigators first received the Steele Reports. The speed with which surveillance of a U.S. person associated with Trump's campaign was authorized – in the face of the unverified Steele Reports and in the absence of a defensive briefing being provided to then-candidate Trump – are difficult to explain compared to the FBI's and Department's actions nearly two years earlier when confronted with

[336] *See* OSC Report of Interview of Field Office-1 Handling Agent-1 on May 5, 2020 ("[P]olitics was a concern" because approval for a certain activity was "inexplicably stalled" and "[CD AD] Coleman's call to [Field Office-1 SAC-1] about the case where he said he didn't want to drag the Bureau into a firestorm."); *see also* OSC Report of Interview of [Field Office-1 SAC-1] on September 10, 2020 at 1 - 2 (although the SAC "was never told why HQ would not support the [sensitive investigative technique]A" and "Coleman and [CD Deputy Assistant Director Robert] Jones alluded to the fact they didn't want a presidential candidate on tape," the SAC attributed the delay not to the candidate involved, but alternatively, to the identity of Foreign Government-2, the turnover in management at FBI Headquarters, or a bias against Field Office-1).

[337] FBI-LP-00000111-112.

corroborated all [illegible] attemp[illegible] inf[illegible] [illegible]ing Clinton, who at the time was still a[illegible] candi[illegible] pres[illegible]

*2. The [illegible] Foreign [illegible] Influe[illegible] [illegible]eign Government-3*

In additi[illegible] ng the F[illegible] foreign i[illegible] [illegible]rts by Foreign Government-2, CHS-A also pr[illegible] ration [illegible] about [illegible] [illegible]eign election influence efforts targeting the C[illegible] ign in [illegible] 2015 [illegible]ly the Trump campaign in March 2016) by a dif[illegible] countr[illegible] G[illegible]).[338] A Foreign Government-3 insider ("Insid[illegible]" [illegible]s kn[illegible] FBI [illegible]n intelligence and criminal connections, h[illegible] HS-A [illegible] meeti[illegible] [illegible]didate Clinton because Insider-1 wanted to prop[illegible] r g" th[illegible] nde[illegible] campaign contributions on behalf of Foreign Go[illegible] exch[illegible] pro[illegible] [illegible]eign Government-3's interests should Clinton [illegible] ident.[339]

Althou[illegible] ation [illegible] ce threat from a different country, the handling a[illegible] A conti[illegible] ork th[illegible] [illegible]der the existing counterintellig[illegible] the thr[illegible] repo[illegible] ng Foreign Government-2. The handling Agent [illegible] ith FB[illegible] the C[illegible] ligence Division at Headquarters to seek to rene[illegible] ise Ill[illegible] ("C[illegible] [illegible]ity the CHS had to make introductions a[illegible] raising [illegible] [illegible]ber 2014 that involved a representative [illegible] Governme[illegible]

Accordi[illegible] A, Insi[illegible] half [illegible] [illegible]overnment-3, sought access through CHS-A [illegible] r cam[illegible] aisin[illegible] [illegible] Fall of 2015.[341] Although CHS-A was initially [illegible] r indi[illegible] iated [illegible]ndraising efforts that Insider-1 could attend, th[illegible] cons[illegible] e ca[illegible] disinvited Insider-1 to the event because of the [illegible] gative [illegible] forei[illegible] might attract.[342] According to CHS-A, the fu[illegible] dact s[illegible] HS-A [illegible] separate meeting for Insider-1.[343] Field Office-1 [illegible] OIA f[illegible] 4 fo[illegible] attend the late November 2015

---

[338] CHS-A Sou[illegible] R – S[illegible] OIA S[illegible] [illegible]roved 11/19/2015); Sub V Serial 400.

[339] CHS-A So[illegible] R – S[illegible] OIA S[illegible] [illegible]roved 11/19/2015).

[340] FBI-AAA-[illegible] seq[illegible] SC R[illegible] [illegible]rview of Field Office-1 Handling Agent-3 on Ap[illegible] a[illegible]3.

[341] CHS-A So[illegible] R- Seri[illegible]

[342] CHS-A So[illegible] R- Seri[illegible] *also* [illegible]-03-0001188 (Email from Headquarters S[illegible] Specia[illegible] Field [illegible]andling Agent-3 & others dated 01/15/2016).

[343] FBI-AAA-[illegible] 3 Email f[illegible] quar[illegible] [illegible]sory Special Agent-4 to Field Office-1 Handli[illegible] & other[illegible] /15/[illegible] -A Source file, Sub R Serial 207. The Office fou[illegible] e the[illegible] Clint[illegible] with Insider-1.

event and make introductions on behalf of Insider-1, but ultimately CHS-A did not attend the event.[344]

CHS-A, however, did attend a fundraiser in January 2016, after providing same-day notice and receiving the approval of his FBI handling agent.[345] CHS-A reported in an email that Insider-1 "got cold feet" and was not going to attend, but the source file report indicates Insider-1 was told by a representative of Clinton not to attend.[346] When Insider-1 decided not to attend, he/she asked CHS-A to deliver a message of support. CHS-A provided the draft message to the handling agent, who received same-day approval from FBI OGC for the CHS to deliver the message at the event scheduled for later that day.[347]

However, without the knowledge or prior approval of the handling agent, CHS-A had made a $2700 campaign contribution (the maximum amount at the time for an individual contribution) prior to the event, which CHS-A indicated he/she "made on [his/her] [credit] card" on behalf of Insider-1.[348] If true, the campaign contribution on behalf of a foreign national would violate Title 52 USC Section 30121 ("Contributions and donations by foreign nationals"). However, despite CHS-A's claim that the contribution was made in his/her personal name, the Federal Election Commission records reviewed did not reveal any contribution in CHS-A's name. Rather, Commission records corroborate a contribution paid by a credit card in the name of a close associate (who was a U.S. person) of CHS-A. CHS-A also told the handling agent that "[t]hey [the campaign] were okay with it. [...] yes they were fully aware from the start" of the contribution being made on behalf of a foreign interest and CHS-A offered to provide a copy of the credit card charges.[349] Despite this offer by CHS-A to provide a copy of the credit card charges, we did not find any indication that the handling agent asked for or otherwise secured a copy.

---

344 *See* FBI-AAA-03-0000514 (Email from Clinesmith to Field Office-1 Handling Agent-3, Headquarters Supervisory Special Agent-4 & others dated 11/19/2015); *see also* OIA Serial 4 dated 11/19/2015; *see also* FBI-AAA-EC-00000983 (Lync exchange between Headquarters Supervisory Special Agent-4 & Field Office-1 Handling Agent-3 dated 01/19/2016) (CHS did not attend the 11/30/2015 event).

345 FBI_DOJ_2019_CFH_005507 at 1-3, 6 (CHS informed handling agent on 1/13/2016: "I just got to DC, will be meeting Hillary today. [Insider-1] was suppose[d] to join me but [Insider-1] got cold feet [...]. [Insider-1] asked me to relay a message and setup a meeting. That should be okay right?" Agent replied on 1/13/2016 that it was fine to deliver that message.)

346 CHS-A Source File Sub R Serial 208.

347 FBI_DOJ_2019_CFH_005507 at 3 ("The message is [head] [of Foreign Government-3] fully supports you and wants closer cooperation once you are president. He has always believed you would be the perfect candidate and has been following your campaigning closely. [Foreign Government-3] and US have a [ ] and is the only standing fort against [third country]. [Insider-1] would like to sit with you and or your staff to discuss regional affairs. If it's possible for me to get a contact or arrange a meeting. Would that be okay?"); *see* CHS-A Source File Sub-V Serial 384, and Sub R Serial 208.

348 FBI_DOJ_2019_CFH_005507 at 7.

349 *Id.* at 6-7.

When interviewed by the Office about this contribution, one of CHS-A's FBI handlers could not explain why this apparent illegal contribution was not documented in FBI records.[350] Although the handling agent at the time asked CHS-A about the payment,[351] there is no indication that the agent documented the contribution in the CHS's source file.[352] Moreover, despite the CHS telling the handling agent that the CHS was going to Insider-1's house "after the event to update [him/her]," [353] there was no follow up by the handling agent to document that in the source file.[354] In fact, the handling agent subsequently told the CHS to stay away from all events relating to Clinton's campaign.[355]

The Counterintelligence Division Unit Chief ("Headquarters Unit Chief-2") also did not recall the campaign contribution, despite being shown an FBINET Lync chat dated at the time of the events between himself and Headquarters Supervisory Special Agent-4, in which Headquarters Unit Chief-2 wrote "just spoke with the [Field Office-1] ASAC" and asked Headquarters Supervisory Special Agent-4, "do we know who made the $2700 donation, CHS, CHS's boss, or CHS on behalf of [Insider-1]? We'll have to have an answer for that by the morning."[356] In 2021, at the time of the Office's interview of Headquarters Unit Chief-2, his SAC was the former ASAC of Field Office-1 with whom the Lync indicated Headquarters Unit Chief-2 had spoken about this matter at the time of the events in January 2016. Field Office-1 Supervisory Special Agent-1, who oversaw the investigation, also had no recollection about why this contribution was not documented in CHS-A's source file, nor considered as reportable unauthorized illegal activity by CHS-A.[357] Also, Field Office-1 ASAC-1 had no recollection of the payment by CHS-A, and did not know why it was not documented in the source file.[358]

Although Field Office-1 had documented reporting from CHS-A regarding the threat to the Clinton campaign, and subsequently to the Trump campaign, of Foreign Government-3's

---

[350] OSC Report of Interview of Field Office-1 Handling Agent-2 on May 5, 2021 at 3.

[351] FBI_DOJ_2019_CFH_005507 at 6 ("I also need to know how the money ($2700) was donated on behalf of [Insider-1]. Did it come out of your pocket? How was it paid? Was there any mention of the donation being on behalf of [Insider-1] BEFORE the contribution was made? Was the money returned?").

[352] OSC Report of Interview of Field Office-1 Handling Agent-3 on September 22, 2020 at 3 ("[Field Office-1 Handling Agent-3] could not recall if he documented the $2700 payment in [the Source File] or not. He did not make a conscious decision to not document the payment.").

[353] FBI_DOJ_2019_CFH_005507 at 2.

[354] OSC Report of Interview of Field Office-1 ASAC-1 on July 7, 2021 at 5 (the handling Agent's ASAC did not know why CHS-A's purported visit to Insider-1 after the January 13, 2016 fundraising event was not documented in an FBI record).

[355] FBI_DOJ_2019_CFH_005507 at 6; *see also* Source file Sub xxx Serial 384.

[356] OSC Report of Interview of Headquarters Unit Chief-2 on April 22, 2021 at 4; FBI-AAA-EC-00000983 (Lync exchange between Headquarters Supervisory Special Agent-4 & Headquarters Unit Chief-2 dated 01/19/2016).

[357] OSC Report of Interview of Field Office-1 Supervisory Special Agent-1 on April 8, 2021 at 5.

[358] OSC Report of Interview of Field Office-1 ASAC-1 on July 7, 2021 at 4 - 5.

foreign election influence efforts, Field Office-1 did not open a separate investigation into this threat.[359] Nor did Field Office-1 "consider this information as to whether it would be a good idea to let [Insider-1] get close to HRC in an operation or that [Insider-1] might be a foreign influence threat to the presidential candidates worthy of continued scrutiny."[360] Field Office-1 also did not document the unauthorized illegal activity by CHS-A in connection with making a campaign contribution purportedly on behalf of Insider-1.[361] Instead, the FBI effectively removed their sole source of insight into this threat when the handling agent, responding to direction, admonished CHS-A:

> do NOT attend any more campaign events, set up meetings, or anything else relating to [Clinton's] campaign. We need to keep you completely away from that situation. I don't know all the details, but it's for your own protection."[362]

Moreover, despite removing their source of insight into this threat, and DAD Archey's belief that "the FBI protects the candidates by doing defensive briefings,"[363] the FBI did not provide the Clinton campaign or the Trump campaign a defensive briefing regarding Foreign Government-3's foreign election influence efforts.[364]

Contrasted with the FBI's rapid opening of Crossfire Hurricane, the FBI appears to have made no effort to investigate the possible illegal campaign contribution (which allegedly was a precursor to the contribution of a significant sum of money by Insider-1 on behalf of Foreign Government-3) or the Clinton campaign's purported acceptance of a campaign contribution that was made by the FBI's own long-term CHS on behalf of Insider-1 and, ultimately, Foreign Government-3.

---

[359] OSC Report of Interview of Field Office-1 Supervisory Special Agent-1 on April 8, 2021 at 4 (The Field Office never opened a counterintelligence case on [Insider-1] because [Insider-1] lived in areas outside Field Office-1's area of responsibility).

[360] OSC Report of Interview of Field Office-1 Supervisory Special Agent-1 on April 8, 2021 at 4.

[361] OSC Report of Interview of Field Office-1 Supervisory Special Agent-1 on April 8, 2021 at 5, (Headquarters Supervisory Analyst-1 "did not know why this action was not documented in a FD-1023 and stated that it should have been because it was Unauthorized Illegal Activity (UIA) and not within the scope of what [CHS-A] was allowed to do in the OIA.")

[362] FBI_DOJ_2019_CFH 005512; *see also* OSC Report of Interview of Field Office-1 Supervisory Special Agent-1 on April 8, 2021 at 5 ("Their plan, however, was to move [CHS-A] away from the political matters so they could fully utilize [CHS-A] in overseas national security matters.").

[363] OSC Report of Interview of David Archey on June 21, 2021 at 4.

[364] This conclusion by the Office is based on the Office's review of available documentation in the source file, Sentinel, and electronic communications of FBI personnel. Neither Archey nor Field Office-1 ASAC-1 recalled this threat reporting nor offered an explanation as to the absence of defensive briefings. *See* OSC Report of Interview of David Archey on June 21, 2021 at 5; *see also* OSC Report of Interview of Field Office-1 ASAC-1 on July 7, 2021 at 5.

### 3. *Alle*[illegible] *ving* [illegible]

Beginn[illegible] 2016 [illegible] ices, the New York Field Office ("NYFO"), the [illegible] Field [illegible] le Rock Field Office ("LRFO"), opened investig[illegible] ssible [illegible] tivi[illegible] the Clinton Foundation.[365] The LRFO case ope[illegible] cation [illegible] product and corroborating financial reporti[illegible] cular [illegible] engaged a federal public official in a flow of ben[illegible], name[illegible] ons were made to a non-profit, under both dire[illegible] contr[illegible] deral [illegible] al, in exchange for favorable government ac[illegible] fluenc[illegible] WFO [illegible] n was opened as a preliminary investigation, b[illegible] ase Ag[illegible] could develop additional information to [illegible] allega[illegible] rece[illegible] d book, *Clinton Cash* by Peter Schweizer, bef[illegible] conv[illegible] gation.[367] Additionally, the LRFO and NY[illegible] ions in[illegible] source reporting that identified foreign govern[illegible] d mad[illegible] to [illegible] utions to the Foundation in exchange for fa[illegible] preferenti[illegible] fro[illegible] [368]

With th[illegible] FBI fiel[illegible] avin[illegible] vestigations related to the Clinton Foundation, the[illegible] ived [illegible] meetings between the field offices, FBI He[illegible] nd ap[illegible] ited [illegible] ney's offices and components from the Depar[illegible] meeti[illegible] vers[illegible] cially important given that the investigations [illegible] g in a[illegible] ar i[illegible] ton was a declared candidate for President. Sev[illegible] meeting[illegible] ribed [illegible] ail below.

On Feb[illegible], a meet[illegible] eld [illegible] Foundation investigations. Present for the [illegible] the FB[illegible] ong[illegible] cutive Assistant Director Randy Coleman, Crim[illegible] tive D[illegible] istan[illegible] e Campbell and Acting OGC Section Chief-[illegible] nt fro[illegible] Criminal Division Assistant Attorney Gene[illegible] well [illegible] nteg[illegible] Chief Ray Hulser.[369] When

---

[365] OSC Repor[illegible] of Ra[illegible] July [illegible]; OSC Report of Interview of Headquarters [illegible] on Janu[illegible] 0 a[illegible] 58A-WF-6930742 Serial 1 (opened 1/29/2[illegible] OJ_20[illegible] 02365 [illegible] 6912913 Serial 1 opened 01-27-2016) (openin[illegible] identi[illegible] ing [illegible] LR-2187489, opened July 2017 and containing [illegible] to 58[illegible] 13); [illegible] 388608 Serial 1 (opened 1/22/2016).

[366] FBI_DOJ_2[illegible] 02365 [illegible]

[367] *See* Email f[illegible] inton [illegible] Case [illegible] WFO ASAC-1 dated 09/01/2017; *see generally*, [illegible] Inte[illegible] FO C[illegible] dation Case Agent-1 on August 20, 2020.

[368] *See* FBI_D[illegible] _002[illegible] fer[illegible] pecific CHS references to an intelligence pr[illegible] uary [illegible] 58A[illegible] 08 Serial 1 at 4. WFO's Opening EC (58A-WF-[illegible] al 1) [illegible] eragi[illegible] m a different pending investigation b[illegible] orpo[illegible] ence [illegible] porting.

[369] OSC Report [illegible] of Act[illegible] Sect[illegible] n Sept. 9, 2020 at 2; OSC Report of Interview of [illegible] eman [illegible] 2, 20[illegible]

interviewed by the Office, Hulser noted, in sum, that the FBI briefing was poorly presented and that there was insufficient predication for at least one of the investigations due to its reliance on allegations contained in a book. Hulser also downplayed the information provided by the NYFO CHS and recalled that the amount involved in the financial reporting was "de minimis."[370]

Although Hulser declined prosecution on behalf of the Public Integrity Section, he told the Office he "made it clear, however, that his decision was not binding on the various U.S. Attorneys' Offices or FBI field divisions."[371] Acting OGC Section Chief-1 recalled that the Department's reaction to the Clinton Foundation briefing was "hostile."[372]

Three weeks later, on February 22, 2016, another meeting was convened at FBI Headquarters to discuss the Foundation investigations.[373] The meeting was chaired by McCabe.[374] Present for the meeting from the FBI were, among others, Coleman, Campbell, and representatives from the affected field offices, including then-WFO Assistant Director-in-Charge ("ADIC") Paul Abbate.[375] Representatives from the Department and the affected U.S. Attorney's offices were also present.[376] At the meeting, McCabe initially directed the field offices to close their cases, but following objections, agreed to reconsider the final disposition of the cases.[377] In his interview with the Office, Abbate described McCabe as "negative," "annoyed," and "angry."[378] According to Abbate, McCabe stated "they [the Department] say there's nothing here" and "why are we even doing this?"[379] At the close of the meeting, Campbell directed that for any overt investigative steps to be taken, the Deputy Director's approval would be required.[380] This restriction on overt investigative activity essentially

---

370 OSC Report of Interview of Ray Hulser on July 8, 2020 at 1-2. We note that the financial reporting concerning the Clinton Foundation was not available to show Hulser at the time of his interview to help refresh any recollections he might have. The Office, however, separately reviewed the material to understand the allegations that caused the reporting to be made in the summer of 2015. The reporting, which in itself is not proof of wrongdoing, was a narrative describing multiple funds transfers, some of which involved international bank accounts that were suspected of possibly facilitating bribery or gratuity violations. The transactions involved occurred between 2012 and 2014, and totaled hundreds of thousands of dollars.

371 *Id.* at 1.

372 OSC Report of Interview of Acting OGC Section Chief-1 on Sept. 9, 2020 at 2.

373 *Id.*

374 *Id.*

375 *Id.*; OSC Report of Interview of Paul Abbate on March 18, 2020 at 2.

376 OSC Report of Interview of Acting OGC Section Chief-1 on Sept. 9, 2020 at 2.

377 *Id.*; OSC Report of Interview of Paul Abbate on March 18, 2020 at 2.

378 OSC Report of Interview of Paul Abbate on March 18, 2020 at 2.

379 *Id.*

380 *Id.*

remained in place until August 2016. Abbate recalled that FBI personnel from the field offices left the meeting frustrated with the limitations placed on them by the Deputy Director.[381]

According to NYFO Assistant Director in Charge Diego Rodriguez, Coleman called him on behalf of Director Comey around May and directed the NYFO to "cease and desist" from the Foundation investigation due to some undisclosed counterintelligence concern.[382] Coleman informed Rodriguez that Comey wanted to consult with Associate Deputy Attorney General David Margolis regarding the referenced counterintelligence matter.[383] The Office was not able to determine what the counterintelligence issue raised by Comey was.[384]

On August 1, 2016, a video teleconference meeting ("VTC") was held wherein the WFO and LRFO cases were directed to be closed and consolidated into the NYFO investigation.[385] During this VTC, the NYFO was given authorization to seek subpoenas from the U.S. Attorneys' offices in the Southern and Eastern Districts of New York ("SDNY" and "EDNY").[386] However, both SDNY and EDNY declined to issue subpoenas to the NYFO, despite previously expressing support for the investigation.[387]

Once again, the investigative actions taken by FBI Headquarters in the Foundation matters contrast with those taken in Crossfire Hurricane. As an initial matter, the NYFO and WFO investigations appear to have been opened as preliminary investigations due to the political sensitivity and their reliance on unvetted hearsay information (the *Clinton Cash* book) and CHS reporting.[388] By contrast, the Crossfire Hurricane investigation was *immediately* opened as a full investigation despite the fact that it was similarly predicated on unvetted hearsay information. Furthermore, while the Department appears to have had legitimate concerns about the Foundation investigation occurring so close to a presidential election, it does not appear that similar concerns were expressed by the Department or FBI regarding the Crossfire Hurricane investigation. Indeed, in short order after opening the Crossfire Hurricane file and its four sub-files, the FBI was having one of its long-time CHSs meet not with just one Trump campaign

---

381 *Id.*

382 OSC Report of Interview of Diego Rodriguez on August 12, 2019 at 2; *see also* OSC Report of Interview of Diego Rodriguez on January 16, 2020 at 1-2.

383 *Id.* at 2.

384 Mr. Margolis unfortunately passed away in July 2016. Comey declined to be interviewed by the Office.

385 58A-NY-6888608 Serial 6; OSC Report of Interview of Headquarters Unit Chief-3 on January 28, 2020 at 3.

386 58A-NY-6888608 Serial 6.

387 OSC Report of Interview of Acting OGC Section Chief-1 on Sept. 9, 2020 at 3; OSC Report of Interview of Diego Rodriguez on January 16, 2020 at 1; *see also* OSC Report of Interview of NYFO Clinton Foundation Case Agent-1 on January 15, 2020 at 1–2; OSC Report of Interview of Patrick Fallon on September 29, 2020 at 2.

388 *See* Email from WFO Clinton Foundation Case Agent-1 to WFO ASAC-1 dated 09/01/2017; *see generally* OSC Report of Interview of WFO Clinton Foundation Case Agent-1 on August 20, 2020.

associate, but meet and record conversations with three such insiders. And a little more than a month after opening the Crossfire Hurricane file on Page, a "senior U.S. law enforcement official" was publicly reported as confirming for Michael Isikoff and *Yahoo! News* that the FBI had Page on its radar screen.[389]

In the end, the perceived difference between the approaches taken and mindsets of FBI personnel central to both the Clinton and Trump matters is well-captured in a February 24, 2016 email between McCabe's Special Assistant Lisa Page and Strzok. Prior to the FBI's interview of Clinton in the investigation of her use of a private email server while she was serving as Secretary of State, the following exchange took place:

> Page: One more thing: [Clinton] may be our next president. The last thing you need [is] going in there loaded for bear. You think she's going to remember or care that it was more doj than fbi?
>
> Strzok: Agreed . . . .[390]

## C. **Investigative Referral of Possible Clinton Campaign Plan**

### *1. Factual background*

The Office also considered as part of its investigation the government's handling of certain intelligence that it received during the summer of 2016. That intelligence concerned the purported "approval by Hillary Clinton on July 26, 2016 of a proposal from one of her foreign policy advisors to vilify Donald Trump by stirring up a scandal claiming interference by the Russian security services."[391] We refer to that intelligence hereafter as the "Clinton Plan intelligence." DNI John Ratcliffe declassified the following information about the Clinton Plan intelligence in September 2020 and conveyed it to the Senate Judiciary Committee:

- In late July 2016, U.S. intelligence agencies obtained insight into Russian intelligence analysis alleging that U.S Presidential candidate Hillary Clinton had approved a campaign plan to stir up a scandal against U.S. Presidential candidate Donald Trump by tying him to Putin and the Russians' hacking of the Democratic National Committee. The IC does not know the accuracy of this allegation or the extent to which the Russian intelligence analysis may reflect exaggeration or fabrication.
- According to his handwritten notes, CIA Director Brennan subsequently briefed President Obama and other senior national security officials on the intelligence, including the "alleged approval by Hillary Clinton on July 26, 2016 of a proposal from one of her foreign policy advisors to vilify Donald Trump by stirring up a scandal claiming interference by Russian security services."

---

389 *See* Isikoff, *Officials Probe Ties.*

390 FBI-0008217 (Office of Professional Responsibility (OPR) letter to Strzok dated Feb. 24, 2016 at 4) FBI-0008217-240 at 0008220.

391 Letter from John Ratcliffe, DNI, to Sen. Lindsay Graham (Sept. 29, 2020) (hereinafter "*Ratcliffe Letter*"); Notes of John O. Brennan, declassified by DNI Ratcliffe on October 6, 2020 (hereinafter "*Brennan Notes*").

- On 07 [illegible] 2[illegible]16, U.S. [illegible] [illegible]arded an investigative referral to FBI Dir[illegible] Comey [illegible] A[illegible] [illegible]tor of Counterintelligence Peter Strzok [illegible] U.S. Pres[illegible] candida[illegible] [illegible]linton's approval of a plan concern[illegible] dent[illegible] Dem[illegible] [illegible]and Russian hackers hampering U.S. ele[illegible] means o[illegible] the [illegible] her use of a private mail server.[illegible]

The Clinton Pl[illegible] was [illegible] the O[illegible] [illegible]stigation for two reasons.

*First*, t[illegible] intel[illegible] [illegible] arguably suggested that private actors affiliated [illegible] Clinton ca[illegible] [illegible]16 to promote a false or exaggerated na[illegible] publi[illegible] gov[illegible] [illegible]encies about Trump's possible ties to Russia. Giv[illegible] [illegible]cant qu[illegible] materi[illegible] [illegible]and other government agencies did in fact receive [illegible] 2[illegible]16 pre[illegible] ectio[illegible] [illegible] afterwards that originated with and/or were fu[illegible] Clinton [illegible] aff[illegible] [illegible]ons (*i.e.*, the Steele Dossier reports, the Alfa Bank a[illegible] and the [illegible] alle[illegible] Clinton Plan intelligence prompted the O[illegible] [illegible]ider (i[illegible] [illegible]ere [illegible] plan by the Clinton campaign to tie Trump to R[illegible] to "s[illegible] [illegible]ndal" [illegible] of the 2016 presidential election, and (ii) if such [illegible], wh[illegible] [illegible]ect o[illegible] [illegible] of that plan was to intentionally provide knowin[illegible] [illegible] or m[illegible] [illegible]form[illegible] FBI or other agencies in furtherance of [illegible]

*Second*, [illegible] Plan i[illegible] was [illegible] relevant to the Office's review and investigation b[illegible] part of [illegible] of i[illegible] that became known to certain U.S. officials at or [illegible] they [illegible] al de[illegible] the Crossfire Hurricane case and in related law en[illegible] intell[illegible] [illegible]ts. [illegible] officials relied, at least in part, on materials p[illegible] [illegible]ded b[illegible] [illegible] ca[illegible] or the DNC when seeking FISA warrants again[illegible] [illegible]n (*i.e.*, [illegible] D[illegible] [illegible] and taking other investigative steps, the Clin[illegible] [illegible]ligence [illegible]ial [illegible] reliability and credibility of those materials. Put[illegible] his i[illegible] [illegible]-take[illegible] [illegible]alue—was arguably highly relevant and exculpator[illegible] [illegible]ould b[illegible] [illegible]llen[illegible] in combination with other facts, to suggest that m[illegible] as the S[illegible] [illegible]er re[illegible] the Alfa Bank allegations (discussed below and in g[illegible] Sec[illegible] [illegible]we[illegible] political effort to smear a political opponent and [illegible] [illegible]urces [illegible] [illegible] law enforcement and intelligence agencies in su[illegible] [illegible]tical ob[illegible] the C[illegible] [illegible]re examined whether, and precisely whe[illegible] U.S. [illegible] enforcem[illegible] intellig[illegible] [illegible]ls became aware of the Clinton Plan intellige[illegible] hey ve[illegible] [illegible]alyzed [illegible] [illegible]ence to understand its potential

---

[392] *Referral M*[illegible]

[393] To be clear[illegible] [illegible] not [illegible] vie[illegible] [illegible]tial existence of a political plan by one campaign [illegible] [illegible]gative [illegible] its [illegible] illegal or criminal in any respect. As prosecutor[illegible] [illegible] remi[illegible] [illegible]ry [illegible] [illegible]an trial, opposition research is commonplace [illegible]on, D.C. [illegible] here [illegible]ed by actors of all political parties, and is not a ba[illegible] itself f[illegible] [illegible]liabili[illegible], only if the evidence supported the latter of the tw[illegible] descri[illegible] [illegible]*i.e.*, i[illegible] an intent by the Clinton campaign or its personnel [illegible] pro[illegible] [illegible]form[illegible] government—would such conduct potentially sup[illegible] charg[illegible]

significance; and whether those officials, in turn, incorporated the intelligence into their decision-making regarding the investigation of individuals who were part of the Trump campaign and had possible ties to Russian election interference efforts.

As was declassified and made public previously, the purported Clinton Plan intelligence was derived from insight that "U.S. intelligence agencies obtained into Russian intelligence analysis."[394] Given the origins of the Clinton Plan intelligence as the product of a foreign adversary, the Office was cognizant of the statement that DNI Ratcliffe made to Senate Judiciary Chairman Lindsey Graham in a September 29, 2020 letter: "The [intelligence community] *does not know the accuracy of this allegation* or the extent to which the Russian intelligence analysis may reflect exaggeration or fabrication."[395]

Recognizing this uncertainty, the Office nevertheless endeavored to investigate the bases for, and credibility of, this intelligence in order to assess its accuracy and its potential implications for the broader matters within our purview.

Given the significance of the Clinton Plan intelligence, and the need to protect sources and methods of the Intelligence Community, we report the results of our investigation in bifurcated fashion. More specifically:

(1) This section describes in unclassified form the circumstances in which U.S. officials received and acted on (or failed to act upon) the Clinton Plan intelligence, as well as the nature and significance of their reactions to it;

(2) The Classified Appendix to this report provides further information about (i) the details of the Clinton Plan intelligence; (ii) facts that heightened the potential relevance of this intelligence to the Office's inquiry; and (iii) the Office's efforts to verify or refute the key claims found in this intelligence.

a. Relevant facts

Before addressing the U.S. government's receipt and handling of the Clinton Plan intelligence, we reiterate below the description of that intelligence as declassified by the DNI in his September 29, 2020 letter to Chairman Graham. Ratcliffe's letter stated, in part, as follows:

> In late July 2016, U.S. intelligence agencies obtained insight into Russian intelligence analysis alleging that U.S Presidential candidate Hillary Clinton had approved a campaign plan to stir up a scandal against U.S. Presidential candidate Donald Trump by tying him to Putin and the Russians' hacking of the Democratic National Committee.[396]

As described herein and in the Classified Appendix, U.S. officials described the Clinton Plan intelligence in various other ways in their official notes and documents. As described more fully in the Classified Appendix, there were specific indications and additional facts that heightened the potential relevance of this intelligence to the Office's inquiry.

---

394 *Ratcliffe Letter.*

395 *Id.* (emphasis added).

396 *Id.*

*i. Receipt of the Clinton Plan intelligence*

The Intelligence Community received the Clinton Plan intelligence in late July 2016.[397] The official who initially received the information immediately recognized its importance— including its relevance to the U.S. presidential election— and acted quickly to make CIA leadership aware of it.[398] Materials obtained from former Director Brennan's office holdings reflect that he personally received a copy of the intelligence.[399] When interviewed, Brennan generally recalled reviewing the materials but stated he did not recall focusing specifically on its assertions regarding the Clinton campaign's purported plan.[400] Brennan recalled instead focusing on Russia's role in hacking the DNC.[401]

On July 28, 2016, Director Brennan met with President Obama and other White House personnel, during which Brennan and the President discussed intelligence relevant to the 2016 presidential election as well as the potential creation of an inter-agency Fusion Cell to synthesize and analyze intelligence about Russian malign influence on the 2016 presidential election.[402] Brennan's recollection was that he spoke with Director Comey on the morning of July 29, 2016, to brief him on his July 28th meeting with the President.[403] Brennan could not recall when he actually saw the Clinton Plan intelligence, but he did not think he had the information when he spoke to Comey on that morning.

Immediately after communicating with the President, Comey, and DNI Clapper to discuss relevant intelligence, Director Brennan and other agency officials took steps to ensure that dissemination of intelligence related to Russia's election interference efforts, including the Clinton Plan intelligence, would be limited to protect sensitive information and prevent leaks.[404] Brennan stated that the inter-agency Fusion Cell, a team to synthesize and analyze pertinent intelligence on Russian malign influence activities related to the presidential election, was put in motion after his meeting with President Obama on July 28th. Email traffic and witness interviews conducted by the Office reflect that at least some CIA personnel believed that the Clinton Plan intelligence led to the decision being made to set up the Fusion Cell.[405]

---

[397] *Id.*; *see also* OSC Report of Interview of IC Officer #6 on Aug. 19, 2020 at 11.

[398] OSC Report of Interview of IC Officer #6 on Aug. 19, 2020 at 4.

[399] OSC Report of Interview of John Brennan on Aug. 21, 2020 at 7-8; 16-17.

[400] *Id.* at 8-9.

[401] *Id.*

[402] OSC Report of Interview of John Brennan on Aug. 21, 2020 at 8; Email from OGA Liaison-1 to OGA employees dated 08/02/2016; Notes of Retired CIA Employee-2 dated 07/28/2016.

[403] OSC Report of Interview of John Brennan on Aug. 21, 2020 at 8.

[404] *Id.*

[405] OSC Report of Interview of I.C. Officer #6 on Aug. 19, 2020 at 4; OSC Report of Interview of I.C. Officer #12 on Dec. 23, 2020 at 3.

*ii. White House briefing*

On August 3, 2016, within days of receiving the Clinton Plan intelligence, Director Brennan met with the President, Vice President and other senior Administration officials, including but not limited to the Attorney General (who participated remotely) and the FBI Director, in the White House Situation Room to discuss Russian election interference efforts.[406] According to Brennan's handwritten notes and his recollections from the meeting, he briefed on relevant intelligence known to date on Russian election interference, including the Clinton Plan intelligence.[407] Specifically, Director Brennan's declassified handwritten notes reflect that he briefed the meeting's participants regarding the "alleged approval by Hillary Clinton on 26 July of a proposal from one of her [campaign] advisors to vilify Donald Trump by stirring up a scandal claiming interference by the Russian security services."[408]

*iii. FBI awareness*

The Office was unable to determine precisely when the FBI first obtained any of the details of the Clinton Plan intelligence (other than Director Comey, who attended the August 3, 2016 briefing). It appears, however, that this occurred no later than August 22, 2016. On that date, an FBI cyber analyst ("Headquarters Analyst-2") emailed a number of FBI employees, including Supervisory Intelligence Analyst Brian Auten and Section Chief Moffa, the most senior intelligence analysts on the Crossfire Hurricane team, to provide an update on Russian intelligence materials.[409] The email included a summary of the contents of the Clinton Plan intelligence.[410] The Office did not identify any replies or follow-up actions taken by FBI personnel as a result of this email.

When interviewed by the Office, Auten recalled that on September 2, 2016 – approximately ten days after Headquarters Analyst-2's email – the official responsible for overseeing the Fusion Cell briefed Auten, Moffa, and other FBI personnel at FBI Headquarters regarding the Clinton Plan intelligence.[411] Auten did not recall any FBI "operational" personnel (*i.e.*, Crossfire Hurricane Agents) being present at the meeting.[412] The official verbally briefed the individuals regarding information that the CIA planned to send to the FBI in a written investigative referral, including the Clinton Plan intelligence information.[413] Auten recalled thinking at the meeting that he wanted to see the formal *Referral Memo* containing the Clinton

---

406 OSC Report of Interview of John Brennan on Aug. 21, 2020 at 7; *Brennan Notes*; Notes of Retired CIA Employee-2 dated August 3, 2016 (brief-back notes of Brennan post-White House meeting).

407 *Brennan Notes.*

408 *Id.*

409 FBI-JCM-0004364 (Email from Headquarters Analyst-2 to Brian Auten, Jonathan Moffa & others dated 08/22/2016.).

410 *Id.*

411 OSC Report of Interview of Brian Auten on July 26, 2021 at 7, 13.

412 *Id.* at 7.

413 *Id.*

Plan intelligen[illegible] t: and [illegible] this [illegible] records reflect that by no later than that same [illegible] ber 2, [illegible] FBI [illegible] rector for Counterintelligence Bill Priestap wa[illegible] of the [illegible] of the [illegible] intelligence as evidenced by his hand-written n[illegible] early [illegible] eting [illegible], DAD Dina Corsi and Acting AD for Cyber Eric [illegible] he Offi[illegible] ble t[illegible] the exact contours of Priestap's knowledge, ho[illegible] t becau[illegible] ned [illegible] ewed by the Office on this subject.[416]

*iv.* [illegible] *al and* [illegible] *ation*

Five da[illegible] September [illegible], the [illegible] ted its *Referral Memo* in response to an FBI requ[illegible] information [illegible] ion Cell.[417] The CIA addressed the *Referral Me*[illegible] FBI Dir[illegible] the [illegible] Deputy Assistant Director Peter Strzok. The *R*[illegible], which [illegible] the [illegible] intelligence, stated, in part:

> Per FBI [illegible] est, CI[illegible] the b[illegible] les of information the CROSS[illegible] CAN[illegible] ll ha[illegible] date [Source revealing informa[illegible]]:
>
> [] An e[illegible] scuss[illegible] ider[illegible] te Hillary Clinton's approv[illegible] ncern[illegible] icent[illegible] e Donald Trump and Russian [illegible] mpering [illegible] ns a[illegible] distracting the public from her use [illegible] mail [illegible] ording [illegible] urces, Guccifer 2.0 is an individ[illegible] of hack[illegible] US o[illegible] ve is tied to Russian intellig[illegible]. Also, [illegible] 2.0 claimed credit for hacking [illegible] atic N[illegible] mitt[illegible] is year.[418]

None o[illegible] sonnel [illegible] to b[illegible] ed could specifically recall receiving this [illegible], nor [illegible] ing anything in response to the *Referral Mem*[illegible] that [illegible] ble [illegible] ivered this *Referral Memo* to the FBI, as he had [illegible] umero[illegible] ral [illegible] nd noted that he typically shared referral memo[illegible] t of the [illegible] gative team, although he did not recall if he did [illegible] tance.[419]

In late S[illegible] 016, hig[illegible] U.S. [illegible] urity officials, including Comey and Clapper, r[illegible] telligen[illegible] on [illegible] ference in the 2016 presidential election that i[illegible] Clinton [illegible] ffice did not identify any further

---

414 *Id.*

415 Handwritte[illegible] W. Pri[illegible] 09/0[illegible]

416 *Id.*

417 *Referral Me*[illegible]

418 *Id.*

419 OSC Repo[illegible] of B[illegible] at 13.

420 *Id.*

421 Intelligenc[illegible] Docu[illegible]

actions that the CIA or FBI took in response to this intelligence product as it related to the Clinton Plan intelligence.

v. *Awareness by the Crossfire Hurricane investigators*

The Office located no evidence that in conducting the Crossfire Hurricane investigation the FBI considered whether and how the Clinton Plan intelligence might impact the investigation. No FBI personnel who were interviewed by the Office recalled Crossfire Hurricane personnel taking any action to vet the Clinton Plan intelligence.[422] For example, Brian Auten stated that he could not recall anything that the FBI did to analyze, or otherwise consider the Clinton Plan intelligence, stating that it was "just one data point."[423]

This stands in sharp contrast to its substantial reliance on the uncorroborated Steele Reports, which at least some FBI personnel appeared to know was likely being funded or promoted by the Clinton campaign. For example:

- During a meeting in London on July 5, 2016, Steele provided his first Report to Handling Agent-1. Handling Agent-1's notes from the meeting reflect that "HC" was aware of his (Steele's) "Brit firm seeking info."[424] While Handling Agent-1 did not have an independent recollection of Steele explicitly stating that "HC" referred to Hillary Clinton, he could think of no other individual – in that context – to whom "HC" could possibly refer.[425]

- On September 23, 2016, Strzok sent a Lync message to Brian Auten regarding the Michael Isikoff article that stated, "Looking at the Yahoo article. I can definitely say at a minimum [Steele's] reports should be viewed as intended to influence as well as to inform."[426]

- On October 11, 2016, Strzok sent a Lync message to OGC attorney Kevin Clinesmith noting that Steele's "unnamed client" was "presumed to be connected to the [Clinton] campaign in some way[.]"[427]

Nor did the Office identify any evidence that the FBI disclosed the contents of the Clinton Plan intelligence to the OI attorneys working on FISA matters related to Crossfire Hurricane. Similarly, the FBI did not disclose any of the Clinton Plan intelligence materials to the FISC (despite relying on the uncorroborated Steele reporting in its FISA applications

---

422 *See, e.g.*, OSC Report of Interview of Headquarters Analyst-2 on Feb. 25, 2020 at 11; OSC Report of Interview of Jonathan Moffa on Feb. 28, 2020 at 2-4.

423 OSC Report of Interview of Brian Auten on July 26, 2021 at 13.

424 Handwritten notes of Handling Agent-1 at 4.

425 OSC Report of Interview of Handling Agent-1 on Mar. 1, 2022 at 2.

426 FBI-AAA-EC-00006182 (Lync Message Exchange between Strzok and Auten dated 09/23/16).

427 FBI-AAA-EC-00006440 (Lync Message Exchange between Strzok and Clinesmith on 10/11/16).

concerning Carter Page), and we uncovered no evidence that anyone at the FBI considered doing so.

The Office showed portions of the Clinton Plan intelligence to a number of individuals who were actively involved in the Crossfire Hurricane investigation. Most advised they had never seen the intelligence before, and some expressed surprise and dismay upon learning of it. For example, the original Supervisory Special Agent on the Crossfire Hurricane investigation, Supervisory Special Agent-1, reviewed the intelligence during one of his interviews with the Office.[428] After reading it, Supervisory Special Agent-1 became visibly upset and emotional, left the interview room with his counsel, and subsequently returned to state emphatically that he had never been apprised of the Clinton Plan intelligence and had never seen the aforementioned *Referral Memo*.[429] Supervisory Special Agent-1 expressed a sense of betrayal that no one had informed him of the intelligence. When the Office cautioned Supervisory Special Agent-1 that we had not verified or corroborated the accuracy of the intelligence and its assertions regarding the Clinton campaign, Supervisory Special Agent-1 responded firmly that regardless of whether its contents were true, he should have been informed of it.[430]

Former FBI General Counsel Baker also reviewed the Clinton Plan intelligence during one of his interviews with the Office.[431] Baker stated that he had neither seen nor heard of the Clinton Plan intelligence or the resulting *Referral Memo* prior to his interview with the Office. He acknowledged the significance of the reporting and explained that had he known of it during the Crossfire Hurricane investigation, he would have viewed in a different and much more skeptical light (i) information the FBI received from Steele concerning Trump's purported ties to Russia and (ii) information received from attorney Michael Sussmann that purported to show a secret communications channel between the Trump Organization and Alfa Bank.[432]

*vi. Other evidence obtained by the Office that appears to be relevant to an analysis of the Clinton Plan intelligence*

As discussed above, according to the declassified Clinton Plan intelligence, on July 26, 2016, Clinton allegedly approved a proposal from one of her foreign policy advisors to tie Trump to Russia as a means of distracting the public from her use of a private email server. The Office interviewed a number of individuals connected with the campaign as part of its investigation into the Clinton Plan intelligence. One foreign policy advisor ("Foreign Policy Advisor-1") stated that she did not specifically remember proposing a "plan" to Clinton or other campaign leadership to "stir up a scandal" by tying Trump to Putin or Russia.[433] Foreign Policy Advisor-1 stated, however, that it was possible that she had proposed ideas on these topics to the campaign's leadership, who may have approved those ideas.[434] Foreign Policy Advisor-1

---

[428] OSC Report of Interview of Supervisory Special Agent-1 on July 22, 2020 at 7.

[429] *Id.*

[430] *Id.*

[431] OSC Report of Interview of James Baker on June 18, 2020 at 4.

[432] *Id.*

[433] OSC Report of Interview of Foreign Policy Advisor-1 on July 21, 2021 at 7.

[434] *Id.*

recalled conversations with others in the campaign expressing their genuine concerns that the DNC hack was a threat to the electoral system, and that Trump and his advisors appeared to have troubling ties to Russia.[435] Foreign Policy Advisor-1 said it was also possible someone proposed an idea of seeking to distract attention from the investigation into Clinton's use of a private email server, but she did not specifically remember any such idea.[436] Foreign Policy Advisor-1 advised that she did not recall the FBI coming up in any campaign conversations she had.[437]

Records obtained from Foreign Policy Advisor-1 reflect that on July 27, 2016 – the day following candidate Clinton's purported authorization of the plan – Foreign Policy Advisor-1 circulated a draft public statement to certain of her colleagues. In the email circulating the draft statement, Foreign Policy Advisor-1 urged her colleagues to sign the draft statement, which criticized Trump for his comments about the NATO alliance and asserted that Trump's public statements concerning NATO were too friendly towards Russia. In her cover email, Foreign Policy Advisor-1 wrote, in part:

> We are writing to enlist your support for the attached public statement. Both of us are Hillary Clinton supporters and advisors but hope that this statement could be signed by a bipartisan group[.] Donald Trump's repeated denigration of the NATO Alliance, his refusal to support our Article 5 obligations to our European allies and his kid glove treatment of Russia and Vladimir Putin are among the most reckless statements made by a Presidential candidate in memory.[438]

During the same week, Clinton's campaign manager, Robby Mook, stated in media interviews that the campaign believed that the Russian government had carried out the DNC hack to assist Trump's electoral chances, and that Trump had made troubling statements concerning Russia.[439]

During an interview of former Secretary Clinton, the Office asked if she had reviewed the information declassified by DNI Ratcliffe regarding her alleged plan to stir up a scandal between Trump and the Russians.[440] Clinton stated it was "really sad," but "I get it, you have to go down every rabbit hole." She said that it "looked like Russian disinformation to me; they're very good at it, you know." Clinton advised that she had a lot of plans to win the campaign, and anything that came into the public domain was available to her.

In addition, the Office interviewed several other former members of the Clinton campaign using declassified materials[441] regarding the purported "plan" approved by Clinton.

---

[435] *Id.*

[436] *Id.*

[437] *Id.*

[438] XXXX-0014561 (Email from Foreign Policy Advisor-1 dated July 27, 2016).

[439] Jeremy Herb, *Mook Suggests Russians Leaked DNC Emails to Help Trump*, Politico (July 24, 2016); Jessie Hellmann, *Clinton Campaign Manager Questions Russian Involvement in Email Leak*, The Hill (July 24, 2016).

[440] OSC Report of Interview of Hillary Clinton on May 11, 2022 at 6.

[441] *See Ratcliffe Letter*.

The campaign C[illegible] John F[illegible] had th[illegible] seen the declassified material before, charact[illegible] information [illegible] alon[illegible] that the campaign was involved in any such "pl[illegible] Sulliva[illegible] paign [illegible]y Advisor, stated that he had not seen the intelli[illegible] before [illegible] other than to say, "that's ridiculous."[443] [illegible] campai[illegible] Trump and Russia, Sullivan could not recal[illegible] ulating [illegible] act negative attention away from Clinton by tyin[illegible] ssia, [illegible] not con[illegible] ule out the possibility.[444] The campaign Com[illegible] Directo[illegible] Palm[illegible] s shown the *Referral Memo*,[445] stated that she [illegible] the [illegible] be[illegible] contents to be "ridiculous," and could not recall [illegible] this [illegible] the [illegible] She stated that Podesta, Mook, Sullivan and he[illegible] aware of [illegible] involv[illegible] een Trump and Russia being conducted by P[illegible] the cam[illegible] firm [illegible] not think Clinton was aware of it, nor did she rec[illegible] tion or [illegible] from [illegible] out the project.[447]

Another [illegible] adv[illegible] gn P[illegible] r-2") confirmed that the campaign was f[illegible] ump [illegible] ut [illegible] due to national security concerns and n[illegible] distr[illegible] fr[illegible] server issue.[448] Foreign Policy Advisor-2 state[illegible] not h[illegible] rsati[illegible] on about a plan involving Trump and Russia duri[illegible] cratic [illegible] that [illegible] remember Clinton approving anything concr[illegible] he wo[illegible] ssari[illegible] involved in such strategy conversations.[449]

The Off[illegible] of cert[illegible] ficati[illegible] ng Foreign Policy Advisor-1 and Foreign Policy [illegible] oweve[illegible] provi[illegible] pport for the notion that the Clinton campai[illegible] ged in [illegible] plan [illegible] 2016 to encourage scrutiny of Trump's potent[illegible] ssia, a[illegible] amp[illegible] ave wanted or expected law enforcement o[illegible] es to a[illegible] t, in[illegible] cluding that the Russians were responsible for [illegible]

For ex[illegible] y 5, 201[illegible] Pol[illegible] -2 sent an email to three other campaign advi[illegible] ual-1,[illegible] l-2,[illegible] idual-3") in which she wrote:

> We're [illegible] ways to [illegible] and [illegible] eat (and scary) piece on Trump [illegible][450] On[illegible] hear[illegible] folks is that the Russia

---

442 OSC Repor[illegible] of Jo[illegible] at 5.

443 OSC Repor[illegible] of Jak[illegible] on [illegible] at 3-4.

444 *Id.*

445 *Referral M*[illegible]

446 OSC Repor[illegible] of Je[illegible] eri[illegible] 2021 at 4.

447 *Id.* at 1-2

448 OSC Repor[illegible] of For[illegible] Ad[illegible] Mar. 28, 2022 at 4.

449 *Id.*

450 In its June [illegible] *Atl*[illegible] ublish[illegible] by Franklin Foer titled "*Putin is Well on His W*[illegible] *the N*[illegible] *y.*"

desk at State has been tracking (and sounding an internal alarm) about parallels between rhetoric/words/methods that Trump uses and Putin-supported European right-wing candidates. I'm told it goes beyond just populist stuff. I'd love to get my hands on details of what they are seeing - can one of you help run this down? I imagine INR or IC [Intelligence Community] types might also have some insight - obviously need to be a bit careful here but eager to get specifics or details.[451]

Foreign Policy Advisor-2 stated that she did not speak with anyone at the State Department about this issue.[452] The information she mentioned in this email regarding the State Department's Russia desk came from an outside advisor who formerly worked at the State Department ("Outside Advisor-1").[453]

In addition, on July 25, 2016, Foreign Policy Advisor-1 had the following text message exchange with Foreign Policy Advisor-2:

[Foreign Policy Advisor-2]: Can you see if [Special Assistant to the President and National Security Council member] will tell you if there is a formal fbi or other investigation into the hack?

[Foreign Policy Advisor-1]: [She] won't say anything more to me. Sorry. Told me [she] went as far as [she] could.

[Foreign Policy Advisor-2]: Ok. Do you have others who might?

[Foreign Policy Advisor-1]: Has [Individual-2] tried [her]? Curious if [she] would react differently to [Individual-2]? I can also try OVP [Office of the Vice President]. They might say more.

[Foreign Policy Advisor-2]: I don't know if he has but can ask. Would also be good to try ovp, and anyone in IC [intelligence community]

[Foreign Policy Advisor-1]: Left messages for OVP but politico just sent me a push notification stating that they are indeed investigating.

[Foreign Policy Advisor-2]: Fbi just put our [sic] statement. Thx[454]

In sum, Foreign Policy Advisor-1's July 27, 2016 email to her colleagues regarding Trump, Russia and NATO – the day after Clinton purportedly approved a plan to tie Trump to Russia – is consistent with the substance of the purported plan. In addition, Foreign Policy

[451] XX_DOJ_000003 (Email from Foreign Policy Advisor-2 dated July 5, 2016).

[452] *Id.*

[453] *Id.*

[454] XX_DOJ_000022-23 (Text message exchange between Foreign Policy Advisor-1 and Foreign Policy Advisor-2 dated 07/25/2016).

Advisor-1's text message exchange with Foreign Policy Advisor-2 supports the notion that at least some officials within the campaign were seeking information about the FBI's response to the DNC hack, which would be consistent with, and a means of furthering, the purported plan. Moreover, the campaign's funding of the Steele Reports and Alfa Bank allegations as described in greater detail in Sections IV.D.1.b.ii and IV.E.1.b provide some additional support for the credibility to the information set forth in the Clinton Plan intelligence.

*vii. Other events occurring at the time of the purported approval of the Clinton Plan intelligence*

As set forth in Section IV.D.1.h.i, some of the significant Steele Dossier reporting related to Carter Page and his alleged role as a conduit for passing Russian information between Paul Manafort and the Trump campaign. This uncorroborated allegation is significantly undercut by the evidence examined by the Office and that, at the time, was in the possession of the Crossfire Hurricane investigators. As discussed below, this evidence was never presented to OI or the FISC at *any time* during the pendency of the Page FISA surveillance.

Furthermore, the evidence gathered by the Office revealed a concerted effort on the part of Fusion GPS in late July 2016 – *i.e.*, the same timeframe the Clinton Plan intelligence was purportedly approved – to communicate with the press regarding the Page allegations in the Steele reporting. For example:

- On July 19, 2016, Peter Fritsch of Fusion GPS emailed Steve LeVine, identified in his signature block as a Washington correspondent for *Quartz*, and asked of LeVine "have you ever come across this cat carter page? He strikes me as a fraud . . . ."[455] Mr. LeVine responded that he knew Page, he (LeVine) was on vacation, but would reach out when he returned.[456]

- On July 22, 2016, Fritsch emailed Franklin Foer of *Slate* stating "now we need to do the next level, which is in the works." Foer responded, "Good deal – what's the next level? And is it a sex scandal?" Fritsch replied, "it's who carter page met with in early july and what they talked about."[457]

- On July 25, 2016, Mark Hosenball of *Reuters* sent Glenn Simpson at Fusion GPS an email stating "if you have stuff on the Carter Page guy, including his most recent Russian excursion, pls. send. Doing two Russian hacking stories today and might be able to do another as early as tomorrow."[458]

---

[455] SCID_00034478.

[456] *Id.*

[457] SCID_00034501. Notably, in an uncorroborated Steele Report dated just three days earlier, in what Steele designated as "Company Intelligence Report 2016/94," dated July 19, 2016, it was alleged that Page had met secretly with "SECHIN and senior Kremlin Internal Affairs official, DIVYEKIN."

[458] SC-00082677.

- On July 26, 2016, Fritsch emailed Jay Solomon of the *Wall Street Journal* and wrote:

  > "OTR the easy scoop waiting for confirmation: that dude carter page met with igor sechin when he went to moscow earlier this month. sechin discussed energy deals and possible lifting of sanctions on himself et al. he also met with a senior kremlin official called divyekin who told page they have good kompromat on hillary and offered to help. he also warned page they have good kompromat on the donald. i know of one person who is chasing this and has asked kremlin re these meets. the response: there was no meeting between sechin and page "at the kremlin." uh, well, ok . . . maybe somewhere else? no comment. needless to say, a senior trump advisor meeting with a former kgb official close to putin, who is on the treasury sanctions list, days before the republican convention and a big russian-backed wikileak would be huge news."[459]

  That same day, Solomon responded, "Page is neither confirming nor denying." Fritsch replied "call adam schiff or difi [in context, Sen. Diane Feinstein] for that matter. i bet they are concerned about what page was doing other than giving a speech over 3 days in moscow."[460]

  Fritsch later emailed Solomon that "its kind of hard to believe that the wsj is ignoring the russia stuff. literally everyone is chasing this [expletive] now."[461]

- Also, on July 26, 2016 – the date of the purported approval of the Clinton Plan intelligence – Fritsch reached back out to Steve LeVine of *Quartz*, and wrote *"[S]o carter page is of some urgency now. Can you talk?"*[462] LeVine replied that he could and asked if Fritsch wanted to talk by phone.[463]

- On that same date, July 26, 2016, Glenn Simpson emailed Jane Mayer of *New Yorker* magazine with the subject line "Carter Page." Simpson wrote, "Jane – I understand that you are interested in him."[464] Two days later, Mayer responded to Simpson advising him that her editor, among others, was "interested in setting up an off the record meeting to discuss stories, and learn more about your research."[465]

---

459 SCID_00034363.

460 *Id.*

461 *Id.* (emphasis added).

462 SCID_00034478 (emphasis added).

463 *Id.*

464 SC-00082579.

465 *Id.*

- On July [illegible] Simpson [illegible] Berk[illegible] [illegible]ployee at Fusion GPS, an email with the [illegible] "carter [illegible] clea[illegible] [illegible]son asked Berkowitz to send "the carter pa[illegible]" to [illegible] [illegible] *Washington Post*.[467] Later that same da[illegible] sent [illegible] [illegible]rter page clear" information.[468]

- Importa[illegible] [illegible]ry ne[illegible] 29, [illegible] [illegible]urger emailed Simpson with subject [illegible] ve ar[illegible] [illegible]k ba[illegible] [illegible]a," and wrote "*That Page met with Se[illegible] [illegible]ov, Th[illegible] [illegible] said one of our Moscow sources.*[illegible] [illegible] respo[illegible] [illegible] and stated "ok."[470] Hamburger then em[illegible] "FYI, [illegible] by [illegible] [illegible]ter who likely doesn't like this story. [illegible] know[illegible]

Thus, i[illegible] [illegible]d mo[illegible] [illegible] the C[illegible] [illegible]rricane investigators used the alleged Page m[illegible] initial [illegible] [illegible]SA applications – a Moscow-based U.S. media sou[illegible] *[illegible]shing*[illegible] [illegible]pea[illegible] [illegible]en able to debunk to its satisfaction the [illegible]gs.

Severa[illegible] on Sep[illegible] 201[illegible] [illegible]ailed Michael Isikoff of *Yahoo! News*. As disc[illegible] on Sep[illegible] 201[illegible] [illegible]s the first journalist to publish an article about th[illegible] [illegible]ings b[illegible] [illegible]ritsch wrote, "Glenn [Simpson] says you may s[illegible] the carter [illegible]? [illegible] I'm gonna stiff-arm someone else chasing..."[472] [illegible] "go[illegible] [illegible]g to [illegible] [Simpson] on [sic] a bit."[473] Thereafter, on S[illegible] 201[illegible] [illegible]sent [illegible] [illegible]d document identified as a transcript of Pa[illegible] 2016 s[illegible] [illegible]

The ab[illegible] [illegible]ails fro[illegible] GPS [illegible] of the media are a sampling of the correspond[illegible] Car[illegible] the [illegible]C-funded Fusion GPS sent to various membe[illegible] [illegible]a fro[illegible] 2015 [illegible]ted date the Clinton Plan intelligence wa[illegible] through [illegible] 201[illegible]

In additi[illegible] s to th[illegible] an i[illegible] [illegible]nd as discussed in detail in Section IV.E.1.c.iii bel[illegible] [illegible]mber [illegible] [illegible]ichae[illegible] [illegible] a lawyer at Perkins Coie, the firm that was then s[illegible] [illegible]sel to [illegible] [illegible]ca[illegible] [illegible]with James Baker, the FBI

---

[466] SC-00082[illegible] [illegible] refer[illegible] [illegible]O'[illegible] [illegible]s to refer to two commercially available datab[illegible] [illegible]vide in[illegible] [illegible] [illegible]hings, individuals, businesses and assets.

[467] *Id.*

[468] *Id.*

[469] SC-000825[illegible] [illegible]dded[illegible]

[470] *Id.*

[471] *Id.*

[472] SCID_000[illegible]

[473] *Id.*

[474] SCID_000[illegible]

General Counsel, at FBI Headquarters in Washington, D.C. Sussmann provided Baker with purported data and "white papers" that allegedly demonstrated a covert communications channel between the Trump Organization and a Russia-based bank, Alfa Bank.[475] Sussmann's billing records reflect that he was regularly billing the Clinton campaign for his work on the Alfa Bank allegations.[476] Importantly, on July 29, 2016 – three days after the purported approval of the Clinton Plan intelligence – Michael Sussmann and Marc Elias, the General Counsel to the Clinton campaign, met with Fusion GPS personnel in Elias's office at Perkins Coie. Sussmann billed his time in this meeting to the Clinton campaign under the category "General Political Advice."[477] Thereafter, on July 31, 2016, Sussmann billed the Clinton campaign for twenty-four minutes with the billing description, "communications with Marc Elias regarding server issue." In compiling and disseminating the Alfa bank allegations, Sussmann consistently met and communicated with Elias.[478]

On October 31, 2016 – a little over one week before the election – multiple media outlets reported that the FBI had received and was investigating allegations concerning a purported secret channel between the Trump Organization and Alfa Bank.[479] On that day, the *New York Times* published an article titled *Investigating Donald Trump, F.B.I. Sees No Clear Link to Russia.*[480] The article stated that the FBI possessed information concerning "what cyber experts said appeared to be a mysterious back channel between the Trump Organization and Alfa Bank."[481] The article further reported that the FBI "had spent weeks examining computer data showing an odd stream of activity to a Trump Organization server," and that the *New York Times* had been provided computer logs that evidenced this activity.[482] The article also noted that the FBI had not found "any conclusive or direct link" between Trump and the Russian government and that "Hillary Clinton's supporters . . . pushed for these investigations."[483] On the same date, *Slate* published an article titled *Was a Trump Server Communicating with Russia?* that likewise discussed at length the allegations that Sussmann provided to the FBI.[484]

Notably, also on that day, *Mother Jones* published David Corn's article titled *A Veteran Spy Has Given the FBI Information Alleging a Russian Operation to Cultivate Donald Trump: Has the Bureau Investigated this Material?*" The *Mother Jones* piece referenced the Foer *Slate*

---

475 Indictment, *United States v. Sussmann*, No. 1:21-cr-00582-CRC (D.D.C. September 16, 2021) (hereinafter "*Sussmann Indictment*" or "*Indictment*") at ¶¶ 3, 27.

476 *Id.* at ¶¶ 4, 20, 24, 25, 26, 29, 37.

477 *Id.* at ¶ 20.

478 *Id.* at ¶¶ 19, 20, 21, 24, 25, 26, 33.

479 *Id.* at ¶ 1.

480 Eric Lichtblau & Steven Lee Myers, *Investigating Donald Trump, F.B.I. Sees No Clear Link to Russia*, N.Y. Times (Oct. 31, 2016).

481 *Id.*

482 *Id.*

483 *Id.*

484 Franklin Foer, *Was a Trump Server Communicating with Russia?*, Slate (Oct. 31, 2016).

article on Alfa Bank and also disclosed that it had reviewed memos prepared by the "former western intelligence official." Corn included information in his October 31, 2016 article that referenced the Isikoff's earlier *Yahoo! News* piece on Carter Page and the Russians. In addition, the Corn article contained allegations that were consistent with those contained in some of the Steele Dossier reports that eventually were published in January 2017 by *BuzzFeed*.[485]

In the months before the publication of these articles, Sussmann had communicated with the media and provided them with the Alfa Bank data and allegations.[486] Sussmann also kept Marc Elias apprised of his efforts, and Elias, in turn, communicated with the Clinton campaign's leadership about potential media coverage of these issues.[487]

On September 1, 2016, Sussmann met with the *New York Times* reporter who published the aforementioned article and billed his time to the Clinton campaign.[488] On September 15, 2016, Elias provided an update to the Clinton campaign regarding the Alfa Bank allegations and the not-yet-published *New York Times* article, sending an email to senior members of the Clinton campaign, which he billed to the campaign as "re: Alfa Article."[489]

On the same day that these articles were published, the Clinton campaign posted a tweet through Clinton's Twitter account that stated: "Computer scientists have apparently uncovered a covert server linking the Trump Organization to a Russian-based Bank."[490] The tweet included a statement from Clinton campaign advisor Jake Sullivan that made reference to the media coverage of the article and stated, in relevant part, that the allegations in the articles "could be the most direct link yet between Donald Trump and Moscow[,] that "[t]his secret hotline may be the key to unlocking the mystery of Trump's ties to Russia[,]" and that "[w]e can only assume that federal authorities will now explore this direct connection between Trump and Russia as part of their existing probe into Russia's meddling in our elections." The fact that the Clinton campaign immediately issued a tweet concerning the articles – after funding the Alfa Bank allegations and receiving foreknowledge of the articles from Sussmann and Elias – tends to

---

[485] According to Glenn Simpson and Peter Fritsch, on September 21, 2016, Steele flew to Washington, D.C. at the urging of Fusion GPS to meet with reporters. *Crime in Progress* at 109. The following day, Simpson and Steele, who was only speaking "on background" with the background information being attributed to a "former, senior western intelligence official," met with reporters in staggered intervals at the Tabard Inn. *Id.* at 109-110. Among the reporters who attended the Tabard presentations were Eric Lichtblau from the *New York Times* and Michael Isikoff of *Yahoo! News*. *Id.* at 110. The next day, September 23, 2016, Isikoff's *Yahoo! News* article focusing on Carter Page and the Russians was published. *Id.* at 111. The article reported that Senate minority leader Harry Reid had written to Director Comey about the need for the FBI to investigate Page and "'significant and disturbing ties' between the Trump campaign and the Kremlin." The article also reported that a "senior U.S. law enforcement official" confirmed that Page was on the radar screen and being looked at. *See* Isikoff, *Officials Probe Ties*.

[486] *Sussmann Indictment* at ¶¶ 24, 25, 26, 27, 33-38.

[487] *Id.* at ¶ 25.

[488] *Id.*

[489] *Id.*

[490] Twitter, @HillaryClinton 10/31/2016 8:36 p.m. Tweet.

support the notion that the Alfa Bank allegations were part of a Clinton campaign plan to tie Trump to Russia.

### 2. *Prosecution decisions*

The aforementioned facts reflect a rather startling and inexplicable failure to adequately consider and incorporate the Clinton Plan intelligence into the FBI's investigative decision-making in the Crossfire Hurricane investigation. Indeed, had the FBI opened the Crossfire Hurricane investigation as an assessment and, in turn, gathered and analyzed data in concert with the information from the Clinton Plan intelligence, it is likely that the information received would have been examined, at a minimum, with a more critical eye. A more deliberative examination would have increased the likelihood of alternative analytical hypotheses and reduced the risk of reputational damage both to the targets of the investigation as well as, ultimately, to the FBI.

The FBI thus failed to act on what should have been – when combined with other, incontrovertible facts – a clear warning sign that the FBI might then be the target of an effort to manipulate or influence the law enforcement process for political purposes during the 2016 presidential election. Indeed, CIA Director Brennan and other intelligence officials recognized the significance of the intelligence by expeditiously briefing it to the President, Vice President, the Director of National Intelligence, the Attorney General, the Director of the FBI, and other senior administration officials.[491] Whether or not the Clinton Plan intelligence was based on reliable or unreliable information, or was ultimately true or false, it should have prompted FBI personnel to immediately undertake an analysis of the information and to act with far greater care and caution when receiving, analyzing, and relying upon materials of partisan origins, such as the Steele Reports and the Alfa Bank allegations. The FBI also should have disseminated the Clinton Plan intelligence more widely among those responsible for the Crossfire Hurricane investigation so that they could effectively incorporate it into their analysis and decision-making, and their representations to the OI attorneys and, ultimately, the FISC.[492]

Whether these failures by U.S. officials amounted to criminal acts, however, is a different question. In order for the above-described facts to give rise to criminal liability under federal civil rights statutes, the Office would need to, for example, identify one or more persons who (i) *knew* the Clinton campaign intended to falsely accuse its opponent with specific information or allegations, (ii) intentionally disregarded a particular civil right of a particular person (such as the right to be free of unreasonable searches or seizures), and (iii) then intentionally aided that effort by taking investigative steps based on those allegations while knowing that they were false.

In order to prove a criminal violation of the false statements and/or obstruction statutes by a government official, the Office would need to prove that the official willfully and intentionally failed to inform the FISC or caused another to fail to inform the FISC of the Clinton Plan intelligence in order to conceal that information from the Court. Similarly, to prove a

---

491 *See Ratcliffe Letter*; *Brennan Notes*.

492 *See* OSC Report of Interview of James Baker on June 11, 2020 at 2 (stating that he would have remembered if he had seen the Clinton Plan intelligence reporting and would have considered it significant); OSC Report of Interview of Supervisory Special Agent-1 on July 22, 2022 at 7.

criminal violati[illegible] jury sta[illegible] Offic[illegible] to prove, among other things, that the officia[illegible] statem[illegible] Cou[illegible] [illegible]ledge of its falsity, rather than as a result of conf[illegible], or f[illegible].[illegible]

Althou[illegible] we [illegible] disregard for the Clinton Plan intelligence an[illegible] firma[illegible] favo[illegible] investigative scrutiny of Trump and his associa[illegible] yield [illegible] ffici[illegible] beyond a reasonable doubt that any FBI or CIA [illegible] intenti[illegible] [illegible]mpaign plan to frame or falsely accuse Trump [illegible] ies to R[illegible] did [illegible]ficient evidence to prove that the omission of the [illegible] intel[illegible] appl[illegible] the FISC was a conscious or intentional dec[illegible] is on[illegible] [illegible]ourt's view of the facts supporting probable cause.[illegible]

Moreo[illegible] [illegible]pted p[illegible] pre[illegible] Clinton Plan intelligence would face what in al[illegible] would b[illegible] ntabl[illegible] [illegible]on issues given the highly sensitive natur[illegible] [illegible]ation i[illegible]

In sum[illegible] [illegible]ent's [illegible] the C[illegible] intelligence may have amounted to a significant [illegible] failur[illegible] [illegible]ling [illegible] which confirmation bias and a tunnel-vision p[illegible] [illegible]stigati[illegible] y hav[illegible] [illegible]vernment personnel to fail to appreciate the [illegible] [illegible] unc[illegible] rep[illegible] by an opposing political campaign was [illegible] [illegible]luen[illegible] [illegible]. It did not, all things considered, however, amo[illegible] [illegible]ble cr[illegible] [illegible]se.

D. **The C[illegible] [illegible]SA [illegible]**

On Apri[illegible] [illegible]kins [illegible] firm [illegible]unsel to the Clinton campaign, "Hillary for Am[illegible] [illegible]ed Fu[illegible] Wa[illegible] [illegible]C.-based investigative firm, to conduct oppos[illegible] on Tru[illegible] is ass[illegible] Shortly thereafter, Fusion GPS hired Christoph[illegible] his U[illegible] firm[illegible] [illegible]ss Intelligence, to investigate Trump's ties t[illegible] the tim[illegible] who [illegible] [illegible]ted that he was formerly an intelligence pr[illegible] the Bri[illegible] [illegible] FBI CHS. Beginning in July 2016 and cont[illegible] Dec[illegible] Ste[illegible] [illegible]on GPS prepared a series of reports containing der[illegible] matio[illegible] [illegible]an Trump and Russia. According to the reports, [illegible] nectio[illegible] Tr[illegible] [illegible]sia ran through campaign manager Paul Manafort [illegible] policy [illegible] rter[illegible]

Steele p[illegible] reports [illegible] the State Department, members of Congress, and [illegible] dia out[illegible] styl[illegible] "Company Intelligence Reports," and each report [illegible] iden[illegible] ber [illegible]ny Intelligence Report 2016/095). Collectively, th[illegible] ame t[illegible] col[illegible] the "Steele Dossier," and we refer to them in this [illegible] "Steel[illegible] [illegible] [illegible]ports." The reports played an

---

[493] *See supra* § [illegible] ing th[illegible] [illegible]*sources Manual*).

[494] Indeed, as [illegible] the CI[illegible] [illegible]ng the information to the attention of the highest [illegible] U.S. go[illegible]

[495] SC-00049[illegible] Ag[illegible] [illegible]

[496] *See supra* [illegible]

important role in applications submitted to the FISC targeting Page, a U.S. person. The FBI relied substantially on the reports to assert probable cause that Page was knowingly engaged in clandestine intelligence activities on behalf of Russia, or knowingly helping another person in such activities. As discussed in more detail below, the FBI was not able to corroborate a single substantive allegation contained in the Steele Reports, despite protracted efforts to do so. The Steele Reports themselves, however, were not the only issue that we considered in connection with the Page FISA applications.

This section begins by discussing probable cause and the Page FISA applications. It then focuses on the Steele Reports and the subsources that Steele allegedly used:

- The FBI's relationship with Steele and its handling of the Steele Reports (Subsection V.D.1.b).
- The prior counterespionage investigation of Igor Danchenko, Steele's primary subsource for his reporting (Subsection V.D.1.c).
- Danchenko's relationship with Charles Dolan, one of Danchenko's subsources (Subsection V.D.1.d).
- The FBI's failure to investigate Dolan's possible role as a subsource for Danchenko (Subsection V.D.1.e).
- Danchenko's purported contact with Sergei Millian, another subsource that Danchenko claimed to have received information from (Subsection V.D.1.f).

This section then turns to other aspects of the Page FISA applications:

- Information about Page's role as a source of another U.S. government agency (Subsection V.D.1.g).
- Meetings between FBI CHSs and Papadopoulos, Page, and a senior Trump campaign official (Subsection V.D.1.h).
- Other shortcomings in the Page FISA applications (Subsection V.D.1.i).

This section concludes with a discussion of the factors that the Office considered in its prosecution and declination decisions related to the Page FISA applications.

A few additional aspects of the FISA applications are discussed in the Classified Appendix.

### 1. *Factual background*

#### a. "Probable Cause" and the Page FISA applications

"Omissions of material fact," the FISC has stated, "were the most prevalent and among the most serious problems with the Page applications."[497] The OIG, for its part, found in its review of the applications targeting Page "at least 17 significant errors or omissions" and "so many basic and fundamental errors."[498] These were "made by three separate, hand-picked teams on one of the most sensitive FBI investigations that was briefed to the highest levels within the

[497] *In re Accuracy Concerns Regarding FBI Matters Submitted to the FISC*, Corrected Op. and Order at 4, Misc. No. 19-02 (FISC Mar. 5, 2020).

[498] *Redacted OIG Review* at xiii-xiv; *see also id.* at 413.

FBI."[499] The *OIG Review* also found that FBI personnel "did not give appropriate attention to facts that cut against probable cause."[500]

Also of concern, and the focus of this section, is that several Crossfire Hurricane investigators were skeptical of the information used in the Page FISA applications and, particularly as time went on, believed that Page *was not* acting as an agent of Russia and *was not* a threat to national security. Nevertheless, despite the surveillance's lack of productivity, FBI management directed the Crossfire Hurricane investigators to renew the Page surveillance three times.

*i. The lead up to the initial Page FISA application*

As has been noted by several individuals, including Deputy Director McCabe, the FISA on Page would not have been authorized without the Steele reporting.[501] Indeed, prior to receipt of the Steele Reports, the FBI had drafted a FISA application on Page that FBI OGC determined lacked sufficient probable cause.[502] Within two days of their eventual receipt by Crossfire Hurricane investigators, however, information from four of the Steele Reports was being used to buttress the probable cause in the initial draft FISA application targeting Page.[503] [504] Yet even prior to the initial application, the Page case agent, Case Agent-1, recognized that the FBI's reliance on the uncorroborated and unvetted Steele Reports could be problematic.

Indeed, on September 27, 2016, Case Agent-1 exchanged the following FBI Lync messages with another employee assisting with Crossfire Hurricane ("Support Operations Specialist-1"):

| | |
|---|---|
| Support Operations Specialist-1: | Hopefully [Steele] can get more detailed info though |

---

499 *Id.* at xiv.

500 *Redacted OIG Review* at 413; *see also id.* at xiii.

501 When asked during his HPSCI testimony whether the initial Page FISA had sufficient probable cause without the Steele Report information, McCabe stated, "Let me be clear. I don't want to rely on implication. My position is that anything less than the package that went to the FISA court would not have been enough. We put in that information that we thought was necessary." U.S. House of Representatives Permanent Select Cmte. On Intelligence Interview of Andrew McCabe on Dec. 19, 2017 at 109.

502 In her interview with the Office, FBI OGC Unit Chief-1 described the probable cause without the Steele reporting as a "close call." OSC Report of Interview of FBI OGC Unit Chief-1 on August 29, 2019 at 6-7. FBI OGC Unit Chief-1 informed the OIG that the Steele reporting "pushed it over." OIG Interview of FBI OGC Unit Chief-1 on June 1, 2018 at 83.

503 FBI-EMAIL-385532 (Email from Case Agent-1 to FBI OGC Unit Chief-1 & Clinesmith dated 9/21/16) (stating that Case Agent-1 had "repackaged the information from the Rome Source [Steele] and put it in the application.")

504 David Laufman, the then-Chief of the Department's Counterespionage and Export Control Section, referred to the FISA targeting Page as "predicated on [the] [Steele] reporting." DOJ-NSD-00060564 (Notes of David Laufman dated 3/27/2017).

| | |
|---|---|
| Case Agent-1: | Yeah, exactly. Dates, times, etc, would be key |
| Support Operations Specialist-1: | Yeah – it just goes down to how confident we are in that reporting |
| Support Operations Specialist-1: | There aren't a WHOLE lot of details in it |
| Case Agent-1: | haha, true. |
| Support Operations Specialist-1: | Which is just what worries me a bit |
| Support Operations Specialist-1: | Hopefully the sources sub-sources are legit |
| Support Operations Specialist-1: | They seem legit based on past reporting |
| Case Agent-1: | Yeah, no kidding. What was strange was that [British Intelligence Services] don't seem to want to deal with the guy. |
| Support Operations Specialist-1: | But there aren't many specifics in this reporting that couldn't be expanded on from open source |
| Case Agent-1: | Not sure why. |
| Support Operations Specialist-1: | Yeah that's weird too |
| Support Operations Specialist-1: | If he has the sub-source network that he claims to have (and the reporting suggests), you would think they'd be interested in him. |
| Support Operations Specialist-1: | Though, maybe these are newly developed since he went to [British Intelligence Services]? |
| Case Agent-1: | Yeah that's the weird thing. [Handling Agent-1] said it was the OC angle and that they're not too interested, but that still seems odd |
| Case Agent-1: | *Who knows. We may have to take a calculated risk with the reporting, if we're pressed for time.*[505] |

This exchange between Case Agent-1 and Support Operations Specialist-1 underscores the fact that Case Agent-1, the principal contributor of the factual information contained in the

[505] FBI-AAA-EC-00008439 (Lync message exchange between Case Agent-1 and Support Operations Specialist-1 dated 09-27-2016) (capitalization in original; emphasis added).

request for the [illegible] [illegible]SA appl[illegible] [illegible]ad cl[illegible] [illegible]ized issues with using the Steele Report informati[illegible] [illegible] unc[illegible] [illegible]natur[illegible] [illegible]gations and the lack of insight into the reliabili[illegible] [illegible]s sub-so[illegible] [illegible]ec, [illegible] [illegible]ced counterintelligence agent like Case Agent-1 w[illegible] [illegible] aware [illegible] [illegible] to ev[illegible] [illegible]edibility and reliability of human source informati[illegible]

The OI [illegible] [illegible]was r[illegible] [illegible] for pr[illegible] initial FISA application ("OI Attorney-1"), re[illegible] [illegible]constan[illegible] [illegible]red to [illegible] FISA and FBI executive management be[illegible] [illegible] the [illegible] [illegible] pr[illegible] [illegible]I Attorney-1 advised the Office that FBI OGC a[illegible] [illegible] Clin[illegible] [illegible]med[illegible] [illegible]rector Comey "wants to know what's going o[illegible] [illegible]puty [illegible] [illegible]Cab[illegible] [illegible] the FBI needed to speak with at DOJ "to get th[illegible] [illegible] McCa[illegible] [illegible]d th[illegible] by the FBI and Comey when he was interviewe[illegible] [illegible] investi[illegible] [illegible]Cab[illegible] [illegible]erviewers that there was a lot of back-and-forth [illegible] Crossfi[illegible] [illegible] inv[illegible] [illegible]nd OI regarding "[w]hen are we going to get it? [illegible] going [illegible] [illegible] and [illegible] repeatedly asked him "where is the FISA, wher[illegible] [illegible]? Wh[illegible] [illegible]s wil[illegible] the Page FISA?" McCabe noted that the FISA w[illegible] [illegible] McC[illegible] [illegible]ly k[illegible] [illegible]wanted.[508]

This rec[illegible] [illegible] is co[illegible] [illegible]ema[illegible] [illegible]d other FBI records in which the inclination on th[illegible] [illegible]partme[illegible] [illegible]d to [illegible] [illegible]usly and FBI executives to move quickly are ma[illegible] [illegible] exam[illegible] [illegible]ber [illegible] [illegible]eeting took place involving AD Priestap, DAD [illegible] [illegible]OGC U[illegible] [illegible] and [illegible] Director's Special Assistant Lisa Page. Page's n[illegible] [illegible] meeti[illegible] [illegible] at D[illegible] [illegible]ant Attorney General Evans had spoken with St[illegible] [illegible] befor[illegible] [illegible] con[illegible] the proposed FISA. Page's notes show the follow[illegible]

- Lots of [illegible] [illegible]e's m[illegible] [illegible] rel[illegible] Hired to do opp. Researc[illegible] [illegible] work [illegible] [illegible]s.
- Don't k[illegible] [illegible] sub-so[illegible] [illegible] th[illegible] [illegible]es are.
- FISA b[illegible] [illegible] policy [illegible]
- Email o[illegible] [illegible]ible] [illegible] [illegible] to [illegible] [illegible]lking to the FBI.[509]

FBI OGC Unit [illegible] [illegible]s fro[illegible] [illegible]mee[illegible] [illegible]hat Evans was concerned that "[Steele] may h[illegible] [illegible]d by [illegible] [illegible]camp[illegible] [illegible]DNC. . . ."[510]

That sa[illegible] [illegible] 7:1[illegible] p.m., [illegible] Uni[illegible] [illegible]ailed OGC attorneys Trisha Anderson and [illegible] [illegible] advis[illegible] [illegible] "We [illegible] concerns to the D[irector] and D[eputy] D[ire[illegible] [illegible]), and [illegible] [illegible]ppor[illegible] [illegible]moving forward despite his

---

[506] OSC Repor[illegible] [illegible]of OI [illegible] [illegible] on Ju[illegible] at 5.

[507] *Id.*

[508] OIG Intervi[illegible] [illegible] McC[illegible] [illegible] 15, [illegible]-09. McCabe, through his counsel, did no[illegible] [illegible] interv[illegible] [illegible] Off[illegible] [illegible]er we offered to narrow the scope of subjects to b[illegible] [illegible]t

[509] FBI-LP-000[illegible] [illegible]handwritte[illegible] [illegible] Lisa P[illegible] [illegible]0/12/16).

[510] E2018002-A[illegible] [illegible]handwri[illegible] [illegible]f FB[illegible] [illegible] Chief-1 dated 10/12/16).

concerns. I just talked to Lisa, and she had reached out to Stu and will inform the DD. We're close to losing our operational window."[511]

Over the next few days, Department and FBI personnel continued to exchange information on questions and needed clarifications in the draft application. On October 18th, Strzok emailed FBI OGC Unit Chief-1 and Clinesmith and asked, "How significant were Bakers [sic] changes back when he reviewed? If the DAG and we (investigative team) are good with the current draft, we need to ram this through. Thanks. I hate these cases."[512] FBI OGC Unit Chief-1 responded shortly thereafter:

> Just talked to Lisa. Baker had a bunch if [sic] comments, but they were not directed to issue Stu's now made a bug [sic] deal about. I think if the investigative team is good with the facts and the DAG is good with the PC, then Andy [McCabe] should push (regardless of Baker's comments.)[513]

The FISC approved the surveillance three days later, on October 21st.

NYFO Case Agent-1, the counterintelligence agent who led the NYFO investigation of Page, was never contacted by the Crossfire Hurricane investigators prior to the submission of the initial Page FISA application.[514] When interviewed by the Office, NYFO Case Agent-1 noted that the NYFO viewed Page as someone "we need[ed] to watch" due to the Russians contacting Page, but she and others were never overly concerned about Page being an intelligence officer for the Russians.[515] At no time during the course of her investigation did NYFO Case Agent-1 consider pursuing a FISA on Page.[516] NYFO Case Agent-1 later read the Page FISA applications and recalled seeing some aspects of her investigation referenced. NYFO Case Agent-1 felt the language used to link Page to the Russians was "a little strong."[517] Nevertheless, NYFO Case Agent-1 assumed the Crossfire Hurricane investigation had uncovered additional information linking Page to the Russians.[518] In fact, the additional information contained in the initial Page FISA application was largely taken from the Steele Reports and carefully selected portions of consensual recordings with an FBI CHS as described below. In retrospect, NYFO Case Agent-1 viewed the Page investigation as a "waste of money."[519]

---

511 FBI-EMAIL-488872 (Email from FBI OGC Unit Chief-1 to Anderson & Clinesmith dated 10/12/16).

512 FBI-EMAIL-483856 (Email from FBI OGC Unit Chief-1 to Strzok, Clinesmith dated 10/18/2016)

513 *Id.* At the time, James Baker was the General Counsel of the FBI and FBI OGC Unit Chief-1's boss.

514 OSC Report of Interview of NYFO Case Agent-1 on Sept. 5, 2019 at 3.

515 *Id.* at 2.

516 *Id.*

517 *Id.* at 4.

518 *See id.*

519 *Id.*

### *ii. The Page FISA application renewals*

In late January 2017, Supervisory Special Agent-1 transferred back to WFO.[520] Supervisory Special Agent-1 was replaced in that position by an experienced counterintelligence agent assigned to WFO ("Supervisory Special Agent-3").[521] In his interview with the Office, Supervisory Special Agent-3 stated that, upon arriving at FBI Headquarters, DAD Jennifer Boone informed him that his primary tasking was to renew the Page FISA application.[522] Despite this tasking, Supervisory Special Agent-3 stated that his investigators did not feel connected to the Page investigation and were excluded from the flow of information and decision-making process, an investigation that, according to Supervisory Special Agent-3, was still managed by the "Triumvirate of control" of the Crossfire Hurricane investigation, namely, Strzok, Auten, and Section Chief Moffa.[523] For example, during the course of their time on Crossfire Hurricane, neither Supervisory Special Agent-3 nor Special Agent-1, an investigator working for Supervisory Special Agent-3, knew that Page had previously served as a source for another government agency.[524] When Special Agent-1 eventually learned this information, he stated that he "felt like a fool."[525] Special Agent-1 also recalled that Supervisory Special Agent-3 would often rhetorically ask his investigators, "what are we even doing here."[526]

Moreover, based on their review of the case file and the lack of evidence obtained from the FISA surveillance, neither Supervisory Special Agent-3 nor his investigators believed that Page was a threat to national security or a witting agent of the Russian government.[527] Special Agent-1 and another agent working for Supervisory Special Agent-3, ("Supervisory Special Agent-2") shared Supervisory Special Agent-3's conclusion that Page was not a witting agent of the Russian government.[528] Special Agent-1 went as far to say that the surveillance on Page was a "dry hole."[529] Nonetheless, Special Agent-1 "assumed" that "somebody above them" possessed important information – unknown to the investigators – that guided the Crossfire Hurricane decision-making.[530] When Supervisory Special Agent-3 informed DAD Boone of his

---

[520] OSC Report of Interview of Supervisory Special Agent-3 on March 18, 2021 at 1.

[521] *Id.*

[522] *Id.* at 2.

[523] *Id.*

[524] OSC Report of Interview of Special Agent-1 on March 21, 2021 at 3; OSC Report of Interview of Supervisory Special Agent-3 on March 18, 2021 at 5.

[525] OSC Report of Interview of Special Agent-1 on March 21, 2021 at 3.

[526] *Id.* at 2.

[527] OSC Report of Interview of Supervisory Special Agent-3 on March 18, 2021 at 2, 5.

[528] OSC Report of Interview of Special Agent-1 on March 21, 2021 at 2; OSC Report of Interview of Supervisory Special Agent-2 on May 5, 2021 at 1.

[529] OSC Report of Interview of Special Agent-1 on March 21, 2021 at 2.

[530] *Id.*

team's assessment, he was largely ignored and directed to continue the FISA renewal process.[531] It was Supervisory Special Agent-3's opinion that Boone was being directed by FBI executive management to continue the FISA surveillance.[532] When interviewed by the Office, Boone did not recall Supervisory Special Agent-3 voicing concerns about the Page FISA, and stated that, if he had, she would have elevated those concerns to AD Bill Priestap.[533] Boone did state, however, that it was not the normal course of business to have the "7th floor" (FBI executive management) intimately involved in an investigation and very unusual to have an investigation run from FBI Headquarters.

Boone did not know why the 7th floor was so involved in this case nor did she know who from the 7th floor was the ultimate decision maker regarding Crossfire Hurricane.[534] Boone did not have direct communication with Deputy Director McCabe, but she understood that McCabe was heavily involved in all aspects of the investigation.[535] Her sense was that Priestap was not in charge and had to get approvals from the 7th floor.[536] On a few occasions, Boone "ran ideas" by Priestap and never heard back from him.[537] Boone recalled occasions when, during Crossfire Hurricane, Priestap would direct field offices to open cases on particular targets associated with the Trump campaign and the field offices would push back due to insufficient predication.[538] During one meeting, Boone and her investigators presented a "Russia Strategy" to Priestap. Boone could sense that Priestap was visibly upset by their strategy and walked out of the meeting.[539]

Supervisory Special Agent-2 signed all three renewals of the Page FISA application.[540] When interviewed by the Office, Supervisory Special Agent-2 stated that, after the initial FISA surveillance of Page, the investigators had "low confidence" that Page was a witting agent of the Russian government.[541] In fact, at the time of the third renewal, Supervisory Special Agent-2 stated that the probability of Page being a witting agent was "very low."[542] Nevertheless, Supervisory Special Agent-2 signed the final renewal because, in his opinion, it was incumbent

---

531 Supervisory Special Agent-3 stated that he developed a sense of "helplessness" and was "powerless" to influence the course of the investigation. OSC Report of Interview of Supervisory Special Agent-3 on March 18, 2021 at 1-2, 4.

532 *Id.* at 4.

533 OSC Report of Interview of Jennifer Boone on July 9, 2021 at 2.

534 *Id.*

535 *Id.*

536 *Id.*

537 *Id.*

538 *Id.*

539 *Id.*

540 OSC Report of Interview of Supervisory Special Agent-2 on May 5, 2021 at 1.

541 *Id.*

542 *Id.* at 2.

on the FBI to e[illegible] curce[illegible] hat P[illegible] a Russian intelligence officer.[543] In essence, it ap[illegible] pervis[illegible] Age[illegible] final renewal of the Page FISA as a "belt and s[illegible] pproac[illegible] ot a Russian agent. For his part, Supervisory S[illegible] told [illegible] ould [illegible] ned the renewal affidavits if he had been the ag[illegible] e fo[illegible] government's assertions.[544] The approach take[illegible] y Sp[illegible] 2, [illegible] agent, is concerning. A U.S. person is an ag[illegible] n pow[illegible] s p[illegible] to believe that the person is knowingly eng[illegible] estine i[illegible] act[illegible] alf of a foreign power, or knowingly hel[illegible] rso[illegible] an affirmative determination. FISA surveilla[illegible] ed f[illegible] s specified in the statute rather than to prove t[illegible] not [illegible] forei[illegible]

*iii. [illegible] FBI [illegible] ollections as of early 2017*

As the [illegible] s as c[illegible], the [illegible] not possess any intelligence showing that a[illegible] ted w[illegible] p ca[illegible] in contact with Russian intelligence of[illegible] he ca[illegible] eed, [illegible] classified documents from early 2017, the FBI'[illegible] show[illegible] pu[illegible] e *New York Times* in February and March 201[illegible] what [illegible] rmer U.S. intelligence officials claimed about [illegible] gn p[illegible] ng i[illegible] any Russian intelligence officers was untrue.[546] [illegible] tifie[illegible] po[illegible] that (i) U.S. law enforcement and intelligence a[illegible] ptec[illegible] atio[illegible] rs of Trump's campaign and other Trump a[illegible] t show[illegible] c[illegible] senior Russian intelligence officials in the [illegible] the el[illegible] for[illegible] ampaign chairman Paul Manafort had [illegible] the in[illegible] cke[illegible] intercepted "calls;" and (iii) the intercepted co[illegible] bet[illegible] as[illegible] Russians had been initially captured by th[illegible]

Howev[illegible] BI do[illegible] ref[illegible] three of these highly concerning cl[illegible] -rel[illegible] s wi[illegible] intelligence were untrue. Indeed, in a contempo[illegible] cue o[illegible] artic[illegible] by Peter Strzok, who was steeped in the [illegible] ssfi[illegible] al[illegible] above-referenced allegations were explicitl[illegible] Strzok[illegible] on [illegible] ions included the following:

- The F[illegible] en any [illegible] f a[illegible] s affiliated with the Trump team in cont[illegible] sian i[illegible] offic[illegible] racterized this allegation as mislea[illegible] curat[illegible] He [illegible] there had been some individuals in cont[illegible] sians, b[illegible] n-governmental, but none of

---

[543] *Id.*

[544] OSC Report [illegible] of Sup[illegible] pe[illegible] n March 18, 2021 at 3.

[545] *See* 50 U.S.[illegible] (A) [illegible] & [illegible]

[546] SENATE-F[illegible] 1163 [illegible] n of Michael Schmidt, Mark Mazzetti & M[illegible] rump [illegible] ed Contacts With Russian Intelligence*, N[illegible] eb. 14, [illegible]

[547] *Id.*

these individuals had an affiliation with Russian intelligence. He also noted previous contact between Carter Page and a Russian intelligence officer, but this contact did not occur during Page's association with the Trump campaign.

- The FBI had no information in its holdings, nor had it received any such information from other members of the Intelligence Community, that Paul Manafort had been a party to a call with any Russian government official. Strzok noted that the Intelligence Community had not provided the FBI with any such information even though the FBI had advised certain agencies of its interest in anything they might hold or collect regarding Manafort.[548]
- Regarding the allegation that the NSA initially captured these communications between Trump campaign officials and Trump associates and the Russians, Strzok repeated that if such communications had been collected by the NSA, the FBI was not aware of that fact.

In a second article published by the *Times* on March 1, 2017, bearing the headline, "Obama Administration Rushed to Preserve Intelligence of Russian Election Hacking," allegations were made that U.S. allies, including two named countries, had provided information describing meetings in European cities between Russian officials and other Russians close to Russian President Putin and associates of Trump. The article also repeated the assertions set forth in its February 14, 2017 article. Again, a review of official FBI documentation shows that Strzok had reviewed and refuted these additional allegations in a second critique.[549] With respect to the March 1, 2017 allegations, Strzok noted that no such information had been received from one of the named countries and that the only information received from the second named country, which was received in response to a specific request from the FBI, related to a woman of Russian descent purportedly having been in contact with former Trump National Security Advisor Michael Flynn. In this second critique, Strzok further noted that with respect to the information provided to the *Times* by the four unnamed former and current officials, the FBI (approximately three weeks after it was first reported) continued to be unaware of any information, other than that provided by Christopher Steele in his dossier reports, alleging contacts between Trump associates and senior Russian intelligence officials.

Thus, the FBI had no intelligence about Trump or others associated with the Trump campaign being in contact with Russian intelligence officers during the campaign at least as of early 2017.

Moreover, significant intelligence information that first became available for the FBI to review in 2018 showed that the Russians had access to sensitive U.S. government information years earlier that would have allowed them to identify Steele's subsources. Indeed, an experienced FBI analyst assessed that as a result of their access to the information, Steele's subsources could have been compromised by the Russians at a point in time prior to the date of

---

[548] *Id.* at 001164.

[549] FBI-EMAIL-428172 (Annotated version of article titled *Obama Administration Rushed to Preserve Intelligence of Russian Election Hacking*, N.Y. Times (Mar. 1, 2017)).

the first Steele dossier report.[550] The review team initially briefed Counterintelligence and Cyber executive management about their findings during a conference call. Following the call, while driving home, Headquarters Analyst-3 was called by Acting Section Chief-2. Acting Section Chief-2 told Headquarters Analyst-3 that they appreciated the team's work, but no more memorandums were to be written.[551] A meeting was then held with Assistant Director Priestap and others. During that meeting, the review team was told to be careful about what they were writing down because issues relating to Steele were under intense scrutiny.[552] Two weeks later, the Deputy Assistant Director for Counterintelligence, Dina Corsi, met with the review team and directed them not to document any recommendations, context, or analysis in the memorandum they were preparing. The instructions, which Headquarters Analyst-3 described as "highly unusual,"[553] concerned the team because analysis is what analysts do. Although the team did not fully adhere to that instruction because of the need to provide context to the team's findings, they did tone down their conclusions in the final memorandum.[554] Headquarters Analyst-3 recalled that a separate briefing on the review was eventually provided by the team in the Deputy Director's conference room, although Headquarters Analyst-3 could not recall if Deputy Director David Bowdich attended the briefing. Headquarters Analyst-3 did know that Bowdich was aware of the review itself.[555]

In this same regard, for a period of time, an FBI OGC attorney ("OGC Attorney-1") was part of the review team and was present for the meeting with Corsi. He confirmed that the team was told not to write any more memoranda or analytical pieces and to provide their findings orally.[556] OGC Attorney-1 remembered being shocked by the directive from Corsi.[557] OGC Attorney-1's recollection was that Corsi was speaking for FBI leadership, but that she did not say exactly who provided the directive. OGC Attorney-1 advised the Office that what Corsi said was not right in any circumstance, and it was the most inappropriate operational or professional statement he had ever heard at the FBI.[558] OGC Attorney-1 stated that the directive from Corsi was "really, really shocking" to him and that he was "appalled" by it. As a result of the incident,

---

[550] OSC Report of Interview of Headquarters Analyst-3 on Dec. 2, 2021 at 1; OSC Report of Interview of Headquarters Analyst-3 on Feb. 19, 2020 at 1.

[551] OSC Report of Interview of Headquarters Analyst-3 on Feb. 19, 2020 at 1.

[552] *Id.*

[553] OSC Report of Interview of Headquarters Analyst-3 on Dec. 2, 2021 at 1. Headquarters Analyst-3 was so concerned about the failure to fully exploit the materials involving Steele subsource information (and the possible need to bring information already exploited to the attention of the FISC) that she raised her concerns about the FBI's lack of action in an email to her supervisor in the hope of having the issues explored further. *See* FBI-0009265 (Email from Headquarters Analyst-3 to FBI employees dated 10/17/2018).

[554] OSC Report of Interview of Headquarters Analyst-3 on Dec. 2, 2021 at 1.

[555] *Id.* at 3.

[556] OSC Report of Interview of OGC Attorney-1 on June 30, 2021 at 3.

[557] *Id.*

[558] *Id.* at 3-4.

he ended up walking away from further participation in the review. OGC Attorney-1 said he felt guilty about leaving, but he felt he had to do it.[559] The record thus reflects that at the time the FBI opened Crossfire Hurricane on July 31, 2016, as noted above in the *SSCI Report*, the Russians already knew about Steele's election investigation,[560] and there is reason to believe that even earlier in time they had access to other highly sensitive information from which the identities of Steele's sources could have been compromised.[561]

Finally, in May 2017, about a month before the submission of the last Page FISA renewal application, Strzok was debating whether to join Special Counsel Mueller's investigation. He texted that he was hesitating about joining, "in part, because of my gut sense and concern there's no big there there."[562] Although the "there" does not appear to have been explicitly identified, it may well have been a reference to the Russia – Trump collusion investigation.[563] In any event, and more generally, the OIG found that, "as the investigation progressed and more information tended to undermine or weaken the assertions in the FISA applications," the FBI "did not reassess the information supporting probable cause."[564]

b. The "Steele dossier"

*i. Christopher Steele – FBI Confidential Human Source*

Beginning in 2010, Christopher Steele started providing information to the FBI on a range of subjects including, but not limited to, Russian oligarchs and corruption in international soccer competition. Steele had been introduced to his eventual FBI CHS handler ("Handling Agent-1") by former DOJ official Bruce Ohr.[565] In 2013, the FBI formally opened Steele as an FBI CHS,[566] and Handling Agent-1 would serve as Steele's primary handler over the course of his service as an FBI source. Steele would eventually be closed as an FBI source in November 2016 for disclosing his status as a CHS while providing information to the media regarding his work with Fusion GPS on behalf of the Clinton campaign and the DNC against Trump.[567]

---

[559] *Id.*; *see also* OSC Report of Interview of Headquarters Analyst-3 on Dec. 2, 2021 at 1.

[560] *See supra* footnotes 252 and 253.

[561] OSC Report of Interview of Headquarters Analyst-3 on Dec. 2, 2021 at 1-2; OSC Report of Interview of OGC Attorney-1 on June 30, 2021 at 2.

[562] U.S. House of Representatives Committee on the Judiciary Interview of Lisa Page on July 13, 2018 at 113.

[563] *See id.* at 113-16 (discussion between Lisa Page and Congressman Ratcliffe as to whether Strzok "had a concern that there was no big there there regarding any collusion . . . between the Trump campaign and Russia"); *see also id.* at 155-56 (discussion of same text from Strzok).

[564] *Redacted OIG Review* at 413.

[565] OSC Report of Interview of Handling Agent-1 on July 2, 2019 at 1.

[566] FBI-0000127 (Source Opening Communication dated 10/30/2013).

[567] FBI-0000237 (Source Closing Communication dated 11/17/2016).

Nevertheless, th[illegible] g Depa[illegible] ial [illegible] a conduit – continued to receive information fro[illegible] e his [illegible] CH[illegible]

*ii. [illegible] irst re[illegible] Steel[illegible] July 2016*

In July [illegible] ng Age[illegible] rvi[illegible] 's Assistant Legal Attaché ("ALAT") in Ro[illegible] early [illegible] Ste[illegible] Handling Agent-1 and requested an urgent meeti[illegible] office[illegible] [569] [illegible] 16, Handling Agent-1 met with Steele in Londo[illegible] provid[illegible] Rep[illegible] dated June 20, 2016.[570] This Report detailed[illegible] thing[illegible] infor[illegible] t Donald Trump's alleged sexual activities durin[illegible] cow an[illegible] ho[illegible] n purportedly had been "feeding" information to T[illegible] aign [illegible] [571] Steele informed Handling Agent-1 that he [illegible] been [illegible] ion C[illegible] t information on Trump, including Trum[illegible] ip wit[illegible] siness dealings with Russia.[572] Steele told Hand[illegible] that [illegible] had [illegible] a law firm and that his ultimate client was "sen[illegible] s' sup[illegible] ton[illegible] Agent-1's notes of this meeting reflect that "HC[illegible] f his [illegible] porti[illegible] ng an interview with the Office, Handling Agen[illegible] n a co[illegible] es fr[illegible] 5, 2016 meeting. As previously noted, while Ha[illegible] 1 did n[illegible] inde[illegible] ollection of Steele explicitly stating that "HC[illegible] Hillar[illegible] co[illegible] no other individual – in that context – to wh[illegible] ld pos[illegible] [575]

Steele c[illegible] or to [illegible] 2016 [illegible] n Handling Agent-1, he and Chris Burrows, his co[illegible] Orbis, [illegible] that [illegible] ation collected by Steele had significant natio[illegible] implicati[illegible] e provided to the FBI and Fusion GPS principal G[illegible] agree[illegible] e Jul[illegible] eeting, Steele informed Handling

---

[568] The Source [illegible] indic[illegible] teele [illegible] s a CHS for disclosing his confidential rel[illegible] the FB[illegible]

[569] OSC Report [illegible] of Han[illegible] 19 at 2.

[570] Steele Sourc[illegible] 22 ("J[illegible] OIG [illegible] Handling Agent-1 on Aug. 30, 2018 at 152-15[illegible]

[571] SCO-10508[illegible] s Know[illegible] C[illegible] "Steele Dossier") at 2-4, (Company Intel[illegible] t 201[illegible]

[572] OSC Report [illegible] of Ha[illegible] 019 at 2.

[573] U.S. House [illegible] ives [illegible] Selec[illegible] Intelligence Interview of Handling Agent-1 on De[illegible] 24-25[illegible] ie[illegible] her Steele on June 5 and 6, 2019 at 26.

[574] Handwritte[illegible] lling [illegible] 4 (C[illegible]

[575] OSC Repor[illegible] of Ha[illegible] 022 at 2.

[576] *OIG Review* [illegible] on to [illegible] he did not approve of the disclosure befo[illegible] House [illegible] ent Select Cmte. On Intelligence Interview of G[illegible] on N[illegible]

Agent-1 that he was working on additional reports for Fusion GPS.[577] As discussed in detail below, following this meeting, Handling Agent-1 contacted NYFO ASAC-1 at the NYFO for guidance about the information Steele had provided.[578]

In his interviews with the Office, Handling Agent-1 stated his initial reaction to Steele's reporting was disbelief.[579] Handling Agent-1 knew that Steele possessed strong feelings against the Russians and their threat to the world, and Steele felt that the possibility of a Trump-compromised presidency would pose a global problem.[580] Furthermore, Steele explained to Handling Agent-1 that the information was gathered at the request of Simpson who was working with an unidentified law firm in the United States for the purpose of acquiring information on Trump and his activities in Russia.[581] In his HPSCI testimony, Handling Agent-1 told the committee that he assumed Steele's tasking was "politically motivated."[582] Notwithstanding his skepticism about the reporting, Handling Agent-1 deemed the allegations to be something he could not arbitrarily discount, particularly since Steele was his CHS and someone in whom he had faith.[583]

On July 19, 2016, Steele sent Handling Agent-1 an additional Report (2016/94) detailing, among other things, an alleged meeting that Trump campaign foreign policy advisor Carter Page had in July 2016 with Igor Sechin, Chairman of Russian energy conglomerate Rosneft, and another such meeting with Igor Divyekin, a senior official in the Russian Presidential Administration. This Report alleged details of (i) Page's conversations with Sechin regarding the lifting of U.S. sanctions, and (ii) Page's conversations with Divyekin about Russia being in possession of compromising information on both candidates Trump and Clinton.[584] On July 28, 2016, Handling Agent-1 forwarded Steele Reports 2016/080 and 2016/94 to NYFO ASAC-1.[585] These Reports – including four additional reports subsequently received by Handling Agent-1 from Steele – only reached the Crossfire Hurricane investigators at FBI Headquarters on September 19, 2016.[586]

---

577 OIG Interview of Christopher Steele on June 5 and 6, 2019 at 7.

578 OSC Report of Interview of Handling Agent-1 on July 2, 2019 at 2.

579 *Id.*

580 *Id.* at 1.

581 *Id.* at 2.

582 U.S. House of Representatives Permanent Select Cmte. On Intelligence Interview of Handling Agent-1 on Dec. 20, 2017 at 25.

583 *Id.*

584 SCO-105084 (Documents Known to the FBI Comprising the "Steele Dossier") at 8 (Company Intelligence Report 2016/94).

585 FBI-EMAIL-130305 (Email from Handling Agent-1 to NYFO ASAC-1 dated 07/28/2016).

586 FBI-EMAIL-129902 (Email from Handling Agent-1 to Supervisory Special Agent-1 on 09/19/2016); FBI-EMAIL-129908 (Email from Handling Agent-1 to Supervisory Special Agent-1 dated 09/19/2016).

*iii. The delay in the FBI's transmission of the Steele Reports to the Crossfire Hurricane investigators*

The Office endeavored to account for the nearly 75 days between when Handling Agent-1 received the initial report from Steele in London and when the reports ultimately were passed to the Crossfire Hurricane team at FBI Headquarters. As discussed more fully below, these issues remain unresolved, and the Office has not received a satisfactory explanation that would account for the unwarranted delay.

The FBI possessed the earliest Steele reporting claiming Russian efforts to assist the Trump campaign more than three weeks prior to the receipt of the information provided by the Australian diplomats concerning George Papadopoulos and the opening of the Crossfire Hurricane investigation on July 31, 2016. The Office's investigation has revealed that – taken in its most favorable light to the FBI – the initial reports provided by Steele to Handling Agent-1 in London on July 5, 2016, and then later in July 2016, met an inexplicable FBI bureaucratic delay. As a consequence, the Reports were not disseminated in a manner that would have allowed experienced FBI counterintelligence experts an early opportunity to examine the reports and subject them to appropriate analysis and scrutiny. The failure to act resulted in a gap in time of approximately 75 days from when Steele initially shared his first report with the FBI on July 5, 2016, and September 19, 2016, when the Crossfire Hurricane investigators appear to have first received six of the Steele Reports. Despite the lack of any corroboration of the Reports' sensational allegations, however, in short order portions of four of the Reports were included in the initial Carter Page FISA application without any further verification or corroboration of the allegations contained therein.

Due to conflicting recollections of those involved, significant gaps exist in our understanding of how and why this delay occurred in analyzing Steele's Reports. As discussed above, after meeting Steele in London on July 5, 2016, Handling Agent-1 returned to Rome with Steele's first report (Report 2016/080). Handling Agent-1 told the Office that he informed his immediate supervisor, ("Italy Legat-1"), about the Steele reporting, which led to a conversation about what to do with the Report.[587] Handling Agent-1 informed Italy Legat-1 that he intended to contact trusted colleagues in the NYFO for advice.[588]

In his interview with the OIG, Steele stated that he re-contacted Handling Agent-1 approximately one-week after their initial meeting on July 5, 2016, to inquire if Handling Agent-1 was interested in receiving additional reports that Steele had prepared.[589] Thereafter, Steele emailed Handling Agent-1 his second Report (2016/94).

On July 13, 2016, one week after receiving the initial Steele Report in London, Handling Agent-1 spoke with NYFO ASAC-1 to inform him of the reporting and to ask for guidance.[590]

---

[587] OSC Report of Interview of Handling Agent-1 on July 2, 2019 at 2.

[588] The NYFO was Handling Agent-1's former office of assignment.

[589] OIG Interview of Christopher Steele on June 5 and 6, 2019 at 8.

[590] FBI-AAA-EC-00001529 (Lync message exchange between Handling Agent-1 and NYFO ASAC-1 dated 07/13/2016).

During that call, Handling Agent-1 summarized his July 5th meeting with Steele and Report 2016/080.[591]

NYFO ASAC-1 told the Office that he was unsure of what to do about the Steele Report, but that he verbally informed both his NYFO Supervisor, Criminal SAC Michael Harpster, and NYFO Chief Division Counsel-1, of the Steele reporting and requested their guidance.[592] NYFO ASAC-1 believed that by informing SAC Harpster he was effectively placing the information in the right hands.[593] According to NYFO ASAC-1, NYFO Chief Division Counsel-1 assigned an Assistant Division Counsel ("NYFO Assistant Division Counsel-1") to handle the matter.[594]

No follow up activity appears to have occurred between the NYFO and Handling Agent-1 until NYFO ASAC-1 called Handling Agent-1 on July 28, 2016, at which time he asked Handling Agent-1 to send the Steele Reports to him.[595] NYFO ASAC-1 could not recall the reason for the two-week delay between his July 13th and July 28th calls with Handling Agent-1.[596] For his part, Handling Agent-1 recalled that in the July 28th call, NYFO ASAC-1 advised him that FBI leadership, including an FBI Headquarters official at the Executive Assistant Director ("EAD") level, was now aware of the existence of the reports.[597] That same day, Handling Agent-1 forwarded to NYFO ASAC-1 Steele Reports 2016/080 and 2016/94.

A few hours after receiving the reports, NYFO ASAC-1 forwarded them to SAC Michael Harpster.[598] Harpster initially told the Office that he recalled receiving the Reports from NYFO ASAC-1, but did not read them in order to avoid taint issues with respect to the Clinton Foundation matter that he was overseeing.[599] Harpster recalled, however, that he immediately forwarded the Reports to his supervisor, Assistant Director-in-Charge ("ADIC") Diego Rodriguez.[600] Harpster told the Office that he had no other involvement with the Steele Reports after he provided them to Rodriguez, and, further, that he could not recall speaking with anyone

---

[591] OSC Report of Interview of Handling Agent-1 on July 2, 2019 at 2.

[592] OSC Report of Interview of NYFO ASAC-1 on July 2, 2019 at 1-2.

[593] *Id.* at 1.

[594] *Id.*

[595] FBI-AAA-EC-00001529 (Lync message exchange between Handling Agent-1 and NYFO ASAC-1 dated 07/28/2016); OSC Report of Interview of Handling Agent-1 on July 2, 2019 at 2.

[596] OSC Report of Interview of NYFO ASAC-1 on July 2, 2019 at 2.

[597] OSC Report of Interview of Handling Agent-1 on July 2, 2019 at 2; U.S. House of Representatives Permanent Select Cmte. on Intelligence Interview of Handling Agent-1 on Dec. 20, 2017 at 31 (but in that interview Handling Agent-1 thought NYFO ASAC-1 told him this during a follow-up call on either July 31, 2016 or Aug. 1, 2016).

[598] FBI-EMAIL-135629 (Email from NYFO ASAC-1 to Harpster dated 07/28/2016).

[599] OSC Report of Interview of Michael Harpster on July 3, 2019.

[600] *Id.* Harpster noted that he did not believe the Steele Reports were appropriately sent to him, but rather that they should have been handled by the FBI's International Operations Division which has responsibility for the activities and intelligence involving the FBI's Legal Attaché offices.

else about the [illegible] According [illegible] figure [illegible] that there may have been a conversation wi[illegible] on this [illegible] the O[illegible] found no record in FBI files to indicate that th[illegible] e email [illegible] gue[illegible]

A review [illegible] ords re[illegible] between [illegible] and July 29, 2016, SAC Harpster was visiting FB[illegible] as "sh[illegible] execu[illegible] ement as part of a career development op[illegible] Reco[illegible] lect [illegible] same day he received the Steele Reports from N[illegible], Ha[illegible] with [illegible] FBI officials at Headquarters.[604] Harpster, howe[illegible] Office [illegible] ld n[illegible] receiving the Steele Reports while at Headquarter[illegible] 2016.[illegible] less, [illegible] ds reflect that Harpster, in fact, received the Re[illegible] YFO A[illegible] July [illegible] The email sent by NYFO ASAC-1 contained the m[illegible] discus[illegible] pl[illegible] also reflect multiple telephone calls between H[illegible] NYFO A[illegible] July [illegible] [607] The first call occurred prior to transmission of [illegible] and the [illegible] occur[illegible] ng NYFO ASAC-1's email to Harpster attach[illegible] ts. FBI [illegible] ords [illegible] a July 28, 2016 call between Harpster and R[illegible] the r[illegible] sent [illegible] ASAC-1 to Harpster. Thus, the records substan[illegible] orate N[illegible] C-1'[illegible] events.

In a sec[illegible] w with [illegible] Harp[illegible] ted that he sent the initial Steele Reports to the [illegible] r Resp[illegible] Servi[illegible] Executive Assistant Director ("EAD") Rand[illegible] Cole[illegible] Ass[illegible] tive Assistant Director ("AEAD") David ("DJ") J[illegible] Harpster [illegible] led th[illegible] with Coleman and Johnson at Headquarters o[illegible] 2016.[609] [illegible] se m[illegible] appeared to Harpster that the FBI officials were [illegible] of the [illegible] ports [illegible] D Coleman appeared to have engaged in pre[illegible] sations [illegible] FBI [illegible] about the reports.[610] During their interviews wit[illegible] neithe[illegible] man [illegible] Johnson could recall any conversation w[illegible] about th[illegible] reports [illegible] did not recall receiving the reports from him.[611] [illegible] his m[illegible] Cole[illegible] hnson, Harpster was scheduled to

---

[601] OSC Repor[illegible] of Mi[illegible] 2019.

[602] OSC Repor[illegible] of Di[illegible] 2019 at 1.

[603] FBI-EMAI[illegible] mail to [illegible]

[604] *Id.*

[605] OSC Repor[illegible] of Mi[illegible] ster [illegible] 2020 at 2.

[606] FBI-EMAI[illegible] mail fr[illegible] ASA[illegible] ster dated 07/28/2016).

[607] Phone Log[illegible] uarters [illegible] se[illegible] entry dated 07/28/2016.

[608] OSC Report [illegible] of M[illegible] ster [illegible] 2020 at 2.

[609] *Id.*

[610] *Id.*

[611] OSC Repor[illegible] of R[illegible] man [illegible] 2019; OSC Report of Interview of David Johnso[illegible] 2020 at [illegible] ort [illegible] of David Johnson on May 6, 2020 at 1.

spend the entire next day (July 29th) in an executive management shadowing exercise with Deputy Director McCabe.[612]

While Harpster was at FBI Headquarters, others in the NYFO were conferring internally to determine what to do with the Steele Reports. On August 3, 2016, NYFO ASAC-1 held a meeting with NYFO Chief Division Counsel-1 and NYFO Assistant Division Counsel-1, as well as NYFO Clinton Foundation Case Agent-2, who at the time was overseeing the NYFO portion of the fraud and corruption allegations involving the Clinton Foundation.[613] When interviewed by the Office, NYFO Assistant Division Counsel-1 advised that he had been asked to provide legal advice on whether the Steele Reports, which he had not yet read, could be relevant to the Clinton Foundation investigation.[614] NYFO Assistant Division Counsel-1 told the Office that he was effectively serving as a "taint" attorney to avoid potential conflicts for the NYFO corruption team if it were to access Steele's reporting.[615] Shortly after this meeting, NYFO Assistant Division Counsel-1 had a discussion with Handling Agent-1 about the Reports.[616] On August 5, 2016, NYFO Assistant Division Counsel-1 received two Steele Reports from Handling Agent-1,[617] and on August 25, 2016, NYFO Assistant Division Counsel-1 had a discussion with Handling Agent-1 about Steele's role as an FBI CHS.[618]

NYFO Assistant Division Counsel-1 ultimately concluded that the Steele Reports appeared to be related exclusively to Trump and were not relevant to the Clinton Foundation investigation.[619] Moreover, NYFO Assistant Division Counsel-1 concluded that the Steele Reports should be examined by FBI counterintelligence personnel.[620] NYFO Assistant Division Counsel-1 subsequently met with the NYFO's ASAC for counterintelligence ("NYFO ASAC-2").[621] NYFO Assistant Division Counsel-1 told the Office that he did not provide copies

[612] FBI-EMAIL-137026 (Email to Harpster on 07/26/2016).

[613] OSC Report of Interview of NYFO ASAC-1 on July 2, 2019 at 2; OSC Report of Interview of NYFO Assistant Division Counsel-1 on Aug. 6, 2019 at 1.

[614] OSC Report of Interview of NYFO Assistant Division Counsel-1 on Aug. 6, 2019 at 1.

[615] *Id.*

[616] Handwritten notes of NYFO Assistant Division Counsel-1 dated 08/04/2016; FBI-AAA-EC-00001529 (Lync message exchange between Handling Agent-1 and NYFO Assistant Division Counsel-1 dated 08/05/2016); FBI-EMAIL-129083 (Email from Handling Agent-1 to NYFO Assistant Division Counsel-1 dated 08/05/2016).

[617] FBI-EMAIL-129199 (Email from Handling Agent-1 to NYFO Assistant Division Counsel-1 dated 08/05/2016).

[618] Handwritten notes of NYFO Assistant Division Counsel-1 dated 08/25/2016; FBI-AAA-EC-00001529 (Lync message exchange between Handling Agent-1 and NYFO Assistant Division Counsel-1 dated 08/25/2016).

[619] OSC Report of Interview of NYFO Assistant Division Counsel-1 on Aug. 6, 2019 at 2.

[620] *Id.*

[621] *Id.*

of the Steele Reports to NYFO ASAC-2 in this meeting, but that NYFO ASAC-2 appeared to already be familiar with the Reports.[622]

On August 29, 2016, NYFO ASAC-2 contacted Case Agent-1, one of the principal agents assigned to Crossfire Hurricane, stating, "We have a taint team in place up here. I am trying to get this reporting released to you so you guys can see it. Just debriefed today."[623] On September 1, 2016, NYFO ASAC-2 connected NYFO Assistant Division Counsel-1 with Case Agent-1 and Supervisory Special Agent-1.[624] In his email to Supervisory Special Agent-1, Case Agent-1, and NYFO Assistant Division Counsel-1, NYFO ASAC-2 explained, "[NYFO Assistant Division Counsel-1] has some information that I believe may directly impact your CROSSFIRE HURRICANE investigation. I would like [NYFO Assistant Divisional Counsel-1] to contact your team and deconflict the reporting."[625] On September 2, 2016, NYFO Assistant Division Counsel-1 emailed Handling Agent-1, NYFO ASAC-2, and NYFO ASAC-1 stating, "I spoke to [Supervisory Special Agent-1] briefly yesterday evening . . . [Supervisory Special Agent-1] has an open matter that touches upon what the CHS provided to you. We decided that he should create a subfile in the matter to serve as a repository for the information the CHS provided to you. It is my understanding that he did this last night."[626] However, Supervisory Special Agent-1 confirmed that Handling Agent-1 was unable to upload the reporting to the case file until September 13, 2016.[627] In his email of the same date to Handling Agent-1, NYFO Assistant Division Counsel-1 and Special Agent-2, Supervisory Special Agent-1 notified Handling Agent-1 in Rome that he (Handling Agent-1) has been added as a case participant to the restricted case file. Supervisory Special Agent-1 followed this with his apology "for not getting this to you earlier, but the initial email I sent almost 10 days ago had a hangfire and didn't go out!"[628]

Also of note is the fact that on August 22, 2016, Glenn Simpson of Fusion GPS asked DOJ official Bruce Ohr to call him.[629] Approximately one hour later, Ohr emailed Handling Agent-1 wanting to "check-in."[630] Ohr and Handling Agent-1 planned to speak by phone on

---

[622] *Id.*

[623] FBI-AAA-EC-00008439 (Lync message exchange between Case Agent-1 and NYFO ASAC-2 dated 08/29/2016).

[624] FBI-EMAIL-018184 (Email from NYFO ASAC-2 to Supervisory Special Agent-1, Case Agent-1, NYFO Assistant Division Counsel-1 dated 09/01/2016).

[625] *Id.*

[626] FBI-EMAIL-129523 (Email from NYFO Assistant Division Counsel-1 to Handling Agent-1, NYFO ASAC-2 and NYFO ASAC-1 dated 09/02/2016).

[627] FBI-EMAIL-018127 (Email from Supervisory Special Agent-1 to Handling Agent-1, Special Agent-2, NYFO Assistant Division Counsel-1 dated 09/13/2016).

[628] *Id.* "Hangfire" appears to refer to an email that gets stuck in a person's outbox and does not transmit.

[629] DocID 0.7.23326.122502 (Email from Simpson to Ohr dated 08/22/2016).

[630] DocID 0.7.23326.122508 (Email from Ohr to Handling Agent-1 dated 08/22/2016); OSC Report of Interview of Handling Agent-1 on July 2, 2019 at 2 (in which Handling Agent-1 informed the Office that he recalled receiving a mid-August 2016 call from Ohr.)

August 24, 2016.[631] During the call, Ohr inquired if the FBI was going to do anything with the information contained in the Steele Reports.[632] Handling Agent-1 told Ohr that a group at FBI Headquarters was working on them.[633]

In multiple interviews with both the Office and the OIG, Supervisory Special Agent-1 stated that he was instructed to call NYFO Assistant Division Counsel-1 by Deputy Director McCabe following a briefing at FBI Headquarters on August 25, 2016.[634] According to Supervisory Special Agent-1, McCabe directed him (Supervisory Special Agent-1) to reach out to the NYFO.[635] In context, McCabe had attended a retirement party in New York City for ADIC Rodriguez the night before.[636] When interviewed by the OIG, however, McCabe stated that he did not recall giving advice to Supervisory Special Agent-1 to call the NYFO.[637]

Ultimately, FBI records reflect that it was not until September 19, 2016, that the Crossfire Hurricane team at FBI Headquarters actually received the first six Steele Reports.[638] These Reports were sent to Supervisory Special Agent-1 by Handling Agent-1 – some 75 days after Handling Agent-1 first received the initial Report from Steele in London. The delayed dissemination within the FBI of the sensational information contained in the Steele Reports is both perplexing and troubling. Indeed, the failure of recollection by FBI personnel concerning the matter certainly raises the question of whether the FBI had misgivings from the start about the provenance and reliability of the Steele Reports. Nevertheless, within two days of their eventual receipt by the Crossfire Hurricane team, information from four of the Steele Reports were being used to support probable cause in the initial FISA application on Carter Page.[639]

---

[631] DocID 0.7.23326.122682 (Email from Ohr to Handling Agent-1 dated 08/24/2016).

[632] OSC Report of Interview of Handling Agent-1 on July 2, 2019 at 2.

[633] *Id.*

[634] OIG interview of Supervisory Special Agent-1 on Sept. 13, 2018 at 69-70; OIG interview of Supervisory Special Agent-1 on Jan. 24, 2019 at 89-97, 101-102; OIG interview of Supervisory Special Agent-1 on Feb. 1, 2019 at 86-88; OSC Report of Interview of Supervisory Special Agent-1 on June 17, 2019 at 3-4; Signed, Sworn Statement by Supervisory Special Agent-1 dated Mar. 3, 2021 at 14.

[635] OSC Report of Interview of Supervisory Special Agent-1 on July 22, 2020 at 3.

[636] FBI-EMAIL-624465 (McCabe calendar entry dated 08/24/2016); FBI-EMAIL-623520 (Email to McCabe dated 07/27/2016).

[637] OIG interview of Andrew McCabe on Aug. 15, 2019 at 191.

[638] FBI-EMAIL-129902 (Email from Handling Agent-1 to Supervisory Special Agent-1 dated 09/19/2016); FBI-EMAIL-129908 (Email from Handling Agent-1 to Supervisory Special Agent-1 dated 09/19/2016).

[639] As has been noted by several individuals, including Deputy Director McCabe, the FISA on Page would not have been authorized without the Steele reporting. Indeed, as discussed above, prior to receipt of the Steele Reports, the FBI had drafted a FISA application on Page that the FBI OGC determined lacked sufficient probable cause.

*iv. [illegible] mber [illegible] ahoo! [illegible] cle*

On Sept [illegible] 16, Mi [illegible] pu [illegible] rticle in *Yahoo! News* titled "U.S. Intel Officials [illegible] tween [illegible] iser [illegible]."[640] The article detailed Carter Page's alleged [illegible] ly 20 [illegible] Sech [illegible] an of Russian energy conglomerate [illegible] gor D [illegible] nior [illegible] e Russian Presidential Administration. [illegible] onta [illegible] tion [illegible] rly identical to Steele Report 2016/94. The in [illegible] he art [illegible] dly [illegible] "well-placed Western intelligence source" and ha [illegible] red b [illegible] I.S. [illegible] nent official." A review of communication [illegible] amo [illegible] onnel revealed that senior investigators, in [illegible] e Agen [illegible] Agent-1, believed the "Western intelligence sou [illegible] e. Fu [illegible] ew [illegible] cations also revealed that members of the [illegible] team [illegible] isap [illegible] at Steele had provided the information to [illegible] leving [illegible],[64] [illegible] action would put the Page FISA application in j [illegible] discus [illegible] detail [illegible] il late in the process, several drafts of the Pa [illegible] icatio [illegible] a fo [illegible] plicitly attributed the information in the *Yahoo!* [illegible] Steel [illegible]

*v. [illegible] ter m [illegible] Stee [illegible]*

On Octo [illegible] Speci [illegible] Actin [illegible] hief-1, and SIA Brian Auten traveled to Ro [illegible] et wi [illegible] Agen [illegible] ele.

During [illegible] he in [illegible] forn [illegible] in sum, that the FBI might be willing to pay [illegible] ss of [illegible] le corroborating evidence of the allegations con [illegible] port [illegible] B [illegible] hed Steele about the need to have an exclusive re [illegible] nship [illegible] is time, the FBI had been made aware of the fa [illegible] had a [illegible] vidi [illegible] ts to the State Department through his acquaintan [illegible] ment [illegible] nath [illegible] In turn, Winer had been providing the [illegible] ong [illegible] U.S. [illegible] ecretary of State for European and Eurasian Affair [illegible] and, [illegible] ary of State Clinton.[644] Notwithstandin [illegible] gs, w [illegible] wed [illegible] e, neither Auten nor Special Agent-2 had an [illegible] n of a [illegible] oncerns with Steele.[645] Further, both Auten an [illegible] t-2 d [illegible] aries [illegible] ber 3, 2016 meeting with Steele,

---

[640] Isikoff, *Offi* [illegible] *ies.*

[641] Strzok told [illegible] ng [sic [illegible] oo a [illegible] | would definitely say at a minimum [Stee [illegible] shoul [illegible] as [illegible] luence as well as to inform." FBI-AAA-EC- [illegible] ync m [illegible] ange [illegible] zok and Auten dated 09/26/2016).

[642] SCO-10164 [illegible] r Spe [illegible] to S [illegible] Special Agent-1, Strzok, Auten, Case Agent-1, [illegible] on Chi [illegible] ted 10/04/2016).

[643] *Id.*; OSC Re [illegible] ew [illegible] Agen [illegible] 2, 2019 at 4.

[644] OSC Report [illegible] of Jo [illegible] 21 at 2-3; OSC Report of Interview of Victoria Nu [illegible] 0, 20 [illegible]

[645] OSC Report [illegible] of Bri [illegible] at 17; OSC Report of Interview of Special Agent- [illegible], 2020 [illegible]

and neither summary addressed concerns about the *Yahoo! News* article or whether the issue had even been raised with Steele.[646]

Auten's summary provided, among others, the following pertinent facts:

- Steele had one primary sub-source who traveled frequently in Russia.
- Most of the primary sub-source's contacts appear to be unwitting of where their information was going.
- Steele's primary sub-source had personal contact with Sergei Millian. Millian appeared to be "Source E" referenced in Report 2016/095 and was possibly "Source D" in Report 2016/080.
- Steele provided the FBI with the names of four U.S. citizens who may have information regarding Russia and Trump: (i) Charles Dolan; (ii) U.S. Person-1; (iii) U.S. Person-2; and (iv) U.S. Person-3.
- Steele reiterated that Russian Presidential Administration Spokesman Dimitry Peskov was heavily involved in the Russia/Trump operation.[647]

*vi. The draft Page FISA applications – Yahoo! News*

In late September 2016, OI Attorney-1 received a draft copy of the initial Carter Page FISA application from FBI OGC attorney Kevin Clinesmith. This draft copy included information contained in the Steele Reports that first had been provided to Crossfire Hurricane team on September 19, 2016. On October 2, 2016, OI Attorney-1 emailed a revised draft FISA application to Case Agent-1, Auten, Supervisory Special Agent-1, OGC attorneys Clinesmith and FBI OGC Unit Chief-1, and OI Unit Chief-1.[648] Embedded in this draft FISA application was a question regarding the FBI's assessment of the *Yahoo! News* article, in particular, whether Steele had been the source for the article. OI Unit Chief-1 told the Office that, prior to that draft being sent, he was so certain that Steele was the source of the *Yahoo! News* leak that he included the information in a footnote of the draft application.[649] Case Agent-1 responded to OI Attorney-1's email, in sum, that it was the FBI's assessment that the *Yahoo! News* information had indeed come from Steele.[650]

---

646 SCO-020139 (Email from Auten to Supervisory Special Agent-1, Moffa & Strzok dated 10/04/2016); SCO-101648 (Email from Special Agent-2 to Supervisory Special Agent-1, Strzok, Auten, Case Agent-1, Acting Section Chief-1 & Handling Agent-1 dated 10/04/2016).

647 SCO-020139 (Email from Auten to Supervisory Special Agent-1, Moffa & Strzok dated 10/04/2016).

648 FBI-EMAIL-557611 (Email from OI Attorney-1 to Case Agent-1, Clinesmith, FBI OGC Unit Chief-1, Auten, Support Operations Specialist-1, Moffa, Supervisory Special Agent-1 & OI Unit Chief-1 dated 10/02/2016).

649 OSC Report of Interview of OI Unit Chief-1 on Oct. 27, 2020 at 1.

650 FBI-EMAIL-381130 (Email from Case Agent-1 to OI Attorney-1 dated 10/03/2016).

Following the Rome trip, several additional drafts of the Page FISA application were circulated between the FBI and OI. Throughout these drafts, a footnote stated, in sum, that Source #1 (Steele) had been the "well-placed Western intelligence source" referenced in the *Yahoo! News* article, but that Steele had been admonished by the FBI and that going forward Source #1 would have an exclusive relationship with the FBI.[651] Notwithstanding this footnote, Deputy Assistant Attorney General Evans continued to have questions about Steele's decision to speak with the press about the same information that he had provided to the FBI.[652] Evans wanted further clarification on whether Steele's decision to speak with the press indicated a potential bias.[653]

On October 14, 2016, Special Agent-2 emailed OI Attorney-1 and stated that Steele had not previously mentioned the leak (to *Yahoo! News*) and "only acknowledged it when the FBI brought it up on October 4."[654] This email is directly contradictory to what both Auten and Special Agent-2 told the Office during their interviews, *i.e.*, that the *Yahoo! News* leak had not been raised with Steele. Despite being interviewed about this issue on two separate occasions by the Office, Special Agent-2 did not provide a satisfactory response to explain the contradiction between his memory of the October 3, 2016 meeting with Steele and his October 14, 2016 email to OI Attorney-1.

The confusing nature of Special Agent-2's email was not lost on OI Attorney-1. Indeed, later on October 14th, OI Attorney-1 sent an email to his supervisor, OI Unit Chief-1, which stated, in part:

> I am waiting to hear back from [first name of Case Agent-1], *but my super keen investigative skills tell me* (based on FBI's earlier comment that only mention of the leak is: "[Source #1] has not mentioned the leak and only acknowledges it when the FBI brought it up on October 4.") *they never asked and don't want to ask.*[655]

On October 14, 2016, OI Attorney-1 circulated a document titled "Source #1 footnote update v.2.docx," and informed the recipients that the document "lists the descriptions we

---

651 *See, e.g.*, DOJ-NSD-00033886 (Email from Evans to Toscas & McCord dated 10/11/2016); DOJ-NSD-00028157 (Email from OI Unit Chief-1 to Case Agent-1, Clinesmith, FBI OGC Unit Chief-1, Auten, Support Operations Specialist-1, Moffa, Supervisory Special Agent-1 & OI Attorney-1 dated 10/11/2016).

652 DOJ-NSD-00018909 (Email from Evans to OI Unit Chief-1, Sanz-Rexach, OI Deputy Section Chief-1 & OI Attorney-1 dated 10/11/2016).

653 *Id.*

654 DOJ-NSD-00024317 (Email from Special Agent-2 to Supervisory Special Agent-1, OI Attorney-1, Case Agent-1, Clinesmith, FBI OGC Unit Chief-1, OI Unit Chief-1, Strzok, Moffa & Page dated 10/14/2016).

655 DOJ-NSD-00030201 (Email from OI Attorney-1 to OI Unit Chief-1 dated 10/14/2016) (emphasis added).

provide in the application about Source #1."[656] The last paragraph of the footnote provided the following:

> As discussed above, Source #1 was hired by a business associate [in context, Glenn Simpson] to conduct research into Candidate #1's ties to Russia. Source #1 provided the results of his research to the business associate, and the FBI assesses that the business associate likely provided this information to the law firm that hired the business associate in the first place. Given that the information contained in the September 23rd News Article generally matches the information about Page that Source #1 discovered during his/her research, the FBI assesses that Source #1's business associate or the law firm that hired the business associate likely provided this information to the press.[657]

Later that day, OI Attorney-1 circulated a new draft of the FISA application containing the Source #1 footnote he provided earlier. This version of the FISA application was then sent to the Office of the Deputy Attorney General ("ODAG") for review.

On October 17, 2016, OI Unit Chief-1 circulated follow-up questions to the FBI that had come from ODAG's review of the updated draft application. One question centered on reconciling the disparity between the current Source #1 footnote – now attributing the leak to Fusion GPS or the Clinton campaign's law firm – with the actual language of the article, *i.e.*, that the information in the article came *directly* from a "well-placed Western intelligence source."[658] Later that evening, Case Agent-1, Supervisory Special Agent-1 and others called OI Unit Chief-1 on the FBI's Top Secret Lync system (the FBI's voice chat platform). This call lasted approximately 16 minutes.[659] Following the call, Supervisory Special Agent-1 emailed OI Unit Chief-1 and stated, in sum, that the FBI had addressed all open questions.[660] OI Unit Chief-1 responded to Supervisory Special Agent-1's email and confirmed that all of the Department's questions had been answered.[661] In their interviews with the Office, however, Supervisory Special Agent-1 and OI Unit Chief-1 had no recollection of what was said in the conversation

---

656 DOJ-NSD-00030255 (Email from OI Attorney-1 to Evans, Sanz-Rexach, OI Deputy Section Chief-1 & OI Unit Chief-1 dated 10/14/2016).

657 *Id.* at 3.

658 DOJ-NSD-00023245 (Email from OI Unit Chief-1to Case Agent-1, Supervisory Special Agent-1, Clinesmith, FBI OGC Unit Chief-1, OI Attorney-1 & Support Operations Specialist-1 dated 10/17/2016).

659 FBI-SMS-0000106 (Outlook archive of Lync call dated 10/17/2016).

660 DOJ-NSD-00023605 (Email from Supervisory Special Agent-1 to OI Unit Chief-1, Case Agent-1, Clinesmith, FBI OGC Unit Chief-1, OI Attorney-1 & Support Operations Specialist-1 dated 10/17/2016).

661 DOJ-NSD-00023603 (Email from OI Unit Chief-1 to Supervisory Special Agent-1, Case Agent-1, Clinesmith, FBI OGC Unit Chief-1, OI Attorney-1 & Support Operations Specialist-1 dated 10/17/2016).

that changed the [illegible] ment [illegible] was [illegible] the *Yahoo! News* article.[662] This failure of re[illegible] an imp[illegible] for [illegible] troubling and made the Office's potential prosec[illegible] matter [illegible]

On Octo[illegible] OI At[illegible] mailed [illegible] t-1 and Clinesmith an updated draft of the Pag[illegible] ation. [illegible] #1 [illegible] provided, in part, and with new language in ital[illegible] ng:

> As discu[illegible] Source [illegible] d by [illegible] associate to conduct research [illegible] te #1'[illegible] sia [illegible] rovided the results of his research [illegible] s asso[illegible] he FB[illegible] that the business associate likely pr[illegible] forma[illegible] aw f[illegible] d the business associate in the first [illegible] *e #1 te[illegible] has [illegible] provided this information to the bu[illegible] te and [illegible] Given* formation contained in the Septemb[illegible] Artic[illegible] mat[illegible] rmation about Page that Source [illegible] during [illegible] earc[illegible] sesses that Source #1's business [illegible] the law [illegible] ired [illegible] associate likely provided this info[illegible] pres[illegible] *also [illegible] whoever gave the informa[illegible] 's sta[illegible] infor[illegible] provided by a "well-placed [illegible] igence [illegible] The F[illegible] believe that Source #1 directly [illegible] nform[illegible] pre[illegible]*

In fact, [illegible] he FB[illegible] the s[illegible] ource #1 told the FBI that he/she only provided th[illegible] on to th[illegible] associ[illegible] FBI" in itself was not accurate because the FB[illegible] at Ste[illegible] ady [illegible] Reports to the State Department.[664] [illegible] f the [illegible] Octo[illegible] SA application contained the identical langua[illegible] in th[illegible] ober [illegible] raft.[665]

The Offi[illegible] ceive [illegible] ans[illegible] question of why the FBI initially believed [illegible] provid[illegible] mat[illegible] *Yahoo! News* and then subsequently ca[illegible] that [illegible] and/o[illegible] n campaign's law firm provided the information [illegible] *ws.* T[illegible] er 2[illegible] le itself says that "a well-placed Western intellig[illegible] [told] [illegible] s" ab[illegible] lligence reports,[666] and one would conclude (assum[illegible] article [illegible] that [illegible] ation came directly from the source and not [illegible] m, a bu[illegible] ociat[illegible] erson. And, in fact, Steele later admitted to the [illegible] ptem[illegible] ober [illegible] and others from Fusion GPS provided journa[illegible] *Yaho[illegible]* with [illegible] ns against Page. Why did the FBI's assessmen[illegible] FB[illegible] men[illegible] as able to provide the Office with

---

[662] OSC Report [illegible] f Su[illegible] ecial [illegible] July 21, 2021 at 1; OSC Report of Interview of [illegible] -1 on [illegible] 20 at [illegible]

[663] FBI-EMAIL-[illegible] ail fro[illegible] ey-1 [illegible] gent-1 & Clinesmith dated 10/18/2016) at [illegible]

[664] FBI-EMAIL-[illegible] ail fro[illegible] M[illegible] , Supervisory Special Agent-1 and two other F[illegible] s date[illegible] 016).

[665] *In re Carter* [illegible] . 16-11[illegible]

[666] Isikoff, *Offi[illegible] Ties.*

an explanation as to why the analysis changed, nor do any of the individuals interviewed recall discussions about it. In his interview with the Office, Auten had no recollection of who told him that Steele was not the source of the *Yahoo! News* article, but Auten said his "contemporaneous understanding" at the time of the Rome meeting was that Handling Agent-1 had provided that information.[667] Handling Agent-1, however, emphatically denied asking Steele about the *Yahoo! News* article and stated that his role in the October 2016 meeting was simply to make introductions.[668]

Given Steele's interactions with *Yahoo! News*, the questions about his potential bias raised by Evans and ODAG were completely justified. It seems reasonable to surmise that the FBI's assessment of the *Yahoo! News* article radically changed in order to protect the FISA application. Again, not a single FBI employee who participated in the October 3, 2016 meeting with Steele, no other employees with whom we spoke who assisted in drafting the initial FISA application, nor OI Unit Chief-1 had any recollection of why the FBI's assessment changed. For his part, OI Attorney-1 told the Office that he deferred to the FBI's assessment of the *Yahoo! News* issue because the FBI was the "owner of the facts."[669] OI Attorney-1 also recalled that the FBI was constantly pressuring OI to advance the FISA.[670] As mentioned above, OI Attorney-1 recalled Clinesmith informing him (OI Attorney-1) that Director Comey "wants to know what's going on," and that the Deputy Director asked who the FBI needed to speak with at the Department "to get this going."[671] OI Attorney-1 opined that in hindsight he should have been less deferential to the FBI given his concerns about the validity of the assessment.[672]

OI Unit Chief-1 told the Office that, in hindsight, the FBI's change in assessment regarding *Yahoo! News*, was "curious."[673] OI Unit Chief-1 stated that, at the time, the FBI's evolution on the assessment made sense to him.[674] Nonetheless, OI Unit Chief-1 told the Office that it would be "troubling" if the FBI never asked Steele about his role in the *Yahoo! News* leak, which no one apparently ever did.[675]

*vii. The Steele Reports are included in the Page FISA application*

As discussed in greater detail below, four Steele Reports (2016/080, 2016/94, 2016/095 and 2016/102) were relied on by the FBI to support probable cause in the initial Page FISA application and three renewals of that application. Before the receipt of the Steele Reports, the

---

667 OSC Report of Interview of Brian Auten on July 26, 2021 at 17.

668 OSC Report of Interview of Handling Agent-1 on Aug. 11, 2021 at 2.

669 OSC Report of Interview of OI Attorney-1 on July 1, 2020 at 2.

670 *Id.* at 7.

671 *Id.* at 2.

672 *Id.*

673 OSC Report of Interview of OI Unit Chief-1 on Oct. 27, 2020 at 2.

674 *Id.*

675 *Id.* at 3.

FBI did not believe that there was sufficient probable cause to apply for a FISA warrant against Page.[676]

Although the FBI had reason to believe that the Steele Reports were opposition research documents commissioned by a law firm and that the candidate's campaign who hired the firm was aware of the Steele Reports, there is nothing in the FBI record to show that this was a consideration or subject of debate prior to the use of the Steele information in the initial FISA application targeting Page. Moreover, not a single substantive allegation pulled from the Steele Reports and used in the initial Page FISA application had been corroborated at the time of the FISA submission – or indeed, to our knowledge, has ever been corroborated by the FBI.[677]

The FBI obtained a total of four FISC orders targeting Page, which authorized intrusive electronic surveillance of Page and physical searches of certain items of his property from October 2016 through September 2017. Each of the FISA applications set forth the FBI's basis for believing that Page was knowingly engaged in clandestine intelligence activities on behalf of Russia, or knowingly helping others in such activities and alleged – based, in part, on the Steele Reports – that (i) Page was part of a "well-developed conspiracy of co-operation" between Trump's campaign and the Russian government (Steele Report 2016/095), (ii) Page allegedly met in July 2016 with Igor Sechin, Chairman of Russian energy conglomerate Rosneft, and Igor Divyekin, a senior official in the Russian Presidential Administration (Steele Report 2016/94), (iii) the Kremlin had for years gathered compromising information on Clinton (Steele Report 2016/080), and (iv) Russia had leaked DNC emails to Wikileaks, an idea concocted by Page and others (Steele Report 2016/102).

As discussed above, in late September 2016, OI Attorney-1 received a copy of a draft request to prepare a FISA application targeting Page from Clinesmith. OI Attorney-1 informed the Office that his subsequent primary responsibility was to "wordsmith" the application and to gather information regarding sources.[678] In this regard, OI Attorney-1 primarily worked with Case Agent-1 and Clinesmith.[679] OI Attorney-1 also told the Office that he was not aware of the fact that a previous draft application had been prepared by the FBI prior to the receipt of the Steele Reports which OGC determined lacked sufficient probable cause to move forward.[680] As discussed above, with respect to the initial application, FBI OGC Unit Chief-1 told the Office that she believed that the initial application was a "close call" but needed more information to meet the probable cause standard.[681] FBI OGC Unit Chief-1 stated that the inclusion of the Steele reporting allowed the FBI to clear the probable cause hurdle in the Page FISA

---

676 *See supra* § IV.D.1.a.i.

677 OSC Report of Interview of Brian Auten on July 26, 2021 at 24, 31; *Danchenko* Tr. 10/11/2022 PM at 75-76, 79-81, 87, 96-97, 111, 115-117, 154; *Danchenko* Tr. 10/12/2022 PM at 550-551; *Danchenko* Tr. 10/13/2022 AM at 671, 700. Notwithstanding this lack of corroboration, the three FISA renewal applications on Page continued to use the Steele reporting to support probable cause.

678 OSC Report of Interview of OI Attorney-1 on July 1, 2020 at 1.

679 *Id.*

680 *Id.*

681 OSC Report of Interview of FBI OGC Unit Chief-1 on Aug. 29, 2019 at 6.

application,[682] and, therefore, FBI OGC Unit Chief-1 approved the transmission of the request to OI.

FBI OGC Unit Chief-1 informed the Office, in sum, that she had no concerns with the inclusion of the Steele reporting in the Page FISA applications. FBI OGC Unit Chief-1, however, was not aware of what, if any, vetting had been done regarding the allegations prior to the submission of the initial application to the FISC.[683] FBI OGC Unit Chief-1 did have some recall that a lack of vetting of the Reports was a concern.[684] Finally, FBI OGC Unit Chief-1 told the Office that there was also some concern that Steele had been hired by a law firm on behalf of the Clinton campaign and the DNC to conduct opposition research on Trump.[685] Despite these concerns, the fact that Steele's information was being financed by the DNC and/or the Clinton campaign was not included in the affidavit's source description of Steele.[686] The failure to provide this information to the FISC was a major omission in that the information clearly had the potential to affect the analysis of any bias in Steele's reporting.

With respect to the Steele Report allegations in the initial FISA application, OI Attorney-1 told the Office that he did not think the FBI was initially concerned with corroborating Steele's reporting, although he recalled that at some point some unknown efforts had been made.[687] Rather than corroborating the allegations, OI Attorney-1 recalled that the FBI's primary focus was on Steele's past reliability as an FBI CHS.[688] In his interview with the Office, Case Agent-1 also noted the importance of Steele's past reliability as reason to include his (Steele's) reporting in the FISA application, but also stated, in sum, that it was essential for the FBI to corroborate the Steele reporting, to include verification of Steele's alleged sub-sources.[689] To that end, the Office directly asked Case Agent-1 whether *any* of Steele's allegations contained in the initial FISA application had been corroborated. Case Agent-1 stated that "he could not recall anything specific that was fully corroborated."[690] Shockingly, Case Agent-1 told the Office that the initial

---

682 *Id.* at 6-7.

683 OSC Report of Interview of FBI OGC Unit Chief-1 on July 23, 2020 at 7.

684 *Id.*

685 *Id.* at 9.

686 A footnote in the FISA application did describe the person who hired Steele. It says this person "never advised [Steele] as to the motivation behind the research into [Trump's] ties to Russia." It went on to say that "[t]he FBI speculates that the . . . person was likely looking for information that could be used to discredit [Trump's] campaign." *In re Carter W. Page*, No. 16-1182, at 15-16 n.8. However, as noted above at page 111, prior to the submission of the initial Page FISA application, the FBI in fact knew Steele had told Handling Agent-1 that Fusion GPS had been hired by a law firm and that his ultimate client was "senior Democrats" supporting Clinton. Moreover, it knew that Handling Agent-1's notes of this meeting reflect that, according to Steele, "HC" (Hillary Clinton) was aware of his (Steele's) reporting.

687 OSC Report of Interview of OI Attorney-1 on July 1, 2020 at 2.

688 *Id.*

689 OSC Report of Interview of Case Agent-1 on Aug. 21, 2019 at 3.

690 *Id.* at 3-4.

FISA applicati[illegible] age wa[illegible] the returns would "self-corroborate."[691] [illegible] over[illegible] ore detail below, the FBI did attempt to inve[illegible] anal[illegible] ltimately was not able to confirm or corroborate [illegible] stanti[illegible].

Notwith[illegible] e obvi[illegible] the Department included these allegations in all [illegible] SA a[illegible] applications *after* Steele's primary sub-so[illegible] chen[illegible] viewed by the FBI, and was not able to provide [illegible] for a[illegible] ided to Steele. To that end, as discussed more [illegible] OI Uni[illegible] primary sub-source had been identified and in[illegible] the FB[illegible] later learned that serious questions arose [illegible] uary [illegible] ko concerning the reliability of his information [illegible] parent[illegible] reports. In OI Unit Chief-1's opinion, he dou[illegible] would [illegible] it renewals of the Page surveillance ha[illegible] it fu[illegible] f the [illegible] etween Steele's reporting and the FBI's intervie[illegible] ko.[692]

*viii. [illegible] entif[illegible] pri[illegible] urce*

During [illegible], 2016 [illegible] med FBI personnel that his reporting was p[illegible] rated b[illegible] ub-[illegible] in turn, relied on his own network of sub-sources [illegible] rmation [illegible] rimary sub-source traveled freely in Russia and a[illegible] well-[illegible][694] St[illegible] er, would not provide the FBI with the name [illegible] sub-s[illegible] te [illegible] 16, the FBI determined that Igor Danchenko, a [illegible] ssian [illegible] n, D.C., was Steele's primary sub-source.[695] Not[illegible] is fa[illegible] nd th[illegible] nt did not correct in the final two FISA applicati[illegible] Page th[illegible] izat[illegible] mary sub-source as being "Russia-based."[696]

*ix. [illegible] chenko*

From 20[illegible] 10, Ig[illegible] nko [illegible] analyst at the Brookings Institution in W[illegible] D.C. wh[illegible] sed [illegible] Russian and Eurasian geo-political and ec[illegible] s.[697] [illegible] car[illegible] oyed at Brookings after writing to Brookings se[illegible] ("Broo[illegible] w-1" [illegible] ings Fellow-2") while a student at the Universit[illegible]. Th[illegible] henko was hired as a research

---

[691] *Id.* at 4.

[692] OSC Repor[illegible] of OI [illegible] 20 at 4.

[693] SCO-02013[illegible] Aute[illegible] isor[illegible] ent-1, Moffa, & Strzok dated 10/04/2016).

[694] *Id.*

[695] OSC Repor[illegible] of Bri[illegible] ated [illegible] 1 at 24.

[696] SCO_10515[illegible] of FIS[illegible] ions [illegible] arter Page).

[697] SCID_0000[illegible] um W[illegible] Da[illegible]

assistant to Brookings Fellow-2.[698] In approximately 2010, Brookings Fellow-1 introduced Danchenko to Christopher Steele.[699] In 2011, Steele retained Danchenko as a contractor for his London-based firm, Orbis Business Intelligence.[700] In his work for Orbis, Danchenko focused primarily on Russian and Eurasian business risk assessment and geopolitical analysis. As discussed above, beginning in June 2016, Steele – using information provided primarily by Danchenko[701] – began to compile and draft the Steele Reports containing unsubstantiated allegations of illicit ties between Trump and the Russian government.

As discussed in more detail below, from January 2017 through October 2020, and as part of its efforts to determine the truth or falsity of specific information in the Steele Reports, the FBI conducted multiple interviews of Danchenko regarding, among other things, the allegations that he provided to Steele that ultimately formed the core of the Steele Reports. During these extensive interviews, Danchenko was unable to provide the FBI with corroborating evidence for any of the substantive allegations contained in the Steele Reports. In fact, Danchenko claimed that the Ritz Carlton allegations he provided to Steele were nothing more than "rumor and speculation," and that most of the information he gathered for Steele was the product of casual conversation with people in his social circle, including those parts of the Steele Reports used in the Page FISA applications.[702]

x. *Danchenko's employment at Danchenko Employer-1 and payments by Steele and others*

During the course of its investigation, the Office gathered evidence related to the unusual process through which Steele paid Danchenko over the course of his work for Orbis. A brief recitation of those facts is included below.

As discussed above, Danchenko informed the FBI during his January 2017 interviews that, in approximately 2011, he began conducting work for Steele's firm, Orbis Business Intelligence.[703] Danchenko described his work with Steele as a "side project []" in addition to his employment in the United States at a Virginia-based venture capital firm.[704]

---

698 OSC Report of Interview of Brookings Fellow-2 dated Nov. 16, 2021 at 1.

699 OSC Report of Interview of Brookings Fellow-1 on Sept. 17, 2021 at 4; SCO-005801 (Interview of Igor Danchenko Electronic Communication dated 02/09/2017) at 5.

700 SCO-005801 (Interview of Igor Danchenko Electronic Communication dated 02/09/2017) at 6.

701 According to Danchenko, he provided 80% of the intelligence and 50% of the analysis contained in the Steele Reports. *Danchenko* Government Exhibit 1502.

702 SCO-005801 (Interview of Igor Danchenko Electronic Communication dated 02/09/2017) at 23, 39; SCO_105282 (CHS Reporting Document dated 06/01/2017).

703 SCO-005801 (Interview of Igor Danchenko Electronic Communication dated 02/09/2017) at 6.

704 *Id.*

In approximately 2014, Danchenko ceased working for the venture capital firm following the firm's declaration of bankruptcy.[705] According to Danchenko, at the time of its bankruptcy, the firm was in the process of sponsoring Danchenko's visa application to remain in the United States.[706] Following this development, Danchenko reached out to an acquaintance in the United States who operated Danchenko Employer-1, a Virginia-based information technology staffing firm.[707] Danchenko stated, in sum, that he was seeking employment at Danchenko Employer-1 in order to extend his visa and remain in the United States.[708] Orbis, due to its United Kingdom-based registration, was unable to sponsor Danchenko in furtherance of his work visa application.[709]

According to Danchenko, the principal of Danchenko Employer-1 informed Danchenko that he would hire him on the condition that Danchenko would be compensated by an outside source – in essence, Danchenko Employer-1 would hire Danchenko to assist with his immigration status, but not fund his salary.[710] Danchenko informed Steele about this arrangement and Steele agreed to pay Danchenko Employer-1 for the work that Danchenko was conducting on behalf of Orbis.[711] During his January 2017 interviews with the FBI, Danchenko described Danchenko Employer-1 as a "contract vehicle" through which Danchenko would be paid for his work on behalf of Orbis.[712] Put plainly, Danchenko Employer-1 was merely a front to allow Danchenko to continue his work on behalf of Orbis, while at the same time allowing him to secure a work visa through alleged employment with a U.S.-based company. As relevant to this investigation, Danchenko Employer-1 Executive-1, an ethnic Russian, described Danchenko as someone who was "boastful . . . having low credibility, *and a person who liked to embellish his purported contacts with the Kremlin.*"[713]

The Office's investigation discovered that Orbis, through a separate New Jersey-based company, paid Danchenko Employer-1 for the work Danchenko performed on behalf of Orbis.[714] In turn, Danchenko Employer-1 provided Danchenko with a salary funded by Orbis.[715] By any measure, this was an extremely odd arrangement given that Danchenko performed no work

---

[705] *Id.* at 4-5.

[706] *Id.* at 8.

[707] *Id.* at 9; OSC Report of Interview of Danchenko Employer-1 Executive-1 on June 30, 2021 at 1.

[708] SCO-005801 (Interview of Igor Danchenko Electronic Communication dated 02/09/2017) at 9.

[709] *Id.* at 8-9.

[710] *Id.* at 9.

[711] *Id.*

[712] *Id.*

[713] OSC Report of Interview of Danchenko Employer-1 Executive-1 on June 30, 2021 at 1 (emphasis added).

[714] OSC Report of Interview of New Jersey-Based Company Executive-1 on Aug. 9, 2021 at 1.

[715] *Id.*

related to Danchenko Employer-1's primary business purpose, *i.e.*, the staffing of information technology and engineering contractors.[716] Nevertheless, Danchenko Employer-1 ultimately sponsored Danchenko's work visa to remain in the United States.[717]

In sworn testimony that Steele provided in litigation in the United Kingdom concerning, among other things, the Steele Reports, Steele stated that he paid his sources an average retainer between $3,000 and $5,000 per month.[718]

Banking and other records also show that from January of 2016 through June 2021, Danchenko received over $436,000 in wire transfers from European businesses, including from Orbis and other entities affiliated with Orbis. These money transfers were in addition to the money that Orbis sent through Danchenko Employer-1 to fund Danchenko's salary.

c. <u>The prior counterespionage investigation of Danchenko and the FBI's failure to account for his possible motivations and allegiance</u>

Danchenko was a known entity to the FBI in December 2016 when he was identified as Steele's primary sub-source. As publicly reported, Danchenko was the subject of an FBI counterespionage investigation from 2009 to 2011.[719] In late 2008, while employed by the Brookings Institution in Washington, D.C., Danchenko engaged two fellow employees ("Brookings Researcher-1" and "Brookings Researcher-2") at a happy hour about whether one of the employees might be willing or able in the future to provide classified information in exchange for money.[720] Brookings Researcher-1 was a research fellow for an influential foreign policy advisor who was about to enter the Obama administration.[721] According to Brookings Researcher-1, Danchenko believed that he (Brookings Researcher-1) might also enter the Obama administration with the foreign policy advisor and have access to classified information. During this exchange, Danchenko informed Brookings Researcher-1 that he (Danchenko) had access to people who would be willing to pay money for classified information.[722] Rightly concerned, Brookings Researcher-1 informed a U.S. government contact at an appropriate government agency about this encounter, and the information was subsequently passed on to the FBI.[723]

---

716 OSC Report of Interview of Danchenko Employer-1 Executive-1 on June 30, 2021 at 1-2.

717 *Id.* at 1.

718 *Steele Transcript* at 171.

719 Andrew Desiderio & Kyle Cheney, *Steele Dossier Sub-Source Was Suspected of Spying for Russia, DOJ Reveals*, Politico, (Sept. 24, 2020); *Danchenko* Tr. 10/13/2022 PM at 876:3-877:18, 886:22-25; SCO_105161 (Summary of Final June 3, 2019 Significant Source Validation Report of Igor Danchenko); SCO-061528 (Letter from William Barr to Lindsey Graham dated Sept. 24, 2020); SCO-061530 (Overview of the Counterintelligence Investigation of Christopher Steele's Primary Sub-Source).

720 SCO_105160 (Summary of Solicitation); OSC Report of Interview of Brookings Researcher-1 on Dec. 1, 2021 at 2.

721 *Id.*

722 *Id.*

723 *Id.*

When interview [illegible] Bro [illegible] ied the details of the interaction with Danchenk [illegible] spect to [illegible] tions [illegible] enko at Brookings, Brookings Researcher-1 de [illegible] enko [illegible] s."[725] The second Brookings employee, Broo [illegible] cher-2, [illegible] FBI. While Brookings Researcher-2 di [illegible] ally re [illegible], he did harbor suspicions that Danchenko was [illegible] Russia [illegible] nce.[726] [illegible] cions were based, in part, on the fact that Danche [illegible] iple [illegible] ed working as a low-level research assista [illegible] gs – th [illegible] that Brookings unwittingly provided Danch [illegible] info [illegible] Russians.[727]

Based o [illegible] t on p [illegible] cher-1, the FBI's Baltimore Field Office initiated [illegible] espion [illegible] enko.[728] Two Baltimore Field Office Agents [illegible] gation [illegible] Case Agent-1" and "Baltimore Case Agent-2") [illegible] who [illegible] ce Analyst (IA) as opposed to a Supervisory IA [illegible] dqua [illegible] investigation. The FBI converted its in [illegible] Danc [illegible] "fu [illegible] on" after learning that Danchenko (i) [illegible] t fied [illegible] BI espionage subjects, and (ii) had previous co [illegible] Russ [illegible] sian intelligence officers.[729] In particular, the F [illegible] at in S [illegible] 006, [illegible] informed one Russian intelligence offi [illegible] an [illegible] tering [illegible] n diplomatic service.[730] Four days later, the in [illegible] fcer co [illegible] ormed him that they could meet that day to wor [illegible] nent [illegible] plans."[731] In October 2006, Danchenko con [illegible] ligen [illegible] can be placed in [the following day's] diplomat [illegible]."[732]

As part [illegible] ation [illegible], [illegible] interviewed several people at Georgetown Un [illegible] new [illegible] nchenko was attempting to obtain another a [illegible] e. C [illegible] U.S. [illegible] had recently interned at an intelligence age [illegible] that D [illegible] sked [illegible] r knowledge of Russian matters

---

[724] SCO-06153 [illegible] the [illegible] tion of Christopher Steele's Primary Sub-so [illegible]

[725] OSC Report [illegible] of Bal [illegible] Ag [illegible]. 13, 2020 at 3.

[726] *Id.* at 2.

[727] *Id.*

[728] SCO-06153 [illegible] of the [illegible] tion of Christopher Steele's Primary Sub-so [illegible]

[729] *Id.*

[730] *Id.* at 2.

[731] OSC Report [illegible] of Ba [illegible] Ag [illegible]. 13, 2020 at 3.

[732] SCO-06153 [illegible] of the [illegible] tion of Christopher Steele's Primary Sub-so [illegible]

every time he encountered her.[733] On one occasion, Danchenko inquired about the person's knowledge of a specific Russian military matter.[734] That same person stated, in sum, that Danchenko informed her that he served in the Russian army and worked with rockets, but at the time worked on "special" matters.[735] Danchenko also told this person that his Russian passport listed him as GRU (the Russian military intelligence service) because of his language skills.[736] Based on these encounters, the individual believed that Danchenko was working for a Russian intelligence service.[737] Another Brookings colleague recalled that in 2008 Danchenko informed her that he (Danchenko) had been absent from work at Brookings because he had been in South Ossetia fighting Georgians.[738] Danchenko also bragged to this colleague about vandalizing the Georgian embassy in Belarus.[739]

Further, as part of its espionage investigation, the FBI determined that Danchenko was an associate of two FBI counterintelligence subjects.[740]

In July 2010, the FBI initiated a FISA request on Danchenko, which was subsequently routed to OI in August 2010.[741] However, the investigation into Danchenko was closed in March 2011 after the FBI incorrectly concluded that Danchenko had left the country.[742] Specifically, the FBI believed that Danchenko and his then-wife had traveled on a one-way ticket to London on September 26, 2010.[743] The Office's investigative efforts revealed that, in fact, Danchenko never boarded the flight to London but, unknown to the FBI, continued to reside in the Washington, D.C. area.[744]

In 2012, after the counterespionage investigation of Danchenko had been closed because he was thought to have left the country, Auten exchanged emails with Baltimore Special Agent-2 regarding Danchenko. Specifically, Auten advised Baltimore Special Agent-2 that Danchenko may not have left the United States as initially believed in September 2010.[745] FBI Baltimore

---

733 SCO-101733 (Human Source Validation Report of Danchenko) at 5.

734 *Id.*

735 *Id.*

736 *Id.*

737 *Id.*

738 *Id.*

739 *Id.*

740 SCO-061528 (Letter from William Barr to Lindsey Graham dated Sept. 24, 2020); SCO-061530 (Overview of the Counterintelligence Investigation of Christopher Steele's Primary Sub-Source); *see also* OSC Report of Interview of Brian Auten on July 26, 2021 at 1.

741 SCO-061530 (Overview of the Counterintelligence Investigation of Christopher Steele's Primary Sub-source) at 2.

742 *Id.* at 1; OSC Report of Interview of Baltimore Special Agent-1 on Aug. 13, 2020 at 2.

743 OSC Report of Interview of Baltimore Case Agent-1 on Aug. 13, 2020 at 4.

744 U.S. Customs and Border Protection Person Encounter List for Igor Danchenko at 5.

745 OSC Report of Interview of Brian Auten on July 26, 2021 at 2.

apparently indicated that it would consider re-opening the investigation into Danchenko, but never did.[746] Thereafter, Auten contacted WFO about re-opening a case on Danchenko, or alternatively, attempting to recruit him as a CHS.[747] Auten, however, cautioned WFO to not "get played back," meaning the Russian intelligence services could be using Danchenko as a double-agent.[748] During his interview with the Office, Auten stated that he did not know what, if any, action WFO took with respect to this information.[749] Ultimately, the case against Danchenko was never reopened by the Baltimore Division and no recruitment effort was undertaken by WFO.

The Special Counsel interviewed both Baltimore Special Agent-1 and Baltimore Special Agent-2. Baltimore Special Agent-1 believed that, based on his review of the case file, Danchenko was connected in some manner to Russian intelligence.[750] Baltimore Special Agent-1 believed that Danchenko was "hiding in plain sight" in the United States while frequently traveling overseas to Europe to be debriefed by Russian intelligence.[751] Baltimore Special Agent-2 stated, in sum, that the counterintelligence case on Danchenko remained unresolved and, in her opinion, "certainly a lot more investigation" should have been conducted on Danchenko.[752]

*i. Danchenko becomes a paid FBI CHS despite the unresolved counterespionage investigation*

Danchenko was interviewed by the FBI in January 2017 following his identification in December 2016 as Steele's primary sub-source. FBI materials reviewed by the Office revealed that the primary purpose for the FBI's initial engagement with Danchenko in January 2017 was to recruit him as a paid CHS.[753] If this recruitment was successful, the FBI planned to mine Danchenko for information that was corroborative of the damaging allegations about President-elect Trump in the Steele Reports.

The FBI initially interviewed Danchenko over the course of three days, January 24-26, 2017.[754] These interviews were conducted pursuant to a grant of letter immunity provided by the Department.[755] The interviews were conducted primarily by Case Agent-1 and Auten. Danchenko was represented by counsel during the entirety of the interviews. As Auten has

---

746 *Id.*

747 *Id.*

748 *Id.*

749 *Id.*

750 OSC Report of Interview of Baltimore Case Agent-1 on Aug. 13, 2020 at 4.

751 *Id.*

752 OSC Report of Interview of Baltimore Special Agent-2 on July 28, 2020 at 5.

753 *See, e.g.*, SCO_105244 (Email from Supervisory Special Agent-3 to Boone, Supervisory Special Agent-2, Special Agent-1, Case Agent-1, & Auten dated 01/12/2017).

754 SCO-005801 (Interview of Igor Danchenko Electronic Communication dated 02/09/2017).

755 Letter from David Laufman to Igor Danchenko dated Jan. 24, 2017.

stated both in interviews with the Office and as a trial witness in *United States v. Danchenko*, 21-CR-245 (E.D Va.), the game plan for the January 2017 interviews was to (i) have Danchenko identify his sources for the allegations contained in the Steele Reports and (ii) provide evidence to corroborate the allegations contained in the Steele Reports.[756] As Auten testified in *Danchenko,* during the January 2017 interviews, Danchenko was not able to provide *any* corroborative evidence related to *any* substantive allegation contained in the Steele Reports – and critically – was unable to corroborate *any* of the FBI's assertions contained in the Carter Page FISA applications.[757]

Nevertheless, following the January 2017 interviews, Crossfire Hurricane leadership reached out to WFO to begin the recruitment of Danchenko as an FBI CHS. SA Kevin Helson, assigned to a counterintelligence squad at WFO, was selected to serve as Danchenko's source handler.[758] According to Helson, he was selected because he was a senior agent with knowledge of Russian matters.[759] In early March 2017, Helson prepared the Danchenko source opening documentation. In preparing those documents, Helson incorrectly noted that there was no "derogatory" information associated with Danchenko and that Danchenko had not been a prior subject of an FBI investigation.[760] This was clearly not true as there had previously been the unresolved Baltimore FBI counterespionage investigation of Danchenko that was only closed because it was believed he had left the country and returned to Russia.

The Office was able to determine that Helson became aware of the counterespionage investigation shortly after completing the source opening documentation, but failed to revise the paperwork because of a purported belief that the prior case on Danchenko was based solely on hearsay.[761] In a November 24, 2020 interview with the Office, Helson was shown a spreadsheet listing Sentinel (the FBI's case management system) searches that he performed on March 7, 2017 – mere days after completing the CHS opening documentation – in which he specifically queried the counterespionage case file on Danchenko.[762] Helson stated that he had no recollection as to why he searched certain serials in that case file, and he advised that he would not have thought Danchenko should be the main subject of that type of espionage case since Danchenko, in Helson's view, was a foreign national without a security clearance.[763] Whatever the reason for not locating and documenting the serious derogatory information, the record is clear the FBI opened Danchenko as a CHS without ever resolving the Baltimore espionage matter or examining the file.

---

[756] OSC Report of Interview of Brian Auten on July 26, 2021 at 21; *Danchenko* Tr. 10/11/2022 PM at 125, 151.

[757] *Danchenko* Tr. 10/11/2022 PM at 154, *Danchenko* Tr. 10/12/2022 PM at 550-551.

[758] OSC Report of Interview of Brian Auten on July 26, 2021 at 21; *Danchenko* Tr.10/11/2022 PM at 152-153.

[759] OSC Report of Interview of Kevin Helson on Nov. 24, 2020 at 1.

[760] *Id.* at 7, 10; SCO-105224 (Source Opening Communication dated 03/07/2017).

[761] OSC Report of Interview of Kevin Helson on Nov. 24, 2020 at 10.

[762] *Id.* at 7.

[763] *Id.*

Despite [illegible] that Dan[illegible] as i[illegible] e opening serial of a counterespiona[illegible] n in [illegible] Helson [illegible] investigators that he was surprised to lea[illegible] n on Ma[illegible] 17 [illegible] ko was indeed the main subject of that counteresp[illegible] Acc[illegible] elson [illegible] rmed him, in sum, that Danchenko ha[illegible] with [illegible] ellig[illegible], and that he had previously pitched someon[illegible] info[illegible] on, however, Auten advised him (Helson) that th[illegible] Danch[illegible] "inte[illegible] was not a significant" matter.[765] Helson informe[illegible] hat he [illegible] reco[illegible] his conversation with Auten. Notably, Auten [illegible] Hel[illegible] had [illegible] ssisted in the Baltimore investigation. [illegible] learned [illegible] terespionage case against Danchenko, he [illegible] ime t[illegible] he [illegible] conferring with the case agents previously assi[illegible] atter. [illegible] as d[illegible] more detail below, Helson did not reach out to Ba[illegible] Agen[illegible] ay 2[illegible] anchenko was being evaluated by the FBI's CH[illegible] Mana[illegible] it ("V[illegible] the VMU raised serious concerns about the prior [illegible] nage ca[illegible]

When th[illegible] ed Hels[illegible] s rea[illegible] rning that Danchenko pitched a colleague for c[illegible] mation[illegible] ke something Danchenko would do, that's how [illegible] rks.' [illegible] furth[illegible] sum, that the fact Danchenko comes off as a [illegible] s desc[illegible] Washington, D.C. In his interviews wit[illegible] lelson [illegible] ally [illegible] f the prior counterespionage investigation o[illegible]

Despite [illegible] d cou[illegible] anchenko and Helson's (and others) appare[illegible] osity [illegible] began operating Danchenko as a paid CHS in M[illegible] As d[illegible] he[illegible] BI and Helson made no further efforts to exami[illegible] ved [illegible] exposed the security issues surrounding Da[illegible] May 20[illegible]

*ii.* [illegible] *exam*[illegible] *ity as a source*

The FB[illegible] spiona[illegible] atio[illegible] enko was raised in May 2019 in the context of a[illegible] e Vali[illegible] ort [illegible] n Danchenko prepared by the FBI's VMU. T[illegible] d se[illegible] rel[illegible] chenko's past associations, behaviors, and [illegible], includ[illegible] or [illegible] d espionage case. In addition to the informatio[illegible] he p[illegible] ; Danchenko's fairly extensive contacts with k[illegible] specte[illegible] tellig[illegible] rs, the HSVR detailed a February 2018 U.S. Cust[illegible] der ("C[illegible] ctio[illegible] nko when he re-entered the United States after bei[illegible] ted Kin[illegible] hich [illegible] er discovered business cards for Russian diplom[illegible] Engl[illegible] HS[illegible] ailed several falsehoods and

---

[764] *Id.* at 7-8.

[765] *Id.* at 7.

[766] *Id.* at 8.

[767] SCO-10522[illegible] ning [illegible] atio[illegible] 7/2017).

[768] SCO-1017[illegible] Source Va[illegible] epor[illegible]

inconsistencies found in Danchenko's visa applications and immigration documents. One member of the VMU with extensive prior service as an Army counterintelligence officer in Europe ("Headquarters Supervisory Analyst-1") expressed grave concerns about the counterespionage case and was strongly of the opinion that Danchenko was connected to Russian intelligence in some manner.[769]

In response to the concerns of Supervisory Analyst-1 and others in the VMU, Helson reached out to Baltimore Special Agent-2 for the *first* time – over two years after he initially learned of the counterespionage case against Danchenko. Helson informed the VMU (and later the Office), that Baltimore Special Agent-2 stated, in sum, that the investigation was premised on "hearsay at best."[770] However, when interviewed by the Office on July 28, 2020, Baltimore Special Agent-2 expressed disbelief when she first learned that Danchenko had been signed up as an FBI source because, among other things, the FBI had not resolved the prior counterespionage case.[771] When informed that Helson stated to the VMU that Baltimore Special Agent-2 had characterized the predication of the counterespionage case as "hearsay at best," Baltimore Special Agent-2 was adamant that she would never have characterized Danchenko's direct pitch to Brookings Researcher -1 for classified information as hearsay.[772] To the contrary, Baltimore Special Agent-2 stated that the information came directly from the individual who was the target of the pitch for classified information.[773] In two subsequent interviews with the Office, Baltimore Special Agent-2 again denied ever telling Helson that the counterespionage case against Danchenko was predicated on "hearsay at best."[774] Baltimore Special Agent-2 confirmed to the Office that the Danchenko counterespionage case would have continued if he had not left the country, as the FBI mistakenly believed he had.[775] When shown Helson's source opening documentation that contained the "no derog" entry, Baltimore Special Agent-2 agreed that the entry was clearly incorrect.[776]

*iii. The VMU's recommendations to WFO and Helson*

The HSVR on Danchenko recommended that he be allowed to remain open as a CHS but recommended that several steps be taken to help mitigate the VMU's substantial concerns about Danchenko. As an initial matter, when asked why the VMU recommended that Danchenko be allowed to remain open given the concerns noted above, several individuals who participated in the HSVR stated that the VMU lacked the institutional ability to do anything more than to make

---

769 OSC Report of Interview of Headquarters Supervisory Analyst-1 on Dec. 8, 2020 at 1, 4; *Danchenko* Tr. 10/13/2022 PM at 890-91.

770 SCO-105324 (Helson memo of May 24, 2019 conversation with Baltimore Special Agent-2 at 1).

771 OSC Report of Interview of Baltimore Special Agent-2 on July 28, 2020 at 3.

772 *Id.*

773 *Id.*

774 OSC Report of Interview of Baltimore Special Agent-2 on Aug. 13, 2020 at 1-2; OSC Report of Interview of Baltimore Special Agent-1 on Dec. 18, 2020 at 1.

775 OSC Report of Interview of Baltimore Special Agent-2 on Aug. 13, 2020 at 1.

776 *Id.* at 2.

recommendations to mitigate CHS issues. One supervisor in the VMU noted that it rarely recommended closure of sources out of a general fear that the field offices would largely be unreceptive to important recommendations designed to enhance source handling issues if the VMU recommended closure of a source.[777] In addition to the serious concern about the prior unresolved counterespionage investigation, the VMU also highlighted numerous problematic areas that warranted attention. For example, Danchenko's background and employment history had noted inconsistencies and omissions; his assessed motivation for providing information to the FBI had changed; his immigration applications omitted certain derogatory information and contained inconsistencies and falsehoods; and, despite his concerns for his personal safety, he traveled frequently to Russia before becoming a CHS. Danchenko also demonstrated knowledge of tradecraft and made contradictory statements, and much of the information he provided appeared to be hearsay that he was unable, despite requests, to validate. The VMU recommended several steps to mitigate these areas, such as administering a polygraph examination,[778] further controls on his reporting, and additional evaluation, but these did not occur. Instead, Helson and WFO ignored nearly all of the VMU's recommendations and continued to operate Danchenko as a CHS until WFO was ordered to close Danchenko in October 2020.[779] In total, the FBI paid Danchenko approximately $220,000 during the 3.5 years that Danchenko was a CHS.[780] FBI counterintelligence personnel at WFO and in the Counterintelligence Division at FBI Headquarters opposed efforts to close Danchenko and delayed doing so. Moreover, the Office learned that the FBI proposed making continued future payments to Danchenko, totaling more than $300,000, while the Office was actively

---

[777] At the time the evaluation was prepared on Danchenko, it was the practice of the VMU not to recommend that a CHS be closed, but rather to make recommendations of things to be done in continuing to operate a source. OSC Report of Interview of Headquarters Supervisory Special Agent-2 on March 2, 2021 at 6-7; OSC Report of Interview of Headquarters Supervisory Analyst-1 on Dec. 8, 2020 at 8. The *CHS Policy Guide*, issued in 2021, now includes requirements that:

- The VMU is to "manage[] the FBI's validation review processes" and "must determine what level of validation review is required for each CHS." *CHS Policy Guide* § 20.1.1.
- The Assistant Director for Intelligence is to approve or deny the reopening of a CHS closed for cause. *Id.* § 18.3.1.
- The Directorate of Intelligence manages the Senior Review Board, whose function is to ensure "comprehensive review by senior FBI officials of the FBI's highest-risk CHSs." *See id.* § 20.5.1.

[778] The FBI uses a polygraph examination as a straightforward and practical way to assess a source's motivations, allegiances, and vulnerabilities.

[779] OSC Report of Interview of Kevin Helson on Nov. 24, 2020 at 19; FBI-AAA-0019898 (Email from Headquarters Supervisory Special Agent-1 to Helson & others dated 10/29/2020).

[780] SCO-105237 (Source Closing Communication dated 10/29/2020).

investigating this matter, which would have been in addition to the $220,000 he had already received.[781]

It is extremely concerning that the FBI failed to deal with the prior *unresolved* counterespionage case on Danchenko. Given Danchenko's known contacts with Russian intelligence officers and his documented prior pitch for classified information, the Crossfire Hurricane team's failure to properly consider and address the espionage case prior to opening Danchenko as a CHS is difficult to explain, particularly given their awareness that Danchenko was the linchpin to the uncorroborated allegations contained in the Steele Reports.

Despite the FBI's awareness of (i) there being significant issues relating to conflicts between what Danchenko had reported to the FBI in January 2017 and thereafter as a paid CHS and what Steele, a long term paid CHS of the FBI, had stated in the "Company Intelligence" reports he provided to the FBI (and others), (ii) Danchenko's troubling history regarding a prior unresolved espionage matter, and (iii) a CHS validation report that raised various red flags concerning Danchenko, the counterintelligence executive managers at the WFO and FBI Headquarters resisted efforts to have Danchenko closed as a source. Instead, management supported continued payments to him, requiring FBI Headquarters approval, of sizable amounts of money and insisted that Danchenko was very valuable to the FBI's counterintelligence program. Interviews conducted by the Office revealed, however, that the Assistant Directors for Counterintelligence in WFO and FBI Headquarters, as well as the FBI's Executive Assistant Director for National Security, made clear that they were not even able to accurately describe the value or contributions of Danchenko that would justify keeping him open, much less making hundreds of thousands of dollars in payments to him. Indeed, the Assistant Director for Counterintelligence at FBI Headquarters thought Danchenko was being paid for information he was providing that corroborated the Steele Dossier reporting, which, of course, was not the case because Danchenko never produced any such evidence.

By (i) ignoring the significance of Danchenko's prior status as a subject of a counterespionage investigation, (ii) failing to resolve the conflict between that history and his role as primary sub-source for the Steele reporting, and (iii) failing to follow through on VMU's recommendations for continued operation of Danchenko as a CHS, Helson and the Counterintelligence Division missed another opportunity to make any needed course corrections to Crossfire Hurricane and in the use of Danchenko as a CHS.

d. Danchenko's relationship with Charles Dolan

When interviewed by the FBI in June 2017, Danchenko failed to disclose the role a U.S.-based individual named Charles Dolan played in the reporting Danchenko provided for inclusion in the Steele Reports. In particular, Danchenko denied that Dolan provided any specific information contained in the Steele Reports.[782] However, Dolan acknowledged to the Office that he provided information to Danchenko related to Paul Manafort's firing as Trump campaign

[781] SCO-105290 (Request for required expenses and lump sum payment Electronic Communication dated 10/21/2020).

[782] *Danchenko* Government Exhibit 171T.

manager.[783] Dol[illegible] [illegible]nitte[illegible] [illegible]tion, which appears in Steele Report 2016/10[illegible] [illegible]ed.[7[illegible]]

As disc[illegible] [illegible]vious [illegible] [illegible] 2016 Rome meeting, Steele provided the FB[illegible] [illegible]es o[illegible] [illegible] who might have information on Trump's conne[illegible] [illegible]. Th[illegible] [illegible] Steele were Washington, D.C.-based individua[illegible] [illegible]an, [illegible] [illegible]-2.[785] An FBI report of a September 18th [illegible] inter[illegible] [illegible]ntioned that Danchenko had drinks with Dol[illegible] [illegible] port i[illegible] [illegible]rthe[illegible] [illegible] on that topic.[786] In the same interview, howe[illegible] [illegible]o sta[illegible] [illegible] the "American political figure associated with [illegible] [illegible] and [illegible] [illegible]" [illegible] in the following paragraph of Steele Report 2[illegible]

> Speakin[illegible] [illegible] also i[illegible] [illegible] 201[illegible] [illegible]can political figure associat[illegible] [illegible] TR[illegible] [illegible]ned the reasons behind Paul Ma[illegible] [illegible]dem[illegible] [illegible] the Ukraine corruption revelati[illegible] [illegible] a par[illegible] [illegible] al[illegible] [illegible]ior players close to TRUM[illegible] [illegible]Mana[illegible] [illegible]is control on strategy and policy f[illegible] [illegible]f par[illegible] [illegible]ard was Manafort's predece[illegible] [illegible]ign m[illegible] [illegible] who hated Manafort persona[illegible] [illegible]d cl[illegible] [illegible] discussed the presiden[illegible] [illegible]on a [illegible].[788]

The foll[illegible] [illegible]disc[illegible] [illegible] role in the Steele reporting and his relationship [illegible] [illegible]nko.

*i. [illegible] Dolan*

Charles [illegible] [illegible]blic r[illegible] [illegible] 2016 was employed by a Washington, D.[illegible] [illegible]c rel[illegible] [illegible] In addition to his work as a public relations [illegible] Dola[illegible] [illegible] Executive Director of the Democratic Go[illegible] [illegible]ation, [illegible] [illegible]ormer President Clinton's 1992 and 1996 presid[illegible] [illegible]igns, a[illegible] [illegible]dvis[illegible] Clinton's 2008 presidential

---

[783] *Danchenko* [illegible] AM [illegible]

[784] *Danchenko* [illegible] AM [illegible]

[785] SCO-02013[illegible] [illegible] Aut[illegible] [illegible]nt-1, Moffa, & Strzok dated 10/04/2016) at [illegible]

[786] SCO-00631[illegible] [illegible] Chr[illegible] [illegible] 2017) at 3.

[787] *Id.* at 17.

[788] SCO-10508[illegible] [illegible]Kno[illegible] [illegible] "Steele Dossier") at 18-19, (Company Inte[illegible] [illegible] 201[illegible] [illegible]tal[illegible] [illegible]ginal).

[789] *Danchenko* [illegible] AM [illegible] 97:[illegible] [illegible]rt of Interview of Charles Dolan on Aug. 31, 20[illegible]

campaign.[790] Moreover, beginning in 1997, President Clinton appointed Dolan to two four-year terms on the State Department's U.S. Advisory Commission on Public Diplomacy.[791] With respect to the 2016 Clinton campaign, Dolan described himself as a "door to door" guy in New Hampshire who did not hold any significant position.[792]

*ii. Dolan's connections to the Kremlin*

In his role as a public relations professional, Dolan spent much of his career interacting with Eurasian clients with a particular focus on Russia. For example, from approximately 1999 through 2004-2005, Dolan was employed by global public relations firm Ketchum Inc. where he assisted with Ketchum's representation of the Russian Federation.[793] Part of Dolan's responsibility on the Russian Federation account consisted of, among other things, monitoring current policy discussions of U.S.-based think tanks and reporting back to the Russian government.[794] Dolan also assisted in media consulting and press operations for the 2006 G8 Summit held in St. Petersburg, Russia.[795] As a senior member of Ketchum's Russian Federation team, Dolan frequently interacted with Russian government officials, including, most importantly, Dimitry Peskov, Press Secretary of the Russian Presidential Administration, and Alex Pavlov, Deputy Press Secretary of the Presidential Administration.[796] Peskov has often been described in media reports as Russian President Putin's "right-hand man."[797] As discussed more below, both Peskov and Pavlov would subsequently feature prominently in the Steele Reports.[798] Additionally, Dolan maintained relationships with Sergei Kislyak, who served as Russian Ambassador to the United States from 2008-2017, and Mikhail Kalugin, the head of the Russian Embassy's Economic Section in Washington, D.C. from 2010-2016. Both Kislyak and Kalugin would also feature prominently in the Steele Reports.[799]

---

[790] *Danchenko* Tr. 10/13/2022 AM at 590:6-592:12; OSC Report of Interview of Charles Dolan on Aug. 31, 2021 at 1.

[791] SCID_00013647 (Charles Dolan kglobal biography).

[792] OSC Report of Interview of Charles Dolan on Nov. 1, 2021 at 1.

[793] OSC Report of Interview of Charles Dolan on Aug. 31, 2021 at 1-2; *Danchenko* Tr. 10/13/2022 AM at 592:14-593:14.

[794] OSC Report of Interview of Charles Dolan on Aug. 31, 2021 at 1-2.

[795] *Id.*

[796] OSC Report of Interview of Charles Dolan on Aug. 31, 2021 at 2; *Danchenko* Tr. 10/13/2022 AM at 593:18-594:21.

[797] Mick Krever, *Putin Aide Predicts Relations 'Renaissance' . . . If Russian 'National Interests' Respected*, CNN (Feb. 27, 2015).

[798] Annotated Steele Dossier at 3, 4, 8, 9, 19, 20.

[799] *Id.* at 15, 19.

*iii. Dolan is introduced to Danchenko in early 2016*

In March 2016, Brookings Fellow-1 introduced Dolan to Danchenko in connection with a potential business opportunity.[800] Specifically, Danchenko had reached out to Brookings Fellow-1 in an attempt to broker business between a U.S.-based public relations firm and his longtime friend, Olga Galkina, an executive at a Cyprus-based computer firm named Servers.com.[801] Danchenko would later inform the FBI that Galkina served as a source of information for allegations contained in the Steele Reports.[802] Brookings Fellow-1 subsequently connected Danchenko and Dolan to discuss a possible business venture between Dolan and Servers.com. In March 2016, Danchenko brokered a meeting between Dolan (and his firm kglobal) and Galkina to discuss a potential business arrangement between kglobal and Servers.com, the latter of which was attempting to enter the U.S. marketplace.[803] Dolan was joined at this meeting by a Washington-based lobbyist ("U.S. Person-2") with whom Dolan had previously worked[804] – and who Steele would later name along with Dolan as a possible source for information on Trump/Russia connections.

Dolan and kglobal would ultimately enter a contractual relationship with Servers.com.[805] As discussed in detail below, Dolan traveled to Cyprus on two occasions in the summer of 2016 to meet with Galkina, Aleksej Gubarev (the principal of Servers.com) and other executives at Servers.com.[806] As a result of this collaboration, Dolan and Danchenko continued to communicate through the Spring of 2016.

In late April 2016, Dolan and Danchenko engaged in separate discussions regarding a potential business collaboration between kglobal and Orbis. For example, on April 29, 2016, Danchenko sent an email to Dolan indicating that Danchenko had passed a letter to Christopher Steele on behalf of Dolan.[807] Specifically, the email sent to Dolan stated that Danchenko had "forwarded your letter" to Steele and Steele's business partner, Christopher Burrows. The email continued, "I'll make sure you gentlemen meet when they are in Washington, or when you are in London." That same day, Danchenko sent an email to Dolan outlining certain work that

---

[800] OSC Report of Interview of Charles Dolan on Aug. 31, 2021 at 2; SCID_00007741 (Email from Danchenko to Dolan dated 03/08/2016).

[801] SCID_00007741 (Email from Danchenko to Dolan dated 03/10/2016). According to their website, Servers.com provides access to computer servers in data centers throughout the world.

[802] SCO-005801 (Interview of Igor Danchenko Electronic Communication dated 02/09/2017) at 16.

[803] SCID_00007741 (Email from Danchenko to Dolan dated 03/10/2016); SCID_00017834 (Email from Galkina to Dolan, U.S. Person-2 on 03/24/2016).

[804] OSC Report of Interview of Charles Dolan on Aug. 31, 2021 at 3

[805] *Id.*

[806] *Id.*

[807] SCID_00006415 (Email from Danchenko to Dolan dated 04/29/2016).

Danchenko was conducting for Orbis. The email attached an Orbis report titled "Intelligence Briefing Note, 'Kompromat' and 'Nadzor' in the Russian Banking Sector."[808]

Beginning in early 2015, a Washington, D.C.-based lawyer and acquaintance of Dolan, ("U.S. Person-1") informed Dolan that he was planning a business conference for October 2016 in Moscow.[809] The conference, titled "Inside the Kremlin," was being sponsored by the Young President's Organization, and was designed to introduce senior international business executives to potential investment opportunities in Russia (the "YPO Conference").[810] To that end, the YPO Conference was to include individuals who could provide insight into the economic, political, diplomatic and cultural aspects of the Russian Federation. The YPO Conference was to be held at the Ritz Carlton hotel in Moscow.[811] U.S. Person-1 enlisted Dolan to participate in the YPO conference because of Dolan's access to senior Russian government officials and his ability to provide analysis of the approaching 2016 U.S. presidential election.[812]

In April 2016, Dolan asked Danchenko to assist Dolan and U.S. Person-1 with the YPO conference, which Danchenko agreed to do.[813] Dolan believed that Danchenko's language skills and his supposed contacts in the Russian government would be of assistance to the conference.[814] Dolan subsequently asked and received permission from U.S. Person-1 to enlist Danchenko to assist with logistics, provide translation services, and present on various relevant topics at the YPO Conference.[815] In preparation for the YPO Conference, Dolan and U.S. Person-1 planned to travel to Moscow in June 2016 to view the Ritz Carlton and other potential sites for the conference (the "June Planning Trip").[816] At the same time, Danchenko informed Dolan that he (Danchenko) would be present in Moscow in June on other business.[817]

On April 30, 2016, Dolan sent an email to a U.S.-based acquaintance and stated, in part, the following:

> Waiting on confirmation for meetings with the Kremlin. If all goes well I will probably leave on the 9th [June] and stop in London to meet with these intelligence guys (another potential project but nothing certain) and leave on the 10th for Moscow and stay for the week.[818]

---

808 SCID_00016038 (Email from Danchenko to Dolan, U.S. Person-2 dated 04/29/2016).

809 SCID_00017536 (Email from U.S. Person-1 to Dolan, others dated 02/11/2015).

810 SCID_00014254 (Email from Dolan to U.S. Person-1 dated 02/12/2015).

811 SCID_00017536 (Email from U.S. Person-1 to Dolan, others dated 02/11/2015) at 2.

812 OSC Report of Interview of U.S. Person-1 on Apr. 13, 2021 at 1-2.

813 SCID_00014427 (Email from Dolan to Danchenko dated 04/11/2016); SCID_00015922 (Email from Danchenko to Dolan dated 04/22/2016).

814 *Danchenko* Tr. 10/13/2022 AM at 610:23 – 611:3.

815 *Danchenko* Tr. 10/13/2022 AM at 611:4-8; 640:1-641:15.

816 SCID_00016172 (Email from U.S. Person-1 to Dolan, others dated 05/21/2016).

817 SCID_00006540 (Email from Danchenko to Dolan dated 06/03/2016).

818 SCID_00004759 (Email from Dolan dated 04/30/2016).

In his in[illegible] the C[illegible] de[illegible] with Steele.[819] Travel records confirm that D[illegible] avel to [illegible] ior t[illegible] anning Trip.[820] In fact, the Office was not [illegible] y def[illegible] nce [illegible] hat Dolan ever met with Steele.

To furth[illegible] the [illegible] nce, [illegible], and October 2016, Dolan and U.S. Person-1 [illegible] t thr[illegible] at th[illegible] mbassy in Washington, D.C., and communicated [illegible] Emba[illegible] ludin[illegible] dor Sergei Kislyak and the Head of the Economi[illegible] hail K[illegible] As [illegible] both Kislyak and Kalugin would feature promin[illegible] Steele Re[illegible] chel[illegible] present at any of these meetings.

In antici[illegible] June [illegible] p to [illegible] olan attempted to communicate with Press Sec[illegible] and D[illegible] Sec[illegible], as well as former Russian President and th[illegible] rister [illegible] dved[illegible] n had previously attended several lunches with M[illegible] he ([illegible] d as [illegible] the Valdai Club in connection with his work a[illegible] (The [illegible] is [illegible] ased think tank that is closely associated with [illegible] ident P[illegible] view[illegible] in the West as a vehicle for Russian propag[illegible] 2016 [illegible] che[illegible] vedev's Press Secretary to have Medvedev spea[illegible] Conf[illegible]

When in[illegible] the FBI [illegible] mber [illegible] noted that his primary sub-source (Danche[illegible] source[illegible] acce[illegible] Peskov.[825] In particular, Steele stated that info[illegible] Repo[illegible] Pes[illegible] d from a "friend of a friend" of his primary sub[illegible] chenk[illegible] in th[illegible], Steele informed the FBI that his primary sub-so[illegible] sub-sour[illegible] cont[illegible] key Pavlov and had conversations with Pavlov ab[illegible] Stee[illegible] FBI th[illegible] entified source was close to then-Russian Prime M[illegible] try M[illegible] (As [illegible] above, Dolan claimed to have met Medvedev on s[illegible] ns.) [illegible] tated [illegible] mary sub-source (Danchenko)

---

819 OSC Repor[illegible] of Ch[illegible] on A[illegible] at 6.

820 U.S. Custom[illegible] Prote[illegible] En[illegible] for Charles Dolan at 1.

821 SCID_0001[illegible] from U[illegible] to [illegible] gin, others dated 05/31/2016); SCID_00016[illegible] U.S. [illegible] Do[illegible] ated 07/15/2016); SCID_00017[illegible] Kalugi[illegible] on-1, [illegible] ers dated 10/14/2016).

822 SCO-00567[illegible] Dola[illegible] 05-2[illegible] Report of Interview of Charles Dolan on Sept. [illegible] SCID_[illegible] (Em[illegible] an to U.S. Person-1 dated 09/30/2016); S[illegible] 33 (Em[illegible] olan [illegible] on-1 dated 06/03/2016); SCID_00014[illegible] Dol[illegible] y 19

823 KG_00020[illegible] Dol[illegible] 28/20[illegible]

824 SCID_0001[illegible] from D[illegible] 05[illegible]

825 SCO-00631[illegible] of Chri[illegible] ele o[illegible] 2017) at 6.

826 *Id.* at 7.

827 *Id.* at 15.

828 *Id.*

would meet Pavlov for drinks when he (the primary sub-source) traveled to Russia.[829] However, as discussed more fully below, the Office found no information to indicate that Danchenko maintained a relationship with Pavlov.

On June 10, 2016, before traveling abroad, Dolan sent an email to a U.S.-based acquaintance reflecting that Dolan and Danchenko had become colleagues. Dolan stated in part:

> On Monday night I fly to Moscow and will meet with a Russian guy [Danchenko] who is working with me on a couple of projects. He also works for a group of former MI 6 guys in London who do intelligence for businesses. Send me your questions and I'll pass them on to Igor. He owes me as his Visa is being held up and I am having a word with the Ambassador.[830]

Shortly thereafter, Dolan sent another email to the U.S.-based acquaintance. In describing Danchenko, Dolan stated: "He is too young for KGB. But I think he worked for FSB. Since he told me he spent two years in Iran. And when I first met him he knew more about me than I did. [winking emoticon]."[831] (The Federal Security Service of the Russian Federation, or "FSB" is the principal security agency of Russia and principal successor agency to the KGB.) When interviewed by the Office, Dolan stated that he was "speculating" about Danchenko's connections to Russian intelligence, and that he was "half joking and half serious."[832]

Dolan was scheduled to be in Moscow for the June Planning Trip from June 13-18, 2016. In connection with the June Planning Trip, Dolan decided to first travel to Cyprus to meet with executives from Servers.com.[833] Dolan departed Washington, D.C. on June 9th, arrived in Moscow on the morning of June 10th, and departed for Cyprus later that afternoon.[834] While in Cyprus, Dolan met with Galkina, Gubarev and the other executives at Servers.com's offices.[835] Dolan then left Cyprus on June 13th and flew to Moscow to attend the June Planning trip.[836]

During the June Planning Trip, Dolan and U.S. Person-1 stayed at the Ritz Carlton in Moscow.[837] On June 14th, Danchenko, who as noted above was already present in Moscow, met Dolan for lunch at a restaurant in Moscow.[838] Dolan and Danchenko took a photograph together in front of the Kremlin, which was later posted by Danchenko on Facebook.[839] According to Dolan, this was the only time he encountered Danchenko on the June Planning Trip, and

---

829 *Id.* at 14.

830 SCID_00000732 (Email from Dolan dated 06/10/2016).

831 SCID_00000735 (Email from Dolan dated 06/10/2016).

832 OSC Report of Interview of Charles Dolan on Sept. 7, 2021 at 1.

833 SCID_00000653 (Email from Dolan to Galkina dated 06/01/2016).

834 SCID_00000726 (Email from Dolan to U.S. Person-1 dated 06/08/2016).

835 SCID_00008141 (Email from Galkina to Dolan dated 06/13/2016).

836 SCID_00000653 (Email from Dolan to Galkina dated 06/01/2016).

837 SCID_00041378 (Email to Dolan dated 06/09/2016).

838 SCID_00000787 (Email from Dolan to U.S. Person-1 dated 06/14/2016).

839 *Danchenko* Government Exhibit 605.

Danchenko did not stay at the Ritz Carlton during the June Planning Trip – a fact that was confirmed by hotel records.[840]

While in Moscow, Dolan and U.S. Person-1 participated in, among other things, (i) a meeting with the German-national general manager of the Ritz Carlton, and at least one female hotel staff member to discuss the logistics of the YPO Conference, (ii) a lunch with the general manager and three hotel staff members who assisted in the preparations for the YPO conference, and (iii) a tour of the hotel.[841]

Dolan told the Office that during the June Planning Trip he met with two deputies from the Russian Presidential Administration Press Office (Dimitry Peskov's Office).[842] According to Dolan, Danchenko was not present for any events at the Ritz Carlton during the June Planning Trip and was not present for his meeting with the deputies from the Press Office.[843] As discussed in detail below, the general manager and other hotel staff members would later appear in the Steele Reports.

On June 15, 2016, Dolan emailed an acquaintance from Moscow: "I'm in Russia making plans to be adopted in the event this mad man [Trump] gets elected."[844] On June 18, 2016, Dolan returned to Washington, D.C.[845]

*iv. Trump's alleged salacious sexual activity at the Ritz Carlton Moscow appears in a Steele Report*

On June 17, 2016, Danchenko flew from Moscow to London and met with Christopher Steele on the following day.[846] Three days later, in Steele Report 2016/080 dated June 20, 2016, an allegation appeared that described salacious sexual activity that Trump allegedly had participated in while a guest at the Ritz Carlton Moscow. The allegation stated, in part:

> According to Source D, where s/he had been present, TRUMP's (perverted) conduct in Moscow included hiring the presidential suite of the Ritz Carlton, where he knew President and Mrs OBAMA (whom he hated) had stayed on one of their official trips to Russia, and defiling the bed where they had slept by employing a number of prostitutes to perform 'golden showers' (urination) shows in front of him. The hotel was known to be under FSB control with microphones and concealed cameras in all the main rooms to record anything they wanted to.

---

840 OSC Report of Interview of Charles Dolan on Aug. 31, 2021 at 5.

841 OSC Report of Interview of U.S. Person-1 on Apr. 13, 2021 at 3; OSC Report of Interview of Charles Dolan on Aug. 31, 2021 at 5-6.

842 OSC Report of Interview of Charles Dolan on Nov. 1, 2021 at 2.

843 *Id.* at 2.

844 KG_0003739 (Email from Dolan dated 06/15/2016).

845 SCID_00000726 (Email from Dolan to U.S. Person-1 dated 06/08/2016).

846 SCO-007286 (Danchenko Facebook messages dated 06/16 to 06/17/2016); SCO-016761 (Facebook message from Danchenko to Galkina dated 06/18/2016); OIG interview of Christopher Steele on June 5 & 6, 2019 at 45.

> The Ritz Carlton episode involving TRUMP reported above was confirmed by Source E, a senior (western) member of staff at the hotel, who said that s/he and several of the staff were aware of it at the time and subsequently. S/he believed it had happened in 2013. Source E provided an introduction for a company ethnic Russian operative to Source F, a female staffer at the hotel when TRUMP had stayed there, who also confirmed the story.[847]

Certain of the information in the June 20, 2016 Steele Report reflected facts that Dolan learned during the June Planning Trip to Moscow. For example, while at the Ritz Carlton, Dolan (1) received a tour of the hotel and (according to Dolan) possibly the Presidential Suite, and (2) met with the senior Western member of staff – in context the general manager – and other staff of the Ritz Carlton. As noted, Danchenko did not stay at the Ritz Carlton in June 2016, but had lunch with Dolan during the June Planning Trip at some other location.

Notably, when interviewed by the Office, U.S. Person-1 recalled he and Dolan took a tour of the Presidential Suite.[848] Following his initial interview with the Office, Dolan called U.S. Person-1 and U.S. Person-1 confirmed that he (U.S. Person-1) and Dolan had in fact taken a tour of the Presidential Suite.[849] During that tour, a hotel staff member told the participants that Trump had previously been a guest in the Presidential Suite.[850] According to U.S. Person-1, the staff member informed them that Donald Trump had stayed in the Suite, but did not mention any sexual or salacious activity.[851] When interviewed by the Office, Dolan's recollection about taking a tour of the Presidential suite at the Ritz Carlton was inconsistent and his recollection vacillated over the course of several interviews. Dolan stated, in sum, that it was possible that he (Dolan) told Danchenko about the Presidential Suite and Trump, but he had no specific recollection of doing so.[852] Dolan was adamant that he never told Danchenko about any salacious sexual activity that occurred in the suite.[853]

The Office also interviewed the then-general Manager of the Ritz-Carlton Moscow. The general manager, a German citizen who does not speak Russian, was described in the Steele Report as a "senior (western) member of staff at the hotel and identified as "Source E."[854] The general manager did not recognize the photograph of Danchenko he was shown by the Office.[855]

---

[847] SCO-105084 (Documents Known to the FBI Comprising the "Steele Dossier") at 3, (Company Intelligence Report 2016/080).

[848] OSC Report of Interview of U.S. Person-1 on Apr. 13, 2021 at 3.

[849] OSC Report of Interview of Charles Dolan on Nov. 1, 2021 at 1.

[850] OSC Report of Interview of U.S. Person-1 on Apr. 13, 2021 at 3.

[851] *Id.* at 3.

[852] OSC Report of Interview of Charles Dolan on Nov. 1, 2021 at 1.

[853] *Id.*

[854] SCO-105084 (Documents Known to the FBI Comprising the "Steele Dossier") at 3, (Company Intelligence Report 2016/080).

[855] OSC Report of Interview of general manager of the Moscow Ritz Carlton on Aug. 9, 2022 at 4.

He also denied [illegible] ledge [illegible] is concerning Trump at any time prior to their be[illegible] in the [illegible] ral manager adamantly denied discussing such [illegible] with, o[illegible] nko, or anyone else.[857] Further, the Office obtai[illegible] from the [illegible] on [illegible] reveal that Trump was a guest at the hotel in 201[illegible] t stay in [illegible] ental [illegible] or at any other time.[858]

When i[illegible] the FBI [illegible] y 201[illegible] ko claimed that he had sourced this informatio[illegible] le stay[illegible] itz-C[illegible] ow during the June Planning Trip.[859] While [illegible] nitially [illegible] I that [illegible] n a guest at the Ritz-Carlton Moscow during [illegible] rning T[illegible] acknowledged that he had visited, but not stayed a[illegible] uring the [illegible] anchenko also claimed that he inquired about [illegible] on alle[illegible] h [illegible] did not deny their validity.[861] Finally, Danch[illegible] BI th[illegible] ed th[illegible] these hotel staff members to Christopher Ste[illegible] Septe[illegible] inter[illegible] also told the FBI that "Source E" and "Source F" [illegible] ves at [illegible] rlton [illegible] ith whom his primary sub-source [Danchenko] p[illegible].[863] T[illegible] s app[illegible] anchenko provided the general manager's info[illegible] Steele. [illegible] also [illegible] that "Source D" – another purported sour[illegible] Carlt[illegible] s – [illegible] ring to Sergei Millian.[864]

In a sub[illegible] 2017 F[illegible] as an FBI CHS), Danchenko again confirmed [illegible] spoke[illegible] man[illegible] out the Ritz-Carlton allegations.[865] In that intervie[illegible] also [illegible] Sour[illegible] robably one of the hotel managers.[866]

---

[856] *Id.* at 6-7.

[857] *Id.*

[858] SCO-10176[illegible] itz Ca[illegible] ds)

[859] SCO-00580[illegible] of Igor [illegible] Ele[illegible] munication dated 02/09/2017) at 38-39.

[860] Transcript [illegible] h Danc[illegible] May [illegible] 27-29.

[861] SCO-00580[illegible] of Igor [illegible] Ele[illegible] munication dated 02/09/2017) at 39.

[862] *Id.*

[863] SCO-00631[illegible] of Chri[illegible] teele [illegible] 2017) at 14.

[864] However, a[illegible] more [illegible], D[illegible] ld the FBI that his purported first contact with M[illegible] 21, 20[illegible] Dan[illegible] the only Orbis person who reported had c[illegible] Millian, [illegible] on [illegible] ould be a source for the Steele Report dated J[illegible] was a[illegible] ity [illegible] 2 (CHS Reporting Document dated May 18, [illegible].

[865] Transcript [illegible] Dan[illegible] May [illegible] 25-27.

[866] *Id.* at 28.

When interviewed by the FBI in September 2017, Christopher Steele stated that "Source D" was in fact Sergei Millian, an individual who was in direct contact with his primary sub-source [Danchenko].[867] However, given that Danchenko repeatedly told the FBI that the *first* and *only* time he allegedly communicated with someone he thought was Millian was late July 2016 when he received an anonymous call from a male with a Russian accent, it would have been impossible for Millian to have been a source of the Ritz Carlton allegations (and other information) to Danchenko in June 2016. Thus, Danchenko's statements to the FBI about having no previous contact with Millian were false, or Danchenko's statements to Steele about Source D were false, or Steele gave knowingly false information to the FBI.[868]

The Office found the general manager's statement that he never met with Danchenko to be credible, especially in light of his well-spoken, thoughtful demeanor, and his confidence in his recollections.

Based on the above analysis, the only person who met with both Danchenko and the Ritz Carlton general manager (and the other managers) during the June Planning Trip was Dolan.

The same Steele Report (2016/080) that contained the Ritz Carlton allegations also contained the following allegation:

> Continuing on this theme, Source G, a senior Kremlin official, confided that the CLINTON dossier was controlled exclusively by senior Kremlin spokesman, Dimitry PESKOV, on the direct instructions of Putin himself. The dossier had not been made available, as yet, inter alia, to any foreigners, including TRUMP and his inner circle. However, PUTIN's intentions with regard to the dossier and future dissemination remained unclear.[869]

When interviewed by the FBI in September 2017, Steele identified "Source G" as Alexey Pavlov[870] – the Deputy Press Secretary for the Russian Presidential Administration. Steele stated, in sum, that this information was collected by his primary sub-source (Danchenko) during a trip to Russia, which, given the date of the Report, would coincide with his June 2016 trip and Dolan's June Planning Trip.

The FBI appears to have never addressed this particular allegation with Danchenko or explored whether Danchenko maintained a relationship with Alexey Pavlov. The Office has not seen any independent evidence to indicate that Danchenko had a relationship with Pavlov. As discussed above, Dolan, however, did have a relationship with Pavlov. Leading up to the June Planning Trip, Dolan attempted to contact Pavlov on several occasions.[871] Dolan, however, stated that he could not recall if he connected with Pavlov prior to or during the June Planning

[867] SCO-006313 (Interview of Christopher Steele on Sept. 18, 2017 at 14).

[868] As discussed below, the Crossfire Hurricane team appears to have never endeavored to resolve this question.

[869] SCO-105084 (Documents Known to the FBI Comprising the "Steele Dossier") at 4, (Company Intelligence Report 2016/080).

[870] SCO-006313 (Interview of Christopher Steele on Sept. 18, 2017) at 14.

[871] SCO-005678 (Email from Dolan dated 06/03/2016); SCID_00000790 (Email from Dolan to Galkina dated 06/14/2016).

Trip.[872] In light of these facts, there appears to be a real likelihood that Dolan was the actual source of much of the Ritz Carlton and Pavlov information contained in the Steele Reports.

*v. Dolan returns to Cyprus in July 2016*

Following the June Planning Trip, Dolan returned to Washington, D.C. where he continued to communicate with both Danchenko and Galkina. In July 2016, Dolan returned to Cyprus to meet with Galkina, Gubarev and other executives at Servers.com.[873] Curiously, Steele was in Cyprus at the same time Dolan was meeting with Galkina and others in Cyprus.[874]

During this July trip and continuing through the fall of 2016, Dolan and Galkina communicated regularly via telephone, email and social media. In several of these communications, Dolan and Galkina discussed their political views, support for Clinton, and Galkina's future employment. For example, during the July 2016 meetings in Cyprus, Dolan gave Galkina an autobiography of Clinton, which he signed and inscribed with the handwritten message, "To my good friend Olga, A Great Democrat."[875] On July 13, 2016, Galkina sent a message to a Russia-based associate and stated that Dolan had written a letter to Dimitry Peskov, the Russian Press Secretary, in support of Galkina's candidacy for a position in the Russian Presidential Administration.[876] In his interviews with the Office, Dolan did not recall the specific position Galkina was referring to, and noted that it was "possible" that he reached out to Peskov on behalf of Galkina, but had no specific recollection of doing so.[877]

On July 22, 2016, Dolan sent an email to Galkina and informed her that he would be attending a reception for Hillary Clinton. Shortly thereafter, Galkina responded: "[T]ell her please she [Clinton] has a big fan in [city name], Cyprus. Can I please ask you to sign for me her (anything)."[878] In August 2016, Galkina sent a message to a Russia-based associate describing Dolan as an "advisor" to Hillary Clinton.[879] Galkina further commented regarding what might happen if Clinton were to win the U.S. presidential election, stating in Russian, "[W]hen Dolan takes me off to the State Department [to handle] issues of the former USSR, then we'll see who is looking good and who is not."[880] In September 2016, Galkina made a similar comment in a

---

872 OSC Report of Interview of Charles Dolan on Aug. 31, 2021 at 4; OSC Report of Interview of Charles Dolan on Sept. 7, 2021 at 2.

873 OSC Report of Interview of Charles Dolan on Aug. 31, 2021 at 3; *Danchenko* Tr. 10/13/2022 AM at 614:3-17.

874 Doc. ID 0.7.23326.102657 (Email from Steele to Bruce Ohr dated 07/01/2016). As discussed more below, SA Kevin Helson speculated that Charles Dolan may have directly communicated with Christopher Steele. The Office, however, uncovered no evidence to support this speculation.

875 SCO-002223 (Galkina Facebook messages dated 07/21/2016).

876 SCO-002228 (Galkina Facebook messages dated 07/13/2016).

877 OSC Report of Interview of Charles Dolan on Nov. 1, 2021 at 2.

878 SCO_002190 (Email from Galkina to Dolan dated July 22, 2016)

879 SCO_002235 (Galkina Facebook messages dated Aug. 21, 2016).

880 *Id.*

message to the same associate, stating in Russian that Dolan would "take me to the State Department if Hillary wins."[881]

On October 15, 2016, Galkina communicated with a Russia-based journalist and stated that because of her [Galkina] "acquaintance with Chuck Dolan and several citizens from the Russian presidential administration," Galkina knew "something and can tell a little about it by voice."[882]

On November 7, 2016 (the day before the 2016 U.S. Presidential election), Galkina emailed Dolan in English and stated, in part:

> I am preparing you some information on former USSR/UIC countries, Igor [Danchenko] possibly told you about that . . . . Tomorrow your country is having a great day, so, as a big Hillary fan, I wish her and all her supporters to have a Victory day. Hope, that someday her book will have one more autograph on it).
>
> Thank you for your help and support,
>
> Best regards,
>
> Olga[883]

When initially interviewed by the Office, Dolan stated that Galkina was the "last person" with whom he would ever discuss U.S. politics.[884] However, in a subsequent interview when confronted with emails and social media messages with Galkina evincing communications about Clinton and the 2016 U.S. presidential election, Dolan admitted that he had some discussions with Galkina about the 2016 election and her support for Clinton.[885] However, in an August 2017 FBI interview, Galkina stated, in sum, that she discussed some of the information contained in the Steele Reports with Dolan.[886] Despite Galkina's identification of Dolan as someone with whom she discussed the Steele Reports, and the fact that Dolan resided in the Washington, D.C. area, the FBI failed to interview Dolan about Galkina's statements concerning the Steele Reports.

*vi. Dolan is a source for certain information in a Steele Report*

At least one allegation contained in a Steele Report dated August 22, 2016 (2016/105), reflected information that Danchenko collected directly from Charles Dolan. In particular, that Report detailed the August 2016 resignation of Trump's campaign manager Manafort and his allegedly strained relationship with Corey Lewandowski. The allegation in the Steele Report stated:

---

[881] SCO_002238 (Galkina Facebook messages dated Sept. 2, 2016).

[882] SCO_076721 (Galkina Facebook messages dated Oct. 15, 2016).

[883] SCID_00001417 (Email from Galkina to Dolan dated 11/07/2016).

[884] OSC Report of Interview of Charles Dolan on Aug. 31, 2021 at 3.

[885] OSC Report of Interview of Charles Dolan on Nov. 1, 2021 at 2.

[886] *Danchenko* Tr. 10/14/2022 AM at 977:3-13.

> Close as [illegible] UMP [illegible] son [illegible] MANAFORT's recent resignati [illegible] revelati [illegible] par [illegible] wanted MANAFORT out for vario [illegible] special [illegible] DC [illegible] remains influential . . . . Speaking [illegible] also in [illegible] 201 [illegible] can political figure associat [illegible] TR [illegible] ned the reasons behind MANAF [illegible] dem [illegible] d it [illegible] the Ukraine corruption revelatio [illegible] d a part [illegible] also, [illegible] ior players close to TRUMP [illegible] MANAF [illegible] prin [illegible] sen his control on strategy and polic [illegible] Of [illegible] mpor [illegible] regard was MANAF [illegible] ecesso [illegible] y LEWANDOWSKI, who hat [illegible] RT pe [illegible] rem [illegible] to TRUMP with whom he discu [illegible] entia [illegible] on a [illegible] s.[887]

This Steele Rep [illegible] nform [illegible] Danc [illegible] gathered directly from Dolan in response to a sp [illegible] In pa [illegible] Aug [illegible], Danchenko emailed Dolan to solicit any "thou [illegible] allega [illegible] Pa [illegible]. In the email, Danchenko also informed Dolan [illegible] chenko [illegible] ing [illegible] against Trump":

> Could yo [illegible] ome [illegible] nafort's resignation and anything [illegible] npaign [illegible] rece [illegible]. Any thought, rumor, allegatio [illegible] ng o [illegible] roje [illegible] mp. I asked [U.S. Person-2 [illegible] is ag [illegible] n't sa [illegible] ough shared a couple of valuabl [illegible]
>
> Thanks [illegible]
>
> Best,
>
> Igor[888]

Danchen [illegible] U.S. P [illegible] Re [illegible] yist and acquaintance of Dolan, who was presen [illegible] g be [illegible] March 2016 regarding the proposed busin [illegible] ween [illegible] Sa [illegible] n connection with a voluntary interview by th [illegible] Perso [illegible] d a [illegible] appears to be referenced by Danchenko abo [illegible] ted, in [illegible]

> I have a [illegible] t Vik [illegible] vic [illegible] Firtash, former Ukrainian presiden [illegible] gas oli [illegible] ctiv [illegible] e Russian oligarchs. The relation [illegible] ed, fo [illegible] here [illegible] dress].
>
> My ques [illegible]
>
> My frien [illegible] [in c [illegible] le] i [illegible] at a number of oligarchs, includin [illegible] ska, [illegible] rim [illegible] try Firtash made certain investm [illegible] S. rea [illegible] be [illegible] . . . And that then they made va [illegible] "go [illegible] ents [illegible] dently in the summer of 2008, ju [illegible] p to t [illegible] ial a [illegible] re Mr. Manafort and also

---

[887] SCO-10508 [illegible] s Know [illegible] H C [illegible] "Steele Dossier") at 18-19, (Company Inte [illegible] rt 2016 [illegible] italiz [illegible] ginal).

[888] SCID_0000 [illegible] from D [illegible] o Do [illegible] 8/19/2016).

> Richard Davis were working for the Republican candidate. Was that the case? What were they trying to achieve? Can these payments- if existed – be viewed as political contributions? I understand it is a sensitive question. I'll be happy to discuss it or other perhaps more general things over a coffee at any time. At my end, I'll be happy to share insights on Russia/FSU.
>
> Thanks a lot!
>
> Kind Regards,
>
> Igor[889]

When interviewed by the FBI in September 2017, Steele stated that his initial entrée into U.S. election-related material dealt with Paul Manafort's connections to Russian and Ukrainian oligarchs. In particular, Steele told the FBI that Manafort owed significant money to these oligarchs and several other Russians.[890] At this time, Steele was working for a different client, Russian oligarch Oleg Deripaska, often referred to as "Putin's Oligarch" in media reporting, on a separate litigation-related issue.[891] This information comports with Danchenko's inquiries to U.S. Person-2 in April 2016. As mentioned above, U.S. Person-2's name was provided by Steele during his October 2016 interview with the FBI as an individual who would have information regarding Trump's connections to Russia.

In any event, on August 19th, Dolan replied to Danchenko, stating in part:

> Let me dig around on Manafort. Pretty sure the new team wanted him gone asap and used today's NYT story to drive a stake in his heart.[892]

On August 20, 2016, Dolan emailed Danchenko the following:

> Hi Igor:
>
> I had a drink with a GOP friend of mine who knows some of the players and got some of what is in this article, which provides even more detail. She also told me that Corey Lewandowski, who hates Manafort and still speaks to Trump regularly played a role. He is said to be doing a happy dance over it. I think the bottom line is that in addition to the Ukraine revelations, a number of people wanted Manafort gone. It is a very sharp elbows crowd.[893]

Dolan attached to the email a link to a *Politico* news article that discussed Manafort's resignation as Trump's campaign manager.[894] Later that day, Danchenko replied to Dolan

---

889 SCO-061675 (Email from Danchenko to U.S. Person-2 dated 04/18/2016).

890 SCO-006313 (Interview of Christopher Steele on Sept. 18, 2017) at 6.

891 Kenneth P. Vogel & Matthew Rosenberg, *Agents Tried to Flip Russian Oligarchs. The Fallout Spread to Trump*, N.Y. Times (Sept. 1, 2018).

892 SCID_00000936 (Email from Dolan to Danchenko dated 08/19/2016).

893 SCID_00000941 (Email from Dolan to Danchenko dated 08/20/2016).

894 Kenneth P. Vogel & Marc Caputo, *Inside the fall of Paul Manafort*, Politico (Aug. 19, 2016).

expressing his appreciation for the information, and stating that their "goals clearly coincide[d]" with regard to Danchenko's efforts to gather derogatory information about Trump.

> Dear Chuck,
>
> Thank you for this. Any additional insights will be much appreciated. It is an important project for me, and our goals clearly coincide. I've been following the Russia trail in Trump's campaign. It is there so what you read in the news is hardly an exaggeration. Some things are less dramatic while others are more than they seem.[895]

Dolan replied to Danchenko with the following: "Thanks! I'll let you know if I hear anything else."[896]

Dolan provided this information regarding Manafort to Danchenko two days before it appeared in the August 22, 2016 Steele Report (2016/105). As reflected above, the information provided by Dolan was substantially the same as the information contained in that Steele Report. In particular: (i) Dolan claimed to have received the information from a "GOP friend," whom the Steele Report describes as a "close associate of Trump"; (ii) in his email, Dolan referred to "Ukraine revelations" about Manafort, which the Steele Report also refers to as the "Ukraine corruption revelations"; (iii) Dolan's email stated that "a number of people wanted Manafort gone," and the Steele Report similarly stated that "several senior players close to TRUMP had wanted Manafort out"; and (iv) Dolan's email stated that "Corey Lewandowski, who hates Manafort and still speaks to Trump regularly played a role" in Manafort's departure, and the Steele Report similarly stated that Manafort's departure was due to "Corey Lewandowski, who hated Manafort personally and remained close to TRUMP."

When interviewed by the Office, Dolan later acknowledged that he never met with a "GOP friend" in relation to the information that he passed to Danchenko but, rather, fabricated the fact of the meeting in his communications with Danchenko.[897] Dolan instead obtained the information about Manafort from public news sources.[898]

According to Dolan, he was not aware at the time of the specifics of Danchenko's "project against Trump," or that Danchenko's reporting would later appear in the Steele Reports.[899] Dolan agreed that the information about Manafort contained in Steele Report 2016/105 appeared to be based on the information he provided to Danchenko.[900] Dolan, however, denied that he had knowingly provided any additional information to Danchenko that appeared in the Steele Reports, but acknowledged that it was possible that he could have been an

---

895 SCID_00006677 (Email from Danchenko to Dolan dated 08/20/2016).

896 SCID_00000938 (Email from Dolan to Danchenko dated 08/20/2016).

897 OSC Report of Interview of Charles Dolan on Nov. 1, 2021 at 3.

898 *Id.*

899 OSC Report of Interview of Charles Dolan on Nov. 1, 2021 at 1; OSC Report of Interview of Charles Dolan on Aug. 31, 2021 at 7; *Danchenko* Tr. 10/13/2022 AM at 641.

900 OSC Report of Interview of Charles Dolan on Sept. 7, 2021 at 2.

unwitting source for the Reports.[901] Nevertheless, as discussed below, Dolan appears to have had access to substantially similar information to that which would later appear in other Steele Reports as well.

*vii. The Kalugin allegation in Steele Report 2016/111*

For example, in connection with the YPO Conference, Dolan and U.S. Person-1 met with Russian Ambassador Sergei Kislyak and Russian diplomat Kalugin, the head of the Russian Embassy's Economic Section in Washington. These meetings took place in May, July, and October 2016.[902] According to Dolan, Danchenko was not present at these meetings.[903] Following the meeting on May 31, 2016, a member of Kalugin's staff, Maria Antonova, sent an email to Dolan and U.S. Person-1 telling them that, among other things, Kalugin would be returning to Moscow in September 2016 and would be replaced by another diplomat, Andrey Bondarev. Specifically, Antonova wrote:

> Mikhail [Kalugin] assumes that the right contact point at the MFA could be Mr. Andrey Bondarev who is the Deputy Head of Economic Section at the Ministry's Department of North America. Andrey will be replacing Mikhail here as the Head of Economic Office this September so it may be useful to start working with him now. Though, we need to double-check first whether he will be in Moscow during your visit. We will get back to you when we have a reply.[904]

Danchenko was not a recipient of the email. On August 19, 2016, Kalugin sent an email to Dolan and others. The email stated, in part:

> Dear Colleagues and Friends,
>
> After six years of Foreign Service in Washington, it feels very timely now to bid farewell and go back home to Moscow for embarking on my new endeavors.
>
> [...]
>
> Let me also take this opportunity and introduce you [to] the new Head of Economic Office, Counselor Mr. Andrey Bondarev. Many of you may remember that Mr. Bondarev since his previous appointment at the Embassy a couple of years ago. Andrey is a talented diplomat and economist with impressive experience in American studies. I'm glad to leave you in a such a good company and have no doubts that you will find common ground very soon.[905]

Again, Danchenko was not a recipient of this email.

---

901 OSC Report of Interview of Charles Dolan on Nov. 1, 2021 at 3.

902 SCID_00016319 (Email from U.S. Person-1 to Dolan, Kalugin, others dated 05/31/2016); SCID_00016626 (Email from U.S. Person-1 to Dolan, others dated 07/15/2016); SCID_00017124 (Email to Kalugin, U.S. Person-1, Dolan, others dated 10/14/2016).

903 OSC Report of Interview of Charles Dolan on Nov. 1, 2021 at 1-2.

904 SCID_00016319 (Email from U.S. Person-1 to Dolan, Kalugin, others dated 05/31/2016).

905 SCO-002194 (Email from Kalugin to various recipients dated 08/19/2016).

A Steele [illegible] d Septem [illegible] contained the following allegation:

> [S]peaki [illegible] y to the [illegible] patri [illegible] Russian MFA official
> reported [illegible] hylac [illegible] a [illegible] a diplomat, Mikhail
> Kalugin, [illegible] ithdra [illegible] shi [illegible] notice because Moscow
> feared [illegible] vement [illegible] pre [illegible] tion operation, including
> the so-c [illegible] pers [illegible] eport [illegible] y), would be exposed in
> the med [illegible] eplac [illegible] rei B [illegible] wever was clean in this
> regard.[illegible]

This alle [illegible] substa [illegible] es [illegible] on that Dolan received in May
and August 201 [illegible] n Em [illegible] M [illegible] a and Kalugin himself, insofar as
Dolan was awa [illegible] in was b [illegible] ced [illegible]. Further, records obtained by the
Office revealed [illegible] ache [illegible] chen [illegible] mber 13, 2016 – the day prior to
the date of the [illegible].[907] C [illegible] the [illegible] enko was initially in Russia but
later traveled t [illegible]

When i [illegible] the F [illegible] y 201 [illegible] nko stated that he had known
Kalugin since 2 [illegible] enk [illegible] to le [illegible] mation about Kalugin's departure
from Kalugin [illegible] the di [illegible] alleg [illegible] g Danchenko in obtaining a new
Russian passpo [illegible] ko fur [illegible] hat [illegible] ribed his replacement, Andrey
Bondarev, as a [illegible] g guy. [illegible] nko [illegible] that his conversation with Kalugin
took place in la [illegible] 6 – w [illegible] pen [illegible] same time in which Dolan
received the em [illegible] bassy [illegible] Ar [illegible] ating that Kalugin was being
replaced in the [illegible] e.[911]

A revie [illegible] ko's [illegible] ds, a [illegible] cial media accounts do not
indicate that D [illegible] ntain [illegible] ship [illegible] n. Moreover, during the January
2017 interview [illegible] provi [illegible] with [illegible] card for Kalugin.[912] The business
card contained [illegible] cell p [illegible] When interviewed by the Office,
Dolan identifie [illegible] iting o [illegible] ss ca [illegible] n.[913]

When S [illegible] erview [illegible] B [illegible] 2017, he stated, in sum, that
Danchenko tol [illegible] (Danch [illegible] learn [illegible] alugin information after bumping

---

[906] SCO-10508 [illegible] s known [illegible] d co [illegible] "Steele Dossier") at 20-22,
(Company Inte [illegible] t 20 [illegible]

[907] AT&T Reco [illegible] /201 [illegible] ords [illegible] ration of only 16 seconds).

[908] SCO-00730 [illegible] Face [illegible] dated [illegible]).

[909] SCO-00580 [illegible] of Igo [illegible] Ele [illegible] munication dated 02/09/2017) at
25.

[910] *Id.* at 27-28.

[911] *Id.* at 26.

[912] SCO-00586 [illegible] of Igo [illegible] Ele [illegible] munication dated 02/09/2017 1A)
at 4.

[913] OSC Repor [illegible] of Ch [illegible] en [illegible] at 2.

into Kalugin on a Moscow street in August 2016 – which was the same time that Dolan received the email from Kalugin indicating that he was leaving for Moscow and being replaced by Andrey Bondarev.[914] However, the Office's investigation has revealed that Danchenko was present in the United States during the entire month of August 2016.[915]

Steele further told the FBI that the information contained in Report 2016/111 was derived from his primary sub-source's [Danchenko's] direct contact with multiple sub-sources.[916] These sub-sources included Alexey Pavlov [Deputy Press Secretary of the Russian Presidential Administration], senior Ministry of Foreign Affairs personnel, and two other unidentified individuals.[917] Steele did not identify the two other individuals. However, as noted above, (i) Charles Dolan maintained a relationship with Alexey Pavlov; (ii) had attempted to reach out to Pavlov in connection with the YPO Conference; and (iii) had met with two deputies from the Press Office during the June Planning Trip. Again, the Office found no evidence showing that Danchenko met directly with Pavlov or had previously maintained a relationship with Pavlov. Indeed, in the months leading up to the YPO conference, it was Dolan – not Danchenko – who had reached out to Pavlov on behalf of both YPO and Olga Galkina.[918] Dolan informed the Office that he would be surprised if Galkina had any contacts in the Kremlin.[919]

When initially interviewed by the Office, Dolan stated, in sum, that he was unsure if he told Danchenko about Kalugin being replaced by Bondarev, but that he had no specific recollection of doing so.[920] In a later interview, Dolan stated, in sum, that he believed there was a low probability that he mentioned the Kalugin departure to Danchenko, but that he could not completely rule out the possibility.[921]

Nevertheless, on February 9, 2018, Dolan sent the following email to three U.S.-based acquaintances:

> Dear boy – you must pay attention. Unlike your pal the short lived National Security Advisor General Flynn, I can remember meeting with Mr. Mikhail KULAGIN [sic][922] several times and would be happy to come forward with details to the FBI and others. There are several other

---

[914] SCO-006313 (Interview of Christopher Steele on Sept. 18, 2017) at 11, 16; SCO-002194 (Email from Kalugin dated 08/19/2016).

[915] U.S. Customs and Border Protection Person Encounter List for Igor Danchenko at 3.

[916] SCO-006313 (Interview of Christopher Steele on Sept. 18, 2017) at 17.

[917] *Id.*

[918] SCO-005678 (Email from Dolan dated 06/03/2016); SCID_00000776 (Email from Dolan to Galkina on 06/13/2016).

[919] OSC Report of Interview of Charles Dolan on Nov. 1, 2021 at 2.

[920] OSC Report of Interview of Charles Dolan on Sept. 7, 2021 at 2.

[921] OSC Report of Interview of Charles Dolan on Nov. 1, 2021 at 1-2.

[922] In Steele Report 2016/111 Mikhail Kalugin's name is misspelled as "Kulagin."

> points in the dossier that are true! Let me know if you need additional clarification.[923]

Dolan attached to the email a BBC News article titled "Trump Russia dossier key claim 'verified.'" In the article, BBC journalist Paul Wood stated that "sources I know and trust have told me the US government identified Kalugin as a spy while he was still at the embassy."[924] In this email, Dolan appears to volunteer that he possesses inside information on the Steele Report allegations concerning Kalugin as well as other information pertaining to the veracity of additional Steele Report allegations.

*viii. The Ivanov allegation contained in Steele Report 2016/111*

An additional allegation appearing in the same Steele Report as the Kalugin allegation (2016/111) concerned the firing of Sergei Ivanov, the then-chief of staff of the Russian Presidential Administration. The allegation stated, in part:

> PUTIN had been receiving conflicting advice on interfering from three separate and expert groups. On one side had been the Russian ambassador to the US, Sergei KISLYAK, and the Ministry of Foreign Affairs, together with an independent and informal network run by presidential foreign policy advisor, Yuri USHAKOV (KISLYAK's predecessor in Washington) who had urged caution and the potential negative impact on Russia from the operation/s. On the other side was former PA Head, Sergei IVANOV, backed by Russian Foreign Intelligence (SVR), who had advised PUTIN that the pro-TRUMP, anti-CLINTON operation/s would be both effective and plausibly deniable with little blowback. The first group/s had been proven right and this had been the catalyst in PUTIN's decision to sack IVANOV (unexpectedly) as PA Head in August. His successor, Anton VAINO, had been selected for the job partly because he had not been involved in the US presidential election operation/s.[925]

This allegation coincided with information that Dolan had received from Galkina regarding changes in the Russian Presidential Administration in the weeks prior to the issuance of Steele Report 2016/111. In particular, on August 12, 2016, the same day that Ivanov was reportedly fired, Galkina sent a Facebook message to Dolan stating, "Russian presidential administration is making significant changes right now."[926] Danchenko was not copied on this message. Minutes later, Dolan and Galkina spoke for approximately 10 minutes.[927] On September 13, 2016 – the

---

[923] KG_0002357 (Email from Dolan dated 02/09/2018).

[924] Paul Wood, *Trump Russia Dossier key claim 'Verified,'* BBC News (Mar. 30, 2017). https://www.bbc.com/news/world-us-canada-39435786.

[925] SCO-105084 (Documents Known to the FBI Comprising the "Steele Dossier") at 20-21, (Company Intelligence Report 2016/111) (capitalization in original).

[926] SCO-002232 (Facebook exchange between Dolan and Galkina dated 08/12/2016).

[927] SCO-101564 (Dolan Facebook entry dated 08/12/2016).

day prior to the date of the Steele Report containing the Ivanov allegation – Dolan called Danchenko.[928] As discussed above, at the time of this call, Danchenko was in Russia.

When interviewed by the FBI in January 2017, the FBI asked Danchenko about the sourcing of this allegation. Danchenko stated that he learned about the allegation involving Ivanov from Galkina and "two other friends."[929] According to the FBI's interview report, Danchenko did not identify the two other "friends," nor did he mention Dolan in connection with the allegation.[930] The FBI interview report does not state whether Danchenko was asked to provide the names of the "two other friends."

When interviewed by the FBI in September 2017, Steele stated that the information in this Report was derived from Danchenko's direct contact with multiple sub-sources, including Alexey Pavlov.[931]

When interviewed by the Office, Dolan initially stated that he never discussed Russian politics with Galkina.[932] When confronted with the Facebook exchange regarding the shakeup in the Russian Presidential Administration, Dolan stated that it was "possible" that he had spoken with Galkina about Ivanov being fired, but, again, had no specific recollection of doing so.[933]

*ix. The YPO Conference – October 2016*

On September 30, 2016, U.S. Person-1 sent Dolan the final draft agenda for the YPO Conference.[934] Dolan replied "Thanks – will send to Peskov."[935] Thereafter, in early October 2016, Dolan and Danchenko made their way separately to Moscow for the YPO Conference. During the January 2017 interviews, Danchenko informed the FBI that he did not collect any information for Steele during the YPO conference.[936] Steele, however, told the FBI that, in fact, two reports (2016/130 and 2016/132) were comprised of information that Danchenko purported to gather during the YPO Conference.[937]

In any event, the YPO Conference featured several Russian government officials including Konstantin Kosachev, a senior member of the Russian Duma (parliament) and Mikhail Kalugin, a member of the Russian Ministry of Foreign Affairs (and, as discussed above, formerly

---

928 AT&T Record dated 09/13/2016. (The records reflect a duration of only 16 seconds).

929 SCO-005801 (Interview of Igor Danchenko Electronic Communication dated 02/09/17) at 45.

930 *Id.*

931 SCO-006313 (Interview of Christopher Steele on Sept. 18, 2017) at 17.

932 OSC Report of Interview of Charles Dolan on Aug. 31, 2021 at 3.

933 OSC Report of Interview of Charles Dolan on Nov. 1, 2021 at 2.

934 SCID_00007020 (Email from U.S. Person-1 to Dolan dated 09/30/2016).

935 SCID_00001127 (Email from Dolan to U.S. Person-1 dated 09/30/2016).

936 SCO-005801 (Interview of Igor Danchenko Electronic Communication dated 02/09/2017) at 49-50.

937 SCO-006313 (Interview of Christopher Steele on Sept. 18, 2017) at 18-19.

assigned to the [illegible] assy in [illegible] n).[938] [illegible] ndarev, another member of the Russian Minist[illegible] Affairs [illegible] the diplomat who replaced Kalugin in Was[illegible] listed [illegible] conference.[939] Dolan informed the Office that [illegible] ference [illegible] A Steele Report dated October 20, 2016 (2016 [illegible] an tw[illegible] the [illegible] rence – contained the following allegation:

> The Kre[illegible] ent [illegible] lead[illegible] TIN Duma figure, Konstan[illegible] EV ([illegible] Fore[illegible] Committee) as an importan[illegible] TRU[illegible] ign-[illegible] on operation. KOSAC[illegible] ausib[illegible] be[illegible] Russian legislature rather th[illegible] had [illegible] ne and by implication, may hav[illegible] meet[illegible] COH[illegible] August.[941]

During the Jan[illegible] views [illegible] to sta[illegible] rmation in the Steele Reports related to Cohen [illegible] came [illegible] ia.[942] [illegible] sistent with what Steele informed the FBI during [illegible] r 201[illegible] [943] H[illegible] discussed more below, when interviewed by [illegible] gust 20[illegible] a can[illegible] g anything about a Cohen meeting in Prag[illegible] the [illegible] o ev[illegible] Cohen had met Russian officials in Prague.[945]

*x. [illegible] ontac[illegible] the [illegible] the YPO Conference*

Upon re[illegible] the Y[illegible] ence in [illegible] ber 2016, Dolan and Danchenko continued to co[illegible] On Oc[illegible] 6, D[illegible] aveled from Moscow to London to meet with Ch[illegible] ele.[946] [illegible] 9, [illegible] enko asked Dolan – who was still in Moscow – to [illegible] ication [illegible] armacy.[947] Dolan agreed that he would collect th[illegible] d del[illegible] nch[illegible] e (Dolan) returned to

---

[938] SCID_0000[illegible] from U[illegible] to [illegible] 09/30/2016) at 4.

[939] SCID_0001[illegible] from U[illegible] dat[illegible] 16) at 11.

[940] OSC Report [illegible] of Ch[illegible] on [illegible] at 2.

[941] SCO-10508[illegible] s Know[illegible] I C[illegible] "Steele Dossier") at 33, (Company Inte[illegible] rt 201[illegible]

[942] SCO-00580[illegible] Igor [illegible] E[illegible] munication dated 02/09/2017) at 30-33.

[943] SCO-00631[illegible] of Chri[illegible] eele [illegible] 2017) at 19-20.

[944] SCO-FBIPE[illegible] (Debr[illegible] ga [illegible] 08/26/2017) at 3.

[945] *See Redacte*[illegible] at 1[illegible]

[946] SCO-00731[illegible] Face[illegible] dat[illegible] 16); SCO-005801 (Interview of Igor Danchenk[illegible] Commu[illegible] ted [illegible] at 49-50.

[947] SCO-10146[illegible] exchang[illegible] Dol[illegible] chenko dated 10/09/2016).

Washington, D.C.[948] Thereafter, on October 18, 2016, Danchenko and Dolan met at kglobal's office in Washington, ostensibly for Danchenko to secure the medication from Dolan.[949]

The day following this meeting at kglobal, two Steele Reports were generated (2016/135 and 2016/136). These reports alleged, among other things, that Cohen was heavily engaged in covering up Trump's ties to Russia, and specifically, to contain further scandals involving Manafort and Page. As discussed above, this Report 2016/136 also contains reference to Konstatin Kosachev. In the January 2017 interviews, Danchenko attributed this information to Galkina. Again, Galkina told the FBI that she was not aware of Cohen's alleged meeting in Prague.

Later, on November 3, 2016, Dolan and Danchenko met for lunch in Washington, D.C.[950] After that, on New Year's Day 2017, Danchenko and Dolan met in a park in Arlington, Virginia.[951] When asked about the circumstances of this meeting, Dolan informed the Office, in sum, that he was looking at Facebook and he noticed that Danchenko had posted a picture with his daughter in the park.[952] Dolan stated that since the park was close to his house, he decided to drive over to meet Danchenko.[953]

On the evening of January 10, 2017, Buzzfeed became the first media outlet to publish the Steele Reports.[954] On the morning of January 11, 2017, Dolan called Danchenko.[955] Dolan stated that he called Danchenko because he had suspicions that Danchenko was behind the Steele Reports based on the fact that, among other things, he learned "it was a London operation" and he knew that Danchenko did due diligence work for Orbis, which was based in London.[956] Dolan also thought Galkina might have been a source for Danchenko given her employment at Servers.com.[957] During the call, Danchenko told Dolan, in sum, that he did not know who was behind the reports, but that he would let Dolan know if he came across any information.[958]

---

948 *Id.* at 1.

949 *Id.* at 3.

950 SCO-101471 (Facebook exchange between Dolan and Danchenko dated 11/02/2016).

951 SCO-101472 (Facebook exchange between Dolan and Danchenko dated 01/01/2017).

952 OSC Report of Interview of Charles Dolan on Nov. 1, 2021 at 3.

953 *Id.*

954 Ken Bensinger, Miriam Elder & Mark Schoofs, *These Reports Allege Trump Has Deep Ties to Russia*, Buzzfeed (Jan. 10, 2017).

955 AT&T Record dated 01/11/2017.

956 *Danchenko* Tr. 10/13/2022 AM at 635; OSC Report of Interview of Charles Dolan on Sept. 7, 2021 at 1.

957 *Danchenko* Tr. 10/13/2022 AM at 635; OSC Report of Interview of Charles Dolan on Sept. 7, 2021 at 2.

958 *Danchenko* Tr. 10/13/2022 AM at 635; OSC Report of Interview of Charles Dolan on Sept. 7, 2021 at 1.

According to Dolan, the January 11, 2017 call was the last time he had contact with Danchenko.[959]

On January 13, 2017, Dolan emailed a U.S.-based acquaintance the following:

> I've been interviewed by the Washington Post and the London Times - three times over the last two days over the MI-6 Dossier on Trump and I know the Russian agent who made the report (He used to work for me). My client in Cyprus has been accused of being the party that organized the hacking. Presently speaking with the barrister in London who is filing a brief against Former British intelligence officer Christopher Steele has been unmasked as the man behind an explosive dossier about US president-elect Donald Trump. Also, in conversation with former British Ambassador who knows Steele. Quite right- Oh what a boring life.[960]

At the time the email was sent, Danchenko was not publicly known to be a source for Steele. When asked by the Office why he referred to Danchenko as a "Russian agent," Dolan initially said that he was being facetious, but then also elaborated that he had suspicions about Danchenko's ties to Russian intelligence.[961]

e. The FBI's failure to investigate Charles Dolan's role as a possible source for the Steele Reports

Information from four Steele Reports (2016/080, 2016/94, 2016/095 and 2016/102) was included in the four FISA applications targeting Page. As discussed above, the FBI was not able to corroborate a single substantive allegation in the Steele Reports. Nevertheless, the Steele Reports would form the foundation for the narrative that a U.S. presidential campaign was actively engaged in "a well-developed conspiracy of co-operation" with a foreign adversary. Danchenko was the primary source of information for this narrative that was weaved throughout the Steele Reports. Indeed, as noted earlier,[962] in his own words to an acquaintance, Danchenko stated that he "collected some 80% of [the] raw intel and [performed] half the analysis for the Chris Steele Dossier."[963] Accordingly, Danchenko's relationship with Dolan and Dolan's proximity to key figures and events that appear in the Steele Reports should have been an ample basis to, at a minimum, interview Dolan. However, as discussed below, Dolan was never interviewed, despite the suggestion from both Steele and Galkina that Dolan could have information related to the Steele Reports and the detailed analysis undertaken by two FBI personnel assigned to the Mueller team.

*i. Danchenko's hesitancy to speak to the FBI about Charles Dolan*

Danchenko did not mention Dolan to the FBI during the January 2017 interviews, despite revealing his (Danchenko's) participation in the YPO Conference in October 2016. Further, in a

---

959 *Danchenko* Tr. 10/13/2022 AM at 636, 653.

960 SCO-002217 (Email from Dolan dated 01/13/2017) (underline in original).

961 OSC Report of Interview of Charles Dolan on Sept. 7, 2021 at 1-2.

962 *See* footnote 701.

963 *Danchenko* Government Exhibit 1502.

June 15, 2017 interview with Helson – which in part focused on Dolan – Danchenko only revealed that he was present with Dolan during the YPO Conference in October 2016.[964] Notably, Danchenko did not inform the FBI that he met with Dolan in Moscow during the June Planning Trip; a material omission given the fact that, according to Steele, Danchenko was collecting information for Steele during that trip.

In a June 2017 interview, Danchenko was also asked if he had spoken to Dolan regarding any allegations contained in the Steele Reports. Danchenko denied that Dolan provided any specific information related to the Steele Reports. In particular, when Helson mentioned Dolan's name during a conversation about individuals who may have contributed to the Steele Reports, the following exchange, in part, occurred:

Helson: Um, because obviously I don't think you're the only . . .

Danchenko: Mm-hmm.

Helson: Person that has been contributing. You may have said one - and this is the other thing we are trying to figure out. [ ... ]

Helson: Do you know a Chuck Dolan?

Danchenko: Do I know Chuck Dolan? Yeah.

Helson: How long have you known him?
[laughing]
[approximately 15 second pause]

Danchenko: I've known Chuck for [pause] I don't know, a couple years maybe.

Helson: Couple years?

Danchenko: But but but but but but but I've known of him for like 12 years.

Helson: Okay.

Danchenko: Uh, 11 years. Because he'd always come to Russia and Ru-Russian – Russian [UI] when he worked for Ketchum.

Helson: Okay.

Danchenko: In like 2006, 2007.

Helson: So that was how far back?

Danchenko: Yeah, when . . .

Helson: And that was with Ketchum?

Danchenko: when – you know – well . . .

Helson: Okay.

Danchenko: uh, Russia organized the G20 and he was on – he worked with Ketchum on the – on the – on Russia power.

---

964 Transcript of June 15, 2017 interview of Danchenko at 42-44.

Helson: [illegible] would [illegible]

Danchenko: [illegible] 's a very [illegible]

Helson: [illegible]

Danchenko: [illegible] Yeah [illegible] Russia [illegible] k he is uh – would be any [illegible] involved [illegible] uh [UI] what I would [illegible] would be [illegible] played [illegible], he's a bit naïve in his, [illegible] ing of [illegible]

Helson: [illegible] so you [illegible] was [illegible] . . but you had never [illegible] to Charles [illegible] anything [illegible] ed up in the dossier right?

Danchenko: [illegible]

Helson: [illegible] can't th[illegible]

Danchenko: We talked [illegible] issues perhaps but no, no, [illegible] thing sp[illegible]

In a later [illegible] conversation [illegible] Helson that Dolan had conducted business with C[illegible] and Ser[illegible] and th[illegible] maintained a professional friendship with Dimitry Pe[illegible] Russian [illegible] FBI reporting document detailing this in[illegible] on ob[illegible] Danch[illegible] "hesitant" about acknowledging his association [illegible] Inde[illegible] interv[illegible] OIG in October 2018, Helson stated that in th[illegible] s meeting [illegible] en I brought up Charles [Dolan] it was very gray, [illegible][968]

Following [illegible] 5, 201[illegible] Helson [illegible] Dolan's name on several other occasions. For [illegible] interv[illegible] October [illegible] Danchenko provided the names of several individu[illegible] ing Dolan, [illegible] concerned [illegible] because of their relationship with the Russian [illegible][969] Dan[illegible] characterized [illegible] Dolan as having too many dubious connections to [illegible] government [illegible] includ[illegible] Peskov and Alexey Pavlov.[970] Additionally, in [illegible] 20, 201[illegible] Danchenko [illegible] stated that Dolan had shared emails about Manafort [illegible] s a and [illegible] Danchenko stated that U.S. Person-2 was someone who [illegible] own about [illegible] on the Steele Reports, because Dolan would ha[illegible] in U.S. [illegible] about [illegible].[971] Helson documented the content of this [illegible] FBI rep[illegible] document [illegible]. Danchenko provided no further information or [illegible] Dolan [illegible] personal [illegible]

---

[965] *Id.* at 40-42.

[966] *Id.* at 43-45.

[967] SCO_10528[illegible] reporting D[illegible] dated [illegible].

[968] OIG Report [illegible] of Kevin [illegible] at 147-48.

[969] SCO_10528[illegible] reporting D[illegible] dated [illegible].

[970] S-00081750[illegible] Reporting [illegible] document [illegible] -2017) at 1.

[971] S-00081750[illegible] Reporting [illegible] document [illegible] 2019) at 2.

*ii. The FBI's failure to interview Charles Dolan*

As discussed above, Dolan first came to the attention of Crossfire Hurricane investigators during Steele's October 2016 interview in Rome.[972] Following that meeting, the Crossfire Hurricane personnel prepared a background report on Dolan.[973] Steele again raised Dolan during a September 2017 interview with the FBI when he indicated that at least one allegation in his reporting was sourced to Dolan.[974] Notwithstanding Steele's October 2016 statements about Dolan, the FBI did not question Danchenko during the January 2017 interviews about Dolan or any of the other U.S. citizens that Steele suggested might have information about Trump and Russia.

*iii. The FBI learns of Dolan's relationship with Olga Galkina*

In the January 2017 interviews, Danchenko informed the FBI that Galkina was a source for several of the allegations contained in the Steele Reports.[975] As testimony in the *Danchenko* trial detailed, following this revelation, in the Spring of 2017, the FBI began to review its databases for information related to Galkina. From its review, the FBI learned, among other things, that (i) Galkina maintained a relationship with Charles Dolan, and (ii) Galkina had met with Dolan, Danchenko and others in Washington, D.C. in March 2016 to discuss a business relationship between Servers.com and kglobal.[976] As discussed more fully below, beginning in the fall of 2017, Mueller Analyst-1, whose assignment was to find corroborating information for the Steele reporting, drafted a lengthy memorandum outlining the FBI's holdings on Galkina as they related to the Steele Reports. Dolan featured prominently in this memorandum because of his connections to, among others, Galkina, Danchenko, and Dimitry Peskov and his work for Servers.com.

Based on the information detailed above, in the late spring and early summer 2017, the FBI began to investigate what, if any, role Dolan played vis-à-vis the Steele Reports. To that end, on June 12, 2017, Auten, who at that time was a member of the Mueller Special Counsel team, sent an email to Helson, another Mueller team member ("Mueller Supervisory Special Agent-1") and others, stating, in part:

Some thoughts –

1. I'm not sure [Danchenko] has ever mentioned his connections with Dolan.
2. I'm positive Danchenko never mentioned that he'd done limiting [*sic*] consulting for Servers.com (i.e. putting Dolan in touch)

---

972 SCO-020139 (Email from Auten to Supervisory Special Agent-1, Moffa, Strzok & others dated 10/04/2016).

973 FBI-0040963 (Intelligence Memo dated 10/06/2016).

974 SCO-006313 (Interview of Christopher Steele on Sept. 18, 2017) at 3, 16-17.

975 SCO-005801 (Interview of Igor Danchenko Electronic Communication dated 02/09/2017) at 13-16.

976 *Danchenko* Tr. 10/14/2022 AM at 946, 948-49.

3. As Dolan is tied to Peskov and Presidential Administration press/communications, who is to say that he vs. Galkina is the "true" subsource for Peskov and PA-related reporting in [Steele].

4. Can we run Dolan through unattrib open source to see if he's done any oppositional political research, etc?

The path of information could have been:

Kremlin → Galkina →[Danchenko] →[Steele]; or,

Kremlin → Dolan → Galkina → [Danchenko] → [Steele]; or,

Kremlin → Dolan → [Danchenko] → [Steele][977]

Three days later, on June 15, 2017, Helson became the first FBI employee to ask Danchenko about his relationship with Dolan – despite the fact that the Crossfire Hurricane team was aware of Dolan's potential connections to the Steele Reports as far back as October 2016 and their direct interactions with Danchenko since January 2017.[978]

*iv. Helson requests to interview Charles Dolan*

Given Danchenko's reluctance to speak about Dolan and information learned from the Mueller Special Counsel team, Helson concluded that an interview of Dolan was a logical investigative step. However, when Helson raised this prospect with the Mueller Special Counsel team, he was explicitly told not to interview Dolan. Helson expressed confidence that Auten was the individual who told Helson to "hold off" on interviewing Dolan.[979] When interviewed by the Office, Auten did not have a recollection of telling Helson not to interview Dolan.[980]

During a July 27, 2021 interview with the Office, Helson stated he aggressively "pushed" the Dolan information to the Mueller Special Counsel team but received very little feedback.[981] Helson believed that Mueller Special Counsel attorney Andrew Weissman and a female attorney he was unfamiliar with were present for at least one briefing Helson provided to the Mueller team in which he shared information regarding Dolan.[982] Helson also stated, in sum, that Dolan should have been further investigated in connection with the Steele Reports, or at a minimum, interviewed, based on the information that was available to the FBI at that time.[983]

In December 2017, Helson shared his concerns about Dolan with Mueller Supervisory Special Agent-1 and Mueller Analyst-1, both part of the Mueller Special Counsel team. For

---

977 FBI-AAA-02-0032414 (Email from Auten to WFO Analyst-1, Helson, Mueller Supervisory Special Agent-1 & Analyst-2 dated 06/12/2017).

978 Transcript of June 15, 2017 interview of Danchenko at 42.

979 OSC Report of Interview of Kevin Helson on July 27, 2021 at 3.

980 OSC Report of Interview of Brian Auten on July 26, 2021 at 20, 22, 25.

981 OSC Report of Interview of Kevin Helson on July 27, 2021 at 3.

982 *Id.* at 1.

983 *Id.* at 1-7.

example, on December 21, 2017, in an FBI Lync chat with Mueller Analyst-1, Helson wrote "I really don't like that guy [Dolan]" and that he (Helson) was "fighting to get them [Mueller Team] interested in what I have here," referring to Dolan.[984] In the same chat, Helson informed Mueller Analyst-1 that he would "keep talking to him [Danchenko] about CD [Charles Dolan]."[985] On January 9, 2018, Helson sent a Lync message to Mueller Analyst-1 stating, "What a little triangle the three of them have [Danchenko], [Galkina] and Dolan."[986] Finally, on January 17, 2018, after reviewing Mueller Analyst-1's memorandum on Galkina, Helson wrote to Mueller Analyst-1, "It really makes CD [Dolan] look like he should be investigated."[987] Indeed, as Helson would later state to the OIG:

> There is an individual we kind of [were] watching pop up a lot and that's Chuck Dolan, formerly with Ketchum Group. He's in the same circles. I'm like, are you sure that, I mean, because it would be classic potential tradecraft [to be] like, if you can get information corroborated by one, you can attribute to one, and mask exactly where you got it, is it because, and I don't think anyone's interviewed [him], because I, at the time I had suggested interviewing Dolan, Special's [Mueller Special Counsel] like no, no, don't, don't go talk to him yet. So, and I never, when they said, stay away, I was like, okay, I don't want to. Because I was concerned, I was like, is Dolan [the source], because, and think there's actual, like when I talked with [Danchenko] about him, he initially was reluctant to bring Dolan up. Then he seemed fond of him in a way.[988]
>
> [. . . .]
>
> So he [Dolan] was in the same, he was in the same events [YPO Conference]. And we're, like, does he [Dolan] go to London, does he talk to, I mean, does Chris Steele got him too? I'm like, and that is a question I have flagged, it's like, when it gets quiet and Dolan is, from what I understand, Dolan doesn't want to be talking at this point. So I want to strike that at some point and, say, cross that off my list of, here's what I would really like to talk about. Or at least interview him [Dolan]. That would be the only one that, I would think, would be a source that could have contributed to the dossier and have attributed it to [Galkina]. And thinks it is too, because he's there too. And it would be, there's more sources to it [Steele Reports] than actually there are. Chris [Steele] hasn't come off of any of them at this point. I mean, I don't want to, that's just a theory that I . . .[989]

---

984 SCO_FBIPROD_026627 (Lync message from Helson to Mueller Analyst-1 dated 12/21/2017).

985 *Id.*

986 SCO_FBIPROD_026631 (Lync message from Helson to Mueller Analyst-1 dated 01/09/2018).

987 SCO_FBIPROD_026632 (Lync message from Helson to Mueller Analyst-1 dated 01/17/2018).

988 OIG Interview of Kevin Helson on Oct. 31, 2018 at 54-55.

989 *Id.* at 56.

Neverth[illegible] ussed [illegible] e was [illegible] ned on Dolan and Dolan was never intervie[illegible] 1

*v.* [illegible] *Supervi*[illegible] *Mueller Analyst-1 investigate* [illegible] *onship* [illegible] *Dolan* [illegible] *ko and Galkina*

Mueller [illegible] Speci[illegible] was a[illegible] e Crossfire Hurricane investigation in [illegible] [9] Sh[illegible] ler, M[illegible] ervisory Special Agent-1 transitioned to [illegible] pecial C[illegible] m. [illegible] ervisory Special Agent-1 was assigned, in par[illegible] validat[illegible] le R[illegible] to verify the reporting or, alternatively, to [illegible] ut the [illegible] as not [illegible] [991] Beginning in July 2017, Mueller Superv[illegible] Agent-1 [illegible] close [illegible] ong others, Mueller Analyst-1. As discussed ab[illegible] Analyst [illegible] joined [illegible] investigation in July 2017, was responsible for [illegible] FBI's [illegible] ter in[illegible] elated to Galkina.[992] During that process, Muell[illegible] y Spec[illegible] and [illegible] alyst-1 discovered, as described in testimony in th[illegible] trial, th[illegible] was [illegible] to both Danchenko and Galkina, and (ii) had ext[illegible] the K[illegible] Russ[illegible] ent officials, including Dimitry Peskov.[993] Mu[illegible] sory S[illegible] t-1 an[illegible] Analyst-1 also conducted open-source searches [illegible] borated [illegible] format[illegible] ed in the FBI's databases.

*vi.* [illegible] *interv*[illegible] *Galk*[illegible]

In Augu[illegible] ller Su[illegible] Speci[illegible] Auten and a Russian speaking agent, ("WFO S[illegible] t-1") tra[illegible] Cypru[illegible] w Galkina.[994] Mueller Supervisory Sp[illegible] testifi[illegible] he D[illegible] ial that the purpose of the interview was t[illegible] Galk[illegible] and Dan[illegible] th information contained in the Steele Reports [illegible] moti[illegible] ing [illegible] g the Cyprus interview, which was conducted [illegible] se of [illegible] Muell[illegible] ry Special Agent-1 stated that Galkina appear[illegible] omi[illegible] questi[illegible] except when she was asked about Dolan. Galkin[illegible] ueller [illegible] Spe[illegible] that she did not want to speak about Dolan.[99] [illegible] d da[illegible] interview [illegible] tated, in sum, that she had spoken with two indivi[illegible] nform[illegible] ould [illegible] in the Steele Reports. One of the individuals Gal[illegible] forma[illegible] Dan[illegible] Galkina initially refused to identify the oth[illegible] [997] L[illegible] interv[illegible] Supervisory Special Agent-1

---

[990] OSC Repor[illegible] of M[illegible] rvisor[illegible] gent-1 on May 1, 2020 at 1.

[991] OSC Repor[illegible] of M[illegible] rvisor[illegible] gent-1 on May 1, 2020 at 1.

[992] *Danchenko* [illegible] 22 AM [illegible]

[993] *Id.* at 946, 9[illegible]

[994] OSC Repor[illegible] of M[illegible] rvisor[illegible] gent-1 on Aug. 31, 2021 at 1; *Danchenko* Tr. [illegible] 2 AM at [illegible]

[995] *Danchenko* [illegible] 22 AM [illegible]

[996] OSC Report [illegible] of M[illegible] rvisor[illegible] gent-1 on Aug. 31, 2021 at 2; *Danchenko* Tr. [illegible] 2 AM at [illegible]

[997] OSC Report [illegible] of M[illegible] lyst-1 [illegible] 2021 at 1.

again pressed Galkina about Dolan.[998] This time, Mueller Supervisory Special Agent-1 directly asked Galkina if Dolan had a connection to the information contained in the Steele Reports and whether Dolan was the second unidentified individual with whom she had discussed Steele Report related information.[999] Before answering, Galkina asked Mueller Supervisory Special Agent-1 to remove her (Mueller Supervisory Special Agent-1's) sunglasses from her face so that Galkina could look Mueller Supervisory Special Agent-1 in the eyes.[1000] Galkina then confirmed to Mueller Supervisory Special Agent-1 that Dolan was the second unidentified individual with whom she had discussed Steele Report information.[1001] Galkina also stated that Dolan was a "big democratic supporter."[1002] As discussed above, in October 2016, Galkina would later inform a friend that because of her [Galkina's] "acquaintance with Chuck Dolan and several citizens from the Russian presidential administration," Galkina knew" something and can tell a little about it by voice."[1003]

*vii. Mueller Supervisory Special Agent-1 and Mueller Analyst-1 push to open a case on Charles Dolan*

Armed with the information provided by Galkina, Mueller Supervisory Special Agent-1 returned to the United States and began to further investigate Galkina and Dolan's involvement, if any, with the Steele Reports. As discussed above, beginning in July 2017, Mueller Analyst-1 assisted Mueller Supervisory Special Agent-1 in vetting the Steele Reports.[1004] As part of that work, Mueller Analyst-1 began researching Galkina's relationships with various individuals possibly connected to the Steele Reports, including Danchenko and Dolan.[1005] In connection with that research, Mueller Analyst-1 began drafting a memorandum to memorialize her findings.[1006]

In or about late August 2017, Mueller Supervisory Special Agent-1 and Mueller Analyst-1 briefed various members of the Mueller Special Counsel investigation about Dolan's relationship with Danchenko and Galkina. Those present for this briefing included Auten, Supervisory Special Agent-2 (Mueller Supervisory Special Agent-1's supervisor), and Jeannie Rhee, a prosecutor on the Mueller Special Counsel team, who, at the time, was leading the Special Counsel's investigation into Russian efforts to influence the 2016 presidential election

---

998 OSC Report of Interview of Mueller Supervisory Special Agent-1 on Aug. 31, 2021 at 1-2.

999 *Id.*; *Danchenko* Tr. 10/14/2022 AM at 977:3-13.

1000 OSC Report of Interview of Mueller Supervisory Special Agent-1 on Aug. 31, 2021 at 1-2; *Danchenko* Tr. 10/14/2022 AM at 977:3-13.

1001 *Danchenko* Tr. 10/14/2022 AM at 977:3-13.

1002 SCO-FBIPROD_022274 (Opening Communication dated 12/14/2017) at 4.

1003 SCO_076721 (Facebook exchange with Galkina dated 10/15/2016).

1004 *Danchenko* Tr. 10/14/2022 AM at 944:11-22.

1005 *Id.* at 945:12-947:16.

1006 *Id.* at 954:12-956:3.

(colloquially known as "Team R").[1007] Following the meeting, Mueller Supervisory Special Agent-1 believed that the team was supportive of continuing to investigate Charles Dolan and what connection, if any, he had to the Steele Reports.[1008]

On September 1, 2017, Mueller Supervisory Special Agent-1 drafted a case opening document for Dolan. The opening document detailed, among other things, (i) Dolan's connections to Danchenko and Galkina, (ii) Dolan's connections to the Democratic party, and (iii) Dolan's connections to the Kremlin.[1009] The document also summarized Danchenko's June 15, 2017 conversation with Helson about Dolan.

Nevertheless, on September 7, 2017, Auten instructed Mueller Analyst-1 to cease all research and analysis related to Dolan.[1010] Later that day, Supervisory Special Agent-2 informed Mueller Analyst-1 that she was being transferred from "Team R" to the Mueller team investigating Paul Manafort (colloquially known as "Team M").[1011] In her interview with the Office, Mueller Analyst-1 recalled that she asked Supervisory Special Agent-2 for permission to continue researching Dolan before moving to "Team M," but that her request was denied.[1012] Nevertheless, as discussed more below, following her transfer, Mueller Analyst-1 continued to refine her memorandum regarding Galkina's connections to, among others, Danchenko and Dolan.[1013]

As noted above, in September 2017, Mueller Supervisory Special Agent-1 participated in the two-day interview of Christopher Steele in which Steele admitted that Dolan "had drinks" with Danchenko and was responsible for at least one allegation in the Steele Reports (regarding

---

1007 OSC Report of Interview of Mueller Analyst-1 on Aug. 16, 2021 at 2, 3; OSC Report of Interview of Mueller Supervisory Special Agent-1 on Aug. 31, 2021 at 4.

1008 OSC Report of Interview of Mueller Supervisory Special Agent-1 on Aug. 31, 2021 at 4.

1009 SCO-FBIPROD_022274 (Opening Communication dated 12/14/2017).

1010 It should be noted that this information provided by Mueller Analyst-1 is corroborated by a contemporaneous timeline she kept of the events at issue during her time with the Mueller Special Counsel team. In her interview with the Office, Mueller Analyst-1 stated that she prepared the contemporaneous timeline in the event she were later interviewed about her role on the Mueller Special Counsel investigation. *See* OSC Report of Interview of Mueller Analyst-1 on Oct. 29, 2021 at 2-3.

1011 OSC Report of Interview of Mueller Analyst-1 on Oct. 29, 2021 at 2.

1012 *Id.* at 2

1013 In her interview with the Special Counsel, Mueller Analyst-1 stated that Auten had made edits to her memorandum, some of which removed information regarding Dolan. Mueller Analyst-1 recalled being frustrated by many of these edits and wondered if the edits were being made by individuals other than Auten and with a political motive. However, Mueller Analyst-1 was unable to provide any evidence to support this speculation. *See* OSC Report of Interview of Mueller Analyst-1 on Aug. 16, 2021 at 5. When interviewed by the Office, Auten recalled that his edits were reflective of his belief that some of the information regarding Dolan was too speculative. *See* OSC Report of Interview of Brian Auten on July 26, 2021.

Manafort's resignation as Trump campaign manager.)[1014] Mueller Supervisory Special Agent-1 stated that they did not probe Steele further about Charles Dolan because the FBI did not want to "show their hand" to Steele.[1015]

On September 22, 2017, Mueller Supervisory Special Agent-1 and Mueller Analyst-1 attended a meeting with Supervisory Special Agent-2, Auten, and attorney Rhee to discuss, among other things, the recently completed interview of Steele.[1016] At various times in September 2017, Mueller Analyst-1 recalled that Rhee opined, in sum, that there was no longer a need to investigate the Steele Reports, because the Reports were not within the scope of the Mueller Special Counsel mandate.[1017] Similarly, Auten told the Office he recalled that in September 2017 Deputy Assistant Director David Archey informed the team that they should cease work on attempting to corroborate the Steele Reports.[1018] This directive given by the Mueller investigation leadership is somewhat surprising given that Director Mueller's broad mandate was to investigate, among other things, Russian election interference in the 2016 presidential election – parameters that clearly would seem to include the Steele Reports. Indeed, as Mueller Analyst-1 noted in her interview with the Office, the Mueller Special Counsel team continued to investigate cases involving non-Russian persons and entities. Thus, Mueller Analyst-1 disagreed with the contention that Dolan fell outside of the Mueller mandate.[1019] In her interview with the Office, Mueller Supervisory Special Agent-1 stated that while she did not recall the "outside the mandate" justification for the denial of the Dolan case opening, it would "surprise" her if that was the reason provided by Mueller team leadership.[1020] This purported position also is curious given that the Steele Reports underpinned, in a significant way, the probable cause contained in the Page FISA applications.

Mueller Supervisory Special Agent-1 also recalled that attorney Rhee, while initially favorable to investigating Dolan, gradually soured on the idea.[1021] In that same vein, in a meeting on October 17, 2017, Supervisory Special Agent-2 informed Mueller Supervisory Special Agent-1, Mueller Analyst-1, and Auten that (i) Dolan fell outside of the Mueller investigation's mandate, (ii) the investigators had too much work and too few resources to focus on Dolan, and (iii) WFO could task Danchenko regarding Dolan.[1022] In fact, Mueller Analyst-1's contemporaneous notes explicitly state that Mueller investigation leadership directed Mueller Analyst-1 and Mueller Supervisory Special Agent-1 to "dedicate no resources to CD

---

[1014] SCO-006313 (Interview of Christopher Steele on Sept. 18, 2017) at 3, 16-17.

[1015] OSC Report of Interview of Mueller Supervisory Special Agent-1 on Aug. 31, 2021 at 2.

[1016] OSC Report of Interview of Mueller Analyst-1 on Oct. 29, 2021 at 3.

[1017] *Id.* at 3-4; Timeline prepared by Mueller Analyst-1.

[1018] OSC Report of Interview of Brian Auten on July 26, 2021 at 19.

[1019] OSC Report of Interview of Mueller Analyst-1 on Oct. 29, 2021 at 7.

[1020] OSC Report of Interview of Mueller Supervisory Special Agent-1 on Aug. 31, 2021 at 5.

[1021] *Id.* at 4.

[1022] OSC Report of Interview of Mueller Analyst-1 on Oct. 29, 2021 at 4; Timeline prepared by Mueller Analyst-1, entry dated Oct. 17, 2017.

[Dolan]."[1023] N[illegible], Supervis[illegible] [illegible] that tangential work on Dolan could be contin[illegible] t wa[illegible] on Dolan would be approved.[1024]

Ultimate[illegible] ory Sp[illegible] -2 inf[illegible] ller Supervisory Special Agent-1 that her request [illegible] e on Do[illegible] en d[illegible] it it was a "higher level decision."[1025] S[illegible] pecial A[illegible] ected [illegible] upervisory Special Agent-1 to delete the case [illegible] Sentin[illegible] pite [illegible] uiries, neither Mueller Supervisory Spe[illegible] nor Mu[illegible] nalyst-1 [illegible] rovided a specific rationale for the denial of th[illegible] ing.[1027] S[illegible] Mueller [illegible] ry Special Agent-1 never learned who ultimately d[illegible] se open[illegible] a Do[illegible] 2017 Lync message exchange, Mueller Analyst[illegible] discu[illegible] se op[illegible] olan. In one message, Mueller Analyst-1 stated, [illegible] sn't go[illegible] EM [illegible] ve Management] decides to do with it, is beyon[illegible] ule, I'[illegible] ume[illegible] – and that's all I can do . . . and serialize the rel[illegible]

During [illegible] with th[illegible] perv[illegible] al Agent-2 opined in retrospect that it was an "[illegible] to op[illegible] and [illegible] should have been, at a minimum, interviewed.[1030] [illegible] to be n[illegible] his i[illegible] ith the Office, Auten stated that he was supporti[illegible] an ins[illegible] of D[illegible] s recollection was corroborated by both Mueller [illegible] Speci[illegible] nd M[illegible] lyst-1.[1032]

*viii. [illegible] pervi[illegible] al Ag[illegible] Mueller Analyst-1 expressed [illegible] about [illegible] ence [illegible] bias in the decision not to open [illegible] Dol[illegible]*

In her int[illegible] the Off[illegible] ller Su[illegible] pecial Agent-1 recalled that she and Mueller An[illegible] ssed w[illegible] ecisi[illegible] en on Dolan was politically motivated, given [illegible] ensive [illegible] s to [illegible] tic party.[1033] Mueller Supervisory Spe[illegible] stated [illegible] not [illegible] decision not to open on Dolan

---

1023 Timeline pr[illegible] Mueller [illegible] ntry [illegible] 7, 2017.

1024 OSC Report [illegible] of M[illegible] st-1 [illegible] 2021 at 4.

1025 OSC Report [illegible] of M[illegible] viso[illegible] gent-1 on Aug. 31, 2021 at 5.

1026 *Id.* at 3.

1027 *Id.* at 5.

1028 *Id.*

1029 SCO_FBIPE[illegible] (Lync [illegible] from [illegible] alyst-1 to Helson dated 12/21/2017).

1030 OSC Repor[illegible] of S[illegible] Speci[illegible] n May 5, 2021 at 7.

1031 OSC Repor[illegible] of B[illegible] Ju[illegible] at 19.

1032 OSC Repor[illegible] of M[illegible] visor[illegible] gent-1 on Aug. 31, 2021 at 3; OSC Report of [illegible] Mueller [illegible] or[illegible] 21 at 6.

1033 OSC Repor[illegible] of M[illegible] visor[illegible] gent-1 on Aug. 31, 2021 at 4-5.

was political, but that she did worry about the optics of the decision, given that Dolan was a prominent Democrat.[1034] Mueller Supervisory Special Agent-1 further stated that she did not witness any explicit political bias during her work with the Mueller Special Counsel team.[1035] Nonetheless, at the time, Mueller Supervisory Special Agent-1 believed that the decision not to open on Dolan would eventually be reviewed by the OIG.[1036]

When interviewed by the Office, Mueller Analyst-1 did speculate that the decision not to open on Dolan was politically motivated. Mueller Analyst-1 speculated that the information on Dolan ran counter to the narrative that the Mueller Special Counsel investigators were cultivating given that Dolan was a former Democratic political operative.[1037] However, Mueller Analyst-1 was unable to provide the Office with definitive evidence to support her belief. Like Mueller Supervisory Special Agent-1, Mueller Analyst-1 believed that the decision not to investigate Dolan would eventually be reviewed by the OIG.[1038] In fact, Mueller Analyst-1 informed the Office that she uploaded her Galkina memorandum to three separate case files on the FBI Sentinel system to ensure that the OIG would have access to the document.[1039]

*ix. The FBI's failure to investigate Dolan*

In sum, save for efforts by Auten, Helson, Mueller Supervisory Special Agent-1, and Mueller Analyst-1, the FBI's failure to complete logical investigative steps concerning what, if any, role Dolan played in the Steele Reports was troubling. As discussed above, the Office has determined that Dolan was a source for at least one allegation in the Steele Reports, and was one of only three U.S. persons named by Steele (in both his October 2016 and September 2017 interviews) who had more information about the reports. If the FBI had learned nothing more about Dolan, Steele's statements alone would have been an ample basis to interview Dolan. Moreover, Mueller Supervisory Special Agent-1, Mueller Analyst-1, and others had uncovered significant information about Dolan – independent from what the Office subsequently unearthed – that potentially connected him to the Steele Reports; this was information that plainly warranted further investigation. In summary, the evidence possessed by the FBI and later elicited during the *Danchenko* trial showed that:

- Dolan maintained a relationship with Danchenko, Steele's primary sub-source for the Steele Reports;
- Dolan maintained relationships with various Russian government officials, including Dimitry Peskov and Alexey Pavlov, both of whom feature prominently in the Steele Reports;

---

1034 *Id.*; OSC Report of Interview of Mueller Analyst-1 on Aug. 16, 2021 at 7.

1035 OSC Report of Interview of Mueller Supervisory Special Agent-1 on Aug. 31, 2021 at 4-5.

1036 *Id.*

1037 OSC Report of Interview of Mueller Analyst-1 on Aug. 16, 2021 at 7.

1038 *Danchenko* Tr. 10/14/2022 AM at 956:1-957:23.

1039 *Id.*

- Dolan was present in Moscow in June 2016, met with the General Manager of the Moscow Ritz Carlton, toured the premises, including the Presidential Suite, and had at least one meeting with Danchenko who also was in Moscow;
- Dolan was present in Moscow with Danchenko in October 2016 – during the time frame Danchenko was gathering information for the Steele Reports;
- Dolan maintained a relationship with Galkina, allegedly a sub-source for Danchenko, and met with Galkina in Cyprus on two occasions in the summer of 2016;
- Dolan performed work for Galkina's former employer, who would later appear in the Steele Reports;
- Galkina admitted to the FBI that she provided Dolan with information that would eventually be in the Steele Reports; and
- Dolan was a prominent and longtime Democratic political operative who vocally supported candidate Clinton;

The FBI interviewed hundreds of individuals through the course of the Crossfire Hurricane and Mueller Special Counsel investigations, and yet, they did not interview Dolan or the other two U.S. persons identified by Steele as early as October 2016. The Office interviewed Dolan on several occasions and he denied being a source of information for the Steele Reports, save for the Manafort campaign-related allegation he provided to Danchenko in August 2016 – an allegation he acknowledged to the Office that he fabricated. Although both Steele and Galkina suggested that Dolan may have information related to the Steele Reports, our investigation was not able to definitively prove that Dolan was the actual source for any additional allegations set forth in the Steele Reports. That said, in light of the foregoing, there does not appear to be an objectively sound reason for the decision that was made not to interview him.

f. Sergei Millian

A particularly disturbing example of the unsupported narratives regarding Trump and Russia – created and pressed by Fusion GPS and Steele – involved a Belarussian-American named Sergei Millian. At the time of his purported involvement in Trump-related matters, Millian was a New York-based real estate broker who from 2006-2016 served as president of the Russian-American Chamber of Commerce. In the course of his employment, Millian had occasion to be involved in some relatively minor listings of Trump Organization properties.

As discussed more fully below, Danchenko claimed to have sourced several of the most serious allegations in the Steele Reports to Millian, including allegations of an ongoing conspiracy between the Trump campaign and Russian officials. Several of these allegations were included in the Page FISA applications. In particular, and perhaps most importantly, Steele Report 2016/095 stated, in part:

> Speaking in confidence to a compatriot *in late July 2016, Source E, an ethnic Russian close associate of Republican US presidential candidate Donald TRUMP,* admitted that there was a well-developed conspiracy of co-operation between them and the Russian leadership. This was managed on the TRUMP side

> by the Republican candidate's campaign manager, Paul MANAFORT, who was using foreign policy advisor, Carter PAGE, and others as intermediaries. The two sides had a mutual interest in defeating Democratic presidential candidate Hillary CLINTON, whom President PUTIN apparently both hated and feared.[1040]

During several interviews with the FBI, Danchenko said that he believed "Source E" in Report 2016/095 referred, at least in part, to Millian. According to Steele, Danchenko was the only one communicating with Millian, and Steele stated that Danchenko had had direct contacts with Millian in New York City and Charleston, South Carolina. On the other hand, Danchenko told the FBI that, although Steele believed that he (Danchenko) had met with Millian, he never did.[1041] Further, Danchenko did not correct Steele in his mistaken belief that Danchenko had met directly with Millian.[1042]

As explained in greater detail below, the spectacular claim contained in Steele Report Number 2016/095 of a "well-developed conspiracy of co-operation" between the Trump campaign and Russian leadership is based entirely on a purported anonymous telephone call Danchenko said he received from someone he had never spoken to before. In particular, the information about the conspiracy was conveyed to him by an anonymous caller who Danchenko told Crossfire Hurricane investigators he believed might have been Millian based on Danchenko's claimed comparison of the caller's voice to a known *YouTube* video featuring Millian.[1043] Yet this unvetted, completely uncorroborated allegation was included in the Page FISA applications, both before and after the FBI learned its provenance from Danchenko himself.

*i. Danchenko's statements to the FBI regarding Millian*

When interviewed by the FBI in January 2017, Danchenko was twice asked to review Steele Report Number 2016/095 and explain where the information came from concerning a well-developed conspiracy between the Trump campaign and Russian leadership and the roles allegedly being played by Manafort and Page. Danchenko told the FBI that the "Source E" information sounded as though it were from a call he had received in late July 2016 from an anonymous caller who Danchenko believed was Sergei Millian. In particular, Danchenko described the following "strange" event:

Danchenko told the FBI that in June or July 2016, he communicated with Alexey Bogdanovsky, a U.S.-based Russian national employee of RIA Novosti (a Russian state-run media outlet) about reaching out to Millian, who Danchenko had never met or spoken with.[1044] Bogdanovsky indicated that his colleague at RIA Novosti, Dimitry Zlodorev, had a relationship

---

[1040] SCO-105084 (Documents Known to the FBI Comprising the "Steele Dossier") at 9 (Company Intelligence Report 2016-095) (capitalization in original; emphasis added).

[1041] SCO_105287 (CHS Reporting Document dated 11/14/2017).

[1042] *Id.*

[1043] *Id.*

[1044] SCO-005801 (Interview of Igor Danchenko Electronic Communication dated 02/09/2017 at 35-36).

with Millian and [illegible] sly int[illegible] [illegible]p.[1045] Bogdanovsky ultimately provided Danch[illegible] [illegible]llian's [illegible] [illegible]hereafter, Danchenko told the FBI that he reac[illegible] Millian [illegible] [illegible]ceive a response back from him.[1047] Danch[illegible] provid[illegible] [illegible]se emails, despite explicit requests to prov[illegible] ds of [illegible] ion [illegible][1048]

Danche[illegible] the FB[illegible] [illegible] receiving no email response from Millian, h[illegible] recei[illegible] [illegible]ll from an anonymous individual who he believe[illegible] Millia[illegible] [illegible] phone call, the caller, who did not identify him[illegible] infe[illegible] [illegible]rump and the Kremlin, (ii) "communicatio[illegible] going [illegible] [illegible]ties, and (iii) Manafort and Page.[1050] The u[illegible] er als[illegible] [illegible] there was nothing bad about the "exchange of in[illegible] weer[illegible] [illegible] information could be good for Russia and dam[illegible] p, alt[illegible] [illegible]nko said that he and the person he believed to be M[illegible] o m[illegible] [illegible] in late July 2016.[1052] Danchenko als[illegible] that h[illegible] [illegible]e July 2016, but that Millian, or the person he be[illegible] Millia[illegible] [illegible]eeting.[1053] As discussed in detail below, Danche[illegible] of ev[illegible] [illegible] York conflict with the relevant record. Neverth[illegible] enko [illegible] [illegible]ad, in fact, never met with Millian in perso[illegible] as n[illegible] Dan[illegible] that Steele mistakenly thought that they had m[illegible] occasi[illegible] [illegible]ally did not correct him on that point.[1055]

---

[1045] *Id.* at 35-36.

[1046] *Id.* at 36.

[1047] *Id.* at 20. In [illegible] 2017 [illegible] [illegible]chenko first told the FBI that he received the lat[illegible] onym[illegible] he believed to be Millian following his ini[illegible] Millia[illegible] [illegible]ko la[illegible] FBI that he received the anonymous call [illegible] nd em[illegible] [illegible] below, given the date of his second email to [illegible] chenk[illegible] [illegible] is inconsistent with the documentary ev[illegible] ed du[illegible] [illegible]stig[illegible]

[1048] *Danchenko* [illegible] 22 AM [illegible]

[1049] SCO-0058[illegible] of Igo[illegible] [illegible] El[illegible] [illegible]munication dated 02/09/2017 at 36-37).

[1050] *Id.* at 20, 37.

[1051] *Id.* at 37.

[1052] *Id.*; SCO_1[illegible] Reporti[illegible] [illegible] 2017).

[1053] SCO-00580[illegible] of Igo[illegible] [illegible] El[illegible] [illegible]munication dated 02/09/2017 at 36).

[1054] SCO_1052[illegible] orting [illegible] dated [illegible]).

[1055] SCO_1052[illegible] orting [illegible] dated [illegible]).

Instead, Danchenko told the FBI that the damaging allegations contained in Steele Report 2016/095 stemmed from the single telephone call from the anonymous individual he believed to be Millian.[1056] The Office did not find any evidence, or uncover any motive, that would explain why Millian, a vocal Trump supporter,[1057] would call a complete stranger and provide damaging information about Trump.

In any event, Danchenko was not able to produce phone records or other evidence to corroborate this alleged call, despite explicit requests by the FBI to do so.[1058] Nor does it appear from FBI records that Crossfire Hurricane personnel pulled and reviewed Danchenko's toll records in an attempt to corroborate his statements regarding an anonymous call. Danchenko surmised during one interview that the purported call may have been received on an encrypted phone "app,"[1059] although a review of his email messages to Millian reflect that he made no mention of having or using any phone apps. Consistent with his inability to keep his narrative straight, Danchenko also later told the FBI that he had a "couple" of calls with Millian.[1060]

Danchenko also told the FBI that "Source D" in Steele Report 2016/080, relating in part to the scandalous Moscow Ritz Carlton allegations against Trump, "could be" referring to Millian.[1061] Danchenko's efforts to partially attribute the Ritz Carlton allegations to Millian support the notion that he fabricated his interaction with Millian. Indeed, as noted above, Danchenko told the FBI that the information he obtained from Millian came from a single, 10-15-minute anonymous phone call that took place in late-July 2016 and was the only time that Danchenko allegedly communicated with Millian. Given that the Steele Report containing those sexual allegations was dated June 20, 2016 – *over a month prior* to Danchenko's alleged call with Millian, the above-described "Source D" (Millian) allegation concerning the Ritz Carlton is highly probative of the fact that there was never such a phone call between Danchenko and Millian.[1062] It would have been impossible for Millian to confirm the Ritz Carlton allegations (and other information) to Danchenko in June 2016 because, as Danchenko repeatedly informed the FBI, the *first* time he allegedly communicated with Millian was late July 2016.

*ii. Steele's statements to the FBI about Millian*

On September 18 and 19, 2017, FBI personnel from the Mueller Special Counsel investigation interviewed Steele. Steele stated, in part, that Danchenko had collected election-

---

[1056] SCO-005801 (Interview of Igor Danchenko Electronic Communication dated 02/09/2017) at 37.

[1057] *E.g., Sergei Millian: Donald Trump will improve relations with Russia*, RIA Novosti (Apr. 13, 2016).

[1058] SCO_105282 (CHS Reporting Document dated 06/01/2017).

[1059] Transcript of March 16, 2017 interview of Danchenko at 106-107.

[1060] SCO_105286 (CHS Reporting Document dated 11/13/2017).

[1061] SCO_105282 (CHS Reporting Document dated 06/01/2017).

[1062] SCO-105084 (Documents Known to the FBI Comprising the "Steele Dossier") at 2-4, (Company Intelligence Report 2016/080).

related material in the United States for Orbis.[1063] As part of that undertaking, Danchenko informed Steele that he met in person with Millian on two or three occasions – in New York and "perhaps" in Charleston, South Carolina.[1064] However, as noted, Danchenko informed the FBI that he had not in fact met with Millian on any occasion and did not correct Steele in that misimpression.[1065]

*iii. The evidence obtained by the Office*

The evidence obtained by the Office shows that Danchenko, in fact, never received a phone call or any information from Millian, and Danchenko never made arrangements to meet with Millian in New York. Rather, the evidence demonstrates that Danchenko fabricated these facts regarding Millian. Indeed, a review of the emails sent by Danchenko to Millian in the summer of 2016 support this conclusion – the same emails Danchenko failed to provide the FBI when interviewed regarding Millian. Those emails are described below.

Danchenko first came to the attention of Millian on May 26, 2016 when Russian journalist Dimitry Zlodorev emailed Millian the following:

> Sergey, hello.
>
> I hope all is well with you and your [sic] are once again in America. It is my recollection you told me that you either have or will have news. Will it be convenient if I call sometime next week?
>
> In addition, my colleagues have an acquaintance, Igor Danchenko, who works here in consulting. Through them, he requested I find out if it is okay to get in touch with you? If I understood correctly, it is about Trump and Russia.
>
> Can I give him your contact information—e-mail, phone, or just e-mail?[1066]

Later that day, Millian replied to Zlodorev that he was leaving for Asia on June 10, 2016 and would call him soon.[1067] Millian's reply does not mention Danchenko.

On July 21, 2016, Danchenko, who appears to have acquired Millian's email address from Zlodorev, sent Millian the following message:

> Colleagues from RIA Novosti gave me your contact information. You spoke to Dimitry Zlodorev about Donald Trump and his trips to Russia. I wanted to ask you: what projects was he looking into or were these just image-building trips for beauty contests? There has been a lot of speculation for months now on this topic. It would be interesting to chat about this topic. It's confidential of course – I don't have any relationship to media, though of course I do have acquaintances here. In any case, it would be interesting if and when possible to chat with you by phone or meet for coffee/beer in Washington or in New York where I will be next

---

[1063] SCO-006313 (Interview of Christopher Steele on Sept. 18, 2017) at 7.

[1064] *Id.*

[1065] SCO_105287 (CHS Reporting Document dated 11/14/2017).

[1066] SC_IDC_0042618 (Email from Zlodorev to Millian dated 05/26/2016).

[1067] SC_IDC_0044205 (Email from Millian to Zlodorev dated 05/26/2016).

> week. I myself am in Washington. It is also possible by e-mail in Russian or in English. I sent to you a request to LinkedIn – there my work is clearer.[1068]

Millian did not respond to Danchenko's July 21, 2016 email. In fact, Millian was traveling in Asia at the time Danchenko sent this email and did not return to New York until the night of July 27, 2016.[1069] Notably, Millian had suspended his cellular phone service effective July 14, 2016 (prior to his travel) and his service was only reconnected effective August 8, 2016.[1070]

On July 26, 2016, Millian emailed Zlodorev the following:

> Dimitry, on Friday I'm returning from Asia. An email came from Igor. Who is that? What sort of person?[1071]

That same day, Zlodorev responded:

> Sergey, hello! Do you remember I said that a friend of my colleague wanted to get acquainted with you? You gave permission to give your email. The way I understand it, this is who this is. He and I are not personally acquainted, though he is, it seems, in my LinkedIn. And I didn't know what he wanted to talk about. If I remember correctly, he works at some think tank in Washington.[1072]

Millian did not respond to Danchenko's July 21, 2016 email.

On August 18, 2016 – more than two weeks *after* Danchenko purportedly received the aforementioned anonymous call and allegedly agreed to meet with Millian in New York – Danchenko again emailed Millian, stating in part: "Hello, Sergey! I wrote you several weeks ago. We are contacts on LinkedIn."[1073] Danchenko then described a real estate deal in Russia and inquired about Millian's interest in the transaction. Danchenko closed the email by stating, "Write, call. My contact information is below."[1074] This email – which post-dated the alleged "late July" call from Millian, clearly reflected that Danchenko had not, in fact, spoken with Millian and did not believe he had done so. Specifically, Danchenko's email did not mention a possible call from Millian and did not discuss plans to meet in New York with Millian.

On August 24, 2016, Danchenko emailed Zlodorev, stating in part:

> Aleksey Bogdanovsky recommended that I get in touch with Sergey Millian. I've read your interviews with him. *But for some reason Sergey doesn't respond.* I already both asked him about TRUMP and also proposed a project in Russia.

---

[1068] SC_IDC_0042660 (Email from Danchenko to Millian dated 07/21/2016).

[1069] SCO-101428 (U.S. Customs and Border Protection Person Encounter List for Sergei Millian at 1).

[1070] SCO-101860 (Verizon Notes on Account 404-667-9319); Verizon Subscriber Records for 404-667-9319.

[1071] SC_IDC_0042661 (Email from Millian to Zlodorev dated 07/26/2016).

[1072] SC_IDC_0042663 (Email from Zlodorev to Millian dated 07/26/2016).

[1073] SC_IDC_0042676 (Email from Danchenko to Millian dated 08/18/2016).

[1074] *Id.*

> What is [illegible] hip [illegible] able to ask him to reply to *me? I* [illegible] *rite* [illegible] *bu*[illegible] *nds I would not like to pester* [illegible] y, you [illegible] also [illegible] re.[1075]

This August 24 [illegible] to Zlod[illegible] made [illegible] at Danchenko had not, in fact, spoken with M[illegible] uly. [illegible] nchen[illegible] did not mention a possible call from Millian, d[illegible] plans [illegible] New [illegible] Millian, and did not inform Zlodorev that M[illegible] show [illegible] alleged [illegible] New York.

Later th[illegible] ev resp[illegible] part:

> Igor, hel[illegible] llian [illegible] ago who Igor Danchenko is. I had [illegible] ier, [illegible] ntly [illegible] that time, he wrote to me from S[illegible] The thi[illegible] bas[illegible] n words, now spends more ti[illegible] an in [illegible] y to [illegible] once again. I simply know th[illegible] ntly [illegible] d [illegible] have forgotten.[1076]

The emails quo[illegible] further [illegible] that [illegible] 21, 2016 and August 24, 2016, Millian did not [illegible] meet [illegible] enko knew he had not received a call from some[illegible] elieve[illegible] ian.

In additi[illegible] 20, th[illegible] dicia[illegible] ee released a heavily redacted report of Danch[illegible] y 201[illegible] [1077] In the report, Danchenko is only identified [illegible] rimary [illegible] acted interview was released, Millian had bee[illegible] ported [illegible] rce f[illegible] ormation in the Steele Reports, including the i[illegible] port[illegible] in [illegible] 2016 alleging that Trump and his campaign were [illegible] "well[illegible] cons[illegible] operation" with Russian officials. The redacted a[illegible] ed inter[illegible] ndic[illegible] "primary subsource" (Danchenko) ha[illegible] ntact[illegible] for [illegible] *i.e.*, Millian, from a journalist who had previ[illegible] ved Mi[illegible] Zlod[illegible] llowing the release of the interview, Mill[illegible] email [illegible] empli[illegible] ver the identity of Steele's primary subsource.[1079] [illegible] 20, D[illegible] was [illegible] name in press reporting as Steele's primar[illegible] On Ju[illegible], Mi[illegible] Zlodorev, stating in part:

> "I belie[illegible] ready [illegible]'s sc[illegible] net address]. Do you rememb[illegible] on? [illegible] nko"

On July [illegible] Millian [illegible] led Z[illegible] following:

---

1075 SCO-0058[illegible] of Ig[illegible] to El[illegible] mmunication dated 02/09/2017 1A) at 2 (emph[illegible] apital[illegible] gina[illegible]

1076 *Id.*

1077 U.S. Sena[illegible] on the [illegible] udic[illegible] ittee Releases Declassified Documents tha[illegible] Und[illegible] D[illegible] FISA Warrants (July 17, 2020).

1078 SENATE-[illegible] 106 [illegible]

1079 SC_IDC_0[illegible] ail from [illegible] Zlo[illegible] 07/17/2020).

1080 SC_IDC_0[illegible] ail from [illegible] Zlo[illegible] 07/19/2020).

> I've been informed that Bogdanovsky travelled to New York with Danchenko at the end of July 2016; Danchenko, supposedly to meet with me (but the meeting didn't take place). Can you inquire with Bogdanovsky whether he remembers something from that trip and whether they touched upon my name in conversation, as well as for what reason Danchenko was travelling to NY? Steele, it seems, made Danchenko the fall guy, but Danchenko himself made several statements that were difficult to understand, for example, about the call with me. Did he tell Bogdanovsky that he communicated with me by phone and on what topic? Thank you! This will clarify a lot for me personally. It's a convoluted story![1081]

These 2020 emails between Millian and Zlodorev again point to the fact that Danchenko did not receive a call from Millian in late-July 2016.

The Office also reviewed phone records for both Danchenko and Millian from 2016 and 2017. Those records reveal no communication between Millian and Danchenko. In fact, the Office was able to identify nearly every call received by Danchenko during the relevant timeframe. Of the small number of calls that could not be identified, none had a duration approaching 10-15 minutes.[1082] Moreover, as noted above, service to Millian's primary cellular telephone number was suspended at the time Danchenko allegedly received the anonymous call. Further, the contention that Danchenko may have received an "anonymous call" from someone he believed to be Millian on an internet-based application was not supported by the evidence obtained by the Office. Indeed, at no time did Danchenko inform Millian that he could be contacted on an internet-based application, to say nothing of the particular application Millian should use. Rather, the evidence did show that when Danchenko wanted to communicate on an internet-based application, he explicitly communicated that to his contacts and identified the application to use.[1083]

With respect to the purported meeting with Millian in New York, the evidence obtained by the Office revealed that Danchenko had planned to travel to New York during the week of July 24, 2016, *prior* to even reaching out to Millian for the first time.[1084] Indeed, the evidence revealed that Danchenko's trip to New York was a sightseeing excursion with his young daughter. In order to credit Danchenko's version of events, one would have to accept that Danchenko, with his young daughter, planned to meet an *unidentified* individual at an *unidentified* bar – in a city of 8 million people – at night.

Finally, the Office interviewed Millian. Millian unequivocally stated that he never met with or spoke with Danchenko.[1085] When asked if he provided the information reflected in the Steele Reports to Danchenko, Millian stated "[t]hat did not happen. One-hundred percent did not

---

[1081] SC_IDC_0043181 (Email from Millian to Zlodorev dated 07/20/2020).

[1082] *Danchenko* Government Exhibit 1603.

[1083] *See, e.g., Danchenko* Government Exhibits 610, 610T, 611, 612, 612T.

[1084] SC_IDC_0003641 (Email from Danchenko dated 07/18/2016).

[1085] OSC Report of Interview of Sergei Millian on Feb. 5, 2022 at 1.

happen."[1086] Millian stated he has received threats to his and his family's safety because of his alleged role in the Steele Reports.[1087]

*iv. Fusion GPS implicates Sergei Millian*

As discussed above, the Office found no evidence that Millian was a source for any of the allegations in the Steele Reports. Given this fact, the Office endeavored to determine the genesis of Millian's implication in the Steele Reports. In particular, what caused Danchenko to first reach out to Millian in late July 2016. To that end, the Office reviewed, among other things, records obtained from Fusion GPS and the public statements of Fusion GPS principals Glenn Simpson and Peter Fritsch.[1088]

Specifically, Fusion GPS records demonstrate that Nellie Ohr first identified Millian as having connections to Trump. Ohr was a Russian-language contractor employed by Fusion GPS and the wife of Department official Bruce Ohr. On April 22, 2016, Nellie Ohr prepared a report for Fusion GPS that set forth, in part, Millian's connections to Trump.[1089] This report was prepared just ten days after Fusion GPS was retained by Perkins Coie to conduct opposition research on Trump, and prior to Steele being retained by Fusion GPS.[1090] Notably, on April 13, 2016 – approximately one week prior to Ohr's report – RIA Novosti published an interview with Millian that was conducted by Dimitry Zlodorev.[1091] In that interview, Millian described his alleged real estate connections to Trump and spoke positively about Trump's candidacy.[1092] Millian was interviewed by RIA Novosti several more times over the course of the summer and

---

[1086] *Id.*

[1087] *Id.* at 4.

[1088] The Office collected various records and statements from Fusion GPS and Fusion GPS employees over the course of its investigation. No one at Fusion GPS, however, would agree to voluntarily speak with the Office. In addition, the DNC and the Clinton campaign asserted attorney-client privilege over a substantial number of Fusion GPS's emails.

[1089] *See* Nellie Ohr, *Report 22 April 2016* at 29.

[1090] Consulting Agreement between Fusion GPS and Perkins Coie was signed on Apr. 11, 2016. SC-00004920 (Consulting Agreement dated Apr. 1, 2016). Steele was approached by Simpson to research Trump in May, 2016. OIG Interview of Christopher Steele on June 5 and 6, 2019 at 11; *Crime in Progress* at 69.

[1091] RIA Novosti, *Sergei Millian: Donald Trump Will Improve Relations with Russia* (translated) (Apr. 13, 2016).

[1092] *Id.*

all of 2016.[1093] On May 7, 2016, Nellie Ohr compiled another report discussing, among other things, Millian.[1094] All told, Ohr prepared at least 12 reports that discussed Sergei Millian.[1095]

Nellie Ohr's reports included Millian's views on how a potential "Trump presidency might affect US-Russia relations."[1096] Notably, Ohr included internet links in the reports to several *YouTube* videos from 2012 featuring Millian.[1097] As discussed above, Danchenko told the FBI that the anonymous caller from late-July 2016 "sounded like Millian" based on a *YouTube* video that Danchenko had previously watched.[1098] The reports prepared by Ohr and others at Fusion GPS were ultimately provided to Crossfire Hurricane investigators by Ohr's husband, Bruce Ohr.[1099]

As discussed above, Fusion GPS approached Steele in May 2016. Prior to his retention, Glenn Simpson met with Steele at Heathrow Airport in London and pitched Steele on the opposition research project.[1100] Approximately one week later, Danchenko contacted RIA Novosti journalists seeking Millian's contact information.[1101] The timing of Danchenko's request to RIA Novosti on the heels of Steele's meeting with Simpson in London strongly supports the inference that Fusion GPS directed Steele to pursue Millian.[1102] Indeed, by the time of Steele's meeting with Simpson, Nellie Ohr had already identified Millian's alleged connections to Trump.

In addition to Ohr, other Fusion GPS employees also appear to have worked on research pertaining to Millian. While the vast majority of the internal Fusion GPS emails were withheld from the Office based on privilege claims by the Clinton campaign or the DNC, the privilege log provided revealed that Fusion GPS employees regularly emailed about Millian, often attaching what appear to be draft memoranda about Millian or forwarding news articles concerning Millian.[1103] For example, on July 1, 2016, Fusion GPS employee Jake Berkowitz emailed a draft

---

1093 *E.g.* Dmitry Zlodorev, *Political scientist: Trump's reform will be based on the principle of Americanism*, RIA Novosti (Aug. 09, 2016); Dmitry Zlodorev, *RATP President: Trump will choose a businessman or military man as vice president of the United States*, RIA Novosti (June 10, 2016).

1094 Nellie Ohr, Weekly Writeup 7 May 2016.

1095 *See, e.g.*, Nellie Ohr, Sergei Millian Compendium Updated 24 September 2016.

1096 Nellie Ohr, *Report 22 April 2016* at 29-34.

1097 *Id.* at 32.

1098 SCO_105287 (CHS Reporting Document dated 11/14/2017)

1099 U.S. House of Representatives Executive Session, Cmte. on the Judiciary Joint with the Cmte. on Government Reform and Oversight, Interview of Bruce Ohr on Aug. 28, 2018 at 7-9.

1100 *Crime in Progress* at 69.

1101 SC_IDC_0042618 (Email from Zlodorev to Millian dated 05/26/2016).

1102 In their book, Simpson and Fritsch state that Steele identified Millian as "one of the key intermediaries between Trump and the Russians." *Crime in Progress* at 97.

1103 Bean LLC/Fusion GPS Privilege Log dated Mar. 11, 2022.

memo entitled "[illegible] an 6.3 [illegible] [illegible] later, on July 13, 2016, Berkowitz forw[illegible] re doc[illegible] enn [illegible]

At the sa[illegible] researc[illegible] n was [illegible] ducted, Fusion GPS was promoting Mill[illegible] ss as a [illegible] rump and Russia. For example, on June 27, 201[illegible] pri[illegible] Fritsch [illegible] mail to Franklin Foer, a reporter at *Slate* magazine, [illegible] ine [illegible] ed:

> this dud[illegible]
>
> https.//r[illegible] m/age[illegible] llia[illegible]
>
> he is cl[illegible] at m[illegible] tate [illegible] iversity is something of a giveaw[illegible]
>
> If you a[illegible], come [illegible]

Fusion [illegible] on [illegible] ared [illegible] substantially in late-July 2016. In fact, between Ju[illegible] and Ju[illegible] Fus[illegible] ployees exchanged several dozen internal emails [illegible] Millian [illegible] n Simpson was in contact with ABC News pro[illegible] Mosk [illegible] y, emails showed that Mosk had been communic[illegible] Millian [illegible] July [illegible][10] During the course of this correspondence, [illegible] that [illegible] s ab[illegible] nned to return to the United States in late July.[1111]

> On July [illegible] Mosk em[illegible] m th[illegible]
>
> Hello S[illegible]
>
> I am wri[illegible] you m[illegible] f Donald Trump or Don Jr. visiting [illegible] your [illegible] with [illegible] Organization? We would very mu[illegible] able [illegible] his p[illegible], and business interests in Russia.

Later that day, [illegible] that [illegible] raph with Trump that had been taken in Miami. [illegible] Mosk ask[illegible] if he [illegible] willing to do an interview with ABC News abo[illegible] ences [illegible] conduct the interview in New

---

[1104] *Id.* at 13.

[1105] *Id.*

[1106] SC-001008[illegible] om Frit[illegible] dated [illegible] 6).

[1107] *Id.*

[1108] Bean LLC/[illegible] Privileg[illegible] d Ma[illegible] at 17-23.

[1109] *See, e.g.*, S[illegible] (Ema[illegible] pson t[illegible] ed 07/27/2016); SC_00082580 (Email from Si[illegible] sk & E[illegible] ated [illegible]).

[1110] SC_IDC_0[illegible] ails betw[illegible] n, Mi[illegible] 07/13-27/2016) at 2-3.

[1111] 0.7.8516.5[illegible] from M[illegible] Mosk [illegible] 2016).

[1112] SC_IDC_0[illegible] ails betw[illegible] n an[illegible] ed 07/13-27/2016) at 1-2.

York. Millian indicated that he would be available to conduct an interview in New York on the "Week-end or next week I can."[1113] While making arrangements with Millian, Mosk emailed Simpson and informed Simpson that he (Mosk) was "making arrangements to interview Millian on camera" and that he and Simpson "should chat."[1114] Millian ultimately was interviewed by Brian Ross of ABC News on July 29, 2016.[1115]

For reasons unknown to the Office, ABC News did not air the Millian interview in its entirety until January 2017, after the Steele Reports became public.[1116] Nevertheless, Fusion GPS continued to send Mosk information about Millian,[1117] including Fusion GPS's comprehensive report on Millian dated June 30, 2016.[1118] On September 13, 2016, Mosk emailed Simpson and Berkowitz and asked "What's the most official thing we have showing Millian tied to Trump? That would make it hard for the Trump org to disavow Millian?"[1119] Berkowitz responded with a screenshot of Millian's Trump Gold Donor card that Millian had posted on his Instagram page.[1120] Throughout the fall of 2016, Fusion GPS continued to communicate with the media about Millian and Trump.[1121]

*v. Fusion GPS attempts to tie Millian to Alfa Bank*

As discussed in detail below, throughout the summer and fall of 2016, Fusion GPS was promoting to the media an allegation of secret computer server communications between the Trump campaign and Russian-based Alfa Bank. In an attempt to tie Millian to the Alfa Bank allegations, Fusion GPS sought the assistance of Perkins Coie attorney Michael Sussmann. In turn, Sussmann contacted technology executive Rodney Joffe to determine if Millian had any ties to Alfa Bank.

On August 20, 2016, Joffe emailed a fellow technology executive ("Tech Company-2 Executive-1") and two academic researchers ("University-1 Researcher-1" and "University-1 Researcher-2") a document titled "birdsnest-1.pdf" that contained "known associates" of

---

1113 *Id.*

1114 SC-00083448 (Email from Simpson to Mosk dated 07/27/2016).

1115 SC_IDC_0044296 (Email from Mosk to Millian, others dated 07/28/2016).

1116 *US-Russia Businessman Claimed Ties to Donald Trump (July 2016)*, ABC News (Jan. 24, 2017). https://abcnews.go.com/Politics/video/us-russia-businessman-claimed-ties-donald-trump-july-45022871

1117 SC-00082251 (Email from Berkowitz to Mosk, Simpson dated 09/19/2016).

1118 SC-00082580 (Email from Simpson to Mosk, Berkowitz dated 07/28/2016).

1119 SC-00082257 (Email from Mosk to Berkowitz, Simpson dated 09/13/2016).

1120 SC-00083205 (Email from Simpson to Mosk, Berkowitz dated 09/13/2016).

1121 *See, e.g.*, SC-00083036 (Email from Simpson to Catherine Belton, Financial Times, dated 09/23/2016); SC-00099806 (Email from Simpson to Belton dated 09/22/2016); SC-00027869 (Email from Mark Hosenball, Reuters to Fritsch, Berkowitz & Simpson dated 11/23/2016); SC-00100363 (Email from Eric Lichtblau, N.Y. Times, to Fritsch & Simpson dated 09/27/2016); SC-00088073 (Email from Simpson to David Corn, Mother Jones dated 11/01/2016); SC-00028499 (Email from Peter H. Stone to Berkowitz dated 11/16/2016).

Trump.[1122] Included in the attached "birdnest-1" document was a description of Millian along with (i) his past mailing addresses, (ii) various email addresses, (iii) websites, and (iv) IP addresses that were associated with Millian.[1123] Joffe described the document as "the result of significant investigative effort of Eyore's[1124] professional team," and informed Tech Company-2 Executive-1, University-1 Researcher-1 and University-1 Researcher-2 that other than Paul Manafort, Millian is "seen as the most likely intermediary" between Trump and Russia. Joffe also specifically called the group's attention to the "Russianamericanchamber.com" website.

On September 22, 2016, Sussman emailed Joffe and attached a document containing IP location information for "Russianamericanchamber.com."[1125] The body of the email was redacted by Perkins Coie based on privilege claims by the Clinton campaign.[1126] On the evening of September 26, 2016, Joffe emailed Sussman a message containing the subject line "As requested."[1127] The body of the email was also redacted by Perkins Coie based on privilege claims by the Clinton campaign.[1128] Sussmann and Joffe exchanged additional emails (withheld for privilege) later that night and into the early morning hours of September 27, 2016.[1129]

Further, on September 27, 2016,[1130] Fritsch and Simpson emailed Millian's website (the Russian-American Chamber of Commerce) IP look-up information to Eric Lichtblau at the New York Times.[1131] As discussed below, during the fall of 2016, Fusion GPS was pressuring Lichtblau to write a story about the Trump/Alfa Bank allegations. In the email, Fritsch pointed out that "Alfa" was the website service provider for Millian's website. However, the Office determined that the relevant IP information does not indicate that "Alfa Bank" is the service provider, but rather Alfa Telecom, a Lebanese-based telecom company, which appears to have no affiliation with Alfa Bank whatsoever.[1132]

---

1122 SC-00000578 (Email from Joffe to Tech Company-2 Executive-1, University-1 Researcher-1, University-1 Researcher-2 dated 08/20/2016).

1123 *Id.* at 5.

1124 The Office was not able to identify the individual referred to as "Eyore."

1125 SC_00109377 (Email from Sussmann to Joffe dated 09/22/2016).

1126 Perkins Coie Privilege Log dated 09/07/2021 at Worksheet 2 row 41.

1127 SC_00109375 (Emails between Joffe and Sussmann dated 09/26-27/2016).

1128 Perkins Coie Privilege Log dated 09/07/2021 at Worksheet 2 rows 45-48.

1129 SC_00109375 (Emails between Joffe and Sussmann dated 09/26-27/2016).

1130 Coincidentally – or not – the day following Sussmann and Joffe's exchange of emails concerning the same information.

1131 SC-00100359 (Email from Fritsch to Lichtblau, Simpson dated 09/27/2016).

1132 *Id.*

*vi. The FBI's conduct concerning Millian*

From September 2007 to March 2011, Sergei Millian served as an FBI CHS.[1133] During that time, Millian reported on matters related to Belarus and Russia.[1134] Following, among other things, Danchenko's revelations concerning Millian, in August 2017, FBI agents attached to the Mueller Special Counsel team began investigating Millian to determine what, if any, involvement Millian had in relation to the Russian Government's efforts to influence the 2016 Presidential Election. On January 17, 2019 the FBI closed its case on Millian noting that "the investigation found no confirmation that [Millian] was directed to engage in activities related to Russian Government efforts to interfere with the 2016 U.S. Presidential Election."[1135]

In their interviews with the Office, both Auten and Helson expressed skepticism about Danchenko's alleged interaction with Millian.[1136] It does not appear, however, that the Crossfire Hurricane investigators made any effort to corroborate Danchenko's version of events. For example, it does not appear that the FBI examined either Danchenko or Millian's phone records. Nor does it appear that the FBI questioned Danchenko about the implausibility of the meeting he supposedly planned with Millian in New York. Lastly, and perhaps most importantly, nobody from the FBI questioned Danchenko about the incongruity between Millian's vocal support for Trump and his alleged statements to Danchenko. Again, in order to credit Danchenko's narrative, one would have to accept that Millian called Danchenko, an individual he did not know, and provided him with damaging information on Trump during a 10-15-minute phone call. In sum, the evidence obtained by the Office simply does not support Danchenko's version of events. Nevertheless, despite the obvious infirmities in Danchenko's narrative, the information allegedly provided by Millian remained in the Page FISA applications through the final renewal in June 2017.

g. <u>The FBI's failure to disclose to OI and include in the Page FISA applications Page's role as a source for another government agency</u>

In addition to the inclusion of highly questionable information in the Page FISA applications, the FBI also failed to include highly relevant information in those applications. As disclosed in the *OIG Review*, one of the serious errors in the four Page FISA applications was the failure to report that Page had been approved as an "operational contact" for at least one other government agency ("OGA") during the period from 2008 to 2013.[1137] The record reflects that the Crossfire Hurricane investigators had been made aware of this relationship months prior to the submission of the initial Page FISA application in October 2016.

In the course of its investigation, the OIG also discovered evidence that, prior to the submission of the fourth and final Page FISA application, the issue of Page's relationship with the OGA was raised with the FBI's OGC by the FBI affiant on that application. In particular, the

---

[1133] *Danchenko* Tr. 10/11/2022 PM at 99-100.

[1134] SCO_105159 (Summary re Sergei Millian).

[1135] SCO_105145 (Case Closing Electronic Communication dated 01/17/2019) at 5.

[1136] OSC Report of Interview of Brian Auten on July 26, 2021 at 21; OSC Report of Interview of Kevin Helson on July 27, 2021 at 3-4.

[1137] *See Redacted OIG Review* at xi, 157-58.

affiant, Superv[illegible] Agent-2 [illegible] Kevin Clinesmith, the OGC attorney who wa[illegible] with the [illegible] gators, on what, if any, relationship Pag[illegible] OG[illegible] d of the other agency, (ii) received a resp[illegible] at Pag[illegible] ship with it during a relevant time period, (iii) alt[illegible] nse to [illegible] sent the altered document to the affiant, which [illegible] relie[illegible] ns to the FISC. After discovering this misconduct, [illegible] nform[illegible] d the Director of the FBI of the matter pursuan[illegible] or G[illegible] er information about Clinesmith's ac[illegible] forth [illegible]

*i.* [illegible] *ey K*[illegible]

From J[illegible] Septe[illegible] Cli[illegible] employed by the FBI's OGC as an Assistant Gene[illegible] the N[illegible] Law Branch.[1140] Among other duties, Clinesm[illegible] BI ag[illegible] ations and worked directly with attorneys in O[illegible]

In the la[illegible] d fall [illegible] igned to provide legal support to FBI personnel [illegible] Cro[illegible] n. In this role, Clinesmith interacted with [illegible] ssues [illegible] e Hurricane effort. In addition, Clinesmith pro[illegible] o the [illegible] gators who worked with OI to prepare the FIS[illegible] seek[illegible] veillance of Page.[1142]

On Aug[illegible] month[illegible] 016, approval of the initial FISA application targ[illegible] e OG[illegible] the [illegible] rricane investigators a memorandum ([illegible] 17 Me[illegible] age had been approved as an "operational c[illegible] OGA [illegible] od 2[illegible]. The Memorandum described the reporting Page [illegible] o the [illegible] is prior contacts with certain Russian intellig[illegible].[1143] [illegible] below, Clinesmith would later claim to the O[illegible] not re[illegible] th Memorandum and that he did not have acces[illegible] GC [illegible].[1144] [illegible] chnically true that the document

---

[1138] *Id.* at 157-5[illegible] Repor[illegible] Special Agent-2 on May 5, 2021 at 3.

[1139] *See Redact*[illegible] at 2[illegible]

[1140] *United Sta*[illegible] *linesm*[illegible] No. 2[illegible] B), (D.D.C.), Doc. 9 (Statement of Offense) at [illegible] his ple[illegible] t, Cli[illegible] reed "to be personally debriefed" by the FBI rega[illegible] I's re[illegible] ny information he possesses . . . that should be [illegible] atten[illegible] FISC [illegible] m John Durham to attorney Justin Shur, *Re: Unit*[illegible] *evin C*[illegible] 0). Clinesmith otherwise declined to be [illegible] the [illegible] oper[illegible] investigation.

[1141] *Id.*

[1142] *United St*[illegible] *lines*[illegible] No. [illegible] B) (D.D.C.), Doc. 1 (Information) at 1-2.

[1143] *Id.* at 2.

[1144] OIG Repor[illegible] of K[illegible] nith [illegible] 2019 at 19.

was not located in OGC space, the document was located at FBI Headquarters and available upon request to Crossfire Hurricane personnel, including Clinesmith.[1145]

The first three Page FISA applications made no reference to Page's prior relationship with the OGA. However, before the FBI's submission of the final FISA application, Page himself publicly stated that he had assisted named government entities in the past.[1146] During the preparation of the final FISA application, the affiant on the proposed application, Supervisory Special Agent-2, asked Clinesmith to ask whether Page had ever been a source for the OGA.[1147]

On June 15, 2017, Clinesmith sent an email to a liaison from the OGA ("OGA Liaison-1") stating:

> We need some clarification on Page. There is an indication that he may be a '[digraph]'[1148] source. This is a fact we would need to disclose in our next FISA renewal . . . To that end, can we get two items from you? 1) Source Check/Is [Page] a source in any capacity? 2) If he is, what is a [digraph] source (or whatever type of source he is)?[1149]

OGA Liaison-1 responded by email that same day and provided Clinesmith with a list (but not copies) of pertinent OGA documents. That list included a reference to the August 17 Memorandum the OGA had previously provided to the Crossfire Hurricane team. The liaison also wrote that the OGA uses

> the [digraph] to show that the encrypted individual . . . is a [U.S. person]. We encrypt the [U.S. persons] when they provide reporting to us. My recollection is that Page was or is . . . [digraph] but the [documents] will explain the details. If you need a formal definition for the FISA, please let me know and we'll work up some language and get it cleared for use.[1150]

Clinesmith responded that same day to OGA Liaison-1 stating, "Thanks so much for the information. We're digging into the [documents] now, but I think the definition of the [digraph] answers our questions."[1151]

At the time of the exchange between Clinesmith and OGA Liaison-1, Supervisory Special Agent-2 was on leave, so Clinesmith forwarded the liaison's email to two other Crossfire Hurricane investigators ("Special Agent-3" and "Supervisory Special Agent-4"). Notably, before forwarding the email, Clinesmith removed his initial email to OGA Liaison-1 that

---

[1145] OSC Report of Interview of Supervisory Special Agent-4 on Nov. 20, 2019 at 4.

[1146] Letter from Carter Page to FBI Director Comey (Sept. 25, 2016).

[1147] *See* OSC interview of Supervisory Special Agent-2 on Oct 17, 2019 at 4.

[1148] The digraph was redacted for classification reasons.

[1149] FBI-EMAIL-444179 (Email from Clinesmith to OGA Liason-1 dated 06/15/2017).

[1150] FBI-EMAIL-444164 (Email from Clinesmith to OGA Liason-1 dated 06/15/2017).

[1151] *Id.*

inquired about Page's status as a source.[1152] That same day, Supervisory Special Agent-4 emailed Clinesmith and OI Unit Chief-1, informing OI Unit Chief-1 that she (Supervisory Special Agent-4) would "pull these [documents] for you tomorrow[.]"[1153] In a subsequent reply to Clinesmith, Supervisory Special Agent-4 suggested that OI Unit Chief-1 may have previously been aware of Page's relationship with the OGA.[1154]

Later that evening, notwithstanding the information he received from OGA Liaison-1, Clinesmith told FBI OGC Unit Chief-1 that Page was not a source, but rather a "U.S. subsource of a source."[1155] Clinesmith also sent an email to OI Attorney-1, the OI attorney working on the Page FISA renewal, and requested a time to talk the following day.[1156]

The next day, Clinesmith and OI Attorney-1 spoke for approximately 30 minutes.[1157] Following the call, Clinesmith forwarded to OI Attorney-1 the June 15, 2017, email from OGA Liaison-1.[1158] Once again, Clinesmith omitted the initial email he sent to the liaison that inquired about Page's status as a source.[1159] When interviewed by the OIG, OI Attorney-1 did not recall the substance of his telephone call with Clinesmith.[1160] However, documents reviewed by the Office reflect that OI Attorney-1 replied to Clinesmith's forward of OGA Liaison-1's email and stated, "thanks I think we are good and no need to carry it any further."[1161] Copying Case Agent-1, Clinesmith replied, "Music to my ears."[1162] The Office has found no evidence to indicate that Case Agent-1 went back to look at the OGA documents after he received OI Attorney-1's guidance on the issue from Clinesmith.

On June 19, 2017, Supervisory Special Agent-2, who had returned from leave, exchanged a series of Lync messages with Clinesmith regarding Page:

Supervisory Special Agent-2: Do we have any update on the [OGA] CHS [that is, Page] request? Also, [Case Agent-1]

---

[1152] FBI-EMAIL-444176 (Email from Clinesmith to OI Unit Chief-1 & Supervisory Special Agent-4 dated 06-15-2017).

[1153] FBI-EMAIL-441659 (Email from Supervisory Special Agent-4 to Clinesmith, OI Unit Chief-1 dated 06/15/2017).

[1154] FBI-EMAIL-441647 (Email from Supervisory Special Agent-4 to Clinesmith & OI Unit Chief-1 dated 06/19/2017).

[1155] FBI-AAA-EC-00006440 (Lync exchange between Clinesmith and FBI OGC Unit Chief-1 dated 06/15/2017).

[1156] FBI-EMAIL-441654 (Email from Clinesmith to OI Attorney-1 dated 06/15/2017).

[1157] FBI-EMAIL-447802 (Lync archive dated 06/16/2017).

[1158] FBI-EMAIL-444161 (Email from Clinesmith to OI Attorney-1 dated 06/16/2017).

[1159] *Id.*

[1160] OIG interview of OI Attorney-1 on Sept. 11, 2019 at 5-9.

[1161] FBI-EMAIL-444159 (Emails between Clinesmith and OI Attorney-1 dated 06/16/2017).

[1162] *Id.*

| | |
|---|---|
| | said [OI Attorney-1] is not so optimistic. |
| Clinesmith: | [OGA] CHS: You are referring to Page? |
| Supervisory Special Agent-2: | Yes. |
| Clinesmith: | He is cleared. |
| Supervisory Special Agent-2: | Cleared to fly? |
| Clinesmith: | [digraph]=Masked USPER.[1163] |
| Supervisory Special Agent-2: | So, he was, and the relationship officially ended? |
| Clinesmith: | So, essentially, the real . . . source was using Page as a [Steele]-like subsource.[1164] |
| Clinesmith: | [Carter Page] was never a source. |
| Supervisory Special Agent-2: | You mean the [OGA] officer? |
| Clinesmith: | Right. Whomever generated the reporting from the [documents]. |
| Clinesmith: | It was just liaison with Page which resulted in reporting, eventually they closed it out as unhelpful. |
| Clinesmith: | So, in discussing with [OI Attorney-1], he agreed we do not need to address it in the FISA. |
| Clinesmith: | [OI Attorney-1] is always Eeyore in drafting these special FISA applications. |
| Supervisory Special Agent-2: | So, Page was a [digraph] or Page was a subsource of the [digraph]. |

[1163] "USPER" is short for "U.S. Person."

[1164] Steele is a reference to Christopher Steele, who prepared certain reports, based on information from subsources. The FISA applications on Page relied, in part, on information taken from those reports.

[illegible] ds like a subsource [illegible] h].

[illegible] OGA] confirmed [illegible] was never a source.

[illegible] Special [illegible]

[illegible] esting good, right?

[illegible] *at we don't have to* [illegible] *footnote.*

[illegible] Special [illegible] eresting they say not [illegible] thought otherwise [illegible] writing . . . I will re- [illegible]

[illegible] another person] [illegible], and you talking to [illegible] son].

[illegible] Special [illegible] you. Do we have [illegible]

[illegible] rward.[1165]

As reflected ab[illegible] told [illegible] -2 that Page "was never a source" and that "[the O[illegible] ed exp[illegible]." When Supervisory Special Agent-2 asked [illegible] had th[illegible] responded he did and that he would forward the em[illegible] A had [illegible]

Immedi[illegible] Lync[illegible] betwe[illegible] th and Supervisory Special Agent-2, Clines[illegible] ed to [illegible] Spe[illegible] a version of OGA Liaison-1's June 15, 2017 e[illegible] g alt[illegible] Clin[illegible] made. The altered email from the liaison read as f[illegible]

> My recol[illegible] Pag[illegible] [dig[illegible] *ot a "source"* but the [docum[illegible] in th[illegible] al definition for the FISA,

[1165] FBI-AAA-[illegible] (Lyn[illegible] betwe[illegible] ith and Supervisory Special Agent-2 dated [illegible] emph[illegible] see [illegible] eport of Interview of Supervisory Special Agent-[illegible] 21 a[illegible] isory [illegible] gent-2 believes Clinesmith lied to him about Page [illegible] the [illegible] please let me know and we'll work up some language and get it cleared for use.[1166]

Clinesmith had altered the original June 15, 2017 email from the liaison by adding the words "and not a source" to the email, thus making it appear that OGA Liaison-1 had written in the email that Page was "not a source" for the OGA. Relying on the altered email, Supervisory Special Agent-2 signed the application that was submitted to the FISC on June 29, 2017.[1167] This final FISA application did not include Page's history or status with the OGA.

The Office's investigators, like the OIG investigators, confirmed with OGA Liaison-1 that she had no recollection of ever having told Clinesmith that Page was not a source for the OGA.[1168]

h. CHS meetings with Papadopoulos, Page, and a third Trump campaign member, the *Yahoo! News* article about Page, and Page's offer to be interviewed

In addition to opening Crossfire Hurricane, the FBI opened or had open investigations of four individuals associated with the Trump campaign.[1169] FBI CHSs or undercover employees ("UCEs") met with two of those individuals (Papadopoulos and Page), as well as with a senior Trump campaign foreign policy official, and recorded many of these meetings.[1170] Many of the omissions and much of the misleading information found in the Page FISA applications, described by the OIG, deserve additional emphasis in this report based on the Office's review of the transcripts and careful review of the actual recorded conversations themselves. Indeed, listening to the recordings and reviewing the transcripts was especially important when considered against the backdrop of an unauthorized disclosure made to *Yahoo! News* about the federal investigation into Page, and Page's subsequent offer to be interviewed by the FBI.

*i. The FBI's engagement with CHS-1 and first consensual recording of Carter Page on August 20, 2016*

Approximately ten days after the Crossfire Hurricane investigation was opened on Page, Case Agent-1 worked to arrange a meeting with CHS-1, a long-term counterintelligence source who the FBI had paid a substantial amount of money over many years. WFO closed CHS-1 for cause in January 2011 for "displaying aggressiveness toward handling Agents as a result of what he/she perceived as not enough compensation . . . and for exhibiting questionable allegiance to

---

[1166] FBI-EMAIL-444157 (Email from Clinesmith to Supervisory Special Agent-2 dated 06/19/2017) (emphasis added).

[1167] *See* OSC Report of Interview of Supervisory Special Agent-2 on May 5, 2021 at 3-4.

[1168] OSC Report of Interview of OGA Liaison-1 on Oct. 3, 2019 at 2.

[1169] *See supra* § IV.A.3.c.

[1170] The *AGG-Dom* lists consensual monitoring as an authorized investigative method that requires legal review. *AGG-Dom* § V.A.4. It defines consensual monitoring as "monitoring of communications for which a court order or warrant is not legally required because of the consent of a party to the communication." *Id.* § VII.A. The party consenting to the monitoring may be an FBI CHS or UCE.

the [intelligence] targets with which CHS-1 maintained contact."[1171] Nevertheless, Case Agent-1 reopened CHS-1 within two months of the CHS's closing and continued to serve as his/her handling agent through the Crossfire Hurricane investigation.[1172] (Case Agent-1 had served as CHS-1's handling agent for most of the five-year period before the opening of Crossfire Hurricane).[1173]

When the FBI approached CHS-1 in August 2016 to determine whether he/she knew Papadopoulos, CHS-1 said that he/she was not familiar with Papadopoulos. However, CHS-1 asked Case Agent-1 and two other FBI employees who were present if the FBI had any interest in Carter Page, with whom CHS-1 had met a month earlier in July 2016.[1174] [1175] The FBI learned that Page had been invited to attend a July 2016 meeting focused on intelligence and global security affairs. Page's attendance at the overseas event occurred just days after his visit to Russia, where he had delivered a commencement address at the New Economic School in Moscow. Given the circumstances and familiarity that CHS-1 had with Page from their recent meeting together at the overseas seminar, the FBI believed CHS-1 could initiate contact with Page without arousing any suspicions.[1176] CHS-1 contacted Page at the behest of the FBI and a meeting was arranged for August 20, 2016, which CHS-1 recorded.[1177] The primary purpose of

---

[1171] FBI-0000812 (Source Closing Communication dated 01/25/2011).

[1172] FBI-0000814 (Source Reopening Communication dated 03/23/2011).

[1173] CHS-1 also maintained relationships with other government agencies, and had likewise been paid for his/her services.

[1174] One individual interviewed by the Office advised that CHS-1 was directly involved in deciding which individuals would be invited to that earlier meeting and had authorized an invitation being sent to Page. OSC Report of Interview of U.S. Person-4 on 06/04/2020 at 1.

[1175] It does not appear that, at that time, CHS-1 disclosed to the Crossfire Hurricane investigators that on May 3, 2016, CHS-1 sent an email to Trump Policy Director-1 that contained his/her resume, spoke of her/his prior political experience regarding foreign policy matters, offered to help Trump in the foreign policy area, and, although stating that he/she was not seeking a position in a Trump administration, said he/she believed it was important to see Trump elected. When the Office asked about the email, CHS-1 said that Page had asked him/her to send it. However, when reminded that he/she had not even met Page until nearly two months later, CHS-1 said he/she probably sent it because he/she thought he/she could be helpful to the campaign regarding a particular country (which was not Russia). OSC Report of Interview of CHS-1 on April 6, 2021 at 3.

Relatedly, shortly after Trump's election in November 2016, CHS-1, while still an FBI CHS, sent a senior Trump transition team member an email offering his/her congratulations on Trump's victory and expressing an interest in assisting the new Administration. *See* Email from CHS-1 to Trump Senior Foreign Policy Advisor-1 dated 11/14/ 2016. We have no information to suggest that the FBI requested CHS-1 to send this email.

[1176] FBI-0016044 (EC "Meeting with CHS to discuss CROSSFIRE HURRICANE" dated Aug. 11, 2016).

[1177] FBI-0002721 (EC "Meeting with CHS-1 to discuss CROSSFIRE HURRICANE" dated 08/12/2016).

the meeting (and three additional consensually recorded meetings with Page made by CHS-1) was to assist in determining whether Page had information relevant to the allegation that predicated the opening of the Crossfire Hurricane investigation.

The first meeting between Page and CHS-1 took place as scheduled on August 20, 2016. Before the meeting, the FBI briefed CHS-1 on the information received from Foreign Government-1 that predicated the opening of Crossfire Hurricane. Because Page and CHS-1 were acquainted from their July meeting, they discussed a number of topics during the August 20th engagement. CHS-1 said that he had once known Manafort, the Trump campaign manager who had resigned the previous day.[1178] Page told CHS-1 that he (Page) had "actually literally never met Manafort . . . never said one word to him."[1179] When Page added that he had sent Manafort a couple of emails, the CHS interrupted him and said, "And he [Manafort] never responded probably." Page then replied, "Never, never responded one word."[1180] Since that time, Page has repeatedly stated that, despite allegations to the contrary, he never met or corresponded with Manafort while they worked on the campaign.[1181] Later in the conversation, Page told CHS-1 that, "I was never from the beginning a Manafort fan . . . ."[1182] Page also said that he believed Manafort might be in some trouble, but he provided no further information regarding the source of the trouble.[1183] Page's statements about Manafort, especially about their having no relationship, seriously undercut the reports from Steele subsequently received by the Crossfire Hurricane investigators that alleged that Page was engaged in a conspiracy with Manafort, the Trump campaign and the Russians.[1184]

Importantly, FBI records reflect that the Crossfire Hurricane investigators apparently failed to determine at that time whether Page's statements to CHS-1 had a basis in fact. Had they done so, investigators would have found that Page had previously sent Manafort one direct email message and copied him on two other messages, none of which Manafort appears to have answered.[1185] This documentary evidence provides significant corroboration of Page's

---

[1178] Transcript of Aug. 20, 2016 conversation between Carter Page and CHS-1 at 40.

[1179] *Id.* at 39.

[1180] *Id.*

[1181] *See* U.S. House of Representatives Permanent Select Cmte. on Intelligence Testimony of Carter Page on Nov. 02, 2017 at 21-22.

[1182] Transcript of conversation between Carter Page and CHS-1 on 08/20/2016 at 136.

[1183] *Id.* at 137-38.

[1184] As noted previously, the first Steele Reports were provided to the FBI by Steele beginning on July 5, 2016. Steele Source File at A-022 ("July 5 rpt"); OIG Interview of Handling Agent-1 on Aug. 30, 2018 at 152-158. For some still unexplained reason, however, members of the Crossfire Hurricane team working on drafting the Page FISA did not receive them until September 19, 2016. FBI-EMAIL-129902 (Email from Handling Agent-1 to Supervisory Special Agent-1 dated 09/19/2016); FBI-EMAIL-129908 (Email from Handling Agent-1 to Supervisory Special Agent-1 dated 09/19/2016).

[1185] Email from Carter Page to Paul Manafort, Sam Clovis & J.D. Gordon dated 07/25/2016; Email from Page to Hope Hicks & Manafort dated 08/15/2016; Email from Page to Hicks & Manafort dated 08/16/2016. Our investigation found no evidence that Manafort responded to statements abou [illegible] and sho [illegible] ised, [illegible] when the FBI was assessing the Steele reporting [illegible] erns [illegible] liabili [illegible] portant piece of that reporting.

In addi [illegible] sing M [illegible] ge an [illegible] so discussed three other topics:

*First*, at [illegible] ts in the [illegible] ion [illegible] ked about a possible "October surprise" being [illegible] y he Trum [illegible] ign.[11] [illegible] ace CHS-1 referenced an October surprise from a [illegible] idential [illegible] nd P [illegible] led that he wanted to know the definition of a [illegible] prise "th [illegible] e's [illegible] ctober surprise in, uh, this year, but you know [illegible] g maybe [illegible] ilarit [illegible] ward the end of their meeting, Page was blunt [illegible] [ ]hat is [illegible] r surp [illegible] e planning?" The recording reflects that thi [illegible] d by [illegible] ghing [illegible] ponded "[W]ell I want to have the conspiracy the [illegible] uh, Ru [illegible] mail [illegible] these 33 thousand, you know." In reply, CHS-1 as [illegible] he Rus [illegible] all th [illegible] y?" and Page stated, "I don't, I-I don't know."[11]

*Second*, [illegible] sed w [illegible] irmal [illegible] certain recent media reports regarding his (P [illegible] ess re [illegible] in Ru [illegible] vertheless, during this meeting and all other su [illegible] orded [illegible] th C [illegible] either implicitly or explicitly denied that tho [illegible] ps were [illegible] Russi [illegible] ent.[1190] Additionally, during all of his meetings wi [illegible] age ne [illegible] d any [illegible] n, evidence, or documentation indicating kno [illegible] relati [illegible] een [illegible] ampaign and the Russian government. R [illegible] meeting [illegible] veral [illegible] during their subsequent meetings, Page told CHS [illegible] wanted [illegible] re al [illegible] en the United States and Russia and Russian Pr [illegible] .[191] A [illegible] id Pa [illegible] anything about the campaign working in co [illegible] Russi [illegible] ent.

*Third*, [illegible] d a di [illegible] ith P [illegible] apadopoulos, asserting that, "someone in [re [illegible] here [illegible] onc [illegible] oulos] who's talking about the Trump campai [illegible] th the [illegible] [119] [illegible] he information passed to the FBI by Australia th [illegible] ls stat [illegible] the ba [illegible] rossfire Hurricane investigation. Page, however [illegible] m or [illegible] ss CH [illegible] uation of a relationship between

---

any of these em [illegible] Page. [illegible] mails [illegible] ined on a thumb drive voluntarily provided to the [illegible] st, 201 [illegible] orney [illegible] g then-President Trump.

[1186] Transcript [illegible] on bet [illegible] Pag [illegible] on 08/20/2016 at 52-53, 71-74, 159-160.

[1187] *Id.* at 53.

[1188] *Id.* at 159-1 [illegible]

[1189] *Id.* at 64-6 [illegible]

[1190] *Id.* at 66; Tr [illegible] f conver [illegible] een C [illegible] and CHS-1 on 10/17/2016 at 17; Transcript of co [illegible] etween [illegible] ge an [illegible] 12/15/2016 at 19-20; Transcript of conversatio [illegible] rter Pa [illegible] S-1 [illegible] 7 at 7, 38, 42-43.

[1191] Transcript [illegible] on bet [illegible] Pag [illegible] on 08/20/2016 at 92-93.

[1192] *Id.* at 95.

the Trump campaign and Russia.[1193] Rather, Page was somewhat dismissive of Papadopoulos's youth and described him as "[having gotten] in some hot water" over comments he (Papadopoulos) made about British Prime Minister David Cameron owing Trump an apology. Again, Page did not display any knowledge of an illicit relationship between the Trump campaign and Russia. Finally, when CHS-1 again tried to elicit information on this subject by stating, "So this fellow Papadopoulos is just, um, a young guy who's . . . [s]aying things that he shouldn't say or what," Page responded by simply stating, "No, he's a fine guy." Again, Page did not state or display any knowledge of an existing relationship between the campaign and Russia despite CHS-1's baited statements designed to elicit such information from Page. Page's recorded statements were significant because this was the first time Crossfire Hurricane investigators had an opportunity to obtain direct evidence that might corroborate or, alternatively, raise questions about the allegations passed on by Australia. In this first recorded conversation, Page did not corroborate this information.

Five days later, a briefing concerning this first recording of Page was held at FBI Headquarters for Deputy Director McCabe, Assistant Director Priestap, General Counsel Baker, Section Chief Strzok, Deputy General Counsel Anderson, and other FBI personnel. In addition to a discussion of the meeting between CHS-1 and Page, excerpts from the recorded meeting were played at the briefing.[1194]

*ii. The receipt of the first Steele Reports, publication of the Yahoo! News article naming Page, and Page's expressed willingness to be interviewed by the FBI*

There were no additional meetings between Page and CHS-1 until almost two months later. In the interim, on September 19, 2016, FBI personnel conducting the Crossfire Hurricane investigation received documents that were represented to be intelligence-type products authored by former British intelligence official Christopher Steele. These documents were part of what has become known collectively as the "Steele Dossier." While other sections of this report discuss in detail Steele and his reporting, two allegations relating to Page are relevant to this section. In particular, one allegation stated that "there was a well-developed conspiracy of co-operation between them [the Trump campaign] and the Russian leadership . . . [that] was managed on the Trump side by . . . Paul MANAFORT, who was using foreign policy advisor Carter PAGE and others as intermediaries."[1195] In that role, Page purportedly served as the liaison or "go between" for Trump campaign Chairman Manafort and Russian officials working with the Trump campaign. This allegation was in stark contrast to, and in direct conflict with, what CHS-1 had recorded Page saying in August. Somewhat inexplicably, in subsequent meetings between CHS-1 and Page, CHS-1 never attempted to re-engage Page on the subject of

[1193] *Id.* at 94-97.

[1194] OSC Report of Interview of James Baker on Feb. 7, 2020, at 12; *see also Redacted OIG Review* at 319-320.

[1195] SCO-105084 (Documents Known to the FBI Comprising the "Steele Dossier") at 9 (Company Intelligence Report 2016/095) (capitalization in original). Interestingly, CHS-1 had met Page in a different country on or about July 12, 2016, approximately one month prior to being approached by the FBI about Page, and Company Intelligence Report 2016/094 implicating Page was dated July 19, 2016.

his relationship with Manafort. Moreover, prior to submitting the initial FISA application to the FISC in October 2016, the Crossfire Hurricane investigators apparently never sought to obtain Page's email or phone records (whether from Page himself or otherwise) to verify or disprove Page's statement about his lack of a relationship with Manafort. As a result, at no time either before or during the electronic surveillance of Page did the FBI resolve the glaring conflict between Page's unequivocal statement regarding Manafort and the critical assertion in the Steele reports that Page served as one of Manafort's liaisons to the Russians.

The second Page-related allegation in the Steele reporting was a claim that, in July 2016, while in Moscow to deliver a speech to the New Economic School, Page had met secretly with Vladimir Putin's ally and Chief Executive Officer of Rosneft, Igor Sechin,[1196] and also with Kremlin Internal Affairs official Igor Divyekin.[1197] In late September, the allegations concerning Page's meetings with Sechin and Divyekin first made their way into the public domain with the publication of an article in *Yahoo! News* authored by Michael Isikoff.[1198] In the article, Mr. Isikoff wrote that Page, an American businessman who had been identified as a foreign policy adviser to then-Presidential candidate Trump, was the subject of an investigation being conducted by U.S. intelligence officials. The officials reportedly were trying to determine if Page was having private communications with senior Russian officials. The article went on to refer to a congressional source and said that "[Page's] talks with senior Russian officials close to President Vladimir Putin were being 'actively monitored and investigated' and that a senior U.S. law enforcement official did not dispute that characterization, stating, 'It's on our radar screen'. . . . It's being looked at.'"[1199] The article credited a "well-placed Western intelligence source" as identifying Sechin and Divyekin, both of whom were alleged to be close to Putin, as individuals with whom Page had met while in Moscow[1200]

Two days after publication of the *Yahoo! News* article, Page sent a letter to FBI Director Comey.[1201] In that letter, Page requested that the FBI promptly end its inquiry into his recent trip to Russia. Page alluded to the fact that he had previously been interviewed by the FBI and

---

[1196] At the time, Rosneft was Russia's largest oil and gas producer. *See* Isikoff, *Officials Probe Ties*.

[1197] SCO-105084 (Documents Known to the FBI Comprising the "Steele Dossier") at 8 (Company Intelligence Report 2016/94).

[1198] Isikoff, *Officials Probe Ties*.

[1199] So far as we were able to determine, the FBI did not refer for investigation this leak of highly sensitive information by a "senior U.S. law enforcement official" relating to an ongoing investigation of a presidential campaign.

[1200] As discussed in greater detail in Section IV.D.1.b.vi, the initial consensus of the FBI's Crossfire Hurricane investigators was that Steele, who himself was an FBI CHS, was the unnamed "Western intelligence source" referenced in the article. However, that consensus, which was set out in footnotes of drafts of the initial Page FISA application, changed for unexplained reasons shortly before the final version of the application was submitted to the FISC. That final version of the application attributed the leak of information not to Steele, but rather to Steele's employer, Fusion GPS.

[1201] Letter from Carter Page to FBI Director Comey (Sept. 25, 2016).

specifically volunteered to speak to any member of the FBI "in the interest of helping them put these outrageous allegations [about him] to rest."[1202] Page denied what he termed "completely false media reports . . . [stating] for the record, I have not met this year with any sanctioned official in Russia." Page also publicly stated that he had "interacted with members of the U.S. intelligence community including the FBI and CIA for many decades."[1203] The FBI, however, did not take Page up on his offer to be interviewed, and, indeed, the Crossfire Hurricane investigators were prohibited by FBI senior executives from approaching Page until former Director Comey finally authorized an interview in March 2017, almost six months after Page's written offer. In this regard, FBI records reflect the following relevant Lync messages:

On October 13, 2016, one week *before* the initial Page FISA application was submitted to the FISC, two Crossfire Hurricane investigators, Case Agent-1 (a principal source of information for the Page FISA application) and Special Agent-2, had the following exchange:

> Case Agent-1: It looks like Mgmt doesn't want us to do an interview, right now.
>
> Special Agent-2: of course not, that would make too much sense...
>
> Case Agent-1: Yeah, exactly. We... were told by [Supervisory Special Agent-1] that *mgmt wants to see what we get from his meeting with [CHS][1204] (Monday) and what we see in the FISA.*[1205]

Shortly thereafter, the following exchange occurred between Special Agent-2 and Supervisory Special Agent-1:

> Special Agent-2: Yeah [Case Agent-1] says no appetite to interview [P]age either. thats [sic] stupid.
>
> Supervisory Special Agent-1: yeah- dude i dont [sic] know why we are even here.[1206]

---

[1202] Other parts of this report discuss the fact that Page had been interviewed several times previously by the FBI, most recently in March 2016, when he was interviewed as a potential trial witness for the government in the prosecution of three Russian nationals in the case known as *U.S. v. Buryakov, et al.*, 1:15-CR-00073 (S.D.N.Y.); *see supra* § IV.A.1.a.

[1203] Letter from Carter Page to FBI Director Comey (Sept. 25, 2016).

[1204] As discussed below, four days after this exchange, on October 17, 2016, Page met with FBI CHS-1, who recorded their conversation. During the meeting, Page explicitly stated that he had not met with Sechin and that he did not even know who Divyekin was. *See* Section IV.D.1.h.iii.

[1205] FBI-AAA-EC-00008439 (Lync message exchange between Case Agent-1 and Special Agent-2 dated 10/13/2016) (emphasis added).

[1206] FBI-AAA-EC-00000365 (Lync message exchange between Special Agent-2 and Supervisory Special Agent-1 on 10/13/2016). FBI records make clear that the decision not to interview Page was being driven by the top-echelon of the FBI, including Comey and McCabe. Six months later, the following exchanges occurred between Crossfire Hurricane personnel:

> Special Agent-3 to Supervisory Special Agent-3: What's the over/under on getting the approval today from the DD [Deputy Director]?

It is clear [illegible] r c mess[illegible] ages [illegible] was frustration on the part of Crossfire Hurric[illegible] tors o[illegible] bility [illegible] a timely interview of Page. It is

---

> Supervis[illegible] gent-3 [illegible] Agen[illegible] one cocktail of choice the approval [illegible] me to [illegible]
>
> Case Ag[illegible] visory [illegible] ent-3 [illegible] think this happens today?
>
> Supervis[illegible] gent-3 [illegible] ent-[illegible] et [Special Agent-3's first name] one cock[illegible] the DD [illegible]
>
> Case Ag[illegible] visory [illegible] ent-3 [illegible] what's the hold up with the DD?
>
> Supervis[illegible] gent-3 [illegible] ent-[illegible] itical sensitivities and the whole timing of [illegible]

FBI-AAA-EC-[illegible] r c mess[illegible] nge [illegible] ervisory Special Agent-3, Special Agent-3 [illegible] nt-1 da[illegible] 017 [illegible]

> Case Ag[illegible] go A[illegible] e we [illegible] interview [Page] this morning, but appar[illegible] DD [illegible]
>
> Chicago [illegible] se A[illegible] reat [illegible]

FBI-AAA-EC-[illegible] r c mess[illegible] nge [illegible] se Agent-1 and Chicago Agent-1 dated 03/08/201[illegible].

> Support [illegible] cialis[illegible] Agen[illegible] the hold up? McCabe?
>
> Case Ag[illegible] t Op[illegible] ecial[illegible] ndering if it's McCabe or if it's Priestap [illegible] ing M[illegible]
>
> Case Ag[illegible] t Op[illegible] ecial[illegible] good with it, waiting to hear from the big g[illegible] going [illegible]
>
> Case Ag[illegible] t Op[illegible] ecial[illegible] been told to follow the letter that he sent to [illegible] can't [illegible] y na[illegible] etc.
>
> Case Ag[illegible] t Op[illegible] ecial[illegible] aiting for the Director to approve, they're in [illegible] ter, s[illegible] ate i[illegible] in the hour
>
> Support [illegible] cialis[illegible] Agen[illegible] re's just been no word from the director? [illegible] lly all [illegible] e wa[illegible]

FBI-AAA-EC-[illegible] nic mess[illegible] nga[illegible] se Agent-1 and Support Operations Spe[illegible] 03/0[illegible]

> Support [illegible] cialis[illegible] Age[illegible] normal investigative step. Who cares wh[illegible] re.
>
> Support [illegible] ecialis[illegible] Age[illegible] [sic] don't want to look political, stop tryin[illegible] olitic[illegible]

FBI-AAA-EC-[illegible] nic mess[illegible] nga[illegible] se Agent-1 and Support Operations Spe[illegible] 03/0[illegible] also clear from the messages sent by Case Agent-1, Special Agent-2, and their supervisor on the investigation, Supervisory Special Agent-1, that the timing and circumstances of the interview were not left to the individuals conducting and supervising the investigation, but rather the decisions on those issues were effectively being made by the Director and Deputy Director of the FBI. In this regard, according to McCabe, "Director Comey was getting daily briefings on this stuff, regularly" and the Director was intimately involved with the team that was working the case.[1207]

We observed that Page's letter to Director Comey was received by the FBI less than one week following the Crossfire Hurricane investigative team's receipt of some of the startling, but uncorroborated, Steele Reports. As noted above, those reports included, among a number of other allegations, specific claims that Page was serving as an intermediary between Manafort and Russian leadership, and that Page had met with both Sechin and Divyekin while travelling to Russia in July 2016.[1208] As to the former, as detailed above, Page had already been recorded on August 20, 2016, informing CHS-1 that he had no relationship with Manafort and, indeed, had never even spoken with him. As to the latter claim, Page would be recorded on October 17, 2016 informing CHS-1 that he had not met with Sechin as reported by Steele and was completely unfamiliar with Divyekin. During this same timeframe, and as set forth in greater detail below, the Crossfire Hurricane investigative team was working with OI to secure authorization from the FISC for a FISA warrant on Page.

An interview of Page at that time, for which he had volunteered, would have undoubtedly been beneficial to the nascent Crossfire Hurricane investigation. As noted, Page had previously been interviewed by the FBI on multiple occasions, unrelated to his work on the Trump campaign,[1209] and there was no indication of any reticence on his part to speak openly and at length with the FBI. Indeed, an interview with Page would have enabled the FBI to explore whatever topics were deemed relevant to the investigation, including, but not limited to, the following:

- Page's assessment of Papadopoulos, whose statement to the Australian diplomats had served as the predication for the Crossfire Hurricane investigation. (At the time Page volunteered to be interviewed, he had already discussed Papadopoulos with CHS-1).
- Page's relationship, if any, with Manafort, Sechin, Divyekin and other persons of interest to the investigators.
- An evaluation of any in-person denials made by Page of the allegations contained in the Isikoff *Yahoo! News* article, which would have served the dual purpose of enabling the FBI to better assess the credibility of the Steele Dossier reporting by obtaining more detailed information about the allegations directly from Page.
- Explore with Page any contact(s) that he knew of or suspected between individuals working on the campaign and any Russian officials. Because he was familiar with

---

1207 OIG Interview of Andrew McCabe dated Aug. 15, 2019 at 33.

1208 SCO-105084 (Documents Known to the FBI Comprising the "Steele Dossier") at 8-10 (Company Intelligence Reports 2016/94 and 2016/095).

1209 *See supra* § IV.A.1.a.

Russia, the FBI might have been better able to assess the credibility of the media reporting on Trump's alleged relationship with Russian officials.

An interview with Page also would have enabled the FBI to better assess the reliability of CHS-1. Finally, if the Crossfire Hurricane investigators believed that Page was not being candid, they could have asked Page to submit to a voluntary polygraph exam and to produce relevant records.

Although there may have been a concern that interviewing Page would adversely affect the FBI's ability to secure a FISA warrant, Page had already denied the allegations in the Isikoff article (and the Steele Reports, which he was not even aware at the time) in his letter to Director Comey. Page again denied the allegations in a September 26, 2016 *Washington Post* article, calling them "garbage."[1210] As previously noted, and discussed in more detail below, in a recorded conversation with CHS-1 on October 17, 2016, four days before the FISA surveillance application was approved, Page explicitly denied meeting with Sechin and Divyekin. All of Page's denials were characterized by the FBI in the initial FISA application, as discussed below, as not credible.[1211] If Page had further denied the allegations in an interview, those denials, too, could have been included in the application. Moreover, again, they also may have succeeded in getting Page to agree to take a voluntary polygraph examination on unresolved issues and areas of concern.

Nevertheless, senior FBI management made the decision not to interview Page and, instead, continued to move forward on the FISA surveillance targeting Page.

Notably, once Comey authorized an interview of Page to go forward in March 2017, Page sat for five voluntary interviews and fully cooperated with the FBI, even going so far as to bring his own PowerPoint presentation to one of the interviews.[1212] In those interviews, consistent with representations he had made to CHS-1 in recorded conversations, Page denied meeting with Sechin and Divyekin. Additionally, and also consistent with what he said to CHS-1, Page denied ever meeting with or speaking to Manafort.

Although the Office recognizes the benefit of hindsight in reviewing investigative decision-making, the failure to promptly conduct a voluntary interview of Page, contemporaneous with his request for such an interview, was a missed opportunity to further assess, on a timely basis and in a different light, the actual value of the Papadopoulos information provided by Australia. It also was a missed opportunity to test the reliability of claims about Page contained in the Steele Reports. Other investigative deficiencies with respect to Page – in the Office's assessment – are discussed further below.

---

[1210] Josh Rogin, *Trump's Russia Adviser Speaks Out, Calls Accusations 'Complete Garbage'*, Wash. Post (Sept. 26, 2016).

[1211] *In re Carter W. Page*, No. 16-1182, at 25-27. The first two denials by Page, in the letter to the Director and the *Washington Post* article, were described as "self-serving" in the FISA affidavit. The latter denial was described as vague statements that minimized his activities.

[1212] FBI Interviews of Carter Page on March 9, 2017, March 10, 2017, March 16, 2017, March 30, 2017 and March 31, 2017.

*iii. The second recording of Page made by CHS-1*

On October 17, 2016, CHS-1 and Page had a second meeting, which was also recorded by CHS-1. Regarding the allegation in the Steele reporting that Page had met with Sechin and Divyekin, Page expressly denied that he met with either one and described the reporting on the matter as lies planted in the media by "[Senator] Harry Reid . . . and the Clinton [campaign] team in Brooklyn."[1213] Additionally, Page stated, "the core lie is that I met with these sanctioned Russian officials . . . several of which I never even met in my entire life."[1214] Later in the conversation, Page also advised CHS-1 that Rosneft (Sechin's company) had denied that a meeting between Page and Sechin had taken place.[1215] Finally, Page referred to a story regarding an interview Trump campaign manager Kellyanne Conway conducted with CNN during which, according to Page, she said that "[Page] is not allowed to talk to the Russians, we-he was never authorized."[1216] In relating this story, Page told CHS-1, "I told everyone in the campaign . . . you know I never actually talked to these people. So, it's just kind of . . . you know, complete lies."[1217]

CHS-1 and Page also discussed Page's alleged meeting with Divyekin. Early in the meeting, neither Page nor CHS-1 could even recall Divyekin's name, with Page wondering whether he may have shaken the hand of some unknown person -- who may have been Divyekin -- after his speech at the New Economic School in Moscow in July 2016. With respect to Divyekin, the following exchange occurred:

CHS-1: And there's another one who worked for, uh--

Page: There's another guy—

CHS-1: --Putin

Page: I have never even heard of, you know, he's like in the inner circle.

CHS-1: What's his name again?

Page: I—I can't even remember. It's so outrageous.

CHS-1: Yeah. Right, he's in the inner circle. He-he works in the Kremlin or something.

---

[1213] Transcript of conversation between Carter Page and CHS-1 on 10/17/2016 at 16. Case Agent-1 told the OIG that the Crossfire Hurricane team never fully transcribed the October 17, 2016, recording, but rather only transcribed certain excerpts taken from the recording. *See Redacted OIG Review* at 321. Our investigation made use of the fully transcribed recording.

[1214] Transcript of conversation between Carter Page and CHS-1 on 10/17/2016 at 17.

[1215] *Id.* at 45 (quoting a Rosneft spokesman's statement in Julia Ioffe, *Who is Carter Page? The Mystery of Trump's Man in Moscow*, Politico (Sept. 23, 2016)).

[1216] David Cohen, *Conway Denies Trump Campaign Ties to Russia Figure*, Politico (Sept. 25, 2106) (quoting Trump campaign manager Kellyanne Conway's statement on CNN's "State of the Union").

[1217] Transcript of conversation between Carter Page and CHS-1 on 10/17/2016 at 107.

Page: [illegible] s, ye[illegible] Again, I—I was asking –I wanted [illegible]le ch[illegible] make sure that it—the graduation, [illegible] u know[illegible] that were, you know, when I was [illegible] nence[illegible] Did I happen to shake hands with [illegible]? L[illegible] ely, you know--they didn't even [illegible] of him [illegible] is like for example, uh, a Senior [illegible] r on [illegible] y're not household names where, [illegible] now . . .[illegible]

Later in the me[illegible] not Pa[illegible] me and the following exchange took place in wh[illegible] ned e[illegible] heard [illegible]:

CHS-1: [illegible] uy…th[illegible] earlier is Devianken [sic].

Page: [illegible] eah, yea[illegible] ght, [illegible] *Never heard of him until-*

CHS-1: [illegible] - I nev[illegible] him.

Page: [illegible] Russ[illegible] he [illegible] who are kind of ins and outs- . . . [illegible] Mos[illegible]

CHS-1: [illegible] don't k[illegible] ther, [illegible]

Page: [illegible] *hear*[illegible] *k*[illegible] nd of again Senior Director on [illegible][1219]

Later i[illegible] ion, [illegible] o a[illegible] o whether Page would be attending the up[illegible] dential [illegible] Nev[illegible] vised that he was taking a break from the campa[illegible] CHS-1 [illegible] you [illegible] uch with the campaign . . . ?" Page responded [illegible] I-I [illegible] out-[illegible] st these FBI investigations and, you know it . . . [illegible] ppropriat[illegible] e m[illegible] ents if I'm still officially affiliated with [illegible] . . . ."[1220]

At the [illegible] eting, [illegible] Page [illegible] he possible establishment of a think tank to be [illegible] London [illegible] Russi[illegible] s with the West, a topic they had briefly discusse[illegible] meetin[illegible] elling [illegible] at he liked the idea, Page said, "[T]he only bi[illegible] ously [illegible] thing[illegible] ow, funding for it . . . ." In response, CHS-[illegible] '[I] w[illegible] the [illegible] probably find funds . . . ."[1221] Returning to th[illegible] later. [illegible] "[W]" [illegible] interesting question [CHS-1's name deleted], [illegible] it is, I d[illegible] say [illegible] open check book, but the Russians would [illegible] " at [illegible] CHS-[illegible] d saying," [T]hey would fund it." Page then resp[illegible] m."[1222]

---

[1218] *Id.* at 18-19.

[1219] *Id.* at 99 (em[illegible] c).

[1220] *Id.* at 78.

[1221] *Id.* at 111.

[1222] *Id.* at 112.

A few hours after this meeting, Supervisory Special Agent-1 contacted Strzok to provide a summary of it (which Supervisory Special Agent-1 had received from Case Agent-1). In that exchange, Supervisory Special Agent-1 informed Strzok that Page "did not deny knowing Sechin," and "*outright denied knowing Divyekin.*"[1223] As an initial matter, Page denied *meeting* with either Sechin or Divyekin, the actual allegation set forth in the Steele Report and contained in the initial Page FISA. Supervisory Special Agent-1, however, accurately relayed Page's "outright" denial that he knew Divyekin. Minutes later, Supervisory Special Agent-1 cut-and-pasted his message to Strzok and sent it to both Brian Auten and Section Chief Moffa. Thus, as of October 17, 2016, a principal source of information for the FISA, Case Agent-1, the two most senior analysts on Crossfire Hurricane, Moffa and Auten, and the Deputy Assistant Director of the Counterintelligence Division, Strzok, were all made aware of the fact that Page explicitly denied knowing Divyekin, and should have been made aware that Page denied meeting with either individual. Nevertheless, Page's exculpatory statements were not included in the initial FISA application signed just four days later.

*iv. Crossfire Hurricane investigators submit the initial FISA application on October 21, 2016*

On October 21, 2016, four days after the second recorded meeting with Page, the Department submitted its initial Page FISA application to the FISC, which the Court granted that same day. (Unbeknownst to the Court at the time, the application contained numerous significant defects, many of which were identified by the OIG).[1224] In support of the application, the FBI made several assertions that directly conflicted with explicit statements made by Page in the two recorded conversations with CHS-1. One such assertion was the FBI's assessment that Page was still likely involved with the Trump campaign despite the facts that (i) Page told CHS-1 that he was taking a break from the campaign;[1225] (ii) campaign officials by then had publicly distanced themselves from Page and his purported contacts with the Russians;[1226] and (iii) the campaign manager had publicly stated that Page was not part of the campaign she was running.[1227] The FISA application attributed this assessment to the fact that because Page was one of the campaign's first foreign policy advisors and had established relationships with other members of the campaign, this would enable him to have continued access to these advisors and he would attempt to exert influence on foreign policy matters, regardless of any formal role he

---

1223 FBI-AAA-EC-00006182 (Lync message exchange between Strzok and Supervisory Special Agent-1 dated 10-17-2016) (emphasis added).

1224 *See Redacted OIG Review* at viii-ix; 413.

1225 Transcript of conversation between Carter Page and CHS-1 on 10/17/2016 at 77-78.

1226 Isikoff, *Officials Probe Ties* (quoting Trump campaign advisers Hope Hicks and Jason Miller).

1227 David Cohen, *Conway Denies Trump Campaign Ties to Russian Figure*, Politico, (Sept. 25, 2016) (quoting Trump Campaign Manager Kellyanne Conway's statement on CNN's "State of the Union").

played in the campaign.[1228] This assertion was unsupported by actual evidence that such continued involvement in the campaign was occurring.[1229]

Additionally, notwithstanding Page's explicit denials to CHS-1 and Director Comey of meeting with either Sechin or Divyekin in July 2016, an uncorroborated claim that had been included in the Steele Reports and publicized in the *Yahoo! News* article,[1230] the FISA application mischaracterized and misrepresented Page's words and actions regarding this subject matter. In particular, the FISA application stated that during his meeting with CHS-1, "Page did not provide any specific details to refute, dispel, or clarify the media reporting [and] he made vague statements that minimized his activities."[1231] This assertion, however, seriously misrepresents Page's recorded statements set forth above.

Finally, even though Page told CHS-1 that he was taking a break from the Trump campaign, the FISA application implies that the opposite was true. It said of Page's discussion on October 17th:

> During this meeting with [CHS-1], Page said that he was no longer officially affiliated with [Trump's] campaign, but added that he may be appearing in a television interview within the next week when he travels to the United Kingdom. According to Page, the interview will be discussing the potential change in U.S. foreign policy as it pertains to Russia and Syria if [Trump] wins the election. Accordingly, although Page claimed that he is no longer officially affiliated with the campaign, the FBI assesses that Page continues to coordinate with the Russian Government, and perhaps others, in efforts to influence the U.S. Presidential election.[1232]

---

[1228] *In re Carter W, Page*, No. 16-1182, at 26-27.

[1229] The initial FISA application on Page contained numerous "assessments" similar to the aforementioned statement which, whether correct or incorrect, conflicted with Page's explicit statements.

[1230] In *Crime in Progress*, authors Glenn Simpson and Peter Fritsch (owners of the investigative firm Fusion GPS that hired Christopher Steele to investigate Trump's relationships in Russia) write about a series of background interviews they arranged with selected journalists, including Michael Isikoff, for Steele to share the results of his research. Simpson and Fritsch wrote that the information provided by Steele was only to be attributed to a "former senior Western intelligence official." *See Crime in Progress,* at 108-112. The Isikoff article, however, identified the person providing the information as a "Western intelligence source." *See* Isikoff, *Officials Probe Ties.* Steele also admitted in an interview with Special Counsel Mueller's Office that he had provided information to the American media, specifically to *Mother Jones*. *See* SCO-006313 (Interview of Christopher Steele on Sept. 18, 2017) at 8. Finally, Steele admitted in testimony given in a civil suit filed in the United Kingdom that in September he and Glenn Simpson had meetings in Washington, D.C. with a number of journalists and shared his information with them. *See Steele Transcript* (Mar. 17, 2020) at 163:14-167:9.

[1231] *In re Carter W, Page*, No. 16-1182, at 27.

[1232] *Id.* at 28.

The Crossfire Hurricane personnel assessed, without citing any particular fact or explaining the basis for the assessment, that this discussion of a possible television interview was somehow evidence that Page was continuing to coordinate with the Russian government, and perhaps others, in an effort to influence the U.S. Presidential election. In support, the application asserted that Page's discussion with CHS-1 during their October 17, 2016 meeting about the possibility of him (Page) doing an interview with a British television personality on the implications of a Trump campaign victory on the relationship of the United States with Russia and Syria belied his statement to CHS-1 that he was taking a break from the campaign.

v. *The third recording of Page*

Approximately two months after the initial Page FISA surveillance warrant was authorized, Page and CHS-1 had a third meeting on December 15, 2016. The meeting covered a number of topics. At the outset of the meeting, CHS-1 initiated a general discussion of the potential Russian think tank in London. After CHS-1 discussed a possible partnership with a particular UK-based entity in establishing the think tank, Page advised CHS-1 that he had been "kind of talking with the New Economic School a little bit . . . and they were actually quite, uh, quite positive." Page went on to note that "they've got a lot of support internally, you know."[1233] When CHS-1 asked whether the "support was from the faculty or from the government or what?" Page responded "[F]rom the government, yeah. High level."[1234] Later Page and CHS-1 had a more general discussion regarding logistics of such a think tank, discussing issues such as funding and location. When CHS-1 noted that "you [Page] said last time we met that, um, can I, you got to, you thought you had the funding lined up . . . you said the Russians are giving you a blank check," Page responded, "Well I, I don't know that I went that far. I-I-I thought there was some support of, you know, certainly, uh, this trip proved it, but I think you know, having an institutional base . . . they said well come back to us with a proposal so you know . . . and they, again, very high level people [Russians] were quite supportive of a [particular type of entity]."[1235] Nevertheless, Page later noted during the conversation that, "some people have warned me, be careful with having too much Russian connection for obvious reasons."[1236] Finally, Page and CHS-1 discussed logistical information about possibly setting up the think tank in London, potentially to be sponsored by a UK entity.[1237]

During this meeting, Page also told CHS-1 that, according to the press, he (Page) was under FBI investigation. Page made this statement in response to an inquiry regarding Page's next trip to Moscow. Page said that he had been invited to Christmas parties at Russian energy companies Gazprom and Rosneft,[1238] but had told them, "I said I-I got enough investigation [Unintelligible] going along . . . ." CHS-1 then asked Page who was investigating him and in

---

[1233] Transcript of conversation between Carter Page and CHS-1 on 12/15/2016 at 8-9.

[1234] *Id.* at 9.

[1235] *Id.* at 24-25.

[1236] *Id.* at 25.

[1237] *Id.* at 25, 59-61.

[1238] *Id.* at 44.

response Page [illegible] FBI th[illegible] [illegible] well that's what the press says, you know, no [illegible] ed m[illegible]

*vi. [illegible] misre[illegible] to [illegible] urricane investigators of his/her [illegible] on wi[illegible] regard [illegible] alleged meeting with Sechin*

Appro[illegible] week a[illegible] ting between Page and CHS-1, Case Agent-1 [illegible] essage [illegible] with [illegible] Special Agent-1. Case Agent-1 advised Supervi[illegible] Agen[illegible] out to him (Case Agent-1) that day and had advise[illegible] -1 tha[illegible] just [illegible] that Page had told CHS-1 that he (Page) had met [illegible] on Pag[illegible] n. When Supervisory Special Agent-1 expres[illegible] eared [illegible] -1's claim, Case Agent-1 responded that [illegible] that [illegible] 's statements after reading Sechin's name i[illegible][1240] In [illegible] ater with a Crossfire Hurricane analyst ("Analy[illegible] Agent-1 [illegible] was trying to determine when Page advised C[illegible] purpo[illegible], whil[illegible] essing skepticism that such a meeting had oc[illegible] Agent-1 [illegible] that Page may exaggerate things about his meeti[illegible] -1 conc[illegible] Case [illegible] dditionally speculating that there would be no be[illegible] n in [illegible] Pag[illegible] theless, neither Case Agent-1 nor Analyst-1 appe[illegible] nsidered [illegible] ration regarding the purported Page/Sechin m[illegible] e co[illegible] Page [illegible] from CHS-1, whose account of the statement b[illegible] st acc[illegible] ly could have been corroborated or disproven b[illegible] ng t[illegible] ber 1[illegible] ording of the conversation. This was an especial[illegible] point [illegible] tors [illegible] ince, as mentioned above, during his October 17, [illegible] g with [illegible] ge ha[illegible] denied having met with Sechin in July 2016. If i[illegible] Pag[illegible] ld [illegible] (Page) had met with Sechin during his mos[illegible] Mos[illegible] form[illegible] have been significant in bolstering susp[illegible] Page a[illegible] ons[illegible] Russians, and also arguably would have given mo[illegible] to the [illegible] Re[illegible] on that Page had met with Sechin in July 2016. [illegible] Dec[illegible] reco[illegible] g clearly shows, however, that

---

[1239] As noted, a[illegible] this th[illegible] g ma[illegible] mber 15, 2016, the FBI and Crossfire Hurri[illegible] el stil[illegible] en [illegible] s offer to be interviewed which he had made back [illegible] 25, 20[illegible]

[1240] Case Agent-[illegible] hed [illegible] day, [illegible] that [Page] told [CHS] that he met with Sechi[illegible]" Su[illegible] pecia[illegible] "Come on." Case Agent-1: "yup, said [CHS] jus[illegible] t yes[illegible] rea[illegible] name in the paper. Supervisory Special Agent-[illegible] that a[illegible] FB[illegible] 008439 (Lync message exchange between Case A[illegible] Superv[illegible] ial Ag[illegible] 12/22/2016).

[1241] Case Agent-[illegible] g to fi[illegible] he [illegible] he met with Sechin." Analyst-1: "man, yeah, I j[illegible] m or [illegible] ma[illegible] they are living in a dream world... that w[illegible] inter[illegible] real[illegible] with him." Analyst-1: "what possible reaso[illegible] hav[illegible] th hi[illegible] es no benefit to him." Case Agent-1: "I real[illegible] exagg[illegible] meeti[illegible] y have been in a meeting where he was 1 of 200 p[illegible] AA-E[illegible] 9 (L[illegible] exchange between Case Agent-1 and Analyst-1 [illegible] 16).

Page made no such statement to CHS-1. Although there was brief discussion by the two about Secretary of State nominee Rex Tillerson's relationship with Sechin,[1242] and the accusation made by Senator Harry Reid that Page had purportedly met with Sechin, which was referenced in a recent *Washington Post* column by Josh Rogin,[1243] Page never advised CHS-1 that he had met with Sechin on a recent post-election trip to Russia. As noted above, Supervisory Special Agent-1 told Case Agent-1 that they needed to listen to the audio of the recording. If, in fact, the Crossfire Hurricane investigators listened to the recording, they either missed this fact or elected not to make it known to the OI lawyers with whom they were working on the Page FISA applications.[1244] In either event, CHS-1's misstatement of an important fact was significant in that information provided to the FBI by CHS-1, again according to Case Agent-1, regarding his conversations with Page was used in all four of the Page FISA applications.

*vii. The first renewal of the Page FISA Warrant surveillance order*

Less than a month after the third recorded meeting between Page and CHS-1, the FBI received authorization from the FISC to continue its surveillance of Page for an additional 90 days. The renewal application, like the application to initiate the surveillance, included misrepresentations and mischaracterizations of the recorded conversations. Additionally, the same errors that were contained in the first FISA application were repeated in the renewal application. As noted in the *OIG Review*, the failure to correct these errors in the first FISA renewal application was repeated in the second and third renewal applications.[1245] Specifically, the OIG noted that the first renewal application omitted information the FBI had received from persons who previously had professional interactions with Steele and who in part questioned both his judgment and his pursuit of individuals with political risk, but no intelligence value.[1246] Moreover, as noted later in the *OIG Review*, another significant error in the renewal applications was the omission of a recorded statement made to a second FBI CHS ("CHS-2") by Papadopoulos. In that recorded conversation, Papadopoulos expressly denied any knowledge of the Trump campaign's involvement in the circumstances surrounding the hack of the DNC computers.[1247]

In addition to those defects, the first renewal application included mischaracterizations about the details of the December 15, 2016, meeting between Page and CHS-1. In particular, it mischaracterized the nature of their discussions concerning the creation of a potential think tank

---

[1242] Transcript of conversation between Carter Page and CHS-1 on 12/15/2016 at 17-18.

[1243] *Id.* at 44-45. This is the allegation that had been referenced in a recent *Washington Post* column by Josh Rogin.

[1244] No records were provided to the Office by the FBI which reflect that the recording had been reviewed and its specific contents were shared with the Department of Justice lawyers working on the Page FISA; *see also FBI Inspection Division Report* at 217 (reflecting that the recording was not reviewed and the investigating agents relied on the CHS's erroneous report of the conversation).

[1245] *See Redacted OIG Review* at xi, 413.

[1246] *See id.* at 182.

[1247] *Id.* at xi-xii.

focusing on Russian relations with the West. An objective reading of the transcript and review of the recordings of the two conversations between Page and CHS-1 on this subject in both the October 17, 2016 meeting and the December 15, 2016 meeting reflect that, although the two engaged in a general discussion about the possibility of establishing such an entity, neither discussed the specific details that would be required for such a project to move forward.[1248] Further, although they generally discussed the possible location of the think tank and possible sources of funding, the renewal application asserted that, "[A]ccording to more recent reporting from [CHS-1] . . ." in the December meeting, "[CHS-1] asked Page for additional information regarding the financials for the proposed think tank. According to [CHS-1], Page initially attempted to distance the think tank from Russian funding. When [CHS-1] reminded Page of his previous statement regarding the 'open checkbook,' Page did not refute his previous comment and provided some reassurance to [CHS-1] about the likelihood of Russian financial support."[1249] That assertion, based on the language in the application, perhaps was premised on information provided to the Crossfire Hurricane investigators by CHS-1, rather than the actual words spoken by Page as captured in CHS-1's recordings of the meetings. As provided to the FISC, however, the assertion is an inaccurate representation of the conversation. As noted above, when CHS-1 stated to Page, "[y]ou said the Russians are giving you a blank check," Page immediately responded, "[W]ell I, I don't know that I went that far. I-I-I thought there was some support . . . ."[1250] The actual language used by Page is inconsistent with CHS-1's assertion to Page that Page had been promised a "blank check" by the Russians. The assertion in the FISA application was, at a minimum, incomplete.

The first renewal application also stated that the FBI assessed that Page's attempts to downplay Russian funding may have been an attempt by him to soften his connection to Russia or, alternatively, may have been the result of an instruction from the Russians not to discuss any possible Russian financial involvement.[1251] There is nothing in the actual conversation between the two men, however, that would give rise to such an assessment. A fair and objective reading of the actual conversation indicates that the source of funding, if any, by the Russians was undetermined, and as also noted above,[1252] according to Page, subject to Page submitting a written proposal. And as previously noted, during this discussion with CHS-1, Page also mentioned that "some people have warned me, be careful with having too much Russian connection for obvious reasons."[1253] Instead of including Page's verbatim statements regarding Russian funding in the application, the FISA application makes assertions about funding that are at odds with what Page actually told CHS-1 as reflected in the recording of the meeting.

Moreover, the renewal application was submitted to the FISC only three weeks after Case Agent-1's conversations with Supervisory Special Agent-1 and Analyst-1 regarding CHS-

---

[1248] *See supra* footnotes 1221, 1222 re 10/17/2016 transcript and footnotes 1233 - 1237 re 12/15/2016 transcript.

[1249] *In re Carter W. Page*, Docket No. 17-52, at 35 (FISC Jan. 12, 2017).

[1250] *See supra* footnote 1235.

[1251] *In re Carter W. Page*, No. 17-52, at 35-36.

[1252] *See supra* footnote 1235.

[1253] *See supra* footnote 1236.

1's misstatement that Page had advised CHS-1 that he (Page) had met with Sechin during a post-election trip to Russia. Because of their apparent skepticism about this claim by CHS-1, this issue should have been brought to the attention of the OI attorneys working on the application, as well as the FISC. However, the Office found no evidence that it was appropriately addressed.[1254]

In a number of instances, the Page FISA applications relied on "assessments" to address what otherwise appeared to be plainly exculpatory statements by Page. Because of the sensitive and classified nature of those portions of one or more of the FISA applications, review of those assessments is set forth in the Classified Appendix to this report.

*viii. The fourth recording of Page made by CHS-1 January 25, 2017*

On January 25, 2017, less than two weeks after the first renewal of the Page FISA surveillance order was granted, CHS-1 met with and recorded Page for the fourth and final time. Importantly, on January 10, 2017, *Buzzfeed News* had published the contents of the Steele Reports. The next day, the *Wall Street Journal* identified "former British MI-6 Intelligence Officer Christopher Steele" as the author of the Reports.[1255] Unsurprisingly, the Reports were a topic of conversation as Page and CHS-1 began their fourth meeting. In response to Page's inquiry as to whether CHS-1 knew "[S]teele . . . the MI-6 guy," CHS-1 responded, "No, I never did. I never met him."[1256] Page then speculated that former MI-6 Director Richard Dearlove, who had attended the same July 2016 gathering that Page and CHS-1 had attended,[1257] must have known Steele. CHS-1 responded, "[Y]eah, Dearlove would know him. I mean Dearlove knew any-everybody in Six, and Six is a small organization."[1258] CHS-1 went on to state that, "[h]e [Steele] certainly produced [laughing] electrifying memoranda, didn't he?" Page responded, "[W]ell, you know. I mean, it's-it's just so false that where [Background Noise] do you begin [Unintelligible]?"[1259] This exchange contained yet another denial by Page of the allegations made about him in the Steele Reports, but this specific denial was never brought to the attention of the FISC in the second and third renewal applications for the Page FISA surveillances.[1260]

During this fourth recorded conversation, Page complained to CHS-1 about being under surveillance by the FBI, comparing his plight to that faced by Martin Luther King, Jr. who had

---

[1254] A review conducted by the Office of various documents, including the first FISA renewal application, the *OIG Review*, and documented interviews of FBI and OI personnel conducted by the Office, do not indicate that the information provided by CHS-1, as allegedly related to him by Page, regarding an alleged Page-Sechin meeting, was discussed beyond the two Lync message exchanges involving FBI employees Case Agent-1, Supervisory Special Agent-1, and Analyst-1 discussed above.

[1255] Bradley Hoe, Michael Rothfeld, and Alan Cullison, *Christopher Steele, Ex- British Intelligence Officer, Said to Have Prepared Dossier on Trump*, Wall St. Journal, (Jan. 11, 2017).

[1256] Transcript of conversation between Carter Page and CHS-1 on 01/25/2017 at 6.

[1257] *Id.* at 7.

[1258] *Id.*

[1259] *Id.*

[1260] *In re Carter W. Page*, Docket No.17-375 (FISC April 7, 2017); *In re Carter W. Page*, No.17-679 (FISC June 29, 2017).

been under FBI [illegible] during [illegible] J. [illegible] served as FBI Director. Page informed CHS-1 [illegible] and [illegible] for exercising their constitutional rights of freedom [illegible] and free [illegible]

Later, CHS-1 [illegible] turned [illegible] ion of the establishment of the possible think tank [illegible] relat[illegible] West and the finances related to such an endeavor [illegible] told Pa[illegible]

CHS-1: [illegible] I think [illegible] Russian money to the table, uh, [illegible] t be able [illegible] money.

Page: [illegible] m.

CHS-1: [illegible] could b[illegible]

Shortly [illegible] CHS-1 [illegible] nk ta[illegible] ain, and the following exchange occurred:

CHS-1: [illegible] the [illegible] ith is the decision whether you [illegible] to crea[illegible] w, once you make that decision [illegible] cou[illegible] onnel, but you should take your [illegible] d-and [illegible]

Page: [illegible] 's th[illegible] ith [illegible] me. And this is why I'm kind of [illegible] and [illegible] month in Moscow. The [illegible] ntum [illegible] Cold War sort of—you know like [illegible] people [illegible] re not un-American.[1264]

Later in [illegible] ion, Pag[illegible] he believed the Russians were "[f]ully on board [illegible] stion[illegible] s, whys, when and hows, you know?"[1265]

CHS-1 a[illegible] discuss[illegible] for starting the think tank, with each discussing [illegible] sors t[illegible] ially suggested $1 million, and CHS-1 suggeste[illegible] not thi[illegible] ould raise even a million "bucks," but said to Page:

CHS-1: [illegible] they [illegible] ould come up with a million and [illegible] ould te[illegible] you [illegible] he doors open for a year with [illegible] nd the[illegible] I can get to add to it.[1266]

---

1261 Transcript o[illegible] betw[illegible] Page [illegible] on 01/25/2017 at 21-22.

1262 *Id.* at 25.

1263 *Id.*

1264 *Id.* at 29-30.

1265 *Id.* at 30.

1266 *Id.* at 33.

A short time later, not hearing any firm commitment from Page regarding the establishment of the think tank, CHS-1 stated, "[I]'m just sort of blue skying here. I'm not trying to, you know, persuade you really to do this."[1267]

The various discussions between Page and CHS-1 regarding the possible creation of the think tank occurred over the course of their four conversations. The first occurred, albeit briefly, in their first meeting on August 20, 2016, with more extensive discussions occurring in their three follow up meetings on October 17, 2016, December 15, 2016, and January 25. However, none of the conversations advanced the establishment of the think tank from the aspirational to the concrete. The FBI's original language referring to the initial discussions between Page and CHS-1 regarding the think tank and the possibility of Russian funding did not change in the first three FISA applications (the original plus two renewal applications).[1268] However, some additional language regarding this issue was added in the final renewal application. In that application, the FBI wrote, "[B]ased on more recent information developed through its ongoing investigation of Page, the FBI now assesses that Page is no longer interested in establishing a think tank, likely due to lack of funding."[1269]

Later in their January 25, 2017 conversation, Page again advised CHS-1 that the stories about him and Russia were false. Page stated that the "[f]alse evidence isn't the fault of the Bureau . . . there's been lots of reports the Bureau sort of pushed back on this. And the fact that they never contacted me says something as well."[1270] Finally, Page told CHS-1 the following regarding the allegations against him:

| | |
|---|---|
| Page: | [Y]ou know, what a complete lie, what a complete sham. |
| CHS-1: | But, you know— |
| Page: | And this is the big fraud. . . . If you look at the narrative that was defined all around using government resources based on completely false evidence... and again false evidence is a crime.[1271] |

Page subsequently told CHS-1, "Let's see where this all started. This all started based on complete utter lies. Right?"[1272]

*ix. The second and third renewals of the Page FISA surveillance*

The Crossfire Hurricane investigators sought a second renewal of the FISA authorization, which was granted by the FISC in April 2017.[1273] While there was only one additional recorded conversation between Page and CHS-1 during the time between the first renewal of the FISA

---

1267 *Id.* at 34.

1268 *In re Carter W. Page*, No. 16-1182, at 28; *In re Carter W. Page*, No. 17-52, at 30; *In re Carter W. Page*, No. 17-375, at 31.

1269 *In re Carter W. Page*, No. 17-679, at 45.

1270 Transcript of conversation between Carter Page and CHS-1 on 01/25/2017 at 41.

1271 *Id.* at 42.

1272 *Id.* at 43.

1273 *In re Carter W. Page*, No. 17-375.

warrant and the second application for a renewal, there were several significant events that occurred in the Crossfire Hurricane investigation during that time. These included the five interviews that the FBI eventually conducted with Page in March 2017. As noted above, these interviews occurred nearly six months after Page wrote to Director Comey volunteering to be interviewed.[1274] Additionally, in late January 2017, the FBI conducted a three-day interview of Steele's primary sub-source, Igor Danchenko, who Steele relied heavily upon to gather information for inclusion in the Steele Reports.[1275] Finally, as discussed below, during that same approximate time period, the FBI made a series of recordings of conversations between a second CHS ("CHS-2") and Papadopoulos. The recordings were made in an effort to capture relevant information about the Australian communication that was the basis for opening Crossfire Hurricane.

At the expiration of the second FISA renewal authority, the Crossfire Hurricane investigators sought, and were granted, a third renewal of authority to conduct additional FISA surveillance of Page.[1276]

As noted previously, however, the Crossfire Hurricane investigators did not correct the errors, omissions, and misrepresentations that were contained in both the original FISA application and the first renewal application at the time they submitted the second and third renewal applications to the FISC.[1277] Moreover, additional significant problems were identified by the OIG (and also in a later investigation conducted by the FBI's Inspection Division)[1278] in the second and third renewal applications.[1279] One of the most significant problems relates to Page's recorded statements telling CHS-1 that he never met with Sechin or Divyekin, his public statements to the same effect, and his statements to the FBI during his five interviews, when compared to information provided to the FISC in the three renewal applications. Because of the sensitive and classified nature of those portions of one or more of the FISA renewal applications, review of this issue is necessarily contained in the Classified Appendix to this report.

*x. Recording of a high-level Trump campaign foreign policy advisor by CHS-1 on September 1, 2016*

In addition to the four recordings CHS-1 made of meetings with Page, CHS-1 also recorded a breakfast meeting he/she had in early September 2016 with a high-level Trump campaign foreign policy advisor ("Trump Senior Foreign Policy Advisor-1") who was not a

---

[1274] Again, Page had volunteered to be interviewed by the FBI just two days after the publication of the *Yahoo! News* article in September 2016 identifying him as the subject of an FBI investigation.

[1275] According to Danchenko himself, he was responsible for gathering approximately 80% of the "intel" in the Steele reporting and producing approximately 50% of the analysis in those reports. *Danchenko* Government Exhibit 1502.

[1276] *In re Carter W. Page*, No. 17-679.

[1277] *See supra* footnotes 1228, 1231 and 1232.

[1278] *See FBI Inspection Division Report* at 367.

[1279] *See supra* footnotes 1249 and 1251 for errors specific to the first renewal application; *see also Redacted OIG Review* at xi-xii, 413 subject of the FBI's investigation. As CHS-1 had a background in policy development through his/her work in several Presidential administrations and campaigns, it was not unusual for CHS-1 to request a meeting with Trump Senior Foreign Policy Advisor-1. A prospective meeting between the two had been discussed beforehand during CHS-1's first meeting with Page, who encouraged CHS-1 to have such a meeting, [1280] and this meeting occurred approximately ten days after CHS-1 first met with Page.

FBI records reflect that, prior to the meeting, there had been discussions among FBI personnel about the sensitivities surrounding meeting with a high-level campaign figure and the need to ensure the conversation would remain focused on topics relevant to the main purpose of the Crossfire Hurricane investigation, namely whether there was evidence of collusion between Russian officials and persons associated with the Trump campaign. Those discussions also covered the possibility that the conversation between CHS-1 and the foreign policy advisor might digress into campaign strategy and tactics, with the FBI personnel involved in the discussions expressing concern that such topics were to be avoided if at all possible.[1281] (We note that Crossfire Hurricane investigators properly recognized that other sensitive topics unrelated to the Crossfire Hurricane investigation might come up in the conversation given CHS-1's background and Trump Senior Foreign Policy Advisor-1's position in the Trump campaign).[1282]

Although there were a number of topics covered by CHS-1 and Trump Senior Foreign Policy Advisor-1 that were unrelated to Crossfire Hurricane, they also discussed several matters that were directly relevant to the investigation.[1283] At one point during the conversation, CHS-1, while referencing his/her prior experience in Presidential campaigns, stated:

CHS-1: [W]e were accused of having an October surprise. What do you guys got going? You have WikiLeaks out there.

Advisor: We have a lot hanging over our head. September 13, State [Department] has to produce those emails, that's a big deal.

CHS-1: You can do something with that?

Advisor: Absolutely.[1284]

---

[1280] Transcript of conversation between Carter Page and CHS-1 on 08/20/2016 at 98.

[1281] *See Redacted OIG Review* at 326-328.

[1282] *Id.* at 327 (wherein former AD Priestap told the OIG that "the team discussed the objectives of having the [CHS] engage with members of the Trump campaign... and the 'need to steer clear' of collecting campaign information 'dealing with policies, plans, staffing decisions, [or] anything related.' Priestap also said that 'it's not always possible...once people start talking' to a source to stay on point because the target of the operation may tell a source about the topic as well as a lot of additional information.")

[1283] The FBI did not transcribe the recording of this meeting so the references to the excerpts of the conversation that follow are identified by timestamp.

[1284] Audio recording of CHS-1 and Trump Senior Foreign Policy Advisor-1's conversation on 09/01/2016 at 09:14:15.

This po[illegible] conversa[illegible] s to [illegible] tended to elicit information from Trump Senior F[illegible] Advi[illegible] any [illegible] the advisor had regarding WikiLeaks' dis[illegible] NC-re[illegible] and [illegible]. Trump Senior Foreign Policy Advisor-1, how[illegible] touch[illegible] ks in [illegible] nse to CHS-1's question, instead focusing on a th[illegible] public[illegible] form[illegible] Clinton's emails by the State Department. Tr[illegible] Foreign [illegible] visor [illegible]-1 that the campaign could "absolutely" ma[illegible] e sour[illegible] ased [illegible] Trump Senior Foreign Policy Advisor-1's res[illegible] S-1's c[illegible] ut th[illegible] issue was not mentioned in any of the FISA app[illegible] r thoug[illegible] Leak[illegible], believed to have been facilitated by R[illegible] gence [illegible] usion [illegible] DNC computers, were mentioned in all four FISA [illegible].[1285]

Later in [illegible] sation, [illegible] Trum[illegible] oreign Policy Advisor-1 briefly discussed Wiki[illegible] Julian [illegible] nd [illegible] d possible Russian influence on the election. Th[illegible] exchang[illegible] ace[illegible]

CHS-1: [illegible] nt pag[illegible] w Y[illegible] about Julian Assange. What can [illegible] to off[illegible] ry [illegible] an influence in the Trump [illegible] gn?

Advisor: [illegible] averag[illegible] s a [illegible] n this city it's a big deal, New [illegible] big dea[illegible] pe[illegible] he average voter, there is no [illegible] ction.[illegible]

Advisor: [illegible] t Rus[illegible] ce, [illegible] ise the level of abstraction [illegible] ss th[illegible] a v[illegible] ion. It is up to each state [illegible] de s[illegible] ke s[illegible] te has secured its [illegible] n.[1287]

CHS-1: [illegible] I am co[illegible] th[illegible] sion that Russia has a hand [illegible] we a[illegible] Carte[illegible] example, he made a [illegible] n in M[illegible] ow [illegible] liar with, and there was a [illegible] the sp[illegible] s a[illegible]

Advisor [illegible] portan[illegible] d m[illegible] campaign, except to say [illegible] erfere[illegible] ectio[illegible][1289]

Although this p[illegible] recor[illegible] tion[illegible] ics which were of interest to the Crossfire Hurri[illegible] ators, [illegible] ssar[illegible] influence; and Page's speech at

---

[1285] *In re Carte*[illegible] c. 16-[illegible] *In re* [illegible] *Page*, No. 17-52, at 7-8; *In re Carter W. Page*, [illegible], at 7-[illegible] er F[illegible] 17-679, at 7-8.

[1286] Audio reco[illegible] 1 an[illegible] io[illegible] cy Advisor-1's conversation on 09/01/2016 09:[illegible]

[1287] *Id.* at 09:48[illegible]

[1288] *Id.* at 09:50[illegible]

[1289] *Id.* at 09:51[illegible]

the New Economic School, there was nothing said or discussed by Trump Senior Foreign Policy Advisor-1 regarding any of these issues that would evidence any type of assistance being provided by the Russians to the Trump campaign. In fact, even though these issues were raised by CHS-1, the advisor did not engage on the prompts or baited statements advanced by CHS-1 to spark confirmation of Russian assistance to the Trump campaign. Again, however, even though this recorded conversation was with a senior foreign policy advisor to the campaign and the tenor of the conversation between CHS-1 and the advisor provided no indication of assistance being provided to the campaign by the Russians, there is no mention of this meeting, nor of anything said by Trump Senior Foreign Policy Advisor-1 at the meeting, in any of the Page FISA applications. Indeed, based on our collection of pertinent FBI records, the actual results of this meeting do not appear to have been memorialized by the FBI in an FBI FD-302 or other substantive report.[1290]

*xi. Recordings of George Papadopoulos by FBI UCEs and CHS-1*

In addition to its recordings of meetings between CHS-1 and Page and CHS-1 and the Trump senior campaign foreign policy advisor, the Crossfire Hurricane investigators also used CHS-1 to record two meetings with Trump campaign foreign policy advisor Papadopoulos (whose statements to the Australian diplomats formed the predication cited in the FBI opening communication for the Crossfire Hurricane investigation).[1291] Papadopoulos had been announced as a Trump campaign foreign policy advisor at the same time as Page in late March 2016. Subsequent to his/her initial meeting with Page on August 20, 2016, CHS-1, whose experience and credentials regarding foreign policy and Presidential campaigns are noted above, arranged for Papadopoulos to visit him/her in September 2016 to discuss the possibility of Papadopoulos writing a research paper on oil, gas and energy-related issues, these fields having been noted as areas of Papadopoulos's expertise when he was announced as one of the Trump campaign's foreign policy advisors.[1292]

Additionally, in connection with CHS-1's two meetings with Papadopoulos, two FBI Undercover Employees ("UCE-1" and "UCE-2") also met and had a total of three conversations with Papadopoulos in September 2016, two of which were recorded. Two of these meetings occurred in a foreign country and the other occurred while Papadopoulos was going to meet with CHS-1.[1293]

When interviewed by the Office, UCE-1 was certain that nothing of substantive value was said to him/her by Papadopoulos.[1294] According to UCE-1, unprompted, Papadopoulos

[1290] *See Redacted OIG Review* at 327-329 (indicating that the FBI did not do anything with this recorded meeting; it was not transcribed; and there was no evidence that the recording was put to any use. The FBI produced no documents regarding this recording to our Office.)

[1291] *Crossfire Hurricane Opening EC*.

[1292] Alan Rappeport, *Top Experts Confounded by Advisers to Donald Trump*, N.Y. Times (Mar. 22, 2016); Jeremy Diamond & Nicole Gaouette, *Donald Trump Unveils Foreign Policy Advisers*, CNN (Mar. 21, 2016).

[1293] OSC Report of Interview of FBI UCE-1 on October 21, 2021.

[1294] The conversation was not recorded by UCE-1.

identified himself as a Trump campaign advisor almost immediately after they began talking and showed him/her a picture of Trump and himself. Papadopoulos also told UCE-1 that he was traveling to meet an individual who UCE-1 subsequently learned was CHS-1. UCE-1 and Papadopoulos had a general conversation about the media reports involving Trump and Russia, with UCE-1 recalling that Papadopoulos laughed off such reports. UCE-1 recalled that Papadopoulos made no mention of Russian election interference efforts during their conversation.[1295] UCE-1 met later with the Crossfire Hurricane investigators and briefed them on the conversation he/she had had with Papadopoulos. He/she did not write a report regarding the encounter with Papadopoulos, explaining that it was common in UCE-1's experience that a case Agent would be briefed on the details of meetings and the case Agent was then responsible for writing the report of the meeting. UCE-1 advised that he/she had never seen any write-up or report of his/her meeting with Papadopoulos.[1296]

On September 14, 2016, Papadopoulos first met with UCE-2, who was posing as an assistant to CHS-1. During their conversation, which UCE-2 recorded, Papadopoulos provided UCE-2 with biographical-type information as well as background information concerning his role in the Trump campaign.[1297] Papadopoulos also bragged to UCE-2 that since his initial selection as a campaign advisor (1) his position in the campaign shifted higher due to campaign management changes,[1298] (2) he was with Trump all the time;[1299] (3) he was famous,[1300] and (4) his name now was global.[1301] One exchange between Papadopoulos and UCE-2 was of particular significance regarding Russia:

| | |
|---|---|
| GP: | The only thing I can't do is any business in Russia, right now, ... Russia has become like a hectic country with the campaign and all the other things. |
| UCE-2: | What [UI] on campaign? |
| GP: | Putin says he likes Trump, Trump says he likes Putin. |
| UCE-2: | Oh yeah, yeah. And that's a problem? |
| GP: | It shouldn't be. But if I do business...I will give you an example. I was supposed to speak at the largest energy conference in Russia later this |

---

1295 OSC Report of Interview of FBI UCE-1 on October 21, 2021 at 2-3.

1296 *Id.* at 3. No such report was produced to our investigators by the FBI and one does not appear to have been written.

1297 The Crossfire Hurricane investigators did not prepare a transcript of this conversation so references to excerpts that follow are to the recording timestamps.

1298 Audio recording of UCE-2 and George Papadopoulos conversation on 09/14/2016 at 19:06:20.

1299 *Id.* at 19:10:44

1300 *Id.* at 19:32:26

1301 *Id.* at 19:57:46.

| | |
|---|---|
| | month... It is so difficult in the U.S. politically right now. So, I can do any country except Russia. |
| UCE-2: | Why is it a problem if you want to build bridges to Russia... why give him [Trump] a hard time about it? |
| GP: | As you said, he wants to build bridges. The media is saying he's bad. What's important is to deal with Russia. |
| UCE-2: | Have you ever been to Russia? |
| GP: | No.[1302] |

The following day, September 15, 2016, Papadopoulos met twice with CHS-1. During the first part of their first conversation, which CHS-1 recorded at the direction of the Crossfire Hurricane investigators, they discussed a variety of topics, including a proposal that CHS-1 made to pay Papadopoulos $3,000 to write a research paper on oil and energy involving Cyprus, Turkey, Greece, Russia and Syria.[1303] After advising Papadopoulos that he/she had met with the Trump campaign's senior foreign policy advisor,[1304] CHS-1 discussed his/her admiration for Trump's realistic view of Russia.[1305] The two then discussed other world affairs involving China, North Korea and Japan.[1306]

Following those discussions, the conversation moved to the campaign when, in an apparent reference to the WikiLeaks disclosures of DNC emails, CHS-1 asked Papadopoulos, "do they have more?" In response, Papadopoulos said, "Public statements of Assange has stated that get ready for October. Whatever that means no one knows but..."[1307] Later in the conversation, in an apparent reference to an "October surprise," the following exchange occurred:

| | |
|---|---|
| CHS-1: | We were frightened to death about those surprises in 1980. |
| GP: | [Laughing] Hillary is not that bad but hope-hopefully for her it is a catastrophe along those lines and ah, it-it likely will... |
| CHS-1: | Yeah. |
| GP: | ...you know a lot of dirt has come out on the Clinton Foundation. |
| CHS-1: | Do you think that's when it will happen? |

[1302] *Id.* at 19:58:52 - 20:01:57

[1303] Transcript of conversation between Papadopoulos and CHS-1 on 09-15-2016 AM at 15. In testimony to the House Judiciary Committee, Papadopoulos confirmed that he had been paid $3,000 for writing the paper. *See* U.S. House Committee on the Judiciary, Interview of George Papadopoulos on 10/25/2018 at 101, 109-110.

[1304] Transcript of conversation between Papadopoulos and CHS-1 on 09-15-2016 AM at 15.

[1305] *Id.* at 14-15.

[1306] *Id.* at 19-31.

[1307] *Id.* at 35-36.

GP: [illegible] be [illegible] health.

CHS-1: [illegible] that's [illegible] health.

GP: [illegible] be [illegible].

CHS-1: [illegible] that [illegible]].

GP: [illegible] yeah [illegible] falsified information, her doctors [illegible] knows when it may be. But the [illegible] of the [illegible] yesterday released a statement that [illegible] did [illegible] to the State [illegible] for herself.

CHS-1: [illegible]ve?

GP: [illegible] That's [illegible] CEO of the Clinton Foundation [illegible] indirectly guilty of providing [illegible] to the [illegible] high-level donors to our [illegible]ation…

Later in [illegible] on, [illegible] discussed what Papadopoulos described as an i[illegible] the [illegible] Affairs to speak in Russia, which he turned down [illegible] just [illegible] the campaign trail…especially with what is go[illegible] lost his job essentially over media allegatio[illegible]…."[1309]

Papado[illegible] mentio[illegible] not going to Russia and discussed Page:

GP: [illegible] last [illegible] was oh now he's going, Carter [illegible] I think [illegible].

GP: [illegible] entire T[illegible] within two weeks of each other. [illegible] he adores his relationship with [illegible] to have happen. [chuckles]

CHS-1: [illegible]s stil[illegible] the Russians.

GP: [illegible] know [illegible] n't know what Carter has told you [illegible] [an[illegible] advisor] has told you but Carter has [illegible] actual[illegible] hasn't actually advised him on [illegible] He [illegible] directly through [another Trump [illegible] policy [illegible]…

CHS-1: [illegible] [JI]

GP: [illegible] media [illegible] whole [illegible]. That's not the reality….[1310]

---

[1308] *Id.* at 36.

[1309] *Id.* at 42.

[1310] *Id.* at 42-43.

A short time later, Papadopoulos described Page as "[A] very nice guy, you know, very smart."[1311]

At no time during this conversation did Papadopoulos mention anything about any support being provided by Russia to the Trump campaign, even when the discussion turned to Julian Assange and WikiLeaks. None of the statements made by Papadopoulos during this first meeting, including the aforementioned subjects of Assange, WikiLeaks, Page, and the prospect of some October surprise, were referenced in the FISA applications.

Later that day, however, in the second meeting between CHS-1 and Papadopoulos, there was an explicit discussion about the allegation which predicated the opening of the Crossfire Hurricane investigation. The Crossfire Hurricane investigative team's interpretation of that conversation, as included in the initial and subsequent Page FISA applications, is unsettling.

Shortly after the meeting began, the two engaged in a discussion about the recent publication of DNC emails by WikiLeaks:

CHS-1: I was going to ask you, did you guys have any idea that, um…you know that the, that the, ah, about the DNC leaks?

GP: Oh no.

CHS-1: Because I thought that was a really significant thing….

GP: And no one has proven that the Russians actually did the hacking….[1312]

After briefly discussing the possibility of other countries being involved in the DNC computer intrusion, the discussion continued:

CHS-1: …[s]o actually what you're saying to me is that you didn't feel like the campaign was able to benefit at all from what the Russians could help with.

GP: What do you mean by [Unintelligible]?

CHS-1: Well, you know, I mean I-I think this is a time when given Hillary's weakness and given her strengths that help from the, from a third party like WikiLeaks for example or some other third party like the Russians, could be incredibly helpful. I mean it makes all the difference.

GP: Well as a campaign, of course, we don't advocate for this type of activity because at the end of the day, it's, ah, illegal. First and foremost, it compromises the U.S. national security and third it sets a very bad precedence.

CHS-1: Yeah.

GP: So, the campaign does not advocate for this, does not support what is happening. The indirect consequences are out of our hands.

CHS-1: Yep. Yep.

---

[1311] *Id.* at 43-44.

[1312] Transcript of conversation between Papadopoulos and CHS-1 on 09-15-2016 PM at 12-13.

| | |
|---|---|
| GP: | That's how, that's the best way I can, ah... |
| CHS-1: | But... |
| GP: | For example, our campaign is not [chuckling] engage or reaching out to WikiLeaks or to the whoever it is to tell them please work with us, collaborate because we don't, no one does that. |
| CHS-1: | Yeah. |
| GP: | Unless there's something going on that I don't know which I don't because I don't think anybody would risk their, their life, ah, potentially going to prison over doing something like that. Um ... because at the end of the day, you know, it's an illegal activity. Espionage is, ah, treason. |
| CHS-1: | Yeah. Well particularly involvement with American elections. |
| GP: | Especially if somebody is collaborating with x-group that no one yet knows who they are... |
| CHS-1: | Yeah. |
| GP: | ...Then... I mean that's why, you know, it became a very big issue when Mr. Trump said, "Russia if you're listening..." Do you remember? |
| CHS-1: | Yeah, I remember that comment. Yeah. |
| GP: | And you know we had to retract it because, of course, he didn't mean for them to actively [chuckles] engage in espionage but the media then took and ran with it.[1313] |

Finally, toward the end of their conversation, CHS-1 broached the subject one more time with Papadopoulos:

| | |
|---|---|
| CHS-1: | [W]ell you know I'm-I'm happy to hear from you that, um, you know that there has been no interference in the campaign from outside groups like WikiLeaks or any of these people. |
| GP: | No. And, and, and to run a shop like that, you know, of course it's illegal. No one's looking to, um, obviously get into trouble like that and, you know, as far as I understand that's, no one's collaborating, there's been no collusion and it's going to remain that way.[1314] |

In this conversation, Papadopoulos clearly stated at several points that he was not aware of the Trump campaign working or collaborating with the Russians in any manner. In fact, he stated three times that such activity by the campaign would be illegal. These statements directly contradicted the underlying premise of the Crossfire Hurricane investigation, namely that a member or members of the Trump campaign might be or were colluding with the Russians regarding the release of information detrimental to the Clinton campaign. These were direct, explicit denials by Papadopoulos of his otherwise vague statements to the Australian diplomats about Russian assistance to the campaign – statements that Australia conveyed may have come

[1313] *Id.* at 17-18

[1314] *Id.* at 27.

from public sources.[1315] As previously discussed, these statements were used to predicate Crossfire Hurricane, the active investigation of unknown members of a Presidential campaign.

Significantly, these explicit, recorded denials of Trump campaign involvement with the Russians came *after* the initial meeting between Page and CHS-1 on August 20, 2016, and *after* the September 1, 2016, meeting between CHS-1 and the Trump campaign senior foreign policy advisor, both of which were recorded at the direction of the FBI and were in the possession of the Crossfire Hurricane investigators. In his conversation with CHS-1, Papadopoulos clearly said that such assistance from the Russians would be illegal. This was arguably the most significant information the FBI had gathered after approximately six weeks of investigative effort to evaluate the information it had received from Australia. Yet the FBI chose to discount the information and assessed it to mean the opposite of what was explicitly said.

As reflected in the *OIG Review*, the FBI chose to adopt an interpretation of Papadopoulos's denials of any knowledge of the Trump campaign's involvement with the Russians in connection with the DNC computer intrusion and subsequent publication of certain DNC emails as being "weird," "rote," "canned," and "rehearsed."[1316] They described Papadopoulos as having "a free flowing conversation" with the CHS that changed "to almost a canned response."[1317] Other comments made to the OIG by Crossfire Hurricane investigators included that the perceived change in tone of the conversation may have been an indication that Papadopoulos had been coached by legal advisors to provide certain responses to CHS-1, notwithstanding the lack of any actual evidence to support such a conclusion.[1318]

In interviews conducted by the Office, two Crossfire Hurricane investigators gave similar responses to what they previously told the OIG. One Agent stated that Papadopoulos's emphatic response to CHS-1's statement of a possible connection between the Trump campaign and the Russians was "curious," so much so that there was a consensus view that Papadopoulos's response may have been rehearsed and was, therefore, not authentic.[1319] Another Crossfire Hurricane investigator briefed several FBI Executives regarding this issue, including Deputy Director McCabe, Assistant Director Priestap, General Counsel Baker, Section Chief Moffa, and the Deputy Director's Special Counsel, Lisa Page, noting that the general consensus of the group after the briefing was that one of the statements made by Papadopoulos in his meeting with CHS-1, which would normally be considered exculpatory, was instead assessed as an outlier and intentionally scripted by him to give a false impression.[1320]

Our investigators listened very carefully to this recording and did not detect any change in Papadopoulos's tone of voice when he made these statements to CHS-1. As the Crossfire Hurricane investigators' interpretation of Papadopoulos's actual words was the exact opposite of what was said, and given how critical those words were to an objective assessment of the

---

[1315] *See supra* footnote 214.

[1316] *See Redacted OIG Review* at 332-333.

[1317] *Id.* at 332.

[1318] *Id.*

[1319] OSC Report of Interview of Case Agent-1 on June 19, 2019 at 3.

[1320] OSC Report of Interview of Supervisory Special Agent-1 on June 17, 2019 at 3.

relationship bet[illegible] p ca[illegible] Russi[illegible] exchange between Papadopoulos a[illegible] ould ha[illegible] ought[illegible] tion of the OI attorneys working with the Crossfi[illegible] person[illegible] Page [illegible] ation. The FBI, however, failed to do so at the ti[illegible] conseq[illegible] FISC [illegible] ot advised of the exculpatory statements). Inc[illegible] rement[illegible] attention of the FISC more than two years later, [illegible] 018, w[illegible] d a filing with the Court pursuant to the [illegible] of Ru[illegible] of Pr[illegible] the United States Foreign Intelligence Sur[illegible] nt, as [illegible] und[illegible] United States Code, Section 1803(g).[1321]

Importan[illegible] ulpat[illegible] ts w[illegible] Papadopoulos more than a month *before* th[illegible] FISA [illegible] was [illegible] the FISC.[1322] Thus, at the time Papadopoulos m[illegible] ed st[illegible] e Cr[illegible] icane investigators were actively involved, or we[illegible] involv[illegible] ng [illegible] plication asserting that there was probable cause [illegible] t Page [illegible] wer.[1323] Further, one Crossfire Hurricane inves[illegible] OIC [illegible] mber 15, 2016 meeting between CHS-1 and Pap[illegible] the [illegible] of F[illegible] s's denials of cooperation with the Russians rem[illegible] of co[illegible] d.[1324] Yet the FBI failed to apprise OI,[1325] a[illegible] the FIS[illegible] sign[illegible] ments.

Finally, [illegible] Pap[illegible] den[illegible] owledge of a relationship between the Ru[illegible] Trum[illegible] it d[illegible] ar that the FBI gave any serious thought to simpl[illegible] him [illegible] he [illegible] etween his unambiguous statements to C[illegible] the [illegible] fficial [illegible] ted concerning a "suggestion" regarding possi[illegible] istan[illegible] am[illegible][1326] [1327] Thus, an opportunity to potentially reso[illegible] ing [illegible] rity [illegible] y on was missed.

---

[1321] *See Redacte*[illegible] at 2[illegible]

[1322] As noted pr[illegible] initial F[illegible] ober 21, 2016.

[1323] The effort t[illegible] al vi[illegible] ur d[illegible] CHS-1/Papadopoulos meetings, Crossfire Hurri[illegible] mbers [illegible] d c[illegible] of the unvetted and uncorroborated [illegible] repo[illegible]

[1324] *See Redacte*[illegible] at 3[illegible]

[1325] OSC Repor[illegible] of O[illegible] on J[illegible] at 6.

[1326] According t[illegible] 1, th[illegible] irect[illegible] rview of Papadopoulos was "kicked around"[illegible] otion[illegible] ing [illegible] e Trump campaign leadership with a briefing [illegible] ligen[illegible] efin[illegible] approaches were taken and the Crossfire Hurri[illegible] ssed f[illegible] its in[illegible] *See* OSC Interview of Case Agent-1 dated J[illegible] at 3.

[1327] As related i[illegible] EC f[illegible] fire [illegible] vestigation, quoting the text exactly as it had [illegible] from [illegible] "[T]h[illegible] suggested [to the Australian diplomats] that [illegible] m ha[illegible] form[illegible] gestion from Russia that it could assist this proce[illegible] onym[illegible] of [illegible] uring the campaign that would be damaging to Mr[illegible] d Pres[illegible] a)."

*xii. Recordings of Papadopoulos by CHS-2*

In addition to the recorded meetings Papadopoulos had with CHS-1 and the FBI UCEs during his trip to meet with CHS-1, he also had numerous conversations which were recorded at the FBI's direction with a second CHS ("CHS-2"). CHS-2 was a longtime acquaintance of Papadopoulos. From the first recorded conversation with CHS-2, which occurred on October 23, 2016, until their last recorded conversation, which occurred on May 6, 2017, CHS-2 made a total of 23 separate recordings for the FBI. CHS-2 challenged Papadopoulos with approximately 200 prompts or baited statements which elicited approximately 174 clearly exculpatory statements from Papadopoulos. While their recorded conversations totaled 120 hours and 17 minutes, covering a wide variety of topics, many of which did not relate to the Crossfire Hurricane investigation, there were a number of conversations that were particularly relevant. Indeed, over the course of their recorded meetings, Papadopoulos repeatedly denied that he, the Trump campaign, and Russia had some type of cooperative relationship. However, as with the statements Papadopoulos made in his monitored conversations with CHS-1, none of Papadopoulos's exculpatory statements to CHS-2 regarding his lack of knowledge of assistance from the Russians to the Trump campaign were included in the succeeding Page FISA renewal applications.[1328]

---

[1328] *See Redacted OIG Review* at 233. The OIG report notes that similar denials made by Papadopoulos in interviews he conducted with the FBI were included in the second and third FISA renewals. However, these denials, submitted as footnote 4 to the two renewals, contained qualifying language regarding the denials. While noting that during his interviews with the FBI Papadopoulos had denied discussing anything related to Russia during his meetings with the Australian officials, the footnote also contains the FBI's belief that the interview responses to FBI questions by Papadopoulos regarding these denials were misleading and incomplete. *See In re Carter W. Page*, No. 17-375, at 11 n.4; *In re Carter W. Page*, No. 17- 679, at 11 n. 4.

With regard to misleading and incomplete information being provided to the FBI, Papadopoulos was subsequently charged in a one-count Information with and convicted of making false statements in violation of 18 U.S.C. § 1001(a)(2). *United States v. George Papadopoulos*, Crim. No. 17-cr-182 (RMD) (D.D.C.), Document 8 (Information). Specifically, during his first interview with the Crossfire Hurricane Agents on January 27, 2017, Papadopoulos told the Agents about an individual associated with a London-based entity who had told him about the Russians having "dirt" on Clinton. Although Papadopoulos provided the FBI with the name of the individual and where he could be contacted, Papadopoulos lied to the Agents about when he had received the information (it was received after not before he was named as a foreign policy advisor to the Trump campaign) and he downplayed his understanding of the individual's connections to Russian government officials. *U.S. v. Papadopoulos* Document 19 (Statement of the Offense) at 1-2. In addition, Papadopoulos misled the Agents about his attempts to use the individual and a female associated with that person to arrange a meeting between the Trump campaign and Russian government officials. *Id.* at 2-3. Ultimately, Papadopoulos pleaded guilty to making false statements. On multiple occasions he then met with, answered questions for, and provided information to the Government, *id.* at 13, and eventually was sentenced to 14 days incarceration. *U.S. v. Papadopoulos* Document 50.

On October 29, 2016, in a conversation with CHS-2 that occurred approximately one week after the initiation of the FISA surveillance on Carter Page and ten days before the election, Papadopoulos and the CHS had the following exchanges:

CHS-2: You think Russia is playing a big game in this election?

GP: No.

CHS-2: Why not?

GP: Why would they?

CHS-2: Don't you think they have special interest?

GP: I do not think so, that's all [expletive].

***

CHS-2: You don't think they hacked the DNC?

CHS-2: Who hacked the [expletive] DNC then?

GP: It could be the Chinese, could be the... Iranians, it could be some Bernie supporters...Could be Anonymous[1329]

***

CHS-2: You don't think anyone from the Trump campaign hacked her emails.

GP: No, no.

CHS-2: You don't think anyone from the Trump campaign had anything to do with [expletive] over at the DNC?

GP: No, I know that for a fact.

CHS-2: How do you know that for a fact?

GP: Because I have been working for them the last nine months that's how I know. And all of this stuff has been happening, what, over the last four months?

CHS-2: But you don't think anyone would have done it like undercover or anything like that?

GP: You know when I was in [Redacted] this [Redacted] and he was like a big advisor...asked me the same question. I told him absolutely not. And he actually was probably going in and tell the CIA or something if I'd have told him something else. I assume that's why he was asking. And I told him absolutely not. There's absolutely no reason... First of all, it is illegal, you know, to do that [expletive] ... No one would put their [expletive] life at risk or

[1329] Transcript of conversation between Papadopoulos and CHS-2 on 10-29-2016 at 157-158.

going to jail for the next 50 years to hack some [expletive] that may mean nothing.[1330]

Later in the conversation, Papadopoulos addressed the topic again, in response to CHS-2's inquiries:

GP: First of all, it is illegal to do that. So, no one in their right mind would, right?[1331]

Finally, the two discussed it one more time:

CHS-2: Do you think maybe Russia would have done... it because they could get away with it?

GP: Any foreign government.

CHS-2: They can get away with it?

GP: Yeah, Yeah, any foreign government.[1332]

The language used by Papadopoulos in his conversation with CHS-2 is consistent with the language he used in his conversation with CHS-1 almost six weeks earlier. Indeed, as noted above, Papadopoulos told CHS-2 that he told CHS-1 (whom he did not identify to CHS-2) the same thing as he was telling CHS-2 regarding allegations about the Trump campaign and Russia. Despite these denials by Papadopoulos to two different CHSs at two different times and places, as captured and memorialized on recordings made at the direction of the FBI, no information from either recorded conversation was brought to the attention of the FISC in the applications for the Page FISA renewals. Notably, these statements were made by Papadopoulos not just to an individual who he was meeting for the first time (CHS-1), but also, as the Crossfire Hurricane investigators well knew, to an individual with whom he had been well-acquainted over a long period of time (CHS-2).

In yet another conversation between CHS-2 and Papadopoulos, which occurred on January 25, 2017 (two weeks after publication of the Steele Reports by *BuzzFeed*, and amid media speculation that Sergei Millian, a person Papadopoulos had met and with whom he corresponded, was the source for some of the allegations in the Steele Reports), Papadopoulos expressed concerns about Millian to CHS-2. In this regard, the following relevant comments were recorded by CHS-2:

16:11:25

GP: I think he [Millian] was trying to get me to say a Trump person was trying to do business on the side with the Russians, that is what I think.

16:58:48

[1330] *Id.* at 159-160 (redaction in original).

[1331] *Id.* at 163.

[1332] *Id.* at 164 (redaction in original).

GP: [illegible] not pa[illegible] [illegible] never been to Russia in [illegible]

17:02:5[illegible]

CHS-2: [illegible] you d[illegible] [illegible] to [illegible] [illegible]letive]?

GP: [illegible]ling y[illegible] [illegible] nothin[illegible]

Papado[illegible] [illegible]al to C[illegible] [illegible]rkin[illegible] [illegible]ussians was not mentioned in the FBI's second c[illegible] [illegible] appl[illegible] [illegible] FIS[illegible] [illegible]n Page.[1334] As noted above, certain denials [illegible] [illegible]adopou[illegible] [illegible] inter[illegible] [illegible]mentioned in a footnote, but the Crossfire Hurr[illegible] [illegible]ported [illegible] [illegible]ved [illegible] [illegible] was misleading in those interviews. Th[illegible] [illegible] Papa[illegible] [illegible] this [illegible] [illegible] with CHS-2, which occurred prior to those t[illegible] [illegible]plica[illegible] [illegible]ubm[illegible] [illegible]ISC, was also omitted from any discussion in th[illegible] [illegible] footn[illegible]

In a thi[illegible] [illegible]tion, wh[illegible] [illegible]ce on [illegible] 2017, Papadopoulos and CHS-2 briefly discuss[illegible] [illegible]porting [illegible] FBI [illegible]n of the Trump campaign and possible conta[illegible] [illegible] a duri[illegible] [illegible] presi[illegible] [illegible]paign. The fact of the investigation h[illegible] [illegible]cly repo[illegible] [illegible]ay [illegible] [illegible]nal testimony given by then-FBI Director Come[illegible] [illegible] March 2[illegible] [illegible]nvers[illegible] [illegible]led the following relevant exchanges:

11:38:3[illegible]

GP: [illegible] are doi[illegible] [illegible]stigat[illegible]

CHS-2: [illegible]ou see [illegible] [illegible]ress?

11:39:3[illegible]

GP: [illegible]y are try[illegible] [illegible]ve th[illegible] [illegible] the campaign were like [illegible] with R[illegible] [illegible]e col[illegible]

[illegible]a [expla[illegible] [illegible] ev[illegible] [illegible]bout, you know? What [illegible] that ev[illegible] [illegible]llud[illegible]

[illegible] means th[illegible] [illegible]iting [illegible]ogether plotting [illegible]tive]. [illegible] [illegible] cr[illegible] [illegible] I ever heard of in my life.

11:39:5[illegible]

CHS-2: [illegible]ough?

GP: [illegible] so. [illegible] [illegible]ot sc[illegible] [illegible]ld be doing that. First of [illegible] would [illegible] [illegible]...Y[illegible] [illegible] I think's going to end up

---

[1333] Audio reco[illegible] [illegible]padopou[illegible] [illegible]S-2 [illegible] on 01/25/2017. References are to timestamps of [illegible]

[1334] The second [illegible] [illegible]val ap[illegible] [illegible] Docket [illegible] submitted to the FISC on April 7, 2017, and the th[illegible] [illegible] 17-67[illegible] [illegible]itted [illegible] on June 29, 2017.

[1335] Matt Apuz[illegible] [illegible] Rosen[illegible] [illegible]mari[illegible] [illegible], *F.B.I Is Investigating Trump's Russia Ties, Co[illegible]* [illegible], N.Y. [illegible] March [illegible]

happening.... I think that it will be like oh some of these guys were talking about but... you know some [expletive] like that. I do not know. What do you think?

CHS-2 I think everyone's [expletive].

11:40:53

GP: No-Even the guy the Congressman who's like focusing the Committee today.... Adam Schiff 'cuz I was watching him after breakfast and he's like if people met with them or are doing business in Russia that's not a crime. The crime that we are looking into is if there was like collusion. Which like I said that would be [expletive] nuts. But, I don't believe it.

CHS-2 You think anyone involved would have been dumb enough to leave a paper trail?

GP: Well, like I said, I don't.... I think it would just be insane. I just don't think anybody would be that psychotic unless they have like medical problems.[1336]

As with previous statements made by Papadopoulos to CHS-1 and CHS-2 which were relevant to the predicating information for the Crossfire Hurricane investigation, none of this additional dialogue, wherein Papadopoulos expressed absolutely no knowledge about Trump campaign/Russia collusion, was mentioned in either the second or third Page renewal applications submitted to the FISC. The omission of these March 20, 2017 statements of Papadopoulos is even more concerning in that he made them the very same day the FBI Director publicly confirmed the Crossfire Hurricane investigation which brought heightened attention to these matters.

Finally, in a fourth conversation between Papadopoulos and CHS-2 on March 31, 2017, they once again briefly discussed possible Russian interference in the 2016 election. The following exchange took place:

14:03:45

CHS-2: Do you think the Russians would come and kill you if you said something? The Russian Mafia?

GP: I have nothing to do with the Russians.

14:14:30

CHS-2: If Russia [expletive] meddled in our elections, what else are they controlling about us? That just makes America look weak.

GP: I still don't believe that [they did].[1337]

---

1336 Audio recording of Papadopoulos and CHS-2 conversation on 03/20/2017. References are to timestamps of recording.

1337 Audio recording of Papadopoulos and CHS-2 conversation on 03/31/2017. References are to timestamps of recording.

As in the earlier instances, these exchanges between Papadopoulos and CHS-2 were not mentioned in the second or third FISA renewal applications targeting Page. Nevertheless, it illustrates a consistency in Papadopoulos's denials that either he individually or, to his knowledge, others in the Trump campaign, colluded or worked in collaboration with the Russians during the 2016 presidential campaign.

These statements of Papadopoulos to two individuals with whom he talked openly and believed he could trust, statements which undercut the legitimate concerns raised by the Australian reporting and which resulted in the opening of the Crossfire Hurricane investigation, along with Page's statements in meetings with CHS-1 on multiple occasions, were deliberately ignored or dismissed by the FBI, preventing other entities, such as the OI and the FISC, from being able to adequately scrutinize the FBI's FISA submissions.

i. <u>Other aspects of the Page FISA applications</u>

*i. Multiple levels of subsources*

Much of the probable cause in the Page applications is based on multiple layers of sub-source reporting. The first surveillance application said of a key informant (Steele) that:

> Source #1 maintains a network of sub-sources, who, in many cases, utilize their own sub-sources. The source reporting in this application, which was provided to the FBI by Source #1, is derived primarily from a [redacted], who uses a network of sub-sources. Thus, *neither Source #1 nor the [redacted] had direct access* to the information being reported by the sub-sources identified herein . . . .[1338]

In other words, much of the information came through at least three people before it reached the FBI.

Referring to Steele's sub-sources, Supervisory Intelligence Analyst Brian Auten stated that he "did not have a good handle on how the sub-sources worked or who had what access to whom." He went on to say that "[b]y late January 2017 . . . [w]e knew we had a three-layer problem regarding Steele's sub-sources."[1339] Moreover, once Danchenko had been interviewed, Crossfire Hurricane investigators knew that Danchenko was not operating a "network of subsources," but rather would talk with people in his social circle about issues and then would report what he learned to Christopher Steele.[1340]

*ii. Reliability of subsources*

One of Source #1's sub-sources reported that there was "a well-developed conspiracy of co-operation." This was quoted twice in the initiation as it was at the heart of the factual

---

[1338] *In re Carter W. Page*, Order No. 16-1182, at 16 n.8 (emphasis added) (bolding in original omitted).

[1339] *FBI Inspection Division Report* at 365-66.

[1340] SCO-005801 (Interview of Igor Danchenko Electronic Communication dated 02-09-2017) at 23, 39.

information.[1341] The sub-source said the conspiracy was "between them [assessed to be individuals involved in Candidate #1's campaign] and the Russian leadership."[1342] This was "managed by Candidate #1's then campaign manager, who was using . . . foreign policy advisor Carter Page as an intermediary."[1343] There is no discussion in the FISA application of the reliability of the sub-source who provided this important information,[1344] and the FBI has secured no evidence that corroborated the allegations.

*iii. Role of campaign manager*

Although the campaign manager was reported to be managing the cooperation with Russia, the application included no other information – such as information about suspicious Russian contacts with the manager – to support that statement. Based on our review, the FBI had no substantive evidence that corroborated this allegation.

*iv. Involvement in criminal activity*

The Page FISA initiation approaches the issue of Page's involvement in criminal activity in a manner consistent with FISA's legislative history:[1345]

> As the activities discussed herein involve Page aiding, abetting, or conspiring with Russian Government officials and elements of the [Russian Intelligence Service] in clandestine intelligence activities, the FBI submits that there is probable cause to believe that such activities *involve or are about to involve* violations of the criminal statutes of the United States, including 18 U.S.C. § 371 (Conspiracy), 18 U.S.C. § 951 (Agents of Foreign Governments) and 22 U.S.C. §§ 612, et seq. (Foreign Agents Registration Act).[1346]

In applying the higher standard of criminal involvement to Page, the application did not discuss the standard, or explain how it was met, beyond what is stated above.

*2. **Prosecution decisions***

In light of the foregoing, the Special Counsel carefully reviewed and analyzed the evidence related to (i) Clinesmith and the altered email; (ii) statements made to the FBI regarding the Steele Reports; (iii) the receipt and dissemination of the Steele Reports; (iv) the *Yahoo! News* article; (v) the use of the Steele Reports in the FISA applications targeting Page; (vi) Igor Danchenko, including the legality of Danchenko's visa arrangement and the FBI's handling of the prior counterespionage investigation of Danchenko; (vii) the recordings of Page,

---

[1341] *In re Carter W. Page*, Order No. 16-1182, at 10, 20. For a discussion of this and other parts of the information used to support probable cause, *see supra* § IV.C.1.

[1342] *Id.* at 20 (brackets in original).

[1343] *Id.*

[1344] *In re Carter W. Page*, Order No. 16-1182, at 19 n.17. Like this footnote, other footnotes describe sub-sources and state that they did not know that their reporting would be directed to the FBI, but the footnotes do not provide any information about the reliability of the sub-sources.

[1345] *See supra* § III.C.1.

[1346] *In re Carter W. Page*, Order No. 16-1182, at 32-33 (emphasis added).

Papadopoulos, [illegible] (vi[illegible] [illegible] FISA applications. In determining wh[illegible] [illegible]ons of [illegible] [illegible]nted criminal prosecution, the Special Counse[illegible] [illegible] he *Pri*[illegible] [illegible]*on*.

a. Ke[illegible] [illegible]h

Not only [illegible] [illegible]ed em[illegible] [illegible], the statement Clinesmith made in the altered er[illegible] [illegible]e insta[illegible] [illegible]Special Agent-2 — that Page was not a source — [illegible] [illegible]. In [illegible] [illegible] for the OGA and had provided direct reporting [illegible] in the [illegible] by the OIG, and as later confirmed when [illegible] by our [illegible]-1 described Page as a "source" under the FBI's [illegible] and s[illegible] [illegible] in the email to assist in providing langu[illegible] [illegible]SA a[illegible] [illegible]as telling Clinesmith that, using the FBI's termi[illegible] [illegible]ad b[illegible] [illegible] As the liaison told the OIG, it was incorrect t[illegible] [illegible] as a[illegible] [illegible][1349] [illegible]lso stated that she saw no basis for Clinesmith [illegible] [illegible]uded, [illegible] [illegible]ns and the August 17th Memorandum, [illegible] [illegible]r had [illegible] [illegible] OGA.[1350] In addition, the liaison said that [illegible] [illegible]call [illegible] [illegible]ons with Clinesmith on this issue.[1351] When [illegible] [illegible]y the [illegible] [illegible] the accuracy of the information that she provide[illegible] [illegible]

The alte[illegible] [illegible] Cli[illegible] [illegible]ably material to the final Page FISA applicatio[illegible] [illegible]eral in[illegible] [illegible]lication process explained in interviews with [illegible] [illegible]ge's [illegible] [illegible]isclosed to the FISC because it bore on whethe[illegible] [illegible]obabl[illegible] [illegible]was acting as an agent of a foreign power. OI Att[illegible] [illegible]hat [illegible] [illegible]nt fact if Page had a relationship with the OGA [illegible] [illegible]d in ti[illegible] [illegible] known Russian intelligence officers that we[illegible] in the [illegible] [illegible] case here, because it would raise the issue of wh[illegible] [illegible] thos[illegible] [illegible] to assist the U.S. government.[1353] Deputy Assista[illegible] [illegible]enera[illegible] [illegible]SA target's relationship with an OGA is typicall[illegible] [illegible]an ap[illegible] [illegible] the information about Page's prior relationsh[illegible] [illegible]GA sh[illegible] [illegible]ause it "goes to the question of where the perso[illegible] [illegible]e[.]"[illegible]

---

[1347] *See Redact*[illegible] at 2[illegible]

[1348] *Id.*

[1349] *Id.* at 251, [illegible]

[1350] *Id.* at 251.

[1351] *Id.*

[1352] *United Stat*[illegible] *linesm*[illegible] [illegible]3) (D.D.C.), Doc. 1 (Statement of Offense) at 6.

[1353] *See Redact*[illegible] at 1[illegible]

[1354] *Id.*

[1355] *Id.* at 159.

Indeed, Clinesmith himself knew that, if Page had been a source with the OGA, that information would need to be disclosed in the FISA application.[1356] Clinesmith acknowledged as much in his original email to OGA Liaison-1, stating "This is a fact we would need to disclose in our next FISA renewal."[1357] Later, when interviewed by the OIG, Clinesmith stated there was "a big, big concern from both [NSD OI] and from the FBI that we had been targeting a source, because that should never happen without us knowing about it."[1358] Clinesmith added that, if it were true, they would "need to provide [the information] to the court" because such information would "drastically change the way that we would handle . . . [the] FISA application."[1359]

Supervisory Special Agent-2 also described the importance of knowing Page's prior relationship with the OGA. According to Supervisory Special Agent-2, "if [Page] was being tasked by another agency, especially if he was being tasked to engage Russians, then it would absolutely be relevant for the Court to know . . . [and] could also seriously impact the predication of our entire investigation which focused on [Page's] close and continuous contact with Russian/Russia-linked individuals."[1360] When interviewed by our Office, Supervisory Special Agent-2 echoed the information he provided to the OIG.[1361]

To that end, Clinesmith was the person that Supervisory Special Agent-2 relied on to resolve the issue of whether Page had been a source for the OGA in the past.[1362] Clinesmith's statement to Supervisory Special Agent-2 that the OGA had said "explicitly" that Page had never been a source was "the confirmation that [he] need[ed]."[1363] According to Supervisory Special Agent-2, the language that Clinesmith inserted into the liaison's email — that Page was "not a source" — was the most important part of the email for him.[1364] Supervisory Special Agent-2 stated, "if they say [Page is] not a source, then you know we're good."[1365] Supervisory Special Agent-2 further stated that if the email from the liaison had not contained the words "not a source" then, for him, the issue would have remained unresolved, and he would have had to seek further clarification. As Supervisory Special Agent-2 told the OIG, "If you take out 'and not a

---

1356 *United States v. Kevin Clinesmith*, Crim. No. 20-cr-165(JEB), (D.D.C.), Doc. 1 (Statement of Offense) at 4.

1357 *Id.* at 4-5.

1358 *Id.* at 4.

1359 *Id.*

1360 *See Redacted OIG Review* at 249.

1361 OSC Report of Interview of Supervisory Special Agent-2 on May 5, 2021 at 3; OSC Report of Interview of Supervisory Special Agent-2 on Oct. 17, 2019 at 3-5.

1362 *See Redacted OIG Review* at 255; OSC Report of Interview of Supervisory Special Agent-2 on Oct. 17, 2019 at 4.

1363 *See Redacted OIG Review* at 253; OSC Report of Interview of Supervisory Special Agent-2 on May 5, 2021 at 3.

1364 *Id.* at 255.

1365 *Id.*

source,' . . . it doesn't really answer the question." Supervisory Special Agent-2 also stated that even a verbal statement from OGA liaison-1 would not have resolved the issue for him.[1366]

As discussed above, the OIG subsequently conducted a review of the FISA applications targeting Page and discovered Clinesmith's conduct in altering the email. When confronted with the altered email by the OIG, Clinesmith initially stated that he was not certain how the alteration occurred, but subsequently acknowledged that he made the change.

The seriousness of the Clinesmith's conduct is highlighted by the FISC's reiteration of the fact that "the government . . . has a heightened duty of candor to the [FISC] in *ex parte* proceedings," and "[t]he FISC 'expects the government to comply with its heightened duty of candor in ex parte proceedings at all times. Candor is fundamental to this Court's effective operation . . .'"[1367] In submissions dated October 25, 2019, and November 27, 2019, the Department provided the FISC with notice of Clinesmith's conduct and the failure to disclose Page's prior relationship with the OGA.[1368]

On August 19, 2020, the Office charged Clinesmith in the United States District Court for the District of Columbia with the felony offense of Making False Statements, in violation of 18 U.S.C. § 1001(a)(3). On that same date, in the case known as *United States v. Kevin Clinesmith*, Crim. No. 20-cr-165(JEB) (D.D.C.), Clinesmith waived indictment and pleaded guilty to a one-count Criminal Information.[1369] On January 29, 2021, Clinesmith was sentenced to a term of 12-months' probation.

Finally, it appears likely that political or personal bias contributed at least to some extent to Clinesmith's conduct in this matter.[1370] As mentioned in the *OIG Review*, Clinesmith had also been investigated by the FBI's Office of Professional Responsibility, and ultimately suspended, for sending improper political messages to other FBI employees.[1371] On the day after the 2016 presidential election, Clinesmith wrote, "I am so stressed about what I could have done differently."[1372] In a later exchange with another FBI colleague, Clinesmith was asked "[i]s it

---

1366 *Id.*

1367 *In Re Accuracy Concerns Regarding FBI Matters Submitted to the FISC*, Docket No. Misc. 19-02, at 2 (FISC Dec. 17, 2019) (citing Docket No. BR 14-01, Op. and Order issued on Mar. 21, 2014, at 8, *available at* *http://repository.library.georgetown.edu/bitstream/handle/10822/1052715/gidc00098.pdf?sequence=1&isAllowed=y,* and Docket No. [Redacted], Mem. Op. and Order issued on Nov. 6, 2015, at 59, *available at* *https://repository.library.georgetown.edu/bitstream/handle/10822/1052707/gid_c_00121.pdf?sequence=1&isAllowed=y*).

1368 *Id.* at 1, n.1.

1369 *United States v. Kevin Clinesmith*, Crim. No. 20-cr-165(JEB) (D.D.C.), Doc. 1 (Information).

1370 *United States v. Kevin Clinesmith*, Crim. No. 20-cr-165(JEB) (D.D.C.), Doc. 22 (Government's Sentencing Memorandum at 14).

1371 *See Redacted OIG Review* at 256, n. 400.

1372 FBI, Office of Professional Responsibility, *Report of Investigation* [of Kevin Clinesmith] at 7 (July 17, 2018).

making you rethink your commitment to the Trump administration[,]" and Clinesmith replied, "Hell no," and then added "Viva le resistance."[1373]

b. Statements made to the FBI regarding the Steele reporting

As an initial matter, despite multiple requests to his counsel, Christopher Steele refused to be voluntarily interviewed by the Office. Steele was hired by Fusion GPS to essentially conduct opposition research against then-candidate Trump in the midst of a U.S. presidential election. While many may find this practice unseemly, political opposition research is a firmly entrenched feature of U.S. electoral politics and existed, in one form or another, since the founding of the nation.

Nonetheless, the Office examined evidence to determine if anyone knowingly passed materially false information to the government, including to the FBI, State Department, or to members of Congress. In his two interviews with the FBI's Crossfire Hurricane investigators and the Mueller investigators (October 2016 and September 2017), Steele provided the FBI with his understanding of how the allegations contained in his reporting were gathered, which, according to Steele, was almost exclusively through the efforts of Igor Danchenko. During those interviews, Steele told the FBI about, among other things, his understanding of Danchenko's sub-sources, the location of those sub-sources, and the time period in which Danchenko purported to collect the information. As discussed above, a significant amount of the information Steele provided to the FBI conflicts with what Danchenko would later tell the FBI in the January 2017 interviews and beyond.

For instance, with respect to the Mikhail Kalugin allegations in Report 2016/111, Steele told the FBI that Danchenko learned of Kalugin being recalled to Moscow after he (Danchenko) randomly bumped into Kalugin on a street in Moscow. For his part, Danchenko informed the FBI that he learned of the Kalugin allegations while Kalugin assisted him with renewing his Russian passport. Danchenko also told the FBI that he (Danchenko) did not provide Steele with the Kremlin's rationale for the recall, *i.e.*, Kalugin's involvement in Russia's efforts to interfere with the U.S. presidential election. By way of another example, Steele told the FBI that Danchenko had personally met with alleged Steele Report source Sergei Millian on at least two occasions. During his interviews with the FBI, Danchenko denied telling Steele that he had met with Millian in person (although he acknowledged knowing that this was Steele's belief and Danchenko did not correct Steele on the matter). Danchenko was adamant about only receiving an anonymous call from a Russian male whom Danchenko believed to be Millian. These are just two examples in which Steele's recollection of events differed significantly from those of Danchenko.

The Office attempted to reconcile these conflicting versions of events but was largely unsuccessful. Indeed, untangling the web of allegations proved difficult given that (i) the Office was unable to interview either Steele or Danchenko, (ii) both Danchenko and Steele said that they destroyed all notes reflecting the content of their meetings and communications, (iii) Danchenko deleted most, if not all, of his emails during the relevant timeframe, and (iv) Danchenko's alleged sub-sources, with the notable exception of Charles Dolan, were all domiciled overseas. Thus, while the Office examined the feasibility of false statements charges

---

[1373] *Id.* at 8.

against any parti [illegible] e crea [illegible] ere was insufficient definitive evidence to war [illegible] such [illegible]

c. The [illegible] ipt an [illegible] tion [illegible] Reports

The win [illegible] cinted [illegible] led to arrive at FBI Headquarters on September 1 [illegible] tainly [illegible] ice was never provided a satisfactory exp [illegible] y the [illegible] orts [illegible] to reach the Crossfire Hurricane investigators. [illegible] ic, FBI [illegible] establish who came into contact with the [illegible] e Se [illegible] of the motivations of those individuals in d [illegible] vance [illegible] Repo [illegible] repeated interviews and good-faith attempts to [illegible] lectio [illegible] orts is littered with failed memories and i [illegible] sion [illegible] The [illegible] thered was not sufficient to prove at trial that any [illegible] intent [illegible] ated [illegible] l statutes in relation to the transmittal of th [illegible] orts. [illegible] nce to establish that any FBI personnel inten [illegible] during [illegible] ews.

d. The [illegible] *ws* ar [illegible]

As noted [illegible] ber 23 [illegible] shed an article in *Yahoo! News* titled "U.S. Intel [illegible] be T [illegible] Tru [illegible] and Kremlin."[1374] The article detailed Page's [illegible] ings w [illegible] and D [illegible] contained information that was nearly identical [illegible] ort 2 [illegible] info [illegible] he article allegedly came from a "well-placed W [illegible] gence so [illegible] had [illegible] ned by a "senior U.S. law enforcement off [illegible] BI's in [illegible] me [illegible] le – an assessment ultimately confirmed by S [illegible] t Steele [illegible] ed [illegible] on to *Yahoo! News.* Understandably, [illegible] review [illegible] plication targeting Page, senior personnel in OI [illegible] ised [illegible] th [illegible] *ws* leak revealed a potential significant bias [illegible] art. O [illegible] ly to [illegible] BI's assessment was that the information in [illegible] had co [illegible] eele.

Again, as [illegible] n deta [illegible] t o [illegible] rk during its October 2016 interview of Ste [illegible] was to [illegible] f Ste [illegible] n the source of the leak to *Yahoo! News.* Followi [illegible] 201 [illegible] seve [illegible] the Page FISA application were circulated that co [illegible] otnote [illegible] hat S [illegible] fact, been the source of information in t [illegible] *ws* arti [illegible] revi [illegible] drafts, Department and OI leadership cont [illegible] the FBI [illegible] er St [illegible] ed a bias given his willingness to speak with the p [illegible] lter, o [illegible] 4, 2 [illegible] fire Hurricane investigator emailed an OI a [illegible] g; that S [illegible] not [illegible] entioned the leak (to *Yahoo! News*) and "only [illegible] ged it w [illegible] BI bre [illegible] n October 4." This is despite the fact that when in [illegible] y the Sp [illegible] se [illegible] articipant in the Rome meeting could not recall [illegible] e *Ya* [illegible] eak [illegible] sed with Steele. Auten, for his part, had a vagu [illegible] n that o [illegible] ant i [illegible] g may have spoken with Steele about the issue [illegible] eetin [illegible] fire [illegible] ersonnel – a contention that participant adam [illegible] l. Neve [illegible] e r [illegible] e Page FISA application contained a foot [illegible] that th [illegible] ned th [illegible] ovided the *Yahoo! News*

---

[1374] *See supra* § [illegible]

information to his business associate who, in turn, passed it on to the law firm that hired the business associate.

Understandably, Department leadership had trouble squaring this assessment with the plain reading of the *Yahoo! News* article which stated that a "well-placed Western intelligence source" (in context, Steele) had provided the information directly to *Yahoo! News*. On October 17, 2016, the FBI conducted a Lync call over Top Secret servers with OI to discuss this issue, and the FBI purported to resolve all the questions raised by Department leadership. During their respective interviews with the Special Counsel, not a single participant in that call could recollect the rationale for the changed assessment. Ultimately, the footnote in the final application submitted to the FISC reflected that Steele had not been responsible for the leak to *Yahoo! News*.

The Office was left to answer the obvious question: How did the FBI's assessment change from the rational assessment that Steele leaked the information to *Yahoo! News* to the unfounded assessment that Steele was not responsible for the leak? Unfortunately, this question remains unanswered. Despite repeated interviews and attempts to refresh recollections, we were left with what investigators and analysts stated were failed memories and, as a consequence, inconsistent versions of events. The Office, however, struggles to credit the failed recollections of those whom the Office interviewed given the import of the information to the ODAG and senior officials in NSD.

In any event, given the dearth of contemporaneous documentary evidence reflecting the events in question, the available evidence was insufficient to definitively establish that any of the participants intentionally (i) submitted false information to the FISC, in violation of 18 U.S.C. §1621(2) (perjury), (ii) provided false statements to the Special Counsel, in violation of 18 U.S.C. §1001(a)(2) (false statements), or (iii) violated the civil rights of Page, in violation of 18 U.S.C. §242 (civil rights violations). Again, the Office was unable to establish that any government officials acted with a criminal intent to violate the law, as opposed to mere negligence or recklessness.

Nevertheless, the FBI's conduct concerning the *Yahoo! News* issue is extremely troubling. Again, the Office is left to speculate that the FBI's unfounded assessment of the *Yahoo! News* information was driven by the pressure emanating from FBI Headquarters executives to commence FISA surveillance of Page. Indeed, OI Attorney-1's contemporaneous email to OI Unit Chief-1 noting that Crossfire Hurricane investigators "never asked and [didn't] want to ask" about the *Yahoo! News* leak encapsulates the Office's findings in this matter.[1375]

e. The use of the Steele Reports in the Page FISA applications

The pressure on Crossfire Hurricane investigators to commence FISA surveillance coverage of Page was palpable in the late summer and early fall of 2016. Indeed, as discussed above in Section IV.D.1.a.i, multiple FBI and Department employees described the unusual interest of high-level FBI executives in the Page FISA application. The inclusion of the unvetted Steele Reports in the Page FISA applications is problematic for the FBI, but the issue for the Special Counsel was whether it constituted a provable federal crime.

At the time of the initial application, not a single substantive allegation contained in Reports 2016/080, 2016/094, 2016/095/ and 2016/102 had been corroborated in any meaningful

---

[1375] *See supra* footnote 655.

way by the FBI. The allegations in those Reports and used in the initial FISA application were not mere ancillary facts that supported substantiated allegations. Rather, they contained extremely serious and indeed shocking allegations to the effect that (i) the Kremlin was supplying the Trump campaign with compromising information on Hillary Clinton (2016/080), (ii) Page, an advisor to the Trump campaign, was actively engaging with Russian officials to discuss the lifting of sanctions against Russia as well as the sharing of compromising information on Hillary Clinton (2016/094), (iii) Page was serving as an intermediary between Trump campaign manager Manafort and Russian officials in what the Steele Reports described as a "well-developed conspiracy" of cooperation (2016/095), and (iv) Russia had released hacked DNC emails to Wikileaks – an idea allegedly conceived of by Page. Again, at the time these serious allegations were put into the Page FISA application, the FBI had not corroborated any of these claims.

As discussed above, the Crossfire Hurricane team received the Steele Reports on September 19, 2016. Approximately two days after receipt, the uncorroborated information from the Steele Reports was inserted into the request for FISA surveillance of Page. The Special Counsel's interviews of the relevant players in the drafting of the Page FISA have all acknowledged that minimal efforts had been undertaken at that point to corroborate the Steele reporting. Rather, to a person, the FBI and Department personnel have all stated that the Steele reporting was deemed reliable based on Steele's prior history as an FBI CHS as well as his past employment with the British intelligence services. While undoubtedly the past performance of a source is an important factor in determining the reliability of information, surely establishing probable cause to accuse a U.S. person, to say nothing of a U.S. presidential campaign advisor, with colluding with a foreign adversary requires, at minimum, some degree of independent corroboration.

Notably, not one of the damning allegations contained in the Steele reporting was ever corroborated: not the salacious allegations of events at the Ritz Carlton in Moscow,[1376] not the allegation of there being a "well-developed conspiracy of co-operation" between Trump and the Russians,[1377] not the allegations of secret meetings involving Page and certain sanctioned Russians (namely, Igor Sechin and Igor Divyekin),[1378] and not the allegation of Page serving as Manafort's conduit for information between the Russians and the Trump campaign.[1379] This is true even after the FBI had offered Steele $1 million or more for such corroboration and after Danchenko was signed up as an FBI CHS and paid more than $220,000 for information on other matters.[1380] In addition, Helson told the Office that, as reflected in reports he had written on

---

[1376] SCO-105084 (Documents Known to the FBI Comprising the "Steele Dossier") at 2-4 (Company Intelligence Report 2016/080).

[1377] *Id.* at 9-10 (Company Intelligence Report 2016/095).

[1378] *Id.* at 8 (Company Intelligence Report 2016/094).

[1379] *Id.* at 9-10 (Company Intelligence Report 2016/095).

[1380] OSC Report of Interview of Brian Auten on July 26, 2021 at 18, 24, 31(When asked if there was any substantive information corroborated from the Steele Reports, Auten advised that there were facts that checked out such as names and positions, but that they were not able to corroborate any of the discrete allegations in the dossier); OSC Report of Interview of Kevin Helson on July 14, 2020 at 5, 14 (Helson remembered asking Danchenko if there were any

March 1, 2017 and March 16, 2017, there had been no corroboration of what Danchenko alleged about the Steele reporting during his three-day interview with the FBI.[1381]

Moreover, Auten told the Office that to the best of his recollection, when they checked with another U.S. intelligence agency on matters relating to the Steele reporting, they received no corroborating information back.[1382] As one long-time counterintelligence expert at that agency told the Office, the Dossier contained unverified allegations from sub-sources who allegedly provided the information, information that the government could not obtain despite its vast intelligence resources and paying millions of dollars for intelligence. Indeed, after the Steele Dossier was leaked and became public, that expert's reaction was to ask the FBI, "You didn't use that, right?"[1383]

One Crossfire Hurricane investigator said out loud what others may have been thinking: The initial FISA application targeting Page was being done in the hope that the returns would "self-corroborate." Here, the pressure from FBI leadership to commence surveillance of Page coupled with the FBI's previous unsuccessful attempt to advance the application against Page provided the Crossfire Hurricane investigators with ample motive to include the unvetted Steele Reports in the FISA application.

Although the evidence assembled by the Office may have been sufficient to meet a negligence standard, in order to prove a criminal violation of Page's civil rights, the government would be required to prove, beyond a reasonable doubt, that one or more persons acted *intentionally* to violate his rights. What in our judgement would be the admissible evidence in such a prosecution did not meet that standard.

In addition, in order to prove a false statement charge under 18 U.S.C. S 1001, such a prosecution would have to rest largely on not what was a provable, affirmative false statement, but rather on material omissions (*e.g.*, Page's relationship with another government agency, Page's exculpatory statements to a long-term FBI CHS, and the like). Given the claimed inability of the principal actors to recall the details of critical conversations, and the lack of evidence as to who was responsible for information that was included or withheld in the FISA applications, the standard of proof beyond a reasonable doubt could not be met. Accordingly, the Office did not seek criminal charges against any FBI or Department personnel in relation to the inclusion of the Steele Reports in the four Page FISA applications presented to the FISC.

f. Igor Danchenko

In November 2021, a grand jury sitting in the Eastern District of Virginia returned an indictment ("Indictment") charging Igor Danchenko with five counts of making false statements

---

statements [in the dossier] that could be proven by emails or other documentation. Danchenko, however, could not provide any corroborating information to support this information because, according to Danchenko, the information stemmed from casual conversations); OSC Report of Interview of Analyst-1 on July 14, 2020 at 19 ("the dossier could not be corroborated" and "no substantive facts in the dossier were corroborated").

1381 OSC Report of Interview of Kevin Helson on July 14, 2020 at 5.

1382 OSC Report of Interview of Brian Auten on July 26, 2021 at 26.

1383 OSC Report of Interview of CIA Employee-1 on July 17, 2019 at 3.

to the FBI. Th[illegible] ents, [illegible] made [illegible] chenko's time as an FBI CHS, related to his ro[illegible] primar[illegible] ce fo[illegible] ts.

*First*, th[illegible] allege[illegible] henk[illegible] ely that he had never communicated [illegible] Dolan [illegible] alleg[illegible] ned in the Steele Reports. As discussed abov[illegible] entary [illegible] early [illegible] Dolan was the source for at least one allegation i[illegible] Repor[illegible] lly, [illegible] tion concerned Manafort's resignation as [illegible] paign [illegible] alleg[illegible] told Danchenko that he sourced from a "GOP fr[illegible] t he to[illegible] tigat[illegible] ething he made up.[1384] The allegations rega[illegible] forme[illegible] f Co[illegible] the Indictment.

*Second*, [illegible] nt alleg[illegible] anche[illegible] stated that, in or about late July 2016, he recei[illegible] ous ph[illegible] om a[illegible] whom Danchenko believed to be Sergei Millian. [illegible] also fa[illegible] that [illegible] phone call, (i) the person he believed to be [illegible] red h[illegible] bout i[illegible] that the Steele Reports later described as de[illegible] a well-[illegible] "cons[illegible] ooperation" between the Trump campaign and [illegible] ials, and [illegible] nchen[illegible] agreed to meet in New York. The available e[illegible] sufficie[illegible] beyo[illegible] nable doubt that Danchenko fabricated thes[illegible] ing Mil[illegible] alleg[illegible] ing Millian formed the bases for Counts Two th[illegible] the Ind[illegible]

Followi[illegible] trial [illegible] the [illegible] the jury, the Court dismissed Count One of t[illegible] t purs[illegible] ral R[illegible] inal Procedure 29. The Court held that Danchenk[illegible] to the F[illegible] ing D[illegible] hat he [Danchenko] never "talked to [Dolan] abo[illegible] t sho[illegible] ne do[illegible] 'literally true" because, in fact, the information abo[illegible] was e[illegible] ver[illegible] than in an actual verbal conversation. T[illegible] nied D[illegible] Rule [illegible] o dismiss related to the remaining counts of the In[illegible] lowi[illegible] f de[illegible], the jury concluded that the case had not been pr[illegible] a reaso[illegible] bt.

In dete[illegible] her to b[illegible] al [illegible] st Danchenko, the Office expected to be able to in[illegible] nal [illegible] ainst [illegible] that supported the charged crimes. Thus, prior to t[illegible] mo[illegible] to in[illegible] rtain evidence as direct evidence of the charged cri[illegible] tively, [illegible] mov[illegible] the evidence as "other act" evidence purs[illegible] Rule [illegible] 404[illegible] Danchenko's motive, intent, plan and absence of [illegible] cide[illegible] ular, [illegible] ought permission to introduce evidence of:

> [illegible] o's u[illegible] se [illegible] the FBI regarding his purported receipt [illegible] refl[illegible] 's [illegible] ous sexual activity at the Ritz Carlto[illegible] scow. [illegible] the [illegible] nned to call as a witness the Germa[illegible] eral m[illegible] he [illegible] identified in the Steele Report 2016/0[illegible] E." Th[illegible] xpec[illegible] ral manager would testify that he (i) had [illegible] n of sp[illegible] h Da[illegible] June 2016 or at any time, (ii) had no kno[illegible] allega[illegible] rth in [illegible] Report before their appearance in

[1384] OSC Repo[illegible] of C[illegible] on [illegible], 2021 at 1.

the media, and (iii) never discussed such allegations with Danchenko or any staff member at the hotel;

(2) Danchenko's uncharged false statements to the FBI reflecting the fact that he never informed friends, associates, and/or sources that he worked for Orbis or Steele and that "you [the FBI] are the first people he's told." In fact, the evidence revealed that Danchenko on multiple occasions communicated and emailed with, among others, Dolan regarding his work for Steele and Orbis, thus potentially opening the door to the receipt and dissemination of Russian disinformation; and

(3) Danchenko's email to a former employer in which Danchenko advised the employer, when necessary, to fabricate sources of information. Specifically, on February 24, 2016, just months before Danchenko began collecting information for the Steele Reports, the employer asked Danchenko to review a report that the employer's company had prepared. Danchenko emailed the employer with certain recommendations to improve the report. One of those recommendations was the following:

> Emphasize sources. Make them bold of CAPITALISED [*sic*]. The more sources the better. If you lack them, use oneself as a source ("[Location redacted]-Washington-based businessman" or whatever) to save the situation and make it look a bit better.[1385]

Danchenko's advice that he attach multiple sources to information and obscure one's own role as a source for information was consistent with Danchenko's alleged false statements in which he denied or fabricated the roles of sources in the Steele Reports.

The Court ruled, however, that the evidence described above was inadmissible at trial. The prosecution was forced to then proceed without the benefit of what it believed in good faith was powerful, admissible evidence under Rule 404(b) of the Federal Rules of Evidence.

g. The legality of Danchenko's visa arrangement

The Office consulted with attorneys and investigators from the Department of Homeland Security, United States Citizenship and Immigration Services ("USCIS") to determine if Danchenko's U.S. visa was obtained through fraudulent pretenses, given, in the Office's view, the unusual circumstances in which an individual lists a U.S.-based employer as the sponsor of the visa application (Danchenko Employer-1), but is in actuality employed by a foreign entity (Orbis) and merely paid by the sponsoring entity for work done on behalf of the foreign employer. The USCIS informed the Office that this arrangement was legal.

The Office also reviewed the evidence of Danchenko's circuitous payment stream to determine if Orbis, Danchenko Employer-1, or other entities engaged in money laundering in violation of 18 U.S.C. § 1956. Given the apparent legality of Danchenko's visa arrangement, however, the Office determined that no specified unlawful activity could be proven.

[1385] SC_IDC_00102430 (Email from Danchenko to Former Danchenko Employer-1 Executive-1 dated 02/24/2016) (capitalization in original).

h. The FBI's handling of the prior counterespionage investigation of Danchenko

The failure of the FBI to assess properly the prior counterespionage investigation of Danchenko is incomprehensible. The investigation related to Danchenko's pitching a person he thought perhaps was going into the Obama administration for classified information. Although the conduct of certain FBI employees was, at best, negligent with respect to the prior investigation of Danchenko and his subsequent use as a CHS, we did not find any evidence that FBI personnel acted with specific intent – which the statute requires – to permit knowingly false information received from Danchenko to continue to be used in FISA applications. Prosecution, therefore, was not supported by the available evidence.

i. The recordings of Page, Papadopoulos and others

The Office carefully reviewed and analyzed the evidence related to, among other things, (i) the FBI's handling of the recordings made by CHSs and UCEs, (ii) the conduct of the CHSs and UCEs in making those recordings, and (iii) the FBI's failure to include key exculpatory material from those recordings in the Page FISA applications. As discussed more fully below, in determining whether the actions of individuals and entities warranted criminal prosecution, the Office adhered to the previously delineated Principles of Federal Prosecution.

*i. CHS-1's recordings of Page*

As discussed throughout this report, one of the key allegations contained in the Steele reporting, and which would later underpin the Page FISA applications, was the existence of "a well-developed conspiracy of co-operation" between the Trump campaign and Russian leadership. This alleged conspiracy purportedly was managed by campaign manager Paul Manafort using Page, and others, as intermediaries with the Russians.[1386] On its face, this was a shocking and serious allegation of collusion between the Trump campaign and the Russian government. However, as discussed in detail above, during the first recorded meeting between Page and CHS-1, Page never once indicated that he maintained a relationship with Manafort – despite several efforts by CHS-1 to establish such a relationship. In fact, Page explicitly denied ever having met or spoken with Manafort. While Page said he had sent a couple of emails to Manafort during his time on the campaign,[1387] he noted that Manafort did not respond to any of these emails. These assertions made by Page could have easily been corroborated through basic investigative steps and legal process, but were never undertaken.

Moreover, as discussed above, the Page FISA applications also relied on uncorroborated allegations from the Steele Reports that Page had met with Igor Sechin and Igor Divyekin in July 2016 to discuss the removal of certain sanctions against the Russian government. In his recorded meetings with CHS-1, however, Page denied meeting with Sechin or Divyekin and further denied even knowing who Divyekin was. Following the release of the *Yahoo! News* article on September 23, 2016 containing these same allegations, Page made similar denials in his letter to Director Comey and volunteered to be interviewed by the FBI regarding the accusations.

---

[1386] SCO-105084 (Documents Known to the FBI Comprising the "Steele Dossier") at 9, "Company Intelligence Report 2016/095" (capitalization in original).

[1387] As previously noted, on one of the emails Manafort was included on the TO: line and he was cc'd on two others.

Despite these recorded exculpatory statements made by Page and the denials contained in his letter to Comey, the FBI submitted its initial Page FISA application on October 21, 2016 containing the uncorroborated Steele Report allegations discussed above. The application inaccurately stated that "Page did not provide any specific details to refute, dispel, or clarify the media reporting [and] he made vague statements that minimized his activities." In fact, the only fair reading of Page's statements to CHS-1 regarding Manafort is that Page explicitly denied meeting or speaking with Manafort about any subject, to say nothing of the allegations regarding collusion with the Russian government. In the same vein, the only fair reading of Page's statements to CHS-1 regarding Sechin and Divyekin is that Page explicitly denied meeting with either individual, and, in fact, had never even heard of Divyekin. These multiple, explicit denials to CHS-1 were not included in the initial Page FISA application or subsequent renewals. Further, during the pendency of the Page FISA renewals, the FBI obtained additional information that should have cast further doubt on the allegations contained in the applications, including, but not limited to (i) Page's denials of the allegations during a series of interviews with the FBI in March 2017, and (ii) the FBI's interview of Steele's primary subsource (Igor Danchenko), which as discussed more fully below, cast further doubt on the nature of any alleged relationship between the Trump campaign and the Russian government.

The Crossfire Hurricane investigators did not correct the errors, omissions, and misrepresentations that were contained in the initial Page FISA application and subsequent renewals. When interviewed by the Office, one of the Crossfire Hurricane investigators stated, without further explanation, that he assessed Page's statements to CHS-1 to be "evasive." Similarly, when interviewed by the OIG, the investigator stated that Page "minimized, he kind of vacillated on some things. So, that's our, that was our, my assessment of what he said." Again, a fair reading of the transcripts of the recorded meetings between Page and CHS-1 reveal that Page was, if nothing else, explicit in his denials regarding Manafort, Sechin, and Divyekin. Based on a review of all the evidence, the Office concluded that the Crossfire Hurricane investigators, while aware of Page's explicit denials regarding the allegations, appear to have chosen to cloak those explicit denials in unsupported assessments to not endanger the viability of the Page FISA applications.

While the evidence assembled by the Office may have been sufficient to meet a negligence standard, in order to prove a criminal violation of Page's civil rights, the Government would be required to prove beyond a reasonable doubt that one or more persons acted *intentionally* to violate those rights. What in our judgement would be the admissible evidence in such a prosecution did not meet that standard.

In addition, in order to prove a false statement or perjury charge, such a prosecution would have to rest largely on not what was a provable, affirmative false statement, but rather on material omissions (*e.g.* Page's exculpatory statements to CHS-1). Given, among other things, (i) the reliance by the investigators on their professional assessments, (ii) the claimed inability to recall the details of important conversations, (iii) the lack of evidence as to who was responsible for information that was included or withheld in the FISA applications, and (iv) the inability to prove intent, the Office concluded that the standard of proof beyond a reasonable doubt could not be met. Accordingly, the Office did not seek criminal charges against any FBI or Department personnel in relation to the Page exculpatory material being withheld from the Page FISA applications.

*ii. [illegible] ...ngs of [illegible]*

The FBI [illegible] ...ed meeti[illegible] ...en P[illegible] ...s and FBI CHSs and UCEs. During the cou[illegible] ...meetings [illegible] ...sian assistance to the Trump campaign, not[illegible] ...repeat[illegible] ...by C[illegible] the WikiLeaks disclosures of DNC emails to [illegible] ...r – an [illegible] ...t fort[illegible] ...e FISA applications. In fact, when asked di[illegible] ...S-1 if [illegible] ...had [illegible] ...nowledge about the WikiLeaks disclosures, Pa[illegible] ...eplied [illegible] ...dopo[illegible] that the campaign "would [not] advocate for th[illegible] ...ivity b[illegible] ...e en[illegible] it's, ah, illegal . . . and compromises [illegible] ...ral secu[illegible] ...pado[illegible] ...ated that this type of activity is "espionage . . [illegible] ...padopo[illegible] ...nials about the campaign's involvement w[illegible] ...eaks d[illegible] These highly probative statements, so[illegible] ...were m[illegible] the i[illegible] ...SA application, were not included in th[illegible] ...r any [illegible] ...ren[illegible] ...aps more importantly, these statements did [illegible] ...yone i[illegible] ...ques[illegible] ...ial predication for Crossfire Hurricane, na[illegible] ...oulos' [illegible] ...tern[illegible] ...ustralian diplomats regarding Russia's offer [illegible] ...to the [illegible] ...paig[illegible]

Similar[illegible] ...exculpa[illegible] ...ments, [illegible] ...re Hurricane investigators chose not to credit P[illegible] ...s state[illegible] ...assess[illegible] ...e "weird," "rote," "canned," "rehearsed," a[illegible] ...ting a[illegible] ...the [illegible] ...egal coaching.[1388] Indeed, when interviewed by [illegible] ...the Cro[illegible] ...ca[illegible] ...repeated that assessment noting that Papadop[illegible] ...nts w[illegible] ...[illegible] therefore not authentic. Likewise, whe[illegible] ...d by th[illegible] ...othe[illegible] ...recalled briefing FBI executives about the Papa[illegible] ...temen[illegible] ...Mc[illegible] ...ted that the statements were deemed to be [illegible] ...a fa[illegible] ...on.

For the [illegible] ...s state[illegible] ...ec[illegible] ...vidence assembled by the Office in relation to the [illegible] the Pap[illegible] ...state[illegible] ...Page FISA application may have been sufficien[illegible] ...egligen[illegible] ...but [illegible] ...ent to bring criminal charges against any FBI [illegible] ...ent pers[illegible]

*iii. [illegible] ...duct o[illegible]*

As disc[illegible] ...on De[illegible] 2016 [illegible] ...d Page had the third of what would eventually be [illegible] ...meeti[illegible] ...mee[illegible] and Page discussed, among other things, the po[illegible] ...n of [illegible] ...ased [illegible] ...ocusing on Russia's relations with the West. Alt[illegible] ...discu[illegible] ...ary o[illegible] ...inee Rex Tillerson's relationship with Igor Sech[illegible] ...efly d[illegible] ...Wash[illegible] ...column mentioning Page's purported rela[illegible] ...Sechin[illegible] ...of [illegible] ...g Sechin and Igor Divyekin was not raised duri[illegible] ...ng. Ne[illegible] ...a fe[illegible] CHS-1 informed Case Agent-1 that Page, in fa[illegible] ...CHS-1 [illegible] ...me[illegible] ...on his most recent trip to Russia. According to C[illegible] ..., CHS-1 [illegible] ...to [illegible] ...formation after reading about Sechin in the [illegible] ...review[illegible] ...nscri[illegible] ...eting and careful listening to the entire recordin[illegible] ...o such [illegible] ...made [illegible][1389] and reviewing the transcript or

---

[1388] *Redacted* [illegible] ...at 332-[illegible]

[1389] Transcript [illegible] ...ion betw[illegible] ...Pag[illegible] ...-1 on 12/15/2016.

listening to the recorded conversation appears to have been a basic step that Case Agent-1 did not take. The Office examined whether CHS-1 made an intentional false statement to the FBI when he provided this information, but was unable to establish that CHS-1 intentionally lied to the FBI.

j. Certification of the FISA applications

The Office also assessed whether there were any criminal violations in the certifications made by senior government officials as part of the Page FISA applications.[1390] The certification addresses the foreign intelligence purpose of the application, such as a purpose of obtaining information "necessary . . . to protect against . . . clandestine intelligence activities by an intelligence service or network of a foreign power or by an agent of a foreign power" or "information with respect to a foreign power or foreign territory that . . . is necessary to . . . the national defense or security of the United States . . . or the conduct of the foreign affairs of the United States."[1391] The official must also certify that the foreign intelligence sought cannot be obtained by normal investigative techniques, and explain the basis for that certification.[1392] The certification of a FISA application does not cover the accuracy of the information in the application itself; that is addressed by a sworn statement from an FBI Agent.[1393]

The certifications met the requirements of FISA. Our investigation did not reveal that any certifier lacked a reasonable basis for believing that the assertions as to the purpose of the application were true. The examples and explanations provided in the certifications strongly supported the assertions that a significant purpose of the applications was to obtain foreign intelligence information.

The certifiers also certified that the foreign intelligence sought could not be obtained by normal investigative techniques. The certifications listed other techniques that might be used to investigate Page. Again, our investigation did not find that any certifier lacked a reasonable basis for believing that the assertions about the use of investigative techniques were true. The certifications explained the basis for the statements logically and in a manner that was relevant to the Page applications.

## E. The Alfa Bank and Yotaphone Allegations

### *1. Factual background – Alfa Bank*

a. Introduction

The Office's investigation identified evidence that certain individuals and entities sought to support the Clinton campaign by promoting allegations to law enforcement and the Intelligence Community related to Trump and his campaign. The Office considered

[1390] *In re Carter W. Page*, No. 16-1182, at 63; *In re Carter W. Page*, No. 17-52, at 76; *In re Carter W. Page*, No. 17-375, at 88; *In re Carter W. Page*, No. 17-679 at 98.

[1391] *See* 50 U.S.C. § 1801(e)(2). The certification requirements are discussed above in Section III.C.3.

[1392] 50 U.S.C. §§ 1804(a)(6)(C) and (a)(6)(E)(ii).

[1393] *See supra* §§ III.C.1; III.C.3.

whether the activities of these individuals or entities, as well as government officials, violated any federal criminal statutes. In particular, we examined the validity of the allegations and whether these individuals or entities conspired with the Clinton campaign to provide false or misleading information to law enforcement and the Intelligence Community.

*First*, the Office identified certain statements that Michael Sussmann made to the FBI and the CIA that the investigation revealed were false. Sussmann was a partner at Perkins Coie, the law firm that served as counsel to the Clinton campaign. A grand jury in the U.S. District Court for the District of Columbia found probable cause to believe that Sussmann lied to an FBI official and returned a one-count indictment charging him with making a materially false statement, in violation of 18 U.S.C. § 1001.[1394]

As set forth in the Indictment, on September 19, 2016 – less than two months before the 2016 election – Sussmann met with FBI General Counsel Baker. Sussmann provided Baker with data and white papers that allegedly demonstrated a covert communications channel between the Trump Organization and Alfa Bank, a Russia-based bank. The Indictment alleged that Sussmann lied in that meeting, falsely stating to Baker that he was not providing information to the FBI on behalf of any client. Instead, the Office's investigation revealed that Sussmann had assembled and conveyed the allegations to the FBI on behalf of two clients, Rodney Joffe, an executive at Tech Company-1[1395] and the Clinton campaign. After a two-week trial, a jury found that the case against Sussmann had not been proven beyond a reasonable doubt.

*Second*, as explained further below, the Office's investigation uncovered evidence of numerous actions by individuals and entities with ties to the Clinton campaign to promote the Alfa Bank allegations to the Intelligence Community and the government. The Office also uncovered evidence that individuals and entities with ties to the Clinton campaign promoted allegations that Trump or his associates were using, in the vicinity of the White House and other locations, one or more telephones from the Russian mobile telephone provider Yotaphone. The Office considered the validity of the allegations and evaluated whether the conduct of these individuals or entities constituted a federal offense and whether admissible evidence would be sufficient to obtain a conviction for such an offense. Ultimately, the Office concluded that our evidence was not sufficient to obtain and sustain a criminal conviction.

The Office also examined the FBI's actions in relation to the Alfa Bank and Yotaphone allegations. In doing so, the investigation assessed whether any FBI or other federal employee conspired with others to promote the allegations in order to benefit the Clinton campaign in a manner that would constitute a federal offense. The Office's investigation did not establish sufficient evidence that any FBI official or employee

---

[1394] *See Sussmann Indictment.*

[1395] *Sussmann* Tr. 05/17/2022 PM at 506:12-17. Tech Company-1 is a U.S. based company that provides internet-related services and products to both commercial and government clients. *Sussmann* Tr. 05/17/2022 PM at 502:2-506:8; OSC Report of Interview of University-1 Researcher-1 on 07/22/2021 at 4; OSC Report of Interview of Tech Company-1 Employee-1 on 02/02/2021 at 1-4.

knowingly and intentionally participated in a conspiracy with others to promote the allegations, to falsify government records, to obstruct justice, or to cause the FBI to open an investigation into them as part of such a conspiracy.

b. Sussmann's attorney-client relationship with the Clinton campaign and Joffe

As part of its investigation, the Office obtained billing records from Perkins Coie related to the firm's representation of various individuals and entities, including the Clinton campaign, Tech Company-1, and Rodney Joffe. The records reflect that Sussmann repeatedly billed the Clinton campaign for his work on the Alfa Bank allegations. In compiling and disseminating these allegations, Sussmann and Joffe also met and communicated with Marc Elias, another partner at Perkins Coie, who was then serving as General Counsel to the Clinton campaign.[1396]

By way of background, in April 2015, the Clinton campaign engaged Perkins Coie and Elias to provide "legal counseling and representation of [the Clinton campaign] in connection to its legal affairs, including the Federal Election Commission and other regulatory requirements and general organizational and compliance matters."[1397] A few months later, the DNC and the Democratic Congressional Campaign Committee engaged Perkins Coie to provide legal advice in connection with the "Federal Election Commission and other regulatory requirements and general organizational and compliance matters."[1398]

After these engagements, in the spring of 2016, Perkins Coie engaged Fusion GPS on behalf of the Clinton campaign. Fusion GPS was a Washington, D.C.-based consulting firm that provided research and strategic intelligence services to clients, including corporations and law firms. As set forth in the letter memorializing that engagement, the purpose was for Fusion to support Perkins Coie's legal advice to clients on "defamation, libel and similar laws in which accuracy is an essential legal element."[1399] Elias explained that Perkins Coie hired Fusion for research and investigative services to assist Elias and Perkins Coie in representing the Clinton campaign.[1400] As part of those services, Fusion provided research and other services that were used to, among other things, promote the Alfa Bank allegations to the media and the FBI.

c. The Alfa Bank allegations

*i. Actions by Sussmann, Perkins Coie, and Joffe to promote the allegations*

The Office's investigation revealed that beginning in late July or early August 2016, Sussmann, Joffe, and agents of the Clinton campaign together assembled and disseminated the Alfa Bank allegations and other derogatory information about Trump and his associates to the media and then to the FBI. Generally speaking, the Alfa Bank allegations pertained to

---

[1396] Joffe and Elias declined to be voluntarily interviewed by the Office.

[1397] *Sussmann* Government Exhibit 301 at 1.

[1398] SCO-021710 (Letter from Perkins Coie Attorney-1 to DNC Official-1 re: Legal Representation dated October 7, 2015) at 1.

[1399] *Sussmann* Government Exhibit 302 at 1.

[1400] *Sussmann* Tr. 05/18/2022 AM at 630:10-634:10.

assertions that [illegible] mail [illegible] d in [illegible] ia was configured to allow email communicatio[illegible] Alfa Ba[illegible] Tru[illegible] ation through a "TOR exit node" (*i.e.*, a [illegible] anon[illegible] Spectrum Health, a U.S.-based healthcare com[illegible] in M[illegible]

Begin[illegible] ramer[illegible] offe [illegible] Sussmann, Fusion GPS, a number of cy[illegible] rs, and [illegible] rnet companies to assemble data and white pape[illegible] ction [illegible] d his access to non-public or proprietary in[illegible] offe a[illegible] the [illegible] f researchers at a U.S.-based university ("U[illegible]) who [illegible] ng large amounts of internet data in connection [illegible] g fed[illegible] men[illegible] ity research contract. Joffe tasked these re[illegible] nine [illegible] connection between Trump and Russia.

In parti[illegible] July [illegible] ugust [illegible] mmenced a project in coordination w[illegible] n and [illegible] "inference" and "narrative" tying Trump t[illegible] exam[illegible] three days in August 2016, Joffe had meetings [illegible] calls [illegible][1401] At about the same time, Joffe began tasking [illegible] oyees [illegible] assemble internet data that would suppor[illegible] ence [illegible][1402] [illegible] essly stated in emails that a purpose of thi[illegible] ple[illegible] VIP[illegible] ently referring to Sussmann, Elias, and the [illegible] paign.[illegible]

Among [illegible] Joff[illegible] f another technology company ("Tech Compa[illegible] ive-1"[illegible] interest in Tech Company-3. Joffe instructe[illegible] pany-[illegible] maintained by his company and another af[illegible] pany[1404] [illegible] ing the online activities of Trump and his associ[illegible] told [illegible] e-1 that he was working with a person at a firm [illegible] ton, [illegible] Clinton campaign and the

---

[1401] *Sussmann* [illegible] Exhib[illegible]

[1402] SC-00000[illegible] m Jo[illegible] her-1 & University-1 Researcher-2 dated 08/03/20[illegible] 0732 [illegible] esearcher-1 to Tech Company-1 Employee-1 & [illegible]/20/[illegible] from Tech Company-2 Executive-1 to Joffe, Un[illegible] earche[illegible] er-2 dated 08/20/2016); SC-00000016 (Em[illegible] ersity-1 [illegible] ty-1 Researcher-2, Joffe & Tech Company-2 Ex[illegible] ed 08[illegible] ail from Joffe to University-1 Researcher-1, [illegible] Researc[illegible] Tech [illegible] Executive-1 dated 08/21/2016).

[1403] SC-00000[illegible] m Jo[illegible] Comp[illegible] cutive-1, University-1 Researcher-1 & University-[illegible] 2 date[illegible] 6).

[1404] The affilia[illegible] was P[illegible] sic[illegible] that, among other things, places or gains access t[illegible] inter[illegible] w it to collect large quantities of internet domai[illegible] ("D[illegible] fro[illegible] globe, which it then sells. *Sussmann* Tr. [illegible] M at [illegible] 98[illegible]

[1405] OSC Repo[illegible] of T[illegible] ny-[illegible] 1 on Aug. 12, 2021 at 2-4; *Sussmann* Tr. [illegible] M at [illegible] 6, [illegible] 1.

Democratic Party. Joffe also provided to Tech Company-3 Executive-1 a document containing the physical addresses, email addresses, Internet Protocol ("IP") addresses, email domains, and other personal information associated with various Trump associates, including information about some spouses and family members (the "Trump Associates List").[1406]

Tech Company-3 Executive-1 was highly uncomfortable with this task.[1407] Still, according to Tech Company-3 Executive-1, he and others complied with the instructions because Joffe was a powerful figure at these companies.[1408] The companies thereafter embarked on a data analysis and opposition research project concerning Trump and his associates, which they codenamed "Crimson Rhino."[1409] As part of the research project, Tech Company-3 Executive-1 and his associates drafted a report that they provided to Joffe. The report's "preliminary result" was that the researchers "observed no connection that clearly indicated direct communications between said individuals and Russia that would imply money transfers from Russia to the United States within the last 90 days."[1410]

Joffe also tasked others, including an employee of Tech Company-1 ("Tech Company-1 Employee-1"), to use resources at his companies to conduct opposition research about Trump.[1411] According to Tech Company-1 Employee-1, one of the services that Tech Company-1 provided was access to domain name system ("DNS") information.[1412] As part of these services, Tech Company-1 stored approximately 150 billion DNS transactions per day, which was approximately five terabytes of data.[1413] Although Tech Company-1 Employee-1 acknowledged that Tech Company-1 did not conduct political research as part of its business operations,[1414] during the 2016 campaign, Joffe asked Tech Company-1 Employee-1 to run searches of Tech Company-1's DNS data logs related to the Alfa Bank allegations.[1415] According to Tech Company-1 Employee-1, this included creating scripts to pull data related to various domains and IP addresses, including the domain trump-

---

[1406] *Sussman* Tr. 5/24/2022 PM at 1996:9-11; SC-00083453. The List included Carter Page, Sergei Millian, Paul Manafort, Richard Burt, Roger Stone, and Peter Petrina.

[1407] *Sussmann* Tr. 05/24/2022 PM at 1996:9-1997:12.

[1408] OSC Report of Interview of Tech Company-3 Executive-1 on Aug. 12, 2021 part 2 at 1.

[1409] *Sussmann* Tr. 05/24/2022 PM at 1997:3-1998:12.

[1410] SC-00083451 (Crimson Rhino paper) at 1.

[1411] OSC Report of Interview of Tech Company-1 Employee-1 on Feb. 2, 2021 at 4-5.

[1412] DNS is a naming system for devices connected to the internet that translates recognizable domain names, *E.g.*, http://www.google.com, to numerical IP addresses, *E.g.*, 123.456.7.89. *Sussmann* Tr. 05/17/2022 AM at 325:4-24. "A DNS look-up tells you that one computer looked up the IP address for a particular domain name." *Sussmann* Tr. 05/17/2022 AM at 339:17-18.

[1413] *Sussmann* Tr. 05/17/2022 PM at 504:11-20.

[1414] *Id.* at 506:9-11.

[1415] *Id.* at 508:4-19.

email.com and various domains that included the phrase "alfa" in them.[1416] Tech Company-1 Employee-1 could not recall conducting any other searches of Tech Company-1's DNS data for political projects or related in any way to specific political organizations, but Tech Company-1 Employee-1 never asked Joffe about the purpose of the project or whether these searches were on behalf a political campaign.[1417] Tech Company-1 Employee-1 has stated, in sum and substance, that he did not ask because he did not want to know.[1418]

Joffe similarly tasked Tech Company-2 Executive-1[1419] and other researchers with conducting opposition research regarding Trump. For instance, Joffe emailed these researchers the same Trump Associates List that he had provided to Tech Company-3 Executive-1.[1420] Among those whom Joffe and Tech Company-2 Executive-1 enlisted were researchers at University-1 who were assigned to a then-pending federal cybersecurity contract with the Defense Advanced Research Projects Agency ("DARPA"). At the time, Joffe was negotiating an agreement between Tech Company-1 and University-1 to sell large amounts of internet data to the university for use under the DARPA contract. The intended purpose of this agreement, and of University-1's sensitive work with DARPA, was to gather and analyze internet metadata to detect malicious cyberattacks.[1421] Both Joffe and Tech Company-2 Executive-1 worked with two of these University-1 researchers, University-1 Researcher-1 and University-1 Researcher-2, to mine internet data to conduct opposition research.

As part of these efforts, Sussmann and Elias began facilitating collaboration and information sharing by Joffe, Fusion GPS, and the Clinton campaign. For example, email records reflect that in August 2016, Sussmann began exchanging emails with personnel from Fusion and Elias containing the subject line, "connecting you all by email."[1422] (The contents of these emails have been withheld pursuant to asserted attorney-client privilege.)[1423]

---

[1416] *Id.* at 511:21-517:17; *Sussmann* Government Exhibits 111, 1600, 1602.

[1417] *Sussmann* Tr. 05/17/2022 PM at 514:14-17, 519:3-10.

[1418] *Id.* at 509:5-9, 519:3-10.

[1419] Tech Company-2 Executive-1 was the president and CEO of another company funded by Joffe. *Sussmann* Tr. 05/24/2022 PM at 1985:8-9; OSC Report of Interview of Tech Company-3 Executive-1 on Aug. 16, 2021 at 2. Tech Company-2 Executive-1 declined to be interviewed by the Office.

[1420] SC-00000578 (Email from Joffe to Tech Company-2 Executive-1, University-1 Researcher-1 & University-1 Researcher-2 dated 08/20/2016).

[1421] OSC Report of Interviews of University-1 Researcher-2 in July, August 2021 at 1.

[1422] SC-00108364 (Email from Sussmann to Simpson, Fritsch & Elias dated 08/11/2016).

[1423] Perkins Coie Privilege Log dated 09/07/2021, sheet 2 at lines 1-5. In the *Sussmann* case, Fusion GPS withheld over 1500 documents, claiming they were covered by attorney-client privilege as they were purportedly prepared to assist Perkins Coie in providing legal advice to law firm's clients, the Clinton campaign and Fusion GPS, in the event that then-candidate Trump sued them for defamation. Before trial, the government challenged their privilege claims and

Later that month, Joffe also began communicating with Fusion GPS personnel.[1424] Email records offered at the *Sussmann* trial and described in further detail below reflect that, in the ensuing months, Fusion GPS employees communicated with news reporters regarding the Alfa Bank allegations and urged them to publish articles about them.

Sussmann took additional steps to integrate the Alfa Bank-related allegations into the Clinton campaign's opposition research efforts. For example, in the summer of 2016, Sussmann met in Perkins Coie's offices with Fusion personnel and with Christopher Steele, whose Dossier-related activities are described above.[1425] Fusion had at the time retained Steele to conduct opposition research.[1426] Sussmann and Steele have each testified separately about the meeting and their accounts differ as to what occurred. Although Sussmann testified before Congress that the purpose of the meeting was to "vet" Steele for the Clinton campaign given Sussmann's knowledge of national security matters, Sussmann never acknowledged discussing the Alfa Bank allegations with Steele and has maintained that the contents of their meeting are privileged.[1427] In contrast, Steele testified under oath in a British legal proceeding that, during the meeting, Sussmann told him about the Alfa Bank allegations.[1428] Steele further testified that, after the meeting, Fusion personnel tasked Steele to research and produce intelligence reports about Alfa Bank, which he did.[1429]

---

successfully moved the Court to inspect a sampling of approximately 38 documents *in camera*. After reviewing the materials and receiving briefing not only from the government and Sussmann's counsel but also from Fusion GPS's counsel, counsel for the DNC and counsel for the Clinton campaign, the Court determined that 22 of 38 emails were improperly withheld as privileged. Specifically, the Court rejected their privilege claims because the emails at issue "solely related to disseminating the information they [Fusion GPS] and others had gathered." *United States v. Sussmann*, 21-CR-582, 5/12/2022 Order at 6-7.

1424 *Sussmann* Government Exhibit 602 (Email from Joffe to Laura Seago & Sussmann dated 08/30/2016). Fusion GPS similarly withheld the contents of such communications as subject to attorney-client privilege. Fusion GPS Supplemental Privilege Log dated 03/22/2021.

1425 U.S. House of Representatives Permanent Select Committee on Intelligence Interview of Michael Sussmann, (Dec. 18, 2017) at 74-75; *Steele Transcript* (Mar. 18, 2020) at 1:18-2:3. *See supra* § IV.D.1.b.

1426 U.S. House of Representatives Permanent Select Cmte. on Intelligence Interview of Glenn Simpson, (Nov. 14, 2017) at 13, 19, 22-25.

1427 U.S. House of Representatives Permanent Select Cmte. on Intelligence Interview of Michael Sussmann, (Dec. 18, 2017) at 75-76.

1428 *Steele Transcript* (Mar. 18, 2020) at 1:23-2:3.

1429 *Steele Transcript* (Mar. 18, 2020) at 1:18-2:6; SCO-105084 (Documents Known to the FBI Comprising the "Steele Dossier") at 23-24 (Company Intelligence Report 2016/112).

Accord[illegible] ment [illegible] pub[illegible]ation, Steele also later provided the substance [illegible] Bank al[illegible] to Sta[illegible]ent personnel, and Fusion GPS and Steele pro[illegible] inform[illegible] ice [illegible]ial at the Department.[1430]

Emails [illegible] rds, and [illegible] ial e[illegible]red at trial show that during approximately [illegible] the pe[illegible] [illegible]ng the FBI about these matters – Sussmann pro[illegible] Alfa Bank [illegible] to [illegible]lau, a reporter for the *New York Times*.[1431]

Law fi[illegible] lect [illegible] Bank allegations to the media, Sussmann app[illegible] his eff[illegible] in [illegible] to have communicated with the Clinton campa[illegible] leade[illegible] [illegible]es.[1432]

Emails [illegible] cord[illegible] the same time period, Sussmann and Joffe wor[illegible] to draf[illegible] paper [illegible]marized the Alfa Bank allegations an[illegible] ussmann [illegible] to the [illegible] his September 19th meeting with James Ba[illegible] in bil[illegible] this paper to the Clinton campaign.[1433] [illegible] and as [illegible] in [illegible] below, Joffe also solicited input on this white p[illegible] Uni[illegible] searc[illegible]

Sussma[illegible] ated a[illegible] of the [illegible]oned researchers into his efforts to disseminate [illegible] Bank alleg[illegible] the [illegible] benefit of the Clinton campaign. For [illegible] mails [illegible] on S[illegible]7, 2016 – two days before his meeting with [illegible] ssman[illegible] Unive[illegible]searcher-2, stating that "[w]e have a mutual [illegible] e,"[1434] [illegible] appea[illegible]ring to Joffe. Soon thereafter, Sussmann spo[illegible] versity [illegible]cher-2. [illegible]g their conversation, Sussmann told Universit[illegible] cher-2 th[illegible] Alfa Bank allegations had been lawfully colle[illegible] lecting [illegible]'s ap[illegible]wledge concerning the data's origins.[1436] Un[illegible] esearch[illegible] said [illegible]sked him to speak with the media about the Alfa [illegible] tions, [illegible]bac[illegible][1437]

---

[1430] *Steele Tran*[illegible] 18, 20[illegible] 5117 (Notes from Meeting with Chris Steele da[illegible] 16); S[illegible] (Em[illegible] Winer and Kavalec dated 10/12&13/2016 [illegible] 792 (F[illegible] of [illegible] 12/12/2016).

[1431] *E.g.*, *Sussm*[illegible] ent E[illegible] 6 (M[illegible] billing entry to HFA dated 09/06/16); SCO[illegible] Michael [illegible] Veri[illegible] at 10; SCO-092711 (Michael Sussmann Veri[illegible] 3; se[illegible] 2022 PM at 725:6-726:25, 747:12-749:14; 05/19/[illegible] 344:24-[illegible] 5:25-[illegible]:8-14.

[1432] SC-00004[illegible] om El[illegible] 09/[illegible]

[1433] *E.g.*, *Sussm*[illegible] ent E[illegible] 6, [illegible]6, 553.22.

[1434] SC-00004[illegible] etwee[illegible] 17-1 E[illegible] & Sussmann dated 09/17/16).

[1435] SCO-0927[illegible] n Veri[illegible] at 5.

[1436] OSC Repo[illegible] s of [illegible] Res[illegible] July, August 2021 at 3, 5.

[1437] *Id.* at 5.

### ii. *Actions by Tech Company-2 Executive-1 and others and additional actions by Joffe*

The Office gathered emails and communications between Joffe, employees of various internet companies, and the other researchers regarding the use of internet data related to the Trump campaign. Among the internet data Joffe and his associates obtained was DNS internet traffic pertaining to (i) Spectrum Health, (ii) Trump Tower, (iii) Trump's Central Park West apartment building, and (iv) the Executive Office of the President ("EOP").

For example, Tech Company-2 Executive-1 referenced the Trump Associates that Joffe had provided:

> *Regarding this whole project, my opinion is that from DNS all we could gain even in the best case is an *inference*.*
>
> *I have not the slightest doubt that illegal money and relationships exist between pro-Russian and pro-Trump, meaning actual people very close to Trump if not himself. . . .*
>
> *But even if we found what Rodney asks us to find in DNS we don't see the money flow, and we don't see the content of some message saying "send me the money here" etc.*
>
> *I could fill out a sales form on two websites, faking the other company's email address in each form, and cause them to appear to communicate with each other in DNS. (And other ways I can think of and I feel sure [University-1 Researcher-2] can think of.)*
>
> *IF Rodney can take the *inference* we gain through this team exercise . . . and cause someone to apply more useful tools of more useful observation or study or questioning ... then work to develop even an inference may be worthwhile.*
>
> *That is how I understood the task. Because Rodney didn't tell me more context or specific things.* What [Cyber Researcher-1] has been digging up is going to wind up being significant. It's just not the case that you can rest assured that Hil[l]ary's opposition research and whatever professional govts and investigative journalists are also digging . . . they just don't all come up with the same things or interpret them the same way. But if you find any benefit in what [he] has done or is doing, you need to say so, to encourage [him]. Because we are both killing ourselves here, every day for weeks.
>
> . . . .
>
> *Trump/ advisor domains I've been using. These include ALL from Rodney's PDF [the Trump Associates List] plus more from [Cyber Researcher-1]'s work . . . .*[1438]

[1438] SC-00000570 (Email from Tech Company-2 Executive-1 to Joffe, University-1 Researcher-1 & University-1 Researcher-2 dated 08/20/2016) (emphases added) (capitalizations in original).

The above email reflects the fact that Joffe's tasking likely triggered or affected the research efforts that ultimately culminated in Sussmann's meeting with Baker. Joffe's response states that the "task is indeed broad" and that the ability to "provide evidence of *anything* that shows an attempt to behave badly" would make "the VIPs . . . happy." According to Joffe, the "VIPs" were looking for a "true story that could be used as the basis for a closer examination," and any interactions between Trump and Alfa Bank "would be jackpot."[1439]

Joffe proceeded to disseminate the Alfa Bank allegations despite having previously expressed and received from others expressions of serious doubts and differing views about their strength, and purposefully crafted a written analysis to conceal the weaknesses of the allegations. For example, on August 21, 2016, Joffe urged the researchers to push forward with additional research concerning Trump, which he stated would "give the base of a very useful narrative." Later in the same email, Joffe expressed his own belief that the "trump-email.com" domain was "a red herring," noting that the host for that domain "is a legitimate valid [customer relationship management] company." Joffe therefore concluded that "we can ignore it, together with others that seem to be part of the marketing world."[1440]

On August 22, 2016, University-1 Researcher-1 expressed his view that Joffe's research project was flawed, stating that:

> Lets [sic] for a moment think of the best case scenario, where we are able to show (somehow) that DNS (MX[1441] or otherwise) communication exists between Trump and R[ussia]. *How do we plan to defend against the criticism that this is not spoofed UDP traffic we are observing?* There is no answer to that. Lets [sic] assume again that they are not smart enough to refute our "best case" scenario. Rodney, you do realize that we will have to expose every trick we have in our bag to even make a very weak association? Letsv [sic] all reflect upon that for a moment. [S]orry folks, but unless we get combine netflow and DNS traffic collected at critical points between suspect organizations, *we cannot technically make any claims that would fly public scrutiny.* This is not a typical attribution problem when the two parties (defenders vs. attackers) are clearly separated. In this case we will have not only the Trump folks trying to sho[o]t this down, but all the privacy freaks trying to come up with a crazy conspiracy theory on how we obtain the data. Sorry to say this, we are nowhere close coming [sic] with a plan to attack this problem that will fly in the public domain. *The only thing that drive* [sic] *us at this point is that we just do not like [Trump]. This will not fly in eyes of*

[1439] SC-00000573 (Email from Joffe to Tech Company-2 Executive-1, University-1 Researcher-1 & University-1 Researcher-2 dated 08/20/2016).

[1440] SC-00000665 (Email from Joffe to University-1 Researcher-1, University-1 Researcher-2 & Tech Company-2 Executive-1 dated 08/21/2016).

[1441] "Mail server." *Sussmann* Government Exhibit 247 at 2.

*public scrutiny. Folks, I am afraid we have tunnel vision.* Time to regroup?[1442]

On September 14, 2016, Joffe solicited the views of the researchers on the white paper, and asked these DNS experts to consider the paper not using their expertise, but conducting the reviews as if they were *not* experts:

> Please read as if you had no prior knowledge or involvement, and you were handed this document as a security expert (NOT a dns expert) and were asked: 'Is this plausible as an explanation?' NOT to be able to say that this is, without doubt, fact, but to merely be plausible. Do NOT spend more than a short while on this (If you spend more than an hour you have failed the assignment). Hopefully less. :)[1443]

University-1 Researcher-1 replied, endorsing Joffe's approach: "A DNS expert would poke several holes to this hypothesis (primarily around visibility, about which very smartly you do not talk about). That being said, I do not think even the top security (non-DNS) researchers can refute your statements. Nice!"[1444] University-1 Researcher-1 explained to our investigators that he endorsed Joffe's approach of downplaying the paper's weaknesses because Joffe was important to the success of the then-pending DARPA contract with University-1, and University-1 Researcher-1 therefore felt pressure to please Joffe.[1445] Apart from this email, however, University-1 Researcher-1 consistently maintained that the Alfa Bank data did not support any definitive conclusions.[1446]

The following morning, University-1 Researcher-2 responded to Joffe by disputing one of the paper's key findings, stating that, "Tor exit nodes, by definition route traffic for all users, since they do not know the origin of the traffic. To say that the Tor exit is exclusively used by Alfa Bank goes too far."[1447] Tech Company-2 Executive-1 responded to Joffe, stating, in part, that the paper's conclusion was "plausible" in the "narrow scope" defined by Joffe, and noting in part that: "if the whitepaper intends to say that there are communications between at least Alfa [Bank] and Trump, which are being intentionally hidden by Alfa [Bank] and Trump, I absolutely believe that is the case."[1448] University-1

---

[1442] SC-00000021 (Email from University-1 Researcher-1 to Tech Company-2 Executive-1, Joffe & University-1 Researcher-2 dated 08/22/2016) (emphasis added).

[1443] SC-00000023 (Email from Joffe to University-1 Researcher-1, University-1 Researcher-2 & Tech Company-2 Executive-1 dated 09/14/16) (capitalization in original).

[1444] SC-00000028 (Email from University-1 Researcher-1 to Joffe, University-1 Researcher-2 & Tech Company-2 Executive-1 dated 09/14/16).

[1445] OSC Report of Interview of University-1 Researcher-1 on July 22, 2021 at 1-2.

[1446] *Id.* at 1; 2-3; 4.

[1447] SC-00000758 (Email from University-1 Researcher-2 to Joffe, University-1 Researcher-1 & Tech Company-2 Executive-1 dated 09/16/2016).

[1448] SC-00000760 (Email from Tech Company-2 Executive-1 to Joffe, University-1 Researcher-1 & University-1 Researcher-2 dated 09/15/16).

Researcher-2 [illegible] same [illegible] ed that there was "a threshold of probable caus[illegible] and [illegible]

On Sep[illegible] 2016, [illegible] -1 emailed these researchers, discussing, an[illegible] ngs, [illegible] ation that there was a TOR exit node at Spectr[illegible] at Alf[illegible] nicate with the Trump organization. [illegible] y-2 [illegible] that University-1 Researcher-2 had given his [illegible] very [illegible] ryone in America were as measured, fair [illegible] what [illegible] e?"[1450] Tech Company-2 Executive-1 c[illegible] she [illegible] lfa Bank has a VPN somehow through mail[illegible] .com. [illegible] re dealing with masterminds of the internet." [illegible] y-2 [illegible] firmly believed that there were communicatio[illegible] e Tr[illegible] Bank and that she did not

> care in [illegible] ether [illegible] PN from Alfa Bank, [TOR] [illegible] ank, [illegible] g to a 3-way connection. Rodne[illegible] cra[illegible] ork to accomplish the goals. [illegible] that m[illegible] my opinion be a mistak[illegible]

Notabl[illegible] hes [illegible] nodes dating back to February 22, 2010. FBI [illegible] engag[illegible] tes between February 22, 2010 and Septembe[illegible] ins[illegible] range of 167.73.x.x (assigned to Spectrum Hea[illegible] ind[illegible] e FBI experts advised that historical TO[illegible] ta co[illegible] hite paper allegation in its entirety and f[illegible] con[illegible] rk makes the described arrangement in[illegible] Even if [illegible] ing the TOR network in the alleged manne[illegible] in [illegible] curity than simply using TOR in its default con[illegible] The ex[illegible] d instead amount to a static proxy with a k[illegible] int th[illegible] elated with traffic to the relatively sma[illegible] guard[illegible] ication or the true source IP much more ea[illegible] ng a [illegible] for each connection as the system is desi[illegible] is e[illegible] re users, at some time, connected to [illegible] Heal[illegible] R and may have even come through the sa[illegible] but [illegible] kind of correlation given the deliberately ra[illegible] of T[illegible][1452]

[1449] SC-0000[illegible] m Un[illegible] ech Company-2 Executive-1, Joffe & University-[illegible] date[illegible]

[1450] SC-00000[illegible] m Te[illegible] to University-1 Researcher-2, Joffe & University-[illegible] date[illegible]

[1451] *Id.*

[1452] *FBI Techn[illegible] Repo[illegible]*

*iii. Sussmann's meeting with the FBI*

The night before he met with Baker, Sussmann sent the following text message to Baker's personal cellphone: "Jim – it's Michael Sussmann. I have something time-sensitive (and sensitive) I need to discuss. Do you have availability for a short meeting tomorrow? *I'm coming on my own – not on behalf of a client or company – want to help the Bureau.* Thanks."[1453] Baker responded: "Ok. I will find a time. What might work for you?"[1454] To which Sussmann replied: "Any time but lunchtime – you name it."[1455]

The next day, Sussmann met with Baker at FBI Headquarters. According to Baker, the meeting occurred in Baker's office and lasted approximately 30 minutes.[1456] No one else was present. Baker explained that Sussmann said during the meeting that he had information regarding a "surreptitious communications channel" between Alfa Bank and the Trump organization and that he stated, "I'm not here on behalf of any particular client."[1457] Baker said that he was "100 percent confident" that Sussmann made this statement during the meeting.[1458] Because Baker considered Sussmann a friend and colleague, Baker believed that the statement was truthful. Baker also stated that Sussmann provided him with thumb drives containing data and "white papers" that explained the covert channel. Baker also noted that Sussmann said that major news organizations were aware of the Alfa Bank allegations and were intent on publishing about the issue relatively soon.[1459] As a result, Baker considered this to be an urgent matter because, if a news organization were to publish the allegations, any secret communications channel would likely disappear.[1460]

Thus, soon after he met with Sussmann, Baker spoke with Assistant Director for Counterintelligence Priestap and Deputy General Counsel Anderson, who handled counterintelligence and cyber matters. Baker believed that Priestap and Anderson needed to be aware of the allegations because they involved a Russian bank purportedly making an effort to communicate with the Trump organization. This "seemed to [Baker], on its face, to be a potential national security threat."[1461] Baker relayed to Priestap and Anderson the details of his meeting, including Sussmann's specific representation that he was not there on behalf of any client and a general explanation of the Alfa Bank allegations. Both Priestap

---

[1453] *Sussmann* Government Exhibit 1500 (James Baker iPhone screenshots) at 4 (emphasis added).

[1454] *Id.*

[1455] *Id.*

[1456] *Sussmann* Tr. 05/19/2022 AM at 840:23-841:19.

[1457] *Id.* at 842:9-14.

[1458] *Id.*

[1459] *Id.* at 845:4-10, 847:21-24.

[1460] *Id.* at 848:3-16.

[1461] *Id.* at 854:6-12.

and Anderson took contemporaneous notes. Priestap wrote in his FBI notebook[1462] that Sussmann "said not doing this for any client":

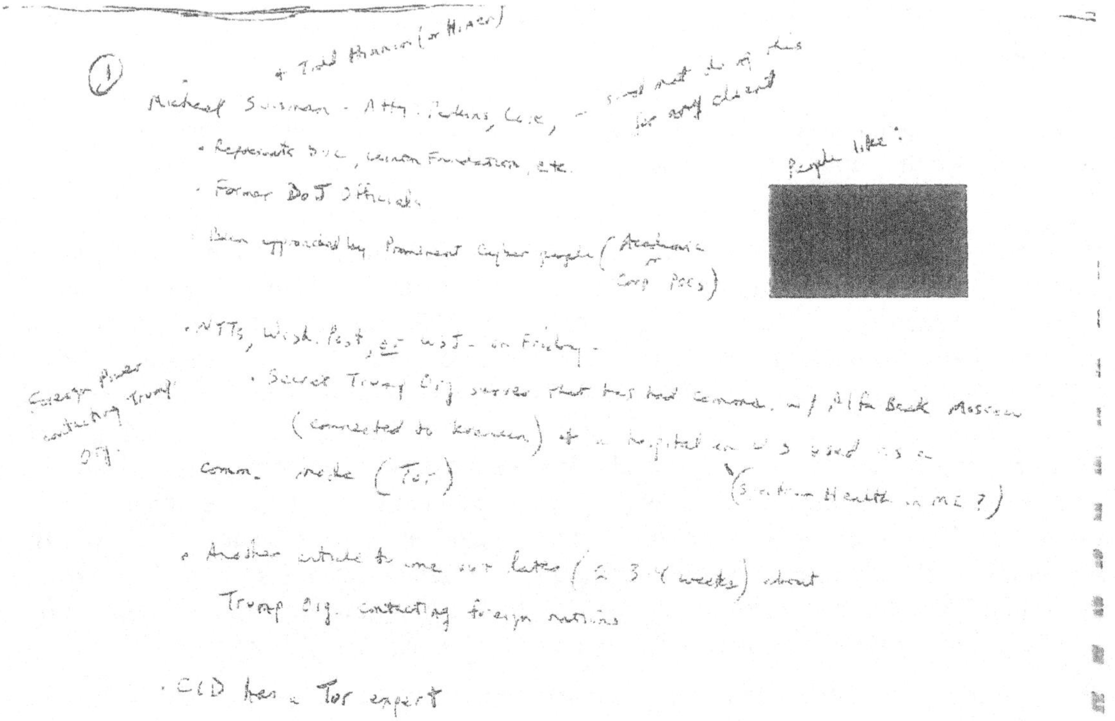


Similarly, Anderson took the following notes,[1463] which stated, in part, "No specific client but group of cyber academics talked w/ him about research":

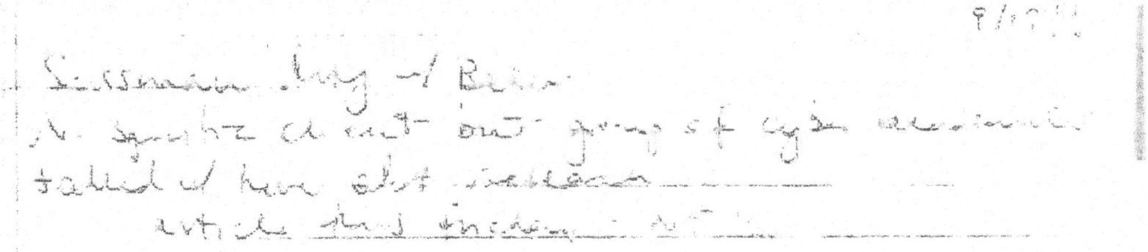


Despite their notes, neither Priestap nor Anderson remembered receiving this information from Baker.[1464] Baker also recalled that he briefed both Director Comey and Deputy Director Andrew McCabe about the Alfa Bank allegations.[1465]

---

[1462] *Sussmann* Government Exhibits 2A, 2B, 2C, 243, 289.

[1463] *Sussmann* Government Exhibits 3A, 242.

[1464] *Sussmann* Tr. 05/23/2022 AM at 1445:22-1446:1; 05/24/2022 AM at 1786:15-25.

[1465] As noted previously, McCabe and Comey declined to be interviewed.

d. The FBI's Alfa Bank investigation

Following his meeting with Sussmann and briefings of FBI leadership, Baker recalled that he gave either Priestap or Strzok the white papers[1466] and thumb drives from Sussmann.[1467] The materials then made their way quickly to the Cyber Division. At trial, an FBI cyber agent ("Cyber Agent-1") testified that the agent and his supervisor ("Cyber Agent-2") were tasked to take custody of the Alfa Bank materials and to obtain signatures for the accompanying chain of custody form.[1468] A review of that form showed that Baker relinquished custody of the materials to Strzok, who then provided the materials to Eric Sporre, the Deputy Assistant Director of the Cyber Division.[1469] According to the form, Sporre thereafter transferred custody to Cyber Agent-2.[1470] Cyber Agent-1 testified that he was able to get signatures from Baker and Sporre for the form, but Strzok was unavailable and someone else obtained his signature.[1471]

i. *The Cyber Division's review of the Alfa Bank allegations*

Following the receipt of the materials, Cyber Agent-2 tasked Cyber Agent-1 to review the data provided on the thumb drives along with the white papers and identify whether there were any "cyber equities," such as an allegation of hacking.[1472] Cyber Agent-2 also tasked Cyber Agent-1 to review the data and compare it to the white paper and provide an assessment as to whether the data supported the white paper's findings.[1473] The white paper that Cyber Agent-1 reviewed, titled "White Paper #1 – Auditable V3,"[1474] contained an initial section titled "Findings" that stated:

> The Trump Organization is using a very unusually-configured 'secret' email server in Pennsylvania for current and ongoing email communications with Alfa Bank (Moscow), and with Alfa Bank (Moscow) through another

---

[1466] At his meeting with Baker, Sussmann provided three white papers to the FBI. Sussmann, Joffe, and possibly others drafted the first paper. *Sussmann* Government Exhibits 11, 319, 327, 331, 382, 553.6, 553.12, 553.16, 553.22; SC-00004255 (Email from Sussmann dated 09/06/2016); SC-00000023 (Email from Joffe to University-1 Researcher-1, University-1 Researcher-2, Tech Company-2 Executive-1 on 09/14/2016). The investigation determined that University-1 Researcher-2 drafted the second paper. Fusion GPS drafted the third paper. *Sussmann* Government Exhibits 687, 688, 689.

[1467] *Sussmann* Tr. 05/19/2022 AM at 878:8-15.

[1468] *Sussmann* Tr. 05/17/2022 AM at 365:20-366:7.

[1469] *Sussmann* Government Exhibit 282.

[1470] *Id.*

[1471] *Sussmann* Tr. 05/17/2022 AM at 370:6-10.

[1472] *Id.* at 371:20-372:4.

[1473] *Id.* at 372:8-24.

[1474] *Sussmann* Government Exhibit 217.

> unusual [illegible] ed ser[illegible] [illegible] Spectrum Health in Michig[illegible]
>
> These [illegible] nfigu[illegible] [illegible]ons between the Trump organi[illegible] la Ba[illegible] [illegible]her systems.
>
> The on[illegible] e xplar[illegible] [illegible]uration is that it shows the Tru[illegible] ation [illegible] multiple sophisticated layers [illegible] n or[illegible] [illegible]derable recent email traffic.

The white pap[illegible] ued th[illegible] domain was "mail1.trump-email.com [wa[illegible] a Pen[illegible] Listrak, which is a reasonably well known C[illegible] er rel[illegible] [illegible]pany that provides large-scale distribution of [illegible] nails [illegible] thousands of recipients hundreds of times a day[illegible]

Within [illegible] eiving [illegible] Cyber Agent-1 and Cyber Agent-2 drafted a rep[illegible] alys[illegible] [illegible]ry stated that they had "assess[ed] th[illegible] [Cy[illegible] report and that the research conducted in t[illegible] als [illegible] ive steps taken and conclusions drawn."[1477] T[illegible] owl[illegible] [illegible]gation of hacking and so there was no reason [illegible] Divi[illegible] [illegible] The report also said that

> it appe[illegible] hat [illegible] wanted to conduct secret [illegible] ce wi[illegible] (or a Russian bank), would [illegible] secre[illegible] l.com', (2) use a domain (trump[illegible] registe[illegible] n, and then (3) commu[illegible] ly to [illegible] ss (as opposed to using TOR o[illegible] s).[1478]

Cyber Agent-[illegible] both [illegible] not agree with the conclusion in the white pape[illegible] ed that [illegible] paper "jumped to some conclusions th[illegible] suppor[illegible] (ii) the methodology was questionable, [illegible] oncl[illegible] ue at all."[1479] In interviews with the Office, bo[illegible] nt-1 [illegible] they were proud of their work because they h[illegible] to th[illegible] their own very different political views.

*ii. [illegible] ng o[illegible]*

After th[illegible] sion[illegible] ferred the matter to a squad in the Chicago F[illegible] espon[illegible] sian counterintelligence and

---

[1475] *Id.* at 3.

[1476] *Sussmann* [illegible] AM [illegible]

[1477] *Sussmann* [illegible] Exhib[illegible]

[1478] *Id.* at 3.

[1479] *Sussmann* [illegible] AM [illegible]

cyber matters. The investigation was referred to a Chicago Field Office Agent ("Chicago Agent-1") who had worked on both the FBI's Mid-Year Examination investigation (the investigation related to Hillary Clinton's email server) and Crossfire Hurricane. Chicago Agent-1 was joined by a new FBI agent, Chicago Agent-2. Chicago Agent-2 was Chicago Agent-1's trainee and was the co-case Agent and primary lead for the Alfa Bank investigation. Chicago Agent-1 and Chicago Agent-2 opened a full investigation "into the network communications between a US-based server and the Russian Alfa Bank organization."[1480] A full investigation, as described above in section III.B.2, may be opened if there is "an articulable factual basis for the investigation that reasonably indicates that . . . [a]n activity constituting a federal crime or a threat to the national security . . . may be occurring."[1481]

According to the case agents and other records obtained during the investigation, it was FBI leadership who decided to open a full investigation. Indeed, two days after the meeting between Baker and Sussmann, Supervisory Special Agent-1, the Crossfire Hurricane supervisor, reached out to Chicago Agent-1. Supervisory Special Agent-1 told Chicago Agent-1 that "people on the 7th floor to include Director are fired up about this server."[1482] Supervisory Special Agent-1 further stated that, if the investigation had not been opened, he would have reached out to Chicago Agent-1's supervisor because "Priestap says it's not an option – we must do it."[1483] Chicago Agent-1 responded that the case team was "opening a CI case today."[1484] Still, the team was already skeptical of the allegations. Chicago Agent-1 noted that the team was "leaning towards this being a false server not attributed to the Trump organization" but that they would "run it down."[1485]

Chicago Agent-1 and Chicago Agent-2 memorialized the opening of the investigation in an EC.[1486] Chicago Agent-1 and Chicago Agent-2 later acknowledged that there were certain errors in this document. Of most importance to the Office was the representation made as to the source of the white papers. The EC stated that "the Department of Justice provided the FBI with a whitepaper that was produced by an anonymous third party."[1487] According to both Chicago Agent-1 and Chicago Agent-2, this

---

[1480] *Sussmann* Government Exhibit 200 (FBI EC from Chicago CG-CY-1, *Opening EC—ALFA BANK* dated 09/23/2016) at 1 (capitalization altered) (hereinafter "*Alfa Bank Opening EC*").

[1481] *AGG-Dom* §§ II.B.3.a; II.B.4.b.i.

[1482] SCO-006608 (Lync messages between Supervisory Special Agent-1 and Chicago Agent-1 dated 09/21/16).

[1483] *Id.*

[1484] *Id.*

[1485] *Sussmann* Government Exhibit 249.

[1486] *Alfa Bank Opening EC.*

[1487] *Id.* at 2 (capitalization altered).

representation was an error, and both recalled that they understood the allegations were presented to the FBI's General Counsel by an anonymous source.[1488]

*iii. The close hold on Sussmann's identity as a source*

In evaluating the FBI's early actions related to the Alfa Bank investigation, one issue that the Office identified was the decision by the FBI to put a "close hold" on Sussmann's identity as the source of the allegations and to prevent its disclosure to the Alfa Bank case team. (A close hold is when the FBI's leadership protects specific information, such as the identity of a source, and prevents the "field" or investigative team from learning that information.) The investigation revealed that multiple members of the Alfa Bank case team were "frustrated" and "concerned" that they were prevented from interviewing the source of the allegations. Accordingly, the Office attempted to determine whether Baker or other senior FBI officials may have protected Sussmann's identity improperly to further the Alfa Bank allegations against Trump for political reasons or to mask Sussmann's ties to the DNC and the Clinton campaign.

During Baker's testimony at the Sussmann trial, and although not remembering having done so, Baker speculated that he may have attempted to protect Sussmann's identity and limited disclosure to only a few senior FBI executives.[1489] According to Baker, if he did so, it was because he considered Sussmann to be a source who "had in their possession very sensitive information that he was willing to give to [the FBI]."[1490] But, again, Baker testified he did not recall whether he had refused to provide this to any specific FBI personnel or who he would have instructed to put a close hold in place. Cyber Agent-1 testified that when he was obtaining Baker's signature on the chain of custody, he could not "distinctly recall what the conversation was" but that he was "frustrated" that Baker did not tell him who had provided the thumb drives.[1491] Cyber Agent-2 told the Office that he and Cyber Agent-1 considered filing a whistleblower claim about Baker's failure to provide the information but ultimately decided that they would not because the data provided was not formal evidence in a criminal proceeding.[1492] The FBI Headquarters Program Manager for the Alfa Bank case team ("Headquarters Supervisory Special Agent-3"), noted that FBI leadership, including Strzok, instructed him not to identify the source to the team.[1493] Headquarters Supervisory Special Agent-3 further explained that he believed that the investigative team did not need to interview the source as a first step and instead should

[1488] *Sussmann* Tr. 05/23/2022 PM at 1645:15-1646:19, 1687:15-1688:12; 05/24/2022 AM at at1820:19-1821:24, 1846:12-1847:7.

[1489] *Sussmann* Tr. 05/19/2022 AM at 879:6-880:13.

[1490] *Id.* at 879:16-880:20.

[1491] *Sussmann* Tr. 05/17/2022 AM at 370:14-19.

[1492] OSC Report of Interview of Cyber Agent-2 on Sept. 16, 2019 at 2.

[1493] OSC Report of Interview of Headquarters Supervisory Special Agent-3 on Dec. 15, 2020 at 2-3, 4, 6.

focus on the data and log files to make a determination as to the validity of the allegations.[1494]

The Office's investigation showed that the Alfa Bank investigative team made multiple requests to learn the identity of the source of the Alfa Bank allegations. Approximately a week after the FBI received the Alfa Bank allegations, Chicago Agent-1 sent Supervisory Special Agent-1 a message requesting that the investigative team interview the source of the white paper.[1495] Approximately a week later, Chicago Agent-1 and his supervisor again made requests to FBI leadership to interview the source of the allegations.[1496] As Chicago Agent-1 explained, this was important to the case team because the investigation had found that the allegations were unsubstantiated, and the team wanted to confirm their findings.[1497] Ultimately, the case team never learned that Sussmann was the source of the allegations nor that he was connected in any way to the DNC and the Clinton campaign.[1498]

The FBI's investigation ultimately concluded that it was unable to substantiate any of the allegations in the white paper that Sussmann provided to Baker:

> FBI Chicago assesses Alfa Bank and Trump Organization related servers almost certainly did not communicate intentionally or covertly, based on the results of an internal examination of Alfa Bank servers by [redacted] and subsequent preventative steps employed by the companies. FBI Chicago has high confidence in this assessment, which is based on a highly reliable sensitive source with excellent access and corroborates FBI investigative activity conducted to date.[1499]

In coming to that conclusion, the investigators took a number of steps. First, they conducted open-source research on the mail1.trump-email.com domain that was identified in the white paper. They learned that the domain was registered to a company called Central Dynamics ("Cendyn") and that the server was housed at a company named Listrak, located in Pennsylvania.[1500] As a result, the FBI reached out to both Cendyn and Listrak to request data and log files from each company and to conduct interviews as well. Both Cendyn and Listrak were compliant with these requests and provided log files and data that was analyzed by FBI analysts on the investigative team. Ultimately, the data and files provided nothing to substantiate the Alfa Bank allegations.[1501] In addition, the FBI reached out to Mandiant, a

---

[1494] *Id.* at 6-7.

[1495] *Sussmann* Government Exhibit 257.

[1496] *Sussmann* Government Exhibit 265.

[1497] *Sussmann* Tr. 05/24/2022 AM at 1841:7-21.

[1498] *Id.* at 1816:19-21.

[1499] SCO-006174 (Examination of Alfa-Bank Servers dated 10/03/2016); *Sussmann* Government Exhibit 233.

[1500] *Sussmann* Tr. 05/24/2022 AM at 1827:17-21.

[1501] *Id.* at 1831:7-13.

cybersecurity [illegible] was hired [illegible] Bank [illegible] an internal investigation and forensic analy[illegible] allega[illegible] and [illegible] the FBI with its findings, which too con[illegible] there wa[illegible] the allegations of a secret communicati[illegible] or any [illegible] of di[illegible] nications between the Alfa Bank servers and Tr[illegible] ation[illegible]

In early [illegible] 6, a[illegible] ailed [illegible] onal Computer Forensics and Training Allia[illegible] Agen[illegible] ntac[illegible] er Division at FBI Headquarters because he ha[illegible] o IP ad[illegible] om [illegible] us source who had requested that the inform[illegible] vided [illegible] [1505] [illegible] to Cyber Agent-3, the anonymous so[illegible] that [illegible] ation [illegible] *New York Times* story involving the upcoming [illegible] Cyb[illegible] was [illegible] contact with Chicago Agent-2. Cyber Agent-3 [illegible] at Chi[illegible] -2 [illegible] e of the information and Cyber Agent-3 interp[illegible] go Age[illegible] onse [illegible] vestigative team was already aware of the i[illegible] [1507] Chi[illegible] t-2 [illegible] hat the case team performed open-source [illegible] se tw[illegible] es th[illegible] in identifying one IP address associated wi[illegible] and [illegible] ss a[illegible] ith a home address in Moscow.[1508]

The O[illegible] igation [illegible] ha[illegible] ous source who provided the two IP addresses t[illegible] nt-3 wa[illegible] Joffe [illegible] likely reason Joffe decided to provide the tw[illegible] s to [illegible] Cyb[illegible] anonymously was to create the appearance of [illegible] n. O[illegible] the [illegible] Office considered was that Joffe and others we[illegible] g to pr[illegible] Alfa [illegible] tions in such a way that the allegations ap[illegible] from [illegible] depen[illegible] es. Indeed, at this time, Joffe himself was a[illegible] [1509]. B[illegible] stanc[illegible] cided to provide the Alfa Bank allegations an[illegible] addres[illegible] er [illegible] ead of his FBI handler, with instructions to[illegible] entity p[illegible] [1510] [illegible] llingness to voluntarily meet with our investigat[illegible] swere[illegible] not [illegible] viding some information to the

---

[1502] *Sussmann* [illegible] 22 PM [illegible] 1651 [illegible]

[1503] *Id.* at 1661 [illegible] -0018 [illegible] rview [illegible] nt representative on 10/13/2016).

[1504] The Natio[illegible] Fore[illegible] aining [illegible] s a nonprofit partnership between the governme[illegible] ndus[illegible] orate [illegible] ate in identifying and disrupting cybercrime. [illegible] f Inter[illegible] er A[illegible] Nov. 18, 2020 at 1.

[1505] OSC Rep[illegible] w of C[illegible] t-3 [illegible] 020 at 1-2.

[1506] SCO-0110[illegible] n Cy[illegible] -3 to [illegible] ervisory Special Agent-1 dated 10/02/2016).

[1507] OSC Rep[illegible] w of C[illegible] 1-3 [illegible] 2020 at 3-4.

[1508] *Sussmann* [illegible] 22 PM [illegible] 3.

[1509] *Sussmann* [illegible] 22 AM [illegible] -216[illegible]

[1510] *Id.* 2167:1[illegible]

FBI through Sussmann and the two IP addresses through Cyber Agent-3, and in both instances to remain anonymous.[1511]

Finally, the Alfa Bank investigators also received information in early October 2016 from a separate CHS regarding the Alfa Bank allegations. Chicago Agent-2 explained that, according to the handler, the CHS had access to the white paper and had made an initial assessment that the allegations were credible but that the data appeared incomplete.[1512] The CHS also explained that he/she had been contacted by University-1 Researcher-2, one of the white paper authors.[1513] In the correspondence from Chicago Agent-2, there is an indication that the FBI was interested in speaking with University-1 Researcher-2,[1514] however, that meeting never occurred.

In January 2017, the FBI closed the Alfa Bank investigation.[1515] Ultimately, the FBI was unable to substantiate any of the allegations in the white paper.[1516]

e. Actions by Fusion GPS to promote the Alfa Bank allegations

The Special Counsel's investigation also uncovered numerous communications in which Fusion GPS leadership and other personnel sought to discuss, advance, and disseminate the Alfa Bank allegations.

As noted, in April 2016, Perkins Coie engaged Fusion GPS in connection with the 2016 election.[1517] As part of Fusion GPS's work on behalf of Perkins Coie and the Clinton campaign, it collected, organized, and promoted opposition research on Trump's ties to Russia.[1518] Perhaps most notably, as described in Section IV.D.1.b, Fusion GPS retained Steele, who compiled the information and reports that became known as the Steele Dossier. Fusion GPS also drafted one of the white papers that Sussmann provided to Baker at their September 19, 2016 meeting. That white paper provided an overview of the parent

---

[1511] It is notable, however, that in November 2016, soon after the presidential election, Joffe emailed a colleague, stating, "I was tentatively offered the top [cybersecurity] job by the Democrats when it looked like they'd win." SC-00029962 (Email from Joffe to Tech Company-1 Employee-2 dated 11/17/2016).

[1512] *Sussmann* Tr. 05/23/2022 PM at 1665:8-16.

[1513] *Id.* at 1665:17-1666:4.

[1514] SCO-007853 (Emails between Chicago Agent-2, Headquarters Supervisory Special Agent-3, Chicago Agent-1, others in October 2016).

[1515] *Sussmann* Government Exhibit 233.

[1516] *Id.*

[1517] *Sussmann* Government Exhibit 302.

[1518] U.S. House of Representatives Permanent Select Cmte. on Intelligence Interview of Glenn Simpson, (Nov. 14, 2017) at 13, 19, 22-25, 59, 101-102; OSC Report of Interview of John Podesta on Jan. 19, 2022 at 2.

company of Alfa Bank and described ties to Russian government officials and certain U.S. persons and entities.[1519]

Following Sussmann's promotion of the Alfa Bank allegations to the FBI, Fusion GPS continued to promote these allegations to various media personnel. For instance, on October 18, 2016 – two weeks before news stories would first appear about the Alfa Bank allegations – Mark Hosenball of *Reuters* emailed Fusion GPS co-founder Peter Fritsch, stating in part, "anything new Russkie/Donald wise?," to which Fritsch responded, "do the [expletive] Alfa Bank secret comms story. It's hugely important. Forget the wikileaks side show."[1520] The reporter replied that the issue with the story was the inability of his "cyber expert colleagues" to confirm that some of the important data was authentic.[1521] Later on that day, Fritsch replied: "It's everyone's problem. Call [University-1 Researcher-2] at [University-1]."[1522]

On October 22, 2016, Franklin Foer, a reporter for *Slate* magazine, emailed University-1 Researcher-2 at his University-1 email address asking for assistance on the "Alfa Bank/Trump story".[1523] A few days later, Fritsch forwarded to Foer a tweet stating that the U.S. Senate Majority Leader had "talked w/ top NatSec officials who say that [the FBI Director] 'possesses explosive information' about Trump's ties to Russia."[1524] Fritsch's email stated: "time to hurry."[1525] Foer replied "Here's the first 250 words," and included in the email a partial draft of an article about Alfa Bank and Trump on which Foer was working for Fritsch's review.[1526] The reporter published an article shortly thereafter.[1527]

On October 31, 2016, media outlets published articles regarding the Alfa Bank allegations and the existence of an FBI investigation.[1528] As previously noted, within hours of these articles, the Clinton campaign issued tweets and public statements concerning the

---

1519 *Sussmann* Government Exhibit 207. The Office has not seen evidence that Fusion was involved in originating the Alfa Bank data or were aware of its origination, but rather only promoted the allegations.

1520 *Sussmann* Government Exhibit 652.

1521 The email said: "[T]he problem with the [Alfa Bank] story at this point is that my cyber expert colleagues cannot satisfy themselves about the authenticity of some of the key data, which they say from what they can tell is NOT public data. We are in contact with your experts via different channels but my colleague [] in Silicon Valley still hasn't got the confidence he says he needs to understand where all the data originated. If you can help more with this pls do. . . ." *Id.*

1522 *Id.*

1523 SC-00018512 (Email from Foer to University-1 Researcher-2 dated 10/22/16).

1524 *Sussmann* Government Exhibit 666.

1525 *Id.*

1526 *Id.*

1527 *Sussmann* Government Exhibit 54.

1528 *Sussmann* Government Exhibit 53; *Sussmann* Government Exhibit 54.

purported existence of a secret communications channel involving the Trump Organization and Alfa Bank.[1529]

f. Actions by the Clinton campaign to promote the Alfa Bank allegations

On October 31, 2016 – about one week before the election – multiple media outlets reported that the FBI had received and was investigating the allegations concerning a purported secret channel between the Trump Organization and Alfa Bank. For example, *Slate* published an article that discussed at length the allegations that Sussmann provided to the FBI.[1530]

Also on that day, the *New York Times* published an article titled *Investigating Donald Trump, F.B.I. Sees No Clear Link to Russia.*[1531] The article discussed information in the possession of the FBI about "what cyber experts said appeared to be a mysterious computer back channel between the Trump Organization and the Alfa Bank."[1532] The article further reported that the FBI had "spent weeks examining computer data showing an odd stream of activity to a Trump Organization server," and that the newspaper had been provided computer logs that evidenced this activity. The article also noted that at the time of the article, the FBI had not found "any conclusive or direct link" between Trump and the Russian government and that "Hillary Clinton's supporters . . . pushed for these investigations."[1533]

As noted above, in the months prior to the publication of these articles, Sussmann had communicated with the media and provided them with the Alfa Bank data and allegations.[1534] Sussmann also kept Elias apprised of his efforts.[1535] Elias, in turn, communicated with the Clinton campaign's leadership about potential media coverage of these issues.[1536]

For example, emails reflect that on September 1, 2016, Sussmann met with the reporter who published the *New York Times* article, Eric Lichtblau.[1537] Sussmann billed his

---

[1529] *Sussmann* Government Exhibit 52; @HillaryClinton 10/31/2016 8:36pm Tweet.

[1530] Franklin Foer, *Was a Trump Server Communicating with Russia?*, Slate (Oct. 31, 2016).

[1531] Eric Lichtblau & Steven Lee Myers, *Investigating Donald Trump, F.B.I. Sees No Clear Link to Russia,* N.Y. Times (Oct. 31, 2016).

[1532] *Id.*

[1533] *Id.*

[1534] *See, e.g., Sussmann* Government Exhibits 553.16, 553.23, 389.

[1535] *E.g., Sussmann* Government Exhibits 307, 327, 331, 367, 553.2, 553.16; *Sussmann* Tr. 05/18/2022 AM at 574:21-575:22.

[1536] *Sussmann* Government Exhibit 377 at 3.

[1537] *Sussmann* Government Exhibit 357; *Sussmann* Government Exhibit 358.

time for the m[illegible] Clinto[illegible] [illegible]der billing description "confidential [illegible] arding [illegible] al p[illegible]

Emails [illegible] ct tha[illegible] be[illegible] [illegible]st one week prior to Sussmann's meeting with [illegible] ann a[illegible] [illegible]out Sussmann's efforts to share the Alfa Bank [illegible] with th[illegible]

In addi[illegible] mbe[illegible] Elia[illegible] [illegible]n update to the Clinton campaign reg[illegible] fa Ba[illegible] [illegible]et-published *New York Times* article, sendin[illegible] Jake [illegible] HFA [illegible]licy Advisor), Robby Mook (HFA Campa[illegible]), John [illegible] HFA [illegible] Chairman), and Jennifer Palmieri (HFA Head o[illegible] ations [illegible] bill[illegible] [illegible]nton campaign as "email correspondenc[illegible] llivan, [illegible] [illegible]lmieri re: Alfa Bank Article."[1541]

On the [illegible] at the [illegible] [illegible]he Clinton campaign posted a tweet through [illegible] ton's [illegible] [illegible]d: "Computer scientists have apparently un[illegible] vert se[illegible] the [illegible]anization to a Russian-based bank."[1542] Th[illegible] ed a [illegible] [illegible]paign advisor Jake Sullivan which made r[illegible] me[illegible] [illegible]ted, in relevant part, that the allegations in [illegible] ould [illegible] dire[illegible] [illegible]etween Donald Trump and Moscow[,] th[illegible] t ho[illegible] the [illegible]cking the mystery of Trump's ties to Russia[illegible] w]e [illegible] sure [illegible]l authorities will now explore this direct co[illegible] een T[illegible] Russ[illegible] their existing probe into Russia's med[illegible] election[illegible]

During [illegible] n tria[illegible] s a[illegible] [illegible] that the HFA campaign did not authorize Sus[illegible] the A[illegible] lleg[illegible] [illegible] FBI. According to Elias and Mook, the ca[illegible] ct trus[illegible] ue to [illegible]nnouncement related to the FBI's Midyea[illegible] stigati[illegible] ng H[illegible]on's use of a private e-mail server during [illegible] Secreta[illegible][1543] [illegible] explained that top Clinton campaign offi[illegible] ware o[illegible] Bank [illegible] and favored providing the allegations to [illegible][1544] M[illegible] not[illegible] [illegible]ad discussed the allegations with Clinton, who [illegible] disse[illegible] the [illegible]dia.[1545] Mook testified that the campaign did [illegible] estion[illegible] ntial [illegible]t the accuracy and reliability of the allegation[illegible] olve[illegible] ut k[illegible] exact origins of the data.[1546]

---

1538 SC-00004[illegible] om Su[illegible] 09[illegible]

1539 SC-00004[illegible] om El[illegible] /09/2[illegible]

1540 "Hillary fo[illegible]

1541 *Sussmann* [illegible] Exhibi[illegible] nt Exhibit 390.

1542 *Sussmann* [illegible] Exhibi[illegible] ary Cl[illegible] 1/2016 8:36pm Tweet.

1543 *Sussmann* [illegible] 22 PM [illegible] 0:[illegible] AM at 1256:2-1257:8.

1544 *Sussmann* [illegible] 22 AM [illegible]-126[illegible]

1545 *Id.* at 126[illegible]

1546 *Id.* at 120[illegible], 1267:2[illegible]

Although the campaign could not substantiate the allegations, they stated that they considered them "concerning" and wanted the media to vet the allegations because of concerns about Trump's association with Russia.[1547] Sullivan and Elias raised Trump's July 2016 "Russia, if you're listening" statement as one reason for the Clinton Campaign's concern about Trump's ties to Russia.[1548]

g. Sussmann's meeting with the CIA

The Office also gathered information related to a post-election meeting that Sussmann had with the CIA. On February 9, 2017, Sussmann provided an updated set of allegations – including the Alfa Bank data and additional allegations relating to Trump – to the CIA. The Office examined Sussmann's interactions with various CIA employees, including how he was able to secure a meeting with the CIA, what occurred during that meeting, and what materials he provided to the CIA.

The investigation revealed that in December 2016, Sussmann reached out to the CIA General Counsel and requested a meeting related to allegations against Trump.[1549] The General Counsel did not take the meeting and suggested to Sussmann that he provide the allegations to the FBI.[1550] Sussmann, however, ignored that suggestion and continued to pursue a meeting. On or about January 31, 2017, Sussmann met with a retired CIA employee ("Retired CIA Employee-1"). During the meeting, Sussmann told Retired CIA Employee-1 that he had a client who wanted to provide information to the CIA about Trump.[1551] Sussmann explained that his client "is an engineer with a number of patents" and was unsure whether his client would reveal his identity to the CIA.[1552] Sussmann further noted that his client did not want to provide this information to the FBI because the client did not trust the FBI and did not believe that the FBI had the requisite resources to deal with the allegations.[1553] Retired CIA Employee-1 also recalled Sussmann's statement that, should the CIA not investigate the allegations, he would provide them to the *New York Times*.[1554] Following the meeting, Retired CIA Employee-1 drafted a memorandum describing the meeting and sent it to active CIA officers, who then scheduled a meeting with Sussmann for early February 2017.[1555]

In the next meeting, Sussmann made a substantially similar statement to the one he had made to Baker regarding the source of the allegations. In particular, Sussmann asserted

---

1547 *Id.* at 1268:4-1269:1; OSC Report of Interview of Jake Sullivan on Nov. 12, 2021 at 2-3.

1548 *Sussmann* Tr. 05/18/2022 PM at 745:2-746:21; OSC Report of Interview of Jake Sullivan on Nov. 12, 2021 at 1-2.

1549 SC-00004549 (Email from Sussmann dated 12/14/2016).

1550 SC-00004559 (Email to Sussmann dated 12/20/2016).

1551 *Sussmann* Tr. 05/20/2022 PM at 1333:3-1334:9; *Sussmann* Government Exhibit 809.

1552 *Sussmann* Tr. 05/20/2022 PM at 1333:3-1334:9; *Sussmann* Government Exhibit 809.

1553 *Sussmann* Tr. 05/20/2022 PM at 1334:15-1335:10; *Sussmann* Government Exhibit 809.

1554 *Sussmann* Tr. 05/20/2022 PM at 1335:22-1336:10; *Sussmann* Government Exhibit 809.

1555 *Sussmann* Government Exhibit 809; SC-00081639 (Email dated 02/08/2017).

that he was not representing a particular client in conveying the above allegations.[1556] Sussmann, however, was in fact continuing to represent at least Joffe – a matter Sussmann subsequently acknowledged under oath in December 2017 testimony before Congress (without identifying the client by name).[1557]

Sussmann provided a similar set of allegations to the CIA that he had previously provided to the FBI. Specifically, Sussmann provided the CIA with an updated version of the Alfa Bank allegations and a new set of allegations that supposedly demonstrated that Trump or his associates were using, in the vicinity of the White House and other locations, one or more telephones from the Russian mobile telephone provider Yotaphone. The Office's investigation revealed that these additional allegations relied, in part, on the DNS traffic data that Joffe and others had assembled pertaining to the Trump Tower, Trump's New York City apartment building, the EOP,[1558] and Spectrum Health. Sussmann provided data to the CIA that he said reflected suspicious DNS lookups by these entities of domains affiliated with Yotaphone.[1559] Sussmann further stated that these lookups demonstrated that Trump or his associates were using a Yotaphone in the vicinity of the White House and other locations.[1560]

The FBI DNS experts with whom we worked also identified certain data and information that cast doubt upon several assertions, inferences, and allegations contained in (i) the above-quoted white papers about the Yotaphone allegations, and (ii) the presentation and Yotaphone-related materials that Sussmann provided to the CIA in 2017. In particular:

- Data files obtained from Tech Company-2, a cyber-security research company, as part of the Office's investigation reflect DNS queries run by Tech Company-2 personnel in 2016, 2017, or later reflect that Yotaphone lookups were far from rare in the United States, and were not unique to, or disproportionately prevalent on, Trump-related networks. Particularly, within the data produced by Tech Company-2, queries from the United States IP addresses accounted for approximately 46% of all yota.ru queries. Queries from Russia accounted for 20%, and queries from Trump-associated IP addresses accounted for less than 0.01%.

- Data files obtained from Tech Company-1, Tech Company-2, and University-1 reflect that Yotaphone-related lookups involving IP addresses assigned to the EOP began long before November or December 2016 and therefore seriously undermine the inference set forth in the white paper that such lookups likely reflected the presence of a Trump transition-team member who was using a Yotaphone in the EOP. In particular, this data reflects that approximately 371 such lookups involving

[1556] *Sussmann* Tr. 05/20/2022 PM at 1366:13-16; *Sussmann* Government Exhibit 814.

[1557] U.S. House of Representatives Permanent Select Cmte. on Intelligence Interview of Michael Sussmann, (Dec. 18, 2017) at 29-30, 54-67.

[1558] "Executive Office of the President."

[1559] *Sussmann* Government Exhibit 817.

[1560] *Id.*

Yotaphone domains and EOP IP addresses occurred *prior* to the 2016 election and, in at least one instance, as early as October 24, 2014.

Two CIA employees ("CIA Employee-2" and "CIA Employee-3") prepared a memorandum summarizing the meeting they had with Sussmann in February 2017. The final version included Sussmann's representation that he was not representing any "particular client."[1561] In their interviews with the Office, both CIA employees specifically recalled Sussmann stating he was not representing a particular client.[1562] [1563]

During the meeting, Sussmann provided two thumb drives and four paper documents that, according to Sussmann, supported the allegations.[1564] The CIA analyzed the allegations and data that Sussmann provided and prepared a report to reflect its findings. The report explained that the analysis was done to examine whether the materials provided demonstrated "technical plausibility" of the following: "do linkages exist to any Russian foreign intelligence service; do linkages exist to Alpha [sic] Bank; are the provided documents/data based upon open source [] tools/activities; and is the provided

---

[1561] *Sussmann* Government Exhibit 814.

[1562] OSC Report of Interview of CIA Employee-2 on Aug. 13, 2020 at 1; OSC Report of Interview of CIA Employee-3 on June 29, 2021 at 3-4.

[1563] Complete resolution of these issues is difficult. The Office's investigation determined that Sussmann's billing practices were irregular. For example, prior to the 2016 election, Sussmann billed all Alfa Bank-related work to the Clinton campaign. Following the election, Sussmann appears to have retroactively billed some of his time for the Alfa Bank-related work to Joffe. The Office did not receive a satisfactory explanation from Perkins Coie for this practice.

Sussmann also engaged in questionable client record keeping. For example, and for reasons unknown, Sussmann's client retention letter to Tech Company-2 Executive-1 was addressed to a "Ms. Tina Wells" with the address of "1200 Pennsylvania Avenue, NW, Washington, D.C. 20004." Sussmann's letter memorializing his joint representation of Joffe and Tech Company-2 Executive-1 was addressed to "Ms. Tina Wells" and "Mr. Bob Hale." *See* Representation letters from Perkins Coie to Rodney Joffe and Tech Company-2 Executive-1 dated 4/12/2017 and 4/13/2017. These fake names are apparent references to the actors who played "Mary Ann" and the "Skipper" on the television series "Gilligan's Island." (Though "Mary Ann" was actually played by Dawn Wells and the "Skipper" was played by Alan Hale.) The address provided for "Ms. Wells" (Tech Company-2 Executive-1) is "1200 Pennsylvania Avenue, NW, Washington, D.C.," which is the William Jefferson Clinton EPA Headquarters and which has no apparent connection to Tech Company-2 Executive-1. The use of false names would appear to prevent a law firm from, among other things, conducting proper conflicts checks.

[1564] The titles of the four documents were: (i) "Network Analysis of Yota-Related Resolution Events"; (ii) "YotaPhone CSV File Collected on December 11th, 2016"; (iii) "Summary of Trump Network Communications"; and (iv) "ONINT on Trump Network Communications." The two thumb drives contained six Comma Separated Value (".CSV") files containing IP addresses, domain names and date/time stamps.

information/da[illegible] [illegible]ly conc[illegible][1566] T[illegible] [illegible]nately concluded that the materials that [illegible] p[illegible]ovide[illegible] [illegible]her "[illegible] plausible" nor did they "withstand tech[illegible] [illegible]" a[illegible] [illegible]at n[illegible] materials showed any linkages between the T[illegible] [illegible]gn or T[illegible] [illegible]ganiz[illegible] [illegible]y Russian foreign intelligence service or Alfa [illegible] [illegible]e rep[illegible] [illegible]led t[illegible] he thumb drives contained hidden data, w[illegible] [illegible] Tech [illegible]-2 E[illegible] name and email address.[1567]

Accor[illegible] [illegible]ann's [illegible] [illegible]pp[illegible] [illegible]ence that his representations to both the FBI an[illegible] [illegible]at he [illegible] [illegible]re o[illegible] [illegible]a client reflect attempts to conceal the rol[illegible] [illegible]lients, [illegible] C[illegible] [illegible]ign and Joffe, in Sussmann's work. Such ev[illegible] [illegible]urther [illegible] [illegible] Sussmann's false statements to two different a[illegible] [illegible] not a [illegible] [illegible]ng but, rather, a deliberate effort to conceal the [illegible] [illegible] of spec[illegible] [illegible]s in[illegible] [illegible] of data and documents to the FBI and CIA.

h. S[illegible] [illegible]gress[illegible] [illegible]

On De[illegible] [illegible]17, S[illegible] [illegible]stifi[illegible] [illegible]th before the HPSCI and addressed his r[illegible] [illegible]ing th[illegible] [illegible]k an[illegible] [illegible] allegations to the FBI and CIA. During t[illegible] [illegible]s, th[illegible] [illegible]exc[illegible] [illegible]rt, occurred:

Questio[illegible] [illegible] Did [illegible] [illegible]y [illegible]s with any other [illegible]strati[illegible] [illegible] reg[illegible] [illegible]nformation you conveyed [illegible]FBI G[illegible] [illegible]cu[illegible] [illegible]A GC? Was there [illegible] else [illegible] [illegible]ted [illegible] for the Federal [illegible]nmen[illegible]

Sussma[illegible] [illegible]t I re[illegible]

Questio[illegible] [illegible] So th[illegible] [illegible]on[illegible] [illegible], I want to ask you, [illegible]was th[illegible] [illegible]on [illegible]

Sussma[illegible] [illegible]form[illegible] [illegible]bou[illegible] [illegible]tions, or potential [illegible]unica[illegible] [illegible]en [illegible] [illegible]own in Russia, and [illegible]ns unk[illegible] [illegible]ia[illegible] Trump Organization.

Questio[illegible] [illegible]ratio[illegible] [illegible]ive[illegible] [illegible] client?

Sussma[illegible]

Questio[illegible] [illegible] info[illegible] [illegible]s r[illegible] [illegible]ou by any other source [illegible] clie[illegible] [illegible]se[illegible]

Sussma[illegible] [illegible]utely.

---

[1565] SCO-0748[illegible] [illegible]ject [illegible]gani[illegible] [illegible]phone and Email Server Network Communicatio[illegible] [illegible]ated C[illegible] [illegible]1).

[1566] *Id.*

[1567] *Id.* at 2.

Question: No, that's fair. So let me ask you this question: When you decided to engage the two principles [sic] one, Mr. Baker in September, and the general counsel of CIA in December, you were doing that on your own volition, based on information another client provided you. Is that correct?

Sussmann: No.

Question: So what was -- so did your client direct you to have those conversations?

Sussmann: Yes.

Question: Okay. And your client also was witting of you going to – in February to disclose the information that individual had provided you?

Sussmann: Yes.

Question: Back to the FBI. You obviously had a conversation or you had a meeting at the FBI with Mr. Baker. Was there anybody else in the room from the FBI in that room with you?

Sussmann: No.

. . . .

Question: Okay. I want to ask you, so you mentioned that your client directed you to have these engagements with the FBI and - and to disseminate the information that client provided you. Is that correct?

Sussmann: Well, I apologize for the double negative. It isn't not correct, but when you say my client directed me, we had a conversation, as lawyers do with their clients, about client needs and objectives and the best course to take for a client. And so it may have been a decision that we came to together. I mean, I don't want to imply that I was sort of directed to do something against my better judgment, or that we were in any sort of conflict, but this was -- I think it's most accurate to say it was done on behalf of my client.[1568]

Sussmann's congressional testimony concealed and obscured the origins and political nature of his work on the Alfa Bank allegations. Moreover, Sussmann's testimony was also misleading in that it conveyed the impression to Congress that Sussmann's only client for the Alfa Bank allegations was Joffe, when in fact he was billing the work to the Clinton campaign. Indeed, during points in the testimony not quoted above, Sussmann was specifically asked if Fusion GPS was his client in these matters.[1569] Sussmann's answer

---

[1568] U.S. House of Representatives Permanent Select Cmte. on Intelligence Interview of Michael Sussmann, (Dec. 18, 2017) at 59-67.

[1569] *Id.* at 74.

failed to disclose or volunteer that Fusion, in fact, had drafted one of the white papers that Sussmann gave to the FBI. Sussmann also failed to mention that the only client billed for Sussmann's pre-election work on those allegations was the Clinton campaign.

i. Perkins Coie's statements to the media

On October 4, 2018, Perkins Coie stated to multiple media outlets that "[w]hen Sussmann met with [the FBI General Counsel] on behalf of a client, it was not connected to the firm's representation of the Hillary Clinton Campaign, the DNC or any Political Law Group client."[1570] The following week, John Devaney, the Managing Partner of Perkins Coie, wrote to the editor of the *Wall Street Journal* and stated, "Mr. Sussmann's meeting with the FBI General [] was on behalf of a client with no connections to either the Clinton campaign, the DNC or any other Political Law Group client."[1571] The Office interviewed Perkins Coie leadership, including Mr. Devaney, regarding their knowledge of Sussmann's promotion of the Alfa Bank allegations and his billing entries related to the Clinton campaign. Each of the Perkins Coie employees denied knowing that Sussmann had in fact billed all of his time related to the Alfa Bank allegations to Clinton campaign.

Sussmann could have easily corrected Perkins Coie's mistaken belief that Sussmann's work on the Alfa Bank allegations "was not connected to the firm's representation of the Hillary Clinton Campaign, the DNC or any Political Law Group client." He chose not to.

j. Providing the Alfa Bank and Yotaphone allegations to Congress

The Office identified documents reflecting that in March and April 2017 – during the months after Sussmann provided the Alfa Bank and Yotaphone allegations to the CIA – the offices of at least two U.S. Senators received similar materials.

On March 22, 2017, Senators Jack Reed and Mark Warner wrote to Director Comey urging the FBI "to conduct an investigation" into reports that "a server belonging to the Trump Organization was purposefully communicating with servers belonging to a major Russian bank and the Spectrum Health organization in Michigan during the 2016 election.[1572] In support of its request, the letter attached an untitled white paper of unknown authorship. The paper included a summary of the Alfa Bank allegations, which was similar in substance to materials that Sussmann had provided to the FBI and CIA."[1573]

---

[1570] *See, e.g., Michael Sussmann, Hillary Clinton Lawyer, Gave FBI Russia Meddling Document*, Wash. Times (Oct. 4, 2018); *Lawyer for Clinton Campaign and DNC Gave FBI Documents for Russia Probe, Sources Say*, Fox News (Oct. 4, 2018).

[1571] John Devaney, *Our Michael Sussmann Is an Honorable Man*, Wall St. J. (Oct. 18, 2018).

[1572] SCO-012000 (Letter from Senators Jack Reed and Mark Warner to Director Comey dated Mar. 22, 2017 and attachment).

[1573] *Id.* at 2-8.

About a month later, Senator Reed sent a second letter to Comey about the Yotaphone allegations.[1574] Like the first letter, this one attached a white paper of unknown authorship.[1575] The paper stated that a small number of Yotaphones are sold globally and a very small number – in the dozens – presently operate in the United States.[1576] The paper noted that a group of internet technical experts had discovered a pattern of Yotaphone-like activity occurring within the Trump Organization and the Spectrum Health networks, which it correlated with Trump campaign and transition team visits to Michigan.[1577] The data also purportedly showed that Yotaphone-like activity continued at the Trump Organization until December 15th when the same activity began within the EOP, from which the experts inferred that the person or persons using this device in the Trump campaign were part of the transition team that began working within the EOP.[1578] The paper concluded that "[g]iven the broad concerns about the Trump campaign's connections to Russia, the existence and activity of the YotaPhone, as described here, stands out as an extraordinary oddity that warrants investigation."[1579]

Finally, on May 8th, a staffer to Senator Reed sent a follow-up memorandum to the FBI's Office of Congressional Affairs.[1580] The memorandum noted that the source of the analysis "insists on remaining anonymous, but is represented by an attorney." It went on to say that "[t]he source is willing, through counsel, to have extensive technical discussions with the Bureau's technical staff to explain the DNS records and the analysis that has been conducted." The memorandum also noted that Senator Reed continued to request that the FBI pursue the allegations and that the source's attorney was Michael Sussmann.[1581]

Because, however, either the FBI or the CIA, or both agencies, had already examined these allegations, the FBI did not take further investigative steps in response to these requests.[1582] The Office did not determine how, or from whom, Senators Reed and Warner received the above-described materials. An executive at Research Organization-1 ("Research Executive-1") appears to have learned about the allegations from Senator Reed's office and thereafter conducted work on these issues in coordination and consultation with Senator Reed's staff. Research Executive-1 was a former FBI analyst and Hill staffer and

---

[1574] SC-00081652 (Letter from Senator Jack Reed to Director Comey dated April 27, 2017 and attachment).

[1575] The paper was titled "An Unusual Russian Phone Operating on Trump Organization Networks and in the Executive Office of the President."

[1576] *Id.* at 1.

[1577] *Id.* at 3.

[1578] *Id.*

[1579] *Id.*

[1580] SC-00081658 (Memorandum from Senator Reed Staffer-1 to FBI Office of Congressional Affairs Employee-1 dated 05/08/2017).

[1581] *Id.*

[1582] SCO_007878 (Email from Moffa to Strzok, others dated 05/31/2017).

the founder of [illegible] Organiz[illegible] [illegible]e-1's activities are further described bel[illegible]

k. <u>Te[illegible] 1's c[illegible] the Clinton campaign</u>

The [illegible] stigati[illegible] that the Clinton campaign and the DNC main[illegible] ught c[illegible] ps with Tech Company-1 personnel, an[illegible] sidered [illegible] roducts and services, at around the same time [illegible] forts t[illegible] he [illegible] d Yotaphone allegations. The campaign and [illegible] rsider[illegible] ble source of data, including telephone met[illegible] re w[illegible] tions regarding Tech Company-1 data.[1583] Th[illegible] mined [illegible] ation [illegible] ring whether the campaign or the DNC main[illegible] ler relati[illegible] with [illegible] any-1 that might have led or contributed to [illegible] Bank [illegible] Although the Office identified multiple insta[illegible] n the [illegible] the [illegible] tained ties or communicated with Tech Compan[illegible] mploy[illegible] not [illegible] idence establishing that any such activities origi[illegible] ffe o[illegible] the [illegible] Yotaphone allegations. Joffe was not copie[illegible] d on [illegible] unic[illegible] he Office did not identify evidence of hi[illegible] f the[illegible] rs. [illegible] not aware of any evidence that the campaign [illegible] used [illegible] ond[illegible] on research (*i.e.*, to gather information re[illegible] pposi[illegible] e, as [illegible] voter information) or otherwise target Trump [illegible] es.[1584]

The [illegible] onsid[illegible] r a[illegible] elated to the Tech Company-1 data constitute[illegible] ampai[illegible] ton campaign by Tech Company-1 or [illegible] criri[illegible] s. [illegible] id not identify any chargeable criminal cond[illegible] gard.

l. <u>C[illegible] ion [illegible] and disseminating the Alfa Bank a[illegible] allegati[illegible]</u>

In ad[illegible] above [illegible] disse[illegible] Alfa Bank and Yotaphone allegations to [illegible] CIA, a[illegible] ss, [illegible] entified other efforts to generate

---

[1583] *See, e.g.*, S[illegible] (Emai[illegible] on C[illegible] fficial-1, to DNC Employee-1 and others, dated 0[illegible] eferen[illegible] Comp[illegible] we use for digital stuff currently"); SC[illegible] Email f[illegible] Emp[illegible] Clinton Campaign Official-1 dated 05/13/2016) ([illegible] we're [illegible] Tec[illegible] 1] too"); SC-00013242 (Email from an emplo[illegible] firm [illegible] ploy[illegible] s dated 05/20/2016) (referencing Tech Compan[illegible] etadat[illegible] 44[illegible] m DNC Employee-2, to representatives [illegible] camp[illegible] others [illegible] 0/2016) (including Tech Company-1 da[illegible] the da[illegible] NC [illegible] test).

[1584] In the cour[illegible] stigati[illegible] fou[illegible] that Tech Company-1 or other private sector [illegible] ted and [illegible] user data, such as telephone data, geolocation da[illegible] kinds [illegible] mati[illegible] , SC-00013383 (Email dated 05/27/2016). [illegible] detai[illegible] rai[illegible] ues that may be of public interest but that are ou[illegible] of th[illegible] We [illegible] day most major campaigns likely buy and use th[illegible] ata.

and disseminate research and other materials relevant to these allegations during the post-election period. These post-election activities included (i) continued efforts by employees of Tech Company-1 and Tech Company-2 (including Tech Company-2 Executive-1) to gather data and information concerning Trump, Russia, and other topics, and (ii) efforts by Research Executive-1 to conduct research and analysis through a non-profit organization that Research Executive-1 created in 2017 with the assistance of former HFA Chairman John Podesta, Fusion GPS founder Glenn Simpson,[1585] and others.

*i. Continued efforts through Joffe-affiliated companies*

Documents and other records that the Office gathered from private entities reflect that during or around the same time period as the aforementioned letters from Senator Reed and afterwards, Joffe was continuing to use Tech Company-1 resources and personnel to discuss research issues relating to Trump and Russia, including the Alfa Bank and Yotaphone allegations.

For example, emails and other evidence reflect that in early 2017 and afterwards, Joffe tasked Tech Company-1 Employee-1 to run searchers over Tech Company-1's DNS traffic to gather additional information concerning the Alfa Bank and Yotaphone allegations. In particular:

- According to Tech Company-1 Employee-1, at or around the time of Trump's inauguration, Tech Company-1 Employee-1 had been running queries for Joffe relating to Trump, including queries concerning Alfa Bank, Yotaphone, and the EOP.[1586] Joffe and Tech Company-1 Employee-1 intended to continue running certain of these queries after Trump's inauguration.[1587] Soon after the inauguration, however, Tech Company-1 Employee-1 and Joffe noticed that Tech Company-1's access to the EOP's DNS traffic had ceased.[1588] Tech Company-1 Employee-1 and Joffe never learned why Tech Company-1 no longer had access to the EOP's DNS data, but it was clear that Tech Company-5, the contractor that handled the EOP's DNS traffic and the company for which Tech Company-1 maintained the EOP's DNS servers, was no longer handling the EOP's data.[1589] The Office was unable to determine the reason such data access ceased.

- During the time period, Joffe also continued to direct Tech Company-1 Employee-1 to run Trump-related searches over Tech Company-1's data, and emails reflect the aforementioned end of Tech Company-1's access to EOP data.

- For example, on February 14, 2017—five days after Sussmann's meeting with the CIA—Joffe emailed Tech Company-1 Employee-1 with the subject line "for obvious reasons. . . ," and stated in the email: "Could you please run a search going back

[1585] Simpson declined to be interviewed by the Office.

[1586] OSC Report of Interview of Tech Company-1 Employee-1 on Feb. 25, 2021 at 2-5.

[1587] *Id.*

[1588] *Id.*

[1589] OSC Report of Interview of Tech Company-1 Employee-1 on July 9, 2021.

from Feb 1 to this moment (or later ;-)) searching for all activity (not just RCODE 0) for wildcard *.yota.* in recursive? Thanks!"[1590]

- That same day, Tech Company-1 Employee-1 uploaded data responsive to Joffe's request to a file transfer site and emailed Joffe: "feb 01-14 uploaded to sftp site... Note that these contain everything, including TLD queries."[1591]

- On the following day, Joffe replied: "[Tech Company-1 Employee-1], looks like no activity for EOP, right? Odd. Could you redo all of Jan so we can see when it disappeared."[1592]

- Later that day, Tech Company-1 Employee-1 responded to Joffe: "yeah – I only looked at a couple of hours on the first day but I noticed the same thing. Most of the recursive traffic was from Comodo address. I think I need to look at overall EOP volumes since Jan 20 to see if there have been significant volume changes."[1593]

- On February 16, 2017 Tech Company-1 Employee-1 emailed Joffe, analyzing location information for three IP addresses that Tech Company-1 Employee-1 had found communicated with Yotaphone IP addresses between January 6, 2017 and January 19, 2017. Tech Company-1 Employee-1 stated, in part:

  > The resolver address in the queries is the address that is dedicated to [Tech Company-5] and was used for EOP traffic. Only the first client address maps to EOP. The others are:
  >
  > [IP address] – Haifa, Israel
  >
  > [IP address] – Madison, Wisconsin
  >
  > [IP address] – amazonaws
  >
  > The timestamps on the records are a bit confusing as well – two queries from two different addresses for the same qname as the exact same second in two different nodes (Chicago and Frankfurt). May be an error in processing but still odd.[1594]

- As of approximately five months later, Tech Company-1 Employee-1 was continuing to run Trump-related searches over Tech Company-1's DNS traffic. In particular, on July 18, 2018, Tech Company-1 Employee-1 emailed Joffe:

  > I have 4 jobs that look specifically for Trump data

---

[1590] SC-00030423 (Email from Joffe to Tech Company-1 Employee-1 dated 02/14/2017).

[1591] SC-00030425 (Email from Joffe to Tech Company-1 Employee-1 dated 02/15/2017).

[1592] *Id.*

[1593] SC-00030424 (Email from Tech Company-1 Employee-1 to Joffe dated 02/15/2017)

[1594] SC-00030427 (Email from Tech Company-1 Employee-1 to Joffe dated 02/16/2017).

- clnt_ip='217.12.97.15' or clnt_ip='217.12.96.15' or clnt_ip='167.73.110.8'
- qname = 'trump1.contact-client.com'
- qname = 'mail1.trump-email.com'
- a query that looks for a bunch of alfa ban.ru domains[1595]

In sum, it appears that efforts to gather and mine data concerning Trump from Tech Company-1's DNS data continued for many months after the 2016 Presidential election.

*ii. Efforts by Research Executive-1 and others*

The Office also gathered information reflecting that, soon after the 2016 election, a number of individuals with ties to the Clinton campaign or Democratic politics met, organized, and executed additional efforts through which they intended to ensure that research and dissemination of materials concerning election interference, including Trump's possible illicit ties to Russia, would continue. These efforts included continued work regarding the Alfa Bank and Yotaphone allegations. As described in further detail below, participants in these activities continued to provide materials to the FBI in an effort to trigger further investigations of Trump's ties to Russia.

In the days immediately after the election, former Clinton campaign Chair Podesta began speaking with associates about a specific potential research project, namely, to create a non-profit organization that would conduct research regarding election interference and would assist the U.S. government and the media in gathering information on this issue.[1596] Podesta spoke and met with Glenn Simpson, Research Executive-1, and others regarding his idea. (Podesta told investigators that he was unaware at that time, or at any time prior to October 2017, that Glenn Simpson and Fusion GPS had carried out opposition work on the Steele Dossier and related matters on behalf of Podesta's prior employer, the Clinton campaign. According to Podesta, he knew during the campaign that Perkins Coie was conducting opposition research for the campaign, but did not know who had been actually conducting that research until October 2017 when he learned specifically that Fusion GPS had been paid by both the campaign and the DNC.)[1597]

In approximately the late 2016 time period, former U.S. Senator Tom Daschle brokered an introduction between Podesta and Research Executive-1—who previously had worked as an FBI analyst, as a Senate Armed Services Committee staffer, and at a private firm founded by Daschle, the Daschle Group. By that time, Research Executive-1 had founded and was running Research Organization-1, which conducted research for private clients.[1598] Podesta assisted Research Executive-1 by helping him contact and vet numerous

---

[1595] SC-00030428 (Email from Tech Company-1 Employee-1 to Joffe dated 07/18/2017).

[1596] OSC Report of Interview of Research Executive-1 on Apr. 14, 2021 at 1.

[1597] OSC Report of Interview of John Podesta on Jan. 19, 2022 at 1-2.

[1598] OSC Report of Interview of Research Executive-1 on Apr. 14, 2021 at 1; OSC Report of Interview of John Podesta on Jan. 19, 2022 at 5.

potential donor [illegible] s: Co[illegible] [illegible] nd Research Executive-1's research on ele[illegible] [illegible] rence.[illegible]

Also, [illegible] time [illegible] search Executive-1 and sought his/her assistan[illegible] 's pro[illegible] ction [illegible] e project. Research Executive-1 and Simpson [illegible] t for c[illegible] In December 2016, Simpson briefed Resea[illegible] 1 on [illegible] concerning Trump's purported ties to Russia [illegible] d con[illegible] According to Research Executive-1, S[illegible] ot me[illegible] R[illegible] utive-1 did not know at this time – that Simpson [illegible] ng w[illegible] kins [illegible] Clinton campaign.[1601]

In Ja[illegible] mps[illegible] -1 again met to discuss the potential resea[illegible] [1602] A[illegible] a result of these discussions, Research Exec[illegible] d Re[illegible] n-profit organization that would continue resea[illegible] n int[illegible] sues, [illegible] Trump's potential ties to Russia.[1603]

Follo[illegible] ation [illegible] ntered into a contract with Fusion GPS a[illegible] ber [illegible] search. Research Organization-2 also maintai[illegible] with [illegible] ss Intelligence, a/k/a "Walsingham [illegible] [1604]

As no[illegible] mong [illegible] Organization-2 conducted, and provided to the [illegible] anal[illegible] Alf[illegible] ations. According to Research Executive-1, h[illegible] aw[illegible] alleg[illegible] Senator Reed's office contacted him [illegible] form [illegible] .[1605] [illegible] Executive-1 learned from a staffer for Sen[illegible] Reed [illegible] – w[illegible] ch Executive-1 knew from his time on the Se[illegible] at th[illegible] who used the name "Max" and who was behi[illegible] ons.[1606] [illegible] also learned that Reed had requested furt[illegible] n fro[illegible] abo[illegible] to investigate this matter because multi[illegible] were [illegible] their view, the FBI was not investigating th[illegible] alleg[illegible] Res[illegible] tive-1 agreed to research the issue through [illegible] ganiza[illegible] on the Alfa Bank matter,

---

[1599] OSC Repo[illegible] of J[illegible] on J[illegible] at 5.

[1600] OSC Repo[illegible] of R[illegible] cuti[illegible] 14, 2021 at 2.

[1601] *Id.* at 1-2.

[1602] *Id.* at 1.

[1603] *Id.* at 1-2.

[1604] *Id.* at 2.

[1605] *Id.* at 2.

[1606] *Id.* at 3.

[1607] *Id.*

Research Executive-1 isolated Fusion GPS from the project for reasons unknown to the Office.[1608]

As a result of receiving this information from the Senate Armed Services Committee, Research Executive-1 met in early 2017 with Sussmann at Perkins Coie's office.[1609] At the meeting, Sussmann discussed the allegations, including media reports concerning them.[1610] According to Research Executive-1, Sussmann did not identify his "client" by name, but stated that he (Sussmann) was dealing with the government on the issue; that he was persuaded by the data; and that he was frustrated by the FBI's dismissal of it.[1611] Sussmann also described to Research Executive-1 his interactions with the media and his frustration with their coverage of it.[1612]

Later that year, Research Executive-1 again met Sussmann at Perkins Coie regarding the Alfa Bank allegations. Sussmann's client, Joffe, was also present at this meeting. During their discussions, Sussmann and Joffe stated that they believed the FBI had sent the Alfa Bank allegations to the wrong investigative team.[1613] Research Executive-1 was told that Joffe was part of a multi-million-dollar program that collected DNS data, which was the source of the data underlying the Alfa Bank allegations.[1614]

During the same time period, Research Executive-1 had assembled an investigative team to examine the Alfa Bank allegations, including a number of DNS experts who had previously worked for multiple U.S. intelligence agencies. Research Executive-1's team tested Joffe's data and conducted their own analysis. The team was skeptical of the Alfa Bank data and found no evidence of a secret channel of communications, but Research Executive-1 said, "it was something."[1615]

Research Executive-1 also learned of the Yotaphone allegations from Sussmann. Research Executive-1's team did some, but not a lot of, work on these allegations. Research Executive-1 told our investigators that he was "totally" skeptical of the Yotaphone assertions.[1616] Research Executive-1 understood that the EOP's computer network was run by the Department of Homeland Security, which contracted out the services to an unknown vendor with access to the data that formed the basis of the Yotaphone allegations.[1617]

---

[1608] *Id.* at 2-3.

[1609] *Id.*

[1610] *Id.*

[1611] *Id.*

[1612] *Id.*

[1613] *Id.* at 3.

[1614] *Id.* at 4.

[1615] *Id.*

[1616] *Id.*

[1617] *Id.* at 3-4.

*iii. Meetings between DARPA and University-1*

In connection with its consideration of the Alfa Bank issue, the Office also gathered information about meetings between certain of the aforementioned University-1 employees and staff members of both the Senate Armed Services Committee and HPSCI. During at least one of these meetings, the participants discussed the Alfa Bank allegations, including the possibility that researchers under DARPA's Enhanced Attribution ("EA") program might assist HPSCI in investigating the allegations.[1618] The Office considered whether these activities might be relevant to a prosecution for contract fraud or abuse of government resources.

In early October 2018, a representative of the Senate Armed Services Committee requested via University-1's Government Affairs representative that researchers affiliated with the EA program provide a briefing to Committee staff members in Washington, D.C. Personnel at University-1 agreed to facilitate such a briefing.[1619]

In late October 2018, another University-1 researcher ("University-1 Researcher-3") and a DARPA Program Manager, ("DARPA Program Manager-1") traveled to Washington, D.C. to provide the briefing. Upon their arrival, University-1 Researcher-3 and DARPA Program Manager-1 met with Reed Staffer-2 and another Committee staffer in the Russell Senate Office Building. At the meeting, which lasted only a short time, University-1 Researcher-3 and DARPA Program Manager-1 provided a broad and brief overview of the EA program – which they understood to be the purpose of the meeting. At the conclusion of the meeting, which had been cut short due to scheduling conflicts, Reed Staffer-2 indicated to University-1 Researcher-3 that he would like to schedule a follow-up meeting with University-1 researchers in attendance so that the Committee staff could receive a more comprehensive briefing on the EA program.[1620]

The following month, in November 2018, University-1 Researcher-3 and University-1 Researcher-2 traveled to Washington, D.C. to provide a second briefing on EA for staffers for the Senate Armed Services Committee. University-1 Researcher-2 recalled that the night before the meeting, he spoke with Joffe, who told him that after the Senate briefing, there was going to be another meeting Joffe wanted him to attend. Joffe told University-1 Researcher-2 that there would be someone to meet him and take him to this other meeting.[1621]

The November 2018 meeting occurred in the Hart Senate Office Building with Reed Staffer-2 and two staffers present. At the meeting, University-1 Researcher-3 and

---

[1618] The Enhanced Attribution program is intended to bring transparency to the actions of malicious cyber actions undertaken by adversaries and other individual cyber operators. *See* https://www.darpa.mil/enhanced-attribution.

[1619] OSC Report of Interview of University-1 Researcher-3 on Aug. 10, 2021 at 2.

[1620] *Id.*

[1621] OSC Report of Interviews of University-1 Researcher-2 in July, Aug. 2021 at 4.

University-1 Researcher-2 gave an unclassified presentation regarding the EA program and the history of DNS.[1622]

Following the meeting in the Senate space, Reed Staffer-2 informed University-1 Researcher-3 and University-1 Researcher-2 that some other people were interested in speaking with them. University-1 Researcher-3 and University-1 Researcher-2 agreed to meet with these other people, who turned out to be HPSCI staffers, but the meeting needed to be quick due to University-1 Researcher-3's schedule. Reed Staffer-2 then brought them into the secure space of the HPSCI.[1623] Before the meeting, University-1 Researcher-3 told Reed Staffer-2 that University-1 Researcher-2 did not possess a security clearance, to which Reed Staffer-2 stated that the briefing would be unclassified.[1624]

After arriving in the HPSCI secure conference room, Reed Staffer-2 introduced University-1 Researcher-3 and University-1 Researcher-2 to several HPSCI staffers. During the meeting, University-1 Researcher-3 and University-1 Researcher-2 began to provide a similar presentation to that which they had given to the Senate staffers. Soon after the start of the presentation, however, the Committee staffers cut University-1 Researcher-3 off and showed him and University-1 Researcher-2 a news article about Trump, Russia, and Alfa Bank that University-1 Researcher-3 had not seen previously.[1625] The staffers asked University-1 Researcher-3 to read the article and said they wanted University-1's help with the matter, and Reed Staffer-2 said University-1 Researcher-3 ". . . could make it easier."[1626]

University-1 Researcher-3 said he responded by saying that it would be inappropriate for a public university to do that, and he suggested they contact DARPA. University-1 Researcher-3 told investigators that Reed Staffer-2 then said, "We are now in charge," and one of the HPSCI staffers said that their boss (Congressman Adam Schiff) would soon take over leadership of HPSCI.[1627] University-1 Researcher-3 took the comment as a mild threat. University-1 Researcher-3 said he then "dragged" University-1 Researcher-2 out of the meeting. University-1 Researcher-2 similarly recalled that University-1 Researcher-3 had quickly ended the meeting.[1628] University-1 Researcher-3 told investigators that he told University-1 Researcher-2, "Don't touch this with a ten foot pole, stay away from this."[1629] University-1 Researcher-3 said he had no recollection of

---

[1622] OSC Report of Interview of University-1 Researcher-3 on Aug. 10, 2021 at 2.

[1623] *Id.*

[1624] *Id.* at 2.

[1625] OSC Report of Interview of University-1 Researcher-3 on Aug. 10, 2021 at 2-3. University-1 Researcher-2 recalled that the staffers showed him articles about Trump's DNS ties to Alfa Bank, and they asked him and University-1 Researcher-3 if there was anything they could do to help with "this." OSC Report of Interviews of University-1 Researcher-2 in July, Aug. 2021 at 4.

[1626] OSC Report of Interview of University-1 Researcher-3 on Aug. 10, 2021 at 3.

[1627] *Id.*

[1628] OSC Report of Interviews of University-1 Researcher-2 in July, Aug. 2021 at 4.

[1629] OSC Report of Interview of University-1 Researcher-3 on Aug. 10, 2021 at 3.

University-1 R[illegible] mention[illegible] he (University-1 Researcher-2) already had do[illegible] sity-1 [illegible] he A[illegible] ated allegations.[1630]

Unive[illegible] archer[illegible] that [illegible] DARPA Program Manager-1 of this request [illegible] CI st[illegible] ding [illegible] ions to the nature of the request.[1631] U[illegible] sear[illegible] is th[illegible] Program Manager-1 listened but did not react su[illegible] to the [illegible].[1632] [illegible] rviewed by the Office, DARPA Program Mana[illegible] learn[illegible] lfa [illegible] ions other than through media reports.[1633] D[illegible] am Ma[illegible] ain[illegible] was unaware of any role that University-1 p[illegible] ved in th[illegible] Bank al[illegible].[1634]

*iv. [illegible] nt Tr[illegible] zati[illegible] omain and Yotaphone data*

This [illegible] t des[illegible] our [illegible] n found with respect to the allegation that [illegible] overt [illegible] ation [illegible] between the Trump Organization and Alfa Bank [illegible] the in[illegible] ve [illegible] interviews of Listrak and Cendyn emplo[illegible] turns [illegible] ation [illegible] was an unusual Russian phone operating on th[illegible] ganiza[illegible] rks a[illegible] Executive Office of the President. We tasked sub[illegible] xperts [illegible] BI's [illegible] hnical Analysis and Operations Section to eval[illegible] these [illegible].

With re[illegible] allega[illegible] here [illegible] t channel of communication between the T[illegible] zation [illegible] Bank, [illegible] t matter experts conducted technical analy[illegible] asse[illegible] the [illegible] S data and information that was provided to the [illegible] A in th[illegible] per[illegible] also interviewed employees at the two contra[illegible] in r[illegible] e tr[illegible] om domain, Cendyn and Listrak. Cend[illegible] er rel[illegible] anag[illegible] eting services provider, registered the [illegible] half [illegible] p Or[illegible] in 2009. The IP address associated wit[illegible], 66.2[illegible] s, a[illegible] rated by Listrak, a subcontractor

---

1630 *Id.*

1631 *Id.*

1632 *Id.*

1633 OSC Repo[illegible] of D[illegible] ram[illegible] on Feb. 11, 2021 at 3.

1634 *Id.*

1635 FBI Cyber [illegible] r Te[illegible] lys[illegible] nical Analysis Report (April 20, 2022) (hereina[illegible] *hnical A[illegible] port* [illegible] 4755). As explained by the FBI experts who as[illegible] is are[illegible] ma[illegible] em) refers to a distributed system of computers o[illegible] hat [illegible] asso[illegible] een domain names and IP addresses. *Pas*[illegible] n indu[illegible] of [illegible] nd aggregating DNS queries at various observ[illegible] rese[illegible] al, [illegible] and security purposes. *FBI Technical Ana*[illegible] t 5-6.

of Cendyn. Listrak provides marketing automation services, including sending bulk email.[1636]

Listrak personnel stated that the Trump Organization's IP address was one of numerous IP addresses assigned to a cluster of four to eight physical servers that handle all outbound email for thousands of Listrak clients. Significantly, Listrak informed us that the IP address and domain used for the Trump Organization were configured to only send *outbound* email.[1637] Moreover, Listrak explained that, as is customary for such services, no one in the Trump Organization had direct technical or system administrator access to Listrak servers.[1638] Indeed, the very notion of a "Trump Server" is a misnomer in that the servers involved did not belong to and were not controlled by the Trump Organization.[1639] To the contrary, the servers belonged to and were controlled by Listrak at all times.[1640] Listrak further stated that it never had, during this time period, a dedicated server (physical or virtual) to handle Trump Organization communications.[1641] Rather, the server that hosted the Trump Organization housed hundreds of other clients and that each server sent millions of emails out for clients.[1642]

Cendyn personnel told us that the Trump Organization's contract with Cendyn for digital and email marketing ended in 2015, but the domain name continued to be registered and pointed to the same IP address.[1643] Moreover, after Cendyn's contract with the Trump Organization expired in 2015, Cendyn continued to use the IP address to send emails out on behalf of other Cendyn clients.[1644] However, there was no data provided at the time, nor is such currently available, that shows which clients were sending email from the IP address during the May through September 2016 time period examined in the white paper.[1645] Cendyn, however, maintained technical control of the domain until March 2017.[1646] Similarly, Listrak maintained complete technical control of its servers during the same May through September 2016 time period.[1647]

---

1636 OSC Report of Interview of Cendyn CEO and CTO on Nov. 17, 2021; OSC Report of Interview of Listrak Employee-1 and personnel on Oct. 27, 2021.

1637 OSC Report of Interview of Listrak Employee-1 and personnel on Oct. 27, 2021 at 1-2.

1638 *Id.*

1639 *Id.*

1640 OSC Report of Interview of Cendyn CEO and CTO on Nov. 17, 2021 at 1-2.

1641 OSC Report of Interview of Listrak Employee-1 and personnel on Oct. 27, 2021 at 1-2.

1642 *Id.*

1643 OSC Report of Interview of Cendyn CEO and CTO on Nov. 7, 2021 at 2.

1644 *Id.*

1645 *Id.* at 1. Cendyn explained that it does not retain these outbound emails, as they are marketing emails, which are wiped from Cendyn's systems within 30 days of being sent.

1646 *Id.* at 2.

1647 OSC Report of Interview of Listrak Employee-1 and personnel on Oct. 27, 2021 at 2.

Because the Trump Organization had no access to the server or any of the systems involved, Listrak personnel told us that the only way any alleged covert communications channel could have existed would be if Listrak employees deliberately modified their mission critical servers with non-standard software or configurations. But they pointed out that making such changes would risk the integrity, reliability or availability of their systems. Moreover, Listrak told us that changing its servers to accommodate incoming messages would completely alter the core structure of its business operations, which is primarily to send outgoing mass marketing emails.[1648] Listrak employees responsible for the design and administration of these servers categorically stated this did not happen and that it would be impossible for it to have happened without their knowledge and without affecting other clients' account functions and operations.[1649]

In addition to investigating the actual ownership and control of the IP address, the Office tasked FBI cyber experts with analyzing the technical claims made in the white paper.[1650] This endeavor included their examination of the list of email addresses and send times for all emails sent from the Listrak email server from May through September 2016, which is the time period the white paper purportedly examined.[1651] The FBI experts also conducted a review of the historical TOR exit node data.[1652]

The technical analysis done by the FBI experts revealed that the data provided by Sussmann to the FBI and used to support Joffe and the cyber researchers' claim that a "very unusual distribution of source IP addresses" was making queries for mail1.trump-email.com was incomplete.[1653] Specifically, the FBI experts determined that there had been a substantial amount of email traffic from the IP address that resulted in a significantly larger volume of DNS queries for the mail1.trump-email.com domain than what Joffe, University-1 Researcher-2 and the cyber researchers reported in the white paper or included on the thumb drives accompanying it.[1654] The FBI experts reviewed all of the outbound email transmissions, including address and send time for all emails sent from the Listrak server

---

1648 *Id.* at 2.

1649 *Id.*

1650 *FBI Technical Analysis Report* at 3-4.

1651 *Id.* at 4, 10-11.

1652 *Id.* at 5-6, 12-13. The Onion Router ("TOR") is an open source global anonymous communications platform, frequently used to access websites without exposing the IP address of the browser to the website or to intermediary observation. TOR publishes a list of TOR exit nodes, which are the last node in a TOR circuit and which provides an unencrypted connection to internet hosts. https://collector.torproject.org/archive/exit-lists/.

1653 Our experts noted that the assertion of the white paper is not only that Alfa Bank and Spectrum Health servers had resolved, or looked up, the domain [mail1.trump-email.com] during a period from May through September of 2016, but that their resolutions accounted for the vast majority of lookups for this domain. *FBI Technical Analysis Report* at 6.

1654 The USB drive that Sussman provided to the FBI on September 19, 2016, which was proffered as data supporting the claims in the white paper, contained 851 records of DNS resolutions for domains ending in trump-email.com. *FBI Technical Analysis Report* at 7.

from May through September 2016, and determined that there had been a total of 134,142 email messages sent between May and August 2016, with the majority sent on May 24 and June 23.[1655] The recipients included a wide range of commercial email services, including Google and Yahoo, as well as corporate email accounts for multiple corporations.[1656]

Similarly, the FBI experts told us that the collection of passive DNS data used to support the claims made in the white paper was also significantly incomplete.[1657] They explained that, given the documented email transmissions from IP address 66.216.133.29 during the covered period, the representative sampling of passive DNS would have necessarily included a much larger volume and distribution of queries from source IP addresses across the internet. In light of this fact, they stated that the passive DNS data that Joffe and his cyber researchers compiled and that Sussmann passed onto the FBI was significantly incomplete, as it included no A-record (hostname to IP address) resolutions corresponding to the outgoing messages from the IP address.[1658] Without further information from those who compiled the white paper data,[1659] the FBI experts stated that it is impossible to determine whether the absence of additional A record resolutions is due to the visibility afforded by the passive DNS operator, the result of the specific queries that the compiling analyst used to query the dataset, or intentional filtering applied by the analyst after retrieval.[1660]

The FBI experts also examined the white paper's claim that a particular "Spectrum Health IP address is a TOR exit node used exclusively by Alfa Bank, *i.e.*, Alfa Bank communications enter a TOR node somewhere in the world and those communications exit, presumably untraceable, at Spectrum Health."[1661] However, the FBI experts assisting us noted that TOR publishes a comprehensive list of exit nodes dating back to February 22, 2010.[1662] The FBI examined this data for dates between February 22, 2010 and September 1, 2021. No instances of IP addresses in the range of 167.73.x.x (assigned to Spectrum Health) were ever indexed as TOR exit nodes.[1663]

---

1655 *Id.*

1656 *Id.*

1657 *Id.* at 11.

1658 *Id.*

1659 The data used for the white paper came from Joffe's companies Packet Forensics and Tech Company-1. As noted above, Joffe declined to be interviewed by the Office, as did Tech Company-2 Executive-1. The 851 records of resolutions on the USB drive were an exact match for a file of resolutions sent from University-1 Researcher-2 to University-1 Researcher-1 on July 29, 2016, which was referred to as "[first name of Tech Company-2 Executive-1]'s data." *Id.* at 7.

1660 *Id.*

1661 *FBI Technical Analysis Report* at 12-13.

1662 https://collector.torproject.org/archive/exit-lists/.

1663 *Id.*

The F[illegible] who exa[illegible] issu[illegible]ed that historical TOR exit node data con[illegible] prove[illegible] paper [illegible]n in its entirety.[1664] Moreover, the FBI exper[illegible]plained [illegible]onst[illegible] TOR network makes the arrangement [illegible] the whi[illegible]pos[illegible]d, they added that even if true or possible, using [illegible] wor[illegible] ne[illegible]e white paper would result in worse anonym[illegible] securi[illegible]ly [illegible] its default configuration.[1665] Rather than al[illegible] undesi[illegible]ic[illegible]tup described in the white paper would create [illegible] with [illegible]dp[illegible]d be more easily traced with traffic to the r[illegible] all num[illegible] which would allow for the identification [illegible]urce [illegible]re ea[illegible]sing a randomly selected exit node for each [illegible] the T[illegible] is [illegible]do.[1666] In simpler terms, the FBI experts told us [illegible] TOR [illegible] the [illegible]scribed by the white paper would make a secret [illegible]ion ch[illegible] eas[illegible]ot harder. And, they further noted that alth[illegible] rely [illegible]re [illegible]s, at some time, connected to both Spectrum [illegible] Alfa B[illegible] TOR, [illegible]ave even come through the same exit nod[illegible]ility in [illegible]dica[illegible] of correlation because of the deliberately ra[illegible] of TO[illegible][1667]

We al[illegible] same [illegible]rts [illegible] white paper on Yotaphones that Sussmann pro[illegible]ther go[illegible]agen[illegible] of Joffe.[1668] This white paper stated that the[illegible]nusual [illegible]nor[illegible]operating on Trump Organization [illegible] in the [illegible] O[illegible] President."[1669] Its claims were based primari[illegible]soluti[illegible] fo[illegible] "client.yota.ru" and "wimax-client.yota.ru" [illegible]3, 201[illegible] an[illegible] from Trump-affiliated networks, cou[illegible] asser[illegible]ch Y[illegible]esolution request activity was rare in the Uni[illegible][1670]

Howe[illegible] experts [illegible]d h[illegible] query data for the yota.ru domains for th[illegible] period [illegible]alyz[illegible]hite paper. Indeed, they examined data [illegible]te pape[illegible]ess to.[1671] In doing so, the FBI experts deter[illegible]ontrary [illegible]ms [illegible]he white paper, the DNS query data actually [illegible]esol[illegible]sts f[illegible]mains were not at all rare from U.S.-based IP [illegible] com[illegible] othe[illegible][1672] These experts further

[1664] *FBI Techn*[illegible] *Repor*[illegible]

[1665] *Id.* at 13.

[1666] *Id.*

[1667] *Id.*

[1668] SC-00001[illegible] Analy[illegible]-Re[illegible]ion Events.

[1669] *Id.*

[1670] *Id.* at 2.

[1671] FBI Cyber [illegible] Operatio[illegible] *m/Yota Observations and Assessment* (un[illegible]inated).

[1672] *Id.*

observed that the DNS query data used to support the white paper claims was deliberately filtered to select only those organizations in the United States with ties to Trump.[1673]

In sum, as a result of our investigation, the FBI experts advised us that actual data and information on YotaPhone resolution requests directly undermined or refuted several conclusions and inferences included in the Yotaphone white paper.[1674]

### 2. *Prosecution decisions*

We identified evidence that certain individuals and entities promoted the Alfa Bank and Yotaphone allegations to the Intelligence Community. We examined the validity of the allegations, conducted technical analyses, and assessed the data and information that was provided to the FBI and CIA. We examined this evidence in considering whether the activities by these individuals and entities, as well as government officials, violated any criminal statutes. In particular, the investigation examined whether these individuals and entities either on their own provided, or conspired with others to provide, false or misleading information to the Intelligence Community.

*First*, and as noted above, we identified certain statements that Sussmann made to the FBI and the CIA that the investigation revealed were false. Given the seriousness of the false statement and its effect on the FBI's investigation, a federal Grand Jury found probable cause to believe that Sussmann had lied to the FBI and charged him with making a false statement to the Bureau, in violation of 18 U.S.C. § 1001.[1675] Ultimately, after a two-week trial, a jury acquitted Sussmann of the false statement charge.

We also considered whether any criminal actions were taken by other persons or entities in furtherance of Sussmann's false statement to the FBI. The evidence gathered in the investigation did not establish that any such actions were taken.

*Second*, our investigation uncovered evidence of actions taken by individuals and entities with ties to the Clinton campaign to promote the Alfa Bank and Yotaphone allegations to the Intelligence Community and Congress. We evaluated whether any of these individuals made a false statement within the meaning of 18 U.S.C. § 1001 and whether admissible evidence would be sufficient to obtain a conviction for such an offense. We also considered whether actions taken by certain persons could have implicated federal election laws. We concluded that the evidence was not sufficient to obtain and sustain a criminal conviction.

We examined as well whether the actions and conduct of Sussmann and various other persons in advancing the Alfa Bank and Yotaphone allegations established a conspiracy to defraud the United States, in violation of 18 U.S.C. § 371. Ultimately, we concluded that our evidence was not sufficient to obtain and sustain a criminal conviction. We did not obtain admissible evidence likely to meet the government's burden to prove beyond a reasonable doubt that the individuals acted "willfully," *i.e.,* with general knowledge of the illegality of their conduct. We faced significant obstacles in obtaining

---

[1673] *Id.*

[1674] *Id.*

[1675] *Sussmann Indictment* at 27.

evidence because many of the individuals and entities involved invoked multiple privileges, including the attorney-client and Fifth Amendment privileges.

*Third*, we examined the FBI's actions in response to the Alfa Bank and Yotaphone allegations. We assessed whether any FBI or other federal official conspired with any other persons in promoting the Alfa Bank allegations to damage the Trump campaign or benefit the Clinton campaign. Our investigation did not find any evidence that any FBI official or employee knowingly and intentionally participated in some type of conspiracy with others to promote the Alfa Bank allegations or cause the FBI to open an investigation. Certain FBI officials, however, declined to be interviewed on the matter, and others professed a lack of recollection of it.

*Finally*, we considered the conduct of third parties and other government officials regarding actions taken following the election that involved the continued promotion of the Alfa Bank and Yotaphone allegations to law enforcement and other government bodies. We did not, however, develop sufficient evidence to charge false statements or conspiracy crimes in connection with any intentional misrepresentations in this regard because it was unclear, in numerous instances, when particular data searches involving the alleged activity at the EOP were run, and when specific data files came into possession of the relevant persons (*i.e.*, whether such data was searched or identified before or after materials were received by the CIA or Congress). In addition, because of the protections of attorney-client privilege and other impediments, we were unable to determine with precision or certainty who authored each of the relevant white papers. Accordingly, we did not charge any individuals[1676] with knowingly providing false information to the government in connection with the Alfa Bank and Yotaphone allegations.

## V. <u>OBSERVATIONS</u>

In making the observations that follow, we are mindful of the benefits hindsight provides and the hazards of possibly being unfair to individuals who were called upon to make decisions under real pressure and in unprecedented circumstances. That said, the objective facts show that the FBI's handling of important aspects of the Crossfire Hurricane matter were seriously deficient. Some FBI employees who were interviewed by our investigators advised that they had significant reservations about aspects of Crossfire Hurricane and tried to convey their misgivings to their superiors. Others had doubts about the investigation, but did not voice their concerns. In some cases, nothing was said because of a sense that there had to be more compelling information in the possession of those closest to the decision-making center of the case than had been made known to them. And there were still other current and former employees who maintained that they did the best they could to take reasonable investigative steps and acted within the FBI's various policies, procedures and guidelines.

As the more complete record now shows, there are specific areas of Crossfire Hurricane activity in which the FBI badly underperformed and failed, not only in its duties to the public, but also in preventing the severe reputational harm that has befallen the FBI as a consequence of Crossfire Hurricane. Importantly, had the Crossfire Hurricane actors faithfully followed their own principles regarding objectivity and integrity, there were clear opportunities to have avoided

[1676] As noted above, the Office charged Sussmann with lying to the FBI when he stated that he was not bringing the Alfa Bank allegations on behalf of any client.

the mistakes and to have prevented the damage resulting from their embrace of seriously flawed information that they failed to analyze and assess properly.

As described in section IV, both the OIG and the FBI's Inspection Division have reviewed aspects of the Crossfire Hurricane investigation into possible collusion between Russia and the Trump campaign and the FISA applications targeting Carter Page. The OIG also conducted a more limited audit of the accuracy of 29 FISA applications that were not connected to Crossfire Hurricane.

In 2020, the Department and the FBI provided the Privacy and Civil Liberties Oversight Board ("PCLOB") 19 of the 29 applications reviewed by the OIG. The PCLOB is an independent agency within the Executive Branch that was established by the 9/11 Commission Act of 2007. The Board's primary mission is to ensure that federal efforts to prevent terrorism are balanced with protecting privacy and civil liberties. The 19 applications were directed at counterterrorism targets and Adam Klein, the former Chairman of the PCLOB, reviewed the 19 applications.[1677]

Following the OIG's review and audit, both the Attorney General and the FISC directed that a number of changes be made. Outside commentators have also recommended numerous changes. In the FISA reform proposals put forth by various individuals and groups, there is division between those that would make all, or many, FISA surveillances more difficult or prohibit certain types of surveillances altogether and those that focus more specifically on the issues raised by the Page applications.

In making our observations, the Office considered but did not include proposals that would curtail the scope or reach of FISA or the FBI's investigative activities. We are concerned about the impact of such proposals in a time of aggressive and hostile terrorist groups and foreign powers. The FBI's priorities include protecting the United States against national security threats.[1678] Inevitably, that involves pursuing some targets and investigations that end up yielding few results. The OIG review of the September 11th attacks noted that "the FBI . . . failed to use the FISA statute fully" and that, in its investigation of Zacarias Moussaoui, a potential "19th hijacker," the deficiencies "included a narrow and conservative interpretation of FISA."[1679] More recently, for reasons that may include the COVID pandemic, the impact of the Page FISA applications, or changes in government priorities, the number of FISC orders using certain FISA authorities reportedly has declined sharply -- from 1184 to 430 -- over a recent four-year period.[1680]

---

[1677] *See* Adam Klein, PCLOB, Chairman's White Paper: *Oversight of the Foreign Intelligence Surveillance Act* (June 2021) (hereinafter "Klein, *White Paper*").

[1678] *See* https://www.fbi.gov/about/mission. *Cf. Sensitive Investigations Memorandum* at 1 ("[T]he Department must respond swiftly and decisively when faced with credible threats to our democratic processes").

[1679] OIG, U.S. Department of Justice, *A Review of the FBI's Handling of Intelligence Information Related to the September 11 Attacks* at 363, 378 (Nov. 2004).

[1680] George Croner, *New Statistics Confirm the Continuing Decline in the Use of National Surveillance Authorities*, Lawfare (May 24, 2022) (describing use of various FISA authorities

Former [illegible] ney [illegible] id K[illegible] that, in amending FISA, "you're doing surgery [illegible] plicated [illegible], "[t]hat may sound trivial, but it's actually ver[illegible] nati[illegible]y."[1681] [illegible], if amendments are not approached from [illegible] perspe[illegible]

> I worry [illegible] too-[illegible] urselves on the other end of the fa[illegible] al-secu[illegible] ving a new inspector general [illegible] -- th[illegible] Department . . . for the prolifer[illegible] pe or [illegible] tions [illegible] lure to stop an attack or other gr[illegible] s com[illegible] security.[1682]

Senator Graham [illegible] same [illegible] ce to lose the ability of the FISA court to operate [illegible] tably [illegible] ed [illegible][1683]

Thus, w[illegible] below [illegible] revie[illegible] IG conducted of the FBI's handling of the [illegible] sen inv[illegible] focu[illegible] ems that appeared both in that investigation an[illegible] Hurrican[illegible] s to assist in the full and complete consi[illegible] litical [illegible] d make FISA applications more understandable [illegible] for th[illegible] nd j[illegible] eview and approve them. We conclude with a [illegible] f bias [illegible] suggest one possible FBI reform for consideration [illegible] artment [illegible] all the many changes that have already been m[illegible] seek [illegible] hem

## A. <u>The OI[illegible] aluati[illegible] the FBI's Counterintelligence Progra[illegible] Hanssen[illegible]</u>

Robert [illegible] "the m[illegible] tory."[1684] For more than 20 years while he was as[illegible] FBI's [illegible] llige[illegible], Hanssen betrayed the United States and gave [illegible] mou[illegible] information, including the identities of do[illegible] sour[illegible] sequently executed by the Soviet Union.[1685] The [illegible] d an [illegible] 's failure to deter and detect Hanssen as a m[illegible] ded th[illegible] did [illegible] detection "because he was a 'master spy'" o[illegible] rdinar[illegible] her because of "longstanding

---

from 2018 to 2[illegible] rlier ye[illegible] log.com/new-statistics-confirm-continuing-decl[illegible] ral-su[illegible] uth[illegible]

[1681] Bryan Tau[illegible] lz, *S[illegible] ebukes FBI Over Handling of Wiretapping of*[illegible] Wall S[illegible] 7, 20[illegible] Kris).

[1682] David Kris, [illegible] *ghts* [illegible] *Report*, Lawfare, Dec. 23, 2019, at 13-15 [illegible] "Kris [illegible]

[1683] Charlie Sav[illegible] *Got a* [illegible] *rity Surveillance. It Was Ugly.* N.Y. Times (D[illegible] ttps[illegible] mes[illegible] 2/11/us/politics/fisa-surveillance-fbi.html?search[illegible]=10.

[1684] OIG, U.S. [illegible] of Jus[illegible] *Performance in Deterring, Detecting, and* [illegible] *the* [illegible] *ert Philip Hanssen* at 6 (Aug. 14, 2003) (her[illegible] *nssen* [illegible]").

[1685] *Id.*

systemic problems in the FBI's counterintelligence program."[1686] For many years, the FBI focused on a specific CIA employee as the potential mole.[1687] Although its initial focus may have been reasonable, as time went on:

> The FBI should have seriously questioned its conclusion that the CIA suspect was a KGB spy and considered opening different lines of investigation. The squad responsible for the case, however, was so committed to the belief that the CIA suspect was a mole that it lost a measure of objectivity . . . . [W]hile FBI management pressed for the investigation to be completed, it did not question the factual premises underlying it."[1688]

One of the OIG's recommendations for the FBI's counterintelligence program in the Hanssen matter was that "supervisors must guard against excessively deferring to line personnel . . . and . . . must ensure that the Department . . . is properly briefed on the strengths and weaknesses of potential espionage prosecutions."[1689] A more cooperative relationship between the Counterintelligence Division and the Department, the OIG explained later, would make it "more likely case agents' analytical and investigative judgments in counterespionage cases will be adequately scrutinized."[1690] Other recommendations similarly concerned greater involvement for Department attorneys, including "a larger oversight role in ensuring the accuracy and fairness of factual assertions in FISA applications and . . . direct access to the case agent and the source information relied on in the application."[1691]

When considering Crossfire Hurricane, some of the OIG's recommendations continue to be relevant, particularly by analogy. Numerous reports clearly state that Russia was trying to influence the 2016 presidential election.[1692] This was also the prevailing view of the media and

---

1686 *Id.* at 10.

1687 *Id.* at 12.

1688 *Id.* at 12-13.

1689 *Id.* at 18.

1690 OIG, U.S. Department of Justice, *A Review of the FBI's Progress in Responding to the Recommendations in the Office of Inspector General Report on Robert Hanssen* at 28 (Sept. 2007) (hereinafter "*Hanssen Progress Review*").

1691 *Hanssen 2003 Review* at 16.

1692 *See, e.g.*, 1 *Mueller Report* at 4 (Russia's Internet Research Agency carried out "a social media campaign designed to provoke and amplify political and social discord in the United States," and the campaign evolved "to a targeted operation that by early 2016 favored candidate Trump and disparaged candidate Clinton"); *Joint Statement from the Department of Homeland Security and Office of the Director of National Intelligence on Election Security* (Oct. 7, 2016) (The Intelligence Community "is confident that the Russian Government directed the recent compromises of e-mails from US persons and institutions, including from US political organizations").

it was widely accepted throughout open source reporting at the time that Russia was to blame for the unlawful intrusion into the DNC servers.[1693]

One of the chief errors from the start of Crossfire Hurricane was the poor analysis the FBI brought to bear on the critical pieces of information that it had gathered, as well as an over-reliance on flawed or incomplete human intelligence that only later was found to be plainly unreliable. In July 2016, the FBI received the most damaging of the Steele Reports but, mysteriously and unfortunately, these reports do not appear to have made their way to the Counterintelligence Division for analysis until after mid-September.[1694] Later in July, Australia provided the information from Papadopoulos to U.S. authorities.[1695] The FBI then appears to have formulated a hypothesis that the Trump campaign, or someone associated with it, was working with the Russians. Neither the *Crossfire Hurricane Opening EC* nor those responsible for the investigation in the Counterintelligence Division or upper management, however, appear to have recognized the crucial need to analyze and then assess the actual ambiguities in Papadopoulos's statements to the Australian diplomats. Instead, the FBI immediately opened a full investigation, an investigation that clearly had the ability to affect an approaching presidential election. Indeed, executive management of the FBI and its Counterintelligence Division appear to have taken the Paragraph Five information at face value in opening the matter as evidenced by the *Opening EC* citing the Paragraph Five information as essentially the sole basis for opening a full investigation on unnamed members of an ongoing presidential campaign. Then, when the Steele reporting finally was received by Crossfire Hurricane personnel in September 2016, it was immediately exploited, with no verification of its sensational allegations, and used in support of its initial request for FISA authority. The Steele reporting would eventually fall apart, but not before it had been continuously adopted by the FBI as supportive of its underlying theory regarding collusion.

The Intelligence Community's *Analytic Standards* say that analysts "must perform their functions with objectivity" and "employ reasoning techniques and practical mechanisms that reveal and mitigate bias."[1696] In the Hanssen investigation, the squad "responsible for the case . . . was so committed to the belief that the CIA suspect was a mole that it lost a measure of objectivity and failed to give adequate consideration to other

---

[1693] *See, e.g.*, David E. Sanger & Nick Corasaniti, *DNC Says Russian Hackers Penetrated Its Files, Including Dossier on Donald Trump*, N.Y. Times (June 14, 2016), https://www.nytimes.com/2016/06/15/us/politics/russian-hackers-dnc-trump.html; Ellen Nakashima, *Russian Government Hackers Penetrated DNC, Stole Opposition Research on Trump*, Wash. Post (June 14, 2016), https://www.washingtonpost.com/world/national-security/Russian-government-hackers-penetrated-dnc-stole-opposition-research-on-trump/2016/06/14; Daniel Strauss, *Russian Government Hackers Broke into DNC Servers, Stole Trump Oppo*, Politico (June 14, 2016), https://www.politico.com/story/2016/06/Russian-government-hackers-broke-into-dnc-servers-stole-trump-oppo-224315.

[1694] *See supra* § IV.D.1.b.iii.

[1695] *See supra* § IV.A.3.

[1696] Intelligence Community Directive 203, *Analytic Standards* at 2 (Jan. 2, 2015). *See supra* § III.B.3.

possibilities.[1697] The *SSCI Russia Report* observed that the FBI's analysts should endeavor "to check assumptions underpinning FBI operations, to apply the rigor of intelligence analysis to assessments and confidential human sources, and to create a culture where questioning previously held assumptions is acceptable and encouraged."[1698] The Office concurs with this recommendation.

Apart from analytic integrity, in seeking FISA authority in Crossfire Hurricane, investigators withheld key pieces of information from the OI attorneys. The OI attorneys are responsible for ensuring the accuracy and fairness of the information presented to the FISC, an impossible task without being provided with relevant information. Both the OIG's review and this review highlight the omissions, errors, and misstatements by FBI personnel, including the withholding of significant exculpatory statements, that should not have occurred had the Crossfire Hurricane investigators considered and treated the Department lawyers as full partners. Rather, Crossfire Hurricane reflects a struggle by OI to obtain straightforward answers about Steele's possible bias and leaks to the media and Page's relationship with another government agency. Nor was OI told about the significant differences between the Steele Reports and the statements Danchenko made to the FBI.

In the follow-on *Hanssen Progress Review*, the OIG quoted a Department official as saying that the Department "still has the occasional fight with the FBI to get full access to information, particularly information pertinent to the reliability of sources relied on in the FISA applications."[1699] The Crossfire Hurricane investigation shows that regrettably these struggles for accuracy and transparency were still occurring in 2016. Moreover, it is certainly to be hoped that, with the new post-Page requirements of the *Sensitive Investigations Memorandum*, the new guidelines governing the FBI's use of human sources, and other significant policy changes, there will not be a recurrence of the serious errors identified by the OIG, the Inspection Division, and our investigation. Absent continual reinforcement by FBI leadership of the need for integrity, accuracy, and objectivity in following these requirements, however, such is not a certainty.

### B. **FBI Investigations**

#### *1. The New York counterintelligence investigation*

When the NYFO opened a counterintelligence investigation of Page in April 2016, at a time when he was a foreign policy adviser to the Trump campaign, the investigation likely should have been treated as a sensitive investigative matter because of Page's role in the campaign. The Attorney General has since addressed this issue in a desirable, though slightly different, way. The Attorney General must approve any investigation of a "senior presidential campaign staff member or advisor." A footnote explains that "this includes any person who has been publicly announced by a campaign as a staffer or member of an official campaign advisory committee or group."[1700]

---

1697 *Hanssen 2003 Review* at 12.

1698 *SSCI Russia Report*, pt. V, at 936.

1699 *Hanssen Progress Review* at 9.

1700 *Sensitive Investigations Memorandum* at 2 & n.3.

## 2. *Pred*[illegible] *Crossfi*[illegible]

The FBI [illegible] Crossfire [illegible] as a full investigation "to determine whe[illegible] al(s) [illegible] with [illegible] campaign are witting of and/or coordinating a[illegible] the C[illegible] of [illegible] As described in section III, the standard for o[illegible] inves[illegible] ctual basis for the investigation that reasonabl[illegible] t... [illegible] federal crime or a threat to the national securi[illegible] *may b*[illegible] stigation may obtain information re[illegible] activi[illegible]

The inf[illegible] the F[illegible] in [illegible] s that a Trump campaign advisor had su[illegible] Aus[illegible] ampaign "had received some kind of sugges[illegible] sia th[illegible] aign. The *OIG Review* found that the FBI m[illegible] nen[illegible] the "articulable factual basis" standard for o[illegible] vestig[illegible] information from Australia, at least when co[illegible] with [illegible] ssia's efforts to interfere with the 2016 U.S. [illegible] that [illegible] onfident, however, that this is the case. Our i[illegible] gathe[illegible] hat a number of those closest to the investigati[illegible] hat th[illegible] been met. For example, both Supervisory Sp[illegible] and [illegible] predication for the investigation a[illegible] Even [illegible] nd approved the *Opening EC*, said that "ther[illegible] this, [illegible] ound."[1705] Strzok's view would seem to dictat[illegible] of th[illegible] , at most, as a preliminary investigation. [illegible] there [illegible] ons to be concerned about the predication of [illegible] ricar[illegible]

Apart f[illegible] to m[illegible] *Dom* for opening a full investigation, [illegible] der [illegible] e least intrusive collection techniques fea[illegible] olicy [illegible] ndment rights are at stake" – which they cle[illegible] maj[illegible] – "the choice and use of investigative [illegible] d be [illegible] inimizes potential infringement of those rights." [illegible] er, th[illegible] [illegible] gment" necessary to achieve an objective.[1707] [illegible] agen[illegible] cision-making and the need to employ the lea[illegible] means [illegible] utions when opening and conducting inv[illegible] order [illegible] ncourage careful evaluation of

---

[1701] *Crossfire F*[illegible] *ening* [illegible]

[1702] *AGG-Dom* [illegible] II.B.4 [illegible]

[1703] *Redacted* [illegible] at 351-[illegible]

[1704] FBI-AAA-[illegible] 5 (Ly[illegible] betw[illegible] isory Special Agent-1 and UK ALAT-1 dated [illegible]

[1705] OSC Repo[illegible] of [illegible] at 2.

[1706] *DIOG* § 4.[illegible]

[1707] *Id.* § 4.1.1.[illegible] omitted[illegible]

facts and circumstances, as well as to assess risk, before proceeding with any investigative activity.

In implementing these standards, the FBI could have taken one or more of the following sensible steps:

- Under the least intrusive standard, rather than opening an investigation with a broad scope ("to determine whether individual(s) associated with the Trump campaign are witting of and/or coordinating activities with the Government of Russia"), the FBI should have focused, at least at the beginning, on Papadopoulos, the alleged source of the information from Australia. On the other hand, the Paragraph Five information was not only connected to Papadopoulos, but also to the campaign as an alleged recipient of "some kind of suggestion from Russia."

- Under the FBI's guidelines, the investigation could have been opened more appropriately as an assessment or preliminary investigation. FBI investigations opened as preliminary investigations, short of full investigations, include time limits and a narrower range of authorized techniques to mitigate risk and avoid unnecessary intrusion. If necessary and appropriate, a lower level of investigative activity may be escalated under the guidelines by converting to a full investigation with supervisory approval.

- In the subsequent investigation of Page under the Crossfire Hurricane umbrella, the FBI could have used additional, less intrusive techniques before seeking authority to conduct electronic surveillance under FISA. The paucity of information collected on key aspects of Page's activities would support such an approach.

Regardless of an investigator's preference for any of these steps, there are now additional requirements that apply to the opening of an investigation like Crossfire Hurricane. The *Sensitive Investigations Memorandum* requires the Attorney General to approve the opening of such an investigation. That an investigation like Crossfire Hurricane should require a concurring decision by the Department, rather than any one component or entity, seems appropriate. We also believe that the proposal described below in E for an identified Department official to challenge all stages of a politically sensitive investigation would be another valuable way of addressing concerns about the opening, continuation and intrusiveness of an investigation like Crossfire Hurricane.

### *3. Opening of individual investigations*

The FBI opened full investigations of Papadopoulos, Page, Flynn, and Manafort in August 2016, as part of Crossfire Hurricane.[1708] Again, in addition to the requirements of the *AGG-Dom* and the *DIOG*, the approval requirements in the *Sensitive Investigations Memorandum* now would apply to these. The proposal in Section V.E would also potentially apply to them.

---

[1708] *See supra* § IV.A.1.e; *Redacted OIG Review* at 59-60.

### 4. *Compartmentation*

Unlike most FBI investigations, which are managed from FBI field offices, Crossfire Hurricane was managed from FBI Headquarters. The information it collected was not shared with or available to others in the FBI, including, as described above, the Directorate of Intelligence. The *OIG Review* says that:

> [B]ecause the information being investigated related to an ongoing presidential election campaign, the Crossfire Hurricane case file was designated as "prohibited" meaning that access to the file was restricted and viewable to only those individuals assigned to work on the investigation. Agents and analysts . . . used covert investigative techniques to ensure information about the investigation remained known only to the team and FBI and Department officials.[1709]

Moreover, at least at times, even those participating in the investigation had limited information available. Supervisory Special Agent-3, who was tasked to supervise the Crossfire Hurricane investigators as a successor to Supervisory Special Agent-1, stated:

> Contributing to the difficulties . . . was how compartmentalized the . . . investigation was, specifically the lack of information sharing between the intelligence analysts and the operational component . . . . Even as the team lead, I only had access to limited information, and from the start of my [temporary duty], I did not have a clear picture of everything going on in the investigation . . . . I was managing the day to day operations of the case without having complete information.[1710]

The investigation's compartmentation, and its unusual structure as a Headquarters investigation, may have limited the amount of oversight that it received. In the past, NSA's collection of the international communications of U.S. citizens and groups was also highly compartmented. A Senate committee chaired by Senator Frank Church investigated this activity. It reported:

> In 1969, NSA formalized the watch list program under the codename MINARET. The program applied not only to alleged foreign influence on domestic dissent, but also to American groups and individuals whose activities "may result in civil disturbances or otherwise subvert the national security of the U.S." At the same time, *NSA instructed its personnel to "restrict the knowledge" that NSA was collecting such information and to keep its name off the disseminated "product."*[1711]

---

[1709] *See Redacted OIG Review* at 58-59.

[1710] *FBI Inspection Division Report* at 290.

[1711] S. Rep. No. 94-755, bk. 3, at 739 (1976) (emphasis added and footnotes omitted).

The report found that "NSA placed more restrictive security controls on MINARET material than it placed on other highly classified foreign intercepts in order to conceal its involvement in activities which were beyond its regular mission."[1712]

In possible contrast to the FBI, the CIA may not have compartmented some of the information that it had. The Office learned at one point from Director Brennan that "[t]here was no effort at the CIA to restrict information because it was potentially embarrassing for Hillary Clinton. . . . Obama just wanted the right people involved."[1713]

In combination, an unusually compartmented investigation bearing on politics will always involve risk, especially when it is the subject of significant media attention. In any event, in opening and conducting a sensitive investigation, the FBI should consider ways to balance the need for secrecy against the need to have a full and informed evaluation of the case. Leaks can cause great harm, but so can a failure to understand the information collected or to take appropriate investigative steps.

*5. **Interaction with the Trump campaign***

On August 11, 2016, the FBI met with CHS-1 who, as described earlier, was a longstanding FBI source. CHS-1 had decided not to join the Trump campaign but told the FBI that he/she was willing to refrain from notifying the campaign about this decision.[1714] The Crossfire Hurricane investigators were pleased or relieved that the source did not want to join the campaign.[1715] But as to whether the FBI encouraged or directed the source to avoid notifying the campaign, the *OIG Review* is less clear. Not notifying the campaign, of course, could in and of itself affect the campaign's staffing decisions or other activities.

On September 1, 2016, CHS-1 met with a high-level Trump campaign official who was not a subject of the Crossfire Hurricane investigation. This meeting was consensually monitored. The OIG notes that "FBI and Department policy did not require that the FBI obtain Department approval to consensually monitor this conversation."[1716]

Also in September 2016, CHS-1 met with Papadopoulos. The *OIG Review* says that, "[t]he OGC Unit Chief told the OIG that because the operation targeted Papadopoulos individually and wasn't directed at anything related to the campaign, she thought that it was appropriate."[1717] If the purpose of CHS-1's meeting with Papadopoulos was not to find out if the

---

[1712] *Id.* at 749.

[1713] OSC Report of Interview of John Brennan on Aug. 21, 2020 at 9 (capitalizations omitted).

[1714] *See Redacted OIG Review* at 315.

[1715] *Id.* at 315-16.

[1716] *Id.* at 327.

[1717] *Id.* at 330; *see also FBI Inspection Division Report* at 178 campaign or an[illegible] behalf [illegible] with Russia, it is hard to know what the purpo[illegible]

### *6. Def[illegible]ings*

The *OI*[illegible] discusses [illegible] decisi[illegible] the candidate Trump or his campaign a de[illegible] ng con[illegible] alleg[illegible] the Crossfire Hurricane team was investigating. [illegible] does no[illegible] whet[illegible] sion was consistent with other decisions that [illegible] made [illegible] or political candidates. There are of course num[illegible] gation[illegible] years [illegible] presidential and congressional candidates or [illegible] includi[illegible] contributions, improper foreign influence, or o[illegible].[1718] [illegible] In 2020, the Department declassified s[illegible] s rel[illegible] 15 i[illegible] of possible illegal campaign contributions. [illegible] ce, the [illegible] ided [illegible] briefing to the Clinton campaign.[1719] [illegible] argued [illegible] decisi[illegible] ide a defensive briefing in that investigation [illegible] Cross[illegible] ane[illegible] n were inconsistent.[1720] President Oba[illegible] have th[illegible] a d[illegible] iefing for the Trump campaign was desirable, [illegible] may [illegible] Crossfire Hurricane.[1721]

As de[illegible] tion [illegible] as [illegible] ed a board, the FIDBB, to address defensive brief[illegible] Attorney Ge[illegible] direct[illegible] to promulgate procedures on this subject; and th[illegible] General [illegible] addi[illegible] cific requirements in connection with politically [illegible] SA ap[illegible] These [illegible] ts, particularly the last one, require a seriou[illegible] n of th[illegible] a ca[illegible] fing, and we support them.

---

[1718] *See, e.g.*, M[illegible] gan, *Fi*[illegible] *ama Sentenced to 12 Years in Prison for For*[illegible] *ams*, [illegible], Feb[illegible] describing "more than $950,000 in unlawful donati[illegible] al con[illegible] Oba[illegible], McCain and many others, nearly all of it from u[illegible] foreign [illegible] *of Rudy Giuliani Convicted over Illegal Campai*[illegible] *ons*, [illegible] (describing conviction involving campaign contr[illegible] behalf [illegible] Montellaro & Myah Ward, *Campaign Fin*[illegible] *Iss*[illegible] *Fin*[illegible] *National's Trump Super PAC Donation*, Poli[illegible] 2022 [illegible] tion made by companies of a Canadian billi[illegible] S. poli[illegible] tted).

[1719] *See supra* [illegible]

[1720] *See, e.g.*, S[illegible] Graha[illegible] *Materials Demonstrate Clear Double Stand*[illegible] *n, Tr*[illegible] *aign*[illegible] 2020), https://www.ju[illegible].gov[illegible] declassified-fbi-materials-demonstrate-c[illegible] standa[illegible] on-t[illegible] aigns.

[1721] The *OIG R*[illegible] ibes se[illegible] ings around the time in 2016 when the FBI opene[illegible] Hurric[illegible] of a[illegible] ken by Deputy FBI Director McCabe, who [illegible] me[illegible] indi[illegible] President Obama stated that the FBI should thi[illegible] ing de[illegible] iefs," [illegible] he did not believe that the Crossfire Hur[illegible] ation [illegible] alia[illegible] been discussed. *Redacted OIG Review* at 76-[illegible] quotat[illegible]).

## C. **FISA Issues**

### 1. *Clarity of applications*

In 2020, the FBI and the Department provided 19 complete FISA applications to the PCLOB for review. Adam Klein, the Chairman of the PCLOB, commented that:

> The applications present the reader (most notably, the FISA court judge) with a great deal of factual information . . . . This information, however, is sometimes repetitive, and the organization does not necessarily facilitate critical analysis. The applications recite many facts related to the target's potential involvement with terrorism. But each fact's relative importance emerges only after very close reading.
>
> . . . .
>
> Overall, these applications provide a great deal of relevant information and generally aim to highlight potential question marks for the court. However, their clarity and organization could be improved . . . .[1722]

Former Chairman Klein has also written that "[s]teps to improve the clarity of applications . . . would help drafters think rigorously about which facts are essential to probable cause, which are merely supportive and why the surveillance is necessary in the first place."[1723] Similarly, the FBI's public strategy says that it will "improve data collection, accessibility, and analysis to better understand, anticipate, and mitigate threats."[1724] Although the PCLOB did not review the applications for surveillance of Page, as the applications did not involve terrorism, some of the *White Paper*'s observations are relevant.

#### a. Transparency of sourcing information

In the Page applications, much of the probable cause information was based on multiple layers of unverified sub-sourcing. Whenever that is the case, there is a greater possibility for bias or exaggerations to proliferate, even under ideal circumstances. We appreciate and support the effort the Department's OI Attorneys made, which may have prevented even larger problems, to describe the sourcing for the Page applications. In any application, the description of the sourcing information is of fundamental importance and should be as transparent as possible. It should include the FBI's insight, or lack thereof, into the

---

1722 Klein, *White Paper* at 12.

1723 Adam Klein, *What the Inspector General's Latest FISA Report Can (and Can't) Tell Us*, Lawfare, Oct. 19, 2021.

1724 *FBI Strategy, Our Four Guiding Principles*, https://www.fbi.gov/about/mission/fbi-strategy (hereinafter "*FBI Strategy*").

reliability of each layer.[1725] This is even more the case where what is described is the central contention of the application.[1726]

In addition, the source and sub-source information might have been easier to understand, and been seen as having more importance, if it had been described in the text of the application rather than in a footnote. Although former Assistant Attorney General Kris correctly notes that the FISC "reads the footnotes" and that "[t]he government's disclosures enabled the court to take Steele's information with a grain of salt,"[1727] we see no reason not to lay out sourcing information as clearly as possible, particularly when it contains subjective assessments.

b. Information from Congress

That a member of Congress is concerned about the activities of a political opponent or someone in another political party or may have written to the Attorney General or the Director of the FBI about those activities, would rarely seem relevant to a discussion of probable cause, unless the member provides specific and credible information that is not available from other sources.[1728]

c. Masking of information

In a FISA application, it is clearly important to protect the identity of sources. This is typically done by giving them a number rather than providing a name. It also may be important to minimize or mask private or derogatory information about someone who is not the target of the application. The broader use of minimized identities, such as describing someone as "Candidate #1" or attributing a news report to "an identified news organization," may not conceal much and may instead make understanding the application more difficult.[1729] It may also (even unintentionally) encourage a reader to think that because one possible step to ensure legality has been taken others have been too. In fact, whether information is minimized or masked has no effect on whether the information itself is accurate and supports a probable cause finding.

d. Use of news reports

Former NSA General Counsel Stewart Baker has urged the FBI to avoid using media reports in FISA applications. The FBI has little knowledge of the reliability of the sources used by reporters, and reliance on press accounts risks shortcutting the process of establishing probable cause. If the FBI uses a media source, it should disclose the name of

---

[1725] *Cf. In re Carter W. Page*, No. 16-1182, at 20 (not addressing reliability of the sub-source information used on that page).

[1726] *See id.* at 10, 20 (providing information from a source that Page was part of "a well-developed conspiracy of co-operation" between the Trump campaign and "Russian leadership").

[1727] David Kris, *The Irony of the Nunes Memo*, Lawfare, Mar. 1, 2018.

[1728] *See In re Carter W. Page*, No. 16-1182, at 23-24 (discussing a news report and including the apparent views of members of Congress).

[1729] *See, e.g., id.* at 22 (minimizing identities).

the source "and any credible claims of bias that have been leveled against the news outlet."[1730] It might also disclose what, if any, efforts it has taken to verify the allegations.

e. Need to share important information

In January 2017, the FBI interviewed Igor Danchenko, Steele's primary sub-source. Danchenko said that Steele "misstated or exaggerated" the sub-source's statements "in multiple sections of the reporting."[1731] NSD, but not OI, was present at the interview.[1732] Because the interview involved an important sub-source used in a FISA application, OI should, at a minimum, have been informed of what the sub-source said.

### 2. *Completeness of applications*

The *OIG Review* concluded that FBI personnel "did not give appropriate attention to facts that cut against probable cause."[1733] The FBI has addressed this issue by requiring that both an agent and a supervisor must affirm that OI "has been apprised of all information that might reasonably call into question the accuracy of the information in the application *or otherwise raise doubts about the requested probable cause findings or the theory of the case*."[1734] The FBI has also pledged that it "will adhere to the rule of law through attention to detail."[1735] Finally, the Attorney General has directed both the FBI and OI to conduct completeness reviews.[1736]

Implementation of the reviews may be difficult. An FBI CHS may have recorded dozens or hundreds of hours of conversations with the target or others engaged in related activities. For example, in the released transcripts of conversations among an FBI CHS, George Papadopoulos, and others, there is clearly a large amount of extraneous information, and it may not always be clear what is being discussed.[1737] Moreover, no one may have listened to all the recordings, or there may not be available transcripts. The FBI may also have a large volume of other raw

---

[1730] Baker, *Partisan Taint in the Trump-Russia Investigation*, Lawfare, Sept. 8, 2020 (hereinafter "Baker, *Partisan Taint*").

[1731] *See Redacted OIG Review* at 187.

[1732] *Id.* at 187 n.336.

[1733] *See Redacted OIG Review* at 413.

[1734] *Wray Declaration* at 3 (emphasis added).

[1735] *FBI Strategy*.

[1736] Attorney General Memorandum, *Augmenting the Internal Compliance Functions of the Federal Bureau of Investigation* at 1-2 (Aug. 31, 2020); *Supplemental Reforms Memorandum* at 3.

[1737] *See* FBI, U.S. Department of Justice, *Verbatim Transcription*, Task Nos. 628389 and 635144 (completed Dec. 22, 2016 and Jan. 9, 2016), *available at* https://www.judiciary.senate.gov/imo/media/doc/2020-05-05%20Submission%20SJC%20SSCI.pdf; FBI, U.S. Department of Justice, *Verbatim Transcription*, Task No. 620098 (completed Nov. 10, 2016), *available at* https://www.judiciary.senate.gov/imo/media/doc/2020-04-24%20Submission%20SJC%20SSCI.pdf. For links to these and other materials, *see* https://www.judiciary.senate.gov/fisa-investigation.

records related [illegible] ation. [illegible] fact [illegible] ake it hard to identify information that "raise[s] do[illegible] requ[illegible] or the theory of the case."

One pos[illegible] mpleme[illegible] requ[illegible] least in part, may be by asking on the FISA veri[illegible] n or el[illegible] f particular kinds of derogatory information abo[illegible] An ex[illegible] FBI has information about financial transa[illegible] r the [illegible] with a foreign power. If the FBI is not aware of [illegible] ion, th[illegible] FISC that the FBI either has no such informati[illegible] may h[illegible] form[illegible] hoosing not to include it. The FISC could then [illegible] absen[illegible] rmation in its assessment of whether the targ[illegible] t of a f[illegible] er.

Moreov[illegible] nstan[illegible] FBI [illegible] iewed data relating to an investigation, or [illegible] still be[illegible] d, O[illegible] to consider whether the FISA application sho[illegible] t fac[illegible]

### 3. *Reli[illegible] FIS[illegible]*

When th[illegible] app[illegible] re ren[illegible] ewing officials may have placed too much relia[illegible] r aut[illegible] General and the FISC. Deputy Attorney Gene[illegible] not[illegible] Page renewal application came to him many d[illegible] rtmen[illegible] prior applications and three different judge[illegible] obab[illegible][1738] [illegible] of the requirements found in the *Supplemental [illegible] randu[illegible]* both [illegible] and renewals of FISA surveillances.[1739] [illegible] som[illegible] d-tea[illegible] es with "partisan risk," might help here.

### 4. *Tim[illegible] reque[illegible]*

Deputy [illegible] rney [illegible] ans [illegible] that the FBI should submit a request to rene[illegible] r ty a[illegible] 45 [illegible] its expiration. In practice, "renewal reque[illegible] e over [illegible] BI to [illegible] week and a half, before the expiration." If t[illegible] ne e[illegible] wo[illegible] ime for the "robust back and forth" needed t[illegible] applic[illegible] mpl[illegible] s proposal would require a significant com[illegible] Departm[illegible] BI la[illegible]

Even if [illegible] time[illegible] ing [illegible] quest, OI may be able to begin acquiring need[illegible] n by req[illegible] fro[illegible] possibly seeking it elsewhere) and asking to m[illegible] 45 da[illegible] expi[illegible] y be worth the effort involved for a sensitive and i[illegible] veilla[illegible]

---

1738 *See Redact[illegible]* at 2[illegible]

1739 *See Supple[illegible] Me[illegible]* [illegible] quirements "[b]efore any application initi[illegible] wing th[illegible] n is submitted to the FISC).

1740 U.S. Senate [illegible] the [illegible] nter[illegible] t Evans – Redacted Version, at 214 (July 31, 2[illegible]

D. **Bias or improper motivation**

The *OIG Review* of Crossfire Hurricane says that "[w]e did not find documentary or testimonial evidence that political bias or improper motivation influenced the FBI's decision to seek FISA authority on Carter Page."[1741] It also says that "[w]hile we did not find documentary or testimonial evidence of intentional misconduct on the part of the [FBI personnel], we also did not receive satisfactory explanations for the errors or problems we identified."[1742] David Kris has catalogued statements in the *OIG Review* like those above and discussed the tension between the statements about the lack of evident bias and the lack of explanation for the problems found.[1743]

In this report we have referred to the possible impact of "confirmation bias" on the Crossfire Hurricane investigation.[1744] Confirmation bias is widely understood as a phenomenon describing how information is processed by individuals and groups. It stands for the general proposition that there is a common human tendency – mostly unintentional – for people to accept information and evidence that is consistent with what they believe to be true, while ignoring or rejecting information that challenges those beliefs. In short, people tend to give more credence to information that supports what they already believe. The effects of confirmation bias can be amplified in groups operating in situations of high stress and under time pressures.[1745]

Throughout the duration of Crossfire Hurricane, facts and circumstances that were inconsistent with the premise that Trump and/or persons associated with the Trump campaign were involved in a collusive or conspiratorial relationship with the Russian government were ignored or simply assessed away. Indeed, as set forth in Sections IVA.2 and 3, from even before the opening of Crossfire Hurricane, some of those most directly involved in the subsequent investigation had (i) expressed their open disdain for Trump, (ii) asked about when they would open an investigation on Trump, and (iii) asserted that they would prevent Trump from becoming President. As discussed throughout this report, our investigation revealed that the stated basis for opening a full investigation "to determine whether individual(s) associated with the Trump campaign [were] witting of and/or coordinating activities with the Government of Russia"[1746] was seriously flawed. Again, the FBI's failure to critically analyze information that ran counter to the narrative of a Trump/Russia collusive relationship exhibited throughout Crossfire Hurricane is extremely troublesome. The evidence of the FBI's confirmation bias in

---

[1741] *See Redacted OIG Review* at vii; *see also id.* at iii-iv (similar statements about opening of Crossfire Hurricane and related investigations).

[1742] *Id.* at xiii; *see also id.* at 414.

[1743] Kris, *Further Thoughts* at 2-5.

[1744] *See, e.g.*, references at pages 18, 98, 305.

[1745] *See generally* ScienceDirect, *Confirmation Bias* (quoting Caleb W. Lack & Jacques Rousseau, *Comprehensive Clinical Psychology* § 11.04.4.1.1 (2d ed. 2022); Shahram Heshmat, *What Is Confirmation Bias?* in *Psychology Today* (Apr. 23, 2015), https://www.psychology today.com/us/blog/science-choice/201504/what-is-confirmation-bias; Bettina J. Cassad & J.E. Luebering, *Confirmation Bias*, in *Encyclopedia Brittanica* (Last updated Mar. 31, 2023).

[1746] *Crossfire Hurricane Opening EC* at 3-4.

the matter, includes, at a minimum, the following information that was simply ignored or in some fashion rationalized away:

- The Australian diplomats told Crossfire Hurricane investigators that Papadopoulos never stated that he had any direct contact with the Russians nor did he provide any explicit information about an offer of assistance.

- There was a complete lack of information from the Intelligence Community that corroborated the hypothesis upon which the Crossfire Hurricane investigation was predicated.

- The FBI generally ignored the significant exculpatory information provided by Carter Page, George Papadopoulos, and Trump Senior Foreign Policy Advisor-1 during recorded conversations with FBI CHSs.

- The FBI failed to pursue investigative leads that were inconsistent with their theory of the case (*e.g.*, Page's recorded denials of having any relationship with Paul Manafort, a fact about which there was available evidence).

- The FBI failed to take Page up on the written offer he made to Director Comey to be interviewed about the allegations contained in Michael Isikoff's *Yahoo! News* article and instead opted to seek FISA surveillance of Page.

- The FBI was willing to make use of the completely unvetted and uncorroborated Steele reporting in multiple FISA applications targeting a U.S. citizen, even after the Crossfire Hurricane investigators had determined that there were major conflicts between the reporting of Steele and his primary sub-source, Igor Danchenko – conflicts the FBI incredibly failed to resolve.

- The Crossfire Hurricane investigators did not even ask Steele about his role in providing information to Michael Isikoff as contained in the September 23, 2016 *Yahoo! News* article – information that essentially accused Carter Page of colluding with the Russians. And thereafter the same investigators demonstrated a willingness to contort the plain language of the article to suggest it was not Steele but Steele's employers who had given the information to Isikoff.

- The FBI ignored the fact that at no time before, during or after Crossfire Hurricane were investigators able to corroborate a single substantive allegation in the Steele dossier reporting.

- There was a complete failure on the part of the FBI to even examine – never mind resolve – the serious counterespionage issues surrounding Steele's primary sub-source, Igor Danchenko.

- The FBI leadership essentially disregarded the Clinton Plan intelligence, which it received at almost the exact same time as the Australian Paragraph Five information. This was despite the fact that at precisely the same time as the Clinton Plan intelligence was received (i) the Clinton campaign made public statements tying the

DNC computer hack to Russian attempts to help Trump get elected, (ii) the FBI was receiving the Clinton campaign-funded Steele Reports, and (iii) the Clinton campaign-funded Alfa Bank allegations were being prepared for delivery to the media and the FBI.

- The Crossfire Hurricane investigators essentially ignored information they had received as early as October 2016 regarding Charles Dolan, a longtime Democratic operative with ties to the Clintons who also possessed significant ties to Russian government figures who would appear in the Steele reporting, and never interviewed him.

- The Crossfire Hurricane investigators provided only partial, and in some instances misleading, information to Department attorneys working on the Page FISA applications while withholding other highly relevant information from those attorneys and the FISC that might cast real doubt on their probable cause assertions.

Finally, the results of the OIG's *Audit of 29 Applications* also establish significant problems in the Page FISA applications, problems that point to bias and other factors. Following the *Audit*, the Department and the FBI "notified the FISC that the 29 applications contained a total of 209 errors, 4 of which they deemed to be material."[1747] We note that because the *Audit* did not look for omitted information – a major issue in the Page applications – the results of the *Audit* and the review of the Page applications are not directly comparable. Nonetheless, at least on the surface, the difference is notable: in the four Page applications, there were a total of 17 material errors and omissions,[1748] far more than the four material errors found in the larger group of 29 non-Page applications.

Given the foregoing, and viewing the facts in a light most favorable to the Crossfire Hurricane investigators, it seems highly likely that, at a minimum, confirmation bias played a significant role in the FBI's acceptance of extraordinarily serious allegations derived from uncorroborated information that had not been subjected to the typical exacting analysis employed by the FBI and other members of the Intelligence Community. In short, it is the Office's assessment that the FBI discounted or willfully ignored material information that did not support the narrative of a collusive relationship between Trump and Russia. Similarly, the *FBI Inspection Division Report* says that the investigators "repeatedly ignore[d] or explain[ed] away evidence contrary to the theory the Trump campaign . . . had conspired with Russia. . . . It appeared that . . . there was a pattern of assuming nefarious intent."[1749] An objective and honest assessment of these strands of information should have caused the FBI to question not only the predication for Crossfire Hurricane, but also to reflect on whether the FBI was being manipulated for political or other purposes. Unfortunately, it did not.

---

[1747] *Audit of 29 Applications* at ii; *see also id.* at 10-11 (listing the material errors found).

[1748] *Redacted OIG Review* at viii – xiii (describing the errors in the Page FISA applications).

[1749] *FBI Inspection Division Report* at 33 n.15, 37.

E. **Possibl** [illegible]

One po[illegible] provid[illegible] itically sensitive investigations would be to id[illegible] ance, a[illegible] who i[illegible] for challenging the steps taken in the investigati[illegible] Baker [illegible] osition for a nonpartisan FBI agent or lawye[illegible] the F[illegible] other stage of the investigation.[illegible] be d[illegible] tig[illegible] ose partisan risk." In Baker's view, the Attor[illegible] rough [illegible] *Memorandum*, has already taken "a good step in[illegible] by r[illegible] tive surveillance and search applications be[illegible] spec[illegible] not involved in the investigation."[illegible] Ad[illegible] d FBI leaders should consider whether a regu[illegible] tce of [illegible] most sensitive cases, whether within the FB[illegible] cratio[illegible] onal Security Division, could serve as an eff[illegible] on c[illegible] bias[illegible] duly delaying time-sensitive applications."[1751]

As a w[illegible] full c[illegible] applications that may present very difficult [illegible] impo[illegible] nd that the Department seriously consider Bake[illegible] for a[illegible] chal[illegible] politically sensitive FISA application and [illegible] s of th[illegible] tion.[1752] [illegible] ng," former Attorney General Levi warned, "[illegible] aken th[illegible] f lif[illegible] peril the realization of the goals we all hold dea[illegible] dure t[illegible] eed that our law is not the instrument of p[illegible] ose."[1753]

---

[1750] Baker, *Pa*[illegible] Baker [illegible] is p[illegible] he career official in more detail in Like It or N[illegible] as a F[illegible] Ref[illegible] Appearance of Partisanship in Intelligence In[illegible] at 12-1[illegible], 20[illegible]

[1751] *White Pap*[illegible]

[1752] Baker also [illegible] t the c[illegible] ne lead in reporting on the investigation t[illegible] nd m[illegible] ship, not after the fact but as it proceeds." *B*[illegible] *Tai*[illegible] aspect of the proposal, at least not without fu[illegible] ation, [illegible] could lead to a politically motivated lea[illegible] ive inv[illegible]

[1753] Edward H[illegible] *ell R*[illegible] 17[illegible] *oted in* U.S. Department of Justice, *FYs 2*[illegible] *Strateg*[illegible] 15[illegible]

# Appendices

Washington Post, *Trump says on Univision he could weaponize FBI, DOJ against his enemies*, Maegan Vazquez, Nov. 10, 2023. During the interview on the Spanish-language TV network, journalist Enrique Acevedo asked Trump if he would weaponize the FBI and Justice Department on his opponents in the same way he claims federal law enforcement agencies have been weaponized against him.

## *Appendices*

This section points to additional resources for news and analysis. We begin with a link to the Justice Integrity Project and its trial coverage. Major stories there typically include appendices with links to then-current news stories, as below. For the excerpt below and others cited here, however, we include only a link to the site with a recommendation to use the Search function, and not a link to the specific story, because those pinpoint links sometimes become broken over time.

Following this section providing sample excerpts from independent, web-based commentators whose archives contain extensive coverage of Special Counsel John Durham's investigation of the FBI and so-called "Russiagate," we provide a letter from U.S. House Judiciary Committee Chair Jim Jordan (R-Ohio) dated June 1, 2013. It provides a roadmap of how Republicans plan to use Durham and his report to advance their partisan political agendas.

**Justice Integrity Project** (https://www.justice-integrity.org). The Justice Integrity Project, co-founded and edited by Andrew Kreig, covered both of Special Counsel John Durham's federal trials of targets of his team's prosecutions, each ending in acquittals. Below is a sample excerpt from Justice Integrity Project trial coverage, with this reporting the acquittal of Michael Sussmann, a respected attorney and cyberlaw expert targeted by Durham and his team:

*At 'Russiagate' Trial, Questions Loom About Special Counsel Durham,* Andrew Kreig, May 29, 2022 (Updated).

With one of the most politically explosive federal prosecutions in years beginning on May 17, U.S. Justice Department Special Counsel John H. Durham's record reveals legal error that undercuts his image as straight-shooting seeker of justice.

In a 2008 ruling that has never been reported by a major news outlet, a New York federal appeals court vacated bribery, wire fraud and racketeering convictions because a team led by Durham, then the Deputy U.S. Attorney in Connecticut (and Acting U.S. attorney for supervising the prosecution), illegally withheld evidence that could have helped federal defendant Charles Spadoni defend himself in a corruption case.

Past performance is relevant now because Durham's three-year probe of alleged illegality pertaining to the 2016 U.S. presidential election is reaching a pivotal and controversial juncture with the trial the of cyberlaw attorney Michael Sussmann on a claim that Sussmann falsely denied that he was representing Democratic nominee Hillary Clinton when he sought to alert FBI general counsel James Baker in the fall of 2016 to suspicions of Russian interference.

Sussmann, his attorneys and some independent commentators have denied wrongdoing and claimed that the prosecution is exceptionally weak and also tainted by political partisanship by Durham, a career prosecutor who was also nominated by President Trump for the political post of U.S. attorney for Connecticut.

Durham's case against Sussmann, a former partner at the DC office of law firm Perkins Coie, has generated substantial interest in the national press, particularly in pro-Trump circles where some Trump supporters regard it as their last best hope to vindicate Trump's 2016 election victory as a purely American popular effort, thereby debunking claims that Russian operatives interfered in the 2016 election to hurt Clinton and other Democratic candidates.

Sussmann and his defenders, on the other hand, have defended his actions as both non-criminal and reasonable, particularly in view of what they see as confirmed threats to the elections process posed by Russians, Trump and their allies. Sussmann's defense lawyers accused Durham, for example, of promoting a "baseless narrative that the Clinton campaign conspired with others to trick the federal government into investigating ties between President Trump and Russia."

Mainstream media outlets that provided heavy coverage of the Durham investigation include the *New York Times*, *Washington Post*, *Politico*, *Wall Street Journal* and *New York Post*, with the latter two Murdoch-owned outlets slanting heavily towards pro-Durham coverage, as have *Fox News* and the *National Review*, among others. The coverage is widely known and otherwise available. So, there is little point in seeking to excerpt any of it here except to note that CNN host Jack Tapper prompted pushback by stating after publication of the Durham

Report that it exone[illegible] Tap[illegible] [illegible]idst of his network's sharp political turn to the [illegible] the lead[illegible] its m[illegible] and top management.

We move no[illegible] sever[illegible] well-credentialed independent analys[illegible] ne a[illegible] Durha[illegible] ith its larger political and historical implicatio[illegible]

The first of th[illegible] mpty[illegible] Wheeler, a national security analyst who holds a [illegible] egree [illegible] ogeth[illegible] ecifics of Durham-related news into a wider narrati[illegible] a daily [illegible] ndic[illegible] sample below, the style is informal if not irrev[illegible] back[illegible] rassroots fundraising effort that has enabled pu[illegible] use of [illegible] ipts [illegible] s with rapid delivery from the courthouse, to enab[illegible] that is [illegible] val[illegible] aders.

**Emptywheel** [illegible] w.em[illegible] net[illegible] cerpt:

*Doo-Doo Pro[illegible] rham [illegible] Kno[illegible] an Anthony Trenga and Two Juries,* Empt[illegible] rcy W[illegible] Ph.D.), [illegible] 23.

There[illegible] g gro[illegible] unsa[illegible] John Durham's conduct that has gotten li[illegible] on.

After [illegible] s has ha[illegible] by [illegible] and one judge, in his report Durham neve[illegible] eate[illegible] tion[illegible] chael Sussmann and Igor Danchenko [illegible] have [illegible] uitt[illegible] one discussion of his prosecutoria[illegible] Durham [illegible] d t[illegible] gations," in his executive summary an[illegible] he st[illegible] act, [illegible] n had made false or fabricated statements. [illegible] his [illegible] ustai[illegible] statements allegations, Durham himself mak[illegible] were [illegible] or un[illegible] by the trial records.

As a[illegible] e rese[illegible] to[illegible] a Bank anomaly found it organically, a[illegible] suspici[illegible] rva[illegible] least three Mueller prosecution[illegible] fort, W[illegible] Cohen, [illegible] an der Zwaan) — that Trump and his asso[illegible] ying a[illegible] ties[illegible] odney Joffe shared the Alfa Bank anoma[illegible] ael Su[illegible]

Suss[illegible] ely pac[illegible] the a[illegible] and asked Fusion GPS what they knew ab[illegible] Bank. He [illegible] ller[illegible] aging-up process to Hillary. The campaign de[illegible] oved [illegible] t in[illegible] vith the NYT.

But th[illegible] the c[illegible] he c[illegible] ussmann blew their big story, by sharing th[illegible] s with [illegible]

Next on our list of recommended resources is the work of Wayne Madsen, author of 23 books and a former U.S. Navy intelligence officer and NSA analyst. He provides near-daily reporting and commentary on investigative topics. The topics frequently include Russian leaders and their sinister working relationships with corrupt far-right and far-left extremists in the United States, most often those allied with Trump. He seldom cites sources and instead relies on a near-uncanny memory and a politically diverse array of U.S. and global informants who are confident he would never identify them. Also, he is a risk-taker in certain of his assessments, as indicated by the sample column below, quoted at length with permission.

**The Wayne Madsen Report** (https://www.waynemadsenreport.com). Sample:

*The Durham Report proves one thing: Trump and his minions are out to gut America's intelligence infrastructure in collusion with the Russians*, May 16, 2023.

The Donald Trump- and William Barr-initiated report on the Robert Mueller special counsel investigation of Russia's 2016 collusion with the Trump campaign is out and one thing is pellucidly clear: Trump and Barr special counsel John Durham, the former U.S. Attorney for the District of Connecticut, took every course possible to expose and damage U.S. intelligence methods and relationships.

Durham's task of investigating the investigators, while producing a big "nothing burger" report, did accomplish what Trump and his associates intended and that was to bring about retribution against the FBI, CIA, National Security Agency, and other U.S. (as well as foreign-allied) intelligence agencies that stood united in exposing deep-seated links between Trump, his Trump Organization, Trump son-in-law Jared Kushner, and various Trump campaign officials, including Paul Manafort, Rick Gates, George Papadopoulos, Roger Stone, and Michael Flynn, all convicted by Mueller.

The Durham Report, which relies on open sources, including right-wing polemicist Peter Schweizer, author of *Clinton Cash*, attempts to re-litigate Durham's failed prosecutions of two figures peripherally associated with the 2016 Hillary Clinton campaign – Michael Sussmann and Igor Danchenko – prosecutions that were themselves a miscarriage of justice.

On December 9, 2019, Durham publicly attacked the report by Department of Justice's Inspector-General Michael Horowitz, which had concluded that there was an "authorized purpose" and "adequate factual predication" for the FBI launching the Crossfire Hurricane investigation into the Trump campaign's connections to Russian intelligence. The report by Special Counsel Robert Mueller also stands in sharp contrast to Durham's political screed masquerading as a special counsel report. The Mueller Report, released in redacted form on March 7, 2019, concluded that, "The Russian government interfered in the 2016 presidential election in sweeping and systematic fashion."

The final report by Durham on his four-year long "investigation," which was nothing more than a wasteful fishing expedition that caught nothing, did manage to expose the U.S. Intelligence Community's working relationships with two members of FIVE EYES intelligence sharing pact – the United Kingdom and Australia and two FIVE EYES Third Party members -- Italy and the Netherlands.

Why would Durham set out to castigate and harm the U.S. Intelligence Community?

The answer lies in his purported ties to the secretive Catholic sect Opus Dei, which was founded in Spain in 1928 by Catholic priest Josemaría Escrivá to serve as a foil to the more liberally-inclined Jesuits. While Opus Dei's membership is secret, there are 93,203 active lay members, in addition to clergy. Seventy percent of the lay members are supernumeraries, who contribute money and "other services" to the sect. Not only Durham, but William Barr, former Trump campaign manager Steve Bannon, Supreme Court Associate Justice Clarence Thomas and his far-right activist wife Gini Thomas, as well as Thomas's colleagues on the bench, Samuel Alito and Amy Coney Barrett, are reported to have links to Opus Dei.

Why would Opus Dei want to cover up the Trump campaign's links to Russia?

It should be recalled that American spy for Russia and the USSR, Robert Hanssen, had been associated with Opus Dei, as had his boss, FBI director Louis Freeh. Moreover, the CIA has long monitored the activities of Opus Dei as a threat to U.S. national security. Hanssen and Freeh were congregants of the Opus Dei-linked St. Catherine of Siena Roman Catholic Church in Great Falls, Virginia, located not far from the CIA headquarters in Langley. St. Catherine is noted for its Latin masses. The congregation has counted among its members former U.S. Senator Rick Santorum and the late Supreme Court Associate Justice Antonin Scalia.

Opus Dei, as a promoter of fascism, is a natural ally for Vladimir Putin, who has embraced global fascism in much the same way that his Soviet predecessors championed global communism.

Declassified CIA files reveal that the CIA tracked Opus Dei influence within the government of Spanish dictator Francisco Franco. One file provides background on the Franco regime suffering from a rivalry in his Cabinet between pro- and anti-Opus Dei factions, stating, "Leaders of the National Movement and some military officers in the cabinet are trying to upset the power of the economic ministers who are linked with the Catholic lay society Opus Dei . . . These ministers are responsible for the present economic program, and their enemies cite present economic difficulties in urging Franco to fire them . . . Franco has stood behind his economic ministers, who represent the Opus Dei planners who brought Spain out of its economic difficulties of the late 1950s."

Another CIA report provides a description of Opus Dei by the Basque terrorist organization ETA: "Opus Dei, a secret, reactionary, despotic sect dedicated to the service of financial and landholding capital, under the concealing cloak of a false philosophical humanism and religious apostolate . . . a combination of select tentacles infiltrated on the cultural, political, economic and military levels within the society [it] "might well be described as a state within a state itself." In 1982, CIA files included a report that the "former head of Milan's Banco Ambrosiano, Robert Calve, whose body was found hanging under Blackfriar's Bridge in London, had attempted to reduce the Vatican's debt to the bank by having Opus Dei assume the debt in its entirety."

In 2019, Barr and Durham traveled to Italy to press Italian law enforcement and intelligence on what their possible role was in what Trump called the "Russia hoax." Barr and Durham visited Rome with a pre-conceived notion that the Italian government helped to set up Trump campaign adviser Papadopoulos in 2016 by passing on information to him that Rome had dirt on Hillary Clinton from emails obtained illegally by Russia, that, in turn, were passed by Moscow to WikiLeaks.

Italian officials, including Prime Minister Giuseppe Conte, insisted they had nothing to contribute to Barr's and Durham's cockamamie theory, but they did hand over to Barr and Durham information on an Italian law enforcement criminal investigation into Trump's suspicious financial dealings. Conte said, "our intelligence is completely unrelated to the so-called Russiagate and that has been made clear."

Did the Italian financial criminal matter, which was briefed to Barr and Durham by Gennaro Vecchione, the chief of the Department of Information for Security (DIS), involve Russia's Alfa Bank, which had operations in Italy and reportedly maintained a server in Trump Tower in New York? Barr and Durham buried the Italian intelligence, and it has yet to see the light of day. The Italian information joins the redacted portions of the Mueller Report in the Justice Department's black hole. Attorney General Merrick Garland has a responsibility to the American public to release the Italian dossier and the blacked-out portions of the Mueller Report.

Durham's malign activities to harm U.S. national security, whether it was on behalf of Trump, Opus Dei, or both, proved too much for his Counsel, former U.S. Attorney for the District of Connecticut Nora Dannehy. In September 2020, Dannehy unexpectedly resigned. It was later reported that Dannehy had objected to Durham's and Barr's handling of certain matters, possibly including Barr and Durham deep-sixing the Italian material on Rome's criminal investigation of Trump.

Nora Dannehy, who is married to Leonard Boyle, the former director of the FBI's Terrorist Screening Center, had good reason to object to Durham's running roughshod over America's most closely-guarded intelligence relationships with other nations as well as his desire to indict FBI Confidential Human Sources (CHS). That may have, in part, contributed [illegible] prose[illegible] Durh[illegible] [illegible]al Counsel office resigning in protest over [illegible] [illegible]ctions.

One [illegible] egregio[illegible] [illegible] findings" contained in his report is his reliance [illegible] intel[illegible] [illegible]ysis [illegible] a non-existent "Clinton Plan" to pin a Russia[illegible] [illegible]rump [illegible] 2016 [illegible]. This Russian disinformation, which insinu[illegible] [illegible] the "Clin[illegible] was [illegible] divert attention from Mrs. Clinton's use [illegible] email [illegible] by Durham as coming from a "trusted fore[illegible] [illegible]out in [illegible] [illegible]er 20[illegible] [illegible]nded by Director of National Intelligence [illegible] Ratcl[illegible] [illegible]ght-w[illegible] [illegible]ter of Trump -- to Senate Judiciary Com[illegible] [illegible]mar[illegible] [illegible]anar[illegible]

Durha[illegible] even ha[illegible] it tha[illegible] [illegible]alled "Clinton Plan" was seeded with Russian [illegible]ion: "[illegible] [illegible]cliffe made to Senate Judiciary Chairman Lin[illegible] [illegible]in a [illegible] 29, [illegible]er: 'The [intelligence community] [illegible] know the [illegible] of th[illegible] or the extent to which the Russian intel[illegible] [illegible]ysis m[illegible] exagg[illegible] fabrication.'" [emphasis added]. Even [illegible]m's ca[illegible] Ju[illegible] [illegible]mittee Chairman Jim Jordan used the "Cli[illegible] - which [illegible] [illegible]ormation masked as an "analysis rep[illegible] Russia[illegible] [illegible] the FBI and other agencies for lying about th[illegible] [illegible]zation[illegible] [illegible]gen[illegible]

The fa[illegible] intellig[illegible] [illegible]luced [illegible]Plan" was relied upon by Durham in an [illegible] gain [illegible] [illegible]nard Benardo, the executive vice presiden[illegible] Soros' [illegible] Society [illegible]s. In yet another example of Durham's pa[illegible] [illegible] expe[illegible] tried [illegible]y subpoenaing Benardo's email that he could [illegible] with [illegible] in [illegible] claim that they had obtained the Clinton Plan [illegible] into Ben[illegible] [illegible] in the fake "Clinton Plan" had been obtain[illegible] from Ru[illegible] [illegible]llig[illegible] Dutch intelligence agency, the General Inte[illegible] Secur[illegible] (AIVD [illegible]ling the fake Clinton Plan, Durham and [illegible] [illegible]rned a [illegible] Third [illegible]ncy and the AIVD was reportedly in[illegible] the [illegible] the[illegible] to U.S. intelligence is strictest confidence h[illegible] [illegible]ealed.

In add[illegible] [illegible]r and D[illegible] [illegible] the Netherlands, they also undermined [illegible] intellige[illegible] [illegible]rshi[illegible] [illegible]tralia. Barr also called Australia's rig[illegible] Prime Min[illegible] [illegible]t Mor[illegible] [illegible]ting for dirt on Trump's opponents. [illegible] targete[illegible] Aus[illegible] [illegible]eign Minister Alexander Downer, who [illegible] [illegible]ing as [illegible] High [illegible]oner in London, was told by a drunken Papa[illegible] during [illegible] May [illegible] [illegible]ncounter in London, about Russian med[illegible] 2016 [illegible] [illegible]ember of Morrison's Liberal Party, repor[illegible] [illegible]act an[illegible] on the [illegible]per diplomatic channels. Durham, wit[illegible] [illegible]s, conc[illegible] [illegible]at the [illegible]ed its Crossfire Hurricane investigation [illegible] camp[illegible] [illegible]d on [illegible]d" information from Downer.

However, it was not Downer's information but that passed to him by Papadopoulos in a London bar that partially served as a predicate for Crossfire Hurricane. Intelligence officers are savvy enough when it comes to drunks spilling secrets in public.

Barr was also in London to ask for help in investigating former MI-6 agent Christopher Steele, the author of the "Steele Dossier" that describes Trump's various connections to Russian intelligence and mob figures. British intelligence was hesitant to cooperate with Barr in his nonsensical pursuit of Steele, at one time MI-6's top Russia expert as one of the more valued members of Her Majesty's Secret Service. The Durham Report also appears to implicate British Prime Minister David Cameron in the bizarre conspiracy theory about a worldwide anti-Trump cabal afoot in 2016.

The repetitive and pedantic Durham Report represents a four-year effort to demonize the networks U.S. intelligence rely upon to maintain national security. Durham sees four U.S. intelligence partners – the UK, Australia, the Netherlands, and Italy – as some secretive plotters to damage Trump. Along with these nations, private intelligence companies used by American and foreign intelligence to conduct open source research and analysis were similarly attacked in the Durham screed. These include Glenn Simpson's Fusion GPS, Christopher Steele's Orbis Business Intelligence, and Charles Dolan of the kglobal [sic] and Ketchum public relations firms (Dolan was the interface with Ritz Carlton Moscow hotel staff, including its German national general manager, that allegedly provided the intelligence that Trump had engaged in what the Durham Report calls "salacious sexual conduct" at the hotel involving prostitutes urinating on each other while on the presidential suite bed where President and Mrs. Obama previously slept during their Moscow state visit), Neustar, Inc. of cyber-security expert Rodney Joffe, the Brookings Institution, the Russian-American Chamber of Commerce in New York, the Perkins Coie law firm that conducted open source research (project Crimson Rhino) on Russian involvement in the 2016 election, the Clinton Foundation, Rodney Joffe's Packet Forensics, and Servers.com, a Cyprus-based computer firm.

Just as the convicted Scooter Libby, the chief of staff for Vice President Dick Cheney who was pardoned by Trump, revealed the identity of CIA clandestine agent Valerie Plame and her Brewster Jennings & Associates cover firm, Durham has seen fit to expose several possible U.S. intelligence business partners to America's enemies. Calls for Durham to be investigated appear warranted given the wide brush that he used to expose U.S. intelligence sources and methods.

Durham's quixotic quest to prove a non-existent conspiracy theory of the Clinton campaign in the persons of campaign chairperson John Podesta, campaign manager Robby Mook, campaign senior policy adviser Jake Sullivan, campaign counsel Marc Elias, and campaign communications director Jennifer Palmieri working together with Attorney General Loretta Lynch, CIA director John Brennan, DNI James Clapper, and the FBI's Andrew McCabe, Peter Strzok, and Lisa Page to tie Trump to Russia falls flat. So, too, does Durham's lame attempt to implicate several journalists in his conspiracy, including Steve LeVine of Quartz, Franklin Foer of Slate, Jane Mayer of New Yorker, ABC News producer Matthew Mosk, Tom Hamburger of The Washington Post, Michael Isikoff of Yahoo! News, David Cohen of Politico, Catherine Belton of the Financial Times, Eric Lichtblau and Steven Lee Myers of The New York Times, Bradley Hoe, Michael Rothfeld, and Alan Cullison of The Wall Street Journal, Paul Wood of the BBC, David Corn of Mother Jones, and Mark Hosenball of Reuters.

Durham's crazy conspiracy theory even involves secretive meetings between journalists and Christopher Steele and Glenn Simpson at Washington's famed Tabard Inn and alleged conspirators using the cover names "Ms. Tina Wells" and "Mr. Bob Hale," which Durham reveals – *<drum roll>* -- are references to the actors who played "Mary Ann" and the "Skipper" on the television series "Gilligan's Island." Durham also reveals that "'Mary Ann' was actually played by Dawn Wells and the 'Skipper' was played by Alan Hale." In reality, the Skipper was played by Alan Hale, Jr. His father, Alan Hale, Sr., was an actor who often appeared in Errol Flynn and Lon Chaney movies. Imagine, a four-year investigation by Durham results in a review of "Gilligan's Island." Perhaps, the Durham Report should forever be known as the "Gilligan Report."

As with everything involving Trump and the Republicans, the name of the game is projection. What Durham wasted four years and millions of dollars of taxpayers' money to come up with is a report that attempts to tie the Clinton campaign, various law enforcement and intelligence officials, foreign nations, private businesses, and journalists in a vast conspiracy to "get Trump." That sort of fiction hasn't been seen from the Republicans since its grand conspiracy of Dominion Voting Systems and Smartmatic, Italian servers, Chinese thermostats and bamboo-infused paper ballots, a deceased Hugo Chavez, and Fox News's own election decision desk all conspiring to ensure Trump's defeat in the 2020 election. That silly conspiracy has cost Fox News a quarter billion dollars in its lawsuit settlement with Dominion. Durham's silly conspiracy theory, on the other hand, has cost the taxpayers $6.5 million that will never be recouped and strongly smells of Opus Dei fascist meddling.

Durham's report also identifies by name several lower-level employees of the FBI and Justice Department, including staffers in Special Counsel Mueller's office. In an era when Trump supporters routinely threaten to kill public officials, this is, perhaps, Durham's greatest crime against the nation. Trump wasted no time in commenting on his Truth Social platform about the Durham Report. He wrote: TREASON! More than a few insane Trump supporters may very well act as judge, jury, and executioner and Durham and his Opus Dei friends will have blood on their hands.

As further context and as a *caveat* to the above column, this editor notes that it is rarely, if ever, possible for an outsider to state with certainty whether high-profile individuals are "members" of Opus Dei. That is because the society uses sophisticated methods to hide its most active adherents and their activities. Opus Dei has been far more successful at hiding them than such powerful societies as the Skull and Bones, the secretive body founded at Yale University in 1832. Even two recent books, *Opus Dei* by Michael Walsh (2004) and *Opus Dei* by John L. Allen, Jr. (2005), failed to identify recent important Americans in the society despite the authors' announced intentions to reveal the facts. In that spirit, even partial revelations and commentary when the objectives are important so long as the research is undertaken in good faith. In this instance, Madsen drew on considerable experience and sourcing to suggest motivations that few other reporters would dare examine.

Finally, we recommend for further study of Durham's work the work of commentator, author, attorney and professor Seth Abramson, who publishes on Substack in addition to his prolific output of books (including the impressive trilogy *Proof of Collusion*, *Proof of Conspiracy* and *Proof of Corruption*), plus his broadcast appearances and social media messaging.

> Proof, (https://sethabramson.substack.com/p). Here is a lengthy excerpt from a commentary in May 2023, which addresses legal issues relevant to former President Trump, whose sinister methods to win election in 2016 and augment power afterward provide much of the material for Abramson's work:
>
> *Investigative Commentary on The Trump Trials, Vol. 15: New Indictments Now Expected; NYC Criminal Trial Date Set; a Finding of Sexual Abuse and Defamation*, Seth Abramson, May 24, 2023. *This new Proof series — authored by a longtime criminal defense attorney and leading Trump biographer — will unpack recent events in the historic trials of disgraced former president Donald Trump.*
>
> Department of Justice Special Counsel Jack Smith is said to be wrapping up the significantly easier part of his two-part remit — the Mar-a-Lago stolen documents probe — and according to the *Wall Street Journal*, Donald Trump and his lawyers expect the former president to be indicted. You can read about this here.
>
> Apparently Trump and his counsel are now so certain he's about to be indicted — potentially for Obstruction of Justice but maybe also, now, given the evidence Smith has that Trump well knew that he could not legally take the documents, under the even-more-serious Espionage Act — that they have made an extraordinary request to meet in private with Attorney General Merrick Garland.
>
> This request is certain to go nowhere, as it would constitute unprecedented interference by Main Justice in the work of one of its special counsels (albeit just the sort of interference Trump eagerly sought from his own DOJ when he was president) and because it includes in its sole paragraph a wholly baseless claim that the famously independent and nonpartisan Smith is in fact some sort of Democratic Party operative, but it does underscore that if Trump were still President of the United States this would be the moment that he'd fire Smith in the same way he repeatedly tried to fire Robert Mueller during the Trump-Russia investigation.

What [illegible] ring ab[illegible] [illegible] that with Trump already under dozens of fel[illegible] ents in [illegible] m; w[illegible] -certainty that he'll soon face federal feloni[illegible] stea[illegible] ossil[illegible] to profit from) classified documents fr[illegible] ite Ho[illegible] ulton [illegible] istrict Attorney Fani Willis apparently p[illegible] dict T[illegible] ugus[illegible] elonies; with Smith currently widening rat[illegible] rowin[illegible] sec[illegible] ederal criminal investigation into Trump ([illegible] lving [illegible] and [illegible] p himself making sure that his Sexual Abus[illegible] ation [illegible] ntin[illegible] the news for the rest of this year and ne[illegible], we'r[illegible] at a p[illegible] candidate who'll be in more civil and crim[illegible] ouble [illegible] ary [illegible] in American history.

Inde[illegible] Gove[illegible] DeSa[illegible] himself to announce his candidacy to[illegible] nesday [illegible] 2023 [illegible] er Spaces event with white supremacist [illegible] d is cle[illegible] ever[illegible] t DeSantis does not expect to beat Trump [illegible] s expec[illegible] nt[illegible] ed out of the 2024 campaign by outside forc[illegible]

# Bibliography

## *The Complete Durham 'Russiagate' Report*

## Books


Abramson, Seth. *Proof of Collusion: How Trump Betrayed America.* Simon & Schuster, 2018.

——— *Proof of Conspiracy: How Trump's International Collusion Is Threatening America.* St. Martin's Press, 2019.

——— *Proof of Corruption: Bribery, Impeachment, and Pandemic in the Age of Trump.* St. Martin's Press, 2020.

——— *Proof of Coup: How the Pentagon Shaped An Insurrection.* Substack, 2022.

Alberta, Tim. *American Carnage: On The Front Lines of the Republican Civil War and the Rise of President Trump.* Harper Collins, 2019.

Allen, John L., Jr. *Opus Dei: An Objective Look Behind the Myths and Reality of the Most Controversial Force in the Catholic Church.* Doubleday, 2005.

Applebaum, Anne. *Autocracy, Inc.: The Dictators Who Want to Run the World.*, Doubleday, 2024

Baker, Peter and Susan Glasser. *Divider: Trump in the White House, 2017-2021.* Doubleday/Penguin Random House, 2022.

Baron, Martin. *Collision of Power: Trump, Bezos, and The Washington Post.* Flatiron Books, 2023.

Bauer, Bob. *The Unraveling: Reflections on Politics without Ethics and Democracy in Crisis.* Rowman & Littlefield, 2024.

Belton, Catherine. *Putin's People: How the KGB Took Back Russia and Then Took On the West*, Farrar, Straus and Giroux, 2020.

Benen, Steve. *Ministry of Truth: Democracy, Reality, and the Republicans' War on the Recent Past*, Mariner Books, 2024.

Berman, Andrew. *Holding the Line: Inside the Nation's Preeminent U.S. Attorney's Office and Its Battle With the Trump Justice Department.* Penguin Press, 2022.

Blackman, Ann and Elaine Shannon. *The Spy Next Door: The Extraordinary Secret Life of Robert Philip Hanssen, the Most Damaging FBI Agent in U.S. History.* Little, Brown and Company, 2008.

Boyd-Barrett, Oliver. *RussiaGate and Propaganda.* Routledge, July 9, 2019.

Browder, Bill. *Red Notice: A True Story of High Finance, Murder, and One Man's Fight for Justice*, Simon & Schuster, 2015.

——— *Freezing Order: A True Story of Money Laundering, Murder, and Surviving Vladimir Putin's Wrath.* Simon & Schuster, 2022.

Campbell, Josh. *Crossfire Hurricane: Inside Donald's War on the FBI.* Algonquin Books, 2019.

Cheney, Liz. *Oath and Honor: A Memoir and a Warning.* Little, Brown and Company, 2023.

Cohen, Bryan Tyler. *Shameless: Republicans' Deliberate Misfunction and the Battle To Preserve Democracy.* Harper, 2024.

Cohen, Michael. *Disloyal: The True Story of the Former Personal Attorney To President Donald J. Trump.* Skyhorse Publishing, 2020.

——— *Revenge: How Donald Trump Weaponized the U.S. Department of Justice Against His Critics.* Melville House, 2022.

Cohen, Stephen F. *War With Russia? From Putin & Ukraine to Trump & Russiagate*, Hot Books, 2022.

Comey, James. *A Higher Loyalty: Truth, Lies, and Leadership.* Flatiron Books, 2018.

Durham, John H and Henry C. Garlander. *The Durham Report: Report on Matters Related to Intelligence Activities and Investigations Arising Out of the 2016 Presidential Campaigns.* May 23, 2023, Independently published.

Fitzpatrick, Robert with Jon Land. *Betrayal: Whitey Bulger and the FBI Agent Who Fought To Bring Him Down.* Tom Doherty Associates, 2011.

Gates, Rick. *Wicked Game: An Insider's Story on How Trump Won, Mueller Failed, and America Lost.* Post Hill Press, 2020.

Gessen, Masha. *The Man Without a Face: The Unlikely Rise of Vladimir Putin*, Riverhead Books, 2013.

Green, Joshua. *Devil's Bargain: Steve Bannon, Donald Trump, and the Storming of the Presidency.* Penguin Press, 2017.

Harding, Luke. *Collusion: Secret Meetings, Dirty Money, and How Russia Helped Donald Trump Win.* Vintage, 2017.

Hill, Fiona and Clifford G. Gaddy, *Mr. Putin: Operative in the Kremlin.* Brookings Institution Press, 2013.

Honig, Elie. *Hatchet Man: How Bill Barr Broke the Prosecutor's Code and Corrupted the Justice Department.* HarperCollins, 2021.

Isikoff, Michael and David Corn. *Russian Roulette: The Inside Story of Putin's War on American and the Election of Donald Trump.* Twelve Books/Hachette Book Group, 2018.

January 6th Committee with introduction by Ari Melber. *January 6 Report.* Harper Paperbacks, 2022.

Karl, Jonathan. *Front Row at the Trump Show.* Dutton/Penguin Random House, 2020.

——— *Betrayal: The Final Act of the Trump Show.* Dutton/Penguin Random House, 2021.

Kinzinger, Adam and Michael D'Antonio. *Renegade: Defending Democracy and Liberty in Our Divided Country.* The Open Field, 2023.

Kushner, Jared. *Breaking History: A White House Memoir.* Broadside Books, 2022.

Lehr, Dick and Gerard O'Neill. *Black Mass: The Irish Mob, The FBI, and A Devil's Deal.* PublicAffairs, 2000.

——— *Whitey: the Life of America's Most Notorious Crime Boss.* Broadway Books/Crown/Random House, 2013.

Leonnig, Carol and Philip Rucker. *I Alone Can Fix It: Donald J. Trump's Catastrophic Final Year.* Penguin Press, 2021.

Levine, Steve. *Putin's Labyrinth: Spies, Murder, and the Dark Heart of the New Russia.* Random House, 2008.

Madsen, Wayne. *Cafe Vaterland: A Novella Set for our Time In Alternate Realty.* WMR Books, 2019.

——— *The Rise of the Fascist Fourth: The Era of Trumpism and the Far-Right.* WMR Books, 2021.

——— *A Parade of New Sovereignties: A Post-Hegemonic World.* WMR Books, 2023.

Manafort, Paul. *Political Prisoner: Persecuted, Prosecuted, but Not Silenced.* Skyhorse Publishing, 2022.

McCabe. Andrew. *The Threat: How the FBI Protects America in the Age of Terror and Trump.* St. Martin's Press, 2019.

McCarthy, Andrew C. *Ball of Collusion: The Plot To Rig an Election and Destroy a Presidency.* Encounter Books, 2019.

Meier, Barry. *Spooked: The Dossier, Black Cube, and the Rise of Private Spies.* Harper Collins, 2021.

Myers, Steven Lee. *The New Tsar: The Rise and Reign of Vladimir Putin.* Alfred A. Knopf, 2015.

Mueller, Robert. *The Mueller Report: Final Special Counsel Report of President Donald J. Trump & Russia Collusion.* Sastrugi Press/Thirteen Colony Press, 2019.

Nance, Malcolm W. *The Plot to Hack America: How Putin's Cyberspies and WikiLeaks Tried to Steal the 2016 Election*, Skyhorse Publishing, 2016.

——— *The Plot to Destroy Democracy: How Putin and His Spies Are Undermining America and Dismantling the West.* Legacy Lit, 2018.

——— *The Plot to Betray America: How Team Trump Embraced Out Enemies, Compromised Our Security, and How We Can Fix It.* Hachette, 2019.

Nelson, Anne. *Shadow Network: Media, Money and the Secret Hub of the Radical Right.* Bloomsbury Publishing, 2019.

Omarosa (Manigault Newman). *Unhinged: An Insider's Account of the Trump White House.* Gallery Books, 2018.

Papadopoulos, George. *Deep State Target: How I Got Caught in the Crosshairs of the Plot to Bring Down President Trump.* Diversion Books, 2019.

Parnas, Lev and Jerry Langton. *Shadow Diplomacy: Lev Parnas' Wild Ride from Brooklyn, NY to Donald Trump's Inner Circle.* Bronxkill Publishing, 2024.

Reeve, Elle. *Black Pill: How I Witnessed the Darkest Corners of the Internet Come to Life, Poison Society, and Capture American Politics.* Atria, 2024

Richardson, Heather Cox. *Democracy Awakening: Notes on the State of America.* Viking, 2023.

Riggleman, Denver. *The Breach: The Untold Story of the Investigation into January 6th.* Henry Holt & Co., 2022.

Rhode, David. *Where Tyranny Begins: The Justice Department, the FBI, and the War on Democracy.* W.W. Norton, 2024.

Sawka, Richard, *Deception: Russiagate and the New Cold War*, Lexington Books, 2021.

Simpson, Glenn and Peter Fritsch. *Crime In Progress: Inside the Steele Dossier and the Fusion GP Investigation of Donald Trump.* Random House, 2019.

Sims, Cliff. *Team of Vipers: My 500 Extraordinary Days in the Trump White House.* Thomas Dunn Books/St. Martin's Press, 2019.

Steele, Christopher. *Unredacted: Russia, Trump, and the Fight for Democracy.* Mariner, 2024.

Stelter, Brian. *Hoax: Donald Trump, Fox News, and the Dangerous Distortion of Truth.* Atria/One Signal Publishers, 2021.

Stone, Roger. *The Making of the President: How Donald Trump Orchestrated a Revolution.* Skyhorse Publishing, 2017.

Strzok, Peter. *Compromised: Counterintelligence and the Threat of Donald J. Trump.* Mariner Books, 2020.

Sullivan, John J. *Midnight in Moscow: A Memoir from the Front Lines of Russia's War Against the West.* Little, Brown and Company, 2024.

Sullivan, Margaret. *Ghosting the News: Local Journalism and the Crisis of American Democracy.* Columbia Global Reports, 2020.

Thomas, Bill and Charles Sutherland. *Red Tape: Adventure Capitalism in the New Russia.* Dutton, 1992.

Unger, Craig. *House of Trump, House of Putin: The Untold Story of Donald Trump and the Russian Mafia.* Dutton, 2018.

——— *American Kompromat: How the KGB Cultivated Donald Trump and Related Tales of Sex, Greed, Power, and Treachery.* Dutton, 2021.

Vise, David A. *The Bureau and the Mole: The Unmasking of Robert Philip Hanssen, the Most Dangerous Double Agent in FBI History.* Atlantic Monthly Press, 2002.

Vogler, Christopher. *The Writer's Journey: Mythic Structure for Writers.* Michael Wiese Productions, 2020.

Walsh, Michael. *Opus Dei: An Investigation Into the Powerful, Secretive Society Within the Catholic Church.* HarperCollins, 2004.

Ward, Vicky. *Kushner, Inc.: Greed. Ambition. Corruption.* St. Martin's Press, 2019.

Weiner, Tim, David Johnston and Neil A. Lewis. *Betrayal: The Story of Aldrich Ames, An American Spy.* Random House, 1995.

Weissmann, Andrew. *Where Law Ends: Inside the Mueller Investigation.* Random House, 2020.

Wise, David. Spy: *The Inside Story of How the FBI's Robert Hanssen Betrayed America.* Random House, 2002.

Wolff, Michael. *Siege: Trump Under Fire.* Henry Holt, 2019.

Woodward, Bob. *War.* Simon & Schuster, 2024.

Woodward, Bob and Robert Costa. *Peril.* Simon & Schuster, 2021.

Zebley, Aaron, James Quarles and Andrew Goldstein. *Interference: The Inside Story of Trump, Russia, and the Mueller Investigation.* Simon & Schuster, 2024.

# Official Reports

## 2023

U.S. Congress [illegible] ciary C[illegible] *[illegible]tter to Attorney General Garland on Jack Smith In[illegible]*, 202[illegible] [illegible]023-2024). (Committee Chair: U.S. Rep. Jim [illegible]) (htt[illegible].house[illegible]/evo-subsites/republicans-judiciary[illegible]es/evo-[illegible]1-jdj-to-garland-re-durham-report.pdf

## 2020

U.S. Congress [illegible] Committee [illegible] Intelligence [illegible] 116-290, Report of the Select Committee [illegible] Intelligence U[illegible] Senate [illegible] Active Measures Campaigns and Interference [illegible] 2016 U.S. [illegible] Volume [illegible]ia's Use of Social Media, with Additional [illegible] 10, 20[illegible] Congress[illegible], 2019-2020). (Committee Chair: U.S. Sen. [illegible], R-NC[illegible] Mark Warner, D-VA). (Redacted Report: [illegible] congress[illegible]PT-116srpt290.pdf).

Abstract (via [illegible] Nebraska [illegible] Digi[illegible]): In 2016, Russian operatives associated [illegible] Petersburg [illegible] Internet [illegible] Agency (IRA) used social media to conduct [illegible] warfare [illegible] designed [illegible]ad disinformation and societal division in [illegible] States [illegible] these operatives used targeted advertising [illegible]onally [illegible]erated content, and social media platforms [illegible] act with [illegible] of millions of social media users in the United [illegible] campaign [illegible]ans on the basis of societal, ideological [illegible] differences [illegible]nts, and was part of a foreign government [illegible] supported [illegible] favor[illegible] in the U.S. presidential election.

The Senate [illegible] on [illegible] undertook [illegible] of these events, consistent with its congressional [illegible] to oversee [illegible] conduct [illegible] the intelligence activities and programs [illegible] United States [illegible] effectiveness of the Intelligence Community [illegible] intelligence [illegible] work of the professional staff of the Committee [illegible] Committee [illegible] drew [illegible]put of cybersecurity professionals, social media [illegible], U.S. [illegible]ment [illegible]nce agencies, and researchers and experts [illegible] work and [illegible] information, hate speech, algorithms, and automation [illegible] ing under [illegible] tee's Technical Advisory Group (TAG). [illegible] found [illegible] IRA [illegible]ence the 2016 U.S. presidential election [illegible] Hillary C[illegible] supporting Donald Trump at the direction [illegible]in. Th[illegible] found [illegible] IRA' s information warfare campaign was broad [illegible] ental [illegible] t of the 2016 presidential election. Further, [illegible]'s an[illegible] IRA [illegible] social media supports the key judgment [illegible] January 6, 20[illegible] Intelligence [illegible] Assessment, "Assessing Russian Activities [illegible] in Re[illegible] Election[illegible] Russia's, goals were to undermine public fa[illegible] democra[illegible] Hillary Clinton,· and harm her electability [illegible] presidency [illegible] Intelligence Community assessed that the [illegible] government [illegible] help [illegible] Trump's election chances when possible [illegible] Secretary [illegible] casting her unfavorably to him," the Committee [illegible] IRA [illegible] and almost invariably supportive of then-[illegible] Trump, ar[illegible] Clinton's campaign.

**2019**

U.S. Department of Justice, Office of the Inspector General, *Review of Four FISA Applications and Other Aspects of the FBI's Crossfire Hurricane Investigation*, Inspector General Michael E. Horowitz, December 9, 2019.

U.S. Department of Justice, Office of the Inspector General, Report of Investigation of Former Federal Bureau of Investigation Director James Comey's Disclosure of Sensitive Investigative Information and Handling of Certain Memoranda, Inspector General Michael E. Horowitz, August 29, 2019.

# News & Commentary

**2024**

**December**

Dec. 2

Meidas Touch Network, *Investigative Commentary: The Big Reason Why Hunter's Pardon is Justified: Kash Patel*, Ron Filipkowski, Dec. 2, 2024. *I've listened to hundreds of interviews of Trump's FBI Director nominee.* I was surprised by some of the reaction from those in the media, the Never Trump (former) Republicans, and a few Democratic elected officials. None of these things address the REAL reason for the pardon: Trump's appointment of Patel, who has ranted and raved for the past four years on every right-wing podcast in America that he was going to get Hunter Biden for things he has never been prosecuted for. Joe takes that threat seriously. Apparently, the critics either do not, or are ignorant and unaware of exactly who Patel is and what he has pledged to do specific to Hunter.

The Bulwark, *Opinion: The Father, the Son, and Kash Patel*, William Kristol, Dec. 2, 2024. *One thing can be bad and another thing can be much worse.* President Biden made a mistake. But the problem with Donald Trump and his appointees isn't that they'll make mistakes. It is that the whole Trump presidency is animated by a plan to create centralized, personalized, unconstrained, and unaccountable power in the president and his agents.

Dec. 1

New York Times, *Biden Pardons His Son Hunter*, Staff Reports, Dec. 1, 2024. After months of vowing to respect the judicial process, President Biden made it clear that his decision was as much personal as it was presidential.

**November**

Nov. 30

New York Times, *Trump Says He Will Nominate Kash Patel to Run F.B.I.*, Devlin Barrett and Maggie Haberman, Nov. 30, 2024. *President-elect Donald J. Trump said on Saturday that he wants to replace*

*Christopher A. Wray, the F.B.I. director, with Kash Patel, a hard-line critic of the bureau who has called for shutting down the agency's Washington headquarters, firing its leadership and bringing the nation's law enforcement agencies "to heel."*

Mr. Trump's planned nomination of Mr. Patel has echoes of his failed attempt to place another partisan firebrand, Matt Gaetz, atop the Justice Department as attorney general. It could run into hurdles in the Senate, which will be called on to confirm him, and is sure to send shock waves through the F.B.I., which Mr. Trump and his allies have come to view as part of a "deep state" conspiracy against him. Mr. Patel has been closely aligned with Mr. Trump's belief that much of the nation's law enforcement and national security establishment needs to be purged of bias and held accountable for what they see as unjustified investigations and prosecutions of Mr. Trump and his allies. Mr. Patel "played a pivotal role in uncovering the Russia, Russia, Russia Hoax, standing as an advocate for truth, accountability and the Constitution," Mr. Trump said in announcing his choice in a social media post. Before leaving office in early 2021, Mr. Trump floated the idea of making Mr. Patel deputy director of either the C.I.A. or the F.B.I. William P. Barr, the attorney general at the time, wrote in his memoir that Mr. Patel would have become deputy F.B.I. director only "over my dead body."

Nov. 28

Washington Post, *Analysis: Trump's plans for disruption, retribution explained through Cabinet picks*, Amber Phillips, Nov. 29, 2024 (print ed.). On some choices, his strategy is clear: Disruption and retribution.

Nov. 27

MSNBC Alex Wagner Tonight, *DOJ braces for corruption of department as Trump prioritizes revenge,* Nov. 27, 2024. David Rohde, national security editor for NBC News, discusses how prosecutors at the Justice Department are preparing to be the subject of weaponized investigations at the hands of Pam Bondi to appease Donald Trump's desire for revenge for efforts to hold him accountable.

Nov. 26

Newsweek, *Adam Schiff Questions If Trump's AG Will Target Jurors Who Indicted Him*, Sonam Sheth, Nov. 26, 2024. *Schiff Reminds His GOP Colleagues The Outcome Of Trump Hush Money Trial.* California U.S. Representative Adam Schiff questioned on Tuesday whether President-elect Donald Trump's next attorney general will go after the grand jurors who voted to indict Trump. "Is she also going to go after the grand jurors who found there was probable cause to believe he was engaged in multiple crimes?" Schiff said on MSNBC, referring to Trump's attorney general nominee, Pam Bondi. During his MSNBC interview on Tuesday, Schiff, who recently won his Senate race in California, mentioned special counsel John Durham, who was tapped to investigate the Justice Department's inquiry into Russia's interference in the 2016 U.S. election. "You can very well see a lot of prosecutors, like Durham, who spend millions of taxpayer dollars to come up with nothing," Schiff told MSNBC's Nicolle Wallace. "Pam Bondi follows through with what she's pledged to do, which is to investigate nonexistent voter fraud, for example, or to go after the prosecutors."

Trump repeatedly suggested arresting Schiff for "treason," though there was no evidence that Schiff had engaged in any wrongdoing. In one post to X, formerly Twitter, Trump demanded that Schiff be "questioned at the highest level for Fraud & Treason," claiming his "lies were made in perhaps the most blatant and sinister manner ever seen in the great Chamber."

["It's clear that Trump wants a whole bunch of John Durhams in the Justice Department," responded MSNBC "Deadline: White House" Host Nicolle Wallace.]

Nov 20

Emptywheel, Analysis: *With Matt Gaetz, Donald Trump's Myth Cannot Fail — It Can Only Be Failed*, Emptywheel (Marcy Wheeler), Nov. 20, 2024. I keep thinking back to this June 2023 exchange between Matt Gaetz and John Durham. It came at the end of Durham's testimony after delivering his report, in which Durham said a lot of inflammatory things, but ultimately concluded that the allegations of Russian interference should have been investigated, but should have been opened at a lower level of investigation.

After four years, Durham blamed Hillary Clinton for things Russians (like those suspected of filling the Christopher Steele dossier with disinformation) had done. But he hadn't done the one thing Republicans needed him to do: assert that the Russian investigation was a hoax. At the end of it, Jim Jordan adopted a tactic he has come to use in his hearings. He took a break for votes, giving staffers a half hour to prepare a rebuttal. And then three Republican members took turns, including Matt Gaetz for his second turn, unrebutted by any Democratic member. Durham fabricated a key part of the theory of his case. He ignored key events — most notably, Trump's invitation for Russia to hack his opponent — that made all the actions of Hillary's people make sense. He relied on a Twitter account as the foundation of his indictment against Igor Danchenko, then whined when such communications were deemed inadmissible without a witness to introduce them.

Yet ultimately, the rules of criminal procedure and some very, very good defense attorneys (no doubt paid with life savings) managed to thwart Durham's efforts to spin from his own fevered imaginations a conspiracy implicating Hillary Clinton....Because reality ultimately debunked Durham's conspiracy theories, Gaetz deemed him to be part of the Deep State.

Nov. 19

Politico, *This Lawyer Has Some Advice for Trump's Would-Be Targets: Take A Vacation*, Ian Ward, Nov. 19, 2024 (print ed.). The first few days and weeks of the Trump administration will signal how serious they will be about going after perceived enemies. Zaid's new clientele — which includes dozens of current and former government officials — have good reason to be concerned. On the campaign trail, Trump promised to carry out a campaign of retribution and revenge against his critics, including specific members of Congress, the media and even the private sector. Trump and his allies have since downplayed these remarks, dismissing them as just so much Trumpian bluster. But Zaid is advising his clients not to take any chances.

Nov. 17

NBC News, *DOJ and FBI officials reach out to lawyers as potential Trump revenge prosecutions loom*, David Rohde and Ken Dilanian, Nov. 17, 2024. Legal experts say Trump's choice for attorney general, Matt Gaetz, signals the president-elect's determination to tightly control the Justice Department and prosecute adversaries. Multiple current and former senior Justice Department and FBI officials have begun reaching out to lawyers in anticipation of being criminally investigated by the Trump administration, according to three people with knowledge of their deliberations.

Nov. 10

Politico, *Law* [illegible] *rump's* [illegible] *dictate Justice Department actions*, Josh Gerstein [illegible] 24. [illegible] says history and law support any president [illegible] start [illegible] etta, who served as legal counsel to Vice Pres[illegible] ence and [illegible] Off[illegible] ement and Budget in the first Trump administ[illegible] Thursd[illegible] no [illegible] ent for any president to stay out of Justice D[illegible] cisions.

Nov. 9

Washington P[illegible] *es pus*[illegible] *Sm*[illegible] *retribution vow*, Isaac Arnsdorf, Perry Stein, Jo[illegible] Sper[illegible] Nov. [illegible] t ed.). Even as Jack Smith moved to wind do[illegible] elec[illegible] ence [illegible] Donald Trump on Friday, House Republi[illegible] tial st[illegible] ecial counsel, setting up an early test of how [illegible] elect's [illegible] out [illegible] t.

House J[illegible] an J[illegible] Ohi[illegible] Barry Loudermilk (R-Georgia) asked Smith's [illegible] e all [illegible] document and election interference probes, [illegible] step [illegible] onal [illegible] aw enforcement investigations and litigation [illegible], the [illegible] an $100 million boosting Trump's campaig[illegible] to the [illegible] posting, "Jack Smith's abuse of the justice s[illegible] go un[illegible] eatedly on the campaign trail to stop Smith's [illegible] d use [illegible] al law enforcement against President Joe Bide[illegible] itics, [illegible] s. He argued without evidence that the fede[illegible] s he fa[illegible] itica[illegible]. In the final weeks of the campaign, Trump s[illegible] quickly [illegible] h and [illegible] eporting him. "He should be thrown out of th[illegible] rump sa[illegible] on "[illegible]," a conservative radio talk show.

Nov. 8

New York T[illegible] *sia C*[illegible] *erence Efforts*, Steven Lee Myers and Julian E[illegible] 8, 20[illegible] did not bother to hide its efforts to influence [illegible] S. pr[illegible] the past. In the final days before Tuesday[illegible] bando[illegible] tense [illegible] ot trying to interfere in the American president[illegible]

The Kre[illegible] tion [illegible] late wave of fabricated videos that targeted [illegible] process [illegible] al ticket but also no longer bothered to hide [illegible] oducing [illegible] claiming election fraud in Arizona was con[illegible] irect[illegible] in [illegible] a Terada, who returned to Russia in 2021 aft[illegible] son [illegible] or money laundering. What impact Russia's i[illegible] ampaign [illegible] year's race, if any, remains uncertain. There is [illegible] gh, th[illegible] azen effort by the Kremlin, one that has left [illegible] overn[illegible] to rebut the falsehoods as they gain populari[illegible] one [illegible] ared [illegible] ade game Whac-a-Mole. This year's election [illegible] w m[illegible] inter[illegible] nd disinformation generally — has become [illegible] erica[illegible] ed social media platforms like X and Telegram [illegible] the co[illegible] itu[illegible] ns of free speech, have opened the door fo[illegible] ence, [illegible] ica[illegible] it. For Russia's leader, Vladimir V. Putin, t[illegible] as a ris[illegible] ng to take

**October**

Oct. 30

New York Times, *Once Top Advisers to Trump, They Now Call Him 'Liar,' 'Fascist' and 'Unfit,'* Michael D. Shear and June Kim, Oct. 30, 2024. *In books, interviews and elsewhere, some of the strongest criticisms of former President Trump have come from those who knew him as commander in chief.* Former President Donald J. Trump often brags about hiring "the best people." But the breadth of the criticism aimed at Mr. Trump, especially from his own former military and national security officials, sets him apart from any modern president. John Kelly, a retired Marine Corps general who served as Mr. Trump's chief of staff, recently called his former boss "an authoritarian," saying he "admires people who are dictators — he has said that. So he certainly falls into the general definition of fascist, for sure." Mark Milley, the country's top military official during the last two years of Mr. Trump's presidency, privately told the journalist Bob Woodward that Mr. Trump is a "fascist to the core" and said his pursuit of another four years in office makes him "the most dangerous person to this country," Mr. Woodward revealed in a recent book.

Mr. Trump and those around him rejected the criticism as little more than sour grapes. The former president has called General Milley a "loser" and worse, and has suggested that the decorated military officer should be executed for treason because of efforts to ease concerns among foreign leaders after the Jan. 6 assault on the Capitol by Mr. Trump's supporters. But the comments from Mr. Kelly and General Milley denigrating Mr. Trump's capacity to serve as commander in chief are particularly striking, even as they echo the sentiments from others across his government and many Republicans outside of his administration.

Sept. 25

Wayne Madsen Report, *Investigative Commentary and Warning: Russia is once again attempting to rig a U.S. election*, Wayne Madsen, Sept. 25, 2024. Multiple intelligence agencies have closely monitored and analyzed Russian interference in elections in democratic nations and have concluded that Russian intelligence has prioritized targeted electoral systems based on a series of factors. The 2024 U.S. election is just as vulnerable to Russian and other malign meddling as in past years. What makes 2024 different is that the Russians can now rely on a number of far-right Donald Trump-supporting conspiracists who have taken control of election machinery in quite a number of election jurisdictions throughout the United States.

Russian election interference has not changed in any major respect, and it continues to employ three methodologies. 1) Interference that targets election infrastructure and voter turnout. Attempts by Trump loyalists to suppress voting this year in Georgia, Texas, Arizona, and other states fit right into this Russian tactic. 2) Interference in the information environment by flooding the information sphere, including social media, with disinformation. Elon Musk's X (former Twitter), Russian FlagTikTok, Instagram, Telegram, WhatsApp, and Facebook (and to a lesser extent Blogspot and LiveJournal) are once again at the forefront of spreading Russian-made disinformation that favors Trump and his Republican loyalists and disparages Democratic candidates. Russia is relying on artificial intelligence to enhance its disinformation campaign targeting 2024 Democratic presidential candidate Kamala Harris with bogus photos, video, and audio, as well as the traditional phony textual news stories. Prior to President Joe Biden withdrawing from the 2024 race, he was the target of a vicious Russia-led and influenced social media campaign that questioned his mental and physical capacities. 3) Erosion of public trust in governments, political leadership, and public institutions. This includes questioning election officials, Secretaries of State of Michigan, Maine, Georgia, Colorado, Arizona, Nevada, Pennsylvania, and Virginia, canvassing boards, and voter registration officers. Russia is suspected of launching hard-to-trace "swatting calls" to U.S. election officials. A swatting call is from someone who calls 9-1-1 or another emergency number to convey to law enforcement that a non-existent crime is occurring at a given address. Police SWAT (Special Weapons and Tactics) teams respond to such calls with guns drawn and ramming devices to break down doors. Artificial intelligence has permitted Russian and other malign actors to imitate the voices of swatting call victims. Overall, Russia and China, in disrupting all facets of the democratic electoral process, are seeking to erode public support for democracy. Russia's first major target: The Netherlands Indications of major Russian election meddling were first caught by the Dutch intelligence service – the General Intelligence and Security Service (AIVD) – in October 2015. The AIVD detected a Kremlin-sponsored hacking group called Pawn Storm (also known as APT28, Cozy Bear, and Fancy Bear) manipulating Netherlands-based, pro-Russian sympathizers, Russian and Russian-speaking eastern Ukrainian expats, and gullible left-wing activists -- led by former Socialist Member of Parliament Harry van Bommel — to nix a yes vote on the April 2016 Dutch referendum on a European Union (EU)–Ukraine trade deal. The referendum resulted in a mere 30 percent turnout with 61 percent voting no on EU-Ukraine association and 38 percent voting yes. The far-right Forum for Democracy, led by Geert Wilders, actively campaigned for a no vote. After the rejection of the Ukraine referendum and understanding the vulnerability of Western electorates to Russian disinformation campaigns, the Kremlin set its sights upon the June 23 Brexit referendum in the United Kingdom that would decide the UK's ongoing membership of the European Union.

Politico Magazine, *Commentary: Russian Disinformation Is Spreading. Europe Could Learn From the US*, Mark Scott, Sept. 25, 2024. *Ongoing tension exists between EU countries about how hard to blunt the threat from Russia and Russian President Vladimir Putin, and no criminal sanction powers are available under the bloc's new digital rulebook.* In the ongoing battle to combat Russian election interference, Washington just showed Brussels what real enforcement looked like — and it didn't take glitzy new social media rules to hobble Moscow's global disinformation machine.

Sept. 9

Meidas Touch Network, *Trump Amplified TENET Media Personalities to Boost Campaign*, J.D. Wolf, Sept. 9, 2024. The group was indicted by the DOJ for being a Russian influence operation

Sept. 7

Washington Post, *Russia's election influence efforts more sophisticated than recent years, officials say*, Ellen Nakashima, Sept. 7, 2024. Moscow is using "authentic U.S. voices" on major social media platforms to "launder" propaganda and divisive narratives aimed at swaying Americans.

Letters From An American, *Commentary: September 6 [Russian Interference In U.S. Elections]*, Heather Cox Richardson, Sept. 7, 2024. One of the things that came to light on Wednesday, in the paperwork the Justice Department unveiled to explain its seizure of 32 internet domains being used by Russian agents in foreign malign influence campaigns, was that the six right-wing U.S. influencers mentioned in the indictments of the Russian operatives are only the tip of the iceberg. Since at least 2022, three Russian companies working with the Kremlin have been trying to change foreign politics in a campaign they called "Doppelganger," covertly spreading Russian government propaganda. "[F]irst and foremost," notes from a meeting with Russian officials about targeting Germany read, "we need to discredit the USA, Great Britain, and NATO." Through fake social media profiles, their operatives posed as Americans or other non-Russians, seeding public conversations with Russian propaganda. In August 2023 they launched the "Good Old USA Project" to target swing-state residents, online gamers, American Jews, and "US citizens of Hispanic descent" to reelect Donald Trump. "They are afraid of losing the American way of life and the 'American dream,'" one of the propagandists wrote. "It is these sentiments that should be exploited in the course of an information campaign in/for the United

States." Using targeted ads on Facebook, they could see how their material was landing and use bots and trolls to push their narrative in comment sections. According to the documents, one of the three companies, Social Design Agency (SDA), monitors and collects information about media organizations and social media influencers. It collected a list of 1,900 "anti-influencers," whose accounts posted material SDA workers thought operated against Russian interests. About 26% of those accounts were based in the U.S. SDA also identified as pro-Russian influencers more than 2,800 people in 81 countries operating on various social media platforms like X, Facebook, and Telegram. Those influencers included "television and radio hosts, politicians, bloggers, journalists, businessmen, professors, think-tank analysts, veterans, professors, and comedians." About 21% of those influencers were in the U.S.

Sept. 6

The New Republic, *Pro-Trump Media Firm Abruptly Folds After Russia Scheme Exposed*, Ellie Quinlan Houghtaling, Sept. 6, 2024. Tenet Media is no more. The conservative media network folded Thursday night, just one day after the Department of Justice unsealed an indictment accusing it of being funded by Russian state-controlled media.

Sept. 5

New York Times, *U.S. Charges American Commentator Who Works for Russian State TV*, Julian E. Barnes and Steven Lee Myers, Sept. 5, 2024. The Justice Department indicted an American commentator for Russian television on Thursday as part of a broader effort by the government to crack down on Russia's attempts to influence American politics ahead of November's presidential election. Dimitri K. Simes, who was an adviser to Donald J. Trump's first presidential campaign, and his wife, Anastasia Simes, were charged with violating economic sanctions against Russia for their work for Channel One, a state-owned television network.

Steady, *Commentary: Feds Say Russia is Meddling Again*, Dan Rather and Team Steady, Sept. 5, 2024. Today Vice President Kamala Harris received the backing of Vladimir Putin. Or at least he gave her a compliment, sort of. Yup, you read that right. At a televised event, Putin said with a hard smirk, Harris has "such an infectious laugh, that it says she's doing well." The timing of his "endorsement" is interesting, and certainly no coincidence, coming just hours after the U.S. accused Russia of an extensive effort to help Donald Trump win the 2024 election. Putin has invested heavily in his admirer and pal Trump. One can assume he would like a return on his money. Just how heavily he's invested became evident when the U.S. Department of Justice yesterday announced the seizure of 32 websites that are allegedly part of a fake news ring run by the Kremlin to tilt the election for Trump; and the indictment of two employees of RT, the Russian state-run news outlet, for covertly funding an American media company that published thousands of pro-Russia and pro-Trump videos on social media. The fake website ring was part of a Russian government-directed "foreign malign influence" campaign known as Doppelgänger. The made-up domain names were meant to confuse visitors into thinking they were on real news sites like The Washington Post. Instead, they were filled with pro-Trump, pro-MAGA propaganda meant to sway American voters as well as squelch support for Ukraine in its war against Russia.

RT funneled nearly $10 million to Tenet Media, a Tennessee-based company that creates far-right video content for social media. Since launching in 2022, Tenet Media has posted more than 2,000 videos, garnering 16 million views on YouTube alone. Benny Johnson, Dave Rubin, and Tim Pool are some of this Russian-financed company's most popular influencers and regularly post pro-Trump content. Today all three issued statements claiming to be victims of the Russian scheme and that they have always maintained editorial control of their content. It happened in

2016 an[illegible]). Here [illegible] in 20[illegible]date of new allegations announced by Attorney [illegible] Merrick Garl[illegible] Russia[illegible] before them the Soviets, have been trying to influence [illegible] elections for [illegible] decade[illegible] much until Donald Trump, during the 2016 cam[illegible] ted th[illegible] help[illegible] to the Mueller report. Lest we forget, the offic[illegible] t docu[illegible] Repo[illegible] Investigation into Russian Interference in the 2[illegible] a. Elec[illegible]

New York T[illegible] *Biden* [illegible] *Tax*[illegible] Thrush and Lauren Herstik, Sept. 5, 2024. Th[illegible] now [illegible] Biden [illegible] to an outcome that once seemed unthink[illegible] time [illegible]

Politico, *Hu*[illegible] *'s next* [illegible]*strategy*, Betsy Woodruff Swan, Sept. 5, 2024 (print [illegible] of pr[illegible] the j[illegible] some of Biden's defense arguments, including tha[illegible] paid [illegible] taxes.

Sept. 4

New York T[illegible] *Accuses* [illegible] *Influence 2024 Election*, Julian E. Barnes, Glenn T[illegible] Steven L[illegible] Sept. 4[illegible] American spy agencies have assessed that the Kre[illegible] former P[illegible] Trump, s[illegible] skeptical of U.S. support for Ukraine.

State Affairs[illegible] *Russians* [illegible] *outlet in Tennessee*, Erik Schelzig and Andy S[illegible] 2024. Aft[illegible] operators in 2022, the television network formerly [illegible] Russia T[illegible] y fun[illegible] conservative content creation company in Tenness[illegible] misinform[illegible] according [illegible] indictment unsealed Wednesday.

Associated [illegible]co, *Tr*[illegible] *Florida* [illegible] *accused of helping Russia sow division, chaos*, Staff Re[illegible] 2024. [illegible] with the African People's Socialist Party an[illegible] ment[illegible] defendants were doing the bidding of the governm[illegible] Pres[illegible] Putin[illegible] ideologically aligned with it. All four are or we[illegible] with th[illegible] People's [illegible] Party and Uhuru Movement, which has location[illegible] burg, Flo[illegible] St. Lo[illegible]

**August**

Aug. 31

SpyTalk, *Pu*[illegible] *Gang*[illegible]*, Says Former US Envoy to Russia John Sullivan*, [illegible] f, Aug[illegible] *Biden*[illegible] *former ambassador, who also chides fellow Republic*[illegible]*ing U*[illegible] the Vietnam War, the top American general [illegible] moreland [illegible] makers in Washington that there was "light a[illegible] tunnel[illegible] lay[illegible] to another seemingly endless war, this one [illegible] John Sul[illegible] served [illegible] Presidents Trump and Biden as ambassador to Russ[illegible] flicker of lig[illegible] only [illegible] darkness. " This is gonna be a bloody sore on [illegible] hope f[illegible] to c[illegible] Sullivan in an interview for the SpyTalk podcast [illegible] asses[illegible] the [illegible] Sullivan is the author of a fascinating new book, *M*[illegible]*w*, th[illegible] his [illegible] overseeing the U.S. Embassy in Russia — "bel[illegible] nes," [illegible] — [illegible] Vladimir Putin launched a naked war of aggressi[illegible] toppling [illegible] Volodymyr Zelensky and turning Ukraine into a R[illegible] state. [illegible] biting [illegible] during which Sullivan was regularly piped [illegible] National [illegible] Council [illegible] calls as the Biden White House mobilized western support to punish Moscow with economic sanctions while rushing billions of dollars worth of military hardware to Ukraine to repel the Russian invaders.

But more than two and half years after Russia's invasion, the war has turned into a gruesome and protracted conflict with no clear path to victory for either side. If that is the case, doesn't that strengthen the argument for a diplomatic "off-ramp," a territorial compromise that ultimately recognizes the harsh reality on the ground that there may be no strategic path for the Ukrainians to expel the Russians from Donbas and Crimea? Sullivan demurs. While he concedes that "it's difficult to imagine at this point the Ukrainians pushing the Russians out," he quickly adds: "When I hear my fellow Republicans, particularly members of Congress who say things like, 'why are we defending Ukraine's borders? I don't care what happens to Ukraine,' they're focusing on the wrong thing. The most important thing for the United States is to oppose Russian aggression."

Aug. 28

New York Times, *Telegram's Loudest Defender: The Global Crypto Industry*, David Yaffe-Bellany, Aug. 28, 2024 (print ed). When the messaging app's founder, Pavel Durov, was arrested, he received a flood of support from a multitrillion-dollar industry that relies on it. Shortly after Pavel Durov, the founder of the messaging app Telegram, was arrested in France on Saturday, the chief executive of the cryptocurrency company Tether called the situation "very concerning." Crypto enthusiasts pledged to support Mr. Durov, posting the hashtag #FreeDurov. Other investors declared that the arrest was an assault on free speech.

Aug. 26

Proof, *Investigative Commentary: Yes, Donald Trump Has Formed a Shadow Government*, Seth Abramson, Aug 16, 2024. Shadow ambassadors. Entire shadow agencies. Tens of thousands of participants, plus a rapidly growing military arm and a 900-page plan to legitimize it all. So what could possibly go wrong?

**July**

July 10

New York Times, *Guest Essay: Trump 2025 Is Coming Into View*, Thomas B. Edsall, July 10, 2024. The combination of recent Supreme Court rulings on presidential power and the Democratic Party's nomination crisis in the wake of President Biden's disastrous debate performance has significantly improved Donald Trump's prospects — not only his odds of once again becoming president but also of enacting a sweeping authoritarian agenda. Trump's debt to the six-member conservative majority on the Supreme Court is twofold. First, their delay. By waiting until the last day of the court's term to issue their decision on Trump's immunity claims, the justices effectively prevented prosecution of federal criminal charges against him before the election. Second, the substance of the July 1 ruling in *Trump v. United States* has convinced Trump and his allies that they will face few legal obstacles if they pursue a radical reconstruction of government — a "second American Revolution," in the words of one loyalist — if Trump regains the White House on Nov. 5.

"In a sweeping decision that constitutionalizes the modern reality of the imperial presidency, the U.S. Supreme Court has established near-total criminal immunity for Donald Trump's official acts while he was president," Noah Feldman, a law professor at Harvard, wrote in a July 2 Bloomberg column, "Emperor Trump?" Luckily for the Democrats, Trump and his allies are undermining their own campaign strategy by pushing onto center stage the most contentious aspects of the MAGA agenda. The controversy over remarks by Kevin Roberts, the president of the Heritage Foundation and the organizer of Project 2025 — a detailed set of policies and proposed appointees for a second Trump administration — epitomizes this development. Roberts boasted of victory during a July 2 appearance on Stephen K. Bannon's "War Room," the day after the Supreme Court issued its immunity decision. "We are in the process of the second American Revolution," Roberts told viewers, adding, more ominously, "which will remain bloodless if the left allows it to be."

**June**

June 10

The Hill, *Trump's calls for political vengeance worry Senate GOP*, Alexander Bolton, June 10, 2024. Some Senate Republicans are expressing concerns over former President Trump's calls for political vengeance after the 2024 election, warning that retaliatory prosecutions will lead the country down a bad road.

June 4

Washington Post, *Trump again suggests political opponents may face prosecution, too*, Hannah Knowles, June 4, 2024. Former president Donald Trump on Tuesday criticized his conviction in New York and suggested that his political opponents might face similar prosecution, even as he also said it would be "terrible" to jail his former rival Hillary Clinton.

**May**

May 22

Citizens for Responsibility and Ethics in Washington (CREW), Investigative Commentary: *Trump has threatened dozens of times to use the government to target political enemies,* Rebecca Jacobs, May 22, 2024. Donald Trump has repeatedly promised to weaponize the federal government during a second administration by pursuing revenge, retaliation and retribution against his political enemies. Because Trump is posting primarily on Truth Social, his newly-public social media company with only a niche following, the extent of his threats have mostly flown under the radar. Trump's attitude can be summed up in one Truth Social post from August, 2023: "IF YOU GO AFTER ME, I'M COMING AFTER YOU!"

CREW analyzed over 13,000 of Trump's Truth Social posts from January 1, 2023 to April 1, 2024, and found that while Trump has recently backed off some of his more violent rhetoric, threatening political opponents has been a consistent fixation for Trump. Since the start of last year, Trump has issued direct or implied threats on Truth Social to use the powers of the federal government to target Joe Biden during a second Trump administration 25 times. Specifically, Trump has threatened him with FBI raids, investigations, indictments and even jail time. But Biden is not Trump's only target. He's also threatened or suggested that the FBI and the Department of Justice should take action against senators, judges, members of Biden's family and even non-governmental organizations. Trump's posts should not be taken as empty threats, but rather as a call to action for Congress to put in place meaningful guardrails against the weaponization of the military and federal government's law enforcement agencies—before it's too late.

**April**

April 18

Letters From An American, *April 18, 2024 [Russian Election Threats To U.S]*, Heather Cox Richardson, April 18, 2024. Yesterday on the social media site X, formerly Twitter, Miles Taylor wrote: "After 2016, I helped lead the US gov[ernmen]t response to Russia's election interference. In 2024, foreign interference will be *worse.* Tech[nology is] more powerful. Adversaries more brazen. American public more susceptible. Political leaders across party lines MUST UNITE against this." Taylor served as chief of staff in the Department of Homeland Security under Trump. Today, Catherine Belton of the Washington Post reported on a secret 2023 document from Russia's Foreign Ministry calling for an "offensive information campaign" and other measures that attack "'a coalition of unfriendly countries' led by the United States. Those measures are designed to affect "the military-political, economic and trade and informational psychological spheres" of Russia's perceived adversaries. The plan is to weaken the United States and convince other countries, particularly those in the North Atlantic Treaty Organization, that the U.S. will not stand by its allies. By weakening those alliances, Russian leaders hope to shift global power by strengthening Russia's ties to China, Iran, and North Korea and filling the vacuum left by the crumbling democratic alliances (although it is not at all clear that China is on board with this plan).

April 9

Wayne Madsen Special Report, *Investigative Commentary: The Russian Bear in the West's Political Houses*, Wayne Madsen, April 9, 2024. *Russian agents and assets permeate Western political systems. Democracy cannot survive with Kremlin stooges acting as modern-day quislings.* In legislatures around the world intelligence agents, assets, and dupes are feverishly working to undermine democratic governance and sowing political chaos. This Kremlin- directed subterfuge is designed to advance the cause of fascism, thrust fascist-oriented political parties into power, and undermine the very fabric of modern liberal democracy. Ever since Russia was documented to have co-opted social media platforms like Facebook and Twitter and data miners like Cambridge Analytica to influence the 2016 Brexit referendum in the United Kingdom and the 2016 presidential election in the United States, Moscow has doubled down on its political influence operations by outright enlisting far-right and some far-left Western politicians to do its bidding. While vehemently denying that Russia interferes in Western elections and popular referendums, Putin has no problem blaming the West for interfering in Russian elections, including his 2024 lopsided 87 percent victory in a quite fraudulent "re- election." Moscow's plan is simple. By subjecting Western and other democracies to unending political chaos, Russia and its allies, most notably China and Iran, are able to extend their political, economic, and military influence far beyond their borders. In this article, we expose Russia's tentacles that reach into practically every national and sub- national legislature in the world and shine a spotlight on the politicians who have sold out their nations to benefit Russia.

The American and British Russiagate Reports: The March 2019 *Report on the Investigation into Russian Interference in the 2016 Presidential Election* and the UK *Parliament Intelligence and Security Committee Report* of July 21, 2020 on Russian interference in the 2016 Brexit referendum and the 2014 Scottish independence referendum contain more than ample evidence of Russia crafting a network of American and British intelligence assets.

**March**

March 12

Meidas Touch [illegible] *Robert Hur* [illegible] *President Biden Couldn't Remember Son's Death,* Th[illegible], March [illegible] *the date of Beau's death according to the interview* [illegible] Special Counsel [illegible] Hur [illegible] ted President Biden for his handling of class[illegible], was [illegible] Rep. [illegible] Dean (D-PA) for the assertion in his report th[illegible] could not [illegible] death of his son Beau, despite the transcri[illegible] view [illegible] who was testifying before the House Judiciary [illegible] was as[illegible] if he [illegible] correct the record. "Your report...says that Mr. [illegible] n't con[illegible] e da[illegible] his son Beau Biden's death," Dean said, "w[illegible] the tr[illegible] ows [illegible] d him the month, and do you know what he [illegible]? He sa[illegible], May [illegible] d you like to correct the record? His memor[illegible] on th[illegible] d the [illegible] mitted to the committee that various other as[illegible] n re[illegible] d [illegible] of his interview with Biden. At one point R[illegible] ll (D-[illegible]) [illegible] ncluding a statement he had made to Biden: "[illegible] have [illegible] and recall," in the report.

Mother Jones [illegible] *Spo[illegible]* [illegible] *Sleazy Assault on Biden,* David Corn, March [illegible] House [illegible] hearin[illegible] by Republicans on Tuesday, Robert Hur—t[illegible] cial cou[illegible] vestig[illegible] nt Joe Biden's retention of classified documen[illegible] a bit of [illegible] ll, [illegible] used his report, which declared there was insu[illegible] nce to [illegible] charg[illegible] den, to slam the president as a crook and to [illegible] mentally [illegible] nt.

Washington [illegible] *script* [illegible] *paints nuanced portrait,* March 12, 2024.

Washington [illegible] *House-Just[illegible]* [illegible] *prepares to testify on Hill,* Perry Stein and Tyler P[illegible], 2024 [illegible] cou[illegible] Hur angered the White House by question[illegible] Biden's [illegible] Biden's handling of classified material after his [illegible] cy. The [illegible] d WH [illegible] nger at Garland, who Biden aides say has over[illegible] cial co[illegible] ate the president's son, Hunter — in a way t[illegible] s insul[illegible] rney [illegible] n some of the Justice Department's toughes[illegible]

March 10

Proof, *Investi[illegible] ory: P[illegible] Said* [illegible] *at Trump Might Get Bonded By Kremlin Allies. N[illegible] ing—* [illegible] Seth Abramson, March 10, 2024. So *Why Is* [illegible] *About* [illegible] ssian bank co-owner Maurice "Hank" Greenb[illegible] and [illegible] ancial patron Evan Greenberg, whose Chubb [illegible] pes [illegible] riminal defendant to the tune of over $91 mil[illegible] big[illegible] the Trump administration is being ignored [illegible] ch in[illegible] ious, still-unapproved bond proposal by Tru[illegible] victor[illegible] know a story has national security implicat[illegible] implie[illegible] ner the presumptive 2024 Republican Party no[illegible] sident of [illegible] Stat[illegible] bought off—lock, stock, and barrel— by the [illegible] ile fo[illegible] resent invading Europe, threatening nuclear [illegible] ng in [illegible]

Washington [illegible] *rrant* [illegible] *credibility issues,* Isaac Stanley-Becker, March [illegible]

March 8

Washington Post, *Opinion: Biden, Republicans and media face critical general election choices*, Jennifer Rubin, March 8, 2024. Mainstream news outlets must decide how to cover the general election. Do they finally cover Trump's obvious defects, zero in on the implications of installing a Vladimir Putin sympathizer and confront the danger of another Jan. 6, 2021, insurrection if Trump loses?

March 7

New York Times, *Mock News Sites With Russian Ties Pop Up in U.S.*, Steven Lee Myers, March 7, 2024. *The fake news organizations, experts say, represent a technological leap in the Kremlin's efforts to spread false and misleading narratives.* Into the depleted field of journalism in America, a handful of websites have appeared in recent weeks with names suggesting a focus on news close to home: D.C. Weekly, the New York News Daily, the Chicago Chronicle and a newer sister publication, the Miami Chronicle. In fact, they are not local news organizations at all. They are Russian creations, researchers and government officials say, meant to mimic actual news organizations to push Kremlin propaganda by interspersing it among an at-times odd mix of stories about crime, politics and culture. While Russia has long sought ways to influence public discourse in the United States, the fake news organizations — at least five, so far — represent a technological leap in its efforts to find new platforms to dupe unsuspecting American readers. The sites, the researchers and officials said, could well be the foundations of an online network primed to surface disinformation ahead of the American presidential election in November.

New York Times, *Lara Trump and Michael Whatley have taken over R.N.C. leadership, tightening Donald Trump's grip on the party*, Michael Gold, March 7, 2024.

March 6

Emptywheel, *Analysis: Kash Patel's Deep State: How Trump Trained the GOP to Hate Rule of Law*, Emptywheel (Marcy Wheeler), March 6, 2024.

March 5

The Hartmann Report, *The Saudi & Putin Scheme for Screwing Biden's Election Hopes*, Thom Hartmann, March 5, 2024.

Wayne Madsen Report, *Investigative Commentary: Beware of Russian-generated fake financial newsletters*, Wayne Madsen, March 5, 2024. Russian on-line disinformation factories have embarked on a different approach to plant anti-Joe Biden and pro-Donald Trump fake news items in the American infosphere. After having baited unsuspecting news consumers with fake news stories purporting to have originated with actual news media organizations, from the *Guardian* of the UK, *Der Spiegel* of Germany, and the *Washington Post*, Russian troll farms are currently inundating email in-boxes with fake financial investment newsletters pushing such false stories as the imminent collapse of the U.S. dollar, a series of U.S. bank failures, and other claptrap aimed at hurting President Biden's re-election chances. One recent fake newsletter, said to be headquartered in Milton, Delaware, hyped a recent "war game" of Russia and China in the Sea of Japan. It noted that the Russian and Chinese war gamers successfully sank a "hostile submarine," read that as American, in the war game and that this is a prelude to a Chinese military attack on Taiwan. Another bogus newsletter, claiming to be based in Palm Beach, Florida, warned that the checking accounts of Americans will soon become worthless as banks switch to "digital dollars." Five banks are singled out in this respect. Another newsletter, claiming to be headquartered in Palm Beach Garden, Florida, states that the Federal Reserve Board has new powers to track every checking account in the nation. These "warnings," of course, are nonsense but they play into Vladimir Putin's hand in creating doubts about the rising U.S.

economy in order to benefit Trump. The Federal Trade Commission and Federal Election Commission could jointly shut down these bogus newsletters. However, the incessant Republican attack on federal regulatory agencies has stymied enforcement of existing laws and regulations.

March 1

Washington Post, *Analysis: Hunter Biden gives House Republicans the rebuttal they didn't want*, Philip Bump, March 1, 2024. Hunter Biden's appearance in front of investigators and members of the House Oversight and Judiciary Committees unfolded a bit like a Bruce Lee movie.

Washington Post, *Opinion: How do you say 'impeachment is dead' in Russian?* Dana Milbank, March 1, 2024. To the extent there ever was life in the impeachment case against the president, it has died after a long illness.

**February**

Feb. 29

Washington Post, *Opinion: Supreme Court order gives Trump's long-shot immunity claim a boost*, Ruth Marcus, Feb. 29, 2024.

Feb. 28

New York Times, *Hunter Biden Calls G.O.P. Impeachment Inquiry a 'Partisan Political Pursuit,'* Luke Broadwater, Feb. 28, 2024. Hunter Biden, the president's son, blasted House Republicans' impeachment inquiry during a closed-door deposition on Wednesday, condemning their investigation as a "partisan political pursuit" that was based on a "false premise" and fueled by "lies."

Washington Post, *Hunter Biden testifies that he never involved his father in business*, Matt Viser and Jacqueline Alemany, Feb. 28, 2024.

The Hartmann Report, *Opinion: Why Won't Our Media Say Donald Trump is America's Modern-Day Benedict Arnold?* Thom Hartmann, Feb. 28, 2024. *Donald Trump needs money. Apparently, many of the documents Trump stole from the White House are still missing.* We are right now in the midst of the third presidential election featuring massive interference from Russian intelligence. Most recently, we found that they sent an agent to the FBI to claim that Biden had taken a bribe in Ukraine: James Comer and Jim Jordan have been running with it, trying to use this Russian disinformation to damage Biden in his run against Trump this fall. Similarly, the 2020 and 2016 elections featured substantial and persistent interventions by Russian intelligence to help get and keep Trump elected. He stole thousands of top-secret (and above) classified documents from the White House, transported them to Florida, and stored them in publicly-accessible locations at Mar-a-Lago. It's the perfect way to hand off intelligence to agents of foreign governments without getting caught. He lied to both the National Archives, the FBI, and the American people about them. And now apparently many are missing. Did Trump sell them already? Prosecutors say that roughly 48,000 people visited Mar-a-Lago between the time in 2021 when Trump brought those documents from Washington to Florida and May 2022, when the FBI finally recovered as many as they could find.

Feb. 26

Politico, *The prospect of a second Trump presidency has the intelligence community on edge*, Erin Banco and John Sakellariadis, Feb. 26, 2024. *Trump sought major changes at the intel agencies in his first term; former officials say he could be more radical in a second.* Former top officials from Donald Trump's administration are warning he is likely to use a second term to overhaul the nation's spy agencies in a way that could lead to an unprecedented level of politicization of intelligence. Trump, who already tried to revamp intelligence agencies during his first term, is likely to re-up those plans — and push even harder to replace people perceived as hostile to his political agenda with inexperienced loyalists, according to interviews with more than a dozen people who worked in his administration. That could empower the former president's top subordinates to shield him from information that doesn't conform with his politics and even change the wording of assessments with which he disagrees, many said.

Politico talked to 18 former officials and analysts who worked in the Trump administration, including political appointees from both parties and career intelligence officers, some who still speak to the former president and his aides and had insight into conversations about his potential second term. "He wants to weaponize the intelligence community. And the fact is you need to look with a 360-degree perspective. He can't just cherry pick what he wants to hear when there are so many U.S. adversaries and countries that don't wish the U.S. well," said Fiona Hill, a top Russia adviser on the National Security Council in Trump's administration who has regularly criticized his policies. "If he guts the intel on one thing, he'll be partially blinding us." Emptywheel, *Analysis: Lesley Wolf Vindicated by Alexander Smirnov Indictment*, Emptywheel (Marcy Wheeler), Feb. 26, 2024. You know who is vindicated by the Alexander Smirnov indictment? Lesley Wolf, who made an effort to prevent Trump's efforts to interfere in the investigation from tainting the investigation into Hunter Biden and then faced death threats because she did so. In the wake of the Alexander Smirnov indictment, the 51 former spooks who wrote a letter stating their opinion that the release of Hunter Biden emails to the NY Post is consistent with a Russian information operation have claimed vindication.

Feb. 23

Mother Jones, *The Smirnov Affair: MAGA Republicans Are Useful Idiots for Russian Intelligence*, David Corn, Feb. 23, 2024. How GOP lawmakers got caught doing Moscow's dirty work. In June 2020, a businessman and fixer named Alexander Smirnov, who was also an FBI informant, passed his handler at the bureau a potentially explosive tip: The owner of Burisma, a Ukrainian energy company, had told him that he had paid $5 million each to Joe Biden and his son Hunter so the elder Biden, then vice president, would stop an investigation into the firm. Last year, that allegation became a key component in the Republican effort to impeach the president. But according to federal prosecutors, it was all a lie. Nine days ago, Smirnov, an Israeli and American citizen who had worked with oligarchs over the years and had been a confidential FBI source for a decade, was indicted for making false statements to federal investigators. Smirnov's indictment is a big deal and blows up a huge chunk of the GOP's impeachment drive. But, more important, his allegedly phony accusation did not occur in a vacuum. It is part of a larger story of the rotten relationship between Russian intelligence and the Trump cosmos.

Washington Post, *Fact Checker Analysis: How a Bill Barr 'assignment' led to a Biden impeachment effort based on a lie*, Glenn Kessler, Feb. 23, 2024. The indictment of Alexander Smirnov, a trusted FBI confidential source, on charges of lying about an alleged Ukrainian bribery scheme involving President Biden and his son Hunter is a new twist in a saga that has its roots in a project launched by then-Attorney General William P. Barr soon after President Donald Trump was impeached for the first time. To some extent, this story mirrors that of the "Steele dossier," a string of unverified and derogatory pieces of information on Trump collected during the 2016 election by a co[illegible] trus[illegible] FBI [illegible] Steele, on behalf of Hillary Clinton's campaig[illegible] mocrat[illegible] reports, leaked to the media, created a firesto[illegible] on by [illegible] abou[illegible] es to Russia — even though much of it turned [illegible] (Ste[illegible] ork.) In the same vein, the Smirnov tale has [illegible] Republ[illegible] targe[illegible]

Feb. 22

Washington [illegible] *The* [illegible] *ly collapsed*, Editorial Board, Feb. 22, 2024. U[illegible] h, H[illegible] icans [illegible] information provided by a "highly credible [illegible] t as [illegible] heir [illegible] ch President Biden. This week, they quietly [illegible] tion [illegible] from [illegible] uments. This one small move speaks volume[illegible] founded [illegible] ade [illegible] nally to be reaching an embarrassing denoue[illegible] counsel [illegible] ss — [illegible] charge of the Justice Department's crimina[illegible] unte[illegible] st we[illegible] ges against Alexander Smirnov. The 43-year-[illegible] citiz[illegible] ors [illegible] deral investigators about the Biden family's [illegible] ings. T[illegible] icial[illegible] laims that the president and his son each so[illegible] r brib[illegible] ainia[illegible] pany Burisma when Mr. Biden was vice pr[illegible] change [illegible] ting [illegible] om scrutiny by Ukraine's national authorit[illegible] Mr. Smi[illegible] "officials associated with Russian intellige[illegible] his in[illegible] igh[illegible] also be lying about Russian officials providi[illegible] on [illegible] Abs[illegible] hat is the point. Either Mr. Smirnov is an ass[illegible] Kreml[illegible] rea[illegible] on about the president, an eerie echo of 2016 [illegible] ferer[illegible] isser[illegible] that, too. Either way, congressional Republi[illegible] d the [illegible] ent in[illegible] words of a fabulist.

Letters from [illegible] *Comm*[illegible] *Bi*[illegible] ather Cox Richardson, Feb. 22, 2024. The cen[illegible] epubli[illegible] r imp[illegible] mocratic president Joe Biden is the allegatio[illegible] his so[illegible] ch [illegible] million bribe from Ukrainian oil and gas com[illegible] when [illegible] as vic[illegible] But in the last week, that accusation has reve[illegible] fferen[illegible] e th[illegible] Republicans.

Feb. 21

Politico, *Ha*[illegible] *legal*[illegible] osh Gerstein and Kyle Cheney, Feb. 21, 2024.

Emptywhee[illegible] *d We*[illegible] *ing on*[illegible] *nder Smirnov's Claims against the Bidens Until H*[illegible] *e*, Em[illegible] r. Mar[illegible]), Feb. 21, 2024.

Hopium, *O*[illegible] *Terr*[illegible] *Republican Party*, Simon Rosenberg, Feb. 21, [illegible]

Washington [illegible] *2024:* [illegible] *mass deportations, detention camps*, Isaac Arnsdo[illegible] f and J[illegible] Feb[illegible]

Feb. 20

Washington [illegible] *charg*[illegible] *bou*[illegible] *imed Russian contacts, feds say*, Devlin Barrett, [illegible] 20[illegible]

Meidas Touch Network, *Commentary: Hunter Biden Attorneys Say Prosecution Confused Sawdust with Cocaine*, Brett Meiselas, Feb. 20, 2024.

Feb. 19

Emptywheel, Analysis: *In Advance of Robert Hur Hit Job, DOJ Updated Public Identification Policy*, Emptywheel (Marcy Wheeler), Feb. 19, 2024.

Emptywheel, *Analysis: How Merrick Garland Mistook a Trump Hitman for a Career Prosecutor*, Emptywheel (Marcy Wheeler), Feb. 19, 2024.

Feb. 17

New York Times, *Indictment of Informant Undercuts G.O.P.'s Impeachment Drive*, Luke Broadwater, Feb. 17, 2024 (print ed.).

Feb. 15

Washington Post, *Former FBI informant charged with lying about Biden business*, Devlin Barrett, Feb. 15, 2024.

New York Times, *U.S. Disrupts Hacking Operation Led by Russian Intelligence*, Eileen Sullivan, Feb. 15, 2021.

Feb. 14

Washington Post, *Special counsel asks Supreme Court to let Trump's D.C. trial proceed*, Ann E. Marimow, Feb. 14, 2024. Federal prosecutors respond to Donald Trump's request to delay trial until after the election by seeking oral argument in March. Special counsel Jack Smith asked the Supreme Court to clear the way for the prosecution of Donald Trump for his efforts to remain in office after losing the 2020 election, pushing back against the former president's claim that he should be shielded from standing trial as he again seeks the White House.

Washington Post, *Election 2024: Biden forcefully condemns Trump's NATO comments as 'un-American,'* Amy B Wang, Feb. 14, 2024.

Feb. 11

New York Times, *Live Updates: Donald Trump said he warned NATO allies to pay their share, or he'd tell Russia to "do whatever the hell they want,"* Michael Gold, Feb. 11, 2024.

New York Times, *Special Counsel Report 'Went Off the Rails,' Biden's Lawyer Says*, Zolan Kanno-Youngs, Feb. 11, 2024.

Feb. 10

Washington Post, *How Justice Dept. special counsel policies let Hur critique Biden's memory*, Perry Stein, Feb. 10, 2024.

Feb. 9

Washington Post, *Special counsel report paints scathing picture of Biden's memory*, Matt Viser and Tyler B. Pager, Feb. 9, 2024.

Feb. 8

Associated Press, *Special counsel: Biden 'willfully' disclosed classified materials, but no criminal charges warranted*, Zeke Miller, Colleen Long, Erick Tucker and Lindsay Whitehurst, Feb. 8, 2024.

Washington Post, *Biden responds angrily to special counsel report questioning his memory*, Matt Viser and Tyler Pager, Feb. 8, 2024.

New York Times, *Opinion: Why MAGA Loves Russia and Hates Ukraine,* David French, Feb. 8, 2024.

Feb. 7

Washington Post, *Putin interview with Tucker Carlson shows Kremlin outreach to Trump's GOP*, Robyn Dixon and Natalia Abbakumova, Feb. 7, 2024.

Feb. 2

Politico, *Special counsel mounts forceful — and unusual — defense of Trump classified documents case*, Josh Gerstein and Kyle Cheney, Feb. 2, 2024.

Feb. 1

Proof, *Investigative Commentary: Last Month's $83.3 Million Civil Jury Verdict Against Donald Trump in Federal Court Raises Historically Serious National Security Concerns*, Seth Abramson, Feb. 1, 2024.

ABC News*, Special counsel questioned witnesses about 2 rooms FBI didn't search inside Trump's Mar-a-Lago residence: Sources*, Katherine Faulders, Mike Levine, and Alexander Mallin, Feb. 1, 2024.

**January**

Jan. 18

New York Times, *Hunter Biden Agrees to Deposition in Impeachment Inquiry*, Karoun Demirjian, Jan. 18, 2024.

Jan. 4

New York Times, *Trump Received Millions From Foreign Governments as President*, Report Finds, Luke Broadwater, Jan. 4, 2024.

## 2023

**December**

Dec. 29

Palm Beach Post, *Lev Parnas didn't testify in Trump Ukraine scandal. Will he appear in Biden impeachment?* Antonio Fins, Dec. 29, 2023. Lev Parnas is telling his side of the story whether a congressional panel wants to listen or not. The man who was a central figure in the 2019 Ukraine scandal that led to the first impeachment of then-President Donald Trump is now revealing insights into and details of the diplomatic impropriety that is, today, at the heart of the current inquiry into President Joe Biden. But it's a message that House Republicans intent on exposing the so-called "Biden crime family" may not be eager to broadcast to the U.S. electorate. "The whole motive and the whole Biden stuff was never about getting justice, and getting to the bottom of Biden criminality or doing an investigation in Ukraine," Parnas said. "It was all about announcing an investigation and using that in the media to be able to destroy the Biden campaign and have Trump win." In December, he will release a book, *Shadow Diplomacy*," and a podcast, "Lev Remembers," will follow. He also is cooperating on a documentary. The common denominator among all the productions is a singular narrative, he said, aimed at "getting the truth out" about what happened with Trump and Ukraine. "It's all because of one individual that wanted to stay in power, that didn't want to relinquish power," he said. "The biggest thing I want our public, and the world, to know is this is not about politics. This is not about what policy you agree upon. It's not about liking Joe Biden," Parnas said. "Trump says it himself: 'I'll be a dictator on day one.' Just listen to his words. He's not lying to you."

Dec. 15

New York Times, *Material From Russia Investigation Went Missing as Trump Left Office*, Maggie Haberman, Julian E. Barnes, Charlie Savage and Jonathan Swan, Dec. 16, 2023 (print ed.).

Dec. 5

Washington Post, *The Trump Cases: Special counsel alleges Trump 'sent' supporters on path to Jan. 6 violence*, Spencer S. Hsu and Devlin Barrett, Dec. 5, 2023.

**November**

Nov. 30

New York Times, *6 Takeaways From Liz Cheney's Book Criticizing Trump and His 'Enablers,'* Peter Baker, Nov. 30, 2023.

Nov. 20

New York Times, *Trump's Dire Words Raise New Fears About His Authoritarian Leanings*, Michael C. Bender and Michael Gold, Nov. 21, 2023 (print ed.).

Nov. 19

Philadelphia Inquirer, *Opinion: Mike Davis wants to cage kids, put Trump enemies in a 'gulag.' He could be our next AG*, Will Bunch, Nov. 19, 2023

Nov. 13

Wayne Madsen Report, *Investigative Commentary: Russia's invasion of legislatures around the world continues sowing chaos in governance*, Nov. 13, 2023.

Nov. 12

Forbes, *Trum[illegible] [illegible]olitical [illegible] [illegible]min' [illegible] [illegible]Day — Echoing Nazi Propaganda*, Sara Dorn, [illegible]

Nov. 10

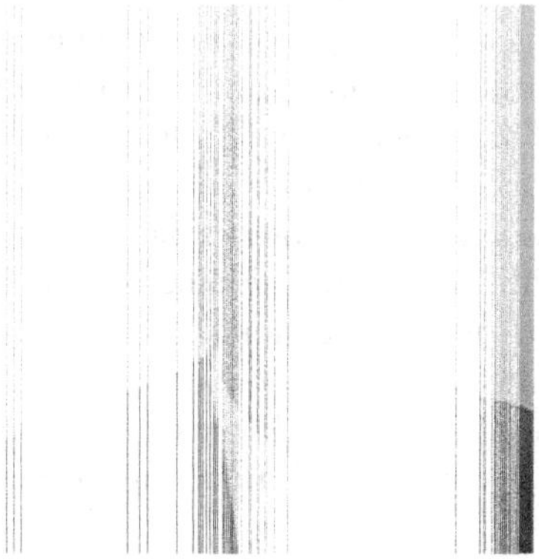

Washington [illegible] [illegible]*ays* [illegible] [illegible] *BI, DOJ against his enemies*, Maegan Vazque[illegible] [illegible] 23. *D*[illegible] [illegible] *panish television giant, the former president also defe*[illegible] [illegible]*ily sep*[illegible] [illegible] [illegible]erview that aired Thursday night on Univisi[illegible] [illegible] [illegible]sident [illegible] [illegible] [illegible] he's elected in 2024, he may use the federal [illegible] [illegible] punis[illegible] [illegible] and [illegible] his administration's separation of migrant [illegible] [illegible] U.S.[illegible] [illegible]ler. [illegible] [illegible]terview on the Spanish-language TV network[illegible] [illegible] rique [illegible] [illegible]ed [illegible] [illegible]ould weaponize the FBI and Justice Depart[illegible] [illegible] [illegible]oneni [illegible] [illegible] [illegible]deral law enforcement agencies have been we[illegible] [illegible] [illegible]rst hi[illegible]

Forbes, *H*[illegible] [illegible] *On C*[illegible] [illegible] [illegible]*mplaints And Clashes With The White House*, [illegible] [illegible]th, [illegible] [illegible] *president's son, is taking a more combative approach* [illegible] *uent* [illegible] *OP* [illegible] *who say he was part of an illegal scheme to use his* [illegible] *enric*[illegible] [illegible] *mber of lawsuits and a congressional ethics complain*[illegible]

Biden f[illegible] [illegible] [illegible]n law[illegible] [illegible] [illegible] former CEO of Overstock, this week alleging [illegible] [illegible] ed th[illegible] [illegible] so[illegible] [illegible] use his father's power to do favors for Iran [illegible] [illegible] exch[illegible] [illegible], an outspoken supporter of former Preside[illegible] [illegible] mp, h[illegible] [illegible] [illegible]acy theories about the 2020 election, Covid-1[illegible] [illegible] alled "[illegible] [illegible] [illegible]). In September, Biden filed lawsuits against [illegible] [illegible], Trump[illegible] [illegible] [illegible]nd Garrett Ziegler, a former Trump aide, fo[illegible] [illegible] rivacy [illegible] [illegible] [illegible] acquired an old personal hard drive of his [illegible] [illegible] sexual [illegible] [illegible] documents and allegedly tampered with, al[illegible] [illegible] its [illegible] [illegible] the media and online. He also sued the own[illegible] [illegible] sho[illegible] [illegible] alle[illegible] [illegible]d off his laptop before its hard drive was give[illegible] [illegible] In July, [illegible] [illegible] rney [illegible] [illegible]nt with the Office of Congressional Ethics [illegible] [illegible] orie [illegible] [illegible] committee hearing displayed large posters [illegible] [illegible] otos [illegible] [illegible] which [illegible] red via the hard drive — engaging in sexual a[illegible] [illegible]; the [illegible] [illegible] evide[illegible] [illegible]s paying for sex and writing it off on his taxe[illegible]

Nov. 8

Associated Press, *House Republicans subpoena Hunter and James Biden as their impeachment inquiry ramps back up*, Farnoush Amiri, Nov. 8, 2023. House Republicans issued subpoenas Wednesday to members of President Joe Biden's family, taking their most aggressive step yet in an impeachment inquiry bitterly opposed by Democrats that is testing the reach of congressional oversight powers. The long-awaited move by Rep. James Comer, the chairman of the House Oversight Committee, to subpoena the president's son Hunter and brother James comes as Republicans look to gain ground in their nearly yearlong investigation. So far, they have failed to uncover evidence directly implicating the president in any wrongdoing. Hunter Biden's attorney Abbe Lowell called the subpoenas "yet another political stunt" and said the investigation has been full of "worn-out, false, baseless, or debunked claims."

Wayne Madsen Report, *Commentary: Kremlin's hand behind anti-Jewish and anti-Israel street action and violence*, Wayne Madsen, Nov. 8, 2023. There is a growing mountain of evidence that Vladimir Putin's Kremlin regime is stoking the flames of anti-Jewish and anti Israel street protests, as well as acts of violence directed against Jews and Jewish synagogues and other targets. Russia, which directed its mercenary Wagner Group to help train certain Hamas forces to carry out the October 7 atrocities in southern Israel -- similar to those employed by Wagner in Bucha, Andriivka, Vorzel and other towns in Ukraine -- hopes that by diverting the attention of the West to the Middle East it will have a freer hand in its war against Ukraine.

Nov. 5

Washington Post, *Trump and his allies are mapping out plans to use the government to punish opponents if he wins in 2024*, Isaac Arnsdorf, Josh Dawsey and Devlin Barrett, Nov. 5, 2023 (print ed.). *Advisers have also discussed deploying the military to quell potential unrest on Inauguration Day. Critics have called the ideas under consideration dangerous and unconstitutional.*

Donald Trump and his allies have begun mapping out specific plans for using the federal government to punish critics and opponents should he win a second term, with the former president naming individuals he wants to investigate or prosecute and his associates drafting plans to potentially invoke the Insurrection Act on his first day in office to allow him to deploy the military against civil demonstrations. In private, Trump has told advisers and friends in recent months that he wants the Justice Department to investigate onetime officials and allies who have become critical of his time in office, including his former chief of staff, John Kelly, and former attorney general William P. Barr, as well as his ex-attorney Ty Cobb and former Joint Chiefs of Staff chairman Gen. Mark A. Milley, according to people who have talked to him, who, like others, spoke on the condition of anonymity to describe private conversations. Critics have called such ideas dangerous and unconstitutional.

Nov. 4

Washington Post, *Trump and his allies are mapping out plans to use the government to punish opponents if he wins in 2024*, Isaac Arnsdorf, Josh Dawsey and Devlin Barrett, Nov. 5, 2023 (print ed.).

Nov. 3

New York Times, *In a Worldwide War of Words, Russia, China and Iran Back Hamas*, Steven Lee Myers and Sheera Frenkel, Nov. 3, 2023. Officials and researchers say the deluge of online propaganda and disinformation is larger than anything seen before. The conflict between Israel and Hamas is fast becoming a world war online. Iran, Russia and, to a lesser degree, China have used state media and the world's major social networking platforms to support Hamas and undercut Israel, while denigrating Israel's principal ally, the United States.

**October**

Oct. 30

Washington Post, *How Russian disinformation toppled government after government in Africa*, Elizabeth Dwoskin, Oct. 30, 2023. *This never-before-told tale reveals how covert online battles in the French-speaking Sahel region led to coups.* When Israeli businessmen Royi Burstien and Lior Chorev touched down in the busy capital of the West African nation of Burkina Faso, they had an urgent message for the country's embattled ruler. The Israelis — one a veteran political operative and the other a former army intelligence officer — had been hired with the mission of keeping the government of President Roch Marc Kaboré in power. Their company, Percepto International, was a pioneer in what's known as the disinformation-for-hire business. They were skilled in deceptive tricks of social media, reeling people into an online world comprised of fake journalists, news outlets and everyday citizens whose posts were intended to bolster support for Kaboré's government and undercut its critics.

But as Percepto began to survey the online landscape across Burkina Faso and the surrounding French-speaking Sahel region of Africa in 2021, they quickly saw that the local political adversaries and Islamic extremists they had been hired to combat were not Kaboré's biggest adversary. The real threat, they concluded, came from Russia, which was running what appeared to be a wide-ranging disinformation campaign aimed at destabilizing Burkina Faso and other democratically-elected governments on its borders. Pro-Russian fake news sites populated YouTube and pro-Russian groups abounded on Facebook. Local influencers used WhatsApp and Telegram groups to organize pro-Russian demonstrations and praise Russian President Vladimir Putin. Facebook fan pages even hailed the Wagner Group, the Russian paramilitary network run by Yevgeniy Prigozhin, the late one-time Putin ally whose Internet Research Agency launched a disinformation campaign in the United States to influence the 2016 presidential election. Three years later, the governments of five former French colonies, including Burkina Faso, have been toppled. The new leaders of two of those countries, Mali and Burkina Faso, are overtly pro-Russian; in a third, Niger, the prime minister installed after a July coup has met recently with the Russian ambassador. In Mali and the Central African Republic, French troops have been replaced with Wagner mercenaries.

Oct. 29

Washington Monthly, *The Prosecutor Who Blew the Whistle on Barr and Durham*, Margaret Carlson and Bill Curry, Oct. 29, 2023. The inspiring tale of Nora Dannehy, Connecticut's newest Supreme Court justice. Calling Durham's bull: Nora Dannehy resigned over her then-boss John Durham's cozy relationship with Trump officials during their investigation into the origins of the Russian collusion probe.

Oct. 15

Emptywheel, *Analysis: Bret Baier's False Claim, the Escort Service, and Former Fox News Pundit Keith Ablow*, Emptywheel (Marcy Wheeler), Oct. 15, 2023. There are a number of things you'd need to do to rule out the possibility of Russian involvement in the process by which a laptop purportedly belonging to Hunter Biden showed up at the Wilmington repair shop of John Paul Mac Isaac, from there to be shared with Rudy Giuliani, who then shared it with three different Murdoch outlets and a ton of other right wing propagandists, many of them members of Congress. One of those would be to rule out that any of the sex workers tied to this escort service [linked to Hunter Biden] had a role in compromising Hunter Biden's digital identity, thereby obtaining credential information that would make it easy to package up a laptop that would be especially useful to those trying to destroy the life of the son of Donald Trump's opponent.

Oct. 12

Wayne Madsen Report, *Commentary: Wagner Group trained Hamas personnel in tactics used in attack on Israel*, Wayne Madsen , Oct 12, 2023. *Russia further isolates itself after new revelations about its support for Hamas.* There is an increasing amount of actionable intelligence that it was Russia, not Iran, that was aware of and partly instrumental in the planning of Hamas's invasion of Israel. The Kremlin also helped engineer other actions designed to throw NATO and other countries off of their footing. These include giving the green light to Azerbaijan to invade the predominantly Armenian enclave of Nagorno-Karabakh and for Serbia to ratchet up border tensions with Kosovo. The Belarusian underground movement has reported that the Wagner Group helped train the Hamas terrorists who invaded Israel and occupied several small towns and kibbutzim in southern Israel near the Gaza border. The Belarusian intelligence specifically pointed to Wagner training Hamas personnel in the use of various assault tactics, including using small unmanned aerial vehicles to drop explosive devices vehicles and other targets. Ukrainian intelligence discovered that Wagner personnel provided Hamas personnel with training in the tactics used in the invasion of Israel in African countries where Wagner maintains a significant presence.

Oct. 11

Wayne Madsen Report, *Commentary: Exposing the Hamas wing of the GOP*, Oct. 11, 2023. The Trumpist Republicans who are crying out that Israel requires more U.S. military assistance but at the expense of current military aid to Ukraine can save their pouting and tears. It may be a dirty secret to the Republicans, but their support base includes a number of white nationalist supporters of Hamas. These include the violent far-right Boogaloo Bois. Although the incident has been conveniently forgotten by the likes of Fox News and other right-wing media outlets, it is important to point out that in 2020 the FBI arrested two members of the Boogaloo Bois for planning to attack government officials and buildings in support of Hamas.

**September**

Sept. 23

New York Times, *The Gun Charges Against Hunter Biden Are Unusual. Here's Why*, Glenn Thrush, Sept. 15, 2023.

Sept. 21

MSNBC, *Former Prosecutor Says She Quit Trump-Russia Probe Over Concerns With Barr*, Nicolle Wallace, Sept. 21, 2023. *'Simply couldn't be part of it.': Fmr. prosecutor breaks silence on quitting Trump-Russia probe.* Former top official at the DOJ Andrew Weissmann and former FBI Counterintelligence Agent Pete Strzok join Nicolle Wallace to discuss federal prosecutor Nora Dannehy comments about her departure from the Durham investigation for the first time since resigning three years ago, confirming it was the politically-driven handling of this investigation that drove her to leave.

Emptywheel, *Analysis: What If Journalists Actually Read Gary Shapley Rather Than Parroting His Testimony?* Emptywheel (Marcy Wheeler), Sept. 21, 2023. There was a really depressing House Judiciary

Commit [illegible] with [illegible] and [illegible]epublicans relentlessly claimed that Hunter [illegible] ting s[illegible] [illegible].S. Attorney investigating him, who wanted [illegible] to fo[illegible] [illegible]al, [illegible]ed Special Counsel status — which should [illegible], that [illegible] [illegible]ary prosecutorial resources against a private [illegible] icans [illegible] [illegible]Garland hadn't interfered in Weiss' investig[illegible] — to [illegible] charge [illegible]en more quickly or more aggressively when th[illegible] was he[illegible] [illegible] hearing not to interfere. Republicans also rep[illegible] and ove[illegible] that [illegible]y — the so-called whistleblower all these R[illegible] in to [illegible] [illegible] addressed in his notes. Those two claims a[illegible] Weiss [illegible] s of [illegible] the two Burisma years Republicans believe i[illegible] st corr[illegible] e, a[illegible] [illegible]uldn't get authority to charge Hunter in the v[illegible] ngeles — [illegible]s had venue.

Sept. 20

CT Mirror, [illegible] *[illegible]ars Bar[illegible]* [illegible] Mark Pazniokas, Sept. 20, 2023. Nora R. Dann[illegible] for [illegible] [illegible]t, broke her long silence Wednesday on why [illegible] rump [illegible] ig[illegible] [illegible]ned from the Department of Justice, calling i[illegible] consc[illegible] [illegible]nation hearing, Dannehy confirmed what m[illegible] ave rep[illegible] saw [illegible]neral William P. Barr as improperly pressuri[illegible] gation [illegible] p[illegible] [illegible]ead of the 2020 presidential election. Danne[illegible] ciary C[illegible] the [illegible]mbly that not only did Barr's request violate [illegible] of Jus[illegible] agai[illegible] [illegible]ting on ongoing investigations or influenc[illegible] but s[illegible] disag[illegible] [illegible]onclusions in a draft interim report. "My co[illegible] not all[illegible] mai[illegible] said. The committee voted 30-4 to recomm[illegible] l Ge[illegible] ly [illegible] [illegible]mination next week when lawmakers are retur[illegible] rd for [illegible] special [illegible]

Hartford C[illegible] *[illegible]proves [illegible]* [illegible] Edmund H. Mahony, Sept. 20, 2023. Commi[illegible] after q[illegible] ut [illegible] [illegible]n investigation. It was the first time Danne[illegible] publ[illegible] [illegible] [illegible]ve the investigative team led by a colleag[illegible] Attor[illegible] [illegible] [illegible]er things, Dannehy said Barr pressed the Dur[illegible] produc[illegible] repo[illegible] [illegible]y critical of the treatment of former Presiden[illegible] Trump [illegible] ared [illegible]nfluenced the outcome of the 2020 presiden[illegible] ad it b[illegible] d. "[illegible]ght and spent my entire career at the Depart[illegible] con[illegible] inv[illegible] [illegible]n objective and apolitical manner," Danne[illegible] p. St[illegible] [illegible]atic co-chairman of the legislature's Judiciar[illegible] at the [illegible] se-ho[illegible] "In the spring and summer of 2020, I had gro[illegible] that th[illegible] investiga[illegible] being conducted in that way."

Law360, *Co[illegible] el Ap[illegible]* [illegible], Christine DeRosa, Sept. 20, 2023. The Co[illegible] ral A[illegible] [illegible] the Judiciary overwhelmingly voted in favor [illegible] Lamon[illegible] ut S[illegible] nominee on Wednesday, setting the stage fo[illegible] ation b[illegible] slatu[illegible]

Sept. 18

Washington [illegible] *[illegible] Biden s[illegible]* [illegible] Barrett, Sept. 18, 2023.

Emptywhee[illegible], *[illegible]ter Bi[illegible]* [illegible] S, [illegible] Marcy Wheeler, Ph.D.), Sept. 18, 2023. I can't [illegible] er whe[illegible] l[illegible]suits [illegible] is filing on behalf of Hunter Biden are prep[illegible] assaul[illegible] inal [illegible]st the President's son. Last week, for example, Lowell alleged that [former Trump White House aide] Garrett Ziegler had criminally hacked an iPhone encrypted on "the laptop" and had altered information on it. Whatever else the lawsuit will do, it will establish that DOJ chose to charge a non-violent recovering addict for owning a gun for 11 days in 2018, but has yet to do anything about the people who've serially compromised the digital life of the President's son. Lowell already has a bunch of other information to substantiate a selective prosecution case.

Sept. 15

Politico, *Hunter Biden's lawyer accuses House Republicans of 'congressional manipulation,'* Betsy Woodruff Swan, Sept. 15, 2023 (print ed.). *The first son's lawyer said House Republicans' "improper interference" is more dangerous than Hunter Biden's prior possession of a gun.* Hunter Biden's lawyer said Thursday that prosecutors caved to House Republicans' political pressure when they secured an indictment of the first son. Just hours after a grand jury indicted Hunter Biden on charges related to gun possession, his top defense attorney, Abbe Lowell, sent a tranche of documents to three congressional committees. The materials were accompanied by a cover letter lambasting the three Republican committee chairs investigating the Biden family. POLITICO obtained the letter and is publishing it here, along with some of the materials. Those materials include a lengthy letter Lowell sent the Justice Department accusing whistleblowers of committing crimes by revealing protected information about the president's son. Lawyers for those whistleblowers have long held that they scrupulously followed the law in making disclosures to Congress. Lowell opened the letter by saying lawmakers were focused solely on trying "to move the needle of political support for the 2024 election" rather than conducting legitimate oversight. And he indicated he believes Hunter Biden's indictment was the result of their pressure. "Your blatant efforts achieved your goal as the U.S. Attorney in Delaware today filed gun charges against our client — charges that are unprecedented when not part of some other criminal conduct and have been found unconstitutional by a federal court of appeals — and who reversed his earlier decision that such charges were not warranted," Lowell wrote. "Your improper interference now affecting a federal prosecutor is a much greater threat to society than the 11 days that Mr. Biden possessed an unloaded gun." The letter marks a major escalation in the fight between the president's son and the Hill Republicans who have made him a focus of their recently announced impeachment inquiry targeting the president.

SFGate, *CT legislature called for special session on state Supreme Court nominee, presidential primary date,* Alexander Soule, Sept. 15, 2023. After tapping former U.S. Attorney Nora Dannehy for the Connecticut Supreme Court, Gov. Ned Lamont issued a proclamation Friday for the Connecticut General Assembly to convene a special session on Tuesday to schedule a public hearing in advance of a formal vote on her nomination. Lamont also plans to issue a second proclamation for a special session in September to consider changing the date for Connecticut's presidential primary, which is now set for the last Tuesday of April.

The Dannehy hearing will be held by the legislature's Judiciary Committee, which is co-chaired by state Sen. Gary Winfield, D-New Haven, and Rep. Steve Stafstrom, D-Bridgeport. If the appointment is approved by the full General Assembly, Dannehy would fill the shoes of Judge Maria Araújo Kahn, who now sits on the U.S. Court of Appeals for the Second Circuit. Dannehy was Lamont's second choice after Sandra Slack Glover withdrew from consideration in May when statements she made in support of U.S. Supreme Court Justice Amy Coney Barrett had surfaced. Dannehy was the first woman to become U.S. Attorney for the District of Connecticut, holding the position from 2008 to 2010. She went on to become deputy attorney general for the state of Connecticut during George Jepsen's initial term as Attorney General, then in 2013 joined Raytheon predecessor company United Technologies Corp., where she was associate general counsel for ethics and compliance. In September 2020, Dannehy attracted national attention in resigning from the U.S. Department of Justice, as a report was being prepared by former U.S. Attorney for the District of Connecticut John Durham on the origins of an FBI investigation into any Russian interference in the 2016 presidential election. At the time, U.S. Sen. Richard Blumenthal stated the "resignation waves a huge red flag about political pressure" by then-U.S. Attorney General William Barr in the runup to the 2020 election.

Washington Post, *Shuffle of Russian military chiefs preceded death of Wagner boss Prigozhin*, Francesca Ebel, Sept. 15, 2023. A day before the airplane disaster that killed Wagner mercenary chief Yevgeniy Prigozhin, Gen. Sergei Surovikin, a Prigozhin ally known as "General Armageddon," was removed as head of Russia's air force.

Sept. 13

Washington Post, *Senior FBI agent disputes some whistleblowers' claims about Hunter Biden probe*, Jacqueline Alemany and Devlin Barrett, Sept. 13, 2023 (print ed.). Thomas Sobocinski, who manages the FBI team investigating Hunter Biden, was interviewed by the House Judiciary Committee.

Emptywheel, *Analysis: Hunter Biden Sues Garrett Ziegler for Hacking His iPhone*, Emptywheel (Marcy Wheeler), Sept. 13, 2023. Hunter Biden just sued Garrett Ziegler for hacking the encrypted compartment on the "Hunter Biden" "laptop" that included his backed up phone.

Emptywheel, *Analysis: By the Time Kevin McCarthy Rolled Out an Impeachment Inquiry, the FBI Had Already Debunked a Key Premise*, Emptywheel (Marcy Wheeler), Sept. 13, 2023. Yesterday morning, in a desperate bid to keep his gavel, Speaker McCarthy directed three committees, including the House Judiciary Committee, to begin an impeachment query. As Philip Bump [of the Washington Post] laid out, only one of McCarthy's justifications for impeachment — that Biden knew more about his son's business than he stated publicly (but not under oath) — has been substantiated; several of the rest have no basis in fact. More importantly, just one relates to Biden's current term as President.

Sept. 1

Hartford Courant, *'Trailblazer for women in the legal profession' Nora Dannehy nominated to CT Supreme Court*, Christopher Keating and Edmund H. Mahony, Sept. 1, 2023. Gov. Ned Lamont nominated well-known lawyer Nora Dannehy to the state Supreme Court on Friday in a family tradition as her father once served on the same court. Dannehy ranks among the state's top lawyers with a long resume that includes serving as former acting U.S. Attorney, deputy state attorney general, and chief counsel to Lamont. Known for avoiding the spotlight, Dannehy, 62, appeared at a press conference with Lamont, Lt. Gov. Susan Bysiewicz, and state Attorney General William Tong. She declined to take any questions from reporters as officials said the questions would be asked by the legislature's judiciary committee in the coming weeks. Dannehy declined to comment Friday when asked by The Courant if she would speak about the Durham probe.

Emptywheel, *Analysis: Trump's "Hunter Biden" "Laptop" Consiglieres Want to Be Paid*, Emptywheel (Marcy Wheeler), Aug. 17, 2023. The question of why Trump is paying for other defendants' legal fees but not (yet) Rudy's may have as much to do with the "Hunter Biden" "laptop" as it does January 6.

**August**

Aug. 14

New York *Times, Sweden Is Not Staying Neutral in Russia's Information War,* Steven Lee Myers, Aug. 14, 2023 (print ed.). The country has empowered a government agency to openly combat online disinformation coming from foreign adversaries, and especially the Kremlin. Facing a tsunami of disinformation about the treatment of Muslims that has in recent months fueled protests from Stockholm to Baghdad, Sweden decided it needed to fight back.

New York Times, *Fast Living and Foreign Dealings: An F.B.I. Spy Hunter's Rise and Fall,* Michael Rothfeld, Adam Goldman and William K. Rashbaum, Aug. 14, 2023. Charles McGonigal had a comfortable life and an influential counterintelligence job in New York. Federal prosecutors suggest it wasn't enough for him.

Aug. 7

Proof, Investigative Commentary: *America Is Getting Worse at Calling Things What They Are, and It's a Big Problem for the January 6 Case Against Donald Trump*, Seth Abramson, Aug. 7 2023. A U.S. law making it counterproductive for the federal government's executive branch to declare a coup has had big repercussions in Egypt and Niger. And after January 6, those chickens are coming home.

> In July 2013, less than a year after Egypt had held its first-ever competitive democratic presidential election, Abdel Fattah el-Sisi staged a military coup there. A decade later, he's still the country's dictator, running a regime as brutally repressive as any on Earth….One of the first people to see this situation as a major political opportunity for Trump was career criminal, white supremacist, and Trump campaign CEO Steve Bannon, who in August 2016, just a few weeks after Trump became the Republican nominee, worked with Kremlin agent George Papadopoulos — who had already told Trump face-to-face, in March 2016, that he had agreed to act as a Kremlin errand-boy in setting up an illicit backchannel between Trump and Vladimir Putin (see Proof of Collusion here) — to now set up a meeting between el-Sisi and Trump.' [G]iven that Putin and el-Sisi would subsequently both become involved in a pro-Trump digital disinformation scheme that violated U.S. federal laws against foreign election interference, it's no surprise that Papadopoulos's partner in this dodgy enterprise was Bannon, who was at the time using his Cambridge Analytica venture to dovetail with an ongoing Kremlin psy-op inside the United States….As detailed in *Proof of Conspiracy* (Macmillan, 2019), just a matter of weeks after Trump entered the 2016 race el-Sisi entered into a transnational criminal conspiracy with several other Middle Eastern leaders aimed at tampering with the U.S. presidential election and ensuring a Trump victory. In fact, the illicit agreement between these men — a group that included el-Sisi's fellow murderous dictators Mohammed bin Salman (of Saudi Arabia) and Mohammed bin Zayed (of the United Arab Emirates) — is now called the "Red Sea Conspiracy" because it was hatched off the coast of Egypt on a yacht anchored in that body of water….Now, a decade later, there's just been an obvious coup in Niger — and once again the United States has a million reasons that all sound very reasonable to not call it what it is. But as we saw in 2013, that's only the first shoe to drop. If anyone in the MAGA wing of the Republican Party feels Niger can be of assistance in re-electing Donald Trump, we can be sure — if past is precedent — that that fact will be exploited.

CNN, *Ex-FBI counterintelligence chief in talks to plead guilty over work he did for Russian oligarch*, Kara Scannell, Kara Scannell, Aug. 7, 2023. The former head of counterintelligence at the FBI's New York office is in talks to plead guilty to charges relating to work he allegedly did for a sanctioned Russian oligarch after leaving the government, according to a court order. Charles McGonigal was indicted earlier this year on charges, including violating US sanctions, conspiracy, and money laundering for working in 2021 with Russian oligarch Oleg Deripaska, who was [illegible] inte[illegible] 201[illegible] [illegible]ntial election. The same day McGon[illegible] [illegible]ed in a [illegible] in [illegible] [illegible]or concealing $225,000 he allegedly received [illegible] [illegible]t Alba[illegible] [illegible] [illegible]Gonigal, who is one of the highest-ranking [illegible] [illegible]ficials [illegible] [illegible] [illegible] pleaded not guilty to both indictme[illegible]

Aug. 6

Wayne Mads[illegible] [illegible] *[illegible]stigat[illegible]* [illegible] *[illegible] makes the Brezhnev Doctrine seem quaint*, W[illegible] [illegible], Aug. [illegible] [illegible] Put[illegible] [illegible]rgets a vulnerable West Africa. Russian [illegible] [illegible]mir Pu[illegible] [illegible] [illegible]v Doctrine and is now applying it not to pr[illegible] [illegible]list co[illegible] [illegible] [illegible]ut to attacking any nation possessin[illegible] [illegible] or m[illegible] [illegible] halt to Russian democracy and in his own [illegible] [illegible] Brezh[illegible] [illegible] [illegible]ne on steroids – Russia reserves the right to i[illegible] [illegible]hat is [illegible] [illegible] The Putin Doctrine has not only been use[illegible] [illegible] [illegible]ssian i[illegible] [illegible] Geor[illegible] [illegible]ne but a continued Russian military presence [illegible] [illegible]nd Ta[illegible] [illegible] Put[illegible] [illegible]so relies on mercenary forces like those of [illegible] [illegible]roup [illegible] [illegible]litary [illegible]gile democracies in Africa. Since 2020, th[illegible] [illegible] over a [illegible] [illegible]oups [illegible]tempts. These have resulted in pro-Russian [illegible] [illegible]es con[illegible] [illegible] in [illegible] Faso, Guinea, and most recently, Niger. Th[illegible] [illegible] attemp[illegible] [illegible]urkin[illegible] [illegible]nea, Niger, Sudan, Chad, Guinea-Bissau, G[illegible] [illegible] [illegible]ao To[illegible] [illegible]ipe [illegible] the fingerprints of Wagner Group and Russ[illegible] [illegible] [illegible] ope[illegible] [illegible]erad[illegible] [illegible]ats.

The m[illegible] [illegible]s elemen[illegible] [illegible] Do[illegible] [illegible]it has a double-headed spear. One is militar[illegible] [illegible] by the [illegible] [illegible]itary [illegible] Group. In the case of the invasion of Ukrai[illegible] [illegible] been e[illegible] [illegible] oth[illegible] [illegible] spear is Wagner chief Yevgeny Prigoz[illegible] [illegible]eration[illegible] [illegible] R[illegible] [illegible] (IRA) and its teams of cyber warrio[illegible] [illegible]ing u[illegible] [illegible] [illegible]he IRA, established in 2013, has softe[illegible] [illegible] with di[illegible] [illegible] [illegible]to Russian military action. This has been t[illegible] [illegible] enfor[illegible] [illegible] [illegible] with Ukraine in both the 2014 Russian [illegible] [illegible] Crim[illegible] [illegible] [illegible] 2022 invasion of Ukraine. In suppo[illegible] [illegible] cou[illegible] [illegible]Wes[illegible] [illegible]A has launched destabilization campai[illegible] [illegible] dem[illegible] [illegible]ected [illegible]ers. The Russian-backed turmoil in West A[illegible] [illegible]s furth[illegible] [illegible] the [illegible]ine in practice. In support of militar[illegible] [illegible] in Mal[illegible] [illegible]aso, G[illegible] Niger, Putin and Prigozhin are able to ma[illegible] [illegible] wag[illegible] [illegible]form[illegible] [illegible]ions designed to turn out into the streets [illegible] [illegible]testers [illegible] [illegible] in Africa are no match for such foreig[illegible] [illegible]ion. [illegible] [illegible] [illegible]ies that can fall victim to the Putin Doctri[illegible] [illegible] democ[illegible] [illegible]s th[illegible] [illegible]ted States, Great Britain, Canada, France[illegible] [illegible] othe[illegible] [illegible] dest[illegible] Russian offensive cyber operations. The Pu[illegible] [illegible] relies o[illegible] [illegible] [illegible]d Trump, Britain's Nigel Farage, French [illegible] [illegible]er Ma[illegible] [illegible]nd o[illegible] [illegible] fascists with large followings to disrup[illegible] [illegible]rocess[illegible] [illegible] elect[illegible] [illegible]tions of votes, and elected legisla[illegible]

Washington [illegible] *[illegible]Trum[illegible] [illegible] [illegible]ernment funding bills*, Paul Kane, Aug. 6, 2023. [illegible] [illegible]t shut[illegible] [illegible]s fa[illegible] [illegible]kers vow to slash funding for Justice Departm[illegible] [illegible]ions in[illegible] [illegible]rump.

Aug. 5

New York Times, *Analysis: How Jack Smith Structured the Trump Election Indictment to Reduce Risks*, Charlie Savage, Aug. 5, 2023 (print ed.). The special counsel layered varied charges atop the same facts, while sidestepping a free-speech question by not charging incitement. In accusing former President Donald J. Trump of conspiring to subvert American democracy, the special counsel, Jack Smith, charged the same story three different ways. The charges are novel applications of criminal laws to unprecedented circumstances, heightening legal risks, but Mr. Smith's tactic gives him multiple paths in obtaining and upholding a guilty verdict.

Aug. 4

New York Times, *Niger's Coup Leaders Sever Ties With France as Detained President Seeks Help*, Elian Peltier, Aug. 4, 2023. Niger's coup leaders on Thursday said that they had severed military ties with France, their country's former colonial ruler, throwing into uncertainty the future of 1,500 French troops based there, in a region of West Africa plagued with coups and Islamist insurgencies. The leaders of the coup also dismissed Niger's ambassadors to France and the United States, another military partner, as well as the ambassadors to Togo and Nigeria, an essential trade partner. In an extraordinary move, the elected president of Niger, who has been locked up in the presidential palace by his own guards for over a week, wrote an opinion column published in The Washington Post calling on the United States and other allies to help restore constitutional order.

Aug. 2

New York Times, *Analysis: Trump's Case Has Broad Implications for American Democracy*, Peter Baker, Aug. 2, 2023 (print ed.). The third indictment finally gets to the heart of the matter: Can a sitting president spread lies to hold onto power even after voters reject him? In the long annals of the republic, the White House has seen its share of perfidy and scandal, presidents who cheated on their wives and cheated the taxpayers, who abused their power and abused the public trust. But not since the framers emerged from Independence Hall on that clear, cool day in Philadelphia 236 years ago has any president who was voted out of office been accused of plotting to hold onto power in an elaborate scheme of deception and intimidation that would lead to violence in the halls of Congress.

Aug. 1

Wayne Madsen Report (WMR), *Investigative Commentary: Wagner chief Prigozhin remains a key player in Africa and Eastern Europe*, Wayne Madsen, Aug. 1, 2023. War clouds looming over western Belarus as Wagner forces dig in. It is becoming more and more obvious that the June 23-24 "revolt" by Wagner Group guns-for-hire in Russia was a staged event that enabled Russian strongman Vladimir Putin to gauge loyalty to him in the upper echelons of the Russian military and among high-ranking apparatchiks in his United Russia political party. Putin's description of the revolt led by his old friend, Wagner chief Yevgeny Prigozhin, as "treason" now appears to have been part of an act. Not only has Prigozhin remained untouched by Putin, but he appeared at the recent Second Russian-African Heads of State Summit in St. Petersburg.

**July**

July 29

Washington Post, *Brazil rejects U.S. extradition request for alleged Russian spy*, Shera Avi-Yonah, July 29, 2023. Brazilian justice officials said Thursday they can't approve a U.S. request to extradite an alleged Russian spy because they have already been processing Moscow's own request for the man. Sergey Cherkasov, 37, was charged by the U.S. Justice Department in March with acting as an illegal agent of a Russian intelligence service while attending Johns Hopkins University's School of Advanced International Studies in Washington as a master's student.

July 28

New York Times, *Trump Faces Major New Charges in Documents Case*, Alan Feuer, Maggie Haberman and Glenn Thrush, July 28, 2023 (print ed). Federal prosecutors on Thursday added major accusations to an indictment charging former President Donald J. Trump with mishandling classified documents after he left office, presenting evidence that he told the property manager of Mar-a-Lago, his private club and residence in Florida, that he wanted security camera footage there to be deleted. The new accusations were revealed in a superseding indictment that named the property manager, Carlos De Oliveira, as a new defendant in the case. The original indictment filed last month in the Southern District of Florida accused Mr. Trump of violating the Espionage Act by illegally holding on to 31 classified documents containing national defense information after he left office.

July 19

Wayne Madsen Report, *Investigative Commentary: The world must coordinate a defense to attacks against representative democracy* (Part 3 in a series), Wayne Madsen, July 19, 2023. In our previous two articles, we reported on the coordinated attacks on national legislatures by far-right forces that were encouraged by an unholy alliance of fascist-rule nations like Russia; "libertarian" high-tech billionaires, including Peter Thiel and Elon Musk; and white nationalist, Nazi, and like-minded political groups in the United States, Germany, Canada, Brazil, and other nations. The attacks on the legislatures of Germany, the United States, Canada, and Brazil were preceded by a few less-known assaults by far-right forces on the legislatures of Macedonia and South Korea. There was also what can best be described as a dry-run attack on the Brazilian Chamber of Deputies on November 16, 2016. Coming just a few days after the election of Donald Trump in the United States, some 50 people smashed a glass door and stormed and occupied the Chamber of Deputies in Brasilia for about three hours. The right-wing protesters demanded that the military stage a coup and rule Brazil by military decree.

July 17

Wayne Madsen Report, *Investigative Commentary: The international plot to attack democratic legislatures,* (Part 1 in a series), Wayne Madsen, July 17, 2023. Current law enforcement and judicial investigations in the United States, Brazil, Germany, and other countries point to a coordinated effort by far-right political parties and politicians – backed by anti-democratic dictatorships in Russia, Saudi Arabia, and – to a lesser extent, China -- to physically attack legislatures in order to bring about fascist rule. The threat to democratic legislatures has not been this severe since the 1930s, which saw a Nazi-led arson attack on the German Reichstag in Berlin in 1933 and the siege by fascists of the French National Assembly in Paris in 1934. The analysis being undertaken by WMR will present the links between the January 6, 2021 attack on the U.S. Congress, the January 2, 2022 arson attack on the South African Parliament, and the January 8, 2023 attack on the Brazilian Congress had more in common than occurring during the month of January. These attacks were closely linked to a vast network of fascist movements backed by far-right political operatives within the U.S. Republican Party and similar parties and organizations in North and South America and Europe.

The arson attack on the South African Parliament had similarities to the 1933 Reichstag fire. Although a mentally ill black man, Zandile Christmas Mafe, was charged with the arson and later confessed to the crime, it turned out that he had links to far-right South Africans who supported the parole of Janusz Waluś, the convicted Polish assassin in 1993 of Chris Hani, the General Secretary of the South African Communist Party and chief of staff of Umkhonto we Sizwe (MK), the armed wing of the African National Congress (ANC). Waluś, who was paroled on December 7, 2022, is barred from leaving South Africa. However, he has become a darling of the far-right, including white nationalist Afrikaners linked to Bannon's global fascist movement, because of Waluś's continued support for racial segregation between blacks and whites.

**June**

June 22

Politico, *Democrats and Republicans clash over Durham testimony on FBI report*, Lucy Hodgman, June 22, 2023 (print ed.). The special counsel testified before the House Judiciary Committee over the details of his 306-page report related to the Trump-Russia probe. Democrats and Republicans on Wednesday sparred over special counsel John Durham's report on the FBI investigation of collusion between Russian officials and Donald Trump's 2016 presidential campaign, rehashing the political implications of both Durham's report and the original Trump-Russia probe. Durham testified for over five hours before the House Judiciary Committee on Wednesday over the details of the 306-page report. Released on May 15, following a four-year investigation, it concluded that the FBI should have launched a preliminary, not a full, investigation into ties between Trump and Russia. Durham also accused the department of a double standard in its probing of foreign interference on Trump's campaign and then-Democratic candidate Hillary Clinton's.

> "I want to emphasize in the strongest terms possible that my colleagues and I carried out our work in good faith with integrity and in the spirit of following the facts wherever they lead without fear of favor," Durham testified. "At no time and in no sense did we act with the purpose to further partisan or political ends." Nevertheless, concern over partisanship dominated the hearing on Wednesday.

Salon, *Analysis: Legal experts: John Durham made false statements to Congress about Trump-Russia probe*, Tatyana Tandanpolie, June 22, 2023. "In a just world, Durham would be investigated," says Harvard Law Prof. Laurence Tribe. Special counsel John Durham, who was appointed by former Attorney General Bill Barr to investigate the FBI's probe into the Trump campaign's alleged collusion with Russia during the 2016 election, made false statements while testifying before the House Judiciary Committee Wednesday, legal experts say. Durham, who House Republicans have heralded over his widely criticized report, misrepresented key parts of the Russia election scandal, "suggesting he was either unfamiliar with basic facts or was purposefully trying to mislead the committee and the American public," according to Mother Jones. "In a just world, Durham would be investigated for the crime of violating 18 U.S.C. § 1001," tweeted Laurence Tribe, a legal scholar and University Professor Emeritus at Harvard Former federal prosecutor Andrew Weissmann, who served on Mueller's team, agreed that Durham made "flat-out wrong statements" about Russia's ties to the campaign and the Trump Tower meeting. But national security attorney Bradley Moss said he does not envision Durham facing any charges. "I get the argument that Durham was, at best, providing misleading assessments here," he wrote, "but I don't see 1001 charges in his future."

June 21

Mother Jones [illegible] *Durham* [illegible] *False* [illegible] *Congress*, David Corn and Dan Friedman [illegible] 23. Th[illegible] [illegible] two essential facts of the Trump-Russia s[illegible] Durham [illegible] appointed by then-Attorney General [illegible] investiga[illegible] [illegible] Trump-Russia scandal and who utterly f[illegible] evid[illegible] before the House Judiciary Commit[illegible] [illegible]sday. [illegible] [illegible]ments to Congress. He might even have lied[illegible] t fou[illegible] [illegible]ld Trump and others hoped would back up [illegible] that [illegible] [illegible]oked up by his enemies within the suppose[illegible] Yet D[illegible] [illegible]front, losing two jury trials unrelated to the c[illegible] [illegible]I's in[illegible] [illegible] from an FBI lawyer who had altered [illegible] [illegible]port a[illegible] [illegible]ner Trump campaign adviser. He prosecu[illegible] [illegible]cials [illegible] [illegible]ials for the supposedly big crime of mountin[illegible] [illegible]itch hu[illegible] [illegible]ven concluded there was justifica[illegible] [illegible] to ha[illegible] [illegible]stigation, just not a full investiga[illegible] [illegible]s att[illegible] [illegible]16 [illegible]ontacts between the Trump campaig[illegible] When [illegible] [illegible]mittee, House Republicans eagerly picked [illegible] [illegible]n his [illegible] which [illegible]uch criticized, and they treated him as a her[illegible] [illegible]estion[illegible] [illegible]mo[illegible] [illegible]ublican members, Durham misrepr[illegible] [illegible]pects [illegible] scan[illegible] [illegible]g he was either unfamiliar with basic facts or [illegible] [illegible]ly trying [illegible] [illegible]nd the American public.

During [illegible] [illegible]stion [illegible] Ad[illegible] [illegible]Calif.) asked Durham about the infamou[illegible] [illegible]d in Tru[illegible] [illegible]hen Donald Trump Jr., Jared Kushne[illegible] [illegible]afort[illegible] [illegible]ign advisers—sat down with an emissary [illegible] govern[illegible] [illegible]had dirt on Hillary Clinton to share. An ema[illegible] [illegible]p Jr. [illegible] [illegible]et up this session informed the candidat[illegible] [illegible]meet[illegible] [illegible]of a[illegible] [illegible]n scheme to help Trump's campaig[illegible] [illegible]smisse[illegible] [illegible]ternat[illegible] [illegible]le get phone calls all the time from individu[illegible] to hav[illegible] [illegible]lik[illegible] [illegible]meeting signaled to Moscow that the Trump [illegible] [illegible]ptive t[illegible] [illegible]dea[illegible] [illegible]ne in the election to boost Trump's chances [illegible] [illegible]presse[illegible] [illegible]t D[illegible] [illegible]t insignificant. "Are you really trying to [illegible] [illegible]mport[illegible] [illegible]h[illegible] [illegible]" he asked. Durham answered: "The more co[illegible] [illegible]s that th[illegible] [illegible] they didn't talk about Mrs. Clinton." [illegible] [illegible]ue. T[illegible] [illegible] [illegible]ounsel Robert Mueller notes that the Russ[illegible] [illegible]lawye[illegible] [illegible] did discuss Clinton: "Participants agreed t[illegible] [illegible]a sta[illegible] [illegible]iff [illegible] [illegible]merican family investment firm] had bro[illegible] [illegible]ws and [illegible] [illegible]that [illegible]he DNC or the Clinton Campaign. She asse[illegible] [illegible]ff bro[illegible] [illegible]gaged [illegible]on and money laundering in both the Unit[illegible] [illegible]Russia." [illegible] no[illegible] Ziff Brothers Investments had engaged [illegible] [illegible]ng.)

Emptywhee[illegible] [illegible] *Strzok* [illegible] *Jokes* [illegible] *about the Clinton Conspiracy Theory Document*, [illegible] (Marc[illegible] [illegible]ane[illegible] [illegible]n Durham fabricated a key aspect of his C[illegible] [illegible]cy theo[illegible] [illegible]aim[illegible] [illegible]ned to make false claims about Donald [illegible] [illegible]n inve[illegible] [illegible]when [illegible]d to make false claims about Trump. [illegible] [illegible]t of th[illegible] [illegible]rging FBI agents because they didn't respond [illegible] [illegible]t a H[illegible] [illegible]had [illegible] by Russia as if it were proof of criminal [illegible] [illegible]ry. He [illegible] [illegible] he provided no proof that any of those FB[illegible] [illegible]nsider[illegible] [illegible] [illegible]ed the referral memo sharing that Russian [illegible]

Emptywheel, Analysis: *In the End, the Leopards Who Launched the Durham Investigation Ate His Face*, Emptywheel (Marcy Wheeler), June 21, 2023. The arc of the hearing should begin with Durham's final answer (in response to an insane rant from Harriet Hageman, Liz Cheney's replacement in Congress), in which Durham claimed that if people believed there is a two-tiered system of justice, the nation cannot stand. Before he provided this answer, Adam Schiff, to whom many Democratic members deferred, had noted that in Durham's comparison of Hillary's treatment by the FBI with Trump's in his report, Durham had completely ignored the way Jim Comey had tanked Hillary's campaign, first in July and then again in October 2016. Durham had ignored, in his treatment, the most consequential events in the 2016 campaign, arguably the decisive set of events. (As I've noted, even CNN concluded that Durham's actual evidence, as opposed to his conclusions, actually shows that even on other investigations, Hillary was treated worse than Trump.) So Durham, after having been called out for ignoring the way the FBI may have decided the election against Hillary, nevertheless reiterated his false claim that he showed the FBI applying a two-tiered system of justice against Trump. Then Durham said that if people believe his false claim, it will sink the nation. With that endpoint in mind, let's review what happened leading up to it.

Emptywheel, *Analysis: Live Twitter Feed of Durham Hearing,* Emptywheel (Marcy Wheeler), June 21, 2023. Jim Jordan starts his hearing with a lie, falsely claiming that Mueller said he had found no collusion. He also flips what happened, suggesting that Trump's coercion of Zelenskyy was the Dems fault.

New York Post, *John Durham hits Nadler for saying Russiagate probe had 'glaring' errors: 'Untrue and offensive,'* Josh Christenson, June 21, 2023. *Durham hearing shows Democrats don't care about democracy after all.* Special counsel John Durham went after House Judiciary Committee ranking member Jerry Nadler (D-NY) Wednesday for accusing his team of "glaring investigative missteps" during its four-year probe of the FBI investigation into alleged collusion between former President Donald Trump's 2016 campaign and Russia. Durham, 73, singled out the Manhattan Democrat during his opening statement at a panel hearing, saying he and his colleagues "carried out our work in good faith, with integrity and in the spirit of following the facts wherever they lead without fear or favor" and that "the findings set forth in this report are serious and deserve attention from the American public and its representatives." "At no time and in no sense did we act with a purpose to further partisan political ends. To the extent that somebody suggests otherwise — that's simply untrue and offensive," he told the House panel of his 306-page report following Nadler's opening remarks.

Nadler, 76, said in his opening remarks that the Durham probe — which found the FBI's investigation of the Trump campaign was "seriously flawed" — was itself "a deeply flawed vessel" and "failed to uncover any wrongdoing." "It may be hard to remember, but at the outset of the Durham investigation, Mr. Durham was a well-respected career prosecutor with a solid reputation," Nadler went on. "The attorney general is supposed to appoint the special counsel to prevent the appearance of politicization in a criminal investigation. Mr. Durham could well have lived up to that expectation. Instead, what we got was a political exercise that operated with ethical ambiguity and existed to perpetuate Donald Trump's unfounded claims."

June 16

Emptywheel, *Analysis: John Durham's Disinformation Problem*, Emptywheel (Marcy Wheeler), June 16, 2023. The only person about whose ties to Christopher Steele John Durham showed no curiosity was Oleg Deripaska. The only person whose ties to the creator of the dossier that led the FBI to adopt false claims against Trump aides that Durham didn't pursue was the guy, on whose behalf, Trump's campaign regularly sent out internal polling data starting in May 2016, the guy, on whose behalf, Trump's campaign manager briefed Russian agent Konstantin Kilimnik on the campaign's plan to win swing states. The 2021 Treasury filing that stated, as fact, that Kilimnik is a, "known Russian Intelligence Services agent implementing influence operations on their behalf," also stated, as fact, that in 2016, "Kilimnik provided the Russian Intelligence Services with sensitive information on polling and campaign strategy," the very same polling data and campaign strategy he obtained from Trump's campaign manager on Oleg Deripaska's behalf. As I've laid out, John Durham never mentioned Kilimnik in his report, not once, to say nothing of how Kilimnik obtained internal polling data and a campaign strategy briefing and delivered it to Russian spies. Everyone else who had the least little tie to Christopher Steele, Durham pursued relentlessly. He charged Igor Danchenko, even though the FBI used Danchenko to, "fish information from Mr. Steele about what Mr. Steele was up to," as the former British spook pursued a second dossier against Trump in 2017. He charged Danchenko even though Danchenko neither wrote the dossier nor shared it (or even knew it was being shared) with the FBI. Durham not only charged Steele's primary source, but he caused Danchenko to be burned as an FBI informant, even though Danchenko's subsource network had reportedly proven incredibly valuable to the FBI. Durham even helped to ensure that the FBI would not pay a significant lump sum payment to Danchenko for his assistance after Republicans in Congress led to his exposure.

June 9

Emptywheel, *Analysis: John Durham's Blind Man's Bluff on DNS Visibility*, Emptywheel (Marcy Wheeler), June 9, 2023.

June 5

Emptywheel, *Analysis: The Dishonest and Incompetent FBI Work John Durham Learned to Love*, Emptywheel (Marcy Wheeler), June 5, 2023.

June 4

Emptywheel, *Analysis: FBI Cyber Division's Enduring Blue Pill Mystery*, Emptywheel (Marcy Wheeler), June 4, 2023.

June 1

Emptywheel, *Analysis: John Durham Fabricated His Basis to Criminalize Oppo Research*, Emptywheel (Marcy Wheeler), June 1, 2023.

**May**

May 25

Mother Jones, *Analysis: John Durham's Report Used Sketchy Intelligence That Might Be Russian Disinformation*, Dan Friedman, May 25, 2023. *Sound familiar?* John Durham's final report blasts the FBI for using the so-called Steele dossier, a compilation of unconfirmed claims about Donald Trump and Russia, without sufficiently considering the chance that Steele's findings contained deliberate Russian falsehoods. But Durham himself relies substantially on a sketchy intelligence product that may be Russian disinformation to push a partisan political narrative. And he does not even note the irony. Durham, the special counsel who former Attorney General Bill Barr selected in 2019 to look into the origins of the FBI's Trump-Russia investigation, may have succeeded in his apparent goal of serving up reheated scraps for a familiar retinue of hardcore Donald Trump defenders to feast on. House Judiciary Chairman Jim Jordan (R-Ohio) announced last week he wants Durham to appear before the committee on Thursday. But that testimony remains unscheduled. The Judiciary Committee did not respond to questions about the delay, which occurred with Durham facing substantial criticism.

Obituaries for his four-year, $7 million investigation have noted Durham's repeated failures to secure courtroom convictions and pointed out how meek his conclusions were compared to the wild expectations of Trump fans. But a different shortcoming in Durham's work—its astounding hypocrisy—may not be getting the attention it deserves. The special counsel's 306-page report refers 65 times to the "Clinton Plan intelligence." That is a claim that Hillary Clinton, on July 26, 2016, approved a plan to "vilify Donald Trump by stirring up a scandal claiming interference by the Russian security services." Where does this supposed intelligence come from? Those very same Russian security services. The report notes that the "Clinton Plan intelligence" came from a "Russian intelligence analysis" that US intelligence agencies got their hands on. Think about that. To figure out how an American presidential campaign supposedly went about attacking a rival campaign, Durham relied on information US intelligence gathered on claims made by Russian intelligence agents about what they supposedly found by spying on Americans. That's a pretty roundabout way to learn the kind of information you'd expect to see in "Playbook." And this game of spy telephone was actually even longer than Durham details. According to the New York Times, US spies obtained their "insight" into Russian intelligence thinking from Dutch intelligence, which was spying on the Russians as the Russians spied on Americans. Durham seems to have found no other confirmation for his "Clinton Plan intelligence." That's reason enough for skepticism. But there is a bigger problem. Russian security services did hack Clinton's campaign to help Trump, according to the entire US intelligence community and the Senate Intelligence Committee. Yet Durham relies on those Russian spies for insight into how Clinton reacted to the hack. That is like the cops citing a bank robber who says the bank framed him. Durham admits that the "Clinton Plan intelligence" may be a "fabrication." Then he cites it anyway, extensively.

May 17

Emptywheel, *Analysis: "Ridiculous:" Durham's Failed Clinton Conspiracy Theory*, Emptywheel (Marcy Wheeler), May 17, 2023. A list of interviews cited in the John Durham report suggests he never really investigated the things he claimed to be investigating -- like the problematic Carter Page FISA applications or the two false statements cases he did charge -- because starting no later than February 2020, he was too busy pursuing a baseless attempt to claim Hillary tried to frame Donald Trump. I put together a very rough list of the interviews that John Durham included in his Report and a table showing the organization of his report. Remember a few things about this list: It won't include everything. Even just among witnesses who testified at trial, Durham was known to have done initial interviews, then threatened them with prosecution, in an often successful attempt to shade their testimony. With others, Durham is being affirmatively misleading by stating that people who did appear before the grand jury were unwilling to be interviewed.

New York Times, *News Analysis: After Years of Political Hype, the Durham Inquiry Failed to Deliver*, Charlie Savage, May 17, 2023. The limping conclusion to John H. Durham's four-year investigation of the Russia inquiry underscores a recurring dilemma in American government: how to shield sensitive law enforcement investigations from politics without creating prosecutors who can run amok, never to be held to account.

Washington Post, *Fact Checker Analysis: The truth about Russia, Trump and the 2016 election*, Glenn Kessler, May 17, 2023. There have been four major investigations into Russian intervention in the 201[illegible] [illegible] election [illegible] subject — a 2019 report released by special [illegible] Robert S. [illegible] department inspector general report, a bipartisan [illegible] the Senate [illegible] released in 2020 by a GOP-controlled Senate, and [illegible] report [illegible] John Durham. All told, the reports add up to [illegible] pages [illegible] contradictory conclusions. But broad the [illegible] produced [illegible] evidence gathered in the lengthy documents [illegible] indictments [illegible] criminal cases.

Mother Jones [illegible] *John* [illegible] David Corn, May 17, 2023. For years, Bill Barr's [illegible] special [illegible] Trump['s] hoax alive. John Durham succeeded [illegible] conventional [illegible] This [illegible] counsel, appointed by then-Attorney General [illegible] handed [illegible] Trump's claim that the FBI's investigation [illegible] Trump-[illegible] had [illegible]" perpetrated by a supposed Deep State cabal [illegible] in the [illegible] with [illegible] against peripheral figures. And the final [illegible] admitted [illegible] revelations within its 316 pages to back up [illegible] assertion [illegible] the FBI [illegible] probe. At the end of the day, the best Durham [illegible] manage [illegible] that [illegible] 2016 should have opened a preliminary [illegible] instead [illegible] investigation [illegible] whoop. After four years of work that cost [illegible] uncovered [illegible] evidence—criminal or otherwise—to cook up a phony [illegible] of Trump [illegible] wrongdoing he cited—which mainly concerned [illegible] use of [illegible] dossier to obtain a surveillance warrant for a single [illegible] campaign [illegible] prior investigation. Durham's crusade [illegible] significant [illegible] undercut all of Trump's claptrap about the FBI [illegible] the [illegible] him in what Trump repeatedly called the "crime [illegible] century."

Yet Durham [illegible] accomplish [illegible] mission [illegible] continued to focus attention on the Great R[illegible] distraction and [illegible] Trump-Russia denialists who have refused [illegible] a fundamental [illegible] campaign: Russia attacked the election [illegible] and [illegible] abetted that assault by denying it was happening [illegible] signaling [illegible] its effort to undermine American democracy [illegible] generated [illegible] and [illegible] purveyors of the Russia hoax. And his nothing [illegible] report has [illegible] years, Trump and his minions have tried mightily [illegible] the [illegible] addressing the Kremlin's covert intervention [illegible] campaign [illegible] several decisive factors in that close contest—[illegible] complicity [illegible] exploitation of this underhanded foreign interference [illegible] relentless [illegible] investigation of these matters was a conspiracy [illegible] wreck [illegible] candidacy, after that failed, to destroy his presidency.

Over and [illegible] claimed [illegible] spied on by the Obama administration [illegible] victimized [illegible]. His goal was obvious: to steer attention [illegible] truth [illegible] White House in part due to a Russian secret [illegible] had [illegible] his defenders brayed about the faults of [illegible] Russia investigation [illegible] from what that probe and subsequent investigations [illegible]. They [illegible] Russia and Trump did during the 2016 campaign [illegible] all of [illegible] investigations [illegible] predicated on the Steele dossier, as if the inaccuracies [illegible] negated what actually transpired. Trump [illegible] claimed that [illegible] inquiry [illegible] kicked off by the tarnished Steele material [illegible] true—[illegible] by Durham during one of the trials he lost. Durham's [illegible] task was [illegible] Trump's theory that the Russia probe was an anti-Trump [illegible]. He [illegible] allegation advanced by Trump and his lapdog [illegible] true [illegible] tradition alive for years. Much of the attention that the Trump-Russia scandal has received in recent times was due to Durham's inquiry. Consequently, the more important subjects of Russia's skullduggery and Trump's deceitful (perhaps treasonous) conduct were subsumed by real and spurious questions about the investigation. With his investigation of the investigation, Durham provided fodder for Trump and his conservative allies. His work exemplifies the so-called "weaponization of government" that Republicans have bemoaned: Barr unleashed a powerful prosecutor to serve Trump's political interests. The court filings Durham submitted and the prosecutions he waged (although failed) offered the Trumpists ammunition to keep their crusade of distraction alive. All of this had nothing to do with the Russian assault and Trump's actions in 2016. But it allowed Trump and the denizens of Foxland to continue to cast the Russia matter as a scandal of investigative abuse, and they ceaselessly predicted that Durham would eventually drop the big one and expose (and indict!) the Deep State evildoers who had manufactured the Russia "hoax."

May 16

Emptywheel, *Analysis: Eight Things Not Mentioned in the Durham Report*, Emptywheel (Marcy Wheeler), May 16, 2023. If John Durham closed just a handful of enormous gaps in his shoddy report, it would all fall apart. There are a whole lot of gaping holes in the Durham Report. Here are eight of the most important things that Durham chose to leave out of his report on his four-year investigation.

1. All mention of the Italian referral on Trump. In January, NYT reported on the many problems with the Durham investigation, none of which shows up in his report. Most importantly, NYT reported that on a trip to Italy, the Italians gave Bill Barr and Durham a tip about crimes Trump may have committed. On one of Mr. Barr and Mr. Durham's trips to Europe, according to people familiar with the matter, Italian officials — while denying any role in setting off the Russia investigation — unexpectedly offered a potentially explosive tip linking Mr. Trump to certain suspected financial crimes. Mr. Barr and Mr. Durham decided that the tip was too serious and credible to ignore. But rather than assign it to another prosecutor, Mr. Barr had Mr. Durham investigate the matter himself — giving him criminal prosecution powers for the first time — even though the possible wrongdoing by Mr. Trump did not fall squarely within Mr. Durham's assignment to scrutinize the origins of the Russia inquiry, the people said. Mr. Durham never filed charges, and it remains unclear what level of an investigation it was, what steps he took, what he learned and whether anyone at the White House ever found out. The extraordinary fact that Mr. Durham opened a criminal investigation that included scrutinizing Mr. Trump has remained secret. By regulation, there should be some investigative result from this investigation in Durham's report. It's not in there.
2. All mention of the conspiracy theories Durham and Barr chased in Europe. The first year or so of the Durham investigation, Bill and John spend traipsing around the world chasing the conspiracy theories George Papadopoulos had floated in a 2018 House Oversight appearance. Barr has confessed they found nothing. But Durham doesn't do that — or even mention the conspiracy theories — in his report. That's important for a number of reasons: because Durham asserts that Congress should have no say in criminal investigations even though they dictated the initial direction of his own, because (as I'll show) Durham badly whitewashes everything having to do with Papadopoulos, and because Durham also doesn't mention the investigative steps he failed to take while running off to Italy to get Joseph Mifsud's Blackberries.
3. Durham's own investigative failures. I've written at length about how Durham's own investigative failures make anything Crossfire Hurricane did look tame by comparison. He failed to get relevant information from DOJ IG or ask Jim Baker to check his iCloud

for what happened to be texts proving Michael Sussmann's defense until after he indicted Sussmann. He never interviewed Papadopoulos, indicted Danchenko relying on what Sergei Millian said on Twitter, and then failed to obtain the messaging app evidence he would need to disprove a call between Millian and Danchenko. Durham focuses, at length, on steps he speculated the FBI didn't take on the Carter Page FISC, but he had more egregious failures to pursue what turned out to be exculpatory information….

May 15

FBI National Press Office, *Statement on Report by Special Counsel John Durham*, May 15, 2023. "The conduct in 2016 and 2017 that Special Counsel Durham examined was the reason that current FBI leadership already implemented dozens of corrective actions, which have now been in place for some time. Had those reforms been in place in 2016, the missteps identified in the report could have been prevented. This report reinforces the importance of ensuring the FBI continues to do its work with the rigor, objectivity, and professionalism the American people deserve and rightly expect."

**February**

Feb. 14

New York Times, *Opinion: Under Trump, Bill Barr and John Durham Made a Mockery of the Rules I Wrote*, Neal K. Katyal, Feb. 14, 2023.

Our Land / Mother Jones, *The Trump-Russia Denialists Still Can't Handle the Truth*, David Corn Feb. 14, 2023. Extreme contrarianism often entails an avoidance of facts. This is especially true for the cadre of Trump-Russia denialists who were recently out in force to bolster and amplify a massive and misguided Columbia Journalism Review critique of the media coverage of the Russia scandal. I've already pointed out what was profoundly wrong with the 24,000-word, four-part series that onetime New York Times reporter Jeff Gerth wrote for CJR. In an act of misdirection, Gerth lambasted the press for overstating the case that Donald Trump directly colluded with the Kremlin and for hyping the unconfirmed Steele dossier. Though Gerth scored some points on these fronts, he curiously ignored the core components of the Trump-Russia affair: Vladimir Putin successfully attacked the 2016 election to help Trump, and Trump aided and abetted this assault by denying or dismissing it. He did not assess how the media reported on these critical matters (a mixed record). Instead, he defined the Russia story only by press coverage of the Steele memos and the question of whether Trump directly schemed with Moscow's covert operators.

Feb. 9

The Bulwark, *Why 'Russiagate' Skeptics Are Cackling—But Shouldn't Be*, Cathy Young, Feb. 9, 2023. *In claiming that the Trump-Russia story was nothing more than a sensation-driven media witch hunt, the revisionists downplay and distort a very ugly story.* Committed skeptics of "Russiagate"—the scandal around Russian interference in the 2016 election with the intent of helping elect Donald Trump, and the Trump campaign's collaboration with this effort—had a good month in January. First, a study released on January 9 concluded that Russian disinformation and propaganda on Twitter, while a real phenomenon, did not significantly affect American attitudes (partly because the notorious Russian bots were, as the Intercept put it, "a small speck when compared to homegrown posters") or influence the results of the 2016 election. Then, on January 30, Columbia Journalism Review published a four-part report on Russiagate with a scathing analysis of media coverage by veteran investigative journalist Jeff Gerth. It concluded that the news media repeatedly fell short of professional standards in their handling of the story, compromising their objectivity and contributing to polarization and erosion of public trust in journalism.

The reaction from the skeptics—a motley crowd that includes everyone from hardcore Donald Trump cultists to anti-anti-Trumpists to critics of America's national security apparatus and various anti-establishment contrarians—was downright exuberant. So is Russiagate really and conclusively debunked as a "hoax" driven by Trump Derangement Syndrome? Hardly. But to explain why will require getting into the weeds. In reality, neither the study, which was conducted by New York University's Center for Social Media and Politics, nor the CJR story, "The Press Versus the President," makes any definitive claims about the substance of Russiagate.

Feb. 5

National Review, *Of Course Jeff Gerth Is Right about Russiagate*, Rich Lowry, Feb. 5, 2023. Finally, a little media accountability. It isn't just that the media failed in covering Russiagate during the Trump years. Since then, they have displayed a near-total unwillingness to examine their role in whipping up a national hysteria based on paranoia and confirmation bias.

Feb. 4

ByLine Times, *Media Criticism: Russia & the US Press: The Article the CJR Didn't Publish*, Duncan Campbell, Feb. 4, 2023. Two and a half years ago, the Columbia Journalism Review refused to publish Duncan Campbell's investigation into The Nation magazine and its apparent support for Vladimir Putin. It is published here in full. In 2018, Duncan Campbell was commissioned by the "voice of journalism" and "watchdog of the press", Columbia Journalism Review (CJR), to write an investigation into the venerable New York magazine The Nation, and its apparent support for Russia's territorial ambitions. In 2020, after a full fact check, legal review and edit, the article was cancelled two days before the scheduled publication. In 2022, months after Putin's full invasion of Ukraine, the CJR again refused to publish the article.

The National Memo, *The Reporter Who Hyped Whitewater Now Backs Trump On 'Russiagate,'* Joe Conason, Feb. 4, 2024. Down at Mar-a-Lago and anywhere else that former President Donald Trump is still venerated, he and his entourage are excited about a publication that has never before drawn his attention. The Columbia Journalism Review has just published a four-part, 24,000-word essay that purports to debunk the Trump-Russia "narrative" — and seeks to blame rising public disdain for the press, among other ills, on The New York Times and The Washington Post for their coverage of that scandal. Its author is Jeff Gerth, a reporter who worked at the Times for three decades..,

Gerth's account is fatally flawed by his omission of critical facts about Trump and Russia, not only in Pulitzer Prize-winning stories published by both newspapers, but in the bipartisan Senate Intelligence Committee report on Russian meddling in the 2016 election as well as the voluminous detail of Russian interference chronicled in the Mueller Report, mendaciously maligned by then-Attorney General William Barr. Like Trump, whom he interviewed twice and treats with kid gloves, Gerth falsely suggests that Special Counsel Robert Mueller somehow exculpated the former president. In fact, Mueller showed that Trump repeatedly obstructed justice to stymie the Russia investigation.

Feb. 2

Mother Jones [illegible] *[illegible]nalism [illegible] [illegible],000 Words on Russiagate and Missed the Point* [illegible] February [illegible] *[illegible]pted takedown of the media's coverage bolsters T[illegible] [illegible]rrative* [illegible] for magicians, is not usually a compon[illegible] criticism [illegible] the coverage of the Trump-Russia scandal [illegible] week [illegible] view, veteran investigative reporter Jeff Ge[illegible] [illegible]ntion [illegible] Russiagate, mirroring Donald Trump's [illegible] the p[illegible] to [illegible]tability for his profound betrayal of the natio[illegible] Gerth's [illegible] a [illegible]rly the New York Times (where he worked [illegible] Gerth [illegible]tering [illegible]ony narrative that there was no Russia s[illegible]ely a [illegible] [illegible]eporters and Trump's enemies in the pres[illegible] stance [illegible] State[illegible]

Jan. 30

Columbia Jo[illegible] [illegible]ew (CJR) [illegible] *[illegible] of Trump* (four-part-series), Jeff Gerth, Ja[illegible] *The pr[illegible]* [illegible] *[illegible], three and four*, with introduction by CJR Edi[illegible] [illegible] Kyle [illegible]

*CJR Editor's* [illegible] *[illegible]ck on* [illegible] *Trum[illegible]* [illegible]r and Publisher Kyle Pope, Jan. 30, 2023. Se[illegible] years [illegible] [illegible]ed dance with Donald Trump, the man wh[illegible] country [illegible] dismissing him, then embracing him as a [illegible] ngs and [illegible] [illegible]forts to catalogue Trump as a threat to the co[illegible] great s[illegible] [illegible] narrative did more to shape Trump's [illegible] the p[illegible] [illegible]siaga[illegible], which included the Steele dossier and the [illegible] among [illegible] [illegible]lted in Pulitzer Prizes as well as embarra[illegible] [illegible]rs and [illegible] the press's pursuit of the Russia story co[illegible] [illegible]t any [illegible] [illegible]ith the press was impossible. For the past yea[illegible] CJR has [illegible] media's coverage of Trump and Russia i[illegible] [illegible], and [illegible] [illegible]nters a new political cycle. Investig[illegible] Jeff G[illegible] [illegible]ople at the center of the story—editors a[illegible] Trump [illegible] oth[illegible] [illegible]t. The result is an encyclopedic look at [illegible] consequ[illegible] [illegible]n media history

Jan. 26

New York Ti[illegible] *[illegible]'s Qu[illegible]* [illegible] *[illegible]iry Unraveled*, Charlie Savage, Adam Goldma[illegible] [illegible]ener, [illegible] Th[illegible] [illegible]ohn Durham at one point veered into a cr[illegible] [illegible]gation [illegible] [illegible]self, even as it failed to find wrongdo[illegible] [illegible]ngs of [illegible] inquiry[illegible]

Jan. 23

The Americ[illegible] [illegible], *Cras[illegible]* *[illegible] Bog[illegible]* [illegible] Beaucar Vlahos, Jan. 23, 2023. Lawmak[illegible] anti-Ru[illegible] [illegible]he invasion of Ukraine. One of the most da[illegible] emerg[illegible] Taib[illegible] "[illegible] Files" is how aggressive congress[illegible]s and [illegible] [illegible]n pushing a cynical narrative that brought [illegible] a gian[illegible] Russian bogeyman that haunts U.S. foreign [illegible] uring in [illegible] [illegible]ing many other acts of narrative and discours[illegible] the "[illegible]"—[illegible] [illegible]s released to Taibbi and other journalist[illegible] of Elo[illegible] [illegible]ober [illegible] the company—show that beginnin[illegible] book [illegible] were [illegible]ordinary pressure to acknowledge and pub[illegible] meddl[illegible] social [illegible]rms throughout the 2016 election.

## 2022

### December

Dec. 16

Washington Post, *Analysis: Elon Musk's 'Twitter files' are an exercise in hypocrisy*, Will Oremus, Dec. 16, 2022. Internal documents show how a small group of executives molded online discourse. Under Musk, that's more of a problem than ever. Elon Musk criticized Twitter's previous regime for suppressing speech it didn't like. Meanwhile, as Twitter's new owner, he has taken to suppressing speech he doesn't like. Over the past two weeks, a group of writers chosen by Elon Musk to review Twitter's previously confidential internal messages has portrayed a handful of unaccountable "trust and safety" executives as making critical decisions about online political speech based partly on their own left-leaning intuitions. The "Twitter files" show the company's former leaders, pre-Musk, at times changing or reinterpreting the company's rules on the fly as they scrambled to react to election misinformation, covid-19 skepticism and the Jan. 6, 2021, attack on the U.S. Capitol.

But there's a glaring irony at the project's core that its authors never acknowledge. If a lack of transparency, accountability or consistency in the processes by which tech giants make far-reaching content moderation decisions is cause for alarm — and it should be — then there is no more egregious example than the one Musk himself has set since buying Twitter for $44 billion in October. This week alone, Musk — who billed himself as a "free-speech absolutist" — permanently banned an account that had been tweeting public data about his private jet, creating a new, ad hoc policy to justify the move. Twitter then began suspending numerous other accounts, including that of rival social network Mastodon and those of several journalists who had criticized the previous suspensions, all without immediate explanation.

### October

Oct. 22

National Review, *Opinion: Waiting for Durham*, Andrew C. McCarthy, Oct. 22, 2022. The special counsel's looming report is the only chance the American people will ever get to hold the Clinton campaign and the FBI accountable for Russiagate.

Oct. 20

Washington Post, *Editorial: John Durham's investigation proved Trump wrong, not right*, Editorial Board, Oct. 20, 2020 (print ed.). At what might be the end of his tenure as Justice Department special counsel, John Durham has failed to fulfill former president Donald Trump's prediction that he would unveil "the crime of the century" in his investigation into the FBI's 2016 Russia probe. Instead, the lawyer mostly confirmed, as others had already concluded, that there was no crime of the century at all.

Washington Post, Analysis: The three-year effort to undercut the Russia probe comes up dry, Philip Bump, Oct. 20, 2020 (print ed.).

Oct. 19

NBC News, *Opinion: Special counsel John Durham's failure belongs to William Barr*, Dennis Aftergut, Oct. 19, 2022. Barr's attempts to rehabilitate his image cannot erase his sad final legacy as a Trump enabler.

The Federalist, *Opinion: Media Shame Durham After Danchenko Verdict, But It's Russia Hoaxers Who Should Be Embarrassed*, Margot Cleveland, Oct. 19, 2022. Jury verdicts are not an indictment of John Durham, and he is not the one who should be embarrassed.

Oct. 18

New York Times, *Acquittal of Russia Analyst Deals Final Blow to Trump-Era Prosecutor*, Charlie Savage and Linda Qiu, Oct. 18, 2022. Igor Danchenko, an analyst who provided much of the research for a notorious dossier of unproven assertions and rumors about former President Donald J. Trump and Russia, was acquitted on Tuesday on four counts of lying to the F.B.I. about one of his sources.

Politico, Durham loses again in court, but trial airs FBI flaws, Josh Gerstein, Oct. 18, 2022

Fox News, Commentary: Danchenko trial: Jury finds Steele dossier source not guilty on all counts, Jake Gibson and Brooke Singman, Oct. 18, 2022.

Washington Times, Primary source of Steele dossier acquitted on charges of lying to the FBI in major defeat for Durham, Jeff Mordock, Oct. 18, 2022

Newsweek, Durham Blasted by Experts After New Acquittal: 'Laughed Out of Court Twice,' Aila Slisco, Week of Oct. 18, 2022.

Oct. 17

Fox News, Opinion: Danchenko trial helps Durham expose how corrupt FBI framed Trump, Gregg Jarrett, Oct. 17, 2022.

Oct. 14

New York Times, *Loss of Steele Dossier Source Damaged National Security, F.B.I. Agent Says*, Adam Goldman, Oct. 14, 2022 (print ed.). The agent denounced the exposure by the Trump Justice Department of Igor Danchenko, who was an F.B.I. informant but is now on trial on charges of lying to investigators.

Emptywheel, *Analysis: Anthony Trenga Smothers The Frothers' Hopes For A Pee Tape Trial ... But Not The Damage Done By Credulous Press*, Emptywheel (Marcy Wheeler), Oct. 5, 2022. Judge Anthony Trenga has refused to let John Durham turn the Igor Danchenko trial into a pee tape circus. Will the journalists who played Durham's clowns last year retract?

**September**

Sept. 14

New York Times, *Durham Inquiry Appears to Wind Down as Grand Jury Expires*, Katie Benner, Adam Goldman and Charlie Savage, Sept. 14, 2022.

Sept. 15

Proof, Investigative Commentary: *DOJ Investigating Ties Between the FBI and the Kremlin Agent Behind 2016 Trump-Russia Collusion*; Jared Kushner May Also Be Implicated, Seth Abramson, Sept. 15, 2022. A new Insider report is here expanded upon by Proof to reveal a potentially harrowing triangle linking Trump's lead agent in Trump-Russia collusion, Putin's lead agent in the same events, and the FBI.

Introduction: The oft-maligned collation of raw intel known as the Steele Dossier, once advertised as "70%" accurate by its curator, Christopher Steele—who said from the outset that his unprocessed data required additional work by U.S. intelligence agents—has so far proven to be about one-third accurate, one-third inaccurate, and one-third unproven, though with each passing year this last third moves closer and closer to falling under "accurate."

**June**

June 1

New York Times, Sussmann Acquittal Raises Question: What Is Durham Actually Trying to Do? Charlie Savage, June 1, 2022.

Mother Jones, *How John Durham's Probe Has Exposed Trump's Russia Con*, David Corn, June 1, 2022. His three-year investigation has so far shown the only hoax was orchestrated by the former president.

Washington Post, *Opinion: A clever effort to try to de-Putinize Trump*, David E. Kendall, June 1, 2022 (print ed.). David E. Kendall, a lawyer at Williams & Connolly, represents 2016 Democratic presidential nominee Hillary Clinton. Well, that was a quick acquittal! The Michael Sussmann prosecution brought by Trump administration special counsel John Durham tried to generate a Clinton-conspiracy bang but ended with a not-guilty-verdict whimper.

The actual case against Sussmann was both narrow and paper-thin from the start. He was charged with lying to the FBI's general counsel in a one-on-one, unrecorded meeting on Sept. 19, 2016, about whom he was speaking for — not on the report he presented about mysterious communications between the Trump Organization and a Vladimir Putin crony's Russian bank (which the FBI later declared unsubstantiated). While the alleged lie was simple, straightforward and could have been explained in two pages, it was encased in 27 pages of dark and inchoate allegations of wrongdoing by a number of Clintonites.

What was the lie? Not that Sussmann provided false evidence of Donald Trump's alleged collusion with the Russians — that was neither alleged nor proven. Not that there was a vast conspiracy to falsely besmirch Trump as seeking Russian assistance — that was neither alleged nor proven. Not that there was a successful deception of the FBI — many witnesses testified they were well aware of Sussmann's many Democratic connections and clients. The Durham indictment charged only that Sussmann had failed to tell the FBI general counsel why he was meeting with him. The jury saw through the fog of misdirection and innuendo in the indictment's overstuffed allegations and quickly returned a not-guilty verdict.

Washington Times, *Durham team seeks redemption with Danchenko trial*, Jeff Mordock, June 1, 2022. Special counsel John Durham's stinging loss in federal court this week cast doubt over the future of his probe of U.S. intelligence community wrongdoing in pursuing Trump-Russia collusion theories, but the Durham team still has a narrow window to redeem themselves.

Even if [illegible] al M[illegible] d wa[illegible] plug on Mr. Durham's investiga[illegible] wait u[illegible] spec[illegible] next trial in October.

## May

### May 31

New York Ti[illegible] Sussn[illegible] ught by Trump-Era Prosecutor, Charlie S[illegible] 1 202[illegible]

Washington [illegible] *Sussma[illegible] alleg[illegible] ump in 2016, acquitted of lying to FBI*, Devlin [illegible] 1 2022 [illegible] ed S[illegible] wyer for Democrats, of lying to the FBI at t[illegible] 2016 [illegible] eat for Special Counsel John Durham, [illegible] ree years [illegible] ral William Barr.

New York M[illegible] ligence [illegible] *ump's Russiagate Theory. Instead He Debunked* [illegible] Chait, [illegible] itor face-plants. Donald Trump and William [illegible] years [illegible] the [illegible] igation was a criminal plot by the FBI. Th[illegible] of Jus[illegible] the Russia investigation was adequate[illegible] but B[illegible] prosecutor, John Durham, who would s[illegible] ever t[illegible] ching its perpetrators to justice.

By 2020, Ba[illegible] g tha[illegible] ght [illegible] he way up to Barack Obama but would b[illegible] accom[illegible] Pr[illegible] a and Vice-President Biden," he said that [illegible] ever th[illegible] d on the information I have today, I don't ex[illegible] m's [illegible] to a[illegible] stigation of either man. Our concern [illegible] l crimin[illegible] ed [illegible] the fall, Barr was reportedly "comm[illegible] Durha[illegible] is in[illegible] tremely seriously and is focused on winning [illegible]."

However fo[illegible], Dur[illegible] win[illegible] ons. His investigation has produced one ext[illegible] – a [illegible] FBI [illegible] Clinesmith* for a likely immaterial error. A[illegible] sing p[illegible] Dur[illegible] his authority by trying to prosecute Michael [illegible] awyer [illegible] Hilla[illegible] hom Durham tried to convict on a single p[illegible] And th[illegible] out [illegible] so pathetically threadbare that it resulted i[illegible] ttal.

### May 24

Politico, *Sus[illegible] alts [illegible] ims*, Josh Gerstein and Kelly Hooper [illegible] The [illegible] sh[illegible] ater this week. The defense for a Democ[illegible] ccused [illegible] he F[illegible] away Tuesday at the prosecution, arguing [illegible] robe t[illegible] ge[illegible] ump-Russia allegations was so shoddy [illegible] hat a[illegible] torney would not have affected the Russia in[illegible]

### May 22

Emptywhee[illegible] *Tweet a[illegible] appeal)*, Emptywheel (Marcy Wheeler [illegible] If y[illegible] ael Sussmann trial anywhere but here and [illegible] would b[illegible] the [illegible] Friday is that former Hillary campaign manager Robby Mook testified that Hillary personally approved of sharing the Alfa Bank story….

Obviously, the frothy right has made it the center of a frenzy to investigate Hillary herself. Surely it will also lead to an investigation of Jake Sullivan. The thing is, legally, the part about investigating wasn't supposed to come into the trial and will be something that, at the very least, Judge Christopher Cooper issues an instruction to the jury on.

This media frenzy was the predictable result of Andrew DeFilippis breaking Cooper's rules. Again.

**February**

Feb. 14

New York Times, Court Filing Started a Furor in Right-Wing Outlets, but Their Narrative Is Off Track, Charlie Savage, Feb. 14, 2022.

**2021**

Sept. 30

New York Times, *Trump Server Mystery Produces Fresh Conflict*, Charlie Savage and Adam Goldman, Sept. 30, 2021.

**2020**

Dec. 1

New York Times, Barr Makes Durham a Special Counsel in a Bid to Entrench Scrutiny of the Russia Inquiry, Charlie Savage, Dec. 1, 2020.

Sept. 11

New York Times, *Top Aide in Review of Russia Inquiry Resigns From Justice Dept.*, Charlie Savage, Katie Benner, Adam Goldman and Neil Vigdor, Sept. 11, 2020.

**2018**

March 10

New London Day, *U.S. Attorney Durham tells mob tales during rare lecture*, Karen Florin, March 10, 2018. Connecticut U.S. Attorney John Durham details his role as a special prosecutor in the Whitey Bulger case at the University of St. Joseph in West Hartford on Monday, March 5, 2018.

United States Attorney John H. Durham has kept such a low profile while handling some of the country's most infamous criminal investigations that he once made New Republic magazine's list of Washington's "most powerful, least famous people." Durham "made his bones," as he would say, prosecuting mobsters, corrupt federal agents and former Connecticut Gov. John G.

Rowland. He's been tapped by United States attorneys general to investigate topics as touchy as alleged torture and coverups during CIA investigations. The 67-year-old Groton resident, nominated as Connecticut's top federal prosecutor by President Donald Trump and endorsed by Republicans and Democrats alike, has confined most of his public speaking to within the four walls of federal courtrooms.

A week after being sworn in, Durham, perhaps realizing that his new role calls for higher visibility, delivered a lecture at the University of St. Joseph in West Hartford, a formerly all-female school that is going all co-ed this year and ratcheting up its criminal justice program.

For about an hour this past Monday, he regaled an audience with an insider's view of the widely publicized investigations that brought down mobsters James "Whitey" Bulger, Stephen "The Rifleman" Flemmi and their corrupted FBI handler, Special Agent John Connolly Jr. It was a case that extended into Connecticut, where gambling venues for the sport jai alai were infiltrated by Bulger's Winter Hill Gang.

Durham's longtime partner in crime-fighting, Deputy Chief State's Attorney Leonard C. Boyle, introduced the U.S. attorney to the university gathering as the person members of the Connecticut bar call when stumped by a legal question. Boyle said Durham has "an extreme work ethic" and is working all the time, whether in the office or at home.

Boyle seemed as amazed as anyone that his friend had agreed to the speaking engagement, since Durham is "notoriously shy about speaking about himself or what he does." The University of St. Joseph's affiliation with the Catholic church may have helped. "Other than an overwhelming commitment to the cause of justice, the two great devotions of John's life are his Catholic faith and his family," Boyle said.

**2017**

July 11

New York Times, *Russian Dirt on Clinton? 'I Love It,' Donald Trump Jr. Said*, Jo Becker, Adam Goldman and Matt Apuzzo, July 11, 2017. Donald Trump Jr. received an email on June 3, 2016, promising dirt on Hillary Clinton. The information was described as being part of Russia's support for his father's presidential bid. His reply? "I love it."

May 15

Washington Post, *Trump revealed highly classified information to Russian foreign minister and ambassador*, Greg Miller and Greg Jaffe, May 15, 2017. President Trump revealed highly classified information to the Russian foreign minister and ambassador in a White House meeting last week, according to current and former U.S. officials, who said Trump's disclosures jeopardized a critical source of intelligence on the Islamic State. The information the president relayed had been provided by a U.S. partner through an intelligence-sharing arrangement considered so sensitive that details have been withheld from allies and tightly restricted even within the U.S. government, officials said.

**2016**

July 27

New York Times, *Donald Trump calls on Russia to find Hillary Clinton's missing emails*, Ashley Parker and David E. Sanger, July 27, 2016.

**2011**

July 2

Justice Integrity Project, *CIA Torture Investigator Plays Powerful But Mysterious Role*, July 2, 2011. John Durham is the career federal prosecutor who made news June 30 when the Justice Department acted on his recommendation to narrow a probe of CIA mistreatment of detainees from 101 to two cases. Our Justice Integrity Project revealed last July that a federal appeals court found in 2008 serious misconduct by a team of federal prosecutors supervised by Durham.

**2010**

Justice Integrity Project, *DOJ Absolves CIA For Destroying Torture Evidence*, Andrew Kreig, Nov. 9, 2010. The Justice Department announced on Tuesday, Nov. 9, 2010 that the CIA's former top clandestine officer and others will not be charged in the destruction of CIA videotapes of interrogations of suspected terrorists. That probe is controversial because of claims that the DOJ covered up wrongdoing by a whitewash investigation of misconduct by CIA and DOJ personnel. Suspicions arose in part because the investigation has been led since 2008 by John Durham, a career Justice Department prosecutor based in Connecticut. The Justice Integrity Project has revealed that courts have found that Durham and another high-ranking colleague were implicated in suppressing evidence in at least two cases.

Nieman Watchdog, Harvard University, *New Questions Raised About Prosecutor Who Cleared Bush Officials in U.S. Attorney Firings*, Andrew Kreig, July 25, 2010. Four days before Nora Dannehy was appointed to investigate the Bush administration's U.S. attorney firing scandal, a team of lawyers she led was found to have illegally suppressed evidence in a major political corruption case. This previously unreported fact calls her entire investigation into question as well as that of a similar investigation by her DOJ colleague, John Durham, of DOJ and CIA decision-making involving torture. (Available at http://www.niemanwatchdog.org/index.cfm?fuseaction=ask_this.view&askthisid=00469)

**2003**

Connecticut Law Tribune, *Attorney's Trial Tactics Impugned*, Kellie A. Wagner, June 23, 2003. *Judge tosses conviction.* Admonishing Deputy U.S. Attorney John Durham's trial tactics, as well as her own failure to maintain courtroom decorum, U.S. District Judge Janet Bond Arterton has taken the extraordinary step of overturning a weapons charge conviction largely on account of prosecutorial misconduct....In granting defendant Anthony Washington's request for a new trial las month, Arterton rebuked Durham for undermining the defense's key witness, while personally vouching for those who took the stand on the prosecution's behalf, maligning defense counsel and his arguments; and alluding to highly prejudicial facts not in evidence.

## Key Figures In 'Russiagate' Research

*Editor's Note:* This roster is to help readers identify those mentioned, omitted or otherwise relevant to the Durham Report. Descriptions draw heavily from Wikipedia entries and their sourcing, augmented by material from the Durham, Mueller and Congressional Reports. Listings are arranged by last name except for major officials listed at the top. Suggestions are welcome for updates in future editions.

### Major Public Officials

**President Donald J. Trump**, born on June 14, 1946, is an American politician, media personality, and businessman who served as the 45th president of the United States from 2017 to 2021.

Trump won the 2016 presidential election as the Republican nominee against Democratic nominee Hillary Clinton via the Electoral College vote, 304 to 227, while losing the popular vote by 2.9 million.

In 2016, Trump won 30 states, including Michigan, Pennsylvania, and Wisconsin, states considered Democratic since the 1990s. Clinton won 20 states and the District of Columbia. Trump's victory marked the return of an undivided Republican government — a Republican White House combined with Republican control of both chambers of Congress.

In January 2017, American intelligence agencies—the CIA, the FBI, and the NSA, represented by the Director of National Intelligence—jointly stated with "high confidence" that the Russian government interfered in the 2016 presidential election to favor the election of Trump. In March 2017, FBI Director James Comey told Congress, "[T]he FBI, as part of our counterintelligence mission, is investigating the Russian government's efforts to interfere in the 2016 presidential election. That includes investigating the nature of any links between individuals associated with the Trump campaign and the Russian government, and whether there was any coordination between the campaign and Russia's efforts."

On May 9, 2017, Trump dismissed Comey.

Many suspicious links between Trump associates and Russian officials and spies were discovered and the relationships between Russians and "team Trump" were widely reported by the press.

Trump is the only American president to have been impeached twice. After he tried to pressure Ukraine in 2019 to investigate Biden, he was impeached in December by the House of Representatives for abuse of power and obstruction of Congress; he was acquitted by the Senate in February 2020. The House impeached him a second time in January 2021 for incitement of insurrection, and the Senate acquitted him the next month.

In his last full day in office, Trump granted 143 pardons and commutations. Those pardoned included three former Republican congressmen, Steve Bannon, Paul Manafort and Roger Stone.

**Attorney General William P. Barr**, born May 23, 1950, served as the 77th and 85th United States attorney general in the administrations of Presidents George H. W. Bush, a former CIA Director, and Donald Trump. Barr worked for the CIA from 1971 to 1977.

In the 1980s, Barr worked for the law firm Shaw, Pittman, Potts & Trowbridge, with one year's work in the White House of the Ronald Reagan administration. Before becoming attorney general in 1991, Barr held numerous other posts within the Department of Justice, including leading the Office of Legal Counsel and serving as deputy attorney general.

Under Barr's advice, President George H. W. Bush in 1992 pardoned six officials involved in the Iran–Contra affair.

From 1994 to 2008, Barr worked for GTE and its successor Verizon Communications, which made him a multimillionaire.

Barr became attorney general for the second time in 2019. During his term, he received criticism from many for his letter on the Mueller report and his interventions in the convictions and sentences of former advisors to President Trump, Roger Stone and Michael Flynn.

On June 1, 2022, Barr was interviewed on Fox News about the verdict in the failed prosecution of Michael Sussmann. He continued to defend Trump by repeating debunked "Russiagate" conspiracy theories about the origins of the Russia investigation by stating that the case against Sussmann "crystallized the central role played by the Hillary campaign in launching, as a dirty trick, the whole Russiagate collusion narrative."

The *Washington Post* noted that the Justice Department traditionally seeks to avoid impugning individuals who are not charged with crimes, and the DOJ is not involved in exposing political "dirty tricks" that have not been found unlawful.

Barr asserted Durham "exposed really dreadful behavior by the supervisors in the FBI, the senior ranks of the FBI, who knowingly use this information to start an investigation of Trump," though the Sussmann case did not relate to how the FBI Crossfire Hurricane investigation began. Although Barr appointed Durham to investigate possible FBI wrongdoing in opening Crossfire Hurricane, Durham's prosecution of Sussmann portrayed the FBI as a victim, rather than a perpetrator, of wrongdoing.

**Special Counsel Robert S. Mueller III**, born in 1944, is an American lawyer who served as the sixth director of the FBI from 2001 to 2013.

Mueller is a registered Republican in Washington, D.C., and was appointed and reappointed to Senate-confirmed positions by presidents George H. W. Bush, Bill Clinton, George W. Bush, and Barack Obama.

On May 17, 2017, Mueller was appointed by Deputy Attorney General Rod Rosenstein as special counsel overseeing an investigation into allegations of Russian interference in the 2016 U.S. presidential election and related matters. He submitted his report to Attorney General William Barr on March 22, 2019. On April 18, the Department of Justice released it. On May 29, he resigned, and the Office of the Special Counsel was closed.

In this capacity, Mueller oversaw the investigation into "any links and/or coordination between the Russian government and individuals associated with the campaign of President Donald Trump, and any matters that arose or may arise directly from the investigation."

Mueller's appointment to oversee the investigation immediately garnered widespread support from both Democrats and Republicans in Congress

On October 30, 2017, Mueller filed charges against former Trump campaign chairman Paul Manafort and campaign co-chairman Rick Gates. The 12 charges include conspiracy to launder money, violations of the 1938 Foreign Agents Registration Act (FARA) as being an unregistered agent of a foreign principal, false and misleading FARA statements, and conspiracy against the United States.

On December 1, 2017, Mueller reached a plea agreement with former national security adviser Michael Flynn, who pleaded guilty to giving false testimony to the FBI about his contacts with Russian ambassador Sergey Kislyak. As part of Flynn's negotiations, his son, Michael G. Flynn, was not expected to be charged, and Flynn was prepared to testify that [illegible] officials [illegible] team [illegible] him to make contact with the Russians.

On February [illegible] Mueller [illegible] 13 Rus[illegible]duals and three Russian companies [illegible] to [illegible] ning Russian propaganda that targeted Dem[illegible] rinee [illegible] ton [illegible]esident-elect Donald Trump.

**Attorney General M[illegible] Garland** [illegible] 52, [illegible]can lawyer and jurist who serves as the 86th U[illegible] attorn[illegible] [illegible] served as a U.S. circuit judge of the Court of Appeal[illegible] trict [illegible] Circ[illegible]97 to 2021. In 2016, President Barack Obama nomi[illegible]rd to th[illegible] Supre[illegible]ut the Republican-led U.S. Senate effectively b[illegible]rd's ap[illegible]nt.

A native of th[illegible]rea, Ga[illegible]University and Harvard Law School, whe[illegible] editor [illegible] rvard [illegible]w. He served as a law clerk [illegible] Henry Fri[illegible] he U[illegible]s Court of Appeals for [illegible] Circuit a[illegible] Sup[illegible] Justice William J. Br[illegible] then [illegible] co[illegible]tion at Arnold & Por[illegible]ch h[illegible] a f[illegible]ecutor in the United State[illegible] of J[illegible] re h[illegible]d the investigatio[illegible]ution [illegible]bers. President Bi[illegible]pointed [illegible] the [illegible] of Appeals in 1997, and [illegible] ved a[illegible] dg[illegible]o 2020.

President Ba[illegible], anoth[illegible]rat, [illegible] Garland to serve as an associate jus[illegible]preme [illegible] Ma[illegible]ill the vacancy created by the death of Ant[illegible] Howe[illegible]ublic[illegible] majority refused to hold a hearing or v[illegible]nina[illegible]pre[illegible]efusal of a Senate majority to consider a S[illegible] nom[illegible]s hig[illegible]versial. President Joe Biden nominated G[illegible]. atto[illegible]al in [illegible]021. He was confirmed by the Senate in a [illegible]rd to[illegible] Ma[illegible]ame year.

Garland's gr[illegible]eft the [illegible]ussi[illegible] in the early 20th century, fleeing antis[illegible]ns in [illegible]w U[illegible]oland. Two of his grandmothe[illegible] were la[illegible]ed i[illegible]aust. After graduating from law school, Garla[illegible] years [illegible]cial [illegible]st for Judge Henry Friendly of the U.S. Cou[illegible] for th[illegible] Circu[illegible]rk City) and then for Justice William J. Br[illegible] the U.S. [illegible] Co[illegible]78 to 1979. After his clerkships, Garland spe[illegible]as a sp[illegible] tan[illegible]orney General Benjamin Civiletti. At t[illegible] Departm[illegible] nds[illegible]ities included the supervision of high-profile [illegible]rorism[illegible] ud[illegible]homa City bombing, Ted Kaczynski (a [illegible] the "U[illegible]r"), [illegible]anta Olympics bombings.

As Attorney General, Garland announced the appointment of Special Counsel Jack Smith to oversee the Trump investigations on Nov. 18, 2022, days after Trump announced his 2024 presidential campaign. Other special counsels Garland appointed include former Trump appointees to the Justice Department Robert K. Hur and David C. Weiss.

**Special Counsel Robert K. Hur**, born in 1973, is an American lawyer who served as the United States Attorney for the District of Maryland from 2018 to 2021. He previously served as Principal Associate Deputy Attorney General with the U.S. Department of Justice. Hur oversaw the 2023-2024 investigation into President Joe Biden's alleged mishandling of classified documents during Biden's time as vice president.

Hur was born in New York City to South Korean parents. He holds degrees from Harvard College, King's College at Cambridge University and Stanford Law School. After law school, Hur was a law clerk for Judge Alex Kozinski of the U.S. Court of Appeals for the Ninth Circuit and for Chief Justice William Rehnquist of the U.S. Supreme Court from 2002 to 2003. He then served as Special Assistant and Counsel to Christopher A. Wray, then Assistant Attorney General in charge of the Justice Department's Criminal Division. Among other posts, he served as a top aide to Rod Rosenstein after Rosenstein became Deputy Attorney General in the Trump Administration, He was a liaison to Special Counsel Robert Mueller's investigation of Russian interference in the 2016 election.

In 2017, President Trump nominated Hur to be U.S. Attorney for Maryland. Following the end of the Trump Administration and Hur's return to private practice with the law firm Gibson Dunn, Attorney General Merrick Garland appointed Hur to oversee investigations into President Joe Biden's alleged mishandling of classified documents during his time as vice president. On February 7, 2024, Garland notified Congress that Hur had concluded his investigation, and no charges were recommended. In Hur's final report, he stated that he found that Biden "willfully retained and disclosed classified materials after his vice presidency when he was a private citizen." He concluded that "no criminal charges are warranted in this matter ... even if there was no policy against charging a sitting president," because the "evidence does not establish Mr. Biden's guilt beyond a reasonable doubt." He also cited Biden's memory as a factor, concluding that "Biden would likely present himself to a jury ... as a sympathetic, well-meaning, elderly man with a poor memory." The White House rebuked Hur's characterization as inappropriate, politicized commentary that veered from standards of unbiased, legal analysis.

**Special Counsel John "Jack" Smith**, born in 1969, is an American attorney who has served in the U.S. Department of Justice as an assistant U.S. attorney, acting U.S. attorney, and head of the department's Public Integrity Section. He was also the chief prosecutor at the Kosovo Specialist

Chambers, an international tribunal at The Hague tasked with investigating and prosecuting war crimes in the Kosovo War.

In November 2022, attorney general Merrick Garland appointed Smith an independent special counsel, responsible for overseeing two preexisting Justice Department criminal investigations into former president Donald Trump, three days after Trump announced his 2024 presidential campaign: one regarding Trump's role in the January 6 U.S. Capitol attack, and the other into alleged mishandling of government records, including classified documents. The documents case resulted in a 37-count indictment of Trump in June 2023 to which three counts were later added in July. In August, the January 6 case resulted in an indictment on four charges.

Smith earned degrees from the State University of New York at Oneonta and Harvard Law School, from which he graduated *cum laude*. From 2008 to 2010, Smith worked as investigation coordinator for the Office of the Prosecutor of the International Criminal Court in The Hague, Netherlands. In that position, he oversaw cases against government officials and militia members accused of war crimes and genocide. In 2010, Smith returned to the U.S. to become chief of the U.S. Department of Justice's Public Integrity Section. On May 7, 2018, Smith was named to a four-year term as chief prosecutor for the Kosovo Specialist Chambers in The Hague, investigating war crimes in the Kosovo War

On June 8, 2023, a grand jury indicted Trump on seven federal criminal charges related to his handling of classified documents. This marked the first time in American history that a serving or former president has been indicted on a federal criminal charge. On August 1, Trump was indicted by a grand jury on four more federal felony counts relating to his attempts to overturn the 2020 presidential election and his conduct during the attack on the Capitol.

**Special Counsel David C. Weiss, born in 1956,** is an American attorney nominated by President Donald Trump to be United States Attorney for the United States District Court for the District of Delaware, and was retained by President Joe Biden. He has served in that office since February 22, 2018.

Weiss received his bachelor's degree from Washington University in St. Louis and his Juris Doctor degree from Widener University School of Law in Delaware.] He clerked for Justice Andrew D. Christie of the Delaware Supreme Court. He then served as an assistant United States Attorney in Delaware from 1986 to 1989, prosecuting violent crimes and white-collar criminal offenses. Leaving the U.S. Attorney's office, he worked as a commercial litigation associate and partner at the Duane Morris firm and as an executive at a financial services firm He

returned to the Delaware U.S. Attorney's office as First Assistant U.S. Attorney in 2007. In this capacity, he served as Acting US Attorney for the District of Delaware from 2009 until the confirmation of Charles Oberly.

Weiss later served as Acting U.S. Attorney for Delaware again during the administration of Donald Trump following the resignation of Oberly. He was subsequently nominated to officially fill that position, and on February 15, 2018, his nomination to be the United States Attorney was confirmed by the Senate by voice vote. He was sworn in on February 22, 2018.

Weiss has been in charge of the investigations into the financial dealings of Hunter Biden and was asked by Biden Administration executives to remain in office. On August 11, 2023, Attorney General Merrick Garland named Weiss as special counsel in the Hunter Biden. On February 14, 2024, he indicted a former FBI informant with lying about President Joe Biden and his son Hunter Biden's involvement in business dealings with Ukrainian energy company Burisma Holdings, undercutting a major aspect of Republicans' impeachment inquiry into the president. Biden's defense counsel has filed papers also seeking dismissal of federal gun possession and tax charges against Hunter Biden because of alleged major irregularities and government misconduct in the long running federal investigations.

## Ru[illegible] Key Fi[illegible]

**Seth Abramson** is th[illegible] Times [illegible] series *Proof of Collusion* (2018), *Proof of Con*[illegible]), *Pro*[illegible] nd *Proof of Coup* (2022). A

[illegible] mer [illegible] nd investigator who taught [illegible] ital jo[illegible] of New Hampshire, he earned a [illegible] gree f[illegible] nd has authored 18 books in [illegible] dition [illegible] s on his *Proof* website and [illegible] e ne[illegible] digital journalism and the law, [illegible] nves[illegible] tionally thorough in its visual portrayal and analy[illegible] ticipa[illegible] an interference with the 2016 U.S. presidential ele[illegible] mest[illegible] to overturn the 2020 election.

**Aras Agalarov** is a R[illegible] h clo[illegible] President Vladimir Putin and Donald Trump's par[illegible] g a M[illegible] Moscow in 2013.

**Emin Agalarov** is so[illegible] arov [illegible] pop[illegible] helped arrange major contributions to the [illegible] nizati[illegible] form at the Miss Universe pageant in Moscow. [illegible] d alo[illegible] fath[illegible] business relationship with Donald Trump and h[illegible] s. He [illegible] 201[illegible] with **Donald Trump Jr.** and Paul Manafort, among o[illegible] p To[illegible] a Russian lawyer allegedly promised emails tha[illegible] harmf[illegible] Cli[illegible] r presidential campaign.

**Aldrich Ames**, born [illegible] forme[illegible] terin[illegible] officer who was convicted of

espiona[illegible] f of the [illegible] in 1994. He is serving a life sentenc[illegible] he po[illegible] deral Correctional Institution in Terre H[illegible] a.[ Am[illegible] npromised more highly classifie[illegible] than [illegible] ert Hanssen, who was arrested seven y[illegible] 001.

**Julian Assange**, fou[illegible] Leaks [illegible] rn editor, publisher and activist whose medi[illegible] Wiki[illegible] pub[illegible] d documents that generated political news. In or[illegible] t pub[illegible] 01[illegible] with five newspapers documents and oth[illegible] ument[illegible] by [illegible] nning, a U.S. Army intelligence analyst.

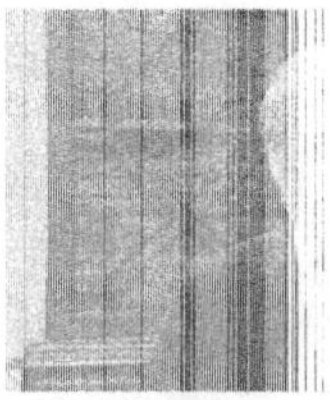

Sw[illegible] vestigated him for years on du[illegible] likel[illegible] inspired claims that he en[illegible] mpa[illegible] nduct during two sexual en[illegible] with [illegible] invited him to sleep with th[illegible] ara[illegible] during a lecture tour. Later, he breached bail in the United Kingdom and obtained refuge in Ecuador's London embassy beginning in 2012.

UK police arrested him in 2019 after Ecuador withdrew his asylum status. The U.S. government unsealed indictments that year and in 2020 charging him with computer intrusion related to Manning's leaks and with violating the Espionage Act of 2017. In June 2023, Assange lost his appeal of an extradition order to face U.S. charges.

During the 2016 U.S. presidential campaign, Assange had been critical of both Hillary Clinton and Donald Trump. But WikiLeaks released during the campaign emails from the Democratic National Committee (DNC) and Clinton Campaign Chairman John Podesta that were especially damaging to Democrats, causing DNC Chairwoman Debbie Wasserman Schultz to resign her post, among other impacts. Special Counsel Robert Mueller attributed the attack on the DNC to 12 Russian GRU military intelligence agents who were indicted for allegedly obtaining the emails and sharing them via the pseudonym Guccifer 2.0 with WikiLeaks and others. Assange has said the Russian government was not the source of the emails.

**Alpha Bank** is the largest of Russia's private banks in Russia. It was founded in 1990 by Russian businessman Mikhail Fridman, who is still the controlling owner as of this writing.

**James A. Baker** was FBI general counsel from 2014 to 2017 and later deputy general counsel of Twitter before being fired by Elon Musk in December 2022. A onetime friend of his former Department of Justice colleague Michael Sussmann, Baker later provided adverse testimony

against Sussmann in Special Counsel John Durham's unsuccessful false statement prosecution, which ended in acquittal.

In December 2017, Baker was replaced as general counsel and reassigned to a different position within the FBI. It was revealed in April 2018, that he was a recipient of at least one Comey memo. In May 2018, Baker resigned from the FBI and joined the Brookings Institution as a fellow, writing for the justice-focused blog, Lawfare.

**Stephen Bannon**, born in 1953, is an American media executive, political strategist, and former investment banker. He served as the White House's chief strategist in the administration of U.S.

president Donald Trump during the first seven months of Trump's term.

Shown before microphones outside the federal courthouse in Washington, DC in a photo by the Justice Integrity Project with his attorney in the background, Bannon is a former executive chairman of Breitbart News and previously served on the board of the now-defunct data-analytics firm

Cambridge Analytica. Bannon became heavily involved in pro-Trump campaign activities, including as the chief executive officer of the campaign. He received appointed as chief strategist and senior counselor to the president following Trump's election. He was forced out eight months later and was rebuked by Trump for highly critical comments about the president quoted by Michael Wolff in the book *Fire and Fury*.

In August 2020, Bannon and three others were arrested on federal charges of conspiracy to commit mail fraud and money laundering in connection with the "We Build the Wall" fundraising campaign.

But Bannon received a pardon from Trump on the president's last day in office before Bannon stood trial. The state of New York later indicted Bannon on similar charges not covered by the pardon. Also, Bannon appealed a separate four-month jail sentence he received for two criminal charges of contempt of Congress for failure to comply with a subpoena by the U.S. House committee investigating the January attack on the Capitol following the 2020 elections.

**Senate Intelligence Committee Chair Richard Burr**, born in 1955, is an American businessman and politician who served as a United States senator from North Carolina from 2005 to 2023. A member of the Republican Party, Burr was previously a member of the United States House of Representatives.

From 2015 to 2020, he chaired the Senate Intelligence Committee. In 2016, he announced that he would not seek reelection in 2022.

Burr was one of seven Republican senators to vote to convict Donald Trump of incitement of insurrection in his second impeachment trial. Burr had been a national security adviser to the Trump campaign and had stated that Trump "aligns perfectly" with the Republican Party.

As chair of the United States Senate Select Committee on Intelligence, Burr led that chamber's investigation into Russian interference in the 2016 United States elections.

*Commissioned Reports*

The Senate Intelligence Committee commissioned two reports that extensively described the Russian campaign to influence social media during the 2016 election.

One report, *The Tactics & Tropes of the Internet Research Agency*, was produced by the New Knowledge cybersecurity company aided by researchers at Columbia University and Canfield Research LLC.

Another, *The IRA, Social Media and Political Polarization in the United States, 2012-2018*, was by the Computational Propaganda Project of Oxford University along with the social media analysis company Graphika. The New Knowledge report highlighted "the energy and imagination" of the Russian effort to "sway American opinion and divide the country", and their focus on African-Americans. The report identified more than 263 million "engagements" (likes, comments, shares, etc.) with Internet Research Agency content and faulted U.S. social media companies for allowing their platforms to be co-opted for foreign propaganda." Examples of efforts included "campaigning for African American voters to boycott elections or follow the wrong voting procedures in 2016," "encouraging extreme right-wing voters to be more confrontational," and "spreading sensationalist, conspiratorial, and other forms of junk political news and misinformation to voters across the political spectrum."

*2020 Senate Committee Report*

On April 21, 2020, the Senate Intelligence Committee released a unanimous, heavily redacted report reviewing the January 2017 intelligence community assessment on Russian interference. The committee felt that the assessment brought a "coherent and well-constructed intelligence basis for the case of unprecedented Russian interference in the 2016 U.S. presidential election", specifically that the interference was unprecedented in its "manner and aggressiveness." The Senate committee heard "specific intelligence reporting to support the assessment that Putin and the Russian Government demonstrated a preference for candidate Trump", and that Putin "approved and directed" the interference.

The committee praised the assessment as an "impressive accomplishment", noting that the assessment "reflects proper analytic tradecraft" despite a limited timeframe. The committee also stated that "interviews with those who drafted and prepared the ICA affirmed that analysts were under no political pressure to reach specific conclusions." A disagreement between the CIA and the NSA of the agencies' confidence level of Russia's preference for Trump "was reasonable, transparent, and openly debated among the agencies and analysts." Additionally, the committee found that the Steele dossier was not used by the assessment to "support any of its analytic judgments."

On August 17, 2020, the Republican-controlled Senate Intelligence Committee released the fifth and final volume of their 996-page report, ending one of the United States "highest-profile congressional inquiries." The Committee report, which was based on three years of investigations, found that the Russian government had engaged in an "extensive campaign" to sabotage the election in favor of Trump, which included assistance from some members of Trump's own advisers. Volume 5 said the Trump administration had used "novel claims" of executive privilege to obstruct the inquiry.

The report sa[illegible] r[illegible]p's 20[illegible] [illegible]ign s[illegible] [illegible]ager to accept Russia's help, however aft[illegible] of th[illegible] [illegible]cting [illegible]telligence Committee Chair Marco Rubio [illegible]ement [illegible] the co[illegible] found absolutely no evidence that then-ca[illegible] [illegible]ald Tru[illegible] ca[illegible] [illegible]ded with the Russian government [illegible] the 20[illegible] [illegible]on."

Burr was one [illegible] Republica[illegible] [illegible]e to [illegible] Trump's second impeachment trial. On Feb[illegible] [illegible] North [illegible] Repu[illegible] [illegible]y censured him for the vote.

**Maria Butina,** born [illegible] Russian [illegible], po[illegible] [illegible]ist, journalist, and former entrepreneur who w[illegible] [illegible] in 201[illegible] [illegible]g as [illegible] [illegible]tered foreign agent of Russia within the United St[illegible] [illegible]work[illegible] [illegible]ssista[illegible] [illegible]sandr Torshin; a former member of the Fede[illegible] [illegible]il, m[illegible] [illegible] ad[illegible] United Russia party, and deputy governor of the Cen[illegible] Russia.

[illegible]e, sh[illegible] [illegible]o infiltrate conservative groups [illegible], inc[illegible] [illegible]ational Rifle Association (as [illegible] one [illegible]ght, adjoining a later mug shot), [illegible] an[illegible] [illegible]omote Russian interests in the [illegible] United S[illegible] [illegible]dential election. In 2013, she [illegible] [illegible]blic[illegible] [illegible]operative Paul Erickson in [illegible] he tw[illegible] close, started dating, and [illegible]y m[illegible] [illegible]ther. In 2015, she emailed him a description [illegible]d proj[illegible] [illegible] [illegible]ublican Party to be friendlier to Russia, throu[illegible] The S[illegible] [illegible]llig[illegible] [illegible]ttee later concluded that she attempted to [illegible] the Tru[illegible] [illegible]ign [illegible] a secret communications back channel with [illegible]

In July 2018, [illegible]ng in W[illegible], D.C[illegible] was arrested by the FBI and charged with [illegible] agen[illegible] [illegible]ssian [illegible]n "without prior notification to the Attorney [illegible] Dece[illegible] [illegible], s[illegible] guilty to felony charges of conspiracy to [illegible] regis[illegible] [illegible]gn a[illegible] Russian state. In April 2019, a federal judge [illegible] her to [illegible] served around five months at Tallahassee [illegible] ection[illegible] [illegible]on. H[illegible] pretrial prison term was counted tow[illegible] [illegible]ence.

She was rele[illegible] [illegible]orte[illegible] [illegible]uss[illegible] [illegible] 2019. She publicly denied being a Russ[illegible] 2021, s[illegible] [illegible]ted [illegible] Duma as a member of the United Russi[illegible]

**Cambridge Analytic**[illegible] [illegible]nalyt[illegible] [illegible]ned [illegible] Republican mega-donor [illegible] Merc[illegible] [illegible] fat[illegible] [illegible]r scientist and hedge fund [illegible] Robe[illegible] [illegible]wh[illegible] [illegible]ned Breitbart News. Cambridge [illegible], based [illegible] ite[illegible] allegedly used illegal tactics to target American voters in the 2016 election. According to former Analytica employee Christopher Wylie, the company's Executive Vice President Steven Bannon, who was also an executive with Breitbart News, oversaw the collection of Facebook data that was used to target American voters. Wylie helped with creation of the company referred to the company as a "psychological warfare tool."

**Kevin Clinesmith** was an FBI attorney assigned to the Mueller probe who resigned in February 2018 after being accused of altering an email during the process of renewing a Foreign Intelligence Surveillance Act (FISA) wiretap warrant against former Trump campaign advisor Carter Page. Clinesmith pleaded guilty to a felony violation in August 2020 for adding the phrase "and not a source" to a statement by a CIA liaison saying that Carter Page had a prior "contact" relationship with the CIA from 2008 to 2013.

On January 29, 2021, Clinesmith was sentenced to 12 months federal probation and 400 hours of community service. The judge stated that Clinesmith "likely believed that what he said about Mr. Page was true" and that he had taken "an inappropriate shortcut." He also said the Inspector General's review did not establish that "political considerations played a role in Clinesmith's actions."

**Hillary Rodham Clinton**, born in 1947**,** was U.S. Secretary of State from 2009 to 2013 after nearly four decades in public service as an advocate, attorney, First Lady in Arkansas and Washington, DC, and U.S. Senator from New York. Shown at right in a 2016 photo by Gage Skidmore, she is the author of several best-selling books, including her memoir *Living History* (2003) and her book on children, *It Takes a Village* (1996).

The Durham Report by Special Counsel John H. Durham made scores of references to a supposed "Clinton Plan" to discredit the Trump Campaign unfairly over Russian ties, an allegation based on inferences that became a central part of Republican efforts to exonerate Trump from allegations of improper Russian ties.

However, Durham failed to charge Clinton or anyone in her circle with talking with her about such a "plan" and trial testimony from Campaign Manager Robby Mook indicated that neither she nor he ever specifically authorized payment for the Steele Dossier, which had been created by Fusion GPS and former British intelligence agent Christopher Steele as subcontractors for the law firm Perkins Coie.

**Sam Clovis** was a Trump 2016 campaign co-chairman and a former Iowa radio talk show host official who largely assembled its list of foreign policy advisors in advance of a meeting with the Washington Post's editorial board on March 21, 2016.

**Michael D. Cohen**, born in 1966, is an American former lawyer who served as an attorney for former U.S. president Donald Trump from 2006 to 2018. Cohen was a vice-president of the

Trump Organization, and the personal counsel to Trump, and was often described by media as Trump's "fixer." He served as co-president of Trump Entertainment and was a board member of the Eric Trump Foundation, a children's health charity. From 2017 to 2018, Cohen was deputy finance chairman of the Republican National Committee.

On December 12, 2018, Cohen was sentenced to three years in federal prison and ordered to pay a $50,000 fine after pleading guilty to tax evasion and campaign-finance violations.

Trump employed Cohen until May 2018, a year after the special counsel investigation into Russian interference in the 2016 United States elections began. The investigation led Cohen to plead guilty on August 21, 2018, to eight counts including campaign finance violations, tax fraud, and bank fraud. Cohen said he violated campaign-finance laws at the direction of Trump and "for the principal purpose of influencing" the 2016 presidential election. In November 2018, Cohen entered a second guilty plea for lying to a Senate committee about efforts to build a Trump Tower in Moscow.

He is the principal of Crisis-X, a crisis management company. Following his release from federal prison on charges stemming from his help to Trump in delivering hush money to porn actress Stormy Daniels, he has testified voluntarily many times as an outspoken critic of corruption and his past life in cooperation with federal and state authorities investigating wrongdoing.

He authored the New York Times No. 1 best-seller *Disloyal: A Memoir* (2020). He hosts the highly rated podcast, *Mea Culpa* and has become a political commentator frequently appearing on major news outlets, partly because of his follow-up book *Revenge* (2022).

**James B. Comey Jr**., born in 1960**,** is an American lawyer who was the seventh Federal Bureau of Investigation director, serving from Sept. 4, 2013 to May 9, 2017. He was a Republican before his appointment, like all FBI Directors so far appointed in the United States. However, he described himself as unaffiliated in 2016. He was preceded in the FBI post by Robert Mueller and succeeded by Christopher A. Wray.

During the administration of President George W. Bush, Comey was the U.S. attorney for the Southern District of New York from January 2002 to December 2003 and later the United States deputy attorney general from December 2003 to August 2005.

Comey's role in the 2016 U.S. presidential election was highly controversial, particularly his comments in July criticizing Hillary Clinton's actions regarding her email server as demonstrating "extreme carelessness" even as Comey announced the end of the FBI's criminal investigation of her emails. Later, Comey announced shortly before the election that the FBI was reopening the probe based on new evidence (which proved too trivial to pursue) even though standard Justice Department practices oppose disparaging announcements against candidates during their campaigns or disparaging anyone if charges are not pursued.

In contrast to the FBI and Comey treatment of Clinton, the FBI failed to announce, leak or otherwise confirm a preliminary national security investigation of the Trump campaign called "Crossfire Hurricane" that launched in August 2016 and explored the possibility of improper influence by Russians during the campaign to help the Trump candidacy.

In late August 2016, the FBI acquired some reports from what would later be known as the Steele Dossier. In late July, the FBI opened an investigation into the Trump campaign. Comey asked President Obama for permission to write an op-ed, which would warn the public that the Russians were interfering in the election. The president denied the request. CIA director John O. Brennan then gave an unusual private briefing on the Russians to Senate Minority Leader Harry Reid; Reid then publicly referred to the briefing. Comey, however, refused to confirm—even in classified congressional briefings—that the Trump Campaign was under investigation. In early October, meetings were held in the White House Situation Room. National Security Advisor Susan Rice argued that the information should be released, while Comey argued that disclosure was no longer needed.

President Donald Trump fired Comey on May 9, 2017 following controversies over the FBI's investigation of Russian influence. In 2018, Justice Department inspector general Michael E. Horowitz's report on the FBI's handling of the Clinton email investigation criticized Comey's actions during the 2016 election. In December 2019, Horowitz released a report finding no political bias against Trump by Comey or other FBI officials. On May 3, 2017, Comey testified before the Senate Judiciary Committee hearing that it "makes me mildly nauseous to think that we might have had some impact on the election," but that "honestly, it wouldn't change the decision" to release the information.

**Igor Danchenko**, born in 1978, is a U.S. resident born in Russia who has worked as a political risk, defense and economics analyst focused on Eurasia. In 2016, he worked for Christopher Steele's Orbis Business Intelligence as the primary sub-source for what became known as the Steele dossier. Also, he worked for the FBI as a paid consultant with a focus on Russia. In November 2021, Special Counsel John Durham and his team obtained a grand jury indictment charging Danchenko with lying to the FBI about the dossier. A federal judge dismissed one charge and a federal jury acquitted Danchenko of remaining charges in October 2022.

**Nora R. Dannehy,** born in 1961, is a former federal prosecutor whom Connecticut Gov. Ned Lamont nominated to fill a vacancy on the Connecticut Supreme Court on Sept. 1, 2023. A

[illegible] league [illegible] Conn[illegible] [illegible]eral prosecutor John H. D[illegible] was ap[illegible] Acting [illegible]tes Attorney for the District of Co[illegible] on Apri[illegible]. She [illegible] woman to hold the office. A gr[illegible] Harvard [illegible]ol, sh[illegible] work for the U.S. Department of Ju[illegible]. Am[illegible] [illegible]ping to win corruption c[illegible] of former [illegible]G. Rowland and former state Tr[illegible] Silv[illegible] Sept. [illegible].S. Attorney General Michael B. M[illegible] ointed [illegible]pecial [illegible] probe the George W. Bush administration's dis[illegible] the fe[illegible]cutor[illegible] to determine if anyone should be prosecuted follo[illegible] investigati[illegible] Insp[illegible]eral and Office of Professional Responsibility of the [illegible] of Ju[illegible] had that political pressure drove the dismissals of at l[illegible] the [illegible] prosecu[illegible]6. Her investigation concluded no prosecutable cri[illegible] were [illegible]ted [illegible] to the removal of David Iglesias, the U.S. attorney for [illegible] and [illegible] was i[illegible] evidence to expand the investigation beyon[illegible] al of Igl[illegible] probe as a whitewash that ignored other flagra[illegible] around [illegible] by the U.S. House Judiciary Committee, includi[illegible] Bush [illegible]ration [illegible] on corruption charges of former Alabama Go[illegible]lman, [illegible] at. Neither Siegelman, other defendants or whist[illegible] were rep[illegible] massive allegations of perjured testimony, [illegible] prosecut[illegible] judge[illegible]ocedural irregularities by a trial judge who failed to [illegible] he be[illegible] the [illegible]eholder of a company receiving a $300 million Bush [illegible] ion fe[illegible] ract [illegible]d to defendants.

Dannehy we[illegible] as C[illegible] Dep[illegible]ey General beginning in 2010 and she retu[illegible] U.S. a[illegible] fice [illegible]icut as counsel to U.S. Attorney John Durha[illegible] Marc[illegible] ater, [illegible]e Durham's deputy on his special coun[illegible] on i[illegible] ins[illegible]robe into Russian interference in the 2016 [illegible] resig[illegible]temb[illegible]nexpectedly. No public explanation [illegible]ning [illegible] anonymous sourced reporting, most notabl[illegible] York T[illegible]nua[illegible]at she had disputed an alleged plan by Durh[illegible] pre[illegible]im[illegible] probe before the U.S. 2020 elections in [illegible] Justice [illegible]nt[illegible]

**DCLeaks**, also know[illegible], was [illegible] esta[illegible]une 2016 responsible for publishing leaks of e[illegible]ging to [illegible]promi[illegible]es in the United States government and mi[illegible] secur[illegible] firm[illegible]ed the site is a front for the Russian cyber-espio[illegible] Fancy [illegible] July 1[illegible] indictment was made against 12 Russian GRU mili[illegible]; it alle[illegible] DCLea[illegible]of a Russian military operation to interfere in the 20[illegible] sidential [illegible].

The Cyberse[illegible]ch firm [illegible]nne[illegible]ed that the DCLeaks project showed the [illegible] Russia[illegible] nce, [illegible]he attack pattern of the GRU hacker group [illegible] and [illegible]sona[illegible]0.

In late June 2016, Guccifer 2.0 informed reporters to visit the DCLeaks website for emails stolen from Democrats. With the WikiLeaks disclosure of additional stolen emails beginning on July 22, 2016, more than 150,000 stolen emails from either personal Gmail addresses or via the DNC that were related to the Hillary Clinton 2016 Presidential campaign were published on the DCLeaks and WikiLeaks websites.

On August 12, 2016, DCLeaks released roughly 300 emails from Republican targets, including the 2016 campaign staff of Arizona Senator John McCain, South Carolina Senator Lindsey Graham, and 2012 presidential candidate and former Minnesota Representative Michele Bachmann. The release included 18 emails from the Illinois Republican Party.

On August 12, 2016, DCLeaks released information about more than 200 Democratic lawmakers, including their personal cellphone numbers. The numerous crank calls that Hillary Clinton received from this disclosure along with the loss of her campaign's email security caused a very severe disruption of her campaign which subsequently changed their contact information on October 7, 2016, by calling each of her contacts one at a time.

In August 2017, U.S. Rep. Dana Rohrabacher, a California Republican, met with Julian Assange in the Ecuadorian Embassy in London to offer Assange a pardon from President Trump if Assange could offer material supporting Seth Rich as the source of email leaks from the Democratic National Committee during 2016 and not Russians. In February 2020, Rohrabacher told Yahoo News his goal during this meeting with Assange was to find evidence for a widely debunked conspiracy theory that WikiLeaks' real source was not Russian intelligence agents for the DNC emails but former DNC staffer Seth Rich.

During November 2017, the Associated Press revealed that the FBI had failed to notify almost all of the persons in the cross hairs of the Kremlin-backed Fancy Bear's attack of 312 prominent government and defense officials who had their emails posted on DCLeaks. The FBI was in violation of its own policy of robustly informing victims of hacking.

The GRU mined Bitcoins to later purchase the DCLeaks domain and operate both the DCLeaks server and Guccifer 2.0 server to distribute information obtained from these hackers in order to discredit and disrupt the Clinton Campaign, the DCCC, and the DNC so that the Bernie Sanders Presidential Campaign, Republican candidates and the Donald Trump Presidential Campaign would benefit during the 2016 election cycle.

They obtained the data about 500,000 voters by breaking into voter verification software and targeting local and state election officials. Although Roger Stone did not know the names of the Russian's sources, he had publicly stated that these Russians were in contact with the Trump Campaign and that he had communicated with them.

**Democratic National Committee** is part of the United States Democratic Party. The committee coordinates strategies to support Democratic Party candidates throughout the country for local, state, and national office, as well as works to establish a "party brand." It organizes the Democratic National Convention held every four years to nominate a candidate for President of the United States and to formulate the party platform. While it provides support for party candidates, it does not have direct authority over elected officials.

DEMOCRATIC NATIONAL COMMITTEE

**Oleg V. Deripaska**, born in 1968, is a Russian billionaire and an industrialist who Deripaska enriched himself on previously state-owned assets that were privatized in the aftermath of the collapse of the Soviet Union. He is the founder of Basic Element, one of Russia's largest industrial groups, and Volnoe Delo, Russia's largest charitable foundation.

He was once Russia's richest man but lost a substantial part of his fortune amid the 2007–08 financial crisis. As of June 2022, his wealth was estimated by Forbes at $3.2 billion.

On 22 March 2017, the Associated Press published a report alleging that Paul Manafort, Donald Trump's former presidential campaign manager, negotiated a $10 million annual contract with Deripaska to promote Russian interests in politics, business, and media coverage in Europe and the United States, starting in 2005. Both Deripaska and Manafort confirmed working together in the past but rejected the contents of the AP story. Manafort argued that his work had been inaccurately presented, and that there was nothing "inappropriate or nefarious" about it.

Responding to the allegations, on 28 March 2017, Deripaska published open letters in the print editions of The Washington Post and The Wall Street Journal in which he denied having signed a $10 million contract with Manafort in order to benefit the Putin government.

On 15 May 2017, Deripaska filed a defamation and libel lawsuit against the Associated Press in U.S. District Court in D.C., arguing that the report falsely claimed that Deripaska had signed a contract with Manafort to advance the goals of the Russian government. The lawsuit was dismissed in October 2017 on the grounds that Deripaska had not disputed "any material facts" in the story by the Associated Press.

While Manafort served within the 2016 U.S. presidential campaign, it is alleged that Manafort, via Kyiv-based operative Konstantin Kilimnik, offered to provide briefings on political developments to Deripaska. Behaviors such as these were seen by writers at *The Atlantic* as an attempt by Manafort "to please an oligarch tied to" Putin's government.

In April 2018, the United States imposed sanctions on Deripaska and 23 other Russian tycoons and officials. The statement of the United States Department of the Treasury said that Deripaska "ha[d] been accused of threatening the lives of business rivals, illegally wiretapping a government official, and taking part in extortion and racketeering."

In January 2023, Charles McGonigal, a former head of counterintelligence in the FBI New York City field office, was charged with conspiring with co-defendant Sergey Shestakov, a former Soviet and Russian diplomat who is a U.S. citizen, to provide services to Deripaska in 2021, in violation of U.S. sanctions imposed on Deripaska in 2018. They allegedly did so by investigating a rival Russian oligarch in return for concealed payments from Deripaska, using shell companies in the contract that outlined the services to be performed, using a forged signature on that contract, and using the same shell companies to send and receive payment from Deripaska.

**Charles Dolan** is a public relations professional who in 2016 was employed by kglobal, a Washington, DC-based public relations firm. Previously, he had served as Executive Director of the Democratic Governors Association and Virginia Chairman of President Clinton's 1992 and 1996 presidential campaigns.

**Alexander Downer**, born in 1951, is an Australian former politician and diplomat who was leader of the Liberal Party from 1994 to 1995, Minister for Foreign Affairs from 1996 to 2007, and High Commissioner to the United Kingdom from 2014 to 2018.

On 10 May 2016, according to The New York Times, Downer and his Australian diplomatic colleague **Erika Thompson** met with George Papadopoulos in London and information from this meeting caused the FBI to open a counterintelligence investigation into Russia's attempts to disrupt the 2016 US Presidential election, and whether there was any involvement by Donald Trump's associates. Downer told The Australian in a 28 April 2018 interview that "nothing [Papadopoulos] said in their meeting indicated Trump himself had been conspiring with the Russians to collect information on Hillary Clinton." Downer remained as High Commissioner until 2018.

In 2019 and 2020, Downer wrote regular columns for the Australian Financial Review. In his column on 1 November 2020 discussing the forthcoming US election (held on 3 November), he declared that if he was eligible to vote in the US (which, he explained, he was not), although "there's no perfect choice", he would vote for Donald Trump.

**Marc Elias** is an American lawyer expert in election law, was head of the political law practice at Perkins Coie, a major law firm.

[illegible] esented [illegible] ocra [illegible] Committee, Democratic [illegible] ial Ca [illegible] ommit [illegible] ratic Congressional Campaign [illegible] ttee, De [illegible] Gove [illegible] ciation, and a number of [illegible] atic m [illegible] Cong [illegible] s represented the leadership of [illegible] d St [illegible] of [illegible] ves and United States Senate.

In April 2015, [illegible] ton e [illegible] s a [illegible] record and general counsel for her 2016 pre [illegible] paig [illegible] g to [illegible] ngton Post, in April 2016, Elias hired Fusion [illegible] alf of [illegible] at [illegible] ommittee and the Clinton campaign to [illegible] esearch [illegible] ulte [illegible] le dossier.

On October [illegible] kins Co [illegible] sed [illegible] rom its client confidentiality obligation. E [illegible] r the b [illegible] lvis [illegible] nerica Vote, an organization founded by [illegible] ouri Se [illegible] State [illegible] der that aims to end voter suppression.

On May 18, [illegible] was cal [illegible] tify b [illegible] s for special counsel John Durham at t [illegible] s form [illegible] ne [illegible] ssmann, who had been charged with making [illegible] ement [illegible] ra [illegible] es Baker during a meeting they had in Septe [illegible] Elias a [illegible] ped [illegible] GPS to conduct opposition research aga [illegible] s opp [illegible] ld T [illegible] rting it was part of a larger effort to pro [illegible] ton ca [illegible] om p [illegible] suits from Trump or others. He said that in r [illegible] high- [illegible] tical [illegible] hired firms that could ensure confidentiali [illegible] eaks t [illegible] ama [illegible] ts.

**Michael T. Flynn**, bo [illegible] is a reti [illegible] d Sta [illegible] eutenant general who was the 24th U.S. National S [illegible] sor fo [illegible] 2 da [illegible] ump administration. He resigned in light of r [illegible] he ha [illegible] ding [illegible] ons with the Russian Federation's Ambas [illegible] Unite [illegible] erge [illegible] lynn's military career included a key role in shaping U [illegible] error [illegible] y a [illegible] ng insurgent networks in the Afghanistan and Ira [illegible] he wa [illegible] ne [illegible] arms, conventional, and special operations senior in [illegible] signm [illegible]

[illegible] er lea [illegible] ilita [illegible] er 2014 he established Flynn [illegible] l Gro [illegible] prov [illegible] gence services for businesses [illegible] gove [illegible] nclu [illegible] key. In December 2015, Flynn [illegible] paid [illegible] d [illegible] ow speech at the ten-year [illegible] nivers [illegible] tion [illegible] ate-controlled Russian [illegible] ernat [illegible] sion [illegible] here he sat next to Russian [illegible] esiden [illegible] Puti [illegible] quet table and in the company [illegible] of s [illegible] wing [illegible] commentators and activists, [illegible] luding [illegible] en [illegible] e Jill Stein. Also seated at the table, as sho [illegible] as Pu [illegible] omm [illegible] aide, Dimitry Peskov.

In February 2016, Flynn became a national security advisor to Trump for his 2016 presidential campaign. In March 2017, Flynn retroactively registered as a foreign agent, acknowledging that in 2016 he had conducted paid lobbying work that may have benefited Turkey's government. On January 22, 2017, Flynn was sworn in as the National Security Advisor. On February 13, 2017, he resigned after information surfaced that he had misled Vice President Mike Pence and others about the nature and content of his communications with Russian ambassador., Flynn's tenure as the National Security Advisor is the shortest in the history of the position.

In December 2017, Flynn formalized a deal with Special Counsel Robert Mueller to plead guilty to a felony count of "willfully and knowingly" making false statements to the FBI about the Kislyak communications and agreed to cooperate with the Special Counsel's investigation.

In June 2019, Flynn dismissed his attorneys and retained Sidney Powell, who on the same day wrote to attorney general Bill Barr seeking his assistance in exonerating Flynn. Powell had discussed the case on Fox News and spoken to President Trump about it on several occasions. Two weeks before his scheduled sentencing, in January 2020, Flynn moved to withdraw his guilty plea, claiming government vindictiveness and breach of the plea agreement. At Barr's direction, the Justice Department filed a court motion to drop all charges against Flynn on May 7, 2020. Presiding federal judge Emmet Sullivan ruled the matter to be placed on hold to solicit amicus curiae briefs from third parties. Powell then asked the DC Circuit Court of Appeals to compel Sullivan to drop the case, but her request was denied. On November 25, 2020, Flynn was issued a presidential pardon by Trump. On December 8, 2020, Judge Sullivan dismissed the criminal case against Flynn, stating he probably would have denied the Justice Department motion to drop the case.

On July 4, 2020, Flynn pledged an oath to the pro-Trump QAnon conspiracy theory, and as Trump sought to overturn the results of the 2020 presidential election in which he was defeated, Flynn suggested the president should suspend the Constitution, silence the press, and hold a new election under military authority. Flynn later met with Trump and their attorney Powell in the Oval Office to discuss the president's options. Trump denied reports that Flynn's martial law idea had been discussed. Flynn has since become a prominent leader in a Christian nationalist movement, organizing and recruiting for what he characterizes as a spiritual and political war.

**Peter Fritsch** co-founded the consultancy Fusion GPS with his former *Wall Street Journal* colleague Glenn Simpson. Fritsch finished his *Journal* career as national security editor based in Washington, DC. He co-authored with Simpson *Crime In Progress* (2019), an account of the Steele Dossier and their 2016 investigation of Donald Trump.

**Fusion GPS** was a political and strategic consultancy co-founded by Glenn Simpson and Peter Fritsch. The *Washington Free Beacon*, a conservative publication financially backed by the conservative billionaire financier Paul Singer, originally hired Fusion GPS to undertake anti-Trump research for the 2016 presidential Republican primaries but ended the relationship as Trump secured the nomination. Fusion GPS then began working with Perkins Coie, whose clients included the Democratic National Committee and the Hillary for President campaign of Democratic nominee Hillary Clinton.

**Olga Galkina** was an executive at Servers.com, a Cyprus-based company, and a source for several allegations in the Steele Dossier, according to Steele Dossier source Igor Danchenko, her friend and also an FBI consultant.

**Richard "Rick" Gates III**, born in 1972, is an American former political consultant and lobbyist who pleaded guilty to conspiracy against the United States for making false statements in the investigation into Russian interference in the 2016 United States elections. He is a longtime business associate of Paul Manafort and served as deputy to Manafort when the latter was campaign manager of the Donald Trump presidential campaign in 2016.

> Gates and Manafort were both indicted in October 2017 on charges related to their consultation work with pro-Russian political figures in Ukraine.
>
> In December 2019, federal prosecutors said they would not oppose a sentence of probation, citing his "extraordinary assistance" in cases that led to the convictions of associates of President Donald Trump, even after receiving "pressure not to cooperate ... including assurances of monetary assistance."
>
> On December 17, 2019, Gates was sentenced to three years of probation, 45 days in jail, and 300 hours of community service. He was also ordered to pay a $20,000 fine. The judge took into account years of financial crimes and deception that continued even after he had agreed to plead guilty and cooperate. Gates accepted responsibility and said, "I greatly regret the mistakes I have made."
>
> After his sentencing, Gates published a memoir, *Wicked Game: An Insider's Story on How Trump Won, Mueller Failed, and America Lost.*

**Valery V. Gerasimov**, born in 1955, is a Russian army general appointed by president Vladimir Putin in 2012 to serve as the Chief of the General Staff of the Russian Armed Forces and First

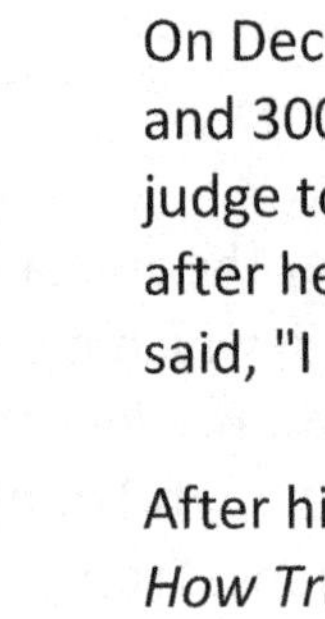

Deputy Minister of Defense, more recently commanding all Russian forces in Ukraine. In 2013, he published an article proposing that Russia adapt its military strategies to wage war using the Internet, hackers and propagandists to foster political divisions among adversaries in the West. His view became known as the "Gerasimov Doctrine.".

**Rudolph William Louis "Rudy" Giuliani,** born May 28, 1944, is an American politician and lawyer who served as the 107th Mayor of New York City from 1994 to 2001, as shown at right. He previously served as the United States Associate Attorney General from 1981 to 1983 and the United States Attorney for the Southern District of New York from 1983 to 1989.

Giuliani led the 1980s federal prosecution of New York City mafia bosses as U.S. Attorney for the Southern District of New York. After a failed campaign for Mayor of New York City in the 1989 election, he succeeded in 1993, and was reelected in 1997, campaigning on a "tough on crime" platform.

Giuliani joined President Donald Trump's personal legal team in April 2018. His activities as Trump's attorney have drawn renewed media scrutiny, in particular due to allegations that he engaged in corruption and profiteering and his promotion of conspiracy theories, most notably about the 2018 and 2020 elections. In late 2019, Giuliani was reportedly under federal investigation for violating lobbying laws, and possibly several other charges, as a central figure in the Trump–Ukraine scandal, which resulted in Trump's first impeachment.

Following the 2020 presidential election, he represented Trump in many lawsuits filed in attempts to overturn the election results, making false and debunked allegations about rigged voting machines, polling place fraud, and an international communist conspiracy. Giuliani spoke at the rally preceding the January 6 United States Capitol attack where he made false claims of voter fraud and called for "trial by combat."

As a consequence, his license to practice law was suspended in New York State in June 2021 and in the District of Columbia in July 2021. In late June 2023, the New York Times reported that he had appeared as a voluntary witness in an ongoing investigation by Justice Department Special Counsel Jack Smith of false election fraud allegations and related crimes stemming from the 2020 U.S. presidential election.

**Robert P. Hanssen**, born in 1944, was an FBI agent who spied for Soviet and Russian intelligence services against the United States from 1979 to 2001. His espionage was described by the Department of Justice as "possibly the worst intelligence disaster in U.S. history."

In 1979, three years after joining the FBI, Hanssen approached the Soviet Main Intelligence Directorate (GRU) to offer his services, beginning his first espionage cycle, lasting until 1981. He restarted his espionage activities in 1985 and continued until 1991, when he ended communications during the collapse of the Soviet Union, fearing he would be exposed. Hanssen restarted communications the next year and continued until his arrest. Throughout his spying, he remained anonymous to the Russians.

Hanssen sold ... of classified documents ... KGB that detailed U.S. strategies in the event ... war, ... weapons technologies, and aspects of the ... counterintelligence program ... spying at the same time as Aldrich Ames ... Both Ames and Hanssen ... compromised the names of KGB agents working ... for the ... executed for their betrayal. Hanssen also ... a multimillion ... tunnel built by the FBI under the Soviet Embassy ... Ames ... 1994 ... these intelligence breaches remained unsolved ... the search ... continued. The FBI paid $7 million to a KGB agent ... a file on a ... mole ... whom the FBI later identified as Hanssen through ... print and ... analysis.

To avoid the death penalty, Hanssen pleaded guilty to fourteen counts of espionage and one of conspiracy to commit espionage. He was sentenced to fifteen life terms without the possibility of parole and was incarcerated ... until his death in 2023.

**Michael E. Horowitz** ... 1962, is an American ... government official. He is the U.S. Department of Justice Inspector General, following ... swearing in. Since 2015, he has also been the chair of the Council of the Inspectors General on Integrity and Efficiency, an organization consisting of ... federal Inspectors General.

... Horowitz announced in January ... that the Inspector General's office would ... review ... related to "allegations of misconduct" ... FBI Director James Comey's handling of the ... investigation ... Hillary Clinton's email practices and whether ... the Department ... employees leaked information improperly ... during the ... 2016 United States presidential election. In ... 2018, ... released ... report, concluding that Peter ... and ... employees "brought discredit to themselves" and to the agency ... found that ... including ... ad hoc decision making and did not follow FBI procedures ... it did not find that he was motivated by any political bias.

Another investigation into the FBI ... Justice Department was launched by Horowitz in March 2018 ... investigation ... the FBI ... Justice Department's filing of four FISA applications ... renewals ... former ... campaign adviser Carter Page and whether ... was ... of the ... process. A redacted version of the report of the ... was ... December ... 2019.

On December ... 2019, Horowitz ... his ... saying that the FBI found 17 "basic and fundamental ... applications ... the Foreign Intelligence Surveillance Court (FISA Court). But the ... did not find political bias ... the investigation of Trump and Russia, nor did ... evidence ... FBI attempted to place people inside the Trump campaign ... report on the ... campaign ...

**Internet Research Agency (IRA),** also known as Glavset, is a Russian company engaged in online propaganda and influence operations on behalf of Russian business and political interests. It is linked to **Yevgeny Prigozhin**, a Russian oligarch, and based in Saint Petersburg, Russia.

The agency was first mentioned in 2016, when a Russian journalist Andrey Zakharov published his investigation into Prigozhin's "troll factory." The January 2017 report issued by the United States Intelligence Community – Assessing Russian Activities and Intentions in Recent US Elections – described the agency as a troll farm: "The likely financier of the so-called Internet Research Agency of professional trolls located in Saint Petersburg is a close ally of [Vladimir] Putin with ties to Russian intelligence," commenting that "they previously were devoted to supporting Russian actions in Ukraine—[and] started to advocate for President-elect Trump as early as December 2015."

The agency has employed fake accounts registered on major social networking sites, discussion boards, online newspaper sites, and video hosting services to promote the Kremlin's interests in domestic and foreign policy including Ukraine and the Middle East as well as attempting to influence the 2016 United States presidential election. More than 1,000 employees reportedly worked in a single building of the agency in 2015.

The extent to which the agency has tried to influence public opinion using social media became better known after a June 2014 *BuzzFeed News* article greatly expanded on government documents published by hackers earlier that year. The Internet Research Agency gained more attention by June 2015, when one of its offices was reported as having data from fake accounts used for biased Internet trolling. Subsequently, there were news reports of individuals receiving monetary compensation for performing these tasks.

On February 16, 2018, a United States grand jury indicted 13 Russian nationals and three Russian entities, including the Internet Research Agency, on charges of violating criminal laws with the intent to interfere "with U.S. elections and political processes," according to the Justice Department.

In February 2023, Yevgeny Prigozhin, the head of the private military company Wagner Group, stated that he founded the IRA: "I've never just been the financier of the Internet Research Agency. I invented it, I created it, I managed it for a long time." The admission came months after Prigozhin had admitted to Russian interference in U.S. elections.

**Michael Isikoff** is chief investigative reporter at *Yahoo News*. He previously worked at the

*Washington Post*, *Newsweek* and NBC News and authored best-selling books on the Clinton presidency and Iraq War. In 2018, he co-authored with David Corn of *Mother Jones* the book *Russian Roulette: The Inside Story of Putin's War on*

*America and the Election of Donald Trump*, expanding on their cutting-edge coverage during the fall of the 2016 presidential campaign.

**Rodney Joffe**, born in South Africa, is an American entrepreneur and cybersecurity expert. He is a recipient of the FBI's Director's Award for Outstanding Cyber Investigation for his role in uncovering the Mariposa botnet.

Joffe is credited with creating web site hosting company Genuity, as well as UltraDNS, a domain name service company which was sold to Neustar in 2006. He retired from Neustar in September, 2021.

In 2016, Joffe was among several web experts who suspected that certain Russian entities were communicating for improper purposes with Trump campaign operatives. Joffe helped compile records purporting to show that activity and passed it on to his attorney, Michael Sussmann.

In a February 2022 court motion related to Michael Sussmann's prosecution, Special Counsel Durham alleged that Joffe and his associates had exploited access his company had through a pending cybersecurity contract with the Executive Office of the President (EOP) to acquire nonpublic government domain name system and other data traffic "for the purpose of gathering derogatory information about Donald Trump." Durham did not allege that any eavesdropping of Trump communications content occurred, and on March 4, 2022, he dropped these claims against Joffe.

A spokesman for Joffe released a statement asserting that his client had lawful access under a contract to analyze White House DNS data for potential security threats. The spokesman stated that Joffe's work was in response to hacks of the EOP in 2015 and of the DNC in 2016, as well as Russian YotaPhone queries in proximity to the EOP and the Trump campaign, which raised "serious and legitimate national security concerns about Russian attempts to infiltrate the 2016 election." According to Joffe's spokesman, "deeply concerned" cybersecurity researchers prepared a report "about the anomalies they found in the data" and shared it with the CIA.

**House Judiciary Committee Chair James D. "Jim" Jordan**, born in 1964, is an American politician serving as the U.S. representative for Ohio's 4th congressional district since 2007. A member of the Republican Party, Jordan is a former collegiate wrestler and college wrestling coach.

Jordan is a founding member of the conservative House Freedom Caucus, serving as its first chair from 2015 to 2017, and as its vice chair since 2017. He was the ranking member of the House Oversight Committee from 2019 to 2020. He vacated that position to become the ranking member of the House Judiciary Committee, of which he became chair in 2023.

Jordan is a close ally of former president Donald Trump. During Trump's presidency, Jordan sought to discredit investigations into Russian interference in the 2016 election and staged a sit-in to prevent a Trump impeachment inquiry hearing over the Trump–Zelenskyy telephone controversy. After Joe Biden won the 2020 presidential election and Trump tried to overturn the election, Jordan supported lawsuits to challenge the election results and voted not to certify the Electoral College results. He refused to cooperate with the U.S. House Select Committee on the January 6 Attack, which subpoenaed him on May 12, 2022.

**Mikhail Kalugin** reportedly worked as head of the Russian Embassy's Economic Section from 2010 to 2016 in Washington, DC. Former British intelligence agent Christopher Steele wrote that Kalugin was brought home to Russia in August 2016 "on short notice because Moscow feared his heavy involvement-in the US presidential election operation...would be exposed in the media there." The U.S. publisher *McClatchy* and U.K. publisher *The Independent* separately reported on the matter in 2017, with *The Independent* reporting that Kalugin denied being a spy.

**Joseph Keith Kellogg Jr.**, born in 1944, is a former United States government official and a retired lieutenant general in the United States Army. He previously served as the National Security Advisor to Vice President Mike Pence, and as the Executive Secretary and Chief of Staff of the United States National Security Council in the Trump administration.

He served as National Security Advisor on an acting basis following the resignation of Michael T. Flynn. In March 2016, the Trump campaign named him as one of Trump's first foreign policy advisors along with several others who included George Papadopoulos,

Kellogg was viewed as a "key witness" in the United States House Select Committee on the January 6 Attack because urged Secret Service to let Vice President Mike Pence to remain at the U.S. Capitol to perform his duties during the Jan. 6 riot. Kellogg was with Trump in the White House as the attack occurred and testified under oath to the committee that the president's staff encouraged the president to take immediate action to quell the unrest, but that he refused.

Kellogg was named a foreign policy advisor to then-presidential candidate Donald Trump in March 2016. On February 13, 2017, following the resignation of National Security Advisor Michael Flynn, Keith Kellogg became the Acting National Security Advisor in the interim of a permanent replacement being appointed.

In April 2018, Vice President Mike Pence chose Kellogg to serve as his national security advisor. According to the White House, Kellogg would continue to serve as an assistant to Trump.

During the 2[illegible] States [illegible] attack [illegible]nded Pence's decision not to leave the Cap[illegible] the Se[illegible] was [illegible]g to get Pence to ride to a safer place, [illegible] on [illegible] Kellogg [illegible] told Anthony Ornato, former Secret Servic[illegible] time [illegible]se De[illegible] of Staff for Operations, why Pence would[illegible] evacuated [illegible] do [illegible]. Leave him where he's at. He's got a job to [illegible] you guys [illegible] You'[illegible] Alaska if you have a chance. Don't do it." [illegible] it cle[illegible] Pence [illegible], even if he needed to remain all night."

Kellogg is vie[illegible] key witne[illegible] the Unit[illegible] House Select Committee on the January 6 At[illegible] he was [illegible] House as the attack occurred. Kellogg testif[illegible] oath to [illegible] mittee [illegible]ber 2021, telling them that the president's st[illegible] urged th[illegible] to [illegible]diate action to quell the unrest, but that he r[illegible]

**Konstantin Kilimnik**, [illegible] 970), is a [illegible] Ukrai[illegible] political consultant. In the United States, he became a[illegible] interest [illegible] the inve[illegible] regarding Russian interference in the 2016 United S[illegible] tions, par[illegible] due to [illegible] with Paul Manafort, an American political consultant, [illegible] campaign [illegible] an for [illegible] Trump.

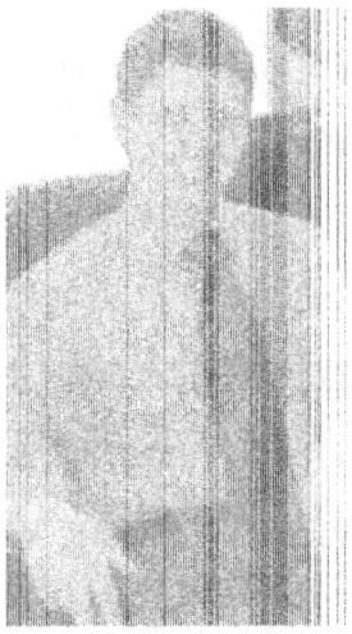

[illegible] 2019 [illegible] report [illegible] Kilimnik was connected to [illegible] ntelligen[illegible] cies, [illegible] August 2020 final report on [illegible] lection in[illegible] te fr[illegible] te Intelligence Committee [illegible] rized [illegible] Russian [illegible]ce officer." In 2017, Kilimnik [illegible] aving ti[illegible] Russian [illegible] agencies. Kilimnik was indicted [illegible] Cou[illegible] Mue[illegible] jury on June 8, 2018 on [illegible] obst[illegible] justic[illegible] spiracy to obstruct justice by [illegible] ng to [illegible] behalf of Manafort.

United States [illegible] a comm[illegible] lys[illegible] March 2021 accused Kilimnik of being one [illegible] es of [illegible] telligen[illegible] romoted and laundered misleading o[illegible] tated [illegible] abo[illegible] "to US media organizations, US officials, [illegible] nt US [illegible], inc[illegible] close to former President Trump and hi[illegible] tation" [illegible] the [illegible] presidential campaign. In April 2021, the U[illegible] Departm[illegible] oned [illegible]r providing Russian intelligence with "sensiti[illegible] n or [illegible] cam[illegible] tegy" provided to him by Manafort fr[illegible] campa[illegible] for [illegible] the false narrative that Ukraine, rather than [illegible] interfe[illegible] 2016

Kilimnik and [illegible] ctively [illegible] Ukraini[illegible]hs and Russian oligarchs who are close to [illegible] and V[illegible] Putin. Al[illegible] orked to ensure that Viktor Yanukovych [illegible] y of Reg[illegible] ld [illegible] eventually sever Ukraine's ties to the United S[illegible] Europe [illegible] Ukraine [illegible]ome much closer to Russia, the Kremlin, and [illegible] Putin.

In its August 2020 final report on the 2016 election interference, the bipartisan Senate Intelligence Committee characterized Kilimnik as a "Russian intelligence officer" who worked with Manafort while he was Trump campaign manager to deflect suspicions of interference away from Russia and onto Ukraine. The report mentions Kilimnik about 800 times, although most of the details about his intelligence connections were redacted. However, the sharing of intelligence with Kilimnik by Manafort and others "represented a grave counterintelligence threat." The committee acquired sufficient evidence to assert that Kilminik may have been involved directly in the plot, not only to hack the Democrats computers, but to pass on the information to WikiLeaks.

**Sergei Kislyak** was the Russian Federation's ambassador to the United States from 2008 to 2017, based in Washington, DC. He developed strong relationships with certain American political leaders, including President Donald Trump.

For example, the *New York Times* published excerpts of an official White House document summarizing Trump's private meeting with Russian foreign minister Sergey Lavrov and the Russian ambassador to the United States, Sergey Kislyak, in the Oval Office in 2017. Trump told Kislyak and Lavrov, according to the report, that he "just fired the head of the FBI. He was crazy, a real nut job."

According to reports, Trump was angry and frustrated when, in the week prior to his dismissal, FBI Director James Comey had revealed in Senate testimony the breadth of the counterintelligence investigation into Russia's effort to sway the 2016 U.S. presidential election. He felt Comey was giving too much attention to the Russia probe and not enough to internal leaks to the press from within the government.

**Jared C. Kushner**, born in 1981, is an American businessman, investor, and former government official. He is the son-in-law of President Donald Trump through his marriage to Ivanka Trump and served as a senior advisor to Trump from 2017 to 2021. He was also Director of the Office of American Innovation.

For much of his career, Kushner worked as a real-estate investor in New York City, especially through the family business, Kushner Companies. He took over the company after his father Charles Kushner was convicted for 18 criminal charges, including illegal campaign contributions, tax evasion, and witness tampering in 2005, although Charles was controversially pardoned by Trump in 2020.

Jared met Ivanka Trump around 2005, and the couple married in 2009. He also became involved in the newspaper industry after purchasing the *New York Observer* in 2006. He was registered as a Democrat and donated to Democratic politicians for much of his life but registered as Independent in 2009 and eventually as Republican in 2018. He played a significant role in the Donald Trump 2016 presidential campaign and was at one point seen as its de facto campaign manager. Around Trump's election, Kushner divested from his family business, but was frequently accused of conflicts of interest as he profited from policy proposals that he himself pushed for within the Trump administration.

He became Senior Advisor to President Trump in 2017, and held the position until Trump left office in 2021. His appointment, like that of his wife to a White House position, prompted critics to decry nepotism.

Since leaving the White House, Kushner founded Affinity Partners, a private equity firm investing in Israeli and American companies expanding in the Middle East, Africa, and Asia.

Kushner's contacts with Russian officials came under scrutiny as part of the larger federal investigation into Russian interference in the election. Before meeting with the Senate and House intelligence committees, Kushner delivered an 11-page document describing his contacts with Russian figures during the campaign and after the election. The *Wall Street Journal* called it "comprehensive disclosure" and said it "introduced a useful precedent to the Trump presidency."

**Eric Lichtblau** is a *New York Times* investigative reporter who won a Pulitzer Prize in 2006 for stories about the NSA's secret wiretapping operations. In the fall of 2016, he researched stories about potential Russian interference in the 2016 election campaign cited during the unsuccessful Durham prosecution of Michael Sussmann. Lichtblau's books include *Bush's Law: The Remaking of American Justice*.

**Sergei Magnitsky** was a tax accountant who accused Moscow law enforcement in 2009 of stealing $230 million in tax rebates from his client, and then was beaten to death in jail.

In 2012, Magnitsky's client, financier Bill Browder, secured passage of the American Magnitsky Act, which imposed sanctions on the officials involved. Russian President Vladimir Putin responded with the Dima Yakovlev Law banning Americans from adopting Russian children.

Putin and others, including Russian-born, U.S-based attorney Natalia Veselnitskaya sought for years to repeal the Magnitsky Act and prevent imposition of sanctions on Russia, including presence at a reputed meeting on June 9, 2016 at the Trump Tower with Donald Trump Jr., Jared Kushner and Trump Campaign Manager Paul Manafort that had been set up by an intermediary claiming she was a
"Russian government attorney" offering incriminating information on Hillary Clinton due to "its government's support for Mr. Trump."

Regarding the meeting, Donald Trump Jr. initially wrote, "I love it" but, in July 2017, said the meeting "was a waste of time." He said that Veselnitskaya used the meeting to criticize the Magnitsky Act. Veselnitskaya herself commented that she mostly talked about Browder's (alleged) misdeeds, whereas the Trump team wanted what she termed "some sort of grenade."

**Paul J. Manafort Jr.**, born in 1949, is an American lobbyist, political consultant, and attorney. A long-time Republican Party campaign consultant, he chaired the Trump presidential campaign from June to August 2016. Manafort had served as an adviser to the U.S. presidential campaigns of Republicans Gerald Ford, Ronald Reagan, George H. W. Bush, and Bob Dole.

In 1980, he co-founded the Washington, D.C.–based lobbying firm Black, Manafort & Stone, along with principals Charles R. Black Jr. and Roger J. Stone, joined by Peter G. Kelly in 1984. Manafort often lobbied on behalf of foreign leaders such as former President of Ukraine Viktor Yanukovych, former dictator of the Philippines Ferdinand Marcos, former dictator of Zaire Mobutu Sese Seko, and Angolan guerrilla leader Jonas Savimbi. Lobbying to serve the interests of foreign governments requires registration with the Justice Department under the Foreign Agents Registration Act (FARA); on June 27, 2017, he retroactively registered as a foreign agent.

On October 27, 2017, Manafort and his business associate Rick Gates were indicted in the U.S. District Court for the District of Columbia on multiple charges arising from his consulting work for the pro-Russian government of Viktor Yanukovych in Ukraine before Yanukovych's overthrow in 2014. The indictment came at the request of Robert Mueller's Special Counsel investigation. In June 2018, additional charges were filed against Manafort for obstruction of justice and witness tampering that are alleged to have occurred while he was under house arrest, and he was ordered to jail.

Manafort was prosecuted in two federal courts. In August 2018, he stood trial in the United States District Court for the Eastern District of Virginia and was convicted on eight charges of tax and bank fraud. Manafort was next prosecuted on ten other charges, but this effort ended in a mistrial with Manafort later admitting his guilt. In the United States District Court for the District of Columbia, Manafort pled guilty to two charges of conspiracy to defraud the United States and witness tampering, while agreeing to cooperate with prosecutors.

On November 26, 2018, Mueller reported that Manafort violated his plea deal by repeatedly lying to investigators. On February 13, 2019, D.C. District Court Judge Amy Berman Jackson concurred, voiding the plea deal. On March 7, 2019, Judge T. S. Ellis III sentenced Manafort to 47 months in prison. On March 13, 2019, Jackson sentenced Manafort to an additional 43 months in prison. Minutes after his sentencing, New York state prosec[illegible] Mana[illegible] six[illegible] felonies. On December 18, 2019, the state cha[illegible] him [illegible] the doctrine of double jeopardy.

The Republi[illegible] Senat[illegible] gence [illegible] concluded in August 2020 that Manafo[illegible] individ[illegible] ted [illegible] intelligence while he was Trump's cam[illegible] ger "r[illegible] counterintelligence threat" by creating opp[illegible] "Russi[illegible] gence [illegible] to exert influence over, and acquire conf[illegible] rmation [illegible] Trump [illegible]."

On May 13, [illegible] fort was [illegible] to h[illegible] ement due to the threat of COVID-19. O[illegible] 23, 2[illegible] Pres[illegible] Trump pardoned Manafort.

Manafort's in[illegible] in Ukr[illegible], when Russian oligarch Oleg Deripaska hi[illegible] Manafort [illegible] ate, to lobby the State Department [illegible] of his [illegible] he could solicit otherwise unavailable [illegible] purchas[illegible] pany, RusAL.

Manafort wo[illegible] advise[illegible] ntial campaign of Yanukovych (and his Part[illegible] during [illegible] time [illegible] December 2004 until the February 20[illegible] presi[illegible] even as the U.S. government (and U.S. Sen[illegible] McCain [illegible] Yanu[illegible] because of his ties to Russia's leader Vladi[illegible] lowin[illegible], [illegible] wrote a memoir entitled *Political Prisoner*, por[illegible] self as [illegible]

**Andrew McCabe**, b[illegible] is an A[illegible] served as the Deputy Director of the FBI from Februa[illegible] March 2[illegible] the [illegible] Director of the FBI from May 9, 2017, to August 2, 2[illegible] serve[illegible] essor [illegible] George Mason University's Schar School of Policy and [illegible]

McCabe [illegible] FBI [illegible] al agent in 1996 and, after [illegible] positio[illegible] easing [illegible] ility, became the acting Director of the FB[illegible] ing J[illegible]'s dismissal by then-President Donald [illegible] McCab[illegible] parted from the FBI on poor terms [illegible] the Trump administration, McCab[illegible] at CNN since 2019.

Attorney Ge[illegible] Sessions [illegible], 2018, 26 hours before his scheduled re[illegible] Session[illegible] his decision on reports from the DOJ Insp[illegible] al and [illegible] iscip[illegible] saying that McCabe had improperly a[illegible] leases [illegible] ation [illegible] *Wall Street Journal* about an investigatio[illegible] Clinton Fo[illegible] agents who questioned him about it on [illegible], thr[illegible] truth. McCabe disputed these charges and [illegible] his firin[illegible] litica[illegible] ed. In September 2019, federal prosecutors recommended McCabe be indicted for actions relating to the leak, but the grand jury did not return an indictment.

In October 2021, McCabe settled with the Justice Department a wrongful termination suit he had filed in August 2019. As part of the settlement, the government agreed to "rescind and vacate" McCabe's termination, correct its records "to reflect that Mr. McCabe was employed continuously by the FBI from July 1996 until he retired on March 19, 2018 as the FBI Deputy Director" in "good standing," restore his pension and other benefits, pay his legal fees and expunge any record of having been fired.

In December 2022, shortly after the appointment of special counsel Jack Smith to investigate former Pres. Trump's mishandling of classified documents, McCabe teamed up with podcaster Allison Gill, of Mueller, She Wrote fame, on a new podcast series, Jack, to follow the case.

**Charles McGonigal** is the former head of counterintelligence in the New York City field office of the FBI. As of March 2023, he is under federal indictment on multiple charges. McGonigal joined the FBI in 1996.

During his tenure at the New York Field Office, he was detailed to the TWA Flight 800 investigation, and later became one of the original case agents assigned to the Russian Illegals Program. McGonigal led the 2010 investigation into the release by WikiLeaks of over 200,000 State Department documents. He also led the investigation into Chelsea Manning's collaboration with WikiLeaks.

In January 2023, McGonigal was arrested and federally indicted on charges of money laundering, making false statements in mandatory disclosures to the FBI, violating U.S. sanctions on Russia, and other counts for allegedly working with Russian oligarch Oleg Deripaska, who had allegedly tasked McGonigal with investigating a Deripaska rival.

The FBI's investigation into McGonigal reportedly began sometime in 2018, after McGonigal was seen meeting with a Russian contact who was under surveillance by British authorities.

**Joseph Mifsud**, born in 1960, is a British-Maltese academic who had dual citizenship in the United Kingdom and Malta. In 2016, he became involved with George Papadopoulos, an advisor to the Donald Trump presidential campaign, and was later accused of being a link between that campaign and Russia. In 2018, he was described as missing, and an Italian court listed his location as "residence unknown."

In March 2016, shortly after George Papadopoulos was named as a foreign policy advisor to the Trump campaign, Mifsud met Papadopoulos in Rome. They later met again in London, where – according to Papadopoulos – Mifsud claimed, "substantial connections to Russian officials" and introduced Papadopoulos to a Russian woman that he falsely claimed was Putin's niece. At a meeting in April, Mifsud told Papadopoulos that he had learned that the Russian government had "dirt" on Hillary Clinton. Mifsud has acknowledged meeting Papadopoulos but denied Papadopoulos's specific allegations.

On 10 May 2016, Papadopoulos repeated the information to the Australian High Commissioner in London, Alexander Downer, who was accompanied by Australian diplomat Erika Thompson, that "the Trump team had received some kind of suggestion from Russia that it could assist this process with the anonymous release of information during the campaign that would be damaging to Mrs Clinton (and President Obama)." Downer later reported to American authorities that Papadopoulos had apparently known about Russia's theft of Democratic National Committee emails before it was publicly reported. Papadopoulos denies having told Downer this. The FBI then launched an investigation into possible connections between Russia and the Trump campaign. Mifsud was interviewed by the FBI in February 2017 while visiting the United States to speak at a conference.

Papadopoulos and other critics of the investigation of Russian interference in the 2016 campaign, such as Republican Congressmen Jim Jordan and Devin Nunes, have suggested Mifsud might be a Western intelligence agent instructed to entrap Papadopoulos in order to justify an investigation.

A December 2019 Justice Department Inspector General report found no evidence Mifsud was an FBI informant, or that his involvement with Papadopoulos was related to any FBI operation. U.S. Attorney General William Barr and U.S. prosecutor John Durham met with Italian intelligence officials in Rome in late September 2019 to learn more about Mifsud and his contacts. Italian officials denied that Italian intelligence services were involved.

According to a filing in a U.S. federal court in the case Democratic National Committee v. Russian Federation in September 2018, Mifsud was "missing and may be deceased."

**Richard W. Miller**, born in 1936, was an FBI agent from 1963 to 1984 and is known as the first FBI agent ever convicted of espionage.

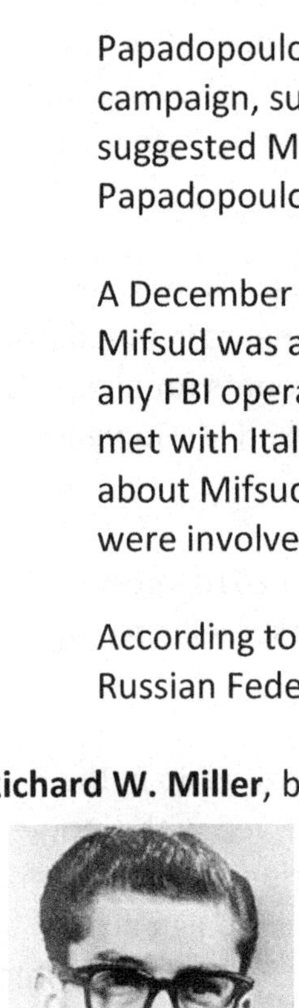

Miller claimed he had been attempting to infiltrate Russian intelligence, which led to a hung jury in his first trial and a conviction and mistrial in his second.

Federal prosecutor Adam Schiff, future chair of the House Intelligence Committee, led the team that won convictions in Miller's third trial in 1993 after presenting evidence that the married father of eight had engaged in a romantic affair beginning in 1984 with a married immigrant from Russia linked to the Soviet KGB spy agency. Evidence showed that Miller had delivered to her classified information, including an FBI counterintelligence manual, in return for sexual favors, $15,000 in cash and $50,000 in gold.

Miller served 13 years of his 20-year sentence and died in 2013.

**Sergei Millian**, born in 1978, is a Belarusian-American businessman and former president of the Russian-American Chamber of Commerce. He has claimed association with Donald Trump and members of Trump's 2016 election campaign, and he was alleged to have been a source for the Steele dossier. Millian has denied being a source.

In November 2021, after the indictment of Steele's primary subsource **Igor Danchenko** for allegedly lying to the FBI about the sources he used in compiling claims for the dossier, the *Washington Post* corrected and removed large portions of their previous articles that had identified Millian as a source.

**Robby Mook**, born in 1979, is an American former political strategist. He was the campaign manager for Hillary Clinton's 2016 presidential campaign. Mook worked for Hillary Clinton's 2008 presidential campaign as a state director in three states.

During testimony given in May 2022 in the trial of Michael Sussmann, Mook testified that Clinton agreed to give a reporter information that connected Trump with Russian Alfa Bank, even though her campaign was uncertain about whether the allegations were true. The statement became a major focus of conservative media even though the trial judge had ruled it as irrelevant and the jury acquitted Sussmann of the charge at issue, an alleged false statement to the FBI when Sussmann sought to pass along a tip about suspected data.

**Jerrold "Jerry" Nadler**, born in 1947, is an American lawyer and politician who since 2023 has served as the U.S. representative for New York's 12th congressional district, which includes central Manhattan. A member of the Democratic Party, he was elected in 1992 to represent the state's 17th congressional district, which was renumbered as the 8th district from 1993 to 2013 and as the 10th district from 2013 to 2023.

Nadler chaired the House Judiciary Committee from 2019 to 2023. In his 17th term in Congress, Nadler is the dean of New York's delegation to the House of Representatives.

Before his el... Congress... served... ns as a New York State Assemblyma... Nadler ... his co... league Carolyn Maloney in a three-way pr... 55% of ... Ma... newly drawn 12th congressional district.

**House Intelligence** Committee **Chair** ... Nunes ... 1973, is an American businessman and po... chief ... officer ... Trump Media & Technology Group. Before resign... the House... joining TMTG, Nunes was first a U.S. congressman fr... from ... 2022.

...member ... Nunes was the chair of the ... Intel... Committee ... 2015 to 2019. He was also a ...member of ... Don... transition team. Nunes's ...er distri... the ... Valley and included most of ...ern T... and ... eastern Fresno County.

...March 20... U.S. Ho... intelligence committee, which Nunes ...ed at ... investigation into possible Russian ...ference ... 2016 ... elections. In February 2018, Nunes public... a four-... ng an FBI conspiracy against Trump. Nunes ...ntly beg... the FBI and the U.S. Justice Department ... abusi... powers ... attempt to hurt Trump. In January 2021, Trump ... Nunes the ... freedom.

In February 2..., who ... the ... transition team, was the first leading House ... to ... community had evidence of contact betw... Trump cam... and R... ...tives. He rejected repeated calls for an in... by a se... committee ... the House should not engage in a "witch hunt" ... this ...'s ...e."

When Trump ... security ... Mich... resigned after it was revealed that he had ... misled V... ...t M... about his communication with Russian offici... said h... ... investigate Flynn's ties to Russia: "From every... I can se... ...rsat... the Russian ambassador—he was doing th... favor, a... ...ould ... for it."

...ch 22, 2... the ... Intelligence Committee's ...iation i... in the 2016 United States ..., Nun... press ... to announce that he had ...d inform... the ...cations of "some members of ...s transit... potentially the president himself" ...en "inci... collec... intelligence community and "widely disse... through... intelligence community. He added that it was legal FISA surveillance, and unrelated to Russia. It was later revealed that it involved Russia and the Trump transition team. The surveillance was of multiple phone conversations between Michael Flynn, a member of the transition team, and Russian Ambassador Sergey Kislyak, which occurred after Flynn sought advice from the Trump transition team at Mar-a-Lago, where they discussed what Flynn should tell Kislyak "about the administration's stance on the sanctions."

*The Nunes Memo*

The Nunes memo (formally titled *Foreign Intelligence Surveillance Act Abuses at the Department of Justice and the Federal Bureau of Investigation*) is a four-page memorandum written for U.S. Representative Devin Nunes by his staff and released to the public by the Republican-controlled House Intelligence Committee on February 2, 2018. The memo alleges that the FBI "may have relied on politically motivated or questionable sources" to obtain a Foreign Intelligence Surveillance Act (FISA) warrant in October 2016 and in three subsequent renewals on Trump adviser Carter Page in the early phases of the FBI's investigation into Russian interference in the 2016 United States elections.

The FBI issued a rare statement expressing "grave concerns" about factual omissions and the accuracy of the memo.

Democrats on the House Intelligence Committee prepared a classified 10-page rebuttal of claims in the Nunes memo. A redacted version of the Democratic memo was ultimately released on February 24.

**Bruce G. Ohr** is a former FBI executive married to Nellie Ohr, a Russian-language expert contractor employed by Fusion GPS. A former associate deputy attorney general and former director of the Organized Crime Drug Enforcement Task Force (OCDETF), as of February 2018 Ohr was working in the Justice Department's Criminal Division. He is an expert on transnational organized crime and has spent most of his career overseeing gang and racketeering-related prosecutions, including Russian organized crime.

Ohr was little-known until 2018, when he became the subject of scrutiny when he was involved in the start of the Russian interference in the 2016 election probe. He was criticized by President Donald Trump, who accused Ohr of abusing his access to sensitive information. No evidence has emerged that Ohr was involved in the initiation of the Russia probe or that Ohr mishandled sensitive information. According to a comprehensive review by ABC News, Ohr "had little impact on the FBI's growing probe into Trump and his associates." The Department of Justice Inspector General reported that Ohr had made "consequential errors in judgment" in failing to inform his supervisors about his role in the investigation.

On September 30, 2020, Ohr retired from his position at DOJ. Ohr had repeated contacts with FBI agents during the fall and winter of 2016–2017, where he shared information he had received from Steele's dossier research. During this time, Ohr failed to inform his supervisors in the Justice Department of his role. An ABC News report stated that Nellie Ohr "was not directly involved in the 'dossier' while she worked for Fusion GPS."

Steele had been an official source of intelligence for the FBI in the Russian-interference probe before the election, until he was terminated as a source in November 2016 for unauthorized contacts with the media.

**Orbis Business Intelligence** is a London-based private intelligence company co-founded in 2009 by former British intelligence agents Christopher Steele and Chris Burrows. Steele had run the Russia desk at the intelligence agency MI6.

**Carter W. Page**, born in 1971, is an American petroleum industry consultant and a former foreign-policy adviser to Donald Trump during his 2016 presidential election campaign. Page is the founder and managing partner of Global Energy Capital, a one-man investment fund and consulting firm specializing in the Russian and Central Asian oil and gas business.

Page was a focus of the 2017 Special Counsel investigation into the many suspicious links between Trump associates and Russian officials and spies and Russian interference on behalf of Trump during the 2016 presidential election. In April 2019, the Mueller report concluded that the investigation did not establish that Page coordinated in Russia's interference efforts.

In December 2019, the Inspector General for the Department of Justice, Michael E. Horowitz, issued a report on his inquiry into the FBI investigation of the 2016 Trump campaign and its ties to Russia. Horowitz found fault with specific aspects of the FBI's conduct, including omissions of facts and false statements to the FISA court when applying for a warrant to conduct surveillance on Page.

**Lisa Page**, a former special assistant to FBI Deputy Director Andrew McCabe, is an American lawyer and cable news commentator who worked with former special counsel Robert Mueller on the Russian disinformation probe.

NBC NEWS
MSNBC

Mueller dismissed Page and former FBI supervisor Peter Strzok from the Russia investigation after text messages between the two criticizing Donald Trump were leaked to reporters.

In 2019, Page sued the Department of Justice and FBI for disclosing the texts, claiming it was a violation of the Privacy Act. Strzok also sued, saying his termination violated his First Amendment Rights and sought reinstatement and back pay. In 2020, she joined NBC News and MSNBC as a national security and legal analyst.

**George D. Papadopoulos**, born in 1987, is former member of the foreign policy advisory panel of Donald Trump's 2016 presidential campaign. On October 5, 2017, Papadopoulos pleaded guilty to a felony charge of making false statements to FBI agents about the timing and the possible significance of his contacts in 2016 relating to U.S.–Russia relations and the Donald Trump presidential campaign. In 2018, he served twelve days in federal prison, then was placed on a 12-month supervised release. During his supervised release from prison, he participated in the filming of a still-unreleased docuseries. In March 2019, Papadopoulos released a book, *Deep State Target: How I Got Caught in the Crosshairs of the Plot to Bring Down President Trump*. He was pardoned by Trump in December 2020.

While living in London, Papadopoulos first reached out to the Trump campaign on August 4, 2015, expressing interest in "an advisory role to Mr. Trump on matters of energy security and U.S. policy in the Eastern Mediterranean." Later, Sam Clovis, who at the time was national co-chairman of Donald Trump's campaign team, approved him as an unpaid adviser.

Employed on March 12, 2016 with the London Centre of International Law Practice (LCILP), Papadopoulos was part of an LCILP visiting delegation to the Link Campus University in Rome, a university associated with Italian intelligence agencies. There he met Joseph Mifsud, a Maltese academic with alleged ties to Russian intelligence who was at the time a teacher at the University of Stirling in Scotland.

On March 21, 2016, in an interview with the editorial board of The Washington Post, Donald Trump announced Papadopoulos as one of his campaign's foreign policy advisers. Trump, reading from a list, said: "He's an oil and energy consultant, excellent guy."

On March 24, Papadopoulos met with Mifsud in London. Papadopoulos said that Mifsud was accompanied by a Russian woman, Olga Polonskaya, whom Mifsud falsely identified as the niece of the Russian President. On the same day, Papadopoulos performed nine internet searches of various combinations attempting to find Olga Polonskaya as a niece of President Putin or former President Medvedev. Mifsud, in a later interview, denied he said this.

On March 31, 2016, Papadopoulos joined candidate Trump as well as Senator Jeff Sessions and other campaign officials for a National Security Meeting at the Trump Hotel in Washington, D.C. Papadopoulos averred that he could facilitate a foreign policy meeting between candidate Trump and Russian President Vladimir Putin.

At a breakfast meeting at the Andaz London Liverpool Street hotel on April 26, 2016, Mifsud told Papadopoulos that he had information that the Russians have "dirt" on Hillary Clinton, thousands of emails.

On May 10, [illegible] con's [illegible] Papadopoulos allegedly told the Australian Hi[illegible]ioner [illegible]ed [illegible]exander Downer, who was accompanie[illegible] an dipl[illegible] at one of the reasons [Trump would win] w[illegible] e Trum[illegible] d re[illegible] e kind of suggestion from Russia that i[illegible] this [illegible] h the [illegible] us release of information during the campaig[illegible] l be da[illegible] M[illegible] nd President Obama).

On July 26, a[illegible] king o[illegible] erve[illegible] me known, Australian officials told the FBI [illegible] 2016 Pa[illegible] los h[illegible] l to Alexander Downer "that the Trump camp[illegible] are th[illegible] gover[illegible] d dirt on Hillary Clinton." This led the Fede[illegible] f Investi[illegible] ope[illegible] intelligence investigation into the Donald T[illegible] lentia[illegible] on [illegible] 6.

In a sentenci[illegible] ndum[illegible] Au[illegible] 18, prosecutors stated that a sentence of [illegible] months [illegible] rranted," noting that Papadopoul[illegible] edly [illegible] stiga[illegible] d not provide "substantial assistance" [illegible] gation, [illegible] his [illegible] rfered with the investigators' ability in the [illegible], 20[illegible] w c[illegible] sud to question and if necessary de[illegible]

Papadopoul[illegible] dently [illegible] beli[illegible] as entrapped by people in various gove[illegible] lligen[illegible] in [illegible] fy FBI surveillance of the Trump camp[illegible]

**Perkins Coie** is a U.S. [illegible] h m[illegible] 20[illegible] offices across the United States and Asia. Partner M[illegible] ved in 2[illegible] e pri[illegible] ney for the Hillary for President campaign and also [illegible] ocratic [illegible] Comm[illegible]). He worked with the consultancy Fusion [illegible]

His partner, [illegible] nan[illegible] in p[illegible] cyberlaw who formerly worked at the U.S. Ju[illegible] tment, [illegible] eavil[illegible] also in researching how emails stolen from [illegible] m prom[illegible] moc[illegible] the campaign seemed to be used by Russ[illegible] aks a[illegible] ls and help Donald Trump's candidacy. S[illegible] o als[illegible] ed [illegible] were experts in Internet traffic, took his susp[illegible] e FBI se[illegible] inves[illegible] t wound up being indicted himself via th[illegible] obe [illegible] of [illegible] ent. A jury acquitted him but not before h[illegible] e't the [illegible] ndu[illegible] egative coverage from the radical right [illegible] cing i[illegible] am[illegible] as the *Wall Street Journal* editorial pag[illegible] ews.

**Earl E. Pitts**, born in [illegible] d the F[illegible] and [illegible] s posts that included work in the agency's Behavi[illegible] Unit [illegible] cad[illegible] ntico, VA. An attorney, he had access to Top Secre[illegible] as we[illegible] wo[illegible] ces for "access to sensitive compartmented inf[illegible] eginn[illegible]

According to an FBI press release in 1996, while in New York, Pitts was given access to "a wide range of sensitive and highly classified operations" that included "recruitment operations involving Russian intelligence officers, double agent operations, operations targeting Russian intelligence officers, true identities of human assets, operations against Russian illegals, defector sources, surveillance schedules of known meet sites, internal policies, documents, and procedures concerning surveillance of Russian intelligence officers, and the identification, targeting, and reporting on known and suspected KGB intelligence officers in the New York area."

Pitts was arrested on Dec 18, 1996 by the FBI and charged with attempted espionage, conspiracy to commit espionage and lesser counts. He entered a plea arrangement in return for a reduced sentence. He claimed that he had a long list of grievances towards the FBI and wanted to "pay them back." The prosecutors recommended a sentence of 24 1/2 years. But U.S. District Judge T.S. Ellis instead sentenced him to 27 years, finding his actions to be especially grievous.

**Yevgeny Prigozhin** founded of the Wagner Group, a private military company engaged in heavy fighting in Ukraine, Africa and Syria in support of Russia's goals. His work has generated allegations of war crimes and a U.S. Justice Department indictment for interference in U.S. elections in 2016.

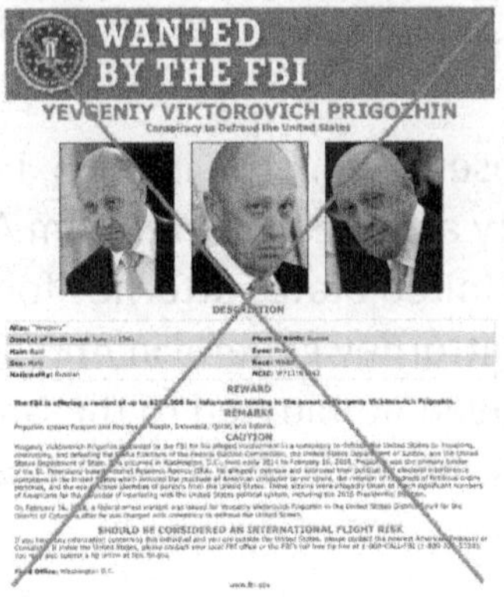


Earlier, he was a criminal who spent time in jail in the Soviet Union in the 1980s for armed robbery and other offenses. After opening a hot dog stand upon release, he evolved the business into catering for the Russian military, leading to a nickname he reportedly hates: "Putin's Chef." Later, he founded the Internet Research Agency, which provided Russian disinformation helping undermine the 2016 U.S. election.

In the spring of 2023, after a hard-won victory for his forces in the Ukrainian battlefield of Bakhmut, he released videos taunting top Russian generals and undertaking what he called defensive operations against their units. Russian authorities issued a warrant for his arrest on treason charges on June 23, prompting Prigozhin to send his army to seize territory in Southern Russia and head towards Moscow in an apparent coup attempt. The situation was temporarily resolved by Prigozhin receiving a pardon and fleeing to Belarus on June 24, 2023.

February 2018, Prigozhin, his Internet Research Agency, another related company, and other connected Russian individuals were indicted by a U.S. grand jury. Prigozhin was charged with funding and organizing operations to interfere with the US political and electoral processes, including the 2016 presidential election, and other crimes, including identity theft. The U.S. State Department later offered a reward of up to $10 million for information about Prigozhin, the Internet Research Agency, and other entities involved in 2016 U.S. election interference. On Nov. 7 2022, Prigozhin said he had interfered in U.S. elections and would continue to interfere in the future.

Throughout 2018, Prigozhin reportedly established numerous interests in Africa via the Wagner Group and approximately 100–200 political consultants. He became involved in such countries as Madagascar, the Central Africa Republic (CAR), the Democratic Republic of the Congo, Angola, Senegal, Rwanda, Sudan, Libya, Guinea, Guinea-Bissau, Zambia, Zimbabwe, Kenya, Cameroon, Côte d'Ivoire, Mozambique, Niger, Nigeria, Chad, South Sudan, and South Africa.
Prigozhin expressed his support for the 2023 Nigerien coup d'état, writing on Telegram "What happened in Niger is nothing other than the struggle of the people of Niger with their colonizers ... who are trying to foist their rules of life on them and their conditions and keep them in the state that Africa was in hundreds of years ago."

Prigozhin went public with harsh criticism of Russia's Ministry of Defense, withdrew Wagner forces from combat in Ukraine, led many of them on a takeover of Russian territory in an advance on Moscow, leading to treason charges against him. He ended the march a reported agreement with Russian leader Vladimir Putin, with treason charges dropped. Prigozhin, along with his Wagner second-in-command and other high-ranking colleagues, died in an airplane crash on Aug. 23, 2023. The airplane, reported either to have exploded or been shot down, was *en route* from Moscow to Saint Petersburg when it crashed, killing all 10 people on board.

**Deputy U.S. Attorney Gen. Deputy Attorney General Rod J. Rosenstein**, born in 1965, is an American attorney who served as the 37th United States deputy attorney general from April 2017 until May 2019. Prior to his appointment, he served as a United States attorney for the District of Maryland. At the time of his confirmation as deputy attorney general in April 2017, he was the longest-serving U.S. attorney. Rosenstein had also been nominated to the United States Court of Appeals for the Fourth Circuit in 2007, but his nomination was never considered by the U.S. Senate.

Following the recusal of Attorney General Jeff Sessions and Comey's dismissal, Rosenstein appointed Robert Mueller as special counsel to investigate the myriad links between Trump associates and Russian officials and spies and related matters. Rosenstein previously assumed authority over the parallel FBI probe after Sessions recused himself over misleading remarks he made to the Senate Committee on the Judiciary during his confirmation process. The *New York Times* reported Rosenstein prevented the FBI and Mueller from investigating Trump's personal and financial dealings in Russia. On November 7, 2018, Trump transferred this oversight to acting US Attorney General Matthew Whitaker.

Rosenstein submitted his resignation as deputy attorney general on April 29, 2019, which took effect on May 11, 2019.

**Felix H. Sater**, born in 1966, is a Russian-American mobster, convicted felon, real estate developer and former managing director of Bayrock Group LLC, a real estate conglomerate based out of New York City. He has been an advisor to corporations such as The Trump Organization, and the Mirax Group.

In 1998, Sater pleaded guilty to his involvement in a $40 million stock fraud scheme orchestrated by the Russian Mafia and became an informant for the Federal Bureau of Investigation (FBI) and federal prosecutors, assisting with organized crime investigations. In 2017, Sater agreed to cooperate with investigators into international money laundering schemes.

During Donald Trump's 2016 presidential campaign, Sater worked with Michael Cohen, former attorney for The Trump Organization, to broker a deal to build a Trump Tower Moscow, asserting to Cohen that he could boost Trump's election prospects through his Russian contacts. On June 21, 2019, Sater was issued a subpoena by the House Intelligence Committee after he refused a request to testify voluntarily. On July 9, 2019, Sater appeared before the House Intelligence Committee, but repeatedly withheld testimony and documents concerning the details of a false joint defense agreement and thus remains under subpoena.

Sater was born in Moscow into a Russian Jewish family, the son of Mikhail Sheferovsky and Rachel Sheferovskaya. According to the FBI, Mikhail Sheferovsky was an underboss for Russian Mafia "boss of bosses," Semion Mogilevich, and was convicted of extorting money from local restaurants, grocery stores, and a medical clinic.

In 1991, Felix Sater smashed a margarita glass in a bar and used it to stab a commodities broker in the face, causing the man to need 110 stitches. For this, Sater was convicted of first-degree assault in 1993. He spent 15 months in prison and was barred by the National Association of Securities Dealers from acting as a broker or otherwise associating with a broker-dealer firm. In January 2022, Sater claimed that the barfight victim had tried to decline pressing charges, but that the U.S. government kept pressing because they wanted cooperation from Sater's father.

Sater joined Bayrock Group LLC as a senior advisor in 2003 at the behest of the company's owner and founder, Tevfik Arif. As a senior advisor, he assisted with several projects, including executive decisions in the Trump SoHo project. He left Bayrock Group LLC in 2008 after the New York Times disclosed his pending criminal case.

Felix Sater ha[illegible]ribed a[illegible]crim[illegible] his links to organized crime and at times [illegible]puted [illegible] authorities.

*Involvement [illegible] Orga[illegible] campaign*

The Trump O[illegible] pursu[illegible]dominium project in Moscow—dubbed the [illegible] Mos[illegible]residential campaign. This project was [illegible] Mich[illegible]ey for the Trump Organization, and from Ja[illegible] May [illegible]orney. Trump signed a nonbinding "[illegible]nt" d[illegible]proceed with the project. The letter, also si[illegible]sian i[illegible] forwarded to Cohen by Sater. He boasted [illegible]out his [illegible]Putin, saying in an email to Cohen on N[illegible] 2015, "[illegible]e president of the USA and we can enginee[illegible]all of [illegible] on this. I will manage this process." H[illegible] that [illegible] for the project through the Russian stat[illegible] Bank, [illegible]ns by the United States government.

In 2010, Sat[illegible]ded bu[illegible]self as "Senior Advisor to Donald Tru[illegible]mail [illegible] In a 2013 sworn affidavit, Trump said "[illegible]e sitt[illegible], I really wouldn't know what he looked like," [illegible]e st[illegible]ve to even think about it. I'm not that fam[illegible]." Tru[illegible]en [illegible]ed several times with Sater, including wh[illegible] priva[illegible]m.

**Former House Intel[illegible]mitte[illegible]** [illegible]n in 1960, is an American lawyer, author, and [illegible]rving [illegible]m California since 2001. A member of the Dem[illegible]y. Schiff [illegible]anent Select Committee on Intelligence from 20[illegible] He wa[illegible]ittee by incoming Republican House Speaker Kevi[illegible] in 202[illegible].

[illegible]graduate[illegible]arvard Law School. As an [illegible]nt U[illegible]uccessfully prosecuted Soviet [illegible]chard [illegible]199[illegible]running for office the following [illegible]He rep[illegible]lif[illegible]ongressional district, which is [illegible]red i[illegible]of Los Angeles.

[illegible]s on [illegible]the [illegible]ropriations Committee, which he joined in [illegible]evious[illegible]reign Affairs Committee.

Schiff was th[illegible]achm[illegible]peachment trial of President Donald Tru[illegible]revio[illegible]impeachment manager in two judicial impe[illegible]ials. O[illegible], 202[illegible]blican-majority House of Representat[illegible] Schi[illegible]y-li[illegible]esolution that called for an investigation into his alleged "falsehoods, misrepresentations and abuses of sensitive information" regarding the 2016 United States presidential election and the first impeachment of Donald Trump. Schiff has denied the censure's allegations, calling them "false and defamatory."

Schiff is a candidate for the United States Senate in the 2024 election to succeed Dianne Feinstein.

Schiff has been a prominent supporter of surveillance reforms, especially in the wake of the leaks of classified intelligence by Edward Snowden.

In December 2018, Schiff suggested that Trump associate Roger Stone might have lied to Congress and said the transcript of his testimony should be forwarded to the Special Counsel. In November 2019, Stone was convicted of lying to Congress.

When he became chair of the House Intelligence Committee in 2019, Schiff took a personal mission to investigate Trump's connections to Russia, separate from the Special Counsel investigation. Schiff came under fire when he demurred when asked if he would accept it if the Special Counsel's investigation concluded that Trump had not colluded with Russia, saying that he had great confidence in Mueller but that "there may be, for example, evidence of collusion or conspiracy that is clear and convincing, but not proof beyond a reasonable doubt," as is needed for a criminal conviction.]

On March 28, 2019, the nine Republican members of the House Intelligence Committee officially called for Schiff to resign due to his allegations that Trump's campaign colluded with Russians in the 2016 election. Schiff responded by accusing the Republican members of tolerating "immoral" and "corrupt" conduct by Trump campaign members and administration appointees.

On June 21, 2023, the House of Representatives censured Schiff in a party-line vote on a resolution that called for an investigation into his alleged "falsehoods, misrepresentations and abuses of sensitive information" about the 2016 United States presidential election and the first impeachment of Donald Trump. Schiff has denied the allegations, calling them "defamatory."

**Joshua A. Schulte**, born in 1988, is a former CIA and NSA employee who was convicted in 2022 of leaking classified documents to WikiLeaks. WikiLeaks published the documents as Vault 7, which the *New York Times* called "the largest loss of classified documents in the agency's history and a huge embarrassment for C.I.A. officials." After his conviction, the Department of Justice called it "one of the most brazen and damaging acts of espionage in American history."

As of July 2023, Schulte was awaiting trial on charges relating to child pornography and copyright infringement.

From January 2010 to May 2010, Schulte was employed as a systems engineer by the NSA, including time spent within the Technology Directorate., He began working for the CIA in May 2010 and was employed within the National Clandestine Service.

By November 2016, Schulte left the CIA to move to New York, and, until his arrest and detention on August 24, 2017, worked as a senior software engineer for Bloomberg LP.

Allegedly motivated by spite and revenge, Schulte stole backup files from a program called Confluence on April 20, 2016. On March 7, 2017, WikiLeaks began to publish content code-named "Vault 7." The confidential documents, dated from 2013 to 2016, included details on the CIA's software capabilities, such as the ability to compromise cars, smart TVs, web browsers, and popular operating systems.

During a raid of Schulte's Manhattan apartment on March 15, 2017, as well as at least one more on March 23, 2017, federal agents allegedly confiscated approximately 60 electronic devices. Afterward investigators allegedly discovered a single classified document as well as over 10,000 images and videos depicting child pornography, including "sadistic and masochistic images and videos of children as young as a few years old who had been brutally sexually assaulted."

**Former U.S. Attorney Gen. Jefferson B. "Jeff" Sessions**, born in 1946, is an American politician and attorney who served as the 84th United States attorney general from 2017 to 2018. A member of the Republican Party, he previously served as United States senator from Alabama from 1997 to 2017 before resigning that position to serve as attorney general in the administration of President Donald Trump.

Sessions was an early supporter of Donald Trump's 2016 presidential campaign; he was nominated by Trump for the post of U.S. attorney general. He was confirmed and sworn in as attorney general in February 2017. In his confirmation hearings, Sessions stated under oath that he did not have contact with Russian officials during the 2016 presidential campaign and that he was unaware of any contact between Trump campaign members and Russian officials.

However, in March 2017, news reports revealed that Sessions had twice met with Russian ambassador Sergey Kislyak in 2016. Sessions later recused himself from any investigations into Russian interference in the 2016 United States elections.

On November 7, 2018, Sessions tendered his resignation at Trump's request following months of public and private conflict with President Trump over his recusal from investigations relating to Russian election interference. Sessions ran in the 2020 Senate election in Alabama to reclaim his old seat, but lost in the Republican primary to Tommy Tuberville, who was supported by President Trump.

**Glenn Simpson**, co-founder with his former *Wall Street Journal* colleague **Peter Fritsch** of the consultancy **Fusion GPS**. He specialized for the Journal in campaign finance, money laundering, tax evasion, securities fraud, and co-authored with Fritsch *Crime In Progress* (2019), an account of the Steele Dossier and their 2016 investigation of Donald Trump.

**Paul Singer**, a billionaire and hedge fund manager, has been a major contributor to conservative organizations and causes. These include the *Washington Free Beacon*, which hired Fusion GPS to conduct opposition research on what it has called "multiple candidates," including Donald Trump, from October 2015 to May 2016 during presidential primary campaign. The *Free Beacon* is reported to have stopped funding this research when Donald Trump had clinched the Republican nomination.

Fusion GPS later hired former British intelligence officer Christopher Steele, who produced research alleging links between the Trump campaign and the Kremlin. Singer has said he was unaware of this dossier until BuzzFeed News published it in January 2017.

**Christopher D. Steele**, born in 1964, is a British former intelligence officer who worked for the Secret Intelligence Service (MI6, a counterpart to the CIA in the United States) from 1987 until his retirement in 2009. He ran the Russia desk at MI6 headquarters in London between 2006 and 2009. In 2009, he co-founded Orbis Business Intelligence, a London-based private intelligence firm.

Steele became controversial after he authored a 35-page series of memos for a controversial political opposition research report later known as the "Steele Dossier." It was prepared for Fusion GPS, a firm hired by an attorney with Perkins Coie associated with the Hillary Clinton 2016 presidential campaign. The dossier claims, based on anonymous sources, that Russia collected a file of compromising information on Donald Trump and that his presidential campaign conspired to cooperate with the Russians in their interference in the 2016 presidential election.

Trump and his allies have falsely claimed the U.S. intelligence community probe into that Russian interference was launched due to Steele's dossier. Contrary to these claims, the Republican-controlled House Intelligence Committee, among many other sources, concluded in an April 2018 report that the probe had been triggered by previous information from Trump adviser George Papadopoulos. The February 2018 Nunes memo, written by staff members for that GOP-led committee, reached the same conclusion.

**Roger J. Stone Jr.**, b [illegible] (show [illegible] 201 [illegible] talk in a photo by Andrew Kreig of the Justice Integr [illegible] is an Am [illegible] conse [illegible] tical consultant and lobbyist. Since the 1970s, Sto [illegible] ed on [illegible] igns [illegible] can politicians, including Richard Nixon, Ronal [illegible] ack Ke [illegible] ole, [illegible] Bush, and Donald Trump. In addition to frequent [illegible] a cam [illegible] ise [illegible] a political lobbyist. In 1980, he co-founded a Wash [illegible] based [illegible] irm [illegible] anafort and Charles R. Black Jr. The firm recruited P [illegible] and w [illegible] Bl [illegible] ort, Stone and Kelly (BMSK) in 1984.

During the 1 [illegible] became [illegible] obbyin [illegible] everaging its White House connections [illegible] gh-pa [illegible] corporations and trade associations, [illegible] oreign [illegible] nts. [illegible] was one of the leading lobbyists for [illegible] mpani [illegible] eign [illegible] ons.

His personal [illegible] ving [illegible] goal [illegible] described as, "a renowned infighter", "a [illegible] ractit [illegible] rd-e [illegible] s" and "a political fixer."

Stone first su [illegible] mp ru [illegible] dent [illegible] 98 while he was Trump's casino business lob [illegible] hingto [illegible]

Stone official [illegible] ump c [illegible] n A [illegible] 15. However, two unnamed associates o [illegible] allege [illegible] olla [illegible] h WikiLeaks founder Julian Assange duri [illegible] presi [illegible] pai [illegible] dit Hillary Clinton. Stone and Assange hav [illegible] e cla [illegible] th [illegible] earch warrants were unsealed in April 2020 w [illegible] conta [illegible] een [illegible] ssange in 2017, and that Stone orchestrate [illegible] fake [illegible] acc [illegible] loggers to run a political influence sch [illegible] ial me [illegible]

On January 25, 2019, Stone was arrested at his Fort Lauderdale, Florida, home in connection with Robert Mueller's Special Counsel investigation and charged in an indictment with witness tampering, obstructing an official proceeding, and five counts of making false statements. In November 2019, a jury convicted him on all seven felony counts. He was sentenced to 40 months in prison. On July 10, 2020, days before Stone was scheduled to report to prison, Trump commuted his sentence. On August 17, 2020, he dropped the appeal of his convictions. Trump pardoned Stone on December 23, 2020.

**Peter P. Strzok**, born in 1970, is a former FBI agent beginning in 1996. As the Deputy Assistant Director of the FBI's Counterintelligence Division on July 30, 2016, he authorized launch of "Crossfire Hurricane," the code name for the agency's probe of potential Russian interference to help the Trump campaign in during the 2016 presidential election. Previously, he had been the chief of the division's Counterespionage Section and led the investigation into Hillary Clinton's use of a personal email server.

In June and July 2017, Strzok worked on Robert Mueller's Special Counsel investigation into any links or coordination between Donald Trump's presidential campaign and the Russian government. In July 2017, Mueller removed Strzok from the Russia investigation after text message exchanges between Strzok and FBI lawyer Lisa Page contained criticisms of Trump and his supporters. News of the text messages led Trump, Republican congressmen and right-wing media to speculate that Strzok participated in a conspiracy to undermine the Trump presidency.

On August 10, 2018, FBI deputy director David Bowdich fired Strzok for the text messages after the FBI's employee disciplinary office had recommended that Strzok only be suspended for 60 days and demoted. On August 6, 2019, Strzok filed a wrongful termination suit against the FBI and the U.S. Department of Justice, asking to be reinstated and awarded back pay. He asserted in the suit that his text messages were "protected political speech", and that the termination violated his First Amendment rights.

In September 2020, Houghton Mifflin Harcourt published Strzok's book, *Compromised: Counterintelligence and the Threat of Donald J. Trump,* which became a *New York Times* and *Washington Post* bestseller. Strzok, who earlier received the FBI's highest award, is currently an adjunct professor at Georgetown University. He also co-hosts a podcast and is a frequent guest commentator on news shows.

**National Security Advisory President Biden Jacob J. "Jake" Sullivan**, born in 1976, is an American political advisor who currently serves as the United States national security advisor to President Joe Biden. He was previously director of policy to President Barack Obama, national security advisor to then Vice President Biden and deputy chief of staff to Secretary Hillary Clinton at the U.S. Department of State.

Sullivan also served as senior advisor to the U.S. federal government at the Iran nuclear negotiations and senior policy advisor to Clinton's 2016 presidential campaign, as well as visiting professor at Yale Law School.

On November 23, 2020, President-elect Biden announced that Sullivan would be appointed as national security advisor. He took office January 20, 2021.

Jake Sullivan was the top National Security advisor to the Clinton 2016 campaign and later chaired the National Security Council for the Biden White House. During the Sussmann trial, the government moved to admit a tweet from Clinton dated Oct. 31, 2016, as evidence, which stated, "Computer scientists have apparently uncovered a covert server linking the Trump Organization to a Russian-based bank."

Clinton also shared a statement from adviser Jake Sullivan that said, "This could be the most direct link yet between Donald Trump and Moscow. Computer scientists have uncovered a covert server linking the Trump Organization to a Russian-based bank."

"This line of communication may help explain Trump's bizarre adoration of Vladimir Putin and endorsement of so many pro-Kremlin positions throughout this campaign," Sullivan's 2016 statement continued. "It raises even more troubling questions in light of Russia's masterminding of hacking efforts that are clearly intended to hurt Hillary Clinton's campaign."

The Durham prosecution team and conservative media focused heavily on the comments while virtually ignoring other evidence that Russians were heavily disrupting the Clinton campaign with stolen emails and other illegal techniques with the vocal encouragement, at the minimum, of various entities associated with the Trump campaign.

**Michael A. Sussmann**, born in 1964, is an American former federal prosecutor and a former partner at the law firm Perkins Coie who focused on privacy and cybersecurity law. Sussmann represented the Democratic National Committee (DNC) and retained CrowdStrike to examine its servers after two Russian hacker groups penetrated DNC networks and stole information during the 2016 U.S. elections.

The Trump administration appointed John Durham as special counsel to investigate the origins of the FBI probe into the many suspicious links between Trump associates and Russian officials and spies. Durham spent more than three years on the investigation and, in 2021, brought a charge of making false statements against Sussmann, accusing him of having lied to the FBI in one meeting in 2016, with no witnesses. Sussman pleaded not guilty. After a jury trial in May 2022, Sussman was found not guilty.

Beginning in 2017, President Donald Trump and his allies alleged the FBI investigation, leading to the Mueller investigation, of possible contacts between his associates and Russian officials was a "hoax" or "witch hunt" that was baselessly initiated by his political enemies.

In May 2019 attorney general Bill Barr appointed U.S. attorney John Durham to investigate the origins of the FBI investigation. Durham's grand jury indicted Sussmann in September 2021, alleging he made a false statement to FBI general counsel James Baker during a meeting they had in September 2016. At the meeting, Sussmann presented what he and others believed was evidence of potential communications between computer servers at the Russian Alfa Bank and the Trump Organization. After Trump became president, the FBI found their claims to be without merit, and they were ignored in the Mueller Report.

The indictment of Sussmann alleges he told Baker he did not represent a client for the purposes of their meeting, when he was actually representing the Hillary Clinton 2016 presidential campaign. Sussman had stated during a 2017 congressional deposition that he sought the meeting with Baker on behalf of an unnamed client, a cybersecurity expert who had analyzed the server communications data. As with the charge against Clinesmith, the charge against Sussmann was unrelated to the opening of the FBI investigation into Trump associates and Russians, which occurred in July 2016, and which was the original basis of Durham's investigation.

After Sussmann's indictment, the *New York Times* reported that in addition to analyzing suspicious communications involving a Trump server, Sussmann and analysts he worked with became aware of data from a YotaPhone — a Russian-made smartphone rarely used in the United States — that had accessed networks serving the White House, Trump Tower and a Michigan hospital company, Spectrum Health. Like the Alfa Bank server, a Spectrum server also communicated with the Trump Organization server. Sussmann notified CIA counterintelligence of the findings in February 2017, but it was not known if they were investigated.

On May 31, 2022, after hearing two weeks of testimony, the jury quickly and unanimously acquitted Sussmann. In a statement issued after being acquitted, Sussman said: "I told the truth to the F.B.I., and the jury clearly recognized that with their unanimous verdict today. Despite being falsely accused, I am relieved that justice ultimately prevailed in this case." Sussmann's defense team said that their client "should never have been charged in the first place" and referred to the case as "a case of extraordinary prosecutorial overreach."

On June 1, 20[illegible] Attorn[illegible] Wil[illegible] was interviewed on Fox News about the ve[illegible] ng M[illegible] repe[illegible] ked conspiracy theories about the origins of [illegible] invest[illegible] case against Sussmann "crystallized t[illegible] role pl[illegible] Hill[illegible] ign in launching, as a dirty trick, the whole Ru[illegible] lusion [illegible]

The *New Yor[illegible]* [illegible] ported [illegible] 2023 [illegible] prosecutors on Durham's team, including his [illegible] leagu[illegible] nnel[illegible] ed to him that the evidence against Suss[illegible] thin [illegible] char[illegible] at an acquittal would undermine [illegible] Durha[illegible] tigat[illegible] enforcement. After Durham pursued the [illegible], one [illegible] ecut[illegible] d in protest while another left for another [illegible]

Durham's pr[illegible] lowed [illegible] ke p[illegible] amounts of information insinuating i[illegible] of the [illegible] nton [illegible] not related to Sussman's prosecution [illegible] harge[illegible] Sus[illegible] secution failed, Barr stated it "accomplish[illegible] far [illegible] tant [illegible] "crystallized the central role played by th[illegible] paign [illegible] ing as[illegible] k the whole Russiagate collusion na[illegible] nning [illegible] s of [illegible]

**Donald Trump Jr.**, b[illegible] s an [illegible] politi[illegible] businessman, author, and former television pr[illegible] is the [illegible] of [illegible] mp, 45th president of the United States from [illegible] and [illegible] le Iv[illegible]

Trump (show[illegible] Skidm[illegible] duri[illegible] speaking event in Phoenix) serves as a t[illegible] xecut[illegible] side[illegible] rump Organization, running the company alo[illegible] ounger [illegible] Eric [illegible] father's presidency, the brothers con[illegible] deals [illegible] men[illegible] n countries, as well as collect payments in [illegible] operti[illegible] reign[illegible] nts, despite a pledge that they would not d[illegible] also se[illegible] board[illegible] ge on his father's TV show *The Apprentice*. [illegible] *Trigg[illegible]* [illegible] 9 a[illegible] *ivilege* in 2020.

Trump was a[illegible] ather [illegible] sider[illegible] gn. He cooperated with Russia in their inter[illegible] e 2016 [illegible] tate[illegible] and had a meeting with a Russian law[illegible] rised d[illegible] form[illegible] ut the campaign of Hillary Clinton in th[illegible] entia[illegible] acc[illegible] number of news reports.

**Jonathan Turley**, bo[illegible] s an A[illegible] torne[illegible] holar, writer, commentator, and legal analyst in [illegible] d pri[illegible] m.

A professor at George Washington University Law School, he has testified in United States Congressional proceedings about constitutional and statutory issues. He has also testified in multiple impeachment hearings and removal trials in Congress, including the impeachment of President Bill Clinton and both the first and second impeachments of President Donald Trump. Turley is a First Amendment advocate and writes frequently on free speech restrictions in the private and public sectors. Turley is a Fox News contributor.

He is a frequent witness before the House and Senate on constitutional and statutory issues, as well as tort reform legislation.

Turley has testified regularly during national controversies. Turley, in his capacity as a constitutional scholar, testified in favor of the Clinton impeachment. He was quoted extensively by congressman James Rogan during the impeachment of Bill Clinton.

On December 4, 2019, Turley testified before the House Judiciary Committee regarding the constitutional grounds for presidential impeachment in the impeachment inquiry against Donald Trump, arguing against a Trump impeachment. It was observed that his prior reasoning for the impeachment of President Bill Clinton contradicted the opinions he shared against the impeachment of President Donald Trump. Turley sought to clarify his positions regarding the two impeachments the next day in an op-ed. Turley noted that in both hearings he stressed that a president could be impeached for non-criminal acts, including abuse of power, and House Judiciary Chairman Jerry Nadler ended the Trump impeachment hearings by quoting him to that effect.

**Craig Unger**, author of a half dozen books, including *American Kompromat: How the KGB Cultivated Donald Trump and Related Tales of Sex, Greed, Power, and Treachery* (2021), as well as the New York Times best-sellers *House of Trump, House of Putin: The Untold Story of Donald Trump and the Russian Mafia* (2021) and *House of Bush, House of Saud* (2004).

His books have explored in-depth Trump's Russian connections, including with powerful and sinister figures in the underworld, as explored in, for example, a chapter entitled "Trump's 59 Russian Connections" in *House of Trump*.

Unger's *American Kompromat* undertakes a deep dive into, among other topics, what he reports as strong links between the conservative Federalist Society, the Catholic Opus Dei secret society founded by the Spanish Fascist Josemaría Escrivá, what he reports as the Opus Dei-linked Catholic Information Center in downtown Washington, DC and, in certain instances, highly prominent federal judges, prosecutors and FBI agents. Unger reports, for example, that FBI agent Robert Hanssen, convicted of spying for the Soviet Union for more than two decades, was revealed after his arrest to have been an Opus Dei member.

**Natalia V. Veselnitskaya**, born in 1975, is a Russian lawyer. Her clients include Pyotr Katsyv, an official in the state-owned Russian Railways, and his son Denis Katsyv, whom she defended against a money laundering charge in New York. On January 8, 2019, she was indicted in the United States with obstruction of justice charges for allegedly having attempted to thwart the Justice Department investigation into the money laundering charges against a client.

Her June 2016 meeting with Donald Trump Jr., Jared Kushner, and Paul Manafort in Trump Tower attracted attention in connection with the Russian interference in the 2016 United States elections, as well as to the role of her business contacts at the research firm Fusion GPS in investigating the interference.

In 2009, Sergei Magnitsky, a tax accountant who had accused Moscow law enforcement of stealing $230 million in tax rebates from his client, was beaten to death in jail. In 2012, Magnitsky's client, Bill Browder, secured passage of the American Magnitsky Act, which imposed sanctions on the officials involved. Russian President Vladimir Putin responded with the Dima Yakovlev Law banning Americans from adopting Russian children.

On June 9, 2016, Veselnitskaya met with Donald Trump Jr., Paul Manafort, and Jared Kushner in Trump Tower, which they scheduled after Emin Agalarov's publicist, Rob Goldstone, told Donald Jr. that she was a "Russian government attorney" offering incriminating information on Hillary Clinton due to "its government's support for Mr. Trump." Regarding the meeting, Trump Jr. initially wrote, "I love it" but, in July 2017, said the meeting "was a waste of time." Donald Trump Jr. said that Veselnitskaya used the meeting to criticize the Magnitsky Act. Veselnitskaya herself commented that she mostly talked about Browder's (alleged) misdeeds, whereas the Trump team wanted what she termed "some sort of grenade."

Also, on or around June 9, prior to and following the Trump Tower meeting, Veselnitskaya met with Fusion GPS co-founder Glenn R. Simpson, ostensibly related to hearings that involved their mutual client Denis Katsyv, concerning charges of Russian tax fraud and money laundering originally uncovered by Magnitsky. The Simpson–Veselnitskaya meetings were denied by Veselnitskaya herself but confirmed by Simpson's lawyer.

**U.S. Rep. Debbie Wasserman Schultz**, , D-Florida, born in 1966, is an American politician serving as the U.S. representative from Florida's 25th congressional district, first elected to Congress in 2004. A member of the Democratic Party, she is a former chair of the Democratic National Committee.

Wasserman Schultz served in the Florida House of Representatives and the Florida Senate and was a national co-chair of Hillary Clinton's 2008 campaign for president. Her district covers much of southern Broward County, including a large part of Fort Lauderdale. It also covers much of northern Miami-Dade County.

On July 28, 2016, she resigned as DNC chair after WikiLeaks released leaked emails showing that she and other members of the DNC staff had seemingly favored Hillary Clinton over Bernie Sanders in the 2016 Democratic primaries in exchange for funding to eliminate the DNC's remaining debt from the 2012 presidential campaign.

**David C. Weiss**, born in 1956, took office in 2018 as U.S. attorney for Delaware after nomination by President Donald Trump. President Joe Biden retained him in office as Weiss continued politically sensitive investigations of the president's son, Hunter Biden. When Republicans and a Trump-nominated federal judge questioned a proposed Weiss plea deal with Hunter Biden on tax and gun charges plea negotiations broke down.

On Aug. 11, 2023, Weiss won appointment from Biden-nominated Attorney General Merrick Garland to become a special counsel investigating the younger Biden and filed federal gun charges the next month against the younger Biden alleging that he possessed a gun for 11 days while a drug user and also made false statements on an application for a gun permit. Biden pleaded not guilty to the charges. Meanwhile, his defense counsel filed a lawsuit against a former Trump administration official and numerous "John Doe" defendants to be named later alleging privacy invasion and hacking of his personal communications devices as part of a conspiracy to make false allegations of corruption and other crimes against him and his father.

**Andrew A. Weissmann**, born in 1958, is an American attorney and professor. He was an Assistant United States Attorney from 1991 to 2002, where he prosecuted high-profile

organized crime cases. He served as a lead prosecutor in Robert S. Mueller's Special Counsel's Office (2017–2019) after previously serving as Justice Department chief of the Fraud Section from 2015 to 2017 and as FBI general counsel.

He is currently a professor at New York University's School of Law and a frequent commentator on news shows. In 2020, he authored *Where Law Ends: Inside the Mueller Investigation.*

**Marcy Wheeler**, Ph... independent ... national security ... analyst who founded the Emptywheel blog that has ... in ... national security and federal law enforcement issues ... decades.

... in-depth ... unmatched in terms of hard-hitting ... decisions, ... timely ..., focuses on legal, ... professional ... political ... dimensions of the Mueller and ... probe ... has ... matters through the years as ... Durham ... destruction of waterboarding ..., Hillary Clinton's ..., the Jan. 6 and election fraud investigations ... pertinent ... the ... omissions of the Durham Report.

Her preview ... Counsel ... Durham's ... House Judiciary Committee testimony, ... June 20... the day ... the hearing, was entitled, *A Guide to the ... John D... Will T...*. It began: "John Durham's investigation ... year eff... the ... make Hillary Clinton — the victim of a ... attack ...

**WikiLeaks** is a publis... media orga... founded ...6. It operates as a non-profit and is funded by do... media ... ships. ... published classified documents and other media provided ... anonymous ... was ... Julian Assange, an Australian editor, publisher, and ... who is ... challen... extradition to the United States over his work with WikiLeaks.

... December 20... has served as its editor-in-chief. ... states ... than ten million documents ... beginning ... December 2022, many of the ... could ... access...

... has released ... documents and media that exposed serious ... of human ... rights.

... 2016 ... campaign, WikiLeaks released ... the Democratic National Committee (DNC) and from Hillary ... campaign ..., the party's national committee ... Clinton in ... primaries ... releases resulted in the resignation of Debbie Wasserman Schultz as ... chairman ... and caused significant harm to the Clinton cam...

During the cam... WikiLeaks ... false ... conspiracy theories about Hillary Clinton, the Democratic Party and ... murder ... Rich, a former DNC staffer. Unfounded ... theories ... by some ... figures and media outlets, hold that Rich ... source ... emails ... killed for working with

WikiLeaks. WikiLeaks popularized conspiracy theories about the Democratic Party and Hillary Clinton, such as tweeting articles which suggested Clinton campaign chairman John Podesta engaged in satanic rituals.

**FBI Director Christopher A. Wray**, born in 1966,is an American attorney who is the eighth and current FBI Director after nomination by President Donald Trump on June 7, 2017 to replace James Comey.

From January 2016 to July 2017, the month of his confirmation, Wray earned $9.2 million working as an attorney for the law firm King & Spalding, significantly more than his salary as FBI Director. According to a calculation from the Wall Street Journal, Wray's net worth in 2017 was estimated to be $23 million to $42 million.

Wray is a Republican, as were each of his predecessors as FBI director since its founding, and a member of the Federalist Society.

**Viktor F. Yanukovych**, born in 1950, is a former politician who served as the fourth president of Ukraine from 2010 until he was removed from office in the Revolution of Dignity in 2014, after months of protests against his presidency. From 2006 to 2007 he was the prime minister of Ukraine. He also served in this post from November 2002 to January 2005, with a short interruption in December 2004. He has lived in exile in Russia since his removal from office in 2014.

In November 2013, a series of events began that led to his ousting as president. Amid economic pressure from Russia, Yanukovych suddenly changed his mind and withdrew from signing an association agreement with the EU, instead accepting a Russian trade deal and loan bailout.

This sparked mass protests against Yanukovych, dubbed the "Euromaidan," which met a harsh response from authorities. The civil unrest peaked in February 2014, when almost 100 protesters were killed by police.

**YotaPhone** was a SmartPhone backed by the Russian company Yota Devices before its bankruptcy was reported in 2019 as stemming from lack of sales and related issues.

# Acknowledgments

This book is dedicated to those prosecutors and judges who inspired me by their force of example to seek justice, not simply victory or similar narrow advantage. I held a front-row seat to observe such powerful lessons as I covered the U.S. Justice Department and federal court system full-time from 1976 to 1981 for the *Hartford Courant*, Connecticut's largest newspaper and the second largest in New England (in terms of staff and circulation) next to the *Boston Globe*.

In simpler times before security concerns isolated officials from the public and reporters, I saw decision-making rendered in a manner far more public-spirited than generally exists today, particularly as evident in the Durham investigation whose arguments form the bulk of this book. The names and actions of these long-ago judges and prosecutors have resonated powerfully with me in this research journey. Before mentioning them I should note that many have died and none, including those few still in office, have had anything to do with this specific research, which is my responsibility.

First in time was the Republican-nominated U.S. Attorney for Connecticut Peter C. Dorsey, later a Reagan-nominated U.S. District Court judge. His successor as U.S. Attorney was the Democratic nominee Richard Blumenthal, later Connecticut's Attorney General and currently a U.S. Senator representing Connecticut. Blumenthal emphasized white-collar crime prosecutions, and he had been a newspaper reporter in one of his first jobs out of college. Partly for such reasons, I came to follow his decision-making in these complex matters especially closely. Among the thoughtful leaders of prosecution teams I reported closely upon in Connecticut were: Thomas P. Smith, later a U.S. Magistrate-Judge; Albert S. Dabrowski, the chief Assistant U.S. attorney in the state and later the chief U.S. Bankruptcy Court judge in Connecticut for 22 years; and Paul E. Coffey, the Justice Department Strike Force on Organized Crime and Racketeering regional leader who led the test prosecution in Hartford for a then-new Racketeering Influenced and Corrupt Organizations (RICO) law before moving on to lead the Strike Force nationally. He served also as Special Counsel in a probe of former CIA Director John Deutch for possessing classified information at home on personal devices.

Presiding over Connecticut's courts were judges strongly committed to public service. They instilled those values in their law clerks, some of whom I interacted with daily as I made my rounds covering court filings, scandals, trials and trends. Particularly impressive were Chief U.S. District Judge T. Emmet Clarie, his colleagues U.S. District Judges M. Joseph Blumenfeld and Jon O. Newman, the latter becoming a longtime U.S. Second Circuit Court of Appeals judge based in New York City. Particularly memorable was this perspective that I recall from a hallway chat with onetime Newman clerk and assistant U.S. attorney, Richard Palmer, a future Connecticut Supreme Court chief justice: "The weight and majesty of the United States government should never be used for a criminal prosecution unless there is strong likelihood of a conviction."

Later, I saw a similar dedication to justice and public service by work from 1990 to 1991 as clerk to U.S. District Judge Mark L. Wolf in Boston, who would continue his corruption-fighting career begun as an aide to U.S. Attorney Gen. Edward Levy and then as a federal prosecutor. As a Reagan-nominated federal trial judge, he initiated an inquiry that exposed the Justice Department's scandalous coddling of such Boston mob informants such as James "Whitey" Bulger. That initiated misconduct inquiries for the behavior of nearly two dozen federal prosecutors and FBI special agents and prompted the judge in later years, particularly as chief federal judge in Massachusetts, repeatedly to warn new presidentially nominated U.S. attorneys that they needed to comply with the law in their litigation decisions. In the spring of 2023, the judge was himself a newsmaker as a witness before the U.S. Senate Judiciary Committee stating that financial circumstances of Supreme Court Associate Justice Clarence Thomas and his wife, Virginia "Ginni" Thomas, had not been adequately shared with the federal court system's administrative body when he had served on it a decade previous.

None of these [illegible] any in[illegible] [illegible]n knowledge of that I was working on it. Any of their imp[illegible] from [illegible]h I well remember.

I recall also [illegible] on a [illegible] in the 19[illegible]al decisions of my newspaper, the *Hartford Courant* wh[illegible] here for [illegible] in th[illegible] early 1980s. Long operating under local ownership, its ed[illegible] a mi[illegible] a concern for consequences. Here is one relevant examp[illegible] appear [illegible] d by today's standards, but it had a purpose: *Courant* Ma[illegible] William [illegible] ple that if someone in public office, including law enforc[illegible] to leak [illegible] and damaging information about someone, the reporter[illegible] should [illegible] why [illegible]older was using power to undertake such a breach of duty. [illegible]ications [illegible]

These lessons [illegible]alism [illegible] also from great teachers. During my undergraduate yea[illegible] Univers[illegible] Alan Bloom required students to read *The Use and Ab*[illegible] written [illegible]een 1873 and 1876. The by-now taped-together paperba[illegible] o stu[illegible] my arms reach near my desk. That book and teacher first [illegible] vital [illegible]king" (which can have many unworthy motives, su[illegible] or ot[illegible]al blackmail) and justice-seeking. "The search for truth [illegible]htlessl[illegible] But it has something great in it only if the seeker has [illegible] condit[illegible] just[illegible]

This is the pla[illegible] ore tra[illegible] contemporaries and the recently departed. My deepest [illegible] colle[illegible] y in the complex research that I have drawn upon. On[illegible] and c[illegible]olific, courageous investigative reporter and author w[illegible] has [illegible] U.S. Navy intelligence officer and NSA analyst to help i[illegible] me and [illegible] darkest realms. Another is the late Barry Sussman, who [illegible]*ington* [illegible] Watergate coverage. Later, as editor of Harvard Univ[illegible]*m W*[illegible] publ[illegible] of my investigative columns, including in 2010 wit[illegible]*s Re*[illegible] *Cleared Bush Officials in U.S. Attorney Firing*, my f[illegible] John [illegible] I thank the directors of the Justice Integrity Proje[illegible] years [illegible] expert guidance on the ways of the world, including c[illegible] about [illegible] reflected in this book: Robert Ames Alden, Ronald [illegible] Edward [illegible] William F. Pepper. I sorely miss those of them who ha[illegible]

I thank also [illegible] electr[illegible] WebResults.com, whose expert and otherwise remarkably [illegible] have [illegible] book and indeed the long-term work of the Justice Integrit[illegible]

Also, I extend [illegible] to the [illegible] nd donors who maintain Wikipedia entries. Drawing on th[illegible] s and [illegible] came a late addition to this book in a long Appendix sectio[illegible] came cl[illegible] like the underlying investigation, would omit or mischa[illegible] mber [illegible] at issue. My thanks is sincere even though I have reporte[illegible] in th[illegible] Wi[illegible]ess. I would like to think, however, that the goal of reporti[illegible] toward [illegible]ng with appreciation positives when they occur.

I am grateful [illegible] family [illegible] who [illegible]must endure the distractions of this kind of research. Per[illegible] way t[illegible] given the passions and potential for violence inherent in so[illegible] ontro[illegible] *not* [illegible]me specifically. This story, after all, relates in part to a vio[illegible] en, wi[illegible]ng literally on the streets near where I work on Pennsylva[illegible] orthw[illegible] ing[illegible]way between the White House and Capitol Hill, and just [illegible] from [illegible] J. Edgar Hoover Building. The site also is halfway betwee[illegible] Trump [illegible] U.S. federal courthouse, where many of the Jan. 6 Capitol ri[illegible] ists [illegible]aring[illegible] often with their supporters present. One of the most prom[illegible] Oath [illegible] leader [illegible]art Rhodes, a military veteran and Yale Law School grad[illegible] d by h[illegible] y as [illegible]te May 2023 just before this book's publication, Rhodes received an 18-year prison term following his conviction at trial (which I covered in person at times) and his unapologetic tirade in court defending his efforts to help keep Donald Trump in office by whatever means necessary.

At that courthouse on Aug. 1, 2023, a landmark in these researches came as I awaited with other reporters the news that a grand jury there on that date had issued a four-count indictment against former President Trump on charges related to the attempt to thwart the certification of 2020 presidential election votes on Jan. 6, 2021. Even such momentous news about a dire threat to the legal framework of the United States constitutes just a step in a process. Many visitors to that courthouse see vivid reminders of that history in the plaque describing how that courthouse and adjoining park are located where U.S. Supreme Court Chief Justice John Marshall, the first in that office, used to live.

My journey to understand the justice system's operations in these matters was prompted by my curiosity in omissions in most news accounts regarding Durham's track record in Connecticut and nationally. These omissions and their implications turned out to hold profound implications for the U.S. justice system, politics, national security and other civic life.

This investigation reveals a chilling tale — and a ray of hope for civic reformers of all political viewpoints.

*The Complete Annotated Durham 'Russiagate' Report* is for those who want to understand the news, not just watch.

Here is what I like to call **KEY**: "**K**nowledge **E**mpowers **Y**ou."

## Praise for *The Complete Durham 'Russiagate' Report*

*Special Counsel John Durham began an investigation in 2019 and, after four years, at a cost of 6.2 million dollars, issued a 306-page report in 2023.*

*The ostensible purpose of the investigation was to determine if the FBI was politically motivated in conducting an investigation into Russia's involvement in the 2016 Presidential election. Donald Trump had claimed that the investigation had been a conspiracy of law enforcers to help Hillary Clinton and to hurt him. Justice Department Inspector General Michael Horowitz found no such motivations but Trump's Attorney General William Barr nonetheless appointed John Durham, U.S. Attorney in Connecticut, as Special Counsel to investigate the FBI's investigation.*

*Durham's report failed to find any conspiracy to damage Donald Trump but nonetheless criticized the FBI for conducting a full investigation "without any actual evidence of collusion" between Russia and the Trump campaign. It acknowledged that a preliminary investigation had been appropriate and noted that there was no FBI rule or practice against a full investigation. It also criticized the FBI for tunnel vision without suggestion how that had produced erroneous conclusions.*

*The book by lawyer-journalist Andrew Kreig examines in intimate detail the motivations and the operations of John Durham in his conducting of the four-year investigation. Kreig concludes, among other things, that the Durham investigation itself was politically motivated and aimed to assist Donald Trump in some of his outrageous accusations against the Justice Department.*

*This careful study is especially relevant today, when the former President hopes to get votes for his re-election by promising if elected to sic the Justice Department on his enemies. Remember Richard Nixon's "Enemy List?" Few thoughts are more disturbing than that such behavior by a President could be legitimate or desirable.*

- **Steven Duke**, Emeritus Professor of Law, Yale Law School

*This five-star case st[illegible]s wide[illegible]mong influencers within the Democratic Party, th[illegible]oriente[illegible]ablis[illegible]d the relevant news media. The author exposes [illegible]edera[illegible]s, en[illegible]by the Trump administration, abused their author[illegible]anear[illegible]rison[illegible]o justifiably sought FBI investigations of Ru[illegible]ce in th[illegible]esid[illegible]ion.*

*Author Andrew Kreig [illegible]rump Ad[illegible]tion S[illegible]sel John Durham to make his case with Dunham's [illegible]306-p[illegible], the[illegible]debunks it with his 13 years of study of Durham's r[illegible]ig's co[illegible]Durh[illegible]cutions shows that juries acquitted every defe[illegible]he p[illegible]dis[illegible]r-year taxpayer-paid probe.*

*This case study is hi[illegible]to cu[illegible]ts re[illegible]in the United States and globally. The proble[illegible]osec[illegible]cting[illegible]inst political opponents is nothing new.*

*As a successful Sout[illegible]ratic G[illegible]ho w[illegible]e able to breech the Republican's "South[illegible]g" as d[illegible]uth[illegible]rs, Clinton and Carter, to challenge President [illegible]Bush, [illegible]ted b[illegible]gned with Karl Rove. (See the CBS-TV 60 Minutes [illegible]b 24, 2[illegible]ndep[illegible]umentary, "Atticus v. Architect, the political assassin[illegible]verno[illegible]imer[illegible]memoir, "Stealing Our Democracy: How th[illegible]ssassin[illegible]gover[illegible]ens our nation."*

*Andrew Kreig, a law[illegible]alist, [illegible]exten[illegible]e "U.S. Attorney Firing Scandal" of 2006. Th[illegible]s tha[illegible]Adm[illegible]had fired their own Republican U.S. Attorneys who [illegible]rosecu[illegible]ats, [illegible]ace at the Justice Department those willing to und[illegible]al dir[illegible].*

*Kreig notes that Joh[illegible]longti[illegible]ue, [illegible]ny, in the Russian-related investigation had pr[illegible]appo[illegible]he B[illegible]stration as independent counsel to investigate the U.[illegible]Firing S[illegible]D was labeled "a whitewash" because she only in[illegible]of th[illegible]Att[illegible]g reminds readers that Democratic Genera[illegible]ajorit[illegible]ecti[illegible]her to the Connecticut Supreme Court with [illegible]ion o[illegible]ocum[illegible]along, get-along careerism that should have require[illegible]e pu[illegible]atio[illegible]r makes clear that the Durham Report is being use[illegible]ns an[illegible]pl[illegible]plate for Republicans who are intent on imprisoni[illegible]en w[illegible]Tru[illegible]ed Special Counsel on a highly dubious basis, and b[illegible]his [illegible]em[illegible]bious basis.*

*Donald Trump has e[illegible]staf[illegible]e Dep[illegible]ith his supporters who would use their powers to [illegible]litica[illegible]fort[illegible]hese problems are not unique to this country. This bo[illegible]w the[illegible]ion[illegible]cently has become operational in elections and suc[illegible]in ot[illegible]n-c[illegible]ocracies, including the United Kingdom, France, U[illegible]Western[illegible].*

*All I can say is: If you want to wake up, America, read "The Complete Annotated Durham 'Russiagate' Report."*

- **Don Siegelman**, Governor of Alabama (1999-2003); Alabama Lt. Governor (1995-1999); Attorney General (1987-1981); and Secretary of State (1979-1987)

*Andrew Kreig provides a thorough and positive education about corruption in the public justice system. I worked in the Fifth-Floor cockpit of the U.S. Justice Department (Office of Legal Counsel), meeting near-daily with Attorney General Robert F. Kennedy on a small team focused on civil rights and anti-corruption during the pivotal year of 1963.*

*I was and am committed to justice, fairness, and law enforcement. Those were clean years in government. "Justice, justice shalt thou pursue" was the reminder over the door to my office. Andrew's writings would have been lead items on my shelf.*

*Like Andrew, I write about the pursuit of justice. My memoir* Lucky Conversations: Visits with the Most Prominent People of the 20th Century *describes my private meetings and conversations on such themes with Martin Luther King Jr., Eleanor Roosevelt, Adlai Stevenson, John Lewis, and Jackie Kennedy, including a JFK visit that included Jackie and the kids on April 11, 1963. That book and my* Whatever Happened To Raoul Wallenberg? *pursue public awareness of federal agency corruption, as does Kreig.*

*Please read his book and gain a better knowledge of what is going on in the USA.*

- **Morris Wolff**, author, human rights advocate and retired law professor whose work included serving on the Senate staff of U.S. Senator John Sherman Cooper of Kentucky when the senator was a Warren Commission member and as Chief Assistant to Philadelphia District Attorney Arlen Specter. In 1960, Wolff founded the first AISEC Secretariat offices in Geneva, building offices in dozens of nations. His next book is a practical guide for young people to pursue high-impact careers in public service.

## Praise for The Justice Integrity Project and *Presidential Puppetry*

*Andrew Kreig was for many years a respected reporter for the Hartford Courant and author of* Spiked. *He went on to lead with distinction the Wireless Communications Association and the Justice Integrity Project. These efforts help provide the intimate knowledge of Washington, national, and global affairs required for such ambitious reporting. A must-read.*

- **Robert Ames Alden**, former president of the National Press Club, co-founder and former president of the National Press Foundation, and former *Washington Post* World News editor

*Andrew Kreig uses his decades of investigative journalism talent to unmask the characters who have manipulated our democratic institutions. His formidable sources and sophisticated insights will enable elected officials, journalists, professors, and voters to evaluate the power interests that were at stake in the 2012 elections and for the future.*

*This is a frightening book that challenges all of us to act bravely. We must rouse ourselves to prevent a small number of wealthy, cynical men from usurping the power that rightfully belongs to the American citizen. He identifies these men, reveals their motives, shows us how they intended to accomplish their goals, and thus puts all of us on notice in this powerful exposé.*

- **Lillian McEwen**, author, *D.C. Unmasked and Undressed,* and former U.S. administrative law judge, prosecutor, and Senate Judiciary Committee counsel under then-Chairman Joseph R. Biden

*This provocative exposé is a clarion call for every American who cherishes belief of personal liberty within a just and democratic society.*

- **Cyril H. Wecht**, M.D. J.D., longtime medical school professor and coroner, author of 60 books and more than 500 professional articles, and widely recognized as one of the world's leading forensic pathologists

*Thought provoking. Controversial. One of those books that inspires readers to look deep beneath the surface.*

- **John Perkins**, best-selling author of *Confessions of an Economic Hit Man* and other books

*Four decades ago, I described shocking abuses of the troops and taxpayers when I went on-the-record with Jack Anderson following my resignation from CIA service in Indochina during the Vietnam era. The situation is far worse now.*

- **John Kelly**, former news editor at NBC-TV and CBS-TV, and former CIA officer

Presidential Puppetry *gives remarkable insight into how our Constitution has disintegrated at the hands of a few secret oligarchs who are calling the shots in domestic and foreign affairs.*

- **John Edward Hurley**, Washington commentator, civic leader, and historian

*Veteran investigative journalist Andrew Kreig delves deep into the underbelly of Washington politics, coming up with startling new revelations that are bound to shake up the status quo.*

- **Dick Russell**, author, *On the Trail of the JFK Assassins*, and other books

*This is clearly the worst of times in many decades, perhaps since the Civil War. The problem that a writer has is that you can write this, explain it, argue it, prove it. But, in the end, the reader and friends have to do something about it.*

- **Sam Smith**, *Progressive Review* publisher, DC Statehood movement co-founder, and author of books that include *Captive Capital* and *Why Bother?*

*National politics has never been a very wholesome game. But the odor of wholesale deception and cynical choreography has been ripening of late into an overpowering stench that our media seems hell-bent on spraying with Febreze. Kreig connects the myriad of dots, from corrupt and cynical jurisprudence, to the ruthlessly edited candidates' playbook, to outright computerized election theft. What emerges is a pointillist "big picture" of terrifying impact. Imagine a Seurat rendition of "The Scream," and you'll get the idea. All of this is well-researched and powerfully written.*

- **Jonathan D. Simon**, Director, Election Defense Alliance and author, *Code Red*

*I love this book. It cuts through the years of bullshit right to the point. It's stunning.*

- **Roger Stone**, consultant to eight GOP presidential campaigns and author of *Nixon's Secrets* and *The Man Who Killed Kennedy*

Presidential Puppetry *is a groundbreaking, comprehensive, masterpiece that leads us down the twisting, turning trail of presidential malfeasance, Constitutional transgression, and outright government criminality while illuminating events that have heretofore gone unreported or under-reported.*

- **Robert S. Finnegan**, Editor, *The Fifth Estate* and former Senior Editor, *The Jakarta Post*, based in Indonesia

## Praise for *Spiked: How Chain Management Corrupted America's Oldest Newspaper*

*Anyone who has bee* [illegible] *will* [illegible] *this compelling book, whether or not they've worke* [illegible] *n. The* [illegible] *pre* [illegible] *ss and downright cowardice so common to newspa* [illegible] *nent* [illegible]

- **John** [illegible] **ur, Pu** [illegible] **per** [illegible]

*Rarely do we get su* [illegible] *book* [illegible] *must read for anyone who cares about the implicatio* [illegible] *pora* [illegible] *country.*

- **Linco** [illegible] **Busin** [illegible]

*A pretty chilling tale* [illegible] *eporte* [illegible]

- **Jona** [illegible] **enior** [illegible] **Medi** [illegible] ***ewsweek***

*Andrew Kreig's case* [illegible] *ctiona* [illegible] *ce.*

- **Ralph** [illegible]

---

## [illegible] S [illegible] th [illegible] tion

*"I came here in 194* [illegible] *hink* [illegible] *so bereft of ideals and ideas. I don't see anything* [illegible] *tha* [illegible] *wrong. Republicans have one goal: To get Obama* [illegible] *hey se* [illegible] *that's all they can do?"*

- **Hele** [illegible] (1920-20 [illegible] correspondent, speaking at a Sara [illegible] Grou [illegible] the [illegible] ress Club, December 7, 2012.

# About the Author-Editor

Washington, DC-based Andrew Kreig directs the Justice Integrity Project (www.justice-integrity.org) and several other organizations in business and civic affairs. As a reporter, he covered both of the major federal trials in 2022 of suspects targeted by Justice Department Special Counsel John Durham, with each defendant absolved by acquittal.

This book's author-editor focused on the Durham probe in part from concerns growing out of his reporting on the U.S. Justice Department fulltime for the *Hartford Courant* from 1976 to 1981. He went on to become a legislative aide, attorney, author, non-profit-executive and public affairs strategist over the next four decades.

In 1987, after resigning from the *Courant* and becoming a free-lance author and legal columnist for *Connecticut Magazine*, he authored *Spiked: How Chain Management Corrupted America's Oldest Newspaper*, which was widely reviewed as a pioneering case study of the damage that news industry profiteering and arrogance can inflict on the public.

After his law school education he became law clerk to U.S. District Court Judge Mark L. Wolf in Boston, worked as an associate attorney in the Latham & Watkins office in Washington, DC and become vice president and general counsel of the Wireless Communications Association. Next, he served as that association's president and CEO from 1996 to 2008 to foster the business and regulatory environment for a new industry worldwide deploying high-speed Internet applications via land-based wireless towers. In 1999, he began two decades as the volunteer co-chair or treasurer of the Fixed Wireless Communications Coalition to advance similar goals. Listed in *Who's Who in the World* and *Who's Who in America* since the mid-1990s, he has lectured on government and business issues on five continents, including as co-keynoter at the 2008 *Futures Summit* of the National Association of Broadcasters.

In 2009, he became a research fellow affiliated with two universities and soon thereafter co-founded the Justice Integrity Project to explore complex legal, political and national security issues.

Reared in Chicago, Arkansas and New York City, he earned a B,A, degree in history from Cornell University, where he was a student newspaper editor, rowing team member and Golden Gloves boxer. He earned law degrees from Yale Law School and the University of Chicago School of Law.

He has been a member of numerous civic and professional groups, including the National Press Club, the Overseas Press Club of America, the News Leaders Association (merged from APME, AOJ and ASNE), the American Society of Journalists and Authors, and the District of Columbia Bar Association.

Made in the USA
Monee, IL
05 November 2026

67385363R00260